FOURTH BOOK OF

Junior Authors
& Illustrators

The Junior Book of Authors

More Junior Authors

Third Book of Junior Authors

Fourth Book of Junior Authors and Illustrators

FOURTH BOOK OF
Junior Authors & Illustrators

EDITED BY DORIS DE MONTREVILLE
AND ELIZABETH D. CRAWFORD

THE H. W. WILSON COMPANY • NEW YORK 1978

Printed in the United States of America

Library of Congress Cataloging in Publication Data
Main entry under title:

Fourth book of junior authors and illustrators.

☐ (Junior authors series)
Continues Third book of junior authors, edited by D. de Montreville and D. Hill.
☐ Includes a cumulative index to the 4 books.
1. Children's literature—Bio-bibliography.
2. Illustrated books, Children's—Bio-bibliography.
I. De Montreville, Doris. II. Crawford, Elizabeth D. III. De Montreville, Doris. Third book of junior authors. IV. Series.
PN1009.A1F6   809'.89282 [B]   78-115
ISBN 0-8242-0568-5

Preface

THIS VOLUME is the latest in the series begun by Stanley J. Kunitz and Howard Haycraft with THE JUNIOR BOOK OF AUTHORS, published in 1934 and revised in 1951. The second volume in the series, MORE JUNIOR AUTHORS, edited by Muriel Fuller, appeared in 1963, and THIRD BOOK OF JUNIOR AUTHORS, edited by Doris de Montreville and Donna Hill, was published in 1972. This latest work includes 242 autobiographical or biographical sketches of authors and illustrators of books for children and young people. Most have come to prominence since the publication of THIRD BOOK OF JUNIOR AUTHORS, but a few are older authors of continuing or renewed popularity who were not in the previous books. The title of the fourth volume has been expanded to reflect the contribution of the illustrators, whose sketches number approximately one third of those in this work.

Preparation for FOURTH BOOK OF JUNIOR AUTHORS AND ILLUSTRATORS was begun in 1972. From a file of 4,500 names of children's authors and illustrators, the editors compiled a preliminary list of 700 to present to an advisory committee of children's book specialists. As a basis for selection, we considered the prizes and awards won, the frequency of appearance of candidates' work on selective lists, the overall quality of the reviews in the major media, or, in some instances, the enduring popularity of a single work, such as *National Velvet*. The votes of two committee members and two editors were required to place a candidate on the master list, and in this way we arrived at a final list of 280 candidates. The advisory committee consisted of Geraldine Clark, Assistant Director for School Library Services for the Board of Education of the City of New York, Mavis W. Davis, Resource Teacher of Libraries for the Elementary Schools of New Rochelle, New York, Mary Elizabeth Ledlie, Coordinator of Youth Services for the Milwaukee (Wisconsin) Public Library, Lavinia Russ, former Children's Book Buyer for Scribner's Bookstore and Children's Book Reviewer for *Publishers Weekly,* and Della Thomas, formerly Director of Oklahoma State University Curriculum Materials Laboratory, now Director, European Studytours in Children's Literature.

Arrangement. Sketches are arranged in alphabetical order by the name appearing most frequently on title pages. Instead of following the system of cross-references in the body of the text provided in earlier volumes in the series, all names and pen-names are cross-referenced in the index at the back of this volume. The index also refers to the earlier books. Phonetic pronunciations of authors' names are given where necessary. When sketches have been translated from another language, this is indicated. The editorial notes appended to most sketches are intended to give additional information not found in the sketch or to provide amplification or clarification. Every effort has been made to avoid perpetuating errors that have been detected in the materials, and when possible we have checked with the biographees themselves for the resolution of conflicts in sources.

Special Features. As in the previous volume, lists of selected works are appended to each sketch and only books published in the United States have been included. Distinguished works published in other countries have been mentioned in the editorial notes, with the English translations of titles given in parentheses. We have tried to list books that have received outstanding notice or which the biographees particularly wished mentioned. Out-of-print titles have been included as well as those currently available. It has not, however, been possible to make a complete listing because of lack of space. Books published for adults have been included only when they have achieved wide popularity with the young readers.

Biographical references appear in the *About* section. These are confined to books and articles in English and ones that seemed most likely to be generally available for research. Critical articles have not been included unless they appeared to shed some useful light on the artistic credo of the subject.

As in THIRD BOOK OF JUNIOR AUTHORS, the signatures of the authors and illustrators willing to permit their use appear, along with photographs when obtainable. When it has not been possible to obtain autobiographical sketches, we have supplied biographical sketches, making an effort to have them written by someone who knew the subject personally or was an authority on his or her work. In such instances credit has been given to the author of the article in the heading of the entry itself. For those sketches otherwise anonymously written, we thank Marilyn L. Archdeacon, Jessica Fitzgerald, Letty Grierson, Jane Matera, Helen Reilly, Matilda Welter, and Refna Wilkin.

Early in 1974, the work was interrupted by the sudden illness and death of Doris de Montreville, who had headed the Teacher's Central Laboratory at Hunter College in New York City for many years. At the time of her death she had completed nearly all the preliminary research for the articles to be included. I have attempted to fill in gaps that existed and to keep up with new material that has appeared as the preparation of the final manuscript stretched out over the passage of time. In carrying on the work I have missed my colleague's sharp eye, her scholar's tenacity in ferreting out the smallest snippet of information, and her inspiration. It was her dearest wish to finish the book she had undertaken. I hope this volume will stand as a suitable memorial to her dedication and concern; it was the goal I kept in mind as I worked.

So many friends, colleagues, editors, and librarians have helped us to gather material or establish connections with hard-to-reach authors and illustrators that a full list here is impossible, but without their assistance this project could never have been completed, and our debt is hereby acknowledged. Special thanks are due to Mrs. Margaret J. Snider, Reference Librarian at the Newton (Massachusetts) Free Library, for her aid in discovering material about the late Mabel C. Bragg and to the correspondents who so graciously offered personal recollections of Miss Bragg: Mrs. Mary G. Gianferante, Mrs. Frank J. Toscano, Mrs. James C. Kennedy, and Miss Madeline W. Cobb.

We have been fortunate in having excellent library resources to draw upon: the New York Public Library, the Teachers' Central Laboratory at Hunter College, the Children's Book Council, the New Haven Free Public Library, the Orange Public Library, and the Art and Architecture Library at Yale University. For the use of their collections and the help of their staffs, particularly of Robin Gottlieb at the Children's Book Council, we are most grateful.

The support and assistance of the editors and staff at the H. W. Wilson Company has been constant and vital, so that it is a pleasure to acknowledge it here, as it is to thank Kenneth Meyer, Pauline Roth, and Refna Wilkin. Each knows the extent of his or her contribution though perhaps not how much I have valued it.

Finally, and most important, no list of acknowledgments can be complete without thanking the authors and illustrators whose sketches are the meat of this work. Without the contribution of their time and talent, there would be no book.

Elizabeth D. Crawford
January 6, 1978

Contents

JOY ADAMSON

January 20, 1910–

AUTHOR OF *Elsa and her Cubs,* etc.

Biographical sketch of Joy-Friederike Victoria Gessner Adamson:

JOY ADAMSON

JOY ADAMSON was born Joy-Friederike Victoria Gessner in Troppau, Silesia. She had ample contact with animals as a girl, for she spent her holidays on a family estate near Vienna. She loved the country and liked to roam, sometimes accompanied by her dog, more often not, because the dog scared away the animals, deer, hares, foxes and other creatures that Joy liked to watch. Shooting and hunting were part of the life there, but when Joy was sixteen she shot for sport for the first time and never cared to repeat the experience.

Her early education was wide-ranging indeed. Her family was musical and Joy could play the piano before she could read. She assumed she would carry on the family tradition, so when she was fifteen she decided to study for the State Diploma for pianists. By the time she was seventeen she realized that she could not be a concert pianist, and since she did not care to teach, she turned to other careers, though she has continued to play for her own pleasure. Among the various interests she followed were sculpture, dressmaking, premedical studies, and shorthand and typing. To each she brought the intensity and dedicated thoroughness that have characterized her later work.

In 1935 her first of three marriages, to the Austrian Victor von Klarwill, interrupted her medical studies. About a year later she went to visit friends in Kenya and fell in love with the country. She felt that she had for the first time encountered a new world that was much bigger than any she had ever dreamed of, for in Europe "everything was dominated by man, whereas in East Africa nature put man in his place and daily I saw around me wonders that surpassed all man-made inventions." She has stayed in Kenya ever since.

In 1938 she married the Swiss botanist Peter Bally. Through him she became fascinated with Kenyan flora. She painted specimens which interested her, and the result was over four thousand paintings, several published books on African wild flowers, exhibitions and collections of her work in Kenya, and, eventually, the Royal Horticultural Society's Grenfell Medal in 1947. Many of her illustrations have been brought together by Kenyan public collections and published in her book *The Peoples of Kenya* (1967), and her own autobiography *Joy Adamson's Africa* (1972).

She was divorced from Bally in 1944 and married George Adamson, a senior game warden at the Serengeti National Park. Her marriage led to an almost continual series of safaris across the 120,000 square miles of Kenya's Northern Frontier district where her husband's responsibilities lay. Opportunties to sketch and observe animal life led to many paintings and drawings and to a series of one-to-one encounters with various animals, which provided the basis of experience for the Elsa books.

Besides Mrs. Adamson's well-known published descriptions of lions and cheetahs, she has pursued longstanding relationships with other animals, notably, a rock hyrax, two baby elephants, an impala, an Arabian oryx, a young buffalo and, fairly recently, a pair of Colobus monkeys. She developed an intensely personal and sympathetic relationship with all except the monkeys, whom she only observed and photographed from a distance.

The long, fascinating saga of the Elsa books and films began in 1956 when George Adamson was forced to shoot a lioness in self-defense. Afterwards they found that the lioness had been defending three cubs. Two were originally given to a Dutch zoo, but one cub, Elsa, they kept. Elsa, who was eventually released when she was twenty-seven months old, later mated with a wild lion; she died in 1961.

Born Free was published in 1960, and led to *Living Free* (1961), the story of Elsa's cubs, and *Forever Free* (1963), telling of Elsa's death and the fate of her cubs. *Born Free* was filmed in 1966 and *Living Free* in 1972. The story was retold for children in *Elsa: The True Story of a Lioness* (1961) and in *Elsa and her Cubs* (1965).

The books describe a relationship of mutual respect which never led to domestication. The main reason, perhaps, for the enormous success of the Elsa books and films (the estimated sale of the three books was thirteen million by 1972) lies in the way they fill the gap between the outright anthropomorphism of the worst of the Disney school of animal writing and the coolly detached prose of the professional zoologist. Joy Adamson reveals personality without any denial of the essential integrity and truth of an animal, and often attains an almost telepathic level of communication.

There were many critics, especially on the Kenyan scene, who felt that reeducating Elsa to the wild state was dangerous—that a wild animal, having been used to humans, would now turn to them as her most desirable prey. The Adamsons justified their action by pointing out the lack of fertility of many wild species in domestic surroundings and the need to restore our wildlife before it is completely destroyed.

Mrs. Adamson has also published studies of a cheetah—in *The Spotted Sphinx* (1969) and in *Pippa's Challenge* (1972), where she discussed the raising of Pippa's cubs. The Pippa stories were adapted for children in *Pippa: the Cheetah and Her Cubs* (1970).

A car accident in 1970 that injured Mrs. Adamson's right hand has virtually ended her painting. She remains, however, a fervent apostle of African wildlife, administering the Elsa wildlife appeal, a registered charity concerned with wildlife conservation in Africa today. The Adamsons have also been instrumental in setting up the Meru National Park in Kenya.

SELECTED WORKS: Born Free, 1960; Elsa: The True Story of a Lioness, 1961; Living Free, 1961; Forever Free, 1963; Elsa and her Cubs, 1965; Pippa: the Cheetah and her Cubs, 1970.

ABOUT: Adamson. Joy Adamson's Africa, 1972; Author's and Writer's Who's Who, 1971; Newquist, Roy, comp. Counterpoint; Who's Who, 1972–73; Who's Who of American Women, 1974–75; Current Biography, 1972; Good Housekeeping February 1972.

ARNOLD ADOFF
July 16, 1935–

Author of *Ma nDa la*, etc.

Biographical sketch of Arnold Adoff:

ARNOLD ADOFF was born in New York City, in the East Bronx, the son of Aaron and Rebecca Adoff. He was always a reader, one of those children who take home armloads of books from the public library and devour them, returning again the following week for another load. He has described his Bronx neighborhood as having "a character—a solid, respectable Jewish middle class, the butcher, the grocer, my father's pharmacy on the corner, the old ladies sitting in front of the stoops, mothers waiting with jars of milk for their kids' afternoon snacks after school before running . . . to play ball." Curious about everything, young Adoff explored the Bronx and later the rest of the city and came to love it "and its potential for power, excitement and discovery." After Stuyvesant High School, City College and Columbia University Graduate School, Adoff began teaching public school in Harlem. He taught for twelve years, during which he took part in Federal education projects at New York University and Connecticut College. His education, which he has characterized as "lily white," hadn't prepared him for teaching Harlem schoolchildren about black history or black culture, so Adoff, who had been writing poetry himself since his teens, began to gather the work of black poets to use in his classes. "I was teaching children who had grown up very much like myself: lower middle class and from a minority. We were not part of the mainstream of American society to which history and literature texts were directed." Since Adoff had always loved poetry—"to collect it, to read it, and to create it"—it was natural for him to put together an anthology. "At age thirty I decided it was time to go beyond my classrooms . . . time to grow up the rest of the way

ARNOLD ADOFF

. . . time to stop *talking* change. Janet Schulman (then at Macmillan) is an old friend, and my wife's first book for children had been accepted there. I showed Jan the material for *I Am the Darker Brother*, and Susan Hirschman took the book." Macmillan published it in 1968 to acclaim on all sides. The American Library Association named it a Notable Book for 1968.

In 1958 Adoff met Virginia Hamilton, who was trying to get started as a writer, at a party in Greenwich Village. "I was writing my poems and she was working on her first (still unpublished) novel. It was a good time to learn to be strong." They married on March 19, 1960. In 1969 the Adoffs moved from New York City to Yellow Springs, Ohio, where Virginia Hamilton's family has lived for several generations. They built a house on family land and settled down to write and raise their two children, a daughter, Leigh Hamilton, and a son, Jaime Levi.

If Adoff is reticent about the personal details of his life, he is passionately articulate about his work and his commitment to it. The move to Yellow Springs ushered in a period of creativity that has resulted in several anthologies and works of his own poetry for children, celebrating the joyousness in a loving family that

Adoff: *AID off*

happens, incidentally, to be biracial. "I am NOT an expert on black life or culture or even black poetry," says Adoff. "I am a continuing student. . . . I think of myself as a pusher—a disseminator of black materials. I seek out opportunities to tell . . . about the work of black poets, writers, educators and historians. . . . I want my anthologies of black American writing to make black kids strong in their knowledge of themselves and their great literary heritage—give them facts and people and power. I also want these black books of mine to give knowledge to white kids so that mutual respect and understanding will come from mutual learning." Adoff insists that black artists be used to illustrate his anthologies of black literature and he refuses to do critical essays on aspects of black literature or life because, he says, "We don't need any more white 'experts' on black anything in this country."

When he is not teaching or lecturing, Adoff works in the mornings. "I take a long time with my books, maybe even two years on an anthology, and so I work on more than one book project at a time. You must mix things up and keep your head interested by changing the pace. I write and rewrite my material many, many times. . . . The key is sitting with it, letting it grow inside, becoming a part of your body for weeks and months and learning to work it over and over." Currently he says, "I am spending a great deal of time on poetry, and the creating of poetry manuscripts for illustration. This work is the continuation of many years of experimentation and development. I am concerned with pushing out the traditional 'frame' of the picture book form; going beyond the traditional prose story format common in books for little kids . . . going beyond the collections of unrelated little poems that make up the majority of the poetry books for young children.

"I am working on my balancing act, much the way a juggler or acrobat would develop his format for the big top show."

"This is the act. Music and meaning in balance. Poetry and, sometimes, poetic prose, in balance and movement. Reality and fantasy, in balance . . . and sometimes, out of balance. Each poem a distinct and alive entity that belongs on its page, and has an intrinsic form and shape that allows it to live on its page. All of the poems of the series interrelated and connected, semantically, poetically, etc., so the semantic line of force creates a 'story' by the time the book is over. . . .

"*Ma nDa la* was the first stop in the published elements of this continuing approach. Spare 'soundings' in series to obliterate the semantic baggage that a word carries with it, and in replacement: a song of joy, and a story of family, and the circle of life.

"*Black Is Brown Is Tan* combines the elements of music and meaning, poetry and poetic prose in a fair balance. Although its extraordinary success is due in large measure to its 'story' of an interracial family situation, it represents to me a breakthrough in the traditional approach to books for young children, in style and form.

"*Make a Circle Keep Us In* is the approach in full bloom. A series of individual, yet interconnected poems, that mean and sing and tell a story of a family, and its day . . . in the end."

The effectiveness of Adoff's commitment to excellence is reflected in the commendations his books have received. Several have been chosen Notable Books for children by the American Library Association: *Malcolm X* (1970); *Black Out Loud* (1970); *Ma nDa la* (1971); *The Poetry of Black America* (1972); and *My Black Me* (1974). *Ma nDa la* was also chosen one of the best books of 1971 by *School Library Journal* and cited as a Brooklyn Art Book for Children in 1975, a citation based upon literary as well as artistic quality.

SELECTED WORKS WRITTEN: Malcolm X, 1970; Ma nDa la, 1971; Black Is Brown Is Tan, 1973; Make a Circle Keep Us In: Poems for a Good Day, 1975; Big Sister Tells Me That I'm Black, 1976; Tornado!, 1977.

SELECTED WORKS EDITED: Black on

Black, 1968; I Am the Darker Brother, 1968; City in All Directions, 1969; Black Out Loud, 1970; Brothers and Sisters, 1970; It Is the Poem Singing into Your Eyes, 1971; The Poetry of Black America, 1973; My Black Me, 1974.

ABOUT: Contemporary Authors, Vol. 41–47; Hopkins, Lee Bennett. More Books by More People; Something about the Author, Vol. 5; Toledo (Ohio) Blade August 26, 1973; Top of the News January 1972.

NAN AGLE

April 13, 1905–

AUTHOR OF *Three Boys and a Lighthouse*, etc.

Autobiographical sketch of Anna Bradford Hayden Agle:

I WAS born in 1905 in Baltimore, Maryland, the youngest of three daughters of Charles Swett and Emily Spencer Hayden—we were and are Ruth, Catherine and Anna Bradford (Nan for short). Our home, Nancy's Fancy, was on Edmondson Avenue and Nunnery Lane in Catonsville. The old country house was large—thirteen rooms, with five open fireplaces—and its dining room had originally been a log cabin. It was a good place to live, seven and one-half acres in all, with an apple orchard, a barn that was fun to play in—a grand barn—and a little stone house on a hill. I wrote about the place and all of the people and animals in *My Animals and Me*.

There was also a field where I kept my pet donkey, Peanuts. I guess everybody in Catonsville knew Peanuts. People would say, "Oh yes, Nancy's Fancy. That's where the gray donkey is." He was the only donkey there and quite a character. I wrote about him in *Kish's Colt*.

I had other animals too, but I was an awful worrywart about animals then, and still am. I feel strongly that we should take care of all other living things—people, animals, trees. I think to hurt anything else needlessly is a terrible thing.

There were always books around our house, and since there wasn't any TV or radio then, my sisters and I read every evening. Mother would go into Pratt Library and come back with bags of books for each of us. My father, a lawyer, was interested in Indians and had many valuable books about them, but it was my grandfather, Edward Spencer, who really collected books. He was the chief editorial writer for the Baltimore *Sun* when he died in 1883 and had written several plays that appeared on Broadway.

Inspired by a wonderful teacher, Miss Emma Weyforth, I started to write in high school, making a thousand mistakes and spelling almost every word wrong. But it was Elizabeth Lewis, the author of a number of children's books, including a Newbery Award winner, who made me want to write seriously. She loved to laugh, really thought a laugh was an important thing. I would tell her stories about Peanuts, and we would laugh like anything. Finally she said, "You must write them down," I did, and that's when I got started, although I never did get those particular stories right until recently in *My Animals and Me*.

I attended Goucher College long enough to be a Delta Gamma and get very sick—and then I decided to go to the Maryland Institute of Art. Actually I had been painting all along. In fact, I have always been doing something, either writing or painting, since I can remember. All our family did. My sisters did biological drawings, and Mother was an excellent photographer. She liked children's portraits particularly, and did her own developing and printing.

While at the Institute, I married Harold Cecil, and our two sons were born in the next few years after my graduation. When the oldest was in the sixth grade and the youngest in the fourth, I started teaching art at Friends School in Baltimore. I had a good time there and rounded out my education by having lunch with ten fourth-grade boys every day for fourteen years. The conversation of young boys is interesting, and much of it has come into my writing. While at Friends I met Ellen Wilson and we started the *Three Boys* series.

I like to do research—to have an idea, hunt for it, and then finally find it—finding the records of graves, the number of children, and that sort of thing. But it's unpleasant sometimes, too. When I was writing *Tarr of Belway Smith*—Tarr is a Labrador retriever who thinks he's the biggest, blackest, most beautiful dog anywhere—I hated having to visit the dog pound to see what it was like for a dog staying there. It depressed me, as it does Tarr in the book.

One of the rewards of writing for children is getting to know them through their letters. I have one regular young correspondent in New Zealand, and another who once wrote that this would probably be the last letter he would send as he was outgrowing me. One little girl in the Bronx, New York, wrote to me, thanking me for writing *Kate and the Apple Tree* for her. She said that before I published it nobody knew she was there.

My sons, Chip and Ridge, are both married now with families of their own. My second husband, John Agle, and I live in a woods outside Baltimore with our marvelous dog Toulouse and all the wild animals and birds. It's a good place to work and think about what next.

———

Nan Agle credits her oldest son with being the inspiration for the *Three Boys* stories. He had been making a book—inspired, perhaps, by her example, as she made little books for Christmas presents—with its own cardboard covers and a story about four brothers who had wonderful adventures together. Nan Agle and Ellen Wilson took up the idea, and *Three Boys and a Lighthouse* was the result, one of the boys having been lost along the way.

Three Boys and a Lighthouse is being used in Germany as an English reader for language study. Seven of Nan Agle's books have been transcribed into Braille.

SELECTED WORKS: Princess Mary of Maryland, 1956; Makon and the Dauphin, 1961; Kate and the Apple Tree, 1965; Joe Bean, 1967; Kish's Colt, 1968; Tarr of Belway Smith, 1969; Maple Street, 1970; My Animals and Me, 1970; K Mouse and Bo Bixby, 1972; Baney's Lake, 1972; Susan's Magic, 1973.

SELECTED WORKS WITH FRANCES ATCHINSON BACON: The Lords Baltimore, 1962; The Ingenious John Banvard, 1966.

SELECTED WORKS WITH ELLEN WILSON: Three Boys and a Lighthouse, 1951; Three Boys and a Tugboat, 1953; Three Boys and a Train, 1956; Three Boys and a Helicopter, 1958; Three Boys and Space, 1962; Three Boys and H₂O, 1968.

ABOUT: Contemporary Authors, Vol. 4; Something about the Author, Vol. 3; Who's Who of American Women, 1972–73.

HELGA AICHINGER

November 29, 1937–

AUTHOR AND ILLUSTRATOR OF *The Shepherd*, etc.

Autobiographical sketch of Helga Aichinger, translated from the German:

BORN in Traun, Austria, a suburb of Linz, whose houses at that time stood in the midst of pastures and fields, I passed a quiet, dreamy childhood with my parents and sisters—a childhood in which even the hard realities of a difficult pe-

Aichinger: *EIK ing er*

riod were occasionally transformed and made radiant. Later, after an unrewarding bread-and-butter job, I was allowed —which would not have been possible without sacrifice—to study calligraphy and typography at the art school in Linz, and here I found the range, understanding, excitement, and possibility of immersing myself in the world of pictures, which is *my* world. Soon I began, self-taught, to develop the technical and formal bases for my work. I also invented my own techniques. I had early success, and here I also learned to know my husband. With him my real intellectual-emotional development began, the unfolding of a shared world, to which for the last several years we have been able to devote ourselves completely, with constant interchange, on a common journey, in our own house in the country. We live among many books and other beautiful things, neighbors to the animals and the trees on the edge of a great forest, on a little stream in a beautiful valley in northern Austria. We have the fields and the orchards to tend, we listen to music a great deal, we sometimes have dear friends in the house, and often the children of our friends. We frequently talk far into the night about a thousand and one problems.

Often I receive letters from all over the world, from people who have become fond of my pictures and want to own them, from children who like my books and ask for new ones. Agreeable questions and requests, which I gladly fill.

Official occasions, even if they bring me joy—like exhibitions, prizes, honors— I avoid if possible. I am a little spoiled by the quiet, and I have never liked to be in the foreground. What I have to say, my pictures and books say.

Our house is no "cloud cuckooland." I know that one cannot let the world go by unheeded. One must not overlook the great sorrow, the folly, the wickedness, and the possibility of hope. One must experience everything, come to terms with it. But one can also work for the good in quiet, gather and fashion strengths that can disclose a deeper reality to a child and encourage him in his best potentialities.

———

Helga Aichinger has received a number of prizes and medals in Europe, including one from the World's Fair in Brussels in 1958 for *Der Rattenfanger* (The Pied Piper), an Honorary Diploma from the International Biennale of Illustration Bratislava (BIB) in 1969, a Gold Medal from BIB in 1971 and the First Prize at the Bologna Book Fair in 1973. She was also named a Highly Commended Ilustrator in the competition for the Hans Christian Andersen Medal in 1974. Miss Aichinger has exhibited in shows all over the world and her work is included in many museum collections, among them the Museum of Modern Art in New York, Stedelijk Museum, Amsterdam, Harvard University Library, and the Klingspor Museum at Offenbach a. M., Germany. Besides book illustration she works in tapestry, glass etching, and makes applique and puppets.

In acknowledging her commendation for the Hans Christian Andersen Award, in a statement printed in *Bookbird*, Miss Aichinger wrote that she thinks her pictures tell more about her work than she can herself, but she goes on to say:

"In order to say something to children

I think it is important to be a child one-self inside, that is, to have remained open and impressionable, capable of experiencing the complete whole even in the smallest thing, of seeing everything as if for the first time.

"I come to grips with our reality again and again and then repeatedly retire to win distance, to filter, to deepen, to collect, to solidify. . . . I don't accept what I encounter and what I experience without criticism, but criticism isn't enough. To accept and do what is necessary, to let the superfluous be, to create reality and not phantoms, to realize that which goes up through me is what it means to be effective from the inside. And actually art begins there where it is a working presence, not merely intentional doing."

SELECTED WORKS WRITTEN AND ILLUSTRATED: The Elephant, the Mouse, and the Flea, 1967; The Shepherd, 1967; The Rain Mouse, 1970; The Rain Man, 1971.

SELECTED WORKS ILLUSTRATED: Jonah and the Great Fish, by Clyde Robert Bulla, 1970; Noah and the Rainbow, by Max Bollinger, 1972; The Boy Who Had Wings, by Jane Yolen, 1974; I Never Saw, by Judson Jerome, 1974.

ABOUT: Contemporary Authors, Vol. 25–28; Something about the Author, Vol. 5; Bookbird No. 1, 1970; No. 3, 1974.

MARTHA ALEXANDER

May 25, 1920–

AUTHOR AND ILLUSTRATOR OF *Nobody Asked Me If I Wanted A Baby Sister,* etc.

Autobiographical sketch of Martha Alexander:

I WAS born in Augusta, Georgia, the second of five girls. Though my family left Georgia when I was nine years old, memories of this period left lasting impressions on me. Before the Civil War, my mother's family owned slaves. When I was a little girl I visited one of them, an old lady ninety-three years old, who had been freed in 1864. She sat in a rocking

chair, wrapped in a quilt, near a wood stove, and told me stories about my grandfather when he was a boy. Another time, I visited the old slave market in Savannah. On the way home I saw a real chain gang working on the road. My feelings about the treatment of black people in the South troubled me. As I grew older I felt embarrassed for having been a part of a culture that permitted and condoned such inhumanity.

In 1929 we moved to Cincinnati, Ohio. I was always quite shy, and going to a new school and speaking with a thick southern accent drew attention to me for the first time and made me very uncomfortable. I lost my accent as quickly as possible. A teacher at my new school was the first person to take an interest in my drawing. The encouragement she gave me was the most important influence in my life up to that time and must have affected my choice of a career later on. In high school my history teacher liked my drawings and let me draw pictures of the subjects we were studying for extra credit. This meant a great deal to me, as I wasn't very interested in history. After high school I enrolled in the Cincinnati Academy of Arts and discovered that I had a talent for drawing which was greater than I had realized. I loved every minute of it and received scholarships every year.

During my four years at the Cincinnati Academy of Arts there were two artists who had a great influence on me. One was Paul Klee. The whimsy and magic of his drawings and paintings fascinated me. The other was Leonardo daVinci, especially his portrait of the *Mona Lisa*. The expression of her face touched me deeply. I longed to be able to express such feeling in my own drawings.

I was married in 1943. Soon after, my husband went overseas in World War II. After the war, we settled in Honolulu with our daughter Kim. Three years later our son Allen was born. During this time I taught silk screen printing and graphics at the Honolulu Academy of Arts, as well as art classes for children. However, I soon realized that I liked doing my own work more than teaching. I sold quite a few of my paintings for children's rooms, several murals for pediatricians' offices, and a variety of collages, mosaics and ceramics.

I was divorced in 1959 and wanted to start a new life somewhere other than in Hawaii. I sent samples and photographs of my work to an old friend who was an illustrator in New York City. She told me she felt sure that I could make a living there as an illustrator. With this encouragement, in 1960 I moved to New York with my two teen-age children.

For the first five years I had quite a struggle supporting myself and my children. I illustrated stories in *Seventeen*, and did fashion and cosmetics illustrations for fashion and women's magazines. Though I got a good deal of satisfaction out of this work, it wasn't what I really wanted to do. I always wanted to illustrate children's books, but was advised that the field was very competitive and low paying compared to magazines.

In 1965 I decided to try children's books in spite of what I had been told. I took my portfolio to Harper and Row and to my surprise was given a book to illustrate almost right away. The first year I illustrated six books. Then I tried my hand at writing my own stories. I had a granddaughter, Lisa, by this time, and some of the things she said and did gave me several ideas for stories. I completed five of these almost at the same time, and four of them were eventually published by the Dial Press. The first was *Out! Out! Out!*, a story without words. My first story with words was *Maybe a Monster*.

Having been so shy and having felt so inarticulate as a child, it seemed almost miraculous that I could write a book. I soon learned that the natural way for me to work was to draw and write almost simultaneously. I never just write a story. I start with a dummy—about thirty pages of blank paper folded in the form of a book—and sketch in pictures and words as they occur to me. While working out the story I am hardly aware of whether I am drawing or writing. Afterwards I am often surprised to see how few words I have used and how much of the story gets told through the pictures. My subject matter comes from my grandchildren, Lisa, Christina, Leslie, Mia and Scott, and from other children. I also use the feelings I remember from my own childhood.

———

Martha Alexander was represented in the American Institute for Graphic Arts Show, 1971–72. Her *Blackboard Bear* was included in the New York *Times Book Review's* Outstanding Books of 1969; *Bobo's Dream* was chosen one of the Best Books of the Year by *School Library Journal* in 1970; and *Sabrina* was an Honor Book in the 1971 *Book World* Children's Spring Book Festival. The American Library Association included *Nobody Asked Me if I Wanted a Baby Sister* in its 1971 List of Children's Books of International Interest, and the Children's Book Council chose it for inclusion in the Children's Book Showcase, 1972.

SELECTED WORKS WRITTEN AND ILLUS-TRATED: Out! Out! Out!, 1968; Maybe a Monster, 1968; Blackboard Bear, 1969; The Story Grandmother Told, 1969; We Never Get to Do Anything, 1970; Bobo's Dream, 1970; Sabrina, 1971; Nobody Asked Me if I Wanted a Baby Sister, 1971; And My Mean Old Mother Will Be Sorry, Blackboard Bear, 1972; No Ducks in *Our* Bathtub, 1973; I'll Protect You from the Jungle Beasts, 1973; I Sure Am Glad to See You, Blackboard Bear, 1976.

SELECTED WORKS ILLUSTRATED: Big Sister and Little Sister, by Charlotte Zolotow, 1966; Maryann's Mud Day, by Janice May Udry, 1967; Elizabeth, by Liesel Skorpen, 1969; Charles, by Liesel Skorpen, 1971; Understood Betsy, by Dorothy Canfield Fisher, 1972; Emily and the Chunky Baby and The Next-Door Dog, by Jean Lexau, 1972; The Wizard of Walnut Street, by Carol Scism, 1973; Too Hot for Ice Cream, by Jean Van Leeuwen, 1974; Mandy's Grandmother, by Liesel Moak Skorpen, 1975; The Everyday Train, by Amy Ehrlich, 1977.

AGNES ALLEN

December 11, 1898–September 15, 1959

and

JACK ALLEN

March 8, 1899–

AUTHOR AND ILLUSTRATOR OF *The Story of Your Home*, etc.

Biographical sketch of Agnes Banister Allen and Cyril Jack Allen by Jack Allen:

I WAS born in Sussex, in the South of England, in the heart of the country, and have remained a country lover ever since. My first ambition was to become a teacher, for which I started training, and had it not been that the First World War left me physically unfit for it, that is what I certainly should have become. My time for the latter part of the First World War was spent as a pilot in the Royal Flying Corps.

After the war, as I could draw and enjoyed it, I entered an art school. My first job was as a commercial artist with a firm of printers and then I went to a national newspaper. This meant a life full of interest, as the work entailed almost everything in design and illustration. It was while an art student that I met Agnes, who was born in London, and in 1928 we were married.

At the time of our marriage Agnes was a secretary in a publisher's office and had started writing herself. Her father was a

AGNES ALLEN

JACK ALLEN

journalist, giving her an even greater incentive. For a time she was editor of a women's magazine.

Soon after our marriage we had a house built about twenty miles south of London so that I was able to commute to work. In 1934 our son David, our only child, was born.

Our house stood in the London bombing area during the Second World War and received the attention of one of Germany's doodle bugs, or flying bombs. This meant hasty and extensive repairs to the roof and long periods of linen windows and no plaster on the ceilings. This meant, too, exciting and unpleasant experiences in town.

It was whilst on holiday that the idea of Agnes's first book resulted from questions asked by David. In the village where we were staying was a "cruck" cottage, a small house built by erecting timbers in the form of an inverted V and joining them by a ridge beam. This interested David, who asked more questions about other buildings. After answering his questions Agnes thought other children might be interested too and wrote *The Story of the Village* which we illustrated between us. This was published by Faber and Faber and, proving a success, was followed by others in a similar vein, amongst them *The Story of Your Home*, which received the Carnegie Medal in 1949.

We spent most of our holidays and whatever other time we could spare visiting museums, art galleries, archaeological sites, and historical towns and cities in Europe for research.

It was truly awe-inspiring to walk around the wonderful buildings and to see the paintings and sculptures of the great masters, whilst handling some of the tools made by prehistoric men and even finding some for ourselves. To see the ashes made by their fires brought them much nearer to us and gave us some understanding of their lives. We were fortunate that we were able to visit the caves in the Dordogne where men had carved the animals to propitiate their gods and give them good fortune in their hunting. We saw the wonderful paintings in the Lascaux Caves before it became necessary to seal them from outside air.

The books meant, too, such diversified times as visits to the Houses of Parliament for *The Story of our Parliament* (published in England, 1949) and wandering around Florence and Rome for a biography of Michelangelo (published in England, 1948). The *Story of Clothes* (published in England, 1955) meant that even I took an interest in historical fashion.

The years we spent together in collaboration were truly wonderful.

SELECTED WORKS: The Story of Your Home, 1950.

MITSUMASA ANNO

March 20, 1926–

AUTHOR AND ILLUSTRATOR OF *Topsy-Turvies: Pictures to Stretch the Imagination*, etc.

Autobiographical sketch of Mitsumasa Anno, translated from the Japanese:

Babyhood—There was a third-class inn in a small town called Tsuwano in western Japan, the usual stars shining up in the sky, farmers and cattlemen gathered from neighboring villages. It was market day. That small inn was filled with the people who had come to market. And I was born in the midst of all that bustle and confusion.

War was imminent in China, and as part of the war preparation the government was encouraging births: in short, I was a product of that policy.

Boyhood—One day a vagabond painter stayed at our inn, and my father asked him to look at my pictures and give some advice. Looking at them intently, the painter said, "The road to art is not an easy, paved one" or something like that, and drew three sparrows as a model for me to copy. This brush drawing did not impress me at all. I told my father I could do much better if I drew my favorite scenes from historic stories, and this made my father very angry. I earnestly desired to become an artist.

Adolescence—I went to a high school far from my hometown. My heart beat when I saw girls in their school uniforms, and drifting clouds in the sky sent me into melancholic moods. I knew something in myself was changing. I was also absorbed in reading any books I could get my hands on. But in 1940, with Japan

Mitsumasa Anno: *Mee tzu MAH sa AHN no*

expanding its war, all those dreams of becoming an artist and the cherished hope of being a professional player of *go* (Japanese checkers) were shattered by a piece of paper from the draft board.

Mid-youth—I went to Paris. The tomb of Van Gogh and books by Escher moved me so much that my headaches recurred —the headaches I developed in the army from being beaten up by the bully a notch above me in rank.

It was this moving experience that motivated me to make my first picture book *Topsy-Turvies,* and then *Upside-Downers; Downside-Uppers and Magical Midnight Circus.*

When I was a child I pictured the world-is-round concept as a rubber ball turned inside out with the people of the different continents living inside the ball. Of course it was a boy's way of imagining, but this kind of imagination, I believe, is another sort of eye for perceiving what things really are.

I suppose my proclivity to see things with this other, imaginative, eye is the source of all the books I have made and will be making both for children and for grown-ups.

———

Mitsumasa Anno's books have been translated into English, French and German. The German edition of *Topsy-Turvies: Pictures to Stretch the Imagination* was among the books commended for the 1973 German Children's and Youth Book Award. The American edition was one of the New York *Times's* choices of best illustrated children's books of the year in 1970, was an American Library Association Notable Book and received a Brooklyn Art Books for Children Citation in 1973, as did *Upside-Downers. Anno's Alphabet* was chosen one of the American Institute of Graphic Arts' Fifty Books of the Year, was an American Library Association Notable Book, and received the Boston *Globe-Horn Book* Award for Illustration in 1975. It was included in the 1976 Children's Book Showcase.

Mitsumasa Anno married Midori Suetsugu on April 1, 1952. They have two children, a boy, Masaichiro, and a girl, Seiko, and live in Tokyo. Besides his painting Mr. Anno often lectures on art and art history for television. He is a member of the Japan Artists Association.

SELECTED WORKS WRITTEN AND ILLUSTRATED: Topsy-Turvies: Pictures to Stretch the Imagination, 1970; Upside-Downers; Downside-Uppers: More Pictures to Stretch the Imagination, 1971; Dr. Anno's Magical Midnight Circus, 1972; Anno's Alphabet: An Adventure in Imagination, 1975; Anno's Counting Book, 1977.

ABOUT: Contemporary Authors, Vol. 49–52; Something about the Author, Vol. 5.

ENRICO ARNO

July 16, 1913–

ILLUSTRATOR OF *The Wicked Enchantment,* etc.

Autobiographical sketch of Enrico Arno:

I WAS born in Mannheim (Germany), an event which apparently induced my parents to leave that place. They moved to Berlin where I lived from the age of six months to twenty-six years and where I went to school and later to the Acad-

Enrico Arno

emy of Arts. My hope was to become the greatest painter of the century; my parents wanted me to become an art teacher. Neither wish was to be fulfilled. The "Nürnberg Laws" declared me a "mongrel in the first degree" (because I had a Jewish mother) and unfit to become a pedagogue; thus my parents' dream went down the drain. As to my own goal, I had to admit that, *hélas*, Picasso had the edge on me. Yet, as there just was nothing that interested me as much as drawing, I applied myself to "applied art"; I worked for two British publishers in London and later went to Italy. For the next seven years I worked for Italian publishers, mainly Mondadori in Milan, and during those years I became much Italianized, including in name.

From 1944 to 1945 I worked for the British Army Education in Rome. There, in Major Morse-Brown's library, I read a book about the colonies in America, and in 1947 I took the first opportunity I could get to go there.

Here I have worked as a book-jacket and record-cover designer, have done many illustrated maps for *Holiday* and *Town and Country,* have illustrated Greek myths and Roman history for *Life,* and a great many children's books.

I am married to Paula Von Haim-

berger, who has provided me with a grown-up daughter from a previous marriage, and with two serendipitous grandsons whose opinions about my work I value greatly, provided they are favorable. Their considered judgment about one of my latest efforts, *Other Worlds, Other Beings* by Stanley Angrist, was "real cool"!

This comment suggested to me that I should stop illustrating books while I was ahead, and so I have now concentrated on film strips for Miller-Brody Productions based on successful children's books, narrated with spoken dialogue, sound effects, and musical accompaniment. My contribution is the visual part: 200 full-color illustrations, still pictures that are shown in synchronization with the text. The first film strip I did was "I, Juan de Pareja" by Elizabeth Borton de Treviño (the story of Velázquez' mulatto assistant). Right now I am finishing the second, "A Wind in the Door" by Madeleine L'Engle, a most imaginative children's sci-fi fantasy that takes place partly in outer space and partly within a blood cell of a sick child —the ending is happy and so am I.

————

Enrico Arno escaped to Italy at the beginning of World War II and worked in Milan until 1943, when the Italian armistice forced him to flee the Nazis. He left for Rome with homemade identification papers, but the Nazis soon followed and Arno was forced to go into hiding until the Liberation. After the war he designed and built himself a house, even to the extent of laying a tile floor and digging his own cistern.

Arno works in many media and uses a wide variety of materials, choosing his technique to harmonize with the work of art as a whole. In addition to book illustration, jacket design for books and records, advertising art and posters, Arno has painted murals and designed a stamp commemorating Fort Ticonderoga which is considered one of the finest examples of philatelic graphic art. He has taught lettering at Pratt Institute and painting at Columbia University.

Fritz Eichenberg, the distinguished graphic artist and teacher, in an appreciation of Arno's work says: "It is not in his makeup to do anything shoddy, no matter for what purpose it may be used. He has done many different things . . . with the same sound craftsmanship, sure taste, and fine sense of design. . . . [He] can perform on every level of his craft without compromise in quality."

The artist's hobby is puppetry.

SELECTED WORKS ILLUSTRATED: The Wicked Enchantment, by Margot Benary-Isbert, 1955; The Story of Gudrun, by E.M. Almedingen, 1967; Men in Armor, by Richard Susskind, 1968; Rough Men, Tough Men, Poems of Action and Adventure, William Cole, ed., 1969; Straight Lines, Parallel Lines, Perpendicular Lines, by Mahnis Charosh, 1970; People of the Short Blue Corn, by Harold Courlander, 1970; Other Worlds, Other Beings, by Stanley W. Angrist, 1973; The Airplane and How It Works, by David Inglis Urquhart, 1973.

ABOUT: Kingman, Lee and others, comps., Illustrators of Children's Books: 1957–1966; American Artist May 1956.

JOSÉ ARUEGO

August 9, 1932–

AUTHOR AND ILLUSTRATOR OF Look What I Can Do, etc.

Autobiographical sketch of José Espiritu Aruego:

IT is amazing every time I think where I am today. To know that all I do is children's books and that the beautiful reward is to be able to do more children's books. Every day I indulge in my fantasies, daydreams and childhood experiences when I work. One thing about my picture books, they always have funny animals doing funny things. Since I work and live alone in my studio apartment I find myself howling and giggling every

time I draw one of these funny characters. Sometimes their expressions are too hilarious so that I get into hysterics from laughing. And for all this joy I am very happy to be in this profession. There was a big change for me in countries and "line of work" when I went into children's books six years ago. I came from the Philippines where the culture and humor are entirely different, and my educational background is that of a lawyer. And yet here I am doing children's books with all kinds of animals jumping in and out. Most of the characters in my books are animals. It seems no matter how I draw them they look funny. I kept asking myself where in my childhood did I develop this happy relationship with the animals I draw. I remember as a child I could not keep a pet. They always died. So whenever I liked an animal, be it a dog, cat, chicken or horse, my parents would arrange it in such a way that the animal was owned by my sister or relatives, but I got to keep it as

José Aruego: HOSE ay ar u AY go

my own. That way I was able to have a healthy pet. I also remember a time when we had three horses (used for transportation), seven dogs and their puppies, six or seven cats and their kittens, a backyard filled with chickens and roosters, a house of pigeons, frogs, tadpoles and ducks in our miniature rice paddies that had a lot of water lilies, and three very fat pigs that belonged to my sister. This was in our small house in the city. Our leftovers from our meals were always put to very good use. My childhood was kept in the company of animals. I still cannot figure out why I took up law. I guess it is because my father is a lawyer, my sister is a lawyer, and all my friends went to law school. All my friends became very successful businessmen, lawyers and politicians. They were all confused when they found out I was doing children's books.

This December [1976] the Philippine government is paying for my trip to the Philippines so I can accept an award (an enormous trophy) as the Outstanding Filipino Abroad in Arts. I find it unbelievable that my children's books and funny animals enabled me to get this prestigious award which is a great honor. Now my friends, lawyer classmates and professors will be more confused than ever.

––––––––

José Aruego was born and grew up in Manila. He received his Bachelor of Arts degree from the University of the Philippines in 1953 and his LL.B. in 1955, but he soon gave up the law and came to New York. He studied art at Parsons School of Design and received a certificate in Graphic Arts and Advertising in 1959. After that came various jobs in design and advertising agencies until he turned his full attention to children's books in 1968. Mr. Aruego has contributed cartoons to a number of magazines and painted a mural at International House in New York City where he met his wife and future collaborator, Ariane Dewey. They were married from 1961 to 1973 and have one son, Juan.

The works of Aruego and Aruego-Dewey frequently appear on lists of outstanding illustrations. The Children's Book Shows mounted by the American Institute of Graphic Arts usually include at least one title: In 1970 it was *Whose Mouse Are You?* by Robert Kraus; in 1971–72, *A Crocodile's Tale, Look What I Can Do* and *Pilyo the Piranha;* and in 1973–74, *Marie Louise and Christophe,* by Natalie Savage Carlson. *Milton the Early Riser,* by Robert Kraus, received a Brooklyn Art Books for Children Citation in 1975 and was chosen for inclusion in the 1974 Society of Illustrators Show. *Whose Mouse Are You?* was an American Library Association Notable Book in 1970, as were *Mushroom in the Rain,* adapted by Mirra Ginsburg, and Robert Kraus's *Owliver* in 1974. *Look What I Can Do* was one of the New York *Times's* choices of best-illustrated books in 1970, and it was also included in the Children's Book Showcase for 1972, as were *The Chick and the Duckling* in 1973 and *Owliver* in 1975.

SELECTED WORKS WRITTEN AND ILLUSTRATED: The King and His Friends, 1969; Juan and the Asuangs, 1970; Symbiosis: A Book of Unusual Friendships, 1970; Look What I Can Do, 1971; Pilyo the Piranha, 1971.

SELECTED WORKS ILLUSTRATED. Parakeets and Peach Pies, by Ray Smith, 1970; Toucans Two, by Jack Prelutsky, 1970; Whose Mouse Are You? by Robert Kraus, 1970; Leo the Late Bloomer, by Robert Kraus, 1971; What Is Pink? by Christina Rossetti, 1971; Good Night, by Elizabeth Coatsworth, 1972.

SELECTED WORKS WRITTEN WITH ARIANE ARUEGO: A Crocodile's Tale, 1972.

SELECTED WORKS ILLUSTRATED WITH ARIANE DEWEY: (as Ariane Aruego) The Chick and the Duckling, by Vladimir G. Suteyev, adapted by Mirra Ginsburg, 1972; (as Ariane Aruego) Milton the Early Riser, by Robert Kraus, 1972; Herman the Helper, by Robert Kraus, 1974; Marie Louise and Christophe, by Natalie Savage Carlson, 1974; Mushroom in the Rain, by Vladimir G. Suteyev, translated and adapted by Mirra Ginsburg, 1974; Owliver, by Robert Kraus, 1974; How the Sun Was Brought Back to the Sky, adapted by Mirra Ginsburg, 1975;

Marie Louise's Heyday, by Natalie Savage
Carlson, 1975; Three Friends, by Robert
Kraus, 1975; Boris Bad Enough, by Robert
Kraus, 1976; Two Greedy Bears, adapted
by Mirra Ginsburg, 1976; If Dragonflies
Make Honey, edited by David Kherdian,
1976.

ABOUT: Contemporary Authors, Vol. 37–
40; Something about the Author, Vol. 6;
Language Arts May 1977; Wilson Library
Bulletin October 1973.

HONOR ARUNDEL

August 15, 1919–June 8, 1973

AUTHOR OF A *Family Failing*, etc.

Biographical sketch of Honor Morfydd
Arundel McCrindle by Joan Lingard:

HONOR ARUNDEL

HONOR ARUNDEL was born and
brought up on a small estate in North
Wales, the fifth in a family of six children; she was educated at a boarding
school in Kent and at Somerville College,
Oxford. When she left Oxford she went
to work in London, first as a typist and
then a journalist on the *Daily Worker*.
During the war she was employed on the
shop floor of an aircraft repair factory;
afterwards she became a film critic,
which resulted, as she said, in her being
put off films for life!

She had three daughters, one by her
first marriage and twins by her second to
the Scottish actor Alex McCrindle. This
marriage was happy and lasting; and I
know that she valued it greatly. In 1953
she moved with her family to Scotland,
to which she became passionately attached. During her last few years she
divided her time between a top flat in
an eighteenth-century building overlooking the esplanade of Edinburgh Castle,
and a cottage in a little village in the
border county of Berwickshire, again
dominated by a castle set on a hill. The
house in Edinburgh was the setting for
The High House, the first of Honor's
books about Emma; the cottage provided the background for *The Longest
Weekend*. She loved going to the cottage, either with her family or alone; it
was there that she appeared to be most

relaxed, and it was this place she
chose to retreat to when she became
seriously ill. In the country she had
peace in which to write and read, to
walk and garden, and in the evenings to
listen to music, one of her greatest pleasures.

It was only relatively late in life—
about ten years before her death—that
she began to write for children. She had
always written poetry and plays, but it
was with her juvenile books that she had
most success and became an established
writer of repute. Of her beginnings in
this field she wrote:

"My first children's book was written
to entertain my two youngest daughters
who had gobbled up all the old favorites
and every Puffin as it came out, ran-
sacked the public library, and still demanded 'something to read.' Our tastes
happily coincided because while we all
enjoyed Impossibility—magic, fairies, the
Borrowers—we hated Improbability—
jewel thieves, secret passages, incognito
princesses. What we wanted more of
were stories about ordinary children who
lived at home, went to school, quar-
relled, had problems with their parents:
domestic realism I suppose you might
call it but with, I hope, an awareness of
social and world problems."

Honor's daughters were her sternest

but most encouraging critics. As they grew older, so did the central characters in her books; and when they entered Edinburgh University, she wrote *The Terrible Temptation*. She was immensely proud of her girls and involved with their lives, without ever seeking to live through them. She was interested in their activities, their friends, their problems, and I believe it was this deep interest which gave her the insight and understanding that illumine her books about teenagers.

Honor wrote with integrity and honor, just as she lived. She was an extremely fine person, having great loyalty to family and friends and a generosity that made her rejoice in the success of others, an attribute not always to be found in writers. I remember her saying, "If one of us does well, then it will be better for all of us." It was she who encouraged me to begin writing for children, to come on to her territory, as it were, and she was genuinely delighted with any success I had.

In addition, her courage was enormous, enabling her to face up to the knowledge of her approaching death. Suspecting, she insisted on knowing, for it had always been her code to face reality squarely and not to shirk the truth. I think she felt that it would have reduced the quality of her life if she had not been able to accept her death with dignity. *The Blanket Word*, in which Jan Meredith's mother dies of cancer, was written after Honor had been told that she had an incurable cancer. She continued to write and be interested in life in all its varieties right up to the end.

Her early death at the age of fifty-three was a sad loss for children's literature as well as for all those who knew and cared for her. Her most fitting memorial is her collection of books, eleven novels for young people, which continue to be read and appreciated all over the world; and I know that, from that alone, she would have taken great comfort.

———

A Family Failing won the Scottish Arts Council's Writing Award in 1972. Although Honor Arundel never received any of the major awards or prizes given for children's books, her work consistently appeared on the lists of the excellent compiled on both sides of the Atlantic.

SELECTED WORKS: The High House, 1968; The Two Sisters, 1969; Emma's Island, 1970; Green Street, 1970; The Longest Weekend, 1970; The Girl in the Opposite Bed, 1971; The Terrible Temptation, 1971; The Amazing Mr. Prothero, 1972; Emma in Love, 1972; A Family Failing, 1972; The Blanket Word, 1973.

ABOUT: Author's and Writer's Who's Who, 1971; Contemporary Authors, Vol. 21–22; Something about the Author, Vol. 4; Junior Bookshelf December 1973; Publishers Weekly July 2, 1973; Signal January 1973.

FRANK ASCH

August 6, 1946–

AUTHOR AND ILLUSTRATOR OF *Elvira Everything*, etc.

Autobiographical sketch of Frank Asch:

I WAS born in New Jersey August 6, 1946. A country kid, I played in the nearby woods, following the brook and splashing water spiders about. In school I vacillated among sitting near the window so I could look out, in the back where I wouldn't be noticed so I could play with marbles under my desk, or up front where I knew I would have to pay attention.

Except for a large apple tree that I drew in first grade, and for which I was effusively praised, I did not receive any encouragement in art or writing until I got to high school. I still remember with pride the day I walked into the art room and saw a whole bulletin board of my drawings entitled FRANK ASCH—ONE-MAN SHOW.

Art school in New York City was a total farce, yet somehow a beautiful one,

Asch: *ASH*

Frank Asch

a hodgepodge of growing up, down and sideways, in and out of galleries and studios, Chinese restaurants and lecture halls. . . .

Since school, I've lived in New York and spent some time in California and India pursuing my interest in yoga.

My book, *Gia and the 100 Dollars Worth of Bubble Gum* reflects that interest, as all my other books reflect some situation or personage in my life. The George in *George's Store* is a lot like my Uncle Jack. Linda is a lot like one of my most cheerful friends. *I Met a Penguin* was inspired by the pet names that I shared with a girl friend. *Elvira Everything* was undoubtedly influenced by the fact that I lived on Ludlow Street, a center for the wholesale toy business and my forthcoming book of poems called *City Sandwich* also comes out of the years I spent living in New York City and the fascination that the city still holds for me. And, of course, I did have a dog called Rebecka.

I have found it very useful in my work to keep in close contact with kids. To that end I have taught in a Montessori preschool, done puppetry and children's theater, and work as a library storyteller.

———

Frank Asch studied at Pratt Institute and Cooper Union, where he received a B.A. in painting. He has also been trained as a Montessori teacher and taught in a Montessori school in New Jersey and in a public grammar school in India. He now lives in Bridgewater, New Jersey, in the house where he was born. With his wife, Janani, who is also a Montessori-trained teacher, Mr. Asch performs in story-theater productions for children in schools and libraries in their neighborhood and nearby states. Calling themselves the Bellybuttons, the Asches write their material themselves, with Mrs. Asch doing the music.

Mr. Asch says that he became interested in children's books while he was at Cooper Union, being first attracted to the subject by the work of Maurice Sendak. His *Yellow, Yellow*, with illustrations by Mark Alan Stamaty, and *Elvira Everything* were each mentioned in the year of their publication in *Publishers Weekly* as children's books to be remembered. Frank Asch's work was also selected for inclusion in the 1971-72 show mounted by the American Institute of Graphic Arts.

SELECTED WORKS WRITTEN AND ILLUS-TRATED: George's Store, 1969; Linda, 1969; Elvira Everything, 1970; The Blue Balloon, 1971; Rebecka, 1972; I Met a Penguin, 1972; In the Eye of the Teddy, 1973; Gia and the Hundred Dollars Worth of Bubble-gum, 1974; Monkey Face, 1977.

SELECTED WORKS WRITTEN: Yellow, Yellow, 1971; Good Lemonade, 1976.

ANN ATWOOD

February 12, 1913–

AUTHOR AND ILLUSTRATOR OF *Haiku: The Mood of Earth*

Autobiographical sketch of Ann Atwood:

IT seems irrelevant to begin by saying, "I was born in a tiny town in the hot southern desert of California." For I

have no recollection of the time, and since that day I have been born many times in many places.

But about my childhood. . . . My mother died in childbirth when I was four, and my father, blind with grief and ill with rheumatic fever, soon married my mother's sister. My stepmother's credo could be stated in one word: duty. This must have made it possible to assume the burden of three small children, a mother paralyzed by a sudden stroke, and a sister who needed to share her home and whose nature stood in direct opposition to hers.

This was our basic household, give or take the comings and goings of aunts and uncles and the annual winter stays of my grandfather, who beat us all at dominoes every night. My stepmother was as stern as my aunt was lenient, and I soon learned what I am sure most children learn, that only secret worlds are safe. As I grew older, I became aware that adults share this same knowledge. My father spent a great deal of his time at home in a cramped, square darkroom three flights up in the attic. He had built everything in it, the long sink, the wooden tanks, the ingenious enlarger. It could be entered through a dark angular maze of narrow walls scented with the

acid smell of hypo and other chemicals. I loved to feel my way through the black passages to find my father rocking a tray under a dim amber light and waiting for images to magically appear on the wet blank paper. He was a silent, sensitive man and his company never failed to comfort me. And though our secret worlds merged in a lightless room, it was my father who taught me to watch the shifting variations of light on an object as one watches the changing expressions on people's faces.

In spite of this magic and mystery I followed a traditional pattern. I took a major in English literature and a minor in education at the University of Redlands. A book of my poems Being Made of Earth was published, and I founded a creative writing class at the adult night school in Riverside. But I was obsessed with light and with the purity of expressions on children's faces, and after attending the Art Center School of Photography in Los Angeles I opened a studio in children's portraiture. My father lived to see the success of this venture and the building of my own studio in San Marino.

Now that life is over and I live by the sea, working out of the deepest center of myself. Writing is extremely difficult for me, as I have not had the long years of a writer's discipline. It was not until my mid fifties that my first book, The Little Circle, with my own brief text, launched me into an entirely unpremeditated career in children's literature. Now, in struggling to write, I find I have shunned words in favor of immediate absorption of experience. I have been satisfied with grasping the essence of things without trying to define them, and this does not make for facile writing. It does, however, serve a photographer well, for light is often closer to truth than language, and when one speaks with light the spirit can be touched without the censorship of the mind. So my books are books of color photographs with narration that seeks to lead the reader as deeply into the picture as he can travel. Sometimes the words seem almost to interrupt and sometimes they seem able to transport thought beyond the boundaries of the pictures. It is this interplay, the ebbing and flowing from words to photographs, that becomes a separate substance finally taking on its own motion and tempo.

This emergence of an independent rhythm seems to apply particularly to filmstrips where the meshing of words and pictures is so tight that one becomes the other. And it is in this unity that I find my deepest satisfaction.

———

Ann Atwood's books and the filmstrips she has made in conjunction with them have received many honors. Among those gathered by *New Moon Cove* was the designation Honor Book for Illustration in the Boston *Globe–Horn Book* Festival in 1969, and the Award for Illustration made by the Southern California Council on Literature for Children and Young People in 1970. *Haiku: The Mood of Earth* was on the *Horn Book* Honor List in 1971 and considered one of the Best Books of the Year by *School Library Journal*. In 1972 the Southern California Council on Literature for Children and Young People gave *Haiku: The Mood of Earth* its first double award for a book and a filmstrip with the citation: "A Distinguished Contribution to the Fusion of Poetry and Photography."

SELECTED WORKS WRITTEN AND ILLUSTRATED: The Little Circle, 1967; New Moon Cove, 1969; The Wild Young Desert, 1970; Haiku: The Mood of Earth, 1971; The Kingdom of the Forest, 1972; My Own Rhythm, 1973; Haiku Vision, 1977.

SELECTED WORKS ILLUSTRATED: Sammy, the Crow Who Remembered, by Elizabeth Hazelton, 1969; (with Erica Anderson) For All That Lives: With Words of Albert Schweitzer, 1975.

Gillian Avery

GILLIAN AVERY

September 30, 1926–

AUTHOR OF *The Elephant War*, etc.
Autobiographical sketch of Gillian Elise Avery Cockshut:

WHEN I am asked why my books all have a Victorian background, the only reason I can find is that the upbringing of middle-class English children in the 1930s more nearly resembled a Victorian than a modern one. We were acutely conscious of class differences (especially differences in accent); we were easily quelled by authority; we were shy and awkward with adults; above all, we took a long time to grow up (I was still preoccupied with my dollshouse when I was thirteen).

I was born in 1926 in Redhill, the rather seedy offshoot of the pleasant old Surrey town of Reigate. Nowadays it is only saved from being an outer ring of London by the North Downs which stand between, but then London seemed much further off, a place to which my father traveled by train every day in a bowler hat and a dark suit, with a beautifully rolled umbrella. We saw very little of him; it was our mother who mattered. She took us on our rare and exciting trips to London and our far more frequent picnics and expeditions in the Surrey countryside. Our world was a small and a very happy one, bounded by the distance that our bikes would carry us (we had no car) or that we could get on a sixpenny bus ride.

We all went to private schools in the district. In middle-class Surrey in the 1930s to send your children to a state school would have meant complete loss of caste, so my parents struggled to pay fees they could ill afford. My school was housed in a splendid Neo-Palladian mansion that an Edwardian millionaire had built for himself, surrounded with superb grounds, and I realize now that the pleasure I got from this has far outweighed the benefits I might have gained from a better education.

My best subject at school had always been English, but nobody knew what I ought to do with this; the school never sent anybody to university and could not have taught up to that level. I thought vaguely that I might become a journalist, but after three years on the local paper, the Surrey *Mirror* (where the staff was endlessly patient and kind) I realized that I must abandon my ambition of Fleet Street and a daily newspaper. Even a weekly paper was too fast for me; what I needed was something that came out once a year. A publisher's office might be more my mark.

So I went first to Chambers's Encyclopaedia, which was then being revised, and then in 1950 to the Clarendon Press at Oxford. What Hollywood had been to some of my contemporaries, Oxford had always been to me. I thought of it with awed fascination and I had never dared hope that I would ever live there, far less that I would ever marry into it, so as to speak. But in 1952 I married Anthony Cockshut, then a research fellow at Balliol College, to whom I owe all the education that I failed to get at school and any knowledge that I have acquired about the Victorian period. (He even tried to teach me Greek and bridge, but I failed him there.) After ten years in Manchester we are back in Oxford where he teaches in the university, where our daughter is an undergraduate. The years in Manchester were on the whole happy ones, though at the time it was a great wrench leaving Oxford. In fact, it

was my homesickness for Oxford that made me settle down to try to evoke it in my first book, *The Warden's Niece*. But as soon as we got back to Oxford I began writing about Manchester!

————

Gillian Avery is married to Anthony Oliver John Cockshut, a fellow at Hertford College, Oxford, and G. M. Young Lecturer in English Literature in the University. Mr. Cockshut's specialty is the Victorian period. Their daughter, who was born in 1957, is Ursula Mary Elise, nicknamed Shenka.

Gillian Avery has steeped herself so deeply in the Victorian period and writes of it with such authority and feeling that her work has been likened to that of the still popular Victorian author E. Nesbit. While she was living in Manchester, where her husband was teaching at Manchester Grammar School, Gillian Avery wrote *A Likely Lad*, a turn-of-the-century story of a Lancashire boy who successfully resists his family's ambitious plans for him and finds his own place in the world. This novel achieved the distinction of being runner-up in 1971 for one of Britain's most prestigious children's book awards, the Carnegie Medal, and winning the other in 1972 when Miss Avery received the Manchester *Guardian*'s Award for Children's Fiction.

Besides her novels, Gillian Avery has compiled five anthologies, written a biography of the well-known nineteenth century author Mrs. Ewing, and is editor of a series of Victorian children's classics. Not surprisingly, she is also a collector of Victorian children's books.

SELECTED WORKS: Victorian People; in Life and Literature, 1970; A Likely Lad, 1971; The Elephant War, 1971; The Italian Spring, 1972; To Tame a Sister, 1973; The Echoing Green: Memories of Victorian Youth, 1974; Ellen and the Queen, 1975.

SELECTED WORKS EDITED: Victorian Doll Stories, 1969.

ABOUT: Author's and Writer's Who's Who, 1963; Contemporary Authors, Vol. 9–10; Manchester Guardian March 23, 1972.

NATALIE BABBITT

July 28, 1932–

AUTHOR AND ILLUSTRATOR OF *The Search for Delicious,* etc.

Autobiographical sketch of Natalie Zane Moore Babbitt:

I WAS born in Ohio in 1932, the middle of the Great Depression, and the first eighteen years of my life were punctuated by family moves here and there within the state in what must have been an effort to recover some of the security we had known before the Crash. There was something indomitable about my parents, however. We always managed to have a good time, and my mother saw most of her careful plans for my sister and me come remarkably close to full realization. She was a promising painter and writer, though she early gave up her ambitions, but she saw to it that my interest in drawing was encouraged in every way.

I did not in those days ever think of writing; I wanted to be an illustrator, specifically an illustrator of books for children, because books played a very large part in my life as a child. I read endlessly, mostly fairy tales and myth, and was read *to,* as well, and those stories made a deep and lasting impression on my imagination. I was blessed with continued encouragement from teachers in secondary school and went on to major in art at Smith College. There was a long wait before my work began, however, for I married Samuel Fisher Babbitt right after my graduation in 1954 and spent the next ten years raising three children up to school age.

My first book was written by my husband, and I made the pictures for it. It seemed like a very promising collaboration. But we came to Clinton, New York, soon after its publication, where my husband took on the many and heavy duties of a college president. So—since he had no more time for writing, I decided I'd have to do it myself.

Now writing is far more important to me than illustrating, for it seems clear that the things I have to say I can say much more effectively with words than I ever could with pictures, in spite of old maxims to the contrary. I spend as much time as I can at my work, every morning when possible, though I must at the same time cope with the constant demands of a messy house, three cats and an uninhibited dog. My children are grown now and have their own lives— Christopher is twenty-one, Tom is eighteen, and Lucy is seventeen—but since I do a little teaching at Kirkland College and have, in addition, certain duties as that strange person, the wife of a college president, I remain something of a juggler.

I am often asked why I do not write books for adults. But this question invariably comes from people who do not understand that only in a child's book can a writer take advantage of the widest range of symbolism, express a basic optimism, and have at his disposal the whole vast richness that only fantasy can offer. By comparison, adult fiction— at least in its present state—seems barren and constricted.

I take my work—and my audience— very seriously and try hard to be a good craftsman. But I have a good time with it, too. For me, at least, it is the most satisfying work in the world.

———

The Search for Delicious was greeted by children's book reviewers on all sides as the first major work of an exciting new talent. This book and Natalie Babbitt's subsequent ones have consistently achieved a place on the major lists of outstanding children's books in the year of their publication. *Kneeknock Rise, The Devil's Storybook, Tuck Everlasting,* and *More Small Poems* (by Valerie Worth, illustrated by Mrs. Babbitt) were all American Library Association Notable Books for Children. *Kneeknock Rise* was a Newbery Honor Book in 1971; *Goody Hall* was chosen an Honor Book in the 1971 *Book World* Children's Spring Book Festival; and *The Devil's Storybook* was nominated for a National Book Award in 1975. In addition, two Babbitt books have been selected for inclusion in the Children's Book Council's Children's Book Showcase: *Goody Hall* in 1972 and *More Small Poems* in 1977.

Mrs. Babbitt (who is distantly related to Zane Grey) teaches writing for children and book illustration at Kirkland College, a women's liberal arts college established in 1966, of which her husband is president.

SELECTED WORKS WRITTEN AND ILLUSTRATED: Dick Foote and the Shark, 1967; Phoebe's Revolt, 1968; The Search for Delicious, 1969; Kneeknock Rise, 1970; The Something, 1970; Goody Hall, 1971; The Devil's Storybook, 1974; Tuck Everlasting, 1975; The Eyes of the Amaryllis, 1977.

SELECTED WORKS ILLUSTRATED: The Forty-ninth Magician, by Samuel Fisher Babbitt, 1966; Small Poems, by Valerie Worth, 1972; More Small Poems, by Valerie Worth, 1976.

ABOUT: Contemporary Authors, Vol. 49–52; Something about the Author, Vol. 6.

ENID BAGNOLD

October 27, 1889–

AUTHOR OF *National Velvet,* etc.

ENID BAGNOLD

Biographical sketch of Enid Algerine Bagnold Jones:

ENID BAGNOLD, born in Rochester, Kent, in 1889, once summed up her career for a reporter as "Simply writing. From the age of nine." It was when she was nine, in fact, that her parents moved to Jamaica (her father was a colonel in the Royal Engineers) and the three years that followed seem to have had a lasting effect on her imagination as a writer.

"The impact of a tropical place on a child of nine," she wrote, "has given me a nostalgia ever since, and has been an underlying thing in my mind that I settle on, like a sort of pollen, whenever my imagination is 'feeding.'"

Perhaps her very first efforts were the poems she remembers writing during the Jamaican period. "My father," she recollected, "was enormously practical, very much of the old school, and when I showed him the poems, he asked me when I'd written them. 'At night, in bed,' I said. 'It's very bad for your health,' he said. 'I want you to promise me not to write more than two a week.'"

Luckily, Miss Bagnold can't have heeded this somewhat dreary prescription, to judge by the steady flow of novels, plays, poems and children's books that bear her name.

When she was twelve, she returned to England and spent the next five years at a school in Godalming (one conducted, incidentally, by the mother of Aldous and Julian Huxley). At the age of seventeen she was sent to a school in Lausanne. This was not a notable success, and she promptly ran away, though in a somewhat decorous fashion, having warned her father of her intention—whereupon he sent a lady courier from Thomas Cook's to escort her home. She remembers herself at this period of her life as being "rather fat and rather highbrow and a bad dancer."

At nineteen she went to study drawing and painting at Walter Sickert's school in Camden Town, London, and about the same time became a suffragette. Her friends at that time included Henry Gaudier-Brzeska, Lovat Fraser, Katherine Mansfield, and Ralph Hodgson.

In 1914, when war broke out, she enrolled in the V.A.D. (Voluntary Aid Detachment) and was assigned to the Royal Herbert Hospital, Woolwich; after two years there, she wrote *A Diary Without Dates*, a novel based on her experiences and critical of the hospital. This was considered a breach of military discipline and resulted in her dismissal. Next, she joined the F.A.N.Y. (First Aid Nursing Yeomanry) and was sent to join the French army as a driver. "Attached to a garage of a hundred French men drivers," she wrote, "our unit led the isolated and rather fantastic life of a dozen men on a boat." Toward the end of the war she became the first woman to be sent as a driver to Verdun. Her wartime experiences were recounted in her novel *The Happy Foreigner*.

In 1920, Enid Bagnold married Sir Roderick Jones, chairman of Reuter's News Agency, and entered into a busy social life which did not, however, stop her from writing for three hours every morning, something she has contrived to do since the age of twenty. Five years after her marriage, she wrote *Serena Blandish*, a novel that so shocked her conservative father that she decided, for his sake, to publish it under the quaintly eighteenth-century pseudonym, "A Lady of Quality." "Soon after the book came out," Miss Bagnold said, "I overheard one man mention the name Blandish to another at a dinner party and asked what they were talking about. 'Not for your young ears, my dear,' one said."

Enid Bagnold has four children, and her two children's books, *Alice and Thomas and Jane* and *National Velvet*, were both illustrated, with a quirky grace, by her daughter Laurian, aged eight at the time of the first book's publication, thirteen by the time *National Velvet* appeared—nearly the same age as Velvet, the spindly, dreamy heroine of the book, a butcher's daughter who yearns for a horse and then, after winning one in a raffle, goes on to win the Grand National. In 1944, the story was made into a Metro-Goldwyn-Mayer film, starring Elizabeth Taylor.

It is as a playwright that Enid Bagnold is best known today, and of her plays the most successful to date has been *The Chalk Garden*, for which she won the Award of Merit for drama of the American Academy of Arts and Letters. A film version of the play appeared in 1964.

A widow since 1962, Enid Bagnold now divides her time between her house in London and one in Rottingdean, in Sussex. She lists her recreations as "gardening, cooking and dressmaking—anything done by my hands."

SELECTED WORKS: Alice and Thomas and Jane, 1931; National Velvet, 1935.

ABOUT: Author's and Writer's Who's Who, 1963; Bagnold, Enid. Enid Bagnold's Autobiography, 1969; Contemporary Authors, Vol. 7–8; Current Biography, 1964; Twentieth Century Authors; Twentieth Century Authors (First Supplement); Something about the Author, Vol. 1; Who's Who in America, 1972–73; Who's Who of American Women, 1972–73; Who's Who of American Women, 1974–75; New Yorker January 19, 1952; Theatre Arts January 1974.

MARGARET BALDERSON

August 9, 1935–

AUTHOR OF *When Jays Fly to Bárbmo.*

Autobiographical sketch of Margaret Balderson:

I WAS born in the western suburbs of Sydney and it was probably because I had few companions of my own age living nearby that I took to scribbling and daydreaming at quite an early age. *When Jays Fly to Bárbmo* was really a direct, though long delayed, result of both these youthful "activities."

I was probably no more than about eight when I first discovered that putting words together could be fun. It could be more than fun—a kind of private adventure, in fact. Looking back I am convinced that only a very few of my other childhood experiences ever equalled this marvelous discovery. I was also probably no more than about eight when someone pointed out to me that the name "Balderson" sounded Norwegian. For some reason I was delighted, and I must have decided there and then that I wanted to go to Norway.

Over the years these two interests developed rather than diminished. I wrote poetry, plays and short stories. I used words with gay abandon, sometimes in impossible combinations, completely disregarding (or perhaps blissfully unaware of) such sobering restraints as discipline, sentence structure, precise meanings of words, current literary fashions and all the other things that one must come to terms with when attempting to write seriously in later life.

Simultaneously I progressed from Asbjörnsen and Moe to Norse myths and legends and from these to Sigrid Undset and Ibsen. Grieg's A minor concerto and "Peer Gynt" were played ad nauseam on the record player. By the time I had discovered that my claim to Norwegian ancestry was pretty remote and that any Norwegian blood that might be flowing through my veins could probably only be detected with a microscope (it seems

MARGARET BALDERSON

that "Balderson" may have dated back to the Viking invasion of England and even this much is not certain), it was already too late.

I went to Norway in 1963 and remained there for the best part of two years. I spent my summers traveling and my winters washing dishes since I am bad at languages and this was one of the few occupations where linguistic expertise was not required. I have washed dishes in many countries. However, towards the end of this two-year period I did manage to get a job in the Tromsö Public Library and so was able to experience something of the long, dark northern winter. This short episode in my life I will never forget.

Up until this time I had no conception of the word "season." In the part of Australia where I came from, spring, summer, autumn and winter all blended into one another with very little apparent change. It grew colder or it grew warmer. A few trees shed their leaves, but these were largely the imported British varieties struggling in suburban back yards. And this was all that ever happened. The people didn't change much, either, from one season to another, and it was the impression of the profound impact that each dramatic Nordic season made upon the personalities of the people of the far north that remained with me long after other memories had dimmed.

I did not go to Norway with the idea of writing a book, but not long after I returned home the idea began to assert itself. There were so many things that I wanted to tell people, but somehow they were not the sort of things that could be adequately expressed in normal conversation. And so *When Jays Fly to Bárbmo* began to take shape.

When I returned to Sydney I found I could no longer live in a concrete jungle. I had lived in too many remote places. I live in a small flat and much of this space is taken up by an old English sheepdog called George, who has found his way into a book. I now live in Mittagong, New South Wales, where I am employed as house mistress/librarian.

———

Margaret Balderson had gone to Europe in 1963 with a group of friends, and once there, decided to branch off to Norway. On her way home she stopped off in Israel to work on a kibbutz for a few months, then made her way back to Australia across Asia. She now works in a library where she is very much involved in the children's section. She is currently working on another novel and when she feels the need to escape, she enjoys going bushwalking.

When Jays Fly to Bárbmo received the Australian Book of the Year Award from the Australian Children's Book Council in 1969. It was runner-up for England's Carnegie Medal the same year. *A Dog Called George* (Oxford, 1975) was highly commended for the Australian Book of the Year Award in 1976.

SELECTED WORKS: When Jays Fly to Bárbmo, 1969.

ABOUT: Contemporary Authors, Vol. 25–28.

"ZACHARY BALL"

June 16, 1897–

AUTHOR OF *Bristle Face*, etc.

Autobiographical sketch of Kelly Ray Masters, who writes under the pen name of "Zachary Ball":

I WAS born in the Blackjack Hills of Missouri some four miles west of the small town of Princeton. When I was six my parents, along with my father's family, moved to Kansas, to farms east of the small town of Altoona, an area called Five Mounds.

At age eight I started to school at the little white one-room Five Mounds School, which was just across the road from our house. And I learned to read the words: "The cat sees the rat." A diphtheria epidemic swept that area that autumn, 1905, and took many children, including my baby sister.

When I was ten my parents moved to Altoona, and I started at town school, and the country boy was very frightened that first day where there was such a monstrous crowd of kids—probably 125. At that age I worked in summer driving town residents' cows to and from pasturage at the edge of town. And I also worked as "water monkey" with a pipeline crew of which my father was foreman.

By the time I was thirteen, we had moved to Kansas City, Missouri, where I attended Van Horn Elementary School. I dropped out of school at the starting of seventh grade to help keep food on the table. I worked at a packing plant, a wooden box factory, and a furniture factory, all located in what was known as the West Bottoms, in Kansas City, Kansas.

We then moved to St. Joseph, Missouri, where I again, at age fifteen, worked in a furniture factory. Then, leaving that job, I went to work as a bellhop at the St. Charles Hotel there. It was located across the street from the Crystal Theater, which booked Orpheum and

"ZACHARY BALL"

Pantages vaudeville with change of program weekly. I never missed a bill change. By some of the hotel help I was called stagestruck, which I was.

I worked at the hotel until the middle of my seventeenth year. That summer a permanent stock company opened an engagement in an airdrome on Fredrick Avenue. Being still stagestruck, I was present at their first performance—and every succeeding one.

By a strange fluke, in two or three weeks I had a job with a small tent repertory show playing Missouri small towns. I was paid four dollars per week, with food furnished and a cot to sleep on, to be on the stage of the little tent theater. I was making more per day as a bellhop—but this was show business!

There followed twenty-five years touring the Midwest with theater and tent "rep" shows, playing week stands. At that time there were some five hundred such tent shows playing from the Mexican to the Canadian borders every summer. Some of my experiences during those years are told in my book *Tent Show*. In addition to the small-town shows, I also played stock engagements in many cities: Denver, Pueblo, Atlanta, Miami, Tampa, and others.

During the last seven years of my acting career, my brother and I played

schools and colleges with small dramatic units. Then Pearl Harbor and gas rationing put an end to our traveling. Untrained in anything except acting, I was then forty-five and a bit old for bellhopping. I started trying to write fiction, with my six grades of formal education. I had always had a desire to write. I got a job delivering morning newspapers in residential areas to sustain my wife, son and myself.

I found fiction writing not too difficult when the understanding came to me that to write a story I was, in imagination, acting in a play and creating the play as I played my part. I had written a few plays in the past, for use with my own show only.

My first sales were to western pulp magazines. Then the Lord put his hand on my shoulder it seemed, and I began selling to *Saturday Evening Post, Collier's, Country Gentleman, Esquire, Blue Book* and several lesser markets.

When the magazines began folding I switched to books for young people, designed for school libraries. I have had seventeen youth books published and two adult novels. My youth books are in school libraries in the United States, Canada, Europe, and Australia.

Now at age seventy-seven, I plug along at writing, and I also spend some time talking to school classes, without charge. My theme is *good* reading, and my efforts stem from a desire to try to encourage kids to become good readers. My heart is very much in this work for I possess a deep and sincere love of kids everywhere.

————

Born Kelly Ray Masters, Zachary Ball assumed his pseudonym when he began his writing career. In 1931 he married Gladys Green and they have two children, a son, Kelly Ray, Jr., and a daughter, Mrs. Charles Becker.

Bristle Face, an Honor Book in the New York *Herald Tribune* Children's Spring Book Festival in 1962 and an American Library Association Notable Book for that year, went on to win the

Dorothy Canfield Fisher Memorial Children's Book Award in 1964 and the William Allen White Children's Book Award in 1965. Subsequently it was filmed by Walt Disney Studios and aired on NBC television.

SELECTED WORKS: Swamp Chief, 1952; Bar Pilot, 1955; Skin Diver, 1956; Young Mike Fink, 1958; North to Abilene, 1960; Salvage Diver, 1961; Kep, 1961; Bristle Face, 1962; Sputters, 1963; Tent Show, 1964.

ABOUT: Author's and Writer's Who's Who, 1971; Contemporary Authors, Vol. 3; Current Biography 1953; Something about the Author, Vol. 3.

BARBARA BARTOS-HÖPPNER

November 4, 1923–

AUTHOR OF *The Cossacks*, etc.

Autobiographical sketch of Barbara Bartos-Höppner, translated from the German:

I BELONG to that generation whose childhood was forcibly ended by the Second World War and who saw themselves transplanted abruptly into the world of the grown-ups. Plans and dreams had to give way to necessities. Only sometimes were they discussed hopefully in the privacy of home. And the more improbable their realization became, the harder I believed in them and the more assiduously I performed the duties that fell to my lot in the family hotel after the death of my father.

I was born in Eckersdorf in Silesia, where on Sunday in Lent there was the joyous custom of singing summer in. With little baskets in one hand, in the other the summer wand, a staff bedecked with colored flowers and ribbons, we children went from house to house to banish winter with our songs and sing the summer in. In 1952—by then I was living in Hamburg—I described such a summer sing out of the memories of my childhood and knew I was then on my way as an author writing of and for young people.

Bartos-Höppner: *BAR toz HERP ner*

That was also the year in which I married my husband, Christoph Bartos, and our son Burghard was born. Since then I have written more than thirty books, and as I write down this number so coolly I wonder how that was ever possible, when I was a housewife and mother too. I might be in the middle of *The Cossacks*, say—in my imagination slipping back four hundred years. The conquest of Siberia might be at stake or I could be standing with the Irish princess Grainne in the Bay of Castelraine and listening to the shriek of the gulls. Wouldn't it be just then that it was time to put the house in order! No, it was far more important to describe how the peat fire that will not burn tastes on the tongue or to follow the track of a bear or to tell of little Marino who climbed every summer to his father in the mountains of the Gran Paradiso, to the eagles, the chamois, and the mountain goats. To be sure, a writing mother certainly has it harder than a writing father, for even if she restricts it to the minimum, the mother still has to look after the family. On that account the first two thirds of each book take ten times as long as the last third, at which point I can no longer be disturbed.

I really wonder that I always embark on the adventure of writing a book again, although I know the difficulties well enough: not to be able to get on with a story at all, for example, or my innate laziness, which is on the lookout for any interruption. At times when I'd like to make an end to a manuscript, any interruption is welcome. A visit somewhere, or the invitation to a reading trip, which then takes me away for weeks at a time from my new house in Nottensdorf, a little village in the vicinity of Hamburg.

Readings are fun. One gets to hear a great deal from the children and from book people. "Why do you write historical books?" "Because for me history is just as living as the present and because I think about how people must have had to deal with their times." Children always want to know quite different things besides: how long it takes to write a book and—practical as they are—how much one earns at it. I found touching the question of one youngster, obviously thinking of his own composition worries, "But what do you do if you write and write and the book will not finish?"

One learns much from these lecture hours, and after the many I have behind me I no longer believe anyone who asserts that children's books are superfluous because the older children, from twelve years up, are ready to go over to grown-up literature. That is to say, I have never believed this. Not because I want to keep on writing books for young people but because I have played so many question-and-answer games with audiences of this age. (Too bad I never once met anyone there who propounded the idea of "superfluous young people's books.")

I like to write—that I should say quietly in closing. Two kinds of writing occasion all kinds of anxiety dreams for me though: blurbs for my books and writing about myself. What is there to confess? In the spring I uncover the roses in our garden, in summer I pick our cherries, in fall I look for hazelnuts under the hedge, and in winter, when I sit by the fireplace, I crack them open for my dog. I think I lead a very ordinary life.

————

The Cossacks received the New York *Herald Tribune* Spring Children's Book Festival Award in 1963 and was an American Library Association Notable Book in the same year. Mrs. Bartos-Höppner's *Die Bucht der schwarzen Boote* (The Bay of the Black Boats) was on the Honors List for the Hans Christian Andersen Award in 1968, and her *Aljoscha und die Bärenmütze* (Aljoscha and the Bearskin Cap) was on the Honor list for the German Children's Book Prize in 1969. Neither of these titles has appeared in the United States.

SELECTED WORKS: The Cossacks, 1963; Save the Khan, 1964; Avalanche Dog, 1967; Storm Over the Caucasus, 1968; Hunters of Siberia, 1969.

ABOUT: Author's and Writer's Who's Who, 1971; Contemporary Authors, Vol. 25–28; Something about the Author, Vol. 5.

NINA BAWDEN

January 19, 1925–

AUTHOR OF *Carrie's War*, etc.

Autobiographical sketch of Nina Mary Mabey Bawden Kark:

I WAS born in an eastern suburb of London, near the docks, and one of my earliest memories is watching my father's ship come in, but being far more interested in a dead pig that was floating, belly upwards, between the ocean liner and the quay. I must have been about four years old because my mother, standing beside me, had my baby brother in her arms, wrapped in a white shawl, and he was born just after my fourth birthday. My mother said, "Look at the ship, can you see Daddy?" but I looked at the dead pig.

My father was a marine engineer and my mother a schoolteacher from a Norfolk village. She hated the dull, flat suburb we lived in and taught me to hate it, but children will find imaginative exercise anywhere and I set the stories I told myself in such unromantic places as the cinder path beside the railway line and a

NINA BAWDEN

shrubbery of dusty laurel bushes at the bottom of our garden.

When I was twelve, the war came. My brother and I were evacuated in a school train, labelled like parcels with our names and addresses hung on cards round our necks, to a mining valley in South Wales. We lived there for three years with a number of foster parents, some nice, some nasty, but chiefly, like Mr. Evans in *Carrie's War*, a mixture of both. Since billets were scarce we had to learn to keep on the right side of our hosts which meant watching them rather more closely and warily than most children need to watch adults. We spent the school holidays with our mother on a Shropshire farm where we were unreservedly, almost lyrically happy. This beautiful county later became the setting for *The White Horse Gang*.

The war, all this time, was something that went on over my head, like adult conversation. When I was seventeen, it came closer: my school returned to London and I finished my education with bombs falling around me. I went to Oxford, took a degree in philosophy, politics, and economics, grew up and got married. Writing had always seemed to me the only possible occupation, and now I began to write in earnest. I published ten novels for adults while my children, Nicholas, Robert, and Perdita,

were born and growing up, but although I often wrote *about* children, I didn't begin to write *for* them until my youngest child was six years old.

I had no intention of writing for any particular age group; I simply wrote the kind of stories I would have liked to read when I was young. Books in which children had adventures, of course—the kind of adventures I had dreamed of, running along the cinder path by the railway, or past the empty park at dusk—but in which the adults were important too, because relationships with adults seemed to be left out of most children's books, and I remembered that when I was young they were most important to me. And I remembered something else, too— something more important, perhaps. Although children inhabit the same world as their parents and teachers, they look at it differently and don't always see what the adults would like them to see. When I write children's books I think of the little girl that was me, standing on the dock side and watching the dead pig in the water, instead of her father's ship coming in.

———

Nina Bawden earned a bachelor's degree with honors from Somerville College, Oxford, in 1946 and a master's degree in 1951. She is a distinguished author of adult books as well as books for children. In 1974 *Carrie's War* was commended for one of Britain's two important children's book awards, the Carnegie Medal, and was a runner-up for the other, the Guardian Award. It was also designated a Notable Book for Children by the American Library Association. In 1976 Miss Bawden won the Guardian Award with *The Peppermint Pig*.

Nina Bawden was married to Austen Steven Kark on August 5, 1954, and has a daughter, Perdita Emily Helena Kark. From a previous marriage she has two sons, Nicholas Bawden and Robert Humphrey Felix Bawden.

She is a member of International P.E.N. and the British Ski Club, a fellow of the Royal Literary Society, and takes an active interest in community affairs as well. Since 1968 she has been a justice of the peace for the County of Surrey.

SELECTED WORKS: Three on the Run, 1965; The White Horse Gang, 1966; The Witch's Daughter, 1966; Handful of Thieves, 1967; Runaway Summer, 1969; Squib, 1971; Carrie's War, 1973; The Peppermint Pig, 1975; Devil by the Sea, 1976.

ABOUT: Jones, Cornelia and Olivia R. Way. British Children's Authors: Interviews at Home; Author's and Writer's Who's Who, 1971; Contemporary Authors, Vol. 17–18; Something about the Author, Vol. 4; Who's Who of American Women, 1974–75; Horn Book June 1974; Signal January 1971.

BYRD BAYLOR

AUTHOR OF *Before You Came This Way,* etc.

Autobiographical sketch of Byrd Baylor:

I HAVE worse faults than not answering biographical questions but not any more consistent ones. I was born in San Antonio. Much of my childhood was spent on ranches in Texas and later in Arizona and Mexico at mines where my father was looking for gold, copper, silver. I must have gone into houses now and then but my memories are all outdoors and I notice now that my books relate to *out*, not in. (I even went to a school in Tucson where I was allowed to sit under a mesquite tree to study.)

I attended the University of Arizona but did not graduate. I live in Tucson now, am not married, have two grown sons.

Sometimes I go other places but the truth is I have to have sun and warmth and mountains so I always come back to the Southwest. Everything (almost everything) I write is regional. Maybe I shouldn't admit it but I never think about what somebody else might like to read. I just write about whatever I care about myself—which usually turns out to be some part of the Southwest. Since I go to Indian ceremonials and search for ancient ruins and Indian treasures (a trea-

sure is an arrowhead, a turquoise bead or a busted pot) and since I happen to feel at home in harsh rough land which has to have its own strange plants and animals and people (me included), these are the things I write about.

———

Byrd Baylor lives in Tucson, Arizona, where she is the executive secretary of the Association of Papago Affairs. Although she has not won a major award, her books have several times come very close to it and they are often to be found on lists of distinguished books. *When Clay Sings,* with illustrations by Tom Bahti, was a Caldecott Honor Book in 1972, as was *The Desert Is Theirs,* illustrated by Peter Parnall, in 1976. *The Desert Is Theirs* was awarded the Fifth Annual Award for Excellence for juvenile literature of the Southwest by the Border Regional Library Association and received Honorable Mention for the New York Academy of Science's 1976 Science Book Award. It also received a Brooklyn Art Books for Children citation for 1977. *Before You Came This Way* was considered an outstanding book of 1969 by the New York *Times,* and *When Clay Sings* was named one of the Best Books for Spring 1972 by *School Library Journal* and was included on the *Horn Book* Honor List. *Before You Came This Way, When Clay Sings, Everybody Needs a Rock, The Desert Is Theirs*, and *Hawk, I'm Your Brother* were all American Library Association Notable Books.

Miss Baylor believes that we cannot strive for the material things in life, that it is the spirit that is necessary for personal development. "Once you make that decision, your whole life opens up and you begin to know what matters and what doesn't." About her work she says, "All the people and places I love most are very free spirited, and that is the feeling I'd like to have in whatever I write."

SELECTED WORKS: Amigo, 1963; One Small Blue Bead, 1965; The Chinese Bug, 1968; Before You Came This Way, 1969; Plink, Plink, Plink, 1971; Coyote Boy, 1972; When Clay Sings, 1972; Sometimes I Dance Mountains, 1973; Everybody Needs a Rock, 1974; They Put on Masks, 1974; The Desert Is Theirs, 1975; Hawk, I'm Your Brother, 1976; We Walk in Sandy Places, 1976.

SELECTED WORKS EDITED: And It Is Still That Way, 1976.

GUNNEL BECKMAN

April 16, 1910–

AUTHOR OF *The Girl Without a Name*, etc.

Autobiographical sketch of Gunnel Torulf Beckman:

I STARTED my writing career as a sob sister in a daily paper in Gothenburg, on the west side of Sweden

It was in the thirties, and I was a very young B.A. from the University of Lund. I was happy to get a job because it was the depression and many of my friends were out of work. A sob sister was the rather flippant term, of American origin, that indicated a person who wrote stories on social themes—a job that was very different from the work I later on in life

GUNNEL BECKMAN

engaged in as a probation officer and as a member of a lay judiciary panel.

As a matter of fact the sobbing didn't come to much. I spent my time with home and fashion—a natural field for a woman journalist at that time. Soon I married the literary and art critic of the newspaper, we had three children, and I got part-time work. And we were very happy in spite of Hitler's roaring and the growing threat of war.

In 1940 Hitler changed our lives. A group of businessmen in Gothenburg started an advertisement boycott of the newspaper because of our editor's bold writing against the Nazis. In a year our excellent little paper was murdered, and we had to move to Stockholm, where my husband later on was the director of a textbook publishing company. And for me, home and fashion changed into only home. We had two more children and there was no domestic help for our old villa in a suburb of Stockholm. My itch to write was soothed by translations and free-lancing—sometimes by writing short stories (oh, how bad!). My dream was to write crime stories, and my model was Craig Rice who in *Home Sweet Homicide* described the smart writing mother who solved mysteries with one hand and took care of her children with the other.

... I filled my residential district with mystery and murder and my garden with villains and rustling leaves.

When I sent the manuscript to the Bonnier publishing house they answered that if I took away all the corpses and police officers, it would be a lovely children's book, a family story!

I did. It was my first book for children, and it was followed by another from our cottage at the Baltic coast. And if the idyllic atmosphere of these books was rather strong, that was due not only to the fact that it was up to date in the fifties to write idyllic children's books, but also to the fact that our family life really was idyllic. After that, my appetite for writing books was whetted. I wrote a bittersweet account of my own childhood as a lonely girl with a governess in an old country mansion in the twenties, with my mother always sick and my father always short of money. . . .

Then at last came the crime story—about a boy who suspects a beloved older friend of drunken driving, a conflict between loyalty and obedience to the law. The next book was the first one translated in English and published in the U.S.—*The Girl Without a Name*—a story about a little Persian girl, suffering from a shock during an earthquake, who comes to Sweden as an adopted child. This period of my authorship ended with a cheerful little book dedicated to my first grandchild.

In 1969 came my first book for what my English publisher calls "new adults." This book was the result of a new climate in the world of authors writing for children and young people. A wind of freedom started blowing in the sixties. One was rather suddenly allowed to write about sex, politics, divorced parents, criminality, etc.—in a word, real life. That meant a great relief and stimulation for all of us who wrote for this category of readers. *Admission to the Feast* is the title of this first novel for new adults, published in U.S. and translated into six languages. It is a story about a nineteen-year-old girl who learns she is suffering from leukemia and knows she has only a short time left to live. She writes a long letter to a friend in the United States, into which she pours her thoughts and feeling, her fear of death. I am glad it was written long before *Love Story* so nobody could talk about plagiarism!

After my children were grown up, I took a more active role in local politics and did some social work in my home town, Solna, a municipality just outside Stockholm. In the book *Try To Understand*, one of the principal characters is an unhappy young girl I met as probation officer. The book is a plea for understanding—understanding of the causes of criminality, understanding between generations, etc. The English title is *A Room of His Own*.

The third of my novels for new adults is called *Mia Alone* and is about a seventeen-year-old high school girl, who thinks she is expecting a baby and her agony and her uncertainty about the right thing to do.

That is what has become of a young sob sister from the thirties.

Gunnel and Birger Beckman were married in 1933. Their five children are Staffan (born 1934), Bjorn (born 1938), Ingar (born 1941), Svante (born 1945), and Susanne (born 1951).

In 1969 Mrs. Beckman won Bonniers' prize for the best book for young people with the manuscript of *Tilltraede till festen*, published in the United States in hard covers as *Admission to the Feast* and in paper as *Nineteen Is too Young to Die*. In the same year she was awarded three thousand kroner by the Swedish Fund for Furtherance of Good Literature.

SELECTED WORKS: The Girl Without A Name, 1970; Admission to the Feast, 1971; A Room of His Own, 1974; Mia Alone, 1975; That Early Spring, 1977.

ABOUT: Contemporary Authors, Vol. 33–36; Something about the Author, Vol. 6.

PURA BELPRÉ

February 2, 1899–

AUTHOR OF *Perez and Martina,* etc.

Autobiographical sketch of Pura Belpré White:

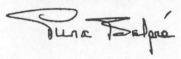

I WAS born in Cidra, Puerto Rico, and baptized in the town of Juana Diaz. My father was a fine raconteur of French descent, blessed with a sense of humor. He was a contractor and often moved about the island. So did his family. It gave us an opportunity to live in different towns and enjoy storytelling, which was a natural pastime.

I was a lover of nature. As a child I lived almost a pastoral existence. I wandered through pathways and fields dotted with color and drenched with morning dew, listening to the wind and watching the awakening of the living creatures. All this storing of beauty and feelings, preserved since childhood, found its way into my writing many years later. It added freshness and richness to the folklore I retold for children.

I entered the University at Rio Piedras in 1920. My year at the university was interrupted by my leaving to attend a sister's wedding in New York City.

Coming to New York City opened a new life for me. In 1921 the head librarian of the 135th Street branch of the New York Public Library in Harlem, Miss Ernestine Rose, thinking that she was getting a Spanish-speaking community, decided to get a Spanish-speaking person to help her organize the work. The offer came to my married sister Elisa, who had taught in Puerto Rico for ten years. Her husband didn't want her to work, and my sister suggested I go instead. I did and liked what I saw. I knew I had found my vocation. I did not return to Puerto Rico. After interviews by the library supervisors, I entered the library system and after various grade examinations was appointed. Thus I became the first Puerto Rican librarian in the New York Public Library. It opened the way to years of in-service training before going to the New York Public Library School in 1926.

While at library school I wrote my first folktale. Mary Gould Davis, the storytelling instructor, suggested that the class write a story. I selected my favorite: *Perez and Martina.* I told the story to the class, and Miss Davis invited me to tell it at her storyteller's meeting. It was a great experience and served as an open door to other symposiums. The approval of the story was a great inspiration to me, and I decided to write the stories I had heard as a child at my home. While I was being trained to become a children's librarian, and when I began to tell stories at the branch, the idea of using my own stories never left me. Therefore, I began to write them down during vacation time.

Miss Rose's dream of a Spanish community didn't materialize, but my experience at the branch was most rewarding. It acquainted me with black culture, and I experienced the black renaissance of art and literature, and the upsurge of poets, novelists, dramatists and musicians. I saw the beginning of what is now the Schomburg collection come into being.

All this experience was left behind when I was transferred to the Seward

Pura Belpré: *POOR a bell PRAY*

Park branch in lower Manhattan, the heart of the Hebrew community. I was again exposed to another culture. Storytelling was an important activity both in the branch and throughout the community. It was here where I built my backlog of stories—stories that served me well over many years. The branch was alive with activities and was thoroughly used by the entire community. I was there two years; then, in 1929, I was transferred to the 115th Street branch in upper Manhattan to develop Spanish work with a Hispanic community growing around the branch.

This truly became the Spanish branch, with a complete program for the children's room as well as for the adult department. Some "firsts" came about here: the first celebration of the Feast of the Three Kings, when the children in Spain and all Hispanic America receive their Christmas presents; the publication of my first story, *Perez and Martina*; and the first story included in a collection. The story was "The Three Magi," included in Anne Eaton's *The Animals' Christmas*, published by Viking Press. *Perez and Martina* was published by Warne and Company. This firm came to publish most of my books in the years that followed. The Spanish version of *Perez and Martina*, and my original story, called *Santiago*, were published by this firm in Spanish. In Spanish and in English, Pantheon published *Ote*, the popular Puerto Rican folktale, a favorite with all the children.

One highly popular activity at the branch was the creation of a puppet theatre. Puppet shows were given in Spanish and English, and the puppets soon took the road to hospitals, schools and, during the summer, the parks.

Communities have a tendency to change. The Spanish community around the 115th Street branch was no different. I found myself transferred to other communities to repeat the work developed at the previous library. Finally, after a stay at the Hamilton Grange branch in upper Manhattan, I was transferred to the Aguilar branch at 170 East 110th Street, in a section named "El Barrio." It is today the oldest Puerto Rican Community, with the only Puerto Rican Museum in the city of New York. While here I was sent by the American Library Association to Cincinnati, Ohio, to read a paper on the "work with the Spanish Speaking Reader in the New York Public Library." The year was 1942. In Cincinnati I met a musicologist, concert violinist and conductor who had been coming to the city to conduct the June Festival of Music. His name was Dr. Clarence Cameron White. A year later he became my husband. Later on, in 1945, I resigned from the library in order to travel and write. In 1961, a widow, I returned to the library as Spanish Children's Specialist in the Office of Children's Services. The special work done in Manhattan and the Bronx formed the basis for what is now the South Bronx Library Project. I worked there as a children's specialist until I retired in March, 1968. In June of the same year I was reappointed on a per diem basis for special services. I am still there. One of the most important projects is a fine traveling puppet theatre which goes everywhere in Manhattan and the Bronx, and on special assignments to Staten Island.

———

What Mrs. White does not say in her sketch is that she is, literally, the mover behind the puppet shows that are such an important part of her Puerto Rican folklore programs. She makes the puppets herself—at first of clay, now of papier-mâché—designs and sews the costumes. Although she had made doll figures as a child, using long mangoes and putting silk hair and faces on them, she did not see her first puppet show until she was an adult. She recognized at once that this was the medium for her, read all she could find, and later took courses as well. Today, besides performing, she has given workshops in storytelling and puppetry at the Museum of Natural History in New York and at New York University. She is in demand as a storyteller and speaker, not only for children but in library schools and schools of education.

Besides her own books, Mrs. White has translated a number of other English-language books into Spanish, among them Munro Leaf's *The Story of Ferdinand* and Elsa Minarik's *Little Bear*. She has provided translations for filmstrips and made a bilingual recording of *Perez and Martina*.

In 1973 the Brooklyn Public Library and The Brooklyn Museum awarded *Santiago* a Brooklyn Art Books for Children Citation. Mrs. White herself received a Citation of Merit from School District Number 7 in the South Bronx for her continuing efforts on behalf of the district's children, and School District Number 16 named its bookmobile for preschool children in her honor: "The Pura Belpré Children's Caravan." Mrs. White was honored by the Instituto de Puerto Rico in Puerto Rico for her contribution to the Puerto Rican culture.

SELECTED WORKS: Perez and Martina, 1961; Juan Bobo and the Queen's Necklace, 1962, reissued 1977; The Tiger and the Rabbit and Other Tales, 1965; Santiago, 1969; Ote, 1969; Dance of the Animals, 1972; Once in Puerto Rico, 1973.

ABOUT: Hopkins, Lee Bennett. Books Are By People.

NATHANIEL BENCHLEY

November 13, 1915–

AUTHOR OF *Gone and Back*, etc.

Autobiographical sketch of Nathaniel Goddard Benchley:

I WAS born November 13, 1915, in Newton, Massachusetts, the first son of Robert and Gertrude (Darling) Benchley. We moved to New York shortly thereafter, where my father became drama critic for the old *Life* and subsequently *The New Yorker*; we moved from the city out to Crestwood and then to Scarsdale, where I spent most of my youth.

I graduated from Phillips Exeter Academy in 1934 and from Harvard College four years later, where—although having majored in English—I got a B.S. degree because of insufficient grounding in Latin (the fault of a progressive day school I'd attended before going to Exeter). So much for my formal education.

My first job was writing a weekly feature piece for Heywood Broun's *Connecticut Nutmeg*; I did that for a month, and then went to the New York *Herald Tribune* as a city reporter with a decrease of ten dollars in salary (thirty-five dollars down to twenty-five). In August 1941 I went on active duty with the Navy in the Public Relations Office, and that job led eventually to duty in destroyers—both American and French—then to PC boats and coastal convoys and, finally, the Pacific.

Early in 1946 I went to *Newsweek* as an assistant editor in the entertainment department, and late the following year I was fired from that job and have been free-lancing ever since. I've done articles, short stories, one play and one movie, and perhaps two dozen or so books, both adult and juvenile.

In 1939 I married Marjorie Bradford, and in 1940 our first son, Peter Bradford, was born. His brother, Nathaniel Robert, was born in 1946.

———

Son of Robert Benchley, the famous humorist, Nathaniel Benchley turned to writing when he finished college because, he says, it seemed the only thing he could do. "There was nothing else for it but to write." He found that having a father already well established had advantages and disadvantages; he received more immediate attention as a writer when he began, but his achievement was then measured against what his father might have done. Benchley dealt with the problem by avoiding his father's kind of writing so that no comparisons could be made. His son Peter, a novelist, continues the family tradition.

In addition to an excellent biography of his father, Benchley has written satirical novels, stories, plays and movie scripts. One of the best known was the popular movie *The Russians Are Coming, the Russians Are Coming*, which Benchley adapted from his novel *The Off-Islanders*.

The setting for *The Off-Islanders* and for several of Nathaniel Benchley's children's books is Nantucket Island where he and his wife live all year around so that Benchley can indulge in his hobbies of fishing, boating and painting landscapes. To his surprise, he sells some of his paintings, though he considers himself an amateur.

Nathaniel Benchley had not written for children until after he moved to Nantucket from New York City. It was part of his "personal battle with TV," he told an interviewer. "I want to get young people in the habit of reading instead of staring at the tube."

That he has succeeded in developing a loyal audience and so won at least a part of the battle is clear from the long list of books Benchley has written and had published. *Bright Candles: A Novel of the Danish Resistance* was an American Library Association Best Book for Young Adults of 1974.

SELECTED WORKS: Oscar Otter, 1966; The Strange Disappearance of Arthur Cluck, 1967; A Ghost Named Fred, 1968; The Several Tricks of Edgar Dolphin, 1970;

The Flying Lesson of Gerald Pelican, 1970; Gone and Back, 1971; Small Wolf, 1972; Only Earth and Sky Last Forever, 1972; Bright Candles: A Novel of the Danish Resistance, 1974; Beyond the Mists, 1975; A Necessary End, 1976; Kilroy and the Gull, 1977.

ABOUT: Author's and Writer's Who's Who, 1971; Contemporary Authors, 1–4; Current Biography, 1953; Something about the Author, Vol. 3; Who's Who in America, 1972–73; World Authors: 1950–1970; Publishers Weekly October 2, 1972.

RAINEY BENNETT

July 20, 1907–

AUTHOR AND ILLUSTRATOR OF *The Secret Hiding Place*, etc.

Autobiographical sketch of Rainey Bennett:

THE road to the publishing of my books was long and winding, though not rough. I was involved with Marshall Field's Christmas newspaper campaign when our girls were very little. (Note: Our son, Tony, wasn't born till later.) Field's slogan was "Christmas is for children." Lots of work for Scott, Foresman in every level save Dick and Jane followed. My illustrations for their *Guide to Modern English* (junior high school) elicited responses from a couple of New York publishing firms. I went to New York with a frail lead or two for books for children. The late Velma V. Varner urged me through my first book—nay, all my authored books. *The Secret Hiding Place* came about through a drawing-painting which showed a little hippo planted on a little mesa-like hill surrounded by big hippos. It was called *The Secret Hiding Place* because the old heavy-heads couldn't look up to see the little one in plain sight. The book is still doing well. I like the Japanese republished version especially well.

So it is. My career is at an end—or is it a beginning?

————

Rainey Bennett [signature]

Rainey Bennett had already enjoyed a long and successful career as an artist before he turned to writing and illustrating children's books. After his graduation from the University of Chicago in 1930, he studied at the Art Institute of Chicago, the Art Students' League, and the George Grosz-Maurice Stern School in New York. He then worked as a muralist, taught off and on at the School of the Art Institute of Chicago, and was engaged in the Federal Art Project in 1935 and 1938. During this period he was holding one-man shows and executing commissions for industrial clients. Among these were two series of watercolors for Nelson A. Rockefeller and Standard Oil of New Jersey that required extensive travel in South America to gather material. Bennett's work hangs in museums across the country, including the Metropolitan Museum of Art, the Art Institute of Chicago, and the Museum of Modern Art.

A habitual winner of awards and prizes, Rainey Bennett carried the habit with him when he began writing children's books. *The Secret Hiding Place* won the New York *Herald Tribune* Children's Spring Book Festival Award for picture books in 1960 and was designated a Notable Book by the American Library Association. The American Institute of Graphic Arts included *After the Sun Goes Down* in its Children's Book Show, 1961–62.

Rainey Bennett was married to the former Ann Port, a dancer, who died in 1975. Their three children, Pamela, Renee, and Anthony, are all grown.

SELECTED WORKS WRITTEN AND ILLUSTRATED: What Do You Think?, 1958; The Secret Hiding Place, 1960; After the Sun Goes Down, 1961.

SELECTED WORKS ILLUSTRATED: Little Chameleon, by Sylvia Cassedy, 1966; Hooray for Pig!, by Carla Stevens, 1974; Holiday Ring, comp. by Adeline Corrigan, 1975; Pig and the Blue Flag, by Carla Stevens, 1977.

ABOUT: Kingman, Lee and others, comps., Illustrators of Children's Books: 1957–1966; Who's Who in America, 1972–73.

BJÖRN BERG

September 17, 1923–

ILLUSTRATOR OF *Old Mrs. Pepperpot*, etc.

Autobiographical sketch of Björn Berg:

MY father, Folke Wson Berg, who is an artist, met my mother Gertrude Olsson, who also painted, at an art school in Munich, Germany in 1923—the same year I was born there.

In 1926 we moved to the United States and stayed nine years in Manhattan, where my brother Sture came into the world. My father was my first teacher. The most important things I know about draftsmanship, he taught me. We had an eight-room apartment on 103rd Street with Swedish-American and other lodgers, restless spirits who left behind them strange memories that I shall try to put in order when the time comes. Most of the population of the district was Irish. It seethed with life.

I spent five years in Public School 54, where our good teacher apologized when she moistened her thumb to turn over the page in our history book. Unfortunately, I don't think we got much further than the Declaration of Independence before I left the U.S.A.

A few hours every week I was let out

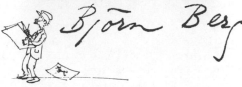

of class, and lucky me, together with other lucky pupils from different schools, kneaded clay and splashed paint quite uninhibitedly. Marvelous!

In this civilized school there was also something called "music appreciation" where we just sat and listened. The goose pimples came out in a very special way whenever Paderewski's recording of *Danse Macabre* was played. And when Rossini galloped over the Alps with William Tell, it tingled all along the spine.

After school we played baseball on the street. The ball often used to bounce down into basements, and there were angry scenes. Sometimes the police came and the whole gang rushed into the nearest doorway, up the stairs, over the roof, down the stairs in another house, out through the door behind the backs of the police, who turned around, whereupon the whole scene was repeated.

My brother and I seldom took part. We mostly stood and threw a ball against a wall or explored Central Park. Or jumped the subway—rather hesitantly as we were nice, well-behaved little children—to Battery Park where extraordinary fish stared at us in the Aquarium.

The town was a jungle full of sounds: Irish reels and jigs, mewing cats, accordion music, roller skates, police sirens. Alarming and mysteriously nocturnal clatter on the iron fire escape at the back of the house. Carousels, organ-grinders. Never quiet. Yes, one minute, I remember. That was when the class had to stand in silence because Edison had died.

Summer was the smell of smoke and garbage . . . and neighboring Irishmen were seen throwing horseshoes in the park on Sundays. My brother and I often popped over to the East Side, where our Uncle Jocke was superintendent in a large apartment block. There we sat for hours, staring at the colored comics that had got down to him in the basement. I think I learned more about pictures there than later at art school.

My father and mother certainly had to struggle quite a bit during those years. They were hard times in the thirties. But Sture and I lived in a rich world full of happenings.

We returned in 1935 to my parents' home country, Sweden. There in my mother's childhood home in the north, I found the surroundings I'd dreamed of when I read Laura Fitinghoff's *Children of the Moor* at the public library in New York. Here there was silence, the cows wandering freely in the forest, blue mountains, silent people, midsummer night, berry-picking in the fall, winter snow, and the newly released torrents of the spring streams.

After a few years of school, terminating at the Academy's School of Etching in Stockholm in the forties, and when the war had finished, I traveled a little in Europe while I sketched on and off and wrote for different newspapers. In Paris, I painted in oils and frescoe at the Ecole des Beaux-Arts, under André Lhote and Fernand Léger.

Since 1952 I've worked as an illustrator for the newspaper, *Dagens Nyheter*, in Stockholm. There have been trips as far afield as India, Ceylon, Russia, Africa, North and South America, Japan and Turkey.

In 1955 I married the textile artist, Eva

Gehlin. Our children are called Olle, Sven, Maja, Torbjörn, and Nils.

The first children's book came in 1954. It was Alf Prøysen's *The Goat that Learned to Count*; then came *Old Mrs. Pepperpot*. My wife, young and beautiful, was said to have a certain resemblance to the old lady. It must have been the bun in her hair then.

In 1963 I illustrated Astrid Lindgren's *Emil in Lönneberga*. Torbjörn was the model. Subsequently I've illustrated children's books interspersed with history and poetry books.

———

Björn Berg has illustrated more than forty books, but his most famous creations are the characters of old Mrs. Pepperpot and a small mischievous boy called Emil, which are favorites in the United States as they are in their native Sweden. In 1971 Berg received the Elsa Beskow Plaque, Sweden's highest honor to an illustrator of children's books, awarded for the body of his work. He was commended for the Hans Christian Andersen Medal in 1972 for his contribution to international children's literature.

SELECTED WORKS ILLUSTRATED: *By Astrid Lindgren*: Emil in the Soup Tureen, 1970; Emil's Pranks, 1971; Emil and Piggy Beast, 1973. *By Alf Prøysen*: Old Mrs. Pepperpot, 1960; Mrs. Pepperpot Again, 1961; Mrs. Pepperpot to the Rescue, 1964; Mrs. Pepperpot in the Magic Wood, 1968; Mrs. Pepperpot's Outing, 1971.

ABOUT: Bookbird No. 4, 1972.

HAROLD BERSON

November 23, 1926–

AUTHOR AND ILLUSTRATOR OF *How The Devil Gets His Due*, etc.

Autobiographical sketch of Harold Berson:

THE first book I ever owned was *A Child's Garden of Verses* by Robert Louis Stevenson. It was illustrated with silhouettes and I read it over and over.

Lines like "I should like to rise and go/ Where the golden apples grow" and "Where in sunshine reaching out/ Eastern cities, miles about/ Are with mosques and minaret/ Among sandy gardens set" are always running through my head at odd moments. Later I read Stevenson's novels and travel writings. I feel close to Stevenson as I do to Edward Lear. I read and reread the poems of John Masefield, particularly "Sea Fever," and pored over the drawings illustrating them by Charles Pears. Most of these books I discovered at the First Street Library in Los Angeles: the Greek legends—Orpheus and Eurydice, Pandora, etc; later on it was Jack London, Melville and Byron, with odd meanderings through "The Knight in the Tiger's Skin," Longfellow, and Tennyson. It was in libraries that I discovered my heroes: Heinrich Schliemann of Mycenae, Sir Arthur Evans of Crete, Champollion, Caillet, etc.

My wife and I enjoy traveling. Most recently Paula and I traveled to Tunisia, Italy and France. We draw and paint on these trips and look for stories to adapt and illustrate. We also draw and paint around New York when time permits. We both love New York, an endlessly fascinating city. We also enjoy going to the ballet.

———

Harold Berson was born and raised in Los Angeles and received a Bachelor of Arts degree from the University of California at Los Angeles in 1953. He had majored in sociology, and after graduation he worked for a time in the Bureau of Public Assistance in Los Angeles until he decided to become an illustrator. Mr. Berson had been drawing ever since childhood, illustrating scenes and characters from the books he read. The idea of being a professional artist hadn't occurred to him, however, until he had a chance to study in Paris on the G.I. Bill. His first commission was given him in 1958, and he estimates that he has illustrated seventy or eighty books since then. His wife Paula is also an artist.

SELECTED WORKS WRITTEN AND ILLUSTRATED: Raminagrobis and the Mice, 1965; Pop Goes the Turnip, 1966; Why the Jackal Won't Speak to the Hedgehog, 1969; Balarin's Goat, 1972; How the Devil Gets His Due, 1972; The Thief Who Hugged a Moonbeam, 1972; Henry Possum, 1973; Larbi and Leila: A Tale of Two Mice, 1974; The Boy, the Baker, the Miller, and More, 1974; A Moose Is Not a Mouse, 1975; I'm Bored, Ma!, 1976; The Rats Who Lived in the Delicatessen, 1976.

SELECTED WORKS ILLUSTRATED: Silver Buttons, by Helen Diehl Olds, 1958; Racketty-Packetty House, by Frances Hodgeson Burnett, 1961; The Bad Child's Book of Beasts, by Hillaire Belloc, 1966; The Dragon that Lived Under Manhattan, by E.W. Hildick, 1970; New Patches for Old, by Barbara K. Walker and Ahmet E. Uysal, 1974; Hang In at the Plate, by Fred Backman, 1974; House Cat, by Ann Finlayson, 1974; Abu Ali, adapted by Dorothy O. Van Woerkom, 1976.

ABOUT: Contemporary Authors, Vol. 33–36; Kingman, Lee, and others, comps. Illustrators of Children's Books: 1957–1966; Something about the Author, Vol. 4.

MARVIN BILECK

March 2, 1920–

ILLUSTRATOR OF *Rain Makes Applesauce,* etc.

Autobiographical sketch of Marvin Bileck:

Bileck: *BILL eck*

MARVIN BILECK

I BELIEVE my first drawings were copies from Felix the Cat and Mickey Mouse. As I think back now, the fact that the animal's eyes, ears and noses were merely circles enabled me to remember and reconstruct them. I also was fascinated by forming "a thing"—by seeing a "living" thing take shape, born out of pencil, paper and thinking. The things I drew were very real to me—I believed in their actual existence. And in this believing, the magic of fiction took root. I could conceive, I could make up people, and this make-believe consumed me. Of course each achievement gave me more confidence to go on and discover for myself, and this, coupled with my mother's encouragement, soon caused me to think of myself as an artist. In Yiddish she would exclaim, "You have hands of gold!"

I was also fortunate in having a wise and thoughtful scoutmaster. He was a civil engineer, but I like to think that his real profession was bringing up boys. He had us out in the woods as often as possible, studying nature and coping with the problems of camping. He had us deeply involved in each activity, whether it was building a lean-to or studying ferns or reptiles, and he instilled in us a respect for all creatures, even the maligned snake. He showed us its ways and how farmers respected a black snake, teaching us a reverence for life and at the same time making us realize how much prejudice is based on rumor. Gentle, a man of few words, C. C. Cook was able to make us aware of the spiritual communion between man and nature. This sensing of life around us is, in my opinion, prerequisite for the artist interested in interpreting stories, poems and the human condition.

My great awakening, or "second birth," occurred at Cooper Union Art School. Here, among serious and dedicated artists, I began to discover the meaning of Art and its relationship to life. I came to understand that aesthetics reside in the realm of the senses and emotions and this principle became my ideal. We became conscious of form. The goal was always to work for and toward the generating and expansion of form. We were all greatly impressed with the principles of expression. I realized that for me self-expression was based upon how much I wanted to shake myself into the nature of another to experience identical feelings, and thus infuse my drawings with these feelings—a translating, interpreting, form-making experience, laden with emotionally charged lines and marks.

We were also shown how decorative art could have form and convey the simplest and most sublime feelings. And I began to dream that I could serve art to children and adults more readily and more widely if my pictures appeared in the pages of a book rather than on the walls of a museum.

For me, drawing is the means of touching through to the heart and soul of all things. I allow my own emotions to heat up what I see, and there the force of passionate imagination begins. The imagination drives the mind and the drawing beyond the limits that ordinary perception allows.

Drawing and making up faces is a life-long obsession. Like an author, the book artist is under the spell of creating people. He is breathless in anticipating how the shaping of various features and their combinations will bring forth "someone." For me drawing from the book always was more satisfying than writing a book report. Drawing was my language and resulted in deriving meaning that made for astonishing deviations from the literal sense. I was fortunate in having English teachers who encouraged this.

I was also enraptured by the melodrama of storytelling. The mounting of suspense parallels the way I pace my drawing, the way I string images about a page, and the way the turning of the pages holds out surprise and wonder. The page is theater, is a stage where place and location of word images to visual images interact for greater effectiveness.

Children's imagery is most meaningful to me because of the joy children get out of things. This joy rubs off on me, and I want a child to enjoy opening a picture book as much as he thrills inside when he walks into a circus tent, want him to think of a drawing of a helmeted policeman as if it were a tin toy that he could pick out of the page and play with. Garcia Lorca says to children in a poem, "What Joy does your divine heart celebrate?" and I believe this is what I address myself to in approaching each page.

———

Marvin Bileck was born and grew up in Passaic, New Jersey. His study at Cooper Union, begun in architecture, was interrupted by four years of Army service during World War II in North Africa, Europe and England. After the war he studied Gothic architecture at the London School of Architecture, then returned to New York and finished his work at Cooper Union. In 1958 Bileck held a Fulbright grant to France where he studied drawing. He has exhibited in the American Institute of Graphic Arts' Fifty Books of the Year and in their Children's Book Shows. *Rain Makes Applesauce* was a Caldecott Honor Book in 1965 and was chosen one of the ten best illustrated books in 1964 by the New York *Times*.

From 1961–67, Mr. Bileck taught drawing, book design and calligraphy at the Philadelphia College of Art. He has been assistant professor of art at Queens College (New York) from 1967 to the present.

SELECTED WORKS ILLUSTRATED: Penny That Rolled Away, by Louis MacNeice, 1954; Sugarplum, by Johanna Johnston, 1955; Nobody's Birthday, by Ann Colver, 1961; Rain Makes Applesauce, by Julian Scheer, 1964; Penny, by Beatrice Schenk de Regniers, 1966; Timi, the Tale of a Griffin, 1970.

ABOUT: Kingman, Lee and others, comps. Illustrators of Children's Books: 1957–1966; Klemin, Diana. The Art of Art for Children's Books; Viguers, Ruth Hill and others, comps. Illustrators of Children's Books: 1946–1956; Who's Who in American Art, 1970, 1973.

ELIZABETH BISHOP

February 8, 1911–

AUTHOR OF *The Ballad of the Burglar of Babylon*, etc.

Autobiographical sketch of Elizabeth Bishop:

I WAS born in Massachusetts. My parents were American and Canadian and I lived for some years and spent many summers with my maternal grandparents in a small village in Nova Scotia. (I have written a few poems and stories about this village and what being a small child there was like.) I grew up, however, mostly in New England, graduated from Walnut Hill School in Natick, Massachusetts, and four years later, from Vassar College.

I have traveled, or perhaps wandered, and lived in many different places: New York, Paris, Key West, Florida (for seven or eight years), Mexico; and from 1952 until 1970 I made Brazil my home, in Petropolis and Rio de Janeiro, and, later, in Ouro Preto in the state of Minas Gerais. I still own a house there. Since I

Elizabeth Bishop

have spent so much time in Brazil, of course I have written quite a bit of poetry about it.

In Brazil I also did some translating from Portuguese. I first translated a real diary, kept during the 1890s by a little girl between the ages of twelve and sixteen. This was published under the title of *The Diary of Helena Morley* (1958). It will be reissued in September 1977 by Ecco Press. It is a fascinating (and educational) book for young people, and very funny as well. (Since I only translated it, I can say this without boasting.)

I taught for the first time at the University of Washington, in Seattle, in 1966. Since the fall of 1970 I have taught seminars in verse-writing and twentieth century poetry at Harvard University, and in the fall term of 1977 I shall be "Berg Professor" at New York University.

The Ballad of the Burglar of Babylon, a rather long poem, a true story, taken from the newspapers in Rio de Janeiro, and episodes of which I actually saw, was published in an edition especially for children, with woodcuts by Anne Grifalconi. But I have never deliberately written with child readers in mind. Some of my poems, and a few prose pieces, seem to have found favor with the editors of anthologies for schoolchildren and high school students and naturally this pleases me. (At present, however, I am extremely tired of the most anthologized of my poems, "The Fish," and I wish very much the anthologists would look through my books for something else. . . .)

———

Elizabeth Bishop was born in Worcester, Massachusetts. As her father died soon after she was born and her mother became ill, she was raised by her maternal grandparents in Nova Scotia and an aunt in Boston.

Reticent about herself and her work, Miss Bishop has accumulated an impressive number of awards and accolades from fellow poets and from critics. Her work has been widely anthologized.

She holds Litt. D.'s from Smith College (1968), Rutgers University (1972), and Brown University (1972). In 1945 Miss Bishop received the Houghton Mifflin Poetry Fellowship, an award of one thousand dollars and publication of her poems *North and South* (1946). A Guggenheim Fellowship was awarded her in 1947. In 1951 she won the first Lucy Martin Donnelly Fellowship, which carried a grant of twenty-five hundred dollars from Bryn Mawr College. That same year she received the American Academy of Arts and Letters Award. Many other honors followed, among them the Pulitzer Prize for Poetry in 1956, the Academy of American Poets Award in 1964, and a National Book Award in 1970. The Brazilian Government honored her with the Order of Rio Branco in 1970. In 1976 she was elected to the American Academy of Arts and Letters and received the Prize for Literature from Books Abroad/Neustadt International and The National Book Critics Circle Award for Poetry.

Elizabeth Bishop served as consultant in poetry to the Library of Congress in 1949–50. In 1966 and again in 1973 she was Visiting Professor of English at the University of Washington. She lectured at Harvard from 1970 to 1973.

The noted critic Louise Bogan said that Elizabeth Bishop's poems are "not in the least showy. They strike no attitudes and have not an ounce of superfluous emotional weight, and they combine an unforced ironic humor with a naturalist's accuracy of observation." Another critic compared Miss Bishop's work to Emily Dickinson's—"wry, witty and shocking, with the same power of singling out the terrifying uncategorizable thatness of a mundane object." "Hers may be a minor voice among the poets of history," wrote Anne Stevenson, "but it is scarcely ever a false one. We listen to it as one might listen to a friend whose exceptional wisdom and honesty we gratefully revere."

SELECTED WORKS: Questions of Travel, 1965; The Ballad of the Burglar of Babylon, 1968; Complete Poems, 1969.

ABOUT: Author's and Writer's Who's Who, 1971; Contemporary Authors, Vol. 7–8; Harte, Barbara and Carolyn Riley. 200 Contemporary Authors; Murphy, Rosalie. Contemporary Poets of the English Language; Stevenson, Anne. Elizabeth Bishop; Twentieth Century Authors (First Supplement); Who's Who in America, 1972–73; Who's Who of American Women, 1972–73, 1974–75; New York Times Book Review May 27, 1956.

MARIE HALUN BLOCH

December 1, 1910–

AUTHOR OF *Aunt America,* etc.

Autobiographical sketch of Marie Halun Bloch:

I WAS born in Ukraine and brought to the United States at the age of four. When I started kindergarten a year later, I did not know a word of English.

My parents fortunately recognized the necessity of mitigating the uprooting I had experienced. They did not cast off our heritage but took care to pass it on to me. I learned who I was. At home we spoke our native tongue and sang our native songs. All through my childhood

Halun Bloch: *ha LUN block*

Marie Hahn Bloch.

my parents strove to acquaint me with the history and literature of Ukraine. They knew that meanwhile, at school, I was learning all of these things about our adopted land. But the dilemma of the immigrant is not an easy one to resolve, either for children or for adults. That is the theme of my book *Marya*.

I was introduced early to literature and storytelling. Even in the old country my grandmother Maria, who of all the people in my life has had the deepest influence upon me, read to me and told me stories, and my parents continued to do so. My father, in particular, was a skillful raconteur. To this day I am able to recall his every word, his every gesture in recounting some incident to guests in our house of an evening, and me sitting long past my bedtime, still as a mouse, so as not to be noticed and sent off to bed. And for a time during my childhood in Cleveland, Ohio, we lived directly across the street from a branch of the public library—surely the best place in town to live!

In school, from grade school through Evanston (Illinois) Township High School, Northwestern University, and the University of Chicago, English and literature were always my favorite sub-

jects. I enjoyed not only the writing of stories and compositions but also the study of language itself, how it worked, what it could be made to do—all those things a writer has to know. While I was still in high school, I became aware of the importance of the unconscious (though I did not name it), without which creative work is scarcely possible. It's no wonder I became a writer. That I had to be was a bit of self-knowledge that came to me very early in life.

Unlike many adults, I remember my own childhood vividly—not events so much as how I felt about various people, about various incidents in my life, and what I thought about the world I was discovering within and without. I can speak to children easily and intimately and that must be one reason that I write for them.

In 1930, while I was attending Northwestern University, I married Donald Beaty Bloch, my English professor. We have one daughter who is married and has two little daughters of her own. They are the delight of my life and I count myself the luckiest of mothers and grandmothers.

My books all stem from my own experiences and my own enthusiasms. A number of years ago, for example, I became greatly interested in earth history. From this interest and a great amount of reading and many field trips came my books *Dinosaurs* and *Mountains on the Move*. In the summers I live in the Colorado mountains. Out of that experience have come my books *Tony of the Ghost Towns* and *The House on Third High*. Developing from my abiding interest in folklore were *Big Steve, Ukranian Folk Tales* (1964), and *Ivanko and the Dragon* (1969), while from my interest in the study of history has come *Bern, Son of Mikula*, a story based upon a medieval legend of Ukraine.

In 1960 I journeyed back to my native land and saw again aunts and uncles who knew me as a child. I met numerous cousins for the first time. This homecoming was a profoundly stirring event for me. Out of that first journey and several since grew my books *Aunt America* and *The Two Worlds of Damyan.*

With each book I write I strive first of all to tell a good story, one that will touch the reader and deepen his understanding of himself. At the same time, probably because of my own fascination with faraway places and long-ago time, I strive to widen the reader's view of our physical world by transporting him to a place or a time that may be new to him. Not surprisingly, my favorite leisure time activity is travel. I have traveled up and down Europe and America, and sometime soon I hope to go to Africa.

———

Marie Halun Bloch is a member of the Ukranian Academy of Arts and Sciences in the United States. Several of her books have been cited as outstanding, among them *Tunnels* which was chosen for the Junior Book Award by the Boy's Club of America in 1955 and *Dinosaurs,* designated one of the New York *Times*'s 100 Best Children's Books in the same year. *Tony of the Ghost Towns* was selected as an Honor Book in the 1956 New York *Herald Tribune* Children's Spring Book Festival. *Aunt America* was named a Notable Book for Children in 1963 by the American Library Association. It was also on the *Horn Book* Fanfare, an annual honors list in 1964, and in 1966 on the Master List for the William Allen White Award. The *Christian Science Monitor* chose *Bern, Son of Mikula* one of the Best Books of the Year in 1972.

SELECTED WORKS: Big Steve, 1952; Tunnels, 1954; Dinosaurs, 1955; Tony of the Ghost Towns, 1956; Marya, 1957; Mountains on the Move, 1960; The Dollhouse Story, 1961; The House on Third High, 1962; Aunt America, 1963; The Two Worlds of Damyan, 1966; Bern, Son of Mikula, 1972.

ABOUT: Author's and Writer's Who's Who, 1971; Contemporary Authors, Vol. 4; Foremost Women in Communications, 1970.

JUDY BLUME

February 12, 1938–

AUTHOR OF *Are You There God? It's Me, Margaret,* etc.

Autobiographical sketch of Judy Sussman Blume Kitchens:

I AM a child of suburbia. I was born in Elizabeth, New Jersey, and grew up in towns very much like the one where Margaret Simon lives in *Are You There God? It's Me, Margaret.* Practically all of my books have suburban East Coast settings because I know them best.

After high school I went to New York University. I planned to be a second grade teacher but following my third year of college I was married to John Blume, an attorney. By the time I graduated I was expecting our first child so my teaching career had to wait. Randy, our daughter, was born on February 22, 1961, and Larry, our son, was born on July 5, 1963. I was quite happy and busy taking care of my family until Larry went off to nursery school. Then I decided I needed something else in my life —something just for me. It wasn't practical to take a teaching job at that time, and I wasn't sure exactly what I wanted to do anyway.

I always shudder when someone asks me how I started writing children's books because the truth is, I'm not sure. It just happened! I know that I used to make up rhyming stories while doing the dinner dishes, and they became my first books (unpublished). They now occupy a special shelf in an out-of-the-way closet, which is where they belong. However, I did learn a lot from them, especially how to interpret letters of rejection.

Next, I took a course at New York University in writing for children, and while I believe that no one can teach you how to write, I did need professional encouragement and found it there. After that things began to happen very fast. I sold several stories to magazines, a picture book was accepted for publication, and I wrote my first book for older readers,

whom she writes, though their very outspokenness may make them unpalatable to some adults. Conspicuously absent from many of the prize and honor lists compiled by critics and librarians, Blume books are well represented when the young readers choose their own favorites. In 1975 the children of Hawaii voted *Are You There God? It's Me, Margaret* the winner of the Nene Award. The same title was also included in the New York *Times* list of Outstanding Books in 1970 and was on the American Library Association's List of Notable Books 1940–1970. *Tales of a Fourth Grade Nothing* received a Sequoyah Children's Book Award, voted by the children of Oklahoma, a Charlie May Simon Children's Book Award, voted by the children of Arkansas, and a Pacific Northwest Library Association Young Readers' Choice Award.

In addition to her books for younger readers, Mrs. Blume produced a novel entitled *Forever* (1975), a frank depiction of a high-school love affair that turns out not to be forever. Although *Forever* was published as an adult book, the critics felt that its natural audience was young adults who may have been Blume fans since the appearance of *Are You There God?* Bearing out their evaluation, a paperback edition appearing in 1976 had sold 600,000 copies within a few months of publication.

Judy Blume's first marriage ended in divorce. She is now married to Tom Kitchens, a physicist, and lives in the mountains of Los Alamos, New Mexico, with her teen-aged children and her calico cat.

SELECTED WORKS: Are You There God? It's Me, Margaret, 1970; Then Again, Maybe I Won't, 1971; Freckle Juice, 1971; Tales of a Fourth Grade Nothing, 1972; It's Not the End of the World, 1972; Otherwise Known as Sheila the Great, 1972; Deenie, 1973; Blubber, 1974; Starring Sally J. Freedman as Herself, 1977.

ABOUT: Contemporary Authors, Vol. 29–32; Something about the Author, Vol. 2; Who's Who of American Women, 1974–75; Elementary English September 1974; New York Times September 29, 1976.

Iggie's House. But it was really the publication of *Are You There God? It's Me, Margaret* that made me feel I might actually become a writer. Margaret's popularity has proved to me that while life styles and goals are constantly changing, feelings remain the same. And that's what I like to write about—feelings.

I get very angry at adults who tell me they want to protect their children from the real world, because that's just an excuse to avoid the issues. I try to be honest in my books. I think young people need to know that others share their feelings—that no matter what your problem is, you're not alone.

With each new book I am learning more about my craft. I still suffer through the first draft, but once that's complete I have lots of fun with my characters. Randy is starting junior high this year and she is urging me to write about older teen-agers. So far I haven't, but who knows? I welcome new challenges!

———

Because she is outspoken about issues and problems that young people have to deal with, Judy Blume's books are exceedingly popular with the audience for

MAX BOLLIGER

April 23, 1929–

AUTHOR OF *David*, etc.

Autobiographical sketch of Max Bolliger, translated from the German:

"OH, you only write for children," people say to me sometimes. They probably think, "He can't do any better." Unfortunately many people still think children's literature is only a subspecies of literature and not to be taken seriously.

But a book for children is neither easier nor more difficult to write than a book for grown-ups. It is different. Someone who writes for children may have experienced his own youth especially intensely and with special memory. Then even as a grown-up he can think back to the child—what he felt, what he loved, what made him anxious, and what relieved the anxiety.

There are stories where I have to consider first whether they are to be comprehensible to small children or big ones. That is a matter of vocabulary. But sometimes I write a story without thinking whether it should be directed to children or grown-ups. I simply write as the story dictates.

Why does one write, really? I don't know why other people write. But if, for some reason or other, I do not get around to working at my writing table for several days, I have a bad conscience, just like a schoolboy who hasn't done his homework. A bad conscience is unbearable. So then I sit myself down again and try to shape and strengthen my ideas with the help of language.

"Why do you think I write?" When I asked this question a child answered, "So you don't have to work anymore." I only wish it were so!

Writing is a hard trade. I am like the children who are supposed to write a composition and sit with pen in mouth before an empty page. What is so difficult? Haven't we all had a good idea now and then? Hasn't everyone thought of a story? The most difficult thing about writing is to find the right words for what one wants to say—the mastery of the language. Sometimes I write a page ten times—a difficult trade indeed.

Max Bolliger was born in the canton of Glarus, Switzerland, and spent his youth in Braunwald. He studied to be a teacher in Aargau and taught for several years in a village school. Having grown interested in the education of the mentally retarded and emotionally disturbed, he then pursued studies in remedial education and psychology. After a further study period in England, he was employed as a special teacher in Luxembourg for a year and a half until he returned to Switzerland. He taught a remedial class in Adliswil, near Zurich, for ten years. Today Max Bolliger is a freelance writer and a regular contributor to television. He lives in Zurich.

David (Germany, 1965) won the German Children's Book Prize in 1966. In 1973 Max Bolliger received the Swiss Children's Book Prize, awarded for the body of his work by the Swiss Teachers' Association. *Mose* (Germany, 1972) was on the Hans Christian Andersen Honor List in 1974.

SELECTED WORKS: David, 1967; Joseph, 1969; Daniel, 1970; The Fireflies, 1970; The Golden Apple, 1970; Noah and the Rainbow, 1972; The Wooden Man, 1974; The Giants' Feast, 1976.

ABOUT: Contemporary Authors, Vol. 25–28; Something about the Author, Vol. 7.

DON BOLOGNESE

January 6, 1934–

and

ELAINE RAPHAEL

March 14, 1933–

ILLUSTRATORS OF *Letters to Horseface,* etc.

Biographical sketch of Donald Alan Bolognese and Elaine Raphael Chionchio Bolognese by Don Bolognese:

ELAINE and I were born in New York. Although I was raised in the Bronx and Elaine in Brooklyn, our experiences were similar. The streets were our playground as well as the meeting place for young and old. The background was World War II and that fostered a strong sense of community. With bond drives, Red Cross posters, etc., there were plenty of opportunities to draw and paint. Art was as natural to us as the other activities of childhood.

We met while students at Cooper Union Art School. There we discovered the value of artists working together. Our instructors were professional book designers and illustrators and through them we were introduced to the world of publishing. This proved to have a profound effect on our careers and our growth. The fact is that without exposure to his peers the artist cannot fully develop. In our case Elaine's talent and mine are complementary. We also try to be objective with each other. And while it is not always easy living with your most perceptive critic, it is instructive and enriching. Artists, as do other people, frequently prefer the easy road. And when early attempts meet with easy suc-cess, it is tempting to be repetitious.

Two of our latest books, *Letters to Horseface* by F. N. Monjo; and *Sam Baker Gone West*, which we wrote ourselves, are illustrative of our resistance to that temptation. Taking the cue from our subject we research, reflect, sketch and interpret. Each project offers another challenge, and as we take on larger and more complex assignments we discover other facets of our talents.

———

Elaine Raphael and Don Bolognese have been married since 1954. They have two daughters and live in New York and Vermont. They have both taught (separately and together) at Pratt Institute, the Cooper Union, New York University, and the Metropolitan Museum of Art's medieval museum, The Cloisters. *Me, Myself and I,* by Gladys Cretan, was included in the Society of Illustrators Show in 1971. *All Upon a Stone,* by Jean C. George, was a Prize Book in the Book World Children's Spring Book Festival in 1971.

SELECTED WORKS WRITTEN AND ILLUS-TRATED BY DON BOLOGNESE: Once Upon a Mountain, 1967; A New Day, 1970; Drawing Horses and Foals, 1977.

SELECTED WORKS ILLUSTRATED BY DON BOLOGNESE: Four Legs and a Tail, by A. D. Jorgensen, 1962; Benjie, by Joan M. Lexau, 1964; The Secret, by Elizabeth Coatsworth, 1965; The Butterfly's Ball and the Grasshopper's Feast, by William Roscoe, 1967; Trail of Apple Blossoms, by Irene Hunt, 1968; Just One More, ed. by Jeanne B. Hardendorff, 1969; Benjie on His Own, by Joan M. Lexau, 1970; All Upon a Stone, by Jean C. George, 1971; All Upon a Sidewalk, by Jean C. George, 1974; Waiting for Cherries, by Ann Himler, 1976; Snorri and the Strangers, by Nathaniel Benchley, 1976; George the Drummer Boy, by Nathaniel Benchley, 1977.

SELECTED WORKS ILLUSTRATED BY ELAINE RAPHAEL: Havelok the Dane, by Ian Seraillier, 1967; Tales of Ancient Egypt, by R. L. Green, 1968; Circus Fun, by Margaret L. Hillert, 1969.

SELECTED WORKS WRITTEN AND ILLUS-TRATED BY DON BOLOGNESE AND ELAINE

Bolognese: *Bo lo NAY see*

RAPHAEL: The Sleepy Watchdogs, 1969;
Sam Baker Gone West, 1977.

SELECTED WORKS ILLUSTRATED BY DON
BOLOGNESE AND ELAINE RAPHAEL: Letters
to Horseface, by F. N. Monjo, 1975;
Knight's Prisoner, by Margaret M. Hodges,
1976.

ABOUT: Kingman, Lee and others, comps.
Illustrators of Children's Books: 1957–1966.

PAUL-JACQUES BONZON

1908–

AUTHOR OF *The Orphans of Simitra*, etc.

Autobiographical sketch of Paul-Jacques
Bonzon, translated from the French:

I WAS born in 1908 in the little village of
Sainte-Marie du Mont (Manche) at the
seashore, right on the spot where American troops landed in 1944. The beach is
now called Utah Beach.

My father was head of the chief administrator's office of the Department of
Manche. He loved drawing and he
passed this love on to me. For many
years I drew and painted.

I studied at the normal school and was
a teacher and later a principal. It was
doubtless this profession that led me to
abandon painting and drawing and influenced me to take up children's literature. During the war I was in the underground in Vercors with young Jewish
children who were separated from their
parents. These children asked me to tell
them stories. I first wrote tales for them.
I published my first book soon after the
war.

I then married, and I have two children who were among my first readers, a
boy Jacques and a girl Isabelle, who is
now an editor in a publishing house. I
live at Valence, a sunny little town in the
Rhône valley. I only leave home to do
research for my books.

I left teaching fifteen years ago to devote myself entirely to literature. I have
written a total of eighty works. One

Paul-Jacques Bonzon: *Paul ZHAHK
baughn ZAUHN*

PAUL-JACQUES BONZON

series is called *The Six Companions,* and
it contains twenty-five titles. The principal hero of this series is a wolf-dog endowed with extraordinary powers of detection. This series and the other works
are translated into nineteen languages
and published in forty countries.

My favorite themes are comradeship,
friendship and devotion. The action often takes place in humble surroundings,
which I like best.

———

The work of Paul-Jacques Bonzon is
better known in France than the United
States. Three of his books have won
French children's book prizes, including
the prestigious Prix Jeunesse, and one of
them has been serialized for French language television. In this country, *The
Orphans of Simitra* was an Honor Book
in the *Herald Tribune* Children's Spring
Book Festival, 1962, and was designated
a Notable Book by the American Library
Association. The same title was included
in the New York *Times* list of one hundred outstanding books of the year in
1962.

SELECTED WORKS: The Orphans of Simitra, 1962; Pursuit in the French Alps,
1963; The Runaway Flying Horse, 1976.

ABOUT: Author's and Writer's Who's Who,
1971.

LÉONCE BOURLIAGUET

January 6, 1895–March 26, 1965

AUTHOR OF *The Guns of Valmy*, etc.

Biographical sketch of Léonce Bourliaguet by Mme. Léonce Bourliaguet,
translated from the French:

LÉONCE BOURLIAGUET

THE only son of a cobbler father, Léonce
Bourliaguet was born on the 6th of January, 1895, in Thiviers, a small city
straddling the provinces of Limousin and
Périgord. In later life he liked to recall
his modest origins and his life among the
rural craftsmen, with their freshness of
outlook, simplicity and picturesque expressions. L.B. himself possessed these
same very earthy qualities.

He studied first in the town of Thiviers, then at normal schools in Péri-
gueux and in Dordogne. At fifteen, at the
very time of his entry into normal school,
his mother died. Orphaned and unused
to the discipline of scholarship, he found
school difficult. He was literary by nature, a philosopher and poet by instinct
and given to imagination and fantasy.
He had trouble conforming to the rigid
strictures of education and was not a
brilliant student, except in French literature.

Those four years were lonely and
dreamy ones, for already L.B. had begun
to display the originality, the independence of spirit, and the nonconformism
that were the essence of his personality.
He found refuge in reading and discovered the intoxication of perceiving and
knowing, of discovering the masters of
thought, the guides to beauty. He began
to show the devotion to style that was
manifest in all his work.

In December 1914, when he was nineteen, Léonce Bourliaguet was inducted
into the 49th Infantry Regiment. Unac-
quainted with life, the idealistic young
man was thrown from his small familiar
world into the vast chaos of war and was
brutally confronted with what he later
called "the terrifying aspect of creation."
His youth and his gallant spirit saved

him from depression. He learned to defend himself through the critical observation of beings and things. He fought
emotion with pleasantry, anguish with
banter, and grew to manifest a charac-
teristically Latin flair for the droll word
in response to the treachery of circumstance, an attitude that became second
nature to him for the rest of his life.

He was taken prisoner April 17, 1916,
interned first in Darmstadt, then sent to
Pomerania. Having been torn from his
books, L.B. now learned to study nature.
He tended cows on the Baltic seashore
and worked on a German farm where he
absorbed the German language and customs at the same time. He encountered a
new world, another language, another
milieu with a lively eye, sharpened wit,
and a sensitive heart. Some of his better
books, *Le Franzmann* (The Frenchie),
La Forêt Sereine (The Serene Forest),
Un Village au Bord de la Mer (A Village
beside the Sea) were the fruit of that
period, which in fact saved him from the
hell of the front lines.

Although he faced the war coura-
geously, with a spirit of patriotism that
struggled with the profound feeling of
human fraternity that he had developed,
he nevertheless retained a horror and
disgust of war, especially the total failure

Léonce Bourliaguet: *LAY onss BOOR*
lia gay

in human relationships it represents, and its beastliness.

Finally, in August 1919 he entered teaching as a rural schoolmaster in the little village of Mialet in Dordogne. Besides the excitement of molding young spirits, he discovered the tranquil joys of trout-fishing. He discovered, too, the joys of family life, for he married a fellow teacher there. In twenty years of marriage, they had three sons: André, Pierre and J. Jacques.

He spent ten years in Mialet, which he always remembered nostalgically because they were simple, happy years. Then his activities led him into preparing to apply for the Inspectorat, which accepted him in 1929. He was the youngest school inspector in France.

In the meantime, for the needs of his classes he had started to "invent stories." But it was only about 1930 that he actually turned toward literature.

By then, he had begun to take the lead in his professional life—which strengthened his knowledge of the world of childhood each day—and in his extremely productive literary life, producing a book each year. Over the years he lived in three departments: Saône et Loire, Ariéze, and Corrèze. He was nicknamed "the Pedestrian" because he used to like to do his inspection tours partly on foot, partly on bicycle, and much more on foot than by bicycle. These tours were one of the chief joys of his life and gave him that knowledge of nature that is shown in his books. "If I had not been an inspector, I would have chosen to be a roadmender," he often said.

Widowed in 1944, he remarried and established a new hearth, with another child, Bruno. He received awards one after another: Prix Jeunesse, Prix Enfance du Monde, Prix Olivier de Serres, Prix Fantasia, Prix de l'Académie Française and, posthumously, the Grand Prix de Caorle.

He retired at sixty-five and moved to a small farmhouse near Brive, which he called "Crickets." He continued writing, still keeping up his walks, in even closer touch with nature. At seventy he was felled by a heart attack, on March 26, 1965, after a life completely devoted to youth.

L.B. was much loved by students who knew he liked them and came to him during inspections with happy faces. He often made them laugh, telling stories, joking with them—he was unequalled in teaching by means of the droll word or anecdote.

His spirit inclined toward a kind of fraternal animism. In his eyes the simplest objects—a broom, a cheesetub, a scarecrow—had a personality, and he introduced them into his charming stories. Nothing was insignificant or without importance: a straying ant, the fluttering of a leaf, the play of a sunbeam were to him "the pattern of observation that will become the honey of dreams." He maintained his compassion even during the hardest adventures of his life, but it was always veiled by humor, by a sort of modesty that concealed his sensitivity. Complete idealist though he was, he knew, too, "that the business of being a star must every so often be boring," and Ariel took a place next to Caliban when L.B. declared, "If I were able, I would do the story of the donkey rolling in the field, trumpeting his joy with his feet in the air."

Three streets in three different cities in France bear the name of Léonce Bourliaguet—in Thiviers, his birthplace; in Brive where he spent a good part of his career; and in Malemort, where he ended his days.

———

Léonce Bourliaguet was awarded numerous prizes and honors for his work in France, and in 1966 *Le Canons de Valmy* (*The Guns of Valmy*) was on the honor list for the Hans Christian Andersen Award. The same year the European Prize of the City of Caorle was awarded posthumously to the author for *Le Canons de Valmy*.

SELECTED WORKS: The Guns of Valmy, 1969.

BIANCA BRADBURY

December 4, 1908–

AUTHOR OF *Two on an Island*, etc.

Autobiographical sketch of Bianca Ryley
Wheeler Bradbury:

BIOGRAPHIES have to start, "I was
born." I was born in Mystic, Connecticut,
and have spent my life in Connecticut,
except for travels abroad. Thus the books
I write are rooted in New England,
where my ancestors started arriving in
the 1600s.

After graduating from Connecticut
College for Women I married Harry B.
Bradbury, a lawyer fresh out of Yale Law
School, and we set ourselves down in
New Milford. The same year my husband was elected to the State Legisla-
ture. After that we switched parties and
continued running for local offices, sometimes winning and sometimes losing.

We started a family and I foresaw
years of being tied to the house. Days
had to be filled with something besides
housework and clubs, and I took to writing, first verse (some of it was poetry),
then short stories, then children's books.
Like many writers for young people I
wrote for our own two boys, starting
with picture books and working up as
the boys grew to "middle age" books.
Now the sons are grown and gone, so I
write for teen-age girls. I had to rediscover my own sex and found I liked it.

We're lucky. We live in the country, in
the woods, and have nightly visitors—
raccoons and skunks and foxes. Sometimes I'm up to my ears in animals because I work with an animal welfare
society which tries to cope with the flood
of unwanted dogs and cats, puppies and
kittens, in seven towns. Animals always
get into my books, and I don't try to keep
them out.

I garden frantically wherever there is a
patch of sun through the trees.

After forty books, writing is a habit
impossible to break. I've messed about
with other centuries, the seventeenth and
nineteenth, but now write in the twenti-

eth on contemporary problems. I dread
the first awful business of spinning a
story out of my head like a spider web
and getting it down in rough draft, but
the rest is pure pleasure—the rewriting
and fussing and typing. I do it between
5:00 and 8:00 A.M., that lovely time when
the day is new.

———

Bianca Bradbury's two sons, William
Wyatt and Michael Ryley, are now
grown up. One is married with a family
of his own. The other is a social worker
with the retarded. Mrs. Bradbury's husband is a former Judge of Probate, now
retired. Besides writing two books a year,
Bianca Bradbury is especially interested
in jazz, sports cars, travel, and the study
of coins.

Two on an Island was designated a
Notable Book by the American Library
Association in 1965 and, in its German
language edition, achieved the Honor
List for the German Children's Book
Prize in 1968. In 1970, the Child Study
Association of America included *Nancy
and Her Johnny-O* among their chil-
dren's books of the year.

SELECTED WORKS: One Kitten Too Many,
1952; Two on an Island, 1965; The Under-
grounders, 1966; Girl in the Middle, 1969;

The Loner, 1970; Nancy and her Johnny-O, 1970; A New Penny, 1971; Those Travers Kids, 1972; My Pretty Girl, 1974; Boy on the Run, 1975; In Her Father's Footsteps, 1976; I'm Vinnie, I'm Me!, 1977.

ABOUT: Contemporary Authors, Vol. 13–14; Foremost Women in Communications, 1970; Something about the Author, Vol. 3.

MABEL CAROLINE BRAGG

September 15, 1870–April 25, 1945

AUTHOR OF *The Little Engine That Could*

Biographical sketch of Mabel Caroline Bragg, whose writing for children was published under the name of "Watty Piper":

"MY work is my life. People refresh me. I enjoy my friends." This remark, made by Mabel Caroline Bragg herself, gives us a little of the flavor of this attractive personality, respected all her working life as a teacher and pioneer in health education, but loved most of all by children for her warmth and concern on their behalf.

Mabel Caroline Bragg was born in Milford, Massachusetts, on September 15, 1870. When she was eight her mother died and she went to live with an aunt in Bristol, Rhode Island; she finished school there and went on to prepare herself for a teaching career.

It seems clear that she was a natural, gifted teacher, one still remembered warmly by past pupils, notably for her humor and energy, her gift for making friends with children, and for her storytelling. She had a strong, compelling voice and the happy knack of bringing the characters in her stories to life.

Her first position was at the Rhode Island State Normal School, from which she had herself graduated in 1889; she taught in normal schools for the next twenty years.

One of her great interests was in the art of speaking well, and she worked hard with her pupils to encourage them to want to speak well too. She told friends that her interest in speech had first been fired by her hatred of her own given name: she had, typically, decided that the only way to deal with it was the positive way—by rolling "Mabel Caroline" so grandly off her tongue that her listener would be stunned into thinking the name an asset.

In 1909 Miss Bragg joined the firm of Newson and Company, publishers of a new reading system. She traveled all over the country to schools that had adopted the system, demonstrating how to teach with it. In 1916 she was made Assistant Superintendent of the Newton (Massachusetts) Public Schools and she threw herself back into the everyday activities of teaching and learning. She also found time to teach educational methods and storytelling in the summer schools at Chautauqua, New York.

Her interest in children and in teaching extended to health education; she realized that to accomplish anything at all, certainly if he were to reach his true potential, a child must be healthy. So successful was she that in 1932 President Hoover sent her to Belgium to demonstrate modern methods of health teaching.

Miss Bragg was, in her time, the author of several books in the field of health education, but it is as the originator of *The Little Engine That Could* that she interests us most today.

The early publishing history of this best seller, first entitled *The Pony Engine*, is very obscure; it is possible that it originally appeared as a Sunday school tract. It first came to light, as far as the records go, in the late twenties when Platt and Munk bought the rights to *The Pony Engine* by Mabel Caroline Bragg from Doubleday, Doran and published it themselves in 1930 as *The Little Engine That Could*—by Watty Piper, with illustrations by Lois Lenski. "Watty Piper" was apparently a Platt and Munk house name; the original story had very likely been revised by a Platt and Munk house editor.

The story, an extremely simple one, is about a trainload of toys and nourishing food for the children on the other side of the mountain, which broke down as it was going up the grade. Although the toys asked every passing engine to help pull them over the mountain, all were too busy or too fine to stop until the little switching engine came along. The little engine wasn't sure it could do the job. As it labored up the mountain, it repeated, with the rhythm of a steam locomotive, the phrase, "I think I can, I think I can, I think I can." And when it succeeded, the puffing became, "I thought I could, I thought I could, I thought I could." These two lines are probably the reason for the story's survival, for they are now a working part of the American language, often used without any conscious associations with *The Little Engine That Could*.

Miss Bragg herself left the Newton School System in 1930 for the School of Education at Boston University, where she held a professorship until her retirement in 1940. She continued to act as an unofficial consultant in education until her death in 1945, enthusiastic to the last in communicating and receiving ideas.

SELECTED WORKS: The Little Engine That Could, 1945.

BARBARA BRENNER
June 26, 1925–

AUTHOR OF *A Snake-Lover's Diary*, etc.

Autobiographical sketch of Barbara Johnes Brenner:

I WAS born in Brooklyn, New York. My mother died when I was a year old and the task of raising me was delegated to my maternal grandparents. I went to live with them on a farm in Suffern, New York, and they proved to be the most loving surrogate parents. I can remember clearly my grandfather, who was a professional gardener, teaching me the scientific names of flowers and plants when I was quite small. His love of nature impressed itself upon me strongly, and I am sure it has colored much of what I write.

Barbara Brenner

My father was a weekend visitor and he never arrived without a gift. Usually it was a book. I grew up with A. A. Milne, Lewis Carroll, the brothers Grimm, and Blackie's *Children's Annual*. I can still recall some of the pages of these beloved friends.

I think that somewhere around the fifth grade one of my teachers suggested that I might have a flair for writing. I took her comment very seriously and from that time thought of myself as a potential author. By the time I was in high school I had honed my skills enough to write the senior play. I also acted in it, but when I saw how badly I interpreted my own words I was confirmed in writing, rather than acting, as a career.

After high school the need for me to have a steady job arose urgently. Writing did not seem to be the steadiest work available, so I put my writing dreams aside. I worked as a saleswoman for awhile, and then as a mathematician for an insurance company. At last I got the chance to do some writing when I got a job as an advertising copywriter.

Shortly after I met my husband in 1946, I started on a new career—illustrator's agent. We married and settled into an apartment in New York, and I continued to represent him and several other artists. But after a few years I began to yearn again for a writing career. When our first son was old enough to go to nursery school, I began to take some free-lance writing assignments. And then I started to write a children's book.

The first book was never published but I learned what not to do by writing it. The second manuscript was accepted by William R. Scott and published in 1957, the year our second son was born. I loved everything about writing for children and decided then that I had found my métier.

I have now written more than thirty books, one for adults, the rest for children from three up through twelve, and one rock musical for children which had a brief run off-Broadway.

If I were asked my favorite kind of writing, I would say it's probably natural science in a fictional setting, like *Lizard Tails and Cactus Spines* and *A Snake-Lover's Diary*. But I also enjoy writing young picture books with a folk-tale or fairy-tale base, like *Little One Inch*, the book my husband and I just completed.

Barbara Brenner attended public schools in Newark, New Jersey, and took courses at Rutgers University, Seton Hall College, and New York University, attending classes at night. She regards writing books for children as challenging though difficult, for her intent is to show that the world is a vastly interesting and exciting place, that it is good to be curious, that biologically we are part of a vast and remarkable chain of life.

Barto Takes the Subway was an Honor Book in the 1961 *Herald Tribune* Children's Spring Book Festival. *A Snake-Lover's Diary* was designated a Notable Book in 1970 by the American Library Association.

Barbara Brenner's rock musical for children, which was produced off-Broadway in 1965, was called *Ostrich Feathers*.

SELECTED WORKS: Barto Takes the Subway, 1961; A Bird in the Family, 1962; The Five Pennies, 1964; The Flying Patchwork Quilt, 1965; Mr. Tall and Mr. Small, 1966; Summer of the Houseboat, 1968; A Snake-Lover's Diary, 1970; Is It Bigger Than a Sparrow?, 1972; If You Were an Ant, 1973; Hemi: A Mule, 1973; Cunningham's Rooster, 1975; Little One Inch, 1977; On the Frontier with Mr. Audubon, 1977.

ABOUT: Contemporary Authors, Vol. 9–10; Foremost Women in Communications, 1970; Something about the Author, Vol. 4.

FRED BRENNER

April 4, 1920–

ILLUSTRATOR OF *A Bird in the Family*, etc.

Autobiographical sketch of Fred Brenner:

ONE of my first childhood memories is of the drone of conversation and the clatter of dishes in a large room filled with people. My mother and father owned a restaurant in Newark, New Jersey. Since they both worked, the restaurant was more my home than our house was; I spent a good part of my early childhood there.

Our restaurant was across the alley from Proctor's Theater, at that time a well-known stop on the vaudeville circuit. Our patrons were frequently actors. During these early years I remember meeting Ethel Merman and Al Jolson and being shown magic tricks by the great Houdini.

But as vivid as these memories are, more vivid is my recall of Franz, the waiter who used to sit with me and draw pictures. Trains were his specialty and they became mine. That was the beginning of my interest in art.

Soon I was drawing everything in sight. By the time I was in high school I had a firm commitment to a career in art. I went to Newark's Arts High School and even before I graduated was attending classes at the Newark School of Fine and Industrial Arts.

My first "art" job was in the advertising

department of Bamberger's Department Store in Newark. As I recall, my artwork at first consisted primarily of drawing lines to indicate the floor under photographs of refrigerators. But I did subsequently get assigned to doing something more substantial. I began to specialize in men's fashion illustration and decorative line illustration.

My career was interrupted by World War II. I enlisted in the Air Force, where I learned to fly a plane and then was assigned to Air Force Intelligence in the Pacific theater. My job was to illustrate an Air Force Intelligence publication and to keep a record, illustrated graphically, of the destruction of Japan.

My wife and I met shortly after I got out of service. I began to free-lance as an illustrator, and she acted as my representative.

After my wife began writing children's books, I became interested in book illustration. It seemed natural for us to work together as well as separately on books, and we have done so. We both particularly enjoy our joint efforts.

Another rewarding aspect of my work has been my teaching experience at Parsons School of Design, an affiliate of the New School for Social Research. Here I have for sixteen years been working with young illustrators. I teach life drawing and fashion illustration, and I conduct a seminar in illustration.

We have two sons—Mark, a biologist, and Carl, a budding composer. Both of the boys have been models for the characters in some of our books, as has our dog, our snake and our iguana lizard.

We are all avid bird watchers, and the backyard of our new home on a lake in Pennsylvania has been arranged to accommodate a variety of avian visitors, which I photograph whenever I get the chance.

SELECTED WORKS ILLUSTRATED: A Bird in the Family, by Barbara Brenner, 1962; The Flying Patchwork Quilt, by Barbara Brenner, 1965; Summer of the Houseboat, by Barbara Brenner, 1968; Rutgers and the Water-Snouts, by Barbara Dana, 1969; The Drinking Gourd, by F. N. Monjo, 1970; The Windmill Summer, by Hila Feil, 1972; If You Were an Ant, by Barbara Brenner, 1973; The Sick Book, by Marie Winn, 1976; A Child's Book of Birds, by Kathleen N. Daly, 1977; Little One Inch, 1977.

HESBA FAY BRINSMEAD

March 15, 1922–

AUTHOR OF *Pastures of the Blue Crane*, etc.

Autobiographical sketch of Hesba Fay Hungerford Brinsmead:

I WAS born in the Blue Mountains of New South Wales. My parents, both trained to be teachers and missionaries, sold all their possessions and took up crown land in this remote part of the mountains in a last bid to save the life of my eldest sister, who suffered an obscure tropic disease as a baby. It worked! Their own uprooting was the price they paid for the baby's life. They were strange country people, for they were both intellectuals in their way—yet doomed to live entirely cut off from the things that would have been mental meat and drink to them. The result was that we all learned to live in a world of books.

HESBA FAY BRINSMEAD

I can remember my father reading Dickens aloud to us when I must have been no more than four years old—also Wells, Thackeray, Bernard Shaw, Kipling, Guy de Maupassant—the lot! We grew up on literature. Our very isolation forced our imaginations to develop. When I was very small indeed, I wrote poetry and announced that I meant to be a writer!

Well, this was not well received. These were the days of the Great Depression. Writers did not make money. Particularly women writers. So I was laughed out of this childish fancy. My mother supervised correspondence lessons at home until high school level; then later on I was talked into beginning a teacher's training course. However, lack of funds intervened. I got mumps, of all things, couldn't work for a while (one worked and studied in those days), and got into debt. So I abandoned the teacher's course and went out West, then to Tasmania as a governess. Still, mind you, I had not entirely abandoned the dream of writing.

I married at twenty, taught in a kindergarten, had two babies, sent them to school, worked with a repertory club, and always felt the sneaking ambition to write. It wasn't until the boys were well established at school that I'd saved enough (from the housekeeping money) to invest in a correspondence course in journalism and a terrible typewriter. Quite suddenly, I was off the ground! I wrote short things for a few years; then, with my own boys teen-age, realized there was a shortage of books for the pre-adults. So I toiled away at *Pastures of the Blue Crane*. Strangely enough, at just about the same time, other writers in other countries were struck with the same idea. In America, *It's Like This, Cat!*; in England, *The Maplin Bird*—so it went. Those books were pioneers of their kind. Today there's a well-established genre: books that do not insult the intelligence of the young reader who stands with one foot in adult territory and one ready to spring away from childhood.

I like to write for the young. My own peers—we've had our chance, and what have we done to the world? Exploited, polluted it—we've done our worst. I like to give what I can to the young ones coming after, and the most important gift is hope. Honesty, sure—and they're entitled to a sense of honor, but surely hope is the seed of the future. If the young ones find it in my books, I'll not have wasted all that paper.

———

Hesba Fay Hungerford's parents had been missionaries in Java before they moved to the Blue Mountains in New South Wales, where Mr. Hungerford had a sawmill and later the local mail run. Mrs. Hungerford was a professional bulb grower. Hesba Fay was the youngest of five children, four girls and a boy.

Before her marriage to Reginald Brinsmead in 1943, she had had stage and voice training, with the idea of becoming a radio announcer. Years later, when her two sons, Bernard Hungerford and Ken Hungerford, were in their teens, she used that training in writing tales for the Australian Broadcasting Corporation, until so many had been used that she was asked not to submit any more for six months. At that point Mrs. Brinsmead turned to writing for young people.

Twice her books have been designated the Australian Children's Book of the Year: in 1965 it was *Pastures of the Blue Crane*, her first novel for teen-agers; in 1972, *Longtime Passing* (Australia, 1971). *Beat of the City* (1966) was specially mentioned and *A Sapphire for September* (Australia, 1967) was commended by the Australian Children's Book Council for the same award. *Season of the Briar* in its German language edition won the Austrian State Prize in 1968 and was also on the Honor List for the German Children's Book Prize that year.

SELECTED WORKS: Pastures of the Blue Crane, 1966; Season of the Briar, 1967; Beat of the City, 1968.

ABOUT: Contemporary Authors, Vol. 21–22; Townsend, John Rowe. A Sense of Story; Bookbird, No. 4, 1969.

GWENDOLYN BROOKS

GWENDOLYN BROOKS

June 7, 1917–

AUTHOR OF *Bronzeville Boys and Girls*, etc.

Biographical sketch of Gwendolyn Elizabeth Brooks Blakely:

GWENDOLYN ELIZABETH BROOKS was born on June 7, 1917, in Topeka, Kansas. Her mother, who had returned to her parents' home to have her child, remained in Kansas for about one month and then with her infant daughter rejoined her husband in Chicago's South Side black ghetto.

The Brookses had moved to the Windy City during the first decade of the twentieth century. Though David Brooks had dreamed of becoming a physician, the young black man could find only menial work and was never able to afford a medical education. Nevertheless he retained all his life a deep love of learning that was shared by his wife, Keziah, who had been an elementary school teacher in Topeka.

Gwendolyn Brooks spent her childhood in a small frame house whose backyard faced a row of tenements. Her family was poor, but her parents provided a rich intellectual atmosphere for Gwendolyn and her younger brother Raymond. Music and books were an integral part of the household, and David Brooks was particularly fond of reading aloud to his children.

At the age of seven Gwendolyn wrote her first verses. Her mother encouraged her and made sure her daughter had the time she needed to read extensively and work to perfect her writing. Being a shy child, Gwendolyn made no close friends. She would spend hours gazing at the clouds from the back porch of her home, dreaming of a glorious future, ignoring the tenements that rose directly in front of her. School and schoolwork did not interest her, and for the most part, she was a mediocre student.

During adolescence, Gwendolyn's awareness of racial prejudice deepened. In high school she noted "nothing overt, but a sort of coldness and controlled hostility among some of the white children who had never met black children except those of their servants." Meanwhile she continued her poetic efforts and came to know the work of such prominent black writers as James Weldon Johnson and Langston Hughes, whom she met when they came to Chicago. When Gwendolyn was thirteen, *American Childhood*, a popular magazine for young people, published her poem "Eventide." She also started a small handwritten newspaper of her own that told the neighborhood gossip. This project was shortlived, but when she was seventeen Gwendolyn became a regular contributor to the *Chicago Defender*. The Negro newspaper printed more than seventy-five of her poems and other writings in its "Lights and Shadows" column.

After graduation from Wilson Junior College during the Depression, Gwendolyn found employment as a secretary for a fraudulent "spiritual advisor," who preyed upon impoverished blacks. This experience brought the young poet into close contact with people undergoing excruciating sufferings during the four months she worked for "Dr." French in the rundown Mecca building, which had formerly been a luxury apartment house. Decades later her experiences furnished the material for her poem "In the Mecca," published in 1968.

In 1939 Miss Brooks married Henry Blakely, a small-businessman in Chicago, and the following year their son Henry was born. Even as she accepted the responsibilities of wife and mother, Gwendolyn Brooks did not abandon her writing. In 1941 she joined a poetry class under the direction of Inez Stark Boulton, an editor of *Poetry* magazine. For two years this class met at Chicago's South Side Community Art Center, and during this time Gwendolyn learned much about modern poetry.

In 1943, 1944 and 1945 Gwendolyn Brooks won first prize for her poetry from the Midwest Writers Conference, and in August 1945 her first book of verse, *A Street in Bronzeville*, was published. The book, which Richard Wright described as "an honest human reaction to the pain that lurks so colorfully in the Black Belt," earned great praise for its author. She was chosen one of *Mademoiselle* magazine's Ten Women of the Year and won an Academy of Arts and Letters award. She also received Guggenheim Fellowships in 1947 and 1948.

Her second book, *Annie Allen*, which expresses the feelings of a woman as daughter, wife and mother, was published in 1949. For this work Miss Brooks was awarded the Pulitzer Prize in 1950, thereby becoming the first black to be so honored. She also won the Eunice Tietjens Memorial Award given by *Poetry* magazine.

Despite the birth of her daughter Nora in 1951, Miss Brooks continued to write prolifically. In 1953 her novel, *Maud Martha*, a series of sketches about a black girl growing up in Chicago, was widely acclaimed. Three years later a children's book, *Bronzeville Boys and Girls*, was published. Each poem in this collection bears the name of a boy or girl and describes the simple and intense feelings of the children of the ghetto.

Gwendolyn Brooks has lectured widely, has taught at several Chicago colleges, and has been named Poet Laureate of Illinois, succeeding Carl Sandburg in that office. In 1977 she was a judge for the National Book Award for poetry. Her poetry, which has appeared in anthologies and in countless periodicals, draws on and captures the life of Chicago's black ghetto, but prior to 1968 her work centered on universal experiences and emotions. Since that date, her tone has grown fiercer and, like many black artists, she has come to concentrate on the black experience as separate and to address herself to a black audience. Recent poems such as "Malcolm X," "Blackstone Rangers," and her autobiography *Report from Part One* (1972) express her new militancy, while her continuing efforts to aid young black writers demonstrate her intense concern that younger voices have the opportunity to be heard.

SELECTED WORKS: Maud Martha, 1953; Bronzeville Boys and Girls, 1956; The Bean Eaters, 1960; In the Mecca, 1968; Riot, 1969; Family Pictures, 1970.

SELECTED WORKS EDITED: A Broadside Treasury, 1965–1970; Jump Bad, 1971; The Black Position, No. 1, 1971; The Black Position, No. 2, 1972; The Black Position, No. 3, 1973.

ABOUT: Adams, Russell L. Great Negroes Past and Present; Cherry, Gwendolyn and others. Portraits in Color; Contemporary Authors, Vol. 1; Current Biography 1950; Dreer, Herman. American Literature by Negro Authors; Drotning, Philip T. and Wesley W. South. Up from the Ghetto; Murphy, Rosalie, ed. Contemporary Poets of the English Language; Rollins, Charlemae. Famous American Negro Poets; Twentieth Century Authors (First Supplement); Who's Who in America, 1972–73; Who's Who in the Midwest, 1970–71; Who's Who of American Women, 1972–73, 1974–75; Ebony July 1968; Saturday Review of Literature May 20, 1950.

ROY BROWN

1921–

AUTHOR OF *A Saturday in Pudney*, etc.

Autobiographical sketch of Roy Brown:

I WAS born in Vancouver, British Columbia, in 1921, but when I was four years old my family returned to England, and I have spent all my life since then, apart from four wartime years abroad in the Royal Air Force, within a short train ride of Central London. Leaving school at the age of fourteen, I took one of my first jobs in London, and I can remember spending most lunch times, packet of sandwiches in hand, seeing how far I could walk in a straight line and back again (not, of course, always choosing the same radial from the center!).

I think it was this somewhat vague exploration that gave me my intense feeling for London—not the London of cathedrals, art galleries and tourist attractions, but the grimier streets and alleys that feature so much in my books. After the war I trained as a teacher and, although it involved a good deal of daily travel (and more walking—better than queuing for buses in the rush hour), I accepted a post in East London at a junior school. It was to be over ten years before my first "real" children's book, *A Saturday in Pudney*, was written, rewritten, rewritten again, and eventually published by Abelard-Schuman, London, yet many of the characters in it were modeled on children I'd taught and people I'd met in those earlier years.

That was in 1966 and other books, all with London settings, have appeared in the United Kingdom and United States at almost yearly intervals. Several have also been translated into German, Italian, Swedish, French and—most recently—Japanese.

In 1969 I took the post of Deputy Head at the well-known Helen Allison School for Autistic Children in Gravesend, Kent. Experience in this very special area of handicap helped to produce *Escape the River*, my fourth novel, which featured a boy character with autistic behavior.

My aim with each novel is to make people, and especially children, as real as possible and to explore their characters against a background of ordinary London life. Most of the stories deal, on the emotional level, with one or more child characters meeting a deeply personal crisis and growing up a little in the course of coping with it.

Two of Roy Brown's books, *A Saturday in Pudney* and *The Day of the Pigeons*, were made into films in England. A third, *The Viaduct*, has twice appeared on British television. *Find*

Debbie was named by *School Library Journal* as one of the best books of 1976. Besides his novels, Roy Brown has written for the popular British television program, "Jackanory," as well as numerous short stories and some non-fiction books, but his novels remain his prime concern.

SELECTED WORKS: A Saturday in Pudney, 1968; The Viaduct, 1968; The Day of the Pigeons, 1969; The Battle of Saint Street, 1971; Escape the River, 1972; Flight of Sparrows, 1973; No Through Road, 1974; The White Sparrow, 1975; Find Debbie, 1976; The Cage, 1977.

KARL BRUCKNER

January 9, 1906–

AUTHOR OF *The Day of the Bomb*, etc.

Autobiographical sketch of Karl Bruckner, translated from the German:

LIKE all my ancestors I was born in Vienna: in 1529 Johannes Karl Bruckner, fought against the Turks who were at that time besieging the city. Vienna is more than two thousand years old. The Celts and the Romans settled here, and the Avars, Huns, Hungarians, Turks, Swedes and French also came. Last of all came the Nazis, and even they were survived by the Viennese, who love to laugh and know how to enjoy life, but who also know how to fight if their freedom is threatened.

But I'm supposed to tell about myself: I was born the son of a book printer on January 9, 1906. My years in primary and secondary school only awakened my wish to become a famous painter or musician. Nevertheless I became an automotive technician, and at twenty-three I was unemployed. In my search for work I tramped through Europe and emigrated to Brazil in 1936. Returning after a two-year stay, rich in experience, I had to exchange civilian clothes for a soldier's uniform at the outbreak of war, though as a convinced pacifist I fought so badly for the "Führer" and his "thousand-year Reich" that at the war's end my chest was bare of any medals at all.

My career as a writer began during the war, and in a rather strange way. In April 1944 I was slightly wounded and stuck in a military hospital. There every night I told my fellow patients an adventure from my journeys. On April 13, 1944, about one o'clock at night, I finished another suspenseful story. Then a comrade called over to me: "Man, that's like a novel. Write it down—you have a talent for writing." On the same day and at the same hour, but two years later, on April 13, 1946, I was working in a newspaper printshop in Vienna— and there I remembered my friend's comment. The next day I began writing my first novel, at the age of forty. I found a publisher who had confidence in my work, although I thought my language and style were so terrible that I refused to let my first work appear, which made my publisher think I was crazy. Two more novels (for adult readers) followed. I improved my vocabulary, wrote more slowly, listened to the cadence of language, and searched for new expressions. In 1948 I wrote my first book for young people; since then I have remained true to this very important branch of literature because I am convinced that if a man reads no books in his youth he will not do it in ripe old age either. Altogether I have written thirty novels. Five of them I did not like too much, and I have not allowed them to be printed; only the best is good enough for the young.

———

As a boy Karl Bruckner was a dreamy child who told fairy tales to himself. Books and literature were not part of his family life, but nevertheless, one year Bruckner's older brother was given a copy of *Robinson Crusoe* for Christmas. The book made a profound impression on young Karl and influenced his dreams for a long time afterwards.

He was a poor student. Though he read widely and spent as much time as he could in museums, his teachers regarded him as a dreamer who would never amount to much. Except for one good year with a beloved teacher, he hated the experience and left school as soon as he could. Then Bruckner went to work in a factory during the day and painted when he got home at night. However, during the worldwide depression his job evaporated and he found himself with time to read and write poetry and to become an opera fan. Hoping to find work, he left Vienna for Berlin, and thence through Europe and South America where he engaged in many different kinds of work before he returned home two years later. By then Bruckner had begun to try to write. He was encouraged by a newspaper editor, but that relationship was short-lived, for soon after, the Nazis came to Vienna, and Bruckner's mentor was a Jew.

After the war, Bruckner worked at odd jobs and dreamed of a political career. He wanted to improve the world, but when he realized how many compromises are demanded for political success, he withdrew again.

His first novel *Das Diamant des Tobias Amberger* (The Diamond of Tobias Amberger) was written in six weeks and received first prize in an Austrian publisher's competition. That was the beginning. Since then Bruckner has written more than twenty-five books. His work has been translated into twenty-three languages and has appeared in eighty-nine foreign editions, a record of which he is justly proud.

Perhaps his best-known book is *Sadako Will Leben* (The Day of the Bomb), a story set amidst the atomic bombing of Hiroshima. The book received the Austrian State Prize for Young People's Books in 1961 and was on the Honors list for the Hans Christian Andersen Award in 1962 and for the German Children's Book Prize in 1963. In addition Bruckner has won the annual Vienna Children's and Youth Book Prize four times. He has been awarded an honorary professorship by his native city for his work in children's literature.

SELECTED WORKS: Golden Pharaoh, 1959; The Day of the Bomb, 1963.

SHEILA BURNFORD

May 11, 1918–

AUTHOR OF *The Incredible Journey*, etc.

Biographical sketch of Sheila Cochrane Burnford, who also uses the pseudonyms "S. D. Burnford" and "Philip Cochrane Every":

SCOTLAND was Sheila Burnford's birthplace and she was educated there, at Harrogate College in Yorkshire, Enland, and in Germany. She grew up in a book-loving home and read widely and without restriction. During the early part of the Second World War, she worked in Royal Naval hospitals and drove an ambulance until family commitments put an end to her active service.

In 1941 she married Dr. David Burnford, at that time a surgeon in the Royal Navy, and spent the later years of the war with her young family in a rambling house in Sussex. During this period, she says, she came to depend on her English bull terrier Bill for company and secu-

SHEILA BURNFORD

rity. "I laugh when I look back upon it, for I used to read to him in the evenings —excerpts from the papers and a long session of Anthony Trollope. There was no one else to listen or to whom I could talk, as the two oldest children were only babies, so the terrier became my captive audience. . . . The extraordinary extent of his recognition of words and phrases, far beyond the normal range, was probably the result of those conversational years."

After the war, the Burnfords, with their three small daughters—and Bill— moved to Canada and settled in Port Arthur in 1948. Bill was lonely when the little girls went off to school, Sheila Burnford recalls, so he was consoled with a new companion, a Siamese kitten named Simon. "They were closer than any other cat-and-dog relationship I have seen, sleeping in the same basket, hunting together, playing; and each assumed some of the other's characteristics." The household was later increased by a Labrador ". . . always a serious, law-abiding gun dog, who never participated in their kitchen raids, or joined them hunting in the woods; but as the terrier's sight began to fail him, the young dog showed the most astonishing perception and tolerance; and it became the accepted custom that he should ac-

company the old terrier on his morning and evening rounds of the neighborhood garbage cans and hydrants, waiting patiently at every place of interest, steering him back on the sidewalk when he would have strayed onto the road, and finally delivering his charge home."

Sheila Burnford had always been interested in writing, and now that her children were at school she decided to try her hand. She began with scripts for the Port Arthur Puppetry Club and then started to write about the Canadian scene for British magazines and periodicals, including *Punch* and *Blackwood's*. A selection of these articles was later published as *The Fields of Noon*.

For some time Sheila Burnford had been thinking of writing a novel about animals, and after Bill the bull terrier died at the age of fifteen, the book began to take shape. "Communication between animals has always fascinated me," Mrs. Burnford writes, "not just the instinctive means, but the day-to-day, individual and original communication that exists even between animals of diversified species when they live harmoniously with common domestic background."

The Incredible Journey, about a terrier, a Labrador retriever and a Siamese cat who journey 250 miles through the Canadian wilderness to reach home, was published in 1963 to great critical and popular acclaim. The book was not intended primarily for children, but children everywhere loved it and it received a number of children's book awards: The Canadian Association of Children's Librarians' Book of the Year Medal in 1963, the Aurianne Award and the Dorothy Canfield Fisher Award the same year, and in 1964 the William Allen White Children's Book Award and the Pacific Northwest Library Association's Young Reader's Choice Award. The book was also included on the 1964 Hans Christian Andersen Honor List. It has been translated into over twenty languages and made into a motion picture by Walt Disney. In 1975 it was included in the American Library Association's reevaluated list of Best Books for

Young Adults entitled "Still Alive in '75."

In 1969 Sheila Burnford's third book, *Without Reserve*, was published. Based on a journal she kept during a number of visits to Cree and Ojibwa reservations, it reflects her interest in the culture and traditions of native peoples. A fascination with birds and marine biology took her on a marine biology expedition to Antarctica in 1968, and this too resulted in a book, *One Woman's Arctic*, published in 1973. In the same year, her children's book *Mr. Noah and the Second Flood* also appeared. Her other interests include flying—she has a pilot's license—hunting, mycology and astronomy. The Burnfords now divide their time between England and Canada.

SELECTED WORKS: The Incredible Journey, 1963; Mr. Noah and the Second Flood, 1973; One Woman's Arctic, 1973.

ABOUT: Contemporary Authors, Vol. 2; Irma McDonough, comp. Profiles from In Review, 1971; Something about the Author, Vol. 3.

OLIVER BUTTERWORTH

May 23, 1915–

AUTHOR OF *The Enormous Egg*, etc.

Autobiographical sketch of Oliver Butterworth:

I GREW up on the outskirts of Hartford, Connecticut, in a place that was pasture and woodlot back in the 1920s, and there were cows just beyond the hurdle fences at the foot of the hill. In the winter we would be snowed in sometimes, and my sister and brother and I would miss school for a day or two until the road was plowed out. After my mother died, my father had to be both parents to us. Sometimes he took us to school on a toboggan.

Later, as the city of Hartford grew bigger, we had more neighbors, the cows disappeared, stores and gas stations began to crop up where corn had grown before, and we took part in the great national experience of the 1920s—the ur-

OLIVER BUTTERWORTH

banization of America. Those childhood memories of the open fields, the long empty road to the "avenue," and the sometime loneliness of a long summer afternoon still cling in my mind.

I went away to boarding school when I was thirteen, living out the long dark winters in the western Connecticut hills with three hundred other boys, learning to work and play together in the strangely fraternal society of a boarding school. After graduation from Dartmouth College in 1937 (where I learned to love the northern New England hills and valleys) I took a job teaching English and Latin to schoolboys who were not visibly enthusiastic about these subjects. I married an athletic young woman and we went on a six-hundred-mile canoeing honeymoon over the border into Canada. In the following years we had four children (three boys and a girl) and built ourselves a summer cabin on a lake in New Hampshire, where we spent many grand summers in a spirit of independence, living happily without electricity or running water, with the children all sharing in the chores.

Then I taught for two years in an elementary school and hit on the idea of writing books for children. The first one was *The Enormous Egg*, which came from our experience with our backyard hens. This was followed by *The Trouble with Jenny's Ear*, coming from the children's experiments with electrical equipment, and my most recent book, *The Narrow Passage*, which grew out of our visit to the famous cave of Lascaux in France.

Our family has enjoyed some splendid trips together. In 1953 we traveled the whole length of the Oregon Trail in a Jeep station wagon, camping out on the still visible camp grounds of the wagon trains, reliving a piece of American history, lying on the Nebraska grass at night by the Platte River, looking up at the stars, thinking of the covered wagon families who looked up at the same stars from the same place more than a hundred years ago.

Then there was the great European Expedition of 1955 and 1956, when we left home for a year and took our four children abroad, living in little villages in Scotland and France and Ireland and Norway, forgetting about school, tutoring the children in math and history and even English, and having wide-eyed experiences like tenting in the Sahara Desert by the pyramids, living in a Norwegian log cabin, and helping to gather in the sheep in the Scottish Highlands.

When the children were a little older, we went to Alaska one summer and lived in the Eskimo village of Point Barrow, the northernmost point of all the United States. We went for rides in the seal-hide umiaks along the shore of the Arctic Ocean, watching the ice floes drifting by and the great whales spouting just off shore.

I have been a teacher so much of my life that I probably try to do a little teaching in my books, telling about things like dinosaurs and caves and crystal radios. But I think what I want most to do is to share my feelings and my ideas, to tell children (and perhaps grown-ups too) about what's precious to me, about the colors of life, the green freedom of leaves and grass, the gray blue of hills and streams, the bone white color of honesty, the flesh tones of the warm pulse of families together, the brown firmness of the ground to sleep on, and the way it stretches from Atlantic to Pacific, and the solid feel of belonging to a land that belongs to you, the blue white of New England winters, the sunshine yellow of springtime, and the true blue of courage to speak up for what you think is right.

I never dreamed when I was young that I would have this chance to tell people about the things that delight me and excite me, and I consider myself incredibly lucky to be able to do it. Sometimes I think I might pinch myself and wake up and find that I had just dreamed about writing books. It seems too good to be true.

Oliver Butterworth married Miriam Brooks in 1940. Their four children are Michael, Timothy, Dan and Kate. Mr. Butterworth now teaches English at Hartford College. He is a trustee of that institution as well as of the Mark Twain Memorial in Hartford. He is a member of the Writer's Group.

The New York *Times* included *The Enormous Egg* in its list of one hundred best children's books published in 1956. *The Trouble with Jenny's Ear* was chosen an Honor Book in the New York *Herald Tribune* Children's Spring Book Festival in 1960.

SELECTED WORKS: The Enormous Egg, 1956; The Trouble with Jenny's Ear, 1960; The Narrow Passage, 1973.

ABOUT: Contemporary Authors, Vol. 4; Something about the Author, Vol. 1; Who's Who in America, 1972–73.

POLLY CAMERON

October 14, 1928–

AUTHOR AND ILLUSTRATOR OF *"I Can't," Said the Ant*, etc.

Autobiographical sketch of Polly McQuiston Cameron:

I WAS born in Walnut Creek, California, and raised in Northern California

Polly Cameron

and at my grandparents' ranch in Arizona, outside of Phoenix. I preferred, of course, the ranch, where life was free and easy, filled with animals and sunshine.

I attended the University of California at Santa Barbara, majoring in Speech with the intention of going into a radio career. My first interest in creating for children was developed out of a children's radio series I wrote, narrated and produced while still in college.

In my third year at school, I lost all interest in formal education, quit school, and retired to the hills of Santa Barbara where I wrote poetry and gardened for a living. But within six months I returned to the ranch in Arizona and got a job in advertising and display, which sparked my first real interest in art.

During the two years I had that job, I designed and built my own house on the ranch. As I look back I wonder how it was accomplished. I had the help of just one friend, who was as much of a house-building novice as I, and we only had evenings and weekends free to work on it.

I lived in the house for only one year, then got the wanderlust and sold it to finance a trip to Europe, which lasted

three and a half years. I bought a car in Paris and drove all over Europe, spent the winter in Majorca until, once again, no more funds. I got a job as a draftsman for an American architectural firm building a giant American air base outside of Casablanca, North Africa. Never having had an art course in my life, it was a job in itself just to bluff my way through, but it was great fun as every destitute American in Paris in the early fifties appeared for a job with questionable references as "draftsman." North Africa has probably not been the same since.

In a year I managed to save enough to return to Paris where I began to paint and to realize that I wanted a career in art. Finally the money ran out again and I had just enough to make it to New York City and no farther.

I put together a design portfolio and began getting free-lance work in almost every aspect of graphic design: book and record jackets, advertising and promotion brochures, magazine illustration, book and catalog design, etc. I was also painting and working in sculpture, exhibiting in New York City and environs.

In 1956 I published my first picture book for very young children, *The Cat Who Thought He Was a Tiger*, which I wrote and illustrated. For me this was the perfect answer for my combined interest in writing and art. It also provided an outlet for my rather bizarre sense of humor, which appears to be at a five- to eight-year-old level. I have since written and illustrated ten books for children and will shortly finish my eleventh. Since 1960, I have also been working as a free-lance graphic art director in educational audiovisual materials.

In 1959 I moved from New York City to a small, absolutely beautiful community of peace and quiet—less than an hour from the city (which I seldom, if ever, visit). Called Sneden's Landing, it's a tiny haven on the Hudson River, with mostly early Revolutionary houses and beautiful gardens. I live in a mid-nineteenth century Victorian-Gothic house overlooking the river, with a brook flowing through the garden and a freshwater spring where George Washington once stopped his troops for water.

In working out the illustration and design of her children's books, Polly Cameron has experimented continually with new techniques. She accounts for this versatility by saying that she is more a designer than an illustrator. In choosing her subjects she occasionally bases her stories on real objects. Thus *The Green Machine* was inspired by Miss Cameron's own classic sports car, a Morgan, and *The Dog Who Grew Too Much* by her own French sheep dog.

In 1960, The American Institute of Graphic Arts made an award to *A Child's Book of Nonsense* for outstanding book design. *"I Can't," Said the Ant* was designated a Notable Book by the American Library Association in 1961.

SELECTED WORKS WRITTEN AND ILLUSTRATED: The Cat Who Thought He Was a Tiger, 1956; The Cat Who Couldn't Purr, 1957; The Dog Who Grew Too Much, 1958; The Boy Who Drew Birds, 1959; A Child's Book of Nonsense, 1960; "I Can't," Said the Ant, 1961; The Two Ton Canary and Other Nonsense Riddles, 1965; The Polly Cameron Picture Book, 1970; The Secret Toy Machine, 1972.

SELECTED WORKS WRITTEN: The Green Machine, 1969.

SELECTED WORKS ILLUSTRATED: Rufus the Red-Necked Hornbill, by Patricia Lauber, 1958.

ABOUT: Contemporary Authors, Vol. 17–18; Foremost Women in Communications, 1970; Kingman, Lee and others, comps. Illustrators of Children's Books: 1957–1966; Something about the Author, Vol. 2.

ERIC CARLE

June 25, 1929–

AUTHOR AND ILLUSTRATOR OF *The Very Hungry Caterpillar*

Autobiographical sketch of Eric Carle:

I WAS born in Syracuse, New York. There I went to kindergarten. I remember large sheets of paper, colorful paints and big brushes. Every morning I set off

ERIC CARLE

to kindergarten with great enthusiasm. When I was six years old, my parents returned to their homeland and relatives in Germany. There I went to school. I remember that we children were given small sheets of paper, a hard pencil, a ruler, an eraser and a warning not to make any mistakes. My enthusiasm for school was considerably reduced.

As a six-year-old boy I had the doubtful privilege of going to school twice, of learning two languages, of coping with two cultures, and adapting myself to two societies. The messages I received during that period of my life were somewhat confused.

I went to school in Germany until I was sixteen. I disliked most of my education with the exception of a wonderful art teacher and a kind and gentle librarian.

I was ten years old when World War II broke out. My father (and best friend) was drafted into the German army. He did not return home until I was eighteen years old. I had missed him especially while he was in a POW camp in Russia from 1945 to 1947.

From 1946 to 1950 I spent four happy and influential years at the Akademie der bildenden Kunste in Stuttgart (Germany). For the first time I felt my horizons expanding and the love for making pictures carrying me on.

From 1950 to 1952 I designed posters for the United States Information Center in Stuttgart. Then I returned to New York and started to work as a graphic designer for the New York *Times*. I was drafted into the U.S. Army the same year and returned to the *Times* after my discharge in 1954. In 1956 I became an art director for a pharmaceutical advertising agency, but I began losing interest in advertising and in 1963 quit my job in order to free-lance as an illustrator.

In the late sixties, several publishing houses asked me to illustrate material for first readers, and I found myself becoming deeply involved in these assignments. I felt something of my own past stirring in me. An unresolved part of my own education needed reworking, and I began to make books—books for myself, books for the child in me, books I had yearned for. I became my own teacher—but this time an understanding one. Since 1968 I have illustrated and written over ten books. *The Very Hungry Caterpillar* has been translated into a dozen languages.

As a child I did not have any children's books aside from a Mickey Mouse and a Flash Gordon book in the United States and a Max and Moritz and Struwelpeter book in Germany. As an adult my interest in children's books has been minimal. And yet I am in the midst of writing and illustrating books for children in all parts of the world. I hope that the children have as much fun looking at my books as I have doing them.

Carle has written of how, as a child, he used to long for a bridge to be built from Germany to America so he could get back "home." He was assured that this was impossible, but now he knows that through children's books such bridges can exist—from country to country and also from the adult artist to his own childhood, and so to other children.

His belief is confirmed by the awards he has collected on both sides of the Atlantic. In 1970 *1, 2, 3 to the Zoo* received the German Children's Book Prize and was also given First Prize for Picture Books at the International Children's Book Fair in Bologna. *The Very Hungry Caterpillar*, having been on the New York *Times* list of the ten best illustrated books of the year in 1969 and included in the 1970 American Institute of Graphic Arts' show of The Best Children's Books, received the 1972 German Children's Book Prize and was singled out for special mention in England and France. The same title was included in a list of best-selling children's books compiled by the Children's Book Council in 1972 and has received a Brooklyn Art Books for Children Citation. *Do You Want to Be My Friend?*, an American Library Association Notable Book in 1971 and designated an Honor Book in the *Book World* Children's Spring Book Festival that year, won the First Prize for Picture Books at Bologna in 1972.

Eric Carle has two children, Cirsten and Rolf. His marriage to Dorothea Wohlenberg ended in divorce.

SELECTED WORKS WRITTEN AND ILLUSTRATED: 1, 2, 3 to the Zoo, 1968; The Very Hungry Caterpillar, 1969; The Tiny Seed, 1970; Do You Want to Be My Friend?, 1971; The Secret Birthday Message, 1972; The Rooster Who Set Out to See the World, 1972; The Very Long Tail, 1972; The Very Long Train, 1972; Have you Seen My Cat?, 1973; I See a Song, 1973; All About Arthur, 1974; The Mixed-Up Chameleon, 1975.

SELECTED WORKS ILLUSTRATED: Why Noah Chose the Dove, retold by Isaac Bashevis Singer, 1974; The Hole in the Dike, retold by Norma B. Green, 1975; Eric Carle's Storybook: Seven Tales by the Brothers Grimm (retold), 1976.

ABOUT: Contemporary Authors, Vol. 25–26; Something about the Author, Vol. 4; Language Arts April 1977.

CAROL CARRICK

May 20, 1935–

AUTHOR OF *The Old Barn*, etc.

Autobiographical sketch of Carol Hatfield Carrick:

AT the time I grew up in a small community on Long Island, New York, it

Carol Carrick

was surrounded by woods, fields, and a pond thriving with dragonflies, tadpoles and discarded goldfish. It was this fortunate setting that started my interest in natural science. I spent many hours identifying wild flowers, collecting cocoons, and fruitlessly searching for information on the care and feeding of tadpoles and baby turtles.

My earliest literary memory is of my mother reading to me. I couldn't wait to learn to read at school. I would spell out every third word of my story books to my mother, and she would patiently tell me what the word was.

I remember getting my first library card. The smell of an old library is still exciting to me. I set myself two impossible tasks—reading all the books there, starting with the A's, and copying the dictionary into a little notebook.

I started writing poems and, with less ease, stories, which always lacked an ending. This is still my problem.

Every summer I withdrew an armload of vacation books from the library to take to my grandmother's on the New Jersey shore. Being very reserved, it was hard to form friendships with the transient children whose parents were renting a cottage for a week or two. Sculpturing sand castles and sea maidens and battling the surf led to dreamy fantasies,

heightened by the exotic sights and smells and sounds of the boardwalk at night.

My imagination was channeled into making drawings, and I was sidetracked into an art career. With the help of a scholarship from Hofstra University on Long Island, I graduated with a B.A. degree in advertising art and worked several years for a magazine, advertising agencies, and free-lancing. This was how I met Donald Carrick in New York City, and it was through blithely "offering" to write a children's book for him to illustrate that I started writing again.

Since I always loved nature and Don is a landscape painter we fell into our own peculiar style of picture book based on the woods and waters around our summer camp in Vermont.

We chose subjects like "The Pond" and made observations and visual notes before starting a story line. Even if I am "only" writing for young children, I am not at ease unless I thoroughly research our material. I feel strongly that even if children are just indirectly learning something from us, our books ought to be accurate. Maybe this is the result of my days of frustrated tadpole-raising.

Moving to the island of Martha's Vineyard, where we spend the school year, may be the inspiration for my books about the life cycles of the lobster, the sand tiger shark, and the octopus.

With the birth of our sons Christopher and, six years later, Paul, solitary canoe rides ended. I began to watch the children instead of birds and butterflies. Their lives resurrected forgotten emotions from my own childhood. With encouragement from Jim Giblin at Seabury, I wrote four "child-scale adventures," starting with *Sleep Out*, and then *The Highest Balloon on the Common* for Greenwillow.

I am now working on my first short novel for older children. To date, it has been my most involving writing experience.

———

The Blue Lobster received honorable

mention for the New York Academy of Science's Children's Science Book Award in 1975.

SELECTED WORKS: The Old Barn, 1966; The Brook, 1967; Swamp Spring, 1969; A Clearing in the Forest, 1970; The Dirt Road, 1970; The Pond, 1970; Sleep Out, 1973; Beach Bird, 1973; Lost in the Storm, 1974; Old Mother Witch, 1975; The Blue Lobster, 1975; The Accident, 1976; The Foundling, 1977; The Highest Balloon on the Common, 1977; Sand Tiger Shark, 1977.

ABOUT: Contemporary Authors, Vol. 45–48; Something about the Author, Vol. 7.

DONALD CARRICK

April 7, 1929–

ILLUSTRATOR OF *The Old Barn*, etc.

Autobiographical sketch of Donald Carrick:

MY early years were spent near several hundred acres of farm land and woodlots bordering the Henry Ford estate in Dearborn, Michigan. I grew up at home with trees and fields, yet never appreciating rivers, which, because of the factories, were like mustard flowing through black banks.

I have always been drawing. It was not until I left the local school for Cass Technical High in Detroit, with its superb staff and the dozens of students who thought as I did, that school finally had a meaning.

Summers and weekends were spent apprenticed to a sign painter. I learned much of the shop craft and traveled around upper Michigan painting billboards. One summer was spent painting a four-story mural for a ginger ale company.

At that time an art career in Detroit meant either designing or advertising. I chose advertising and began to develop the skills necessary to paint happy people and backgrounds for the exquisite airbrush renderings of cars.

Scholarships to the Colorado Springs Fine Arts Center and The Art Students

League in New York replaced the studio drawing board for an easel.

The Korean War draft sent me to Germany. All off-duty time was spent tracking down all the buildings and museums I had studied in art history class. I felt right at home.

Back in New York I worked in another advertising art studio for money to return to Europe. Although I found the work terrible, the practical knowledge of production and color separation gave me a foundation for books that I've never regretted.

The next years were spent painting in Spain and Greece, a winter of study at the Vienna Academy of Fine Art, and working in New York. At this time I began to exhibit paintings in New York and, over the years, have had many one-man shows.

Robert Goldston asked me to illustrate one of his children's history books, *The Civil War in Spain*. It was the first of several books we did together. Each one convinced me more that illustrating books was what I had always looked for.

An editor suggested I try a book on my own. I impressed my wife, Carol, to write our first picture book, *The Old Barn*. This was followed shortly by our first son, Christopher.

I satisfied a lifelong urge by building

a cabin in Vermont, complete with field-stone fireplace. Later I illustrated *A Clearing in the Forest*, which Carol based on our experience.

Together with the Vermont landscape, my painting continued to filter into several nature books, *Swamp Spring* and *The Brook* among others.

My love of trees and of building cropped up again in the first book I wrote. *The Tree* was a heady experience as I realized the dimensions possible when one is completely in control of a book.

I always work from life and like to know as much about a book's subject as possible. A crayfish lived in our turkey roaster while we worked on *The Pond*, two turtles occupied the bathtub for *Turtle Pond*, and I captured a vole and a lobster to observe for long periods while illustrating *Bear Mouse* and *The Blue Lobster*.

Our second son, Paul, made the New York apartment shrink. We had been visiting Martha's Vineyard each summer on the way to Vermont. While making preliminary drawings on the Vineyard for *Beach Bird*, we decided to move there.

Now the ocean, the sun, and fogs are working their way into new books, like *Lost in the Storm*, *Walls Are to Be Walked*, and *A Wet and Sandy Day*.

Donald Carrick was represented in the 1970 show mounted by the American Institute of Graphic Arts. *Bear Mouse*, *Lost in the Storm*, and *The Blue Lobster* were selected for inclusion in the Children's Book Showcase in 1974, 1975, and 1976 respectively.

SELECTED WORKS WRITTEN AND ILLUS-TRATED: The Tree, 1971; Drip Drop, 1973; The Deer in the Pasture, 1976.

SELECTED WORKS ILLUSTRATED: The Civil War in Spain, by Robert Goldston, 1966; The Old Barn, by Carol Carrick, 1966; The Brook, by Carol Carrick, 1967; Swamp Spring, by Carol Carrick, 1969; A Clearing in the Forest, by Carol Carrick, 1970; The Pond, by Carol Carrick, 1970; Turtle Pond, by Berniece Freschet, 1971;

Beach Bird, by Carol Carrick, 1973; Bear Mouse, by Berniece Freschet, 1973; Lost in the Storm, by Carol Carrick, 1974; Grizzly Bear, by Berniece Freschet, 1975; The Blue Lobster, by Carol Carrick, 1975; The Accident, by Carol Carrick, 1976; Wind, Sand and Sky, by Rebecca Caudill, 1976; A Wet and Sandy Day, by Joanne Ryder, 1977; Walls Are To Be Walked, by Nathan Zimelman, 1977.

ABOUT: Contemporary Authors, Vol. 53–56; Something about the Author, Vol. 7.

MARY ELLEN CHASE

February 24, 1887–July 28, 1973

AUTHOR OF *Sailing the Seven Seas*, etc.

Biographical sketch of Mary Ellen Chase:

MARY ELLEN CHASE was born in the seacoast village of Blue Hill, Maine, which was founded by her ancestors in 1692. She was the second of eight children of Edith (Lord) Chase and Judge Edward Everett Chase. Her mother, whose family were preachers and teachers, filled her with a love of books and was, she wrote later, "my first and always my best teacher." Her father's family were seafarers who had sailed all over the world, often with their families, on the great clipper ships. Her paternal grandmother, whom she described as "the most alive person I ever knew," used to tell the children vivid stories of being shipwrecked on her honeymoon, of ordinary days at sea, of foreign harbors and cities. These stories became the material of some of Miss Chase's best works.

Her elementary school years were spent in the village school her father and grandfather had attended and were enriched by her mother's magic with words and dramatizations and her father's passion for memorizing great works, plus his strong belief in the dignity and need of manual labor for everyone, to "straighten out one's thought." When Mary Ellen was thirteen she went to Blue Hill Academy, where excellent teachers drilled her in Latin, Greek, English and mathematics. She entered the

MARY ELLEN CHASE

University of Maine in 1904 and continued happily in all but mathematics, whereupon her father, deciding she needed the discipline of teaching, found a job for her. For ten dollars a week she taught school in the small town of South Brooksville, then known as Bucks Harbor, Maine, and the next year, in West Brooksville. She returned to college in the autumn of 1907 having learned the value of time, the fun of studying, and the thrill of thinking for herself. It was at this time she sold her first short story to *American Boy* for seventeen dollars.

Having been appointed to a teaching fellowship during her last two years of college, she was well prepared for a teaching career when she received her A.B. from the University of Maine in 1909. With ten dollars in her purse and ninety pinned inside her suit, the small-town girl set out by Pullman for Chicago and Clark's Teaching Agency. Mr. Clark placed her in the Hillside Home School in Spring Green, Wisconsin, run by Ellen and Jane Lloyd-Jones, relatives of Frank Lloyd Wright, who had designed one of the school buildings. Here she lived and taught for three inspiring years. Many years later she said of the Lloyd-Joneses: "Whatever vision or imagination I have been able to give to my teaching in the years since then, I owe to two women in a Wisconsin valley thirty years ago."

Ambition then took her to Mrs. Moffat's fashionable School for Girls in Chicago, where she taught "odds and ends," and was kept so busy as private secretary and personal attendant to the duty-minded Mrs. Moffat that she had little time or energy left for her philosophy and history seminars at the University of Chicago. In the spring of 1913 she sailed to Germany to study the language. She returned to Mrs. Moffat's three months later, a far better German teacher. She had, however, contracted a cough which grew worse when she went home to Maine at her father's death in February of 1914.

Doctors sent her to Bozeman, Montana, for her health, where she slept outdoors and had time to become intoxicated with books and thoughts and writing, and to discover she was "never less alone than when alone." A story published in this period earned her one hundred and fifty dollars. When her health improved, she taught in Bozeman schools until she entered the University of Minnesota as a graduate student in English. There she received her M.A. in 1918, and her Ph.D. in 1922. She stayed on as associate professor for four years.

Lecturing, writing for Sunday School magazines, teaching night courses at the university extension and a class in advanced composition at the College of St. Catherine added to her income and experience. Her contacts with the nuns at St. Catherine's, where she spent three summers, satisfied a longing to follow her chosen profession in conjunction with the life of the spirit, a combination Mary Ellen Chase felt was essential to any life well lived.

In 1926, when President William Allen Neilson of Smith College offered her an associate professorship, she was eager to head back east to Northampton, Massachusetts, "a superior town," where a woman teacher might advance.

Extremely popular as a teacher, her courses at Smith bore the simple label,

"Chase." Many of her devoted students still cherish her notes and invitations to tea. Miss Chase was appointed full professor in 1929 and professor emeritus in 1955.

President Neilson arranged days free of teaching so that she and other faculty members might continue writing and lecturing. Mary Ellen Chase rewarded his belief in her by emerging as a leader of the Maine school of writers, along with her early friend and guide Sarah Orne Jewett. Lecturing took her to far corners of the America she loved, with Ohio the state she most enjoyed, possibly because it was most like her own New England. The chance acquaintances and glimpses of different lives gave her material for her writing.

She wrote in odd moments, on trains and stopovers, but much of her best work was done at her summer home, "Windswept," at Petit Manan Point, Maine, and in Grantchester, in Cambridgeshire, England, where she lived for two years, 1935 and 1936. Walking trips through the small villages of southern England resulted in her humorous essays on English weather, trees, manners, food, etc., as well as in settings for stories. A prolific writer of magazine and newspaper articles, book reviews, textbooks, scriptural works, short stories and novels, Miss Chase never kept a complete listing of her published works.

She died in a nursing home in her beloved Northampton at the age of eighty-six.

Mary Ellen Chase was elected to Phi Beta Kappa in 1920 and continued to gather honors throughout the rest of her distinguished academic career. She held an impressive number of honorary degrees: Litt.D. from the University of Maine (1928) and from Bowdoin College (1933); L.H.D. from Colby College (1937), Northeastern University (1947), Smith College (1949), and Wilson College (1957); and LL.D. from Goucher College (1960).

In the commercial world of publishing she also made her mark with more than thirty books for adults and children and numerous articles and stories. In 1931 her story "Salesmanship" won the Pictorial Review Prize of twenty-five hundred dollars.

SELECTED WORKS: Sailing the Seven Seas, 1958; Donald McKay and the Clipper Ships, 1959; The Fishing Fleets of New England, 1961; Victoria: A Pigeon in a Pram, 1963; Dolly Moses: the Cat and the Clam Chowder, 1964; Richard Mansfield, the Prince of Donkeys, 1964; A Journey to Boston, 1965; The Story of Lighthouses, 1965; A Walk on an Iceberg, 1966.

ABOUT: Contemporary Authors, Vol. 15–16; Cournos, John, and Sybil Norton, eds. Famous Modern American Novelists; Current Biography, 1940; The National Cyclopedia of American Biography, Vol. I; Stone, Irving and Richard Kennedy, eds. We Speak for Ourselves; Twentieth Century Authors; Twentieth Century Authors (First Supplement); Wagenknecht, Edward Charles, ed. When I Was a Child; Warfel, Harry Redclay. American Novelists of Today; Who's Who in America, 1970–71; Who's Who of American Women, 1974–75; New York Times July 31, 1973; Publishers Weekly August 20, 1973; Scholastic April 17, 1937; February 26, 1940; Time June 27, 1955; Wilson Library Bulletin February 1934; Yale Review September 1940.

SELINA CHÖNZ

AUTHOR OF *A Bell for Ursli*, etc.

Autobiographical sketch of Selina Chönz, translated from the German:

YEARS ago, when I was a young girl, I was a teacher at the kindergarten college in Zurich. When I was leaving to marry I wanted to show my pupils how to carry on with the education of small children, but there was a great lack of good picture books. I knew it was necessary to produce some, something of the best one could give to children. I married and came back to the Engadine, my homeland, a valley in the Swiss Alps, and I noticed then, as I do now again, how many war pictures children have to look at! I wanted to show children of the Swiss towns and of our mountain valleys

Chönz: *KURNTZ*

Selina Chönz

that the honest and simple life in a small world still exists. Fairy tales are beautiful stories, but reality is visible and it too can be beautiful.

I was lucky to find a good but unknown painter to illustrate the tale I wrote, to help me realize my dream. But when I was ready to show it to my editor, he was upset. He said nobody in all of Switzerland would print a picture book like the one I wanted. I felt that only the best is good enough for children: seven colors, the best paper, bound in board covers! The editor saw it as a book for art connoisseurs. It would be too expensive to print and nobody would buy it. So I went to work to find societies that took subscriptions for some thousands of copies. So the book *A Bell for Ursli* was printed, and it sold out in two months.

Ursli's village is Guarda, where I live too. It is small, with only one hundred and twenty inhabitants. The school has only twelve children up to eleven years old, so the older children must go to school in a larger village every day by postal truck, even in winter when there is much snow. Our village children all speak two or three languages, Romansh, German, and often Italian as well. Romansh is like Latin and is the speech of the family. German is the speech in school. Italian is like Romansh, and one learns it easily from the children who speak Italian at home.

A farm boy, Ursli must start helping his father when he is very young. The father shows him how to do the work in the farmhouse and field, so children learn early how one must help.

The houses in the village are especially beautiful. In summer many tourists come to Guarda to see the village. Ursli's house is the way all houses were in the Engadine at one time. It is white with scratched drawings, called graffiti, which are made when the house is painted, but the drawings are always the same as the original drawings made when the house was built. The village is as it was five hundred years ago. The streets are paved with round stones, as large as apples, so that they hurt to walk on unless one has shoes with thick soles. In every house there is a stall with cows and goats and sheep and a horse. Now the farmers also have small machines for mowing, and tractors to bring the hay home. There are few horses and oxen anymore.

Ursli has a twin sister, called Florina, which means "flower" in English. The name Ursli means "little bear." Florina helps mother in the house, but she must also go haying in summer and carry the basket with lunch to the field. She feeds the cats and the chickens. Here girls learn knitting and embroidery in school. They also have a cooking school. They pick berries so that their mother can make jam. They also look for mushrooms in the forest, which will be dried for use in winter.

In our village the farmers have two houses. One house is rented in summer as a vacation house. Then the families from the cities come to the houses and live there in the good mountain air for three weeks if it is hot in the city. We have a little ski lift and a little pond by the hotel. There is a store and a cheese shop. We can buy everything here except clothes, which we get in the city or order from a catalog.

I have written three books about our little village, which have flown out into the world in nine languages including

Japanese and Arabic. The illustrator is Alois Carigiet, an artist and painter, who lives not far from me and wants to give children a beautiful present from our homeland.

———

SELECTED WORKS: A Bell for Ursli, 1953; Florina and the Wild Bird, 1953; The Snowstorm, 1958.

KAY CHORAO

January 7, 1937–

AUTHOR AND ILLUSTRATOR OF A *Magic Eye for Ida*, etc.

Autobiographical sketch of Ann McKay Sproat Chorao:

MY actual birth took place in Elkhart, Indiana, so that my grandfather might be the attending doctor. But after that event I was promptly moved to my real home which, for the first eight years, was Indianapolis, Indiana.

My clearest memories of that period were of watching my brother's 16-milli-meter movies in our basement (my old highchair was the balcony), and of munching on pumpkin seeds we dried out every year after Halloween on our furnace pipes. I also remember sitting in a variety of holes in our back yard—I was determined to dig to China—or of dangling upside down on a jungle gym. On seeing my bare feet dangling one day, a friend of my mother's commented that you could grow potatoes between my toes. The idea intrigued me.

My literary inclinations at that time were quite nonexistent, although my brother, who was an avid reader, often read books out loud to me. He intro-duced me to the Oz books and the Uncle Wiggly books, which I have since intro-duced to my own children. But between bouts of staring at my toes to see if they were sprouting potatoes (and my name was Sproat, which inspired the neighbor-

KAY CHORAO

hood children to chant, "Kay Sproat is sprouting") I did develop a passion for drawing.

At the age of five I mainly drew fire trucks and Snow White, but the interest continued and grew as I did, with the strongest urge and satisfaction being the representation of people, especially young children.

We moved to Cleveland, Ohio, when I was almost nine, and that was home until I went to college. My years in Cleveland were ordinary growing-up years in a suburban setting. In fourth grade I went to a country school (eigh-teen children in the entire school), but when it was learned that our recesses were stretched into the afternoons, that my teacher's popularity was enhanced by the fact that she supplied us with caps for our cap guns, and that my wobbly abilities in arithmetic had slipped a grade level, I was enrolled in a private school called Laurel. There I acquired a more appropriate education and was en-couraged in a newly discovered interest in writing and, especially, in my old love for drawing and painting.

My four years in college were spent at Wheaton College in Norton, Massachu-setts (B.A., History of Art). The year following graduation I enrolled in the Chelsea School of Art in London, En-

Chorao: *shoe ROW*

gland, where the training was disciplined and classical, a great relief after the American approach to draw as large, loosely and "expressively" as possible.

At Chelsea I met my husband, who was also an art student. We married in 1960 and moved briefly to San Francisco. However, a year later we moved to New York, and here we have stayed ever since, except for summers when we go to Canada.

Our three sons were born in 1962 (Jamie), 1964 (Peter) and 1968 (Ian).

While Jamie and Peter were still babies, I revived the old interest in writing I had harbored since Laurel. I remember sitting in the park, balancing a spiral notebook on my knee while I kept one watchful eye on the sandbox. Enough rejection slips accumulated for these children's stories to paper a small room, but among the rejections were some acceptance checks from a juvenile magazine.

With this modest encouragement, I decided to go to night school and study children's book illustration, in the hope that I might illustrate my own work. I enrolled in the School of Visual Arts night school and studied under Niels Bodecker and Edward Gorey. With their help I assembled a portfolio which I carried around from publishing house to publishing house for five years. During that period editors were friendly and encouraging, but no one wanted to take a chance on someone totally unknown. Every night I sat on a small balcony, which my husband built for the purpose, and drew endless pictures, illustrated poems and kept renewing and revising the contents of my portfolio.

I did some educational film strips and a television commercial, but no book manuscripts were offered, nor were any of mine accepted, until 1971. In the spring of that year Farrar, Straus and Giroux decided to publish *The Repair of Uncle Toe*. It came out in the spring of 1972.

Since that spring, I have been kept very busy, illustrating my own and other people's books.

My sons are not officially allowed on the balcony, where I continue to work, but they do creep up occasionally and offer their unvarnished opinions. At the moment they are in unanimous agreement that Marvel Comics are vastly superior to their mother's work, but they see a glimmer of hope for me. And I, meanwhile, work happily and gratefully for less biased young eyes.

Kay Chorao has always gone by the nickname Kay, though her legal name is Ann. Her second book, *A Magic Eye for Ida*, was chosen by *School Library Journal* as one of the best books of 1973. The American Institute of Graphic Arts picked *Ralph and the Queen's Bathtub* for inclusion in its 1973–74 Children's Book Show. However, Mrs. Chorao's best known work to date is doubtless her illustrations for *Albert's Toothache*, Barbara Williams' story of a young turtle who complains of a toothache in spite of his elders' insistence that it's impossible because turtles have no teeth. The book was an American Library Association Notable Book in 1974, was designated one of the Fifty Best Books of the Year by the American Institute of Graphic Arts, was included in the Society of Illustrators Annual Exhibit in 1975, and the Children's Book Showcase the same year.

SELECTED WORKS WRITTEN AND ILLUSTRATED: The Repair of Uncle Toe, 1972; A Magic Eye for Ida, 1973; Ida Makes a Movie, 1974; Ralph and the Queen's Bathtub, 1974; Maudie's Umbrella, 1975; Molly's Moe, 1976; Lester's Overnight, 1977.

SELECTED WORKS ILLUSTRATED: My Mama Says There Aren't Any Zombies, Ghosts, Vampires, Creatures, Demons, Monsters, Fiends, Goblins or Things, by Judith Viorst, 1973; Albert's Toothache, by Barbara Williams, 1974; The Witch's Egg, by Madeleine Edmondson, 1974; Henrietta, the Wild Woman of Borneo, by Winifred Rosen Casey, 1975; Kevin's Grandma, by Barbara Williams, 1975; Someday, Said Mitchell, by Barbara Williams, 1976; Monster Poems, ed. by Daisy Wallace, 1976; Clyde Monster, by Robert L. Crowe, 1976; The Hunt for Rabbit's Galosh, by Ann

Schweninger, 1976; Frankenstein's Dog, by Jan Wahl, 1977; I'm Terrific, by Marjorie Weinman Sharmat, 1977; That's Enough for One Day, J.P.!, by Susan Pearson, 1977.

ABOUT: Contemporary Authors, Vol. 49–52; Something about the Author, Vol. 8.

"JOHN CHRISTOPHER"

1922–

AUTHOR OF *The White Mountains*, etc.

Autobiographical sketch of Samuel Youd, who writes books for young people under the name of "John Christopher"

"JOHN CHRISTOPHER"

I WAS born not far from Liverpool, on the borderline between two villages (as they were then) of Huyton and Knowsley, and lived in Lancashire until my family moved to Hampshire when I was ten years old. I was educated at Peter Symonds School, Winchester.

On being demobilized by the army in 1946, I was given a grant by the Rockefeller Foundation, which enabled me to write full time for a year. Subsequently I wrote in my spare time, but since 1958 have been a professional writer in the strictest sense of the term: apart from a very occasional short story, the income on which my family and I must live derives from novels alone.

This is a hazardous way of making a living, particularly for someone who is married and has five children of school age. There have been occasional strokes of good fortune, but in between there are years in which income remains well below essential outgoings. I have written novels under several names, and of several different kinds, including light comedy, detective thrillers, even two with cricket backgrounds. My early novels were more serious in intent and published under my own name. I continued to write these until a couple of years ago, and they were published, though with little success. I have had to abandon them since my American publisher understandably refused to go on with a course that was even more financially

disastrous to him than it was to me. As a result of his decision, the last of these books, published in 1963, netted me two hundred and twenty-five pounds after deduction of agent's commission: scarcely adequate to keep a family of seven for half a year.

The relatively more successful Christopher novels began as science fiction and are commonly given that label. They are, in fact, adventure stories involving a study of human reactions to severe environmental stresses. Thus, while in some action has taken place in a world denuded of grasses or against the menace of extraterrestrial entities capable of taking over the minds and personalities of their victims, others have dealt with people trapped in underground caves or forced to trek across the Greenland ice pack from an icebound ship. *The Long Winter*, starting from the premise of a new ice age, was in fact concerned with the ironic possibilities of the whites of northern Europe fleeing as refugees to an arrogant and rich black Africa.

————

John Christopher came to writing for young people after he was well established as an author of science fiction for adults. Approached by a British publisher to write an adventure story for boys, he refused, not believing in commissioned books. Later, however, he wrote the story anyway and, after several revisions, it was published on both sides of the Atlantic as *The White Mountains*, the first in what was to become the Tripods trilogy. Writing about this experience later, Christopher says that the reason for the manuscript's requiring so much revision "was that I had gone into it with the feeling, unexplained, but now dreadfully apparent, that it was 'only a juvenile.' One did not need to work at it in the way one would work at a novel written for adults. My editor's penetrating criticisms brought me up sharply to the realization of what I had done. . . . What I have learned is that writing for children is at least as exacting and concentration-demanding as writing for adults. But one can addd another word: stimulating. It is the form of writing which I can now least imagine giving up."

The White Mountains was followed by *The City of Gold and Lead* and *The Pool of Fire*. Together the books of the trilogy were runners-up for Britain's prestigious Guardian Award in 1969, an award Christopher won in 1971 with *The Guardians*. In the United States *The Guardians* received a Christopher Award in 1970. A German translation of this book, entitled *Die Wächter*, received the German Children's Book Prize in 1976.

The author, who shuns personal publicity, is married to a physicist and science editor. They have one son and four daughters and live on the Channel island of Guernsey. Until he gave up his full-time job to devote himself to writing full time, Christopher had worked in the industrial diamond industry.

SELECTED WORKS: The White Mountains, 1967; The City of Gold and Lead, 1967; The Pool of Fire, 1968; The Lotus Caves, 1969; The Guardians, 1970; The Prince in Waiting, 1970; Beyond the Burning Lands, 1971; The Sword of the Spirits, 1972; Dom and Va, 1973; Wild Jack, 1974.

ABOUT: Townsend, John Rowe. A Sense of Story; World Authors: 1950–1970; Saturday Evening Post April 27, 1957; Signal January 1971.

JACQUELINE CHWAST

January 1, 1932–

AUTHOR AND ILLUSTRATOR OF *When the Baby-sitter Didn't Come*, etc.

Autobiographical sketch of Jacqueline Weiner Chwast:

I ALWAYS enjoyed drawing. It was one of those things I did well enough as a child to be praised for by adults. I also enjoyed singing, but was asked by some of those same adults not to bother. I believe I continue to draw for the pleasure it gives me to do it and for the reward of other people's interest in it.

I kept company in my childhood with figures, animals, tables set with food, and houses which I drew, then cut from paper. Now cut paper is the technique, besides drawing, that I use to illustrate books and magazine articles.

I chose to do illustration as my profession but doing so was more of a natural flow than a deliberate choice, since I'd spent all my life recording impressions and expressing myself through drawings. I only continued, and made my business, what I'd been doing naturally.

I studied at the Arts High School and then graduated from the Newark School of Fine and Industrial Art in Newark, New Jersey.

I wanted to work in children's books because it is an area of commercial art where I can use my imagination, my sense of aesthetics, and most important to me, it is an expression and interpretation of human life around me.

I also like the idea that the book may be the reason that some child and adult are sharing a close time together. My daughters and I used the book as a starting place for discussions that led to many other subjects.

I spend a lot of time in bookstores and

Chwast: *KWAHST*

Jacqueline Chwast

museums looking at other artists' work—
hoping to be influenced.

———

Jacqueline Chwast was born and grew
up in Newark, New Jersey, and moved
to New York at twenty-two. She continued her education with various evening courses at the Art Students League,
but what she really wanted was to get
into publishing. Finally she landed a
staff job with a small children's book
publisher, now defunct. The art director
there gave her a chance and commissioned her to illustrate a picture book for
the firm to publish, but a mean trick of
fate blocked her early debut as a children's book illustrator. She turned her
completed artwork in on a Friday only
to come to work Monday morning and
discover that a fire over the weekend had
burned out the office, her illustrations
along with everything else.

When the firm folded not long after
that, Mrs. Chwast went on to free-lance
outside the children's book field. Her first
book commission was Myra Cohn Livingston's *Whispers and Other Poems*,
which was included in the American Institute of Graphic Arts Children's Book
Show 1958–60. Other commissions fol-

lowed. To date there have been more
than thirty books, and two of them were
also written by Mrs. Chwast. *When the
Baby-sitter Didn't Come* told of the mis-
adventures of two little girls and their
beleaguered mother on an "ordinary"
shopping trip. *How Mr. Berry Found a
Home and Happiness Forever* tells of a
bachelor who is given so many pets that
he has to look for another apartment.
She has another book working in her
mind now and has no objection, she says,
to doing others if the right idea comes
along. As well as books, Jacqueline
Chwast also illustrates magazine articles.
She likes to keep both kinds of work going at once because of the contrast between the two—books take a great deal
of thought and planning, while articles
offer an opportunity for quick, sharp
sidelights.

Mrs. Chwast lives in New York City
with her daughters, Eve Raina (born
October 9, 1958) and Pamela Ileen (born
June 27, 1961). She spends part of each
summer in the country and she lists her
pleasures, besides work, as walking—in
the city and in the country—and talking
to people.

SELECTED WORKS WRITTEN AND ILLUS-
TRATED: When the Baby-sitter Didn't
Come, 1967; How Mr. Berry Found a
Home and Happiness Forever, 1968.

SELECTED WORKS ILLUSTRATED: Whispers and Other Poems, by Myra Cohn Livingston, 1958; I Like You, by Sandol Stoddard Warburg, 1970; A Present From a
Bird, by Jay Williams, 1971; Iggy, by Marcia Newfield, 1972; Play with the Wind, by
Howard Everett Smith, 1972; Timber Tales,
by Mary Dawson, 1973; Sing Song Scup-
pernong, by Jeanne B. Hardendorff, 1974;
Fire, by Gail Kay Haines, 1975; Picnics and
Parades, by Leonore Klein, 1976; I Like Old
Clothes, by Mary Ann Hoberman, 1976;
Don't Throw Another One, Dover!, by Beverly Keller, 1976.

ABOUT: Contemporary Authors, Vol. 49–
52; Kingman, Lee and others, comps. Illus-
trators of Children's Books: 1957–1966;
Something about the Author, Vol. 6;
Graphis No. 162, 1972; Print November–
December 1971.

SEYMOUR CHWAST

ILLUSTRATOR OF *Still Another Alphabet Book*, etc.

Biographical sketch of Seymour Chwast:

SEYMOUR CHWAST was born in New York's Bronx and grew up in the Coney Island section of Brooklyn. He always drew. One of his earliest memories is accompanying his mother to the beauty parlor and, on a piece of cardboard with a mascara pencil, drawing a portrait of a lady with beautiful hair. Walt Disney was his idol; he dreamed of following in his footsteps and becoming a cartoonist until he went to Abraham Lincoln High School and encountered a gifted art teacher, Leon Friend. Friend introduced his students to the work of avant-garde artists and designers and demonstrated the wide range of possibilities that lay beyond cartooning. Under Friend's aegis, Chwast began entering poster and design contests while he was still in high school. By the time he was ready for art school he had a firm foundation in design.

Chwast has said that he chose Cooper Union Art School in New York City mainly because it was free. He was introduced to printmaking and became fascinated by the medium. Later he studied with Antonio Frasconi, and the woodcut and woodcut techniques became important tools of expression for him. At Cooper Union Chwast also became interested in typography and developed the desire to use his "talents in design, typography, drawing and anything else rather than one particular area." It was also while he was at Cooper Union that Chwast met fellow student Milton Glaser and formed a friendship out of which grew the celebrated Push Pin Studios.

After graduation Chwast, Glaser and two other Cooper Union artists, Edward Sorel and Reynold Ruffins, shared a studio for free-lance work while all held full-time jobs elsewhere. Glaser left to accept a Fulbright Scholarship to Italy, but the other three began to publish a

periodic promotion piece, which they first called *The Monthly Graphic*, later *The Push Pin Almanack*. Intended to advertise the talents of its creators, the *Almanack* was sent to art directors in the advertising and publishing fields and anyone else who might be interested in the group's services. When Glaser returned from Italy, he too became involved in the *Almanack*, and Chwast, Glaser and Sorel then set up the Push Pin Studios in 1954. Sorel left after about a year, but the two remaining partners continued the business, with a number of other designers and artists involved at various times, for more than twenty years. The studio continued to publish its periodic promotion piece, the title changed to *The Push Pin Graphic*, which became a showcase for the work of Chwast, Glaser and members of the studio.

The Push Pin Studio has become one of the most celebrated phenomena in the design field, credited with changing the look of visual communication in America and the rest of the world. Mentioned in the major design journals, in tones of awe and admiration, possibly tinged with envy, the work of the studio and of Chwast is characterized as innovative, daring, fresh, creative, trend-setting, original and flexible. The vogue for nine-

Chwast: *KWHAST*

teenth and early twentieth century design and typography so much in evidence today can be said to be largely due to the Push Pin influence. Chwast himself has been quoted as saying that he can't think of anything suitable for a graphic setting that has occurred after 1950.

The breadth of his interests is reflected in the variety of work Chwast tackles: posters, packages, films, book and record jackets, magazine and book illustration, brochures. "Discovery is a thing that excites me," he has said. "To find it in my own work doesn't happen very often, but when it does it's a beautiful thing."

Chwast has achieved distinction in many areas. His posters are in the collection of the Museum of Modern Art in New York. He has exhibited at the American Institute of Graphic Arts, the Art Directors' Clubs of New York and Chicago, and the Society of Illustrators, among others. In 1970 Push Pin Studios was honored by a retrospective exhibition by the Louvre—the first ever accorded a design studio by that institution —which toured the major cities of Europe and went on to Tokyo and São Paulo. *Idea*, the Japanese magazine, accorded Chwast a whole special issue in October 1973. Recently he was honored with the Cooper Union Citation for Excellence.

In the world of children's books, too, Chwast has made an impact whenever he has turned his attention in that direction. *Sara's Granny and the Groodle* was chosen one of the best-illustrated books of 1969 by the New York *Times*. *Still Another Alphabet Book* was one of the American Institute of Graphic Arts' Fifty Books in 1969 as were *Still Another Children's Book* and *The Pancake King* in 1971 and *The House That Jack Built* in 1973. *The Pancake King* was included in the Institute's Children's Book Show in 1971–72 and was one of twenty U.S. entries to the Biennale of Illustrations Bratislava in 1973. *The House That Jack Built* and *The Flip-Flap Mother Goooooose* were both included in the AIGA Children's Book Show in 1973–74.

Seymour Chwast has been characterized by one writer as a "reserved, ruddy-faced, All-American boy, averagely built, soft-spoken and completely given over to graphic family interests," by another as "an enemy of stylistic complacency or platitudinous thinking." He claims the influence of George Grosz, Saul Steinberg, Ben Shahn, Klee, Rouault and Picasso, and designers Cassandre, Reiner and Rand. Critics mention John Held, Jr., Antonio Frasconi, and *New Yorker* cartoonist Gardner Rea as well.

Chwast lives in New York with his wife Paula and has two daughters by his first marriage.

SELECTED WORKS WRITTEN AND ILLUSTRATED: Still Another Alphabet Book, with Martin Stephen Moskof, 1969; Still Another Number Book, with Martin Stephen Moskof, 1971; Flip-Flap Limerickricks, 1972; Flip-Flap Mother Goooooose, 1972; Still Another Children's Book, with Martin Stephen Moskof, 1972; The House That Jack Built, 1973.

SELECTED WORKS ILLUSTRATED: Sara's Granny and the Groodle, by Joan Gill, 1969; Finding a Poem, by Eve Merriam, 1970; The Pancake King, by Phyllis La-Farge, 1971; Sleepy Ida and Other Nonsense Poems, by Steven Kroll, 1977.

ABOUT: Smith, Bryan H., ed. The Penrose Graphic Arts International, 1975, Vol. 68; American Artist September 1958; October 1971; Art and Artists September 1970; Graphis No. 102, 1962; No. 133, 1967; No. 175, 1974–75; Idea October 1973; Print November 1973.

ARTHUR C. CLARKE

December 16, 1917–

AUTHOR OF *Childhood's End*, etc.

Biographical sketch of Arthur Charles Clarke:

ARTHUR C. CLARKE, who has been aptly termed the science fiction writer's science fiction writer, was born in the English coastal town of Minehead on December 16, 1917, and spent his childhood on his parents' farm in Somerset. His introduction to science came when he was ten years old and his father gave him a picture card from a package of

ARTHUR C. CLARKE

cigarettes showing a prehistoric reptile. He proceeded to collect avidly every other card in the series and maintained his interest in prehistory until, at the age of twelve, he discovered astronomy and began a lifelong fascination with outer space. When he was thirteen he built a telescope from cardboard tubes and discarded lenses and spent hours mapping the moon.

Graduating from grammar school in the middle of the depression, Clarke could not afford to continue his education. Always good in mathematics, he became an auditor in His Majesty's Exchequer and Audit Department in London. There he encountered other people who shared his enthusiasm for outer space, and he became an active member of the recently formed British Interplanetary Society. In his early teens he had discovered American science fiction magazines. These so fascinated him that, he later recalled, "I used to haunt Woolworth's in my youth to pick up issues that I had missed." At this time he began to contribute to the mimeographed science fiction magazine, *Novae Terrae*.

In 1938 Clarke sold his first articles to a new science fiction magazine, *Tales of Wonder*. His initial professional efforts were summaries of existing knowledge about the planetary system and the possibility of space travel. That same year

Clarke also wrote three fictional works which appeared in mimeographed periodicals that had considerable circulation among science fiction fans.

World War II interrupted Clarke's budding literary career. Serving in the Royal Air Force from 1941 to 1946, he became an instructor in radar and later on the first Ground Controlled Approach system to be introduced to Britain. These experiences fired his imagination, and in 1945 in an article for *Wireless World*, he outlined a plan for a satellite communications system. Clarke's article made little impression then, and he did not pursue his idea. Almost two decades later, however, with the launching of Syncom II, the first synchronous television satellite, Clarke's visionary proposal became a reality.

At the end of the war Clarke entered King's College, London. He graduated in two years, receiving his B.Sc. degree with first class honors in physics and in pure and applied mathematics. After a term of graduate study he obtained a position as an assistant editor of *Science Abstracts*.

The British Interplanetary Society had languished during the war. Clarke was largely responsible for revitalizing it and served as its president for several years. Meanwhile, his career as a writer gained momentum. In 1946 he sold several stories to an American magazine, and in 1948 his novel, *Against the Fall of Night*, appeared in another American science fiction publication. Throughout 1949 Clarke contributed to major science fiction magazines, and in 1950 his first nonfiction book, *Interplanetary Flight*, a work about the dawn of the space age, was published.

By 1951 Clarke was able to leave his editing job to devote himself to his writing. His second nonfiction effort, *The Exploration of Space*, was a Book-of-the-Month Club selection in 1952. The following year Clarke published several novels. His *Islands in the Sky*, a story about community life in space stations, has since appealed to countless thousands of young people, while *Child-*

hood's End caused Clarke to be compared with such science fiction writers as Olaf Stapledon, C. S. Lewis and H. G. Wells.

With Mike Wilson, a former *Life* photographer, Clarke set out in 1954 to explore the Great Barrier Reef of Australia. During this expedition both men became so enchanted with the island nation of Ceylon (later renamed Sri Lanka) that they made it their permanent home. During the 1950s and 1960s they did extensive skin diving off the island's coast. These experiences inspired Clarke to write a number of articles and books about diving and about the mysteries of the ocean. The best known is the science fiction novel, *The Deep Range*, which details the operation of an undersea farm where killer whales act as "sheep dogs."

In the mid-1960s Clarke began his most famous undertaking, *2001: A Space Odyssey*. In conceiving the movie, Clarke and coauthor and producer-director Stanley Kubrick tried to evoke an awareness of a being absolutely different from anything humanly known. Their effort was of such a dimension that Clarke once remarked, "If this film can be completely understood then we will have failed." The highly symbolic and visually breathtaking *2001* opened in 1968; it received high praise, attracted huge audiences, and won Oscar nominations for its two authors.

Clarke received UNESCO's Kalinga Prize in 1961, awarded for excellence in scientific writing, and the Franklin Institute's Stuart Ballantine medal in 1963, in recognition of his 1945 proposal for satellite communications. He won the Robert Ball Award of the Aviation Space Writers' Association in 1965, the AAAS-Westinghouse Science Writing Prize in 1969, and the Nebula Award for the best science fiction novella in 1973. *Rendezvous with Rama* was on the American Library Association's list of Best Books for Young Adults for 1973, as was *Imperial Earth* for 1976. The author of hundreds of fiction and nonfiction articles, stories and books on outer space, Clarke has seen his prophecy of man traveling to the moon become a reality. But then, he believes that "anything that is theoretically possible will be achieved in practice." It is this faith in the future, perhaps, that accounts for the special appeal his work has for young people.

SELECTED WORKS: Boy Beneath the Sea, with Mike Wilson, 1958; The Challenge of the Sea, 1960; Indian Ocean Adventure, with Mike Wilson, 1961; The First Five Fathoms, with Mike Wilson, 1961; Childhood's End, 1963; Indian Ocean Treasure, with Mike Wilson, 1964; Man and Space, with the Editors of *Life*, 1964; 2001: A Space Odyssey, with Stanley Kubrick, 1968; Rendezvous with Rama, 1973; Imperial Earth, 1975.

ABOUT: Author's and Writer's Who's Who, 1971; Contemporary Authors, Vol. 4; Current Biography, 1966; Moskowitz, Sam. Seekers of Tomorrow, 1966; Twentieth Century Authors (First Supplement), 1955; Who's Who, 1971–72; Who's Who in America, 1972–73; New Yorker August 9, 1964; May 27, 1967; Newsweek October 30, 1961; Publishers Weekly September 10, 1973; Readers' Digest April, 1969; Senior Scholastic May 9, 1968; Time July 19, 1968; Wilson Library Bulletin March, 1963.

MAVIS THORPE CLARK

AUTHOR OF *The Min Min*, etc.

Autobiographical sketch of Mavis Thorpe Clark Latham:

WHEN I was about eight I wrote some short short fairy tales which my eldest sister Vi typed out and made look like a book, the pages being held together with blue tape. Because of this I knew very early in life that I wanted to be a writer. I wrote my first full-length manuscript when I was fourteen, while studying for my Intermediate Certificate at the Methodist Ladies' College, Melbourne. This story was not published in book form, but it did appear in the children's pages of the *Australasian*, an Australian weekly newspaper of that time. My first book in hard covers was published when I was eighteen and was an adventure story for boys.

My father, John Thorpe Clark, was a Scotsman who migrated to Australia as

Mavis Thorpe Clark

a young man, and my mother was born in Wales but came to Australia as a baby. There were no known writers on either side of the family but, as the belated last of five children, I was given every encouragement by both parents, particularly by my mother, who was herself a dreamer of dreams. I married young and my husband, Harold Latham, continued that encouragement.

However, for some time after marriage I wrote only adult short stories, articles and radio plays, as a full-length book seemed too great a task to combine with running a home and looking after my two daughters, Beverly Jeanne and Ronda Fay. Today I am so grateful that I kept on writing—even short pieces—during those busy years, for I believe that writing, of all the human talents, rusts and corrodes more quickly than any other if left lying unused.

As my daughters grew older, I started writing children's books again. Sometimes I am asked why all my novels (I also write adult biography) are for children. I think it is because I find myself constantly drawn to situations which involve children or, rather, young people. My last eight books have been for the teen-ager, perhaps the most important age group in the world today.

Some of my earlier books have an his-

torical setting, dealing with the colonizing of Australia in the first half of last century. This was because unusual backgrounds for stories have always appealed to me, not only in the books I write but also in those I read. But now I am writing of what is happening in Australia today, for this is a land where there are still isolated frontiers and pioneers are still to be found.

Although I was born in Melbourne, Victoria, and grew up in the city, I have always loved the country, especially the Outback. For many years now, I have been able to spend extensive periods of time in such out-of-the-way places as the desertlike opal fields of Coober Pedy, where some of the world's finest opal is mined, or the iron ore mining towns of Tom Price and Dampier on the west coast of Western Australia, or on sheep stations at the edge of the Victoria Desert in South Australia. Recently I was in Darwin, in the Northern Territory, and the exciting Ord River area of the Kimberly cattle- and cotton-growing country. My last book *The Hundred Islands* is set on the islands of Bass Strait.

I travelled many thousands of miles in search of material, criss-crossing this vast country from east to west and north to south. Latterly my companion has been either my daughter, Ronda, or a woman friend, who has acted as co-driver.

Adult biography also attracts me and if I ever give up writing for young people—which is most unlikely—it will be to concentrate on this field. The two biographies I have published to date have been extremely rewarding projects, especially *Pastor Doug*, the story of the Aboriginal leader, Sir Douglas Ralph Nucholls, who was for a short time Governor of South Australia. This book led me into deep research of the Aborigines and their problems, thereby widening my horizon and developing my appreciation of the universality of man.

For me there is tremendous reward in making friends in out-of-the-way places, and glimpsing lives that are lived so simply yet so richly with the earth of the world's oldest continent. Another reward is to have had three of my books put into Braille: *Pastor Doug* by the Victorian Institute for the Blind; *The Min-Min* by the New South Wales Education Department; and *Blue Above the Trees* by the Central Library of Great Britain.

I work in a small room at the rear of my home. One wall is almost all window and looks out on a stretch of lawn completely surrounded with shrubs and trees, including gum-trees and a tall pine. Possums scamper here at night and love the fruit of the two old apple trees.

Mavis Thorpe Clark has written more than twenty books for children, sixteen of them novels. The Children's Book Council of Australia chose *The Min-Min* Book of the Year in 1966–67 and cited *The Brown Land Was Green* (Australia, 1966) as Highly Commended for the same award in the same year. *Blue Above the Trees* was Commended the following year. The German-language editions of *Spark of Opal* (Australia, 1968) and *Iron Mountain* received the German Children's Book Prize in 1971 and 1973 respectively.

Mavis Thorpe Clark is a member of International P.E.N. and has served as president and as vice-president of the Australia Centre.

SELECTED WORKS: The Min-Min, 1969; Blue Above the Trees, 1969; Iron Mountain, 1971; Wildfire, 1974; If the Earth Falls In, 1975; The Sky Is Free, 1976.

ABOUT: Contemporary Authors, Vol. 57–60; Something about the Author, Vol. 8; Who's Who in Australia, 1971; 1974; Bookbird No. 3, 1967.

ELIZABETH CLEAVER

November 19, 1939–

ILLUSTRATOR OF *The Wind Has Wings*, etc.

Autobiographical sketch of Elizabeth Ann Mrazik Cleaver:

I WAS born in Montreal where I received most of my education, except for several years in the 1950s when my fam-

ELIZABETH CLEAVER

ily lived in Hungary. Here I attended secondary school. I have studied at Sir George Williams University in Montreal and the School of Art and Design and Ecole des Beaux Arts. In 1967 during a celebration of Young Canada's Book Week at Boys and Girls House, Toronto, I was invited to illustrate my first book, a manuscript of Canadian poetry for children, *The Wind Has Wings*. Since that time, I have become involved with many projects, ideas and books. I have researched and worked with the children at Baker Lake in the Northwest Territories, adapting Eskimo legends to shadow puppetry.

I have always enjoyed cutting with scissors and I still have the scar to prove that I cut my leg for the sake of art even before I went to school. I still enjoy tearing and cutting paper and not using a brush. Collage is a way of making art by cutting, pasting and tearing. From this description it sounds as if I play and do not work at all. How misleading! Making pictures is demanding work. It is creative play if you like, but one has to use the mind, the hands, the eyes and the heart to create a picture.

It was at Sárospatak, Hungary, in the seventeenth century that Comenius wrote the *Orbis Pictus*, the first illustrated book ever used in schools, and translated into English in 1658. Parenthetically, I should mention that Sárospatak occupies an outstanding place among the historically and culturally significant towns of Northern Hungary. The College of Sárospatak was founded in 1531. It was at this college that I was fortunate enough to study for three years.

Picture books are a world. To create a world one has to be alive. By alive I mean to have dreams, to have desires, to have ideas, to love. Only if one is alive can one create pictures. There is also a Chinese saying that if you want to paint a tree, you must first become a tree. This is only one aspect of creative play. There is the other, the play with materials, the exploration of fresh possibilities of expression in the medium employed, whether collage, oil or wood.

To understand the development of the picture book it is necessary to have a knowledge and respect for art history as well as technique on the part of the artist. Since art is a language and the artist's expression is different from period to period, this language must be constantly refreshed.

Picture books are a major vehicle for self-expression. They reflect the character of the artist, which is influenced by his cultural environment and by the spoken language of his milieu. In my work, the ideas for the pictures for *The Wind Has Wings, Poems From Canada* came from the poems. Poets draw pictures too; they do it with words instead of paint, pencils, collage. Like the artist, poets describe things in an exciting way, the way the imagination sees things. While working on a picture book I live in two worlds: the imaginary and the real one. Imagination and memory play a great part in my work.

The preparation and conception of the illustrations for the Indian legends, *The Mountain Goats of Temlaham* and *How Summer Came to Canada*, was a long one. It was necessary to study particular tribes. To study their culture, their paintings, and sculpture, metalwork, weaving. Through imagination and research I have tried to create the ceremonies the Indians had.

The preparation and conception of *The Miraculous Hind* took a year to complete. This legend is based on actual historical events that took place on the borders of Europe and Asia 1500 years ago. It was transmitted orally for centuries before it was written down. The pictures and the retelling were created with great feeling and love. I tried to think back to my impressions of the few years I spent in Hungary, the customs, the landscape, the spirit that I know is Hungarian. My Hungarian cultural background certainly influenced me. Since this legend originated 1500 years ago, it was necessary to read and study paintings, drawings, engravings, photographs and contemporary representations of original ethnographic material housed in The Royal Ontario Museum. I chose the legend of the Miraculous Hind because of its universal appeal and because I found it most beautiful to illustrate. I love fairy tales, myths and legends; they are my "inner world," the world I love and want to re-create.

I love to tell a story through pictures. While making my pictures I have a dialogue with them. In my work words have their importance, but at times they have to compete with the picture.

There is a saying that a picture is worth a thousand words. But before it can have value we have to put these thousand words into it. We have to invent them, live them and love them.

It is hard sometimes to realize what is put into a book. Of the many elements what I believe to be of most importance is the spirit and love we put into it. Of course a book is never created alone but with the spirit and influence of many people we have known.

––––––

In 1971 Elizabeth Cleaver received the first Amelia Frances Howard-Gibbon Medal awarded by the Canadian Association of Children's Librarians for outstanding illustration. The award was made for her illustrations to *The Wind*

Has Wings, by Mary Alice Downie and
Barbara Robertson. Receiving Honorable Mention for the same award were
two other books illustrated by Elizabeth
Cleaver: *How Summer Came to Canada*
and *The Mountain Goats of Temlaham,*
both with texts by William Toye.

Mrs. Cleaver represented Canada at
the International Book Year Commonwealth Book Fair in London in 1972 and
exhibited at the Commonwealth Art Gallery there. She was Canada's entry for
the Hans Christian Andersen Award in
1972 and received a Highly Commended
citation.

Elizabeth Cleaver held a Canada
Council Arts Bursary Award in 1971–72
and also received Canada Council travel
grants for study throughout Europe, Turkey, Iran and the Canadian Arctic. She
was invited by the National Film Board
of Canada to prepare a film strip from a
legend of her choosing. The film strip,
The Miraculous Hind, was released in
1972 and subsequently published (in
Canada) as a book *The Miraculous
Hind/La Biche Miraculeuse* in 1973. In
1974, the Canadian Association of Children's Librarians awarded the book its
highest award, the Best Book of the Year
for Children.

Mrs. Cleaver has also designed
shadow puppets for Eskimo legends and
fables for The Centaur Theatre in Montreal. She owns her own press and is interested in producing illustrated books
for children in limited editions. She has
illustrated two books not yet available
in the United States: *Canadian Wonder
Tales* collected by Cyrus Macmillan
(1974) and *The Witch of the North*
adapted by Mary Alice Downie (1975).

SELECTED WORKS ILLUSTRATED: The
Wind Has Wings: Poems from Canada, ed.
by Mary Alice Downie and Barbara Robertson, 1968; How Summer Came to Canada,
by William Toye, 1969; The Mountain
Goats of Temlaham, by William Toye, 1969.

ABOUT: Bookbird No. 1, 1973; In Review
Winter 1972; Winter 1974.

VERA CLEAVER
January 6, 1919
and
BILL CLEAVER
March 24, 1920

AUTHORS OF *Where The Lilies Bloom,*
etc.

Autobiographical sketch of Vera A. and
   William J. Cleaver by Bill Cleaver:

IN our thirty-third year of marriage we
live now in a two-story house on a hill
in Winter Haven, Florida. My office is
downstairs and Vera's is upstairs. Our
front windows command a fine view of
a deep, wide lake. Since this is karst
country I suspect this body of clear,
spring-fed water began as a sinkhole.

I am a native of Seattle, Washington,
the second child of two in my family.
Vera was born at Virgil, South Dakota,
the fifth child of nine. Our early, formal
educations were checkerboard. My parents were divorced when I was five and
I was sent to British Columbia to attend
a private school. Vera began her schooling at Kennebec, South Dakota. Each of
us was moved around quite a bit in our
young lives, so to package this question
of education we now have a simple
answer to cover the whole bill: We are
graduates of the public libraries of the
United States of America.

Some random notes about ourselves:

Books we like: This is a hard one because we find what we liked yesterday is
disappointing today. The writings of
Kenneth Roberts, Peter Freuchen, Joseph Wood Krutch, Thornton Wilder,
Rachel Carson, J. Krishnamurti and
Lewis Carroll have survived our tastes.

About nature: We have a great affection for it. We don't collect it because
we don't collect anything except words
and ideas and books. Don't like butterflies on pins or stuffed animals and fish
and birds, don't like to see wild plants in
tame gardens. Insects deserve more of
human good will than they are getting.

About social gatherings: To us they

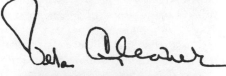

Bill Cleaver

his type is, I wish he'd go back to his corner and leave me to mine.

About work: We would rather be dead than not be able to write. Even in our earliest childhoods we knew we were going to be what we are today. We think we won't ever be rich. From time to time, when circumstances seem right for it, we prepare ourselves to go live under a tree or a bridge. We wouldn't trade being what we are for anything.

About our own books: We think our best is yet to come. Our writing has passed through several stages, and we've been criticized and acclaimed for it. The goal is to create in such a way as to make people who read what we write recognize themselves and say, "This is me and being here on this paper in this situation is what it feels like." Our aim is to produce work that will assist the student in refining his tastes in language that may be relished, respected, recognized as being something of worth. To us, any book, whether for adults or for children, without an outlook on life or a philosophy is worthless.

Under a great variety of circumstances we have lived in a number of places in the United States, Europe and Japan. Memories of these places and their peoples are intense; we've both been blessed with good memories.

From time to time we are asked this question: What do you consider the most important element in fiction for children?

Our answer: We don't believe your question should be qualified. Let us answer it as if you had asked what we consider the most important element in fiction, and not qualify it by saying "for children." For us the most important element in fiction is truth to human nature and truth to the human condition.

————

seem a waste of time. Usually there is someone present who wants to start an argument with us concerning: (1) His child's inability to grasp what he reads; (2) The lack of "important" issues in our books; (3) The lack of quality education in our schools; (4) The cost of schools and libraries; (5) His hard life as opposed to our easy ones. On and on. This fellow usually challenges us to admit we are great literary brains, and this is very boring indeed. My thinking on

Ever since they began publishing for children, the Cleavers' work has been met with critical accolades and awards. Cleaver books have consistently been included in the annual lists of best books compiled by the New York *Times Book Review, School Library Journal, Horn Book* magazine, and *Publishers Weekly*. In addition, *Where the Lilies Bloom* was an American Library Association Notable Book, was nominated for a National Book Award, and was a runner-up for the Boston *Globe-Horn Book* Award in 1970. It has also been made into a successful film, a somewhat rare occurrence with a book written for young people. A second Cleaver book, *Grover*, also was nominated for a National Book Award, in 1971, as was *The Whys and Wherefores of Littabelle Lee* in 1974. In 1977 the Cleavers received a Golden Spur Award for the best juvenile fiction from the Western Writers of America. The award was given for *Dust of the Earth*.

The Cleavers, who met and married during World War II, had sold over 250 stories to pulp magazines before they turned to a genre that would allow them more scope for their talents. Both have always been readers. Vera recalls that when she discovered the library, she and her family parted ways, since they were not book-oriented.

The Cleavers work out their ideas together, talking over characters and plot until every detail is clear to them. This process may take as long as six months before Vera is ready to sit down and start the actual writing. "When the characters and the plot are clear and defined, they practically dictate the words to me," she has said. When asked if Bill were critical of what she writes, she observed that he sometimes pointed to a sign he had made and left beside her typewriter. It reads "Don't Be So Serious."

SELECTED WORKS: Ellen Grae, 1967; Lady Ellen Grae, 1968; Where The Lilies Bloom, 1969; Grover, 1970; The Mimosa Tree, 1970; I Would Rather Be A Turnip, 1971; The Mock Revolt, 1971; Delpha Green & Company, 1972; The Whys and Wherefores of Littabelle Lee, 1973; Me Too, 1973; Dust of the Earth, 1975; Trial Valley, 1977.

ABOUT: Publishers Weekly January 19, 1970; Top of the News June 1976.

ELEANOR CLYMER

AUTHOR OF *My Brother Stevie*, etc.

Autobiographical sketch of Eleanor Lowenton Clymer, who also writes under the name "Elizabeth Kinsey":

I WAS born in New York City and spent most of my life there, living at different times in each of the five boroughs. My taste for stories came from my mother. She didn't know much about home management, but she could at any moment recite poetry, sing Russian folk songs, tell stories which she made up, or read to us from the books in the glass-fronted bookcase.

When I was about six I began to make up my own poems and stories. I soon found out that the library had many more books than the bookcase, and I decided, like Janey Moffat, that I was going to read them all.

Living in New York in those days meant freedom to wander all over the city, to explore the big park and the river fronts and the crowded streets, to ride on the ferryboats and the elevated railroad and the tops of the double-decker buses, and to climb and camp on the Palisades across the Hudson.

In high school I wrote for the school magazine, the *Washington Irving Sketch-Book*, and discovered the thrill of editing it. There also I was introduced to the biological sciences by an unusual teacher. I planned to write a history of science someday. With a small microscope I watched the tiny creatures in jars of stagnant water, and at the Museum of Natural History I studied the bones of the dinosaurs. These interests stayed with me through college, first Barnard, then the University of Wisconsin.

Later, at New York University, I studied story writing with a great teacher, Sylvia Chatfield Bates. All this time I was learning to write, but it wasn't till I married and had a child that I rediscovered my real interest: children's books.

This happened at the Bank Street

Eleanor Clymer

School, where Lucy Sprague Mitchell was teaching the writers' workshop. This woman was revolutionizing children's literature, urging her students to listen to children's language, watch their play, and find out what made sense to them as they grew. I have been writing children's books ever since.

My first books were for the very young, based on the everyday life of the children I knew. As those children grew older I tried to write what would please them—stories about baseball, airplanes, photography, pets. Some books were written under the pen name of Elizabeth Kinsey. Then I went back to an earlier interest and wrote several books about the history of science.

About ten years ago I began to feel that something was missing from my books, some feeling of my own. C. S. Lewis said that if you have something to say, the best way to say it is in a book for children. I had things I really wanted to say, but I hadn't settled on a way to say them.

That was when I wrote *My Brother Stevie*. I wanted to tell what a real child might have said if she had been telling about her life. It wasn't my own life, of course, but the feelings and the setting were things I was familiar with.

Children's emotions and problems in dealing with an adult world are very real and deep, and I felt that perhaps children would be willing to read a book that told it as it was. At the same time an adult writing for children should not present the world as too threatening or hopeless. So though the book did not have a happy ending, it did end on a hopeful note.

That was the first of several books about the city. Though I live in a small country village now, I find myself going back to the city that I knew well in the past.

I have also been able to travel in the last few years. My interest in archaeology led me to visit ancient Indian ruins and then to write about present-day Indians. I'm not an authority on Indian culture, but I think human feelings must be much the same everywhere. So it is permissible to write about Indian children, and perhaps help other children to understand and admire them. *The Spider, the Cave, and the Pottery Bowl* is a story about Hopi children.

My son is grown up now. He is a newspaperman, as his father used to be. And I have a young granddaughter, who is a devourer of stories and is starting to read them for herself.

———

A prolific author, Eleanor Clymer has written more than fifty books. *My Brother Stevie* was an American Library Association Notable Book in 1967 and won the Woodward School Award in 1968. *The Spider, the Cave, and the Pottery Bowl* received an award for its authentic portrayal of the Southwest from the Border Regional Library Association of El Paso, Texas. *Luke Was There* received the Children's Book Award from the Child Study Association of America/Wel-Met, Inc. in 1974 and was filmed for presentation in 1975.

Eleanor Lowenton married Kinsey Clymer in 1933. The Clymers have one son, Adam.

SELECTED WORKS: Search for a Living Fossil, 1963; My Brother Stevie, 1968; The Big Pile of Dirt, 1968; The Second Greatest Invention, 1969; We Lived in the Almont, 1970; The Spider, the Cave, and the Pottery Bowl, 1971; Me and the Eggman, 1972; Luke Was There, 1973; Leave Horatio Alone, 1974; Engine Number Seven, 1975; Hamburgers—and Ice Cream for Dessert, 1975; Horatio's Birthday, 1976.

ABOUT: Contemporary Authors, Vol. 61–64.

ALAN E. COBER

May 18, 1935–

ILLUSTRATOR OF *Mister Corbett's Ghost,* etc.

Autobiographical sketch of Alan E. Cober:

MY first recollections are sitting on the floor having my portrait done in pastels. I remember being near the window holding a purple crayon. I was eighteen months old at the time, in 1936. You would think this the reason I was to become an artist. Maybe it was. I have an artist uncle, the black sheep of the family, whom everyone said I looked and acted like. My father was a criminal lawyer, so I was forbidden to become a criminal and became an artist, a sensitive individual.

In 1952, when I wanted to go to art school, artists were thought of as worse than criminals, since criminals worked. Things have gotten better. Artists are now respected. The respect for people, honesty and social consciousness instilled in me by my parents has grown and finally instilled itself in my work. My drawings of prisons, retarded children, and aged have been produced as a book, *The Forgotten Society.*

I was born in New York City and we lived there until 1942, when we moved to Liberty, New York. I loved it there—the hunting pants, the cold air, the high-top boots, high wool socks with the red band on top to be folded over the boots, and racing down the big hill in my pedal car.

We returned to New York City in 1944 and settled in the Bronx. I lived there until I was drafted into the Army in 1958. I loved to play baseball, football and various other sports. I thought I was a natural athlete until I skied at the University of Vermont, where I went to college. I had a tryout with the Chicago Cubs when I was seventeen years old.

In the army, I taught and worked as an artist in the Special Warfare School at Fort Bragg. I returned home in 1960 and lived in Greenwich Village. I remet my wife Ellen (whom I had first met when I was seventeen). We married in 1961, moved to Riverdale, then on to Ossining, New York, where we have lived in a house built in 1824 for the past thirteen years. We have two children, Leslie (1963), an artist, and Peter (1964), an architect of dog houses and a soccer player. We are all collectors, so the house is filled with American Folk Art, painted boxes and furniture, antique toys, lead soldiers (Peter's), and animals (Leslie's). We summer in Cape Cod and love it. Most of my time is involved in traveling on assignments and lectures and just drawing. I am now working on a show—a life-sized circus and a book of portraits from the circus.

———

Alan Cober studied at the University of Vermont with the idea of becoming a lawyer like his father but gave it up after two years when an art instructor assured him he had talent. He then returned to New York and entered the School of Visual Arts. Later he also studied at the Graphic Arts Division of Pratt Institute and the New School.

Ever since he began drawing professionally Alan Cober's work has won numerous accolades and medals—he estimates that he has about two hundred awards from various art directors' clubs and organizations. In 1965 he was chosen Artist of the Year by the Artists Guild of New York. *Mister Corbett's Ghost*, by Leon Garfield, and Natalia Belting's *Winter's Eve* were on the New York *Times*' best-illustrated list in 1968 and 1969. Cober has twice received Gold Medals from the Society of Illustrators, in 1968 for *Beowulf* and in 1972 for *Pigeon Man*, by Jean-Pierre Abraham. *The Fire Plume*, edited by John Bierhorst, was chosen one of the Fifty Best Books in 1970 by the American Institute of Graphic Arts and was also on the AIGA's list of the seventy-five best children's books published from 1965 to 1972. In 1976 the same book was included in the AIGA's Bias-Free Illustration Show. In 1973 the School of Visual Arts awarded Alan Cober its Outstanding Achievement Award.

In addition to illustrating books for children, Cober works in advertising, fashion, and magazine illustration. "I love to draw," he says. "I keep searching, keep looking for new ways . . . I'm always looking for new things to do . . . I worry about each job. I hope to keep worrying, and maybe they will continue to be close to good."

SELECTED WORKS ILLUSTRATED: Mister Corbett's Ghost, by Leon Garfield, 1968; The Fire Plume, edited by John Bierhorst, 1969; Winter's Eve, by Natalia Belting, 1969; Escape, by Ota Hofman, 1970; The Dark is Rising, by Susan Cooper, 1973; The Tiger's Bones and Other Plays for Children, by Ted Hughes, 1974; Aaron's Door, by Miska Miles, 1977.

ABOUT: Kingman, Lee and others, comps. Illustrators of Children's Books, 1957–1966; American Artist June 1966, April 1972.

WILLIAM COLE

November 20, 1919–

AUTHOR OF *That Pest Jonathan*, etc.

Autobiographical sketch of William Rossa Cole:

I'VE never met any other writers who were born where I was, on Staten Island. I grew up on the shore of New York Harbor, from which I could see the Statue of Liberty and the towers of lower Manhattan. I didn't do much reading until I was in my early teens, when I discovered the novels of P. G. Wodehouse and Thorne Smith, and read all of them. Then I began haunting secondhand junk shops and Salvation Army warehouses, buying books for ten cents and a quarter. My introduction to poetry was a huge anthology, with the covers off, which I paid ten cents for. I read everything in it and marked the page numbers of poems I liked on the last blank page of the book, a habit I still have.

The book that really got me onto literature was a collection of quotations, *The Golden Treasury of the World's Wit and Wisdom*, by Norman Lockridge. This was simply a collection of wise and witty things said by every writer you could think of over the centuries. I had bought it for $1.98 at a Times Square remainder shop when I was sixteen, and I marked everything in it, more or less giving grades to the quotations—"Excellent!" "Good!" "True!" "Untrue!" "To be thought about," etc. Without knowing I did so, I must have memorized a couple of hundred of those quotations, for I find that I've used them from time to time ever since. They also set me to reading further in the works of the writers I particularly admired: Shaw, Wilde, Wells, La Rochefoucauld, Balzac.

My formal education stopped after

high school, where I wasn't by any means a star pupil, although I did well in English.

After high school I did nothing but read and slop around for a few years—the depression was on and I couldn't find a job in New York. When I was eighteen I got work in a delicatessen in Rye, New York, and from that, after six months, moved down the street to a job in the Rye Book Shop, where I made twelve dollars a week until I was raised to twenty dollars as manager. Then World War II got me, and I spent four years in the Infantry. I was slightly wounded in France and had an exciting time in the Battle of the Bulge.

When I got out of the army in 1946 I luckily stumbled on a job as Publicity Director for the publisher, Alfred A. Knopf. After eleven years of that, I moved on to Simon and Schuster as Publicity Director and part-time editor. Early in my Knopf years I put together a collection of cartoons from the English magazine *Punch*, and eventually found a publisher for it. I followed that with a collection of humorous prose and poetry from the same magazine, and then an editor asked me to do a book of funny poems for children, which I did, with

some success. Then I *really* started to do anthologies and have brought out between two and six every year since, making a total of forty-two. I've also written ten books for young children and have had quite a bit of light verse published in magazines and anthologies.

My main interest in the world is poetry, and I have a personal library of some three thousand volumes of it. I can do almost any anthology from my own library and from clippings that I hoard away daily in bulging files. I am delighted to be an anthologist, for I am doing for my living what I would be doing anyway for my personal delight. I live in the heart of Manhattan, on upper Times Square, and spend as much time as I can in Ireland where I am well received, mainly because my mother's father was a famous Fenian leader, Jeremiah O'Donovan Rossa. I have four wonderful children, each of whom has a wonderful name: two girls, Cambria and Jeremy, and two boys, Williams and Rossa.

———

William Cole is a poet, columnist and reviewer, whose articles have appeared in such magazines as the *New Yorker*, the *Atlantic, Harper's,* and the New York *Times* Book Review. It is as an anthologist that William Cole is best known, however. His anthologies for young people have been consistently praised. *I Went to The Animal Fair* was an American Library Association Notable Book in 1958, as was *Beastly Boys and Ghastly Girls* in 1964. *I Went to The Animal Fair* was also included in the American Library Association's List of Notable Children's Books 1940–59.

Since 1963 William Cole has had his own publishing imprint, first with Walker and Company and currently with Viking Press, publishing books by W. H. Auden, Louis Kronenberger, Maurice Dolbier, and others. He has been associated with the National Book Awards since their founding, serving as chairman of the NBA Committee for two years. He is also a member of American

P.E.N., and the Poetry Society of America.

His wife, the former Peggy Bennett, is also a writer.

SELECTED WORKS: Frances Face-Maker, 1963; What's Good for a Six-Year-Old?, 1965; What's Good for a Four-Year-Old?, 1967; What's Good for a Five-Year-Old?, 1969; That Pest Jonathan, 1970; Aunt Bella's Umbrella, 1970; A Book of Animal Poems, 1973; What's Good for a Three-Year-Old?, 1974; Knock Knocks, the Most Ever, 1976; A Boy Named Mary Jane and Other Silly Verse, 1977; Knock Knocks You've Never Heard Before, 1977.

SELECTED WORKS COMPILED: Humorous Poetry for Children, 1955; I Went to the Animal Fair, 1958; The Birds and the Beasts Were There, 1963; Beastly Boys and Ghastly Girls, 1964; Oh What Nonsense, 1966; Oh, How Silly!, 1970; Oh, That's Ridiculous, 1972.

ABOUT: Contemporary Authors, Vol. 9–10; Newquist, Roy, comp. Counterpoint; Library Journal May 1960.

Gladys Conklin

GLADYS CONKLIN

May 30, 1903–

AUTHOR OF *I Like Butterflies*, etc.

Autobiographical sketch of Gladys Plemon Conklin:

I WAS born in the woods near Harpster, Idaho, on May 30, 1903, the second of five children. A few years later, my father filed on a sagebrush-and-sand homestead in Two Rivers, Washington, where I began my education in a two-room school. Always I had an inquisitive interest in the outdoors. The sagebrush and sand didn't offer anything spectacular, but there were gopher snakes and horned toads to play with and the mighty Columbia River to look at and wonder about. Where did it come from and where was it going?

About age ten, I began writing nature essays and small stories for the *Washington Farmer* magazine and for my Sunday School paper. I was still going to a two-room school in my second year of high school when a teacher suggested that I go into town to a larger high school and plan on college. Town was only four miles away, but these were horse-and-buggy days and there were deep sandy roads. This teacher also suggested that I plan to be a librarian as I could never find enough books to read.

I found a family in town to live with and then went on to major in library science at the University of Washington in Seattle. I graduated in 1926, and the day after graduation I sailed for California and began work as a children's librarian in Ventura. At a young age I had decided to get a college degree so I could travel, staying only two years in one place. From Ventura I went to New York City and stayed three years, going to Europe for two months during the second summer. Then back to California and the Los Angeles Public Library.

The traveling came to an end when I married Irving Conklin and inherited a son and a daughter. Today there are four grandchildren and two great-grandsons in the family. With no traveling to distract me, the writing urge came to the surface again. As a result I have a small, choice collection of rejection notes from the top children's editors of that time.

We tried farming for a few years and had a grade A goat dairy in Oregon. It was my lucky day when we returned to civilization and came to the San Francisco Bay area. The small town of Hayward was looking for a children's librarian. A Library Bug Club developed, and I was soon learning with the youngsters how to raise life cycles of butterflies, ant lions, lacewings, and nearly every kind of insect we could find.

The urge to write was developing again with the Bug Club work, and I couldn't resist it. I picked my publisher carefully as I wanted to write factual nature books for the very young. My first effort, *I Like Caterpillars*, was accepted at once and published by Holiday House in 1958. I thought there might be three or four more books, and rather to my amazement, they are still coming. Number twenty-three will be out in 1977.

I had wanted to go to Africa since my high school days and finally joined a safari in 1970. On returning home my exuberance over the trip carried me rapidly through three books: *Giraffe Lives in Africa*, *Elephants of Africa*, and *The Lion Family*.

I find research stimulating and part of the fun of writing. I go to university libraries for research even when writing a book for five-to-eight-year-olds. The five-year-olds today enjoy a book that is full of meaty information.

After spending half a lifetime as a librarian, it has been difficult to think of myself as an author. Being included in *Junior Authors* should make the transition complete.

————

Besides writing a number of books, Gladys Conklin has been active professionally as well. She is a member of the American Library Association, The Women's National Book Association, the Association of California Librarians, of which she was president in 1952, and the Catholic Library Association, over which she presided in 1963.

She has traveled extensively in Mexico as well as in Europe and Africa. Mrs. Conklin is now retired.

SELECTED WORKS: I Like Caterpillars, 1958; I Like Butterflies, 1960; The Bug Club Book, 1966; How Insects Grow, 1969; Giraffe Lives in Africa, 1971; Elephants of Africa, 1972; The Lion Family, 1973; Fairy Rings and Other Mushrooms, 1973; Journey of the Gray Whales, 1974; I Like Beetles, 1975; Cheetahs, The Swift Hunters, 1976; I Watch Flies, 1977; The Octopus and Other Cephalopods, 1977.

ABOUT: Contemporary Authors, Vol. 2; Foremost Women in Communications, 1970; Something about the Author, Vol. 2.

ELIZABETH K. COOPER

February 16, 1916–

AUTHOR OF *Science in Your Own Back Yard*, etc.

Autobiographical sketch of Elizabeth Keyser Cooper:

THOUGH recollections of things long past may be deceptive, I know my early years were happy. My brother and I played in the big, high-ceilinged rooms of the house in Erie, Pennsylvania, where I was born. We had gardens to dig in, trees to climb, and hiding places in an old coach house where two rather terrifying ponies were stabled.

On summer evenings we ate ice cream on the porch and watched fireflies in the hedges. My mother often read aloud to us, and my father taught us to recite poetry. Books and music were important in our home, but the only music we heard in those early years came from records played on an Edison gramophone in the parlor.

As far as I know, no one in my family had ever been an author, artist or musician. To this day I have no idea why, by age eight, I knew that I was going to write. In the beginning I fancied myself as a poet, and my first "book," handwritten in a Webster nickle notebook, was a collection of original verses, rhymed and unrhymed, complete with "Notes on the Life of Elizabeth as a Child"—written, as I recall, to save trouble for my future biographers!

By the time I was eleven, prose had replaced poetry, and I was writing for an audience. I spent most of the summer on a "novel," *The Winsome Weeper*,

Elizabeth K. Cooper

which I read aloud to parents, aunts and uncles. They applauded, and so I kept on writing.

When we moved to Cleveland everything changed, and soon we became a one-parent family. We survived largely because of opportunities and institutions found only in big cities. On Sundays my mother took us children to the Museum of Art. We also attended symphony concerts, and opera when the Metropolitan came to town each year. I spent my Saturdays at the public library, where among the many books I devoured was one that captivated me completely. Its title was *Five Hundred Things a Bright Boy Can Do*, and it introduced me to the wonders of science.

For a while I was shy and lonely in the big Cleveland school I attended. Then, one Monday morning I appeared with the first half of a story, *The Mystery of the Pink Tomato*, with illustrations. The manuscript was passed around the class, surreptitiously at first, and I promised the concluding half for the following week. Eventually everyone, including the teacher, became involved in the Pink Tomato menace. My lonely time was over, and for the rest of the year I was the class mystery writer, turning out such attention-getters as *The Summer*

Visitor's Revenge and *The Poison Ivy Bathing Suit*.

I continued to write fiction all through school and college and in the early years of my marriage. My husband and I collaborated on plays that were produced on NBC radio, scenarios for motion pictures, and some long dramas that were never seen on Broadway. At the same time, I was becoming increasingly involved with science, and also with children and their sense of wonder, a feeling I understood and shared. As I taught, learned from, and explored with children, I began to write for them. I still do. I always will.

———

After Elizabeth Cooper received her bachelor's degree from Western Reserve University, where she was elected to Phi Beta Kappa, she taught school, first in Cleveland, then in New York at the Ethical Culture Schools. While there she collaborated with her colleague, Herbert Zim, on *Minerals*, thus launching a long and distinguished writing career. She has twelve children's science books to her credit, all of them still in print, and in recent years has been deeply engaged in writing elementary school science textbooks as well.

From New York Mrs. Cooper went on to the University of California at Los Angeles, where she earned her M.A. in 1945 and Ed.D. in 1947. She taught on the elementary and college levels and was a school administrator before turning to writing full time.

Her work has consistently received high praise for its freshness and lucidity. In 1958 *Science in Your Own Back Yard* was honored with The Thomas Alva Edison Award for Best Children's Science Book.

Elizabeth Keyser married Clancy Cooper, an actor and producer, in 1935. They have one son, Padraic, a photographer who has collaborated with his mother on several books, and two granddaughters, Deirdre and Allison. The Coopers traveled widely, living abroad for several months at a time. Now a widow, Mrs. Cooper lives in Los Angeles.

SELECTED WORKS: Minerals (with Herbert Zim), 1943; Science in Your Own Back Yard, 1958; Discovering Chemistry, 1959; Science on the Shores and Banks, 1960; Silkworms and Science, 1961; And Everything Nice, 1966; The Fish from Japan, 1969; A Tree is Something Wonderful (with Padraic Cooper), 1972; Sweet and Delicious (with Padraic Cooper), 1973.

ABOUT: Contemporary Authors, Vol. 4; Contemporary Authors. Vol. 33–36.

SUSAN COOPER

May 23, 1935–

AUTHOR OF *The Grey King*, etc.

Autobiographical sketch of Susan Mary Cooper Grant:

LIKE my books, I'm mostly English, partly Welsh. I had two homes in Britain: one in Buckinghamshire, twenty miles from London where I was born and raised; the other in Aberdovey, North Wales, my grandmother's village, in which my parents have now lived for the last fifteen years.

In 1963 I married an American with three teen-age children and moved to Winchester, Massachusetts. The teenagers are grown up now, and we have Jonathan (1966) and Kate (1967) instead.

I discovered I was a writer when I was about eight. Life was noisy at the time, being punctuated by World War II bombs, but we paid no great attention, my younger brother Rod and I. (He's a writer too: very funny thrillers.) It was only twenty-five years later that the bombs echoed again, in a book I wrote called *Dawn of Fear*.

I went to Oxford, took a degree in English, and edited the university newspaper. Then I became a reporter and feature writer for the *Sunday Times* in London, and had a wonderful time exploring odd corners of life for seven years. I wrote an adult novel and my first children's book, *Over Sea, Under Stone*; then I came to America.

I wrote three more adult books. But nothing could quite blot out my homesickness, which was possibly the reason for my discovering that *Over Sea, Under Stone* was in fact the first of five books in a sequence of fantasies for children called *The Dark is Rising*.

The nonsense stories I make up for my own children are quite different from the books I write. The books aren't written *for* children, or for anyone in particular; they simply appear and grow, out of the great jumble of English and Celtic myth and legend that my subconscious has acquired over the years.

In spite of all the hard work involved, it always seems to me rather like the way a splendid crop of mushrooms can spring up overnight in an empty pasture: a wonderful magic for which one is grateful without quite understanding how, or from where, it came.

———

Though the number of Susan Cooper's books for children is not large, her work has attracted favorable attention from the first, culminating in her winning the Newbery Medal for *The Grey King* in 1976. Her first book, *Over Sea, Under*

Stone, was included on the *Horn Book's* Honor List in 1967. *Dawn of Fear* was also honored by *Horn Book* and was an American Library Association Notable Book for Children in 1970, as were *The Dark is Rising* for 1973, and *The Grey King* for 1975. *The Dark is Rising* won the Boston *Globe-Horn Book Award,* was a Newbery Honor Book, and a runner-up for England's Carnegie Medal, all in 1973. In 1976 *The Grey King* was a runner-up for the Carnegie Medal and won the Tir Na N-Og Award for the best children's book of the year in English with Welsh background.

Susan Cooper says she travels "a good deal," annually making visits home to Britain and to the British Virgin Islands, where she and her husband own a "small remote house in which we spend much of the summer, and in which I do a great deal of work."

SELECTED WORKS: Over Sea, Under Stone, 1966; Dawn of Fear, 1970; The Dark is Rising, 1973; Greenwitch, 1974; The Grey King, 1975; Silver on the Tree, 1977.

ABOUT: Authors and Writers; Contemporary Authors, Vol. 29–32; Something about the Author, Vol. 4; Christian Science Monitor May 12, 1976; Horn Book August 1976.

SCOTT CORBETT

July 27, 1913–

AUTHOR OF *Cutlass Island,* etc.

Autobiographical sketch of Scott Corbett:

I HAVE always been fond of travel, almost as fond as I am of staying home. At any rate, the first thing I ever sold was written while I was traveling on a trolley car in Kansas City, Missouri, where I was born and raised.

It was a parody poem, and brought me what was then the princely sum of six dollars from a magazine called *College Humor.*

At that time I was in college myself, and I have made my living as a writer ever since, except for one period from 1943 to 1946 during World War II when I was invited by our government to make my living as a soldier in the 42nd Infantry (Rainbow) Division.

This line of work included travel opportunities to France and southern Germany, so it was not all bad. Before the war I had been living in New York City with my wife and infant daughter. After the war we lived there for five more years and then, helped by the sale of a book to the movies, we moved to East Dennis, Massachusetts, on Cape Cod.

Up to that time I had only written for adults—magazine pieces, books, a little radio and TV material—and not until we had lived on Cape Cod for seven years and were about to move to Providence, Rhode Island, did I finally have sense enough to start writing books for children. I have been happily writing them ever since, about forty of them in all.

Until we moved to Providence I had never taught school a day in my life, but I had the colossal nerve to teach English at Moses Brown, a preparatory school, for the next eight years. To be perfectly honest, I only taught two classes a day, in the mornings, and wrote books in the afternoons.

This was most enjoyable, and I might still be teaching if there were hours enough in the day. By then, however, the business of producing books and the urge to travel made it necessary to end my brief career in the classroom.

In 1965–66 my wife and I spent eight and a half months going around the world on freighters, with long stops in Hong Kong, Taiwan, Japan, Greece and Italy. Most freighters carry only twelve passengers and stop at many out-of-the-way ports to unload or take on cargo. We have made many more trips on freighters since then, including a trip around South America (through the Strait of Magellan) and trips to the Mediterranean and the Orient. During the past ten years we have spent a total of more than a year's time actually at sea. Several of my books have been written during these trips.

My stories often involve something drawn from my own childhood. The first of my Trick books, *The Lemonade Trick*, begins in a small public park where I often played as a boy. A book called *The Red Room Riddle* accurately pictures a segment of my boyhood, though I am thankful to say I never experienced the events that follow (it is a ghost story).

Although I received a B.J. (Bachelor of Journalism) degree from the University of Missouri's School of Journalism, I never went into newspaper work except as an army newspaper editor and reporter. What I have found I like to do best is tell stories which I hope will entertain boys and girls, who are my idea of a good audience.

My signature is the result of being left-handed and lazy. I could not think of an easier way to cross all four t's at once.

———

Scott Corbett married Elizabeth Grosvenor Pierce in 1940. They have one daughter, Florence Lee. His book, *Cutlass Island*, won the Edgar Allan Poe Award as the best mystery for children written in 1962, and *The Mystery Man* received a nomination in 1970. In 1976 the children of Missouri voted for *The Home Run Trick* to receive the Mark Twain Award.

SELECTED WORKS: The Lemonade Trick, 1960; Cutlass Island, 1962; Pippa Passes, 1966; Diamonds Are Trouble, 1967; The Mystery Man, 1970; The Red Room Riddle, 1972; The Home Run Trick, 1973; The Hockey Trick, 1974; The Great McGonnigle's Gray Ghost, 1975; Captain Butcher's Body, 1976; The Great McGonnigle's Key Play, 1976; The Hockey Girls, 1976; The Hangman's Ghost, 1977.

ABOUT: Author's and Writer's Who's Who, 1971; Contemporary Authors, Vol. 3; Something about the Author, Vol. 2.

MARGARET COSGROVE

June 3, 1926–

AUTHOR AND ILLUSTRATOR OF *Wonders of the Tree World*, etc.

Autobiographical sketch of Margaret Leota Cosgrove:

SOMETIMES I can scarcely believe that I ever lived such a life as I lived when a child. Whatever the problems we have, whatever the unhappinesses, if any, in childhood or adulthood, what do they matter if one has some good early days to build on? I lived a double life. First, there was the small town in the northwestern corner of Ohio, Sylvania, where I was born. It always seemed to me that, by some natural order of things, it took exactly one year to complete a cycle of adventure and make rounds in town. A certain sidewalk on the other side of town to skate on in a certain week in May, a certain tree in someone's yard we hadn't gotten around to climbing for a full twelve months, or a spooky place to explore annually—and then it was October already and time to get down to the swamp west of town to walk on the half-submerged planks. I had roots.

And then my father's work as an engineer in the Federal Power Commission began taking him to other cities late in the depression, so my mother took my little sister and me to join him so we could all be together, at a time when mobility in middle-class, small-town families was rare. This was my other life, and I became a city child for a year or so at a time. There were new ideas to

Margaret L. Cosgrove

how books were made, however, I studied anatomy and other sciences and embarked on a new life as a medical illustrator.

At some point or other I sat on the grass in Central Park, and the first book I wrote and illustrated, *Wonders of the Tree World*, evolved. I did like fantasy and imagination, but in one of those pendulum-swings of the publishing world I was instructed by a few editors that fantasy was not good for children; it was science, realism and fact they wanted. I happened to be much interested in biology and already had a few books half written in my head (which have since been published). Now, because I like people too much to live the often solitary life of a writer and illustrator completely, I teach art mornings in the happy atmosphere of the Spence School. I still haven't written and illustrated the books I dream of, but maybe I'll succeed someday.

———

encounter and adaptations to be made. I still believe that most families should maintain and nurture their roots, but there are some questing and restless children who need extra stimulations to thrive on.

After high school I nearly went to college, but decided to make a stopover at the Chicago Art Institute because my fingers kept tingling and I had to draw and paint for a while. Most students there were debating issues and discussing Life, and I felt, by the end of two years there, that I had to go out and find out what was meant by Life, and left to enter nurses' training, in an excellent hospital of the old style, where black stockings and seven-day weeks still prevailed. I became another sort of person for a while, and if I lost a few crucial years that might have made me a better artist and writer, I discovered a little of what I had been looking for and am deeply grateful for those years.

But my fingers began tingling badly again, and I came to New York, doing a few odd jobs and mostly just trying to get my fill of drawing pictures. It was then that the memory of certain books, bought by good parents and cherished in childhood, came back to stand out like beacons on dark nights—something of value. Not having the slightest idea of

Besides Ohio, Margaret Cosgrove lived in Illinois, Vermont and New Jersey as a child. Always inclined toward art, she writes that when she was a child, art "was mostly a matter of storing up impressions and ideas rather than of execution and expression." Now, in her writing and illustrating of her own books, she strives for "an approach that is neither over-popularizing and exploiting the natural sciences in general, nor the presentation of a textbook."

Until she left to free-lance and to write her own books, Margaret Cosgrove was a medical illustrator at Roosevelt Hospital in New York City, where she now lives.

SELECTED WORKS: Wonders of the Tree World, 1953; Wonders of Your Senses, 1959; Wonders Under a Microscope, 1959; Strange Worlds Under a Microscope, 1962; Your Hospital, a Modern Miracle, 1962; Eggs and What Happens Inside Them, 1966; Plants in Time, Their History and Mystery, 1967; Bone for Bone, 1968; Seeds, Embryos, and Sex, 1970; Messages and Voices: the Communication of Animals, 1974; Wintertime for Animals, 1975:

ABOUT: Contemporary Authors, Vol. 9–10; Kingman, Lee and others, comps. Illustrators of Children's Books, 1957–1966.

LEONARD COTTRELL

May 21, 1913–October 6, 1974

AUTHOR OF *The Warrior Pharaohs*, etc.

Autobiographical sketch of Leonard Eric Cottrell, written shortly before his death:

I WAS born in 1913 in the village of Tettenhall, Staffordshire, England, and spent the first twenty-eight years of my life in the industrial city of Birmingham. My father, an engineer, first stirred my interest in antiquity. I remember, when I was ten, reading the newspaper articles he brought home describing the discovery of Tutankhamun's tomb, and also a moment when, visiting Tewkesbury Abbey, he pointed to the roof and said, "Leonard, when those stones were laid men wore chain mail."

Suddenly the dull history books I was reading at school came to life. I realized for the first time that one could actually *touch* things which had been made some nine hundred or more years ago, that the people about whom I had been reading, such as William the Conqueror, were real people, as real as I was. I read prodigiously, and was totally uninterested in school activities such as football, cricket, athletics, etc. History and English were the only subjects which absorbed me. At the age of fifteen I determined to become a writer, although I had taken the scientific side at school (King Edward's Grammar School, Birmingham) and left without taking the examinations which might have led me to a University.

At first I wanted to become a journalist, but as this would have entailed me starting on a small provincial newspaper, some way from home, my mother forbade it. So I went into advertising as a copywriter, which I detested. In my spare time I read Dryden, Pope, Addison, Steele, Johnson, and other eighteenth century writers, but was not at-

LEONARD COTTRELL

tracted to novelists such as Dickens and Thackeray, or by the literature of the nineteenth century generally, except for some of the poetry, e.g., that of Browning, Keats and Shelley. I also read a great many Greek and Roman authors in translation.

I toured the English countryside on my motorcycle, exploring prehistoric stone circles, burial mounds of the Bronze Age, medieval and Renaissance monuments, in fact anything up to the eighteenth century. On these journeys I was often accompanied by the girl whom I eventually married, Miss Doris Swain, though this marriage was dissolved in 1962.

In 1937, after gaining experience in writing articles on historical subjects for the motoring press, I wrote my first "Feature Programme" or documentary for the British Broadcasting Corporation. It was followed by several others which I wrote in my spare time. Then came the Second World War. I wanted to be an R.A.F. pilot but was rejected on medical grounds. The BBC invited me to join their staff in 1942 and I reveled in the experience of meeting fellow writers, actors and producers. Later I became a writer-producer myself, at first concentrating on documentaries about the war. In 1944 I became a war correspondent attached to the Royal Air Force and wrote programs about the war in Italy. My interest in flying was such that when the war ended I persuaded the BBC to let me report on the expansion of civil aviation, and this led me to many countries and about one and a half million miles of flying.

On one such journey I visited Egypt and saw for the first time the Pyramids, the Valley of the Kings and other Egyptian antiquities about which I had read with such enthusiasm. Round about this time, 1947, I persuaded the BBC to let me write and produce a series of programs about great archaeological discoveries and so, during the process of research, I met a number of distinguished scholars. These documentary broadcasts met with such success that I was invited by the late John Pudney, the poet, to undertake a book called *The Lost Pharaohs.*

This was followed, at short intervals, by other books such as *The Bull of Minos, The Anvil of Civilization, Life under the Pharaohs,* and many others. To date I have written thirty-six books and am engaged on two more, both to be published in the United States.

I have never pretended to be an archaeologist, though nowadays I am often regarded as one. I am essentially a writer *about* archaeology and travel. My function, as I see it, is to act as a kind of middleman between the pure scholar and the educated layman or, in some cases, the child. Having much of the child in myself I find it easy and enjoyable to write for young people, and such books as *The Warrior Pharaohs, The Secrets of Tutankhamun's Tomb* and *Reading the Past* have had considerable success in Britain and America. I have no children myself.

In 1954 I joined the staff of BBC Television as writer-director but was never allowed to produce programs on my favorite topic, archaeology. So I left the BBC in 1958, went to live in the beautiful county of Westmorland, in the country, and concentrated entirely on authorship, though I did, and still do, contribute occasional documentaries for

the BBC. Also by this time I had become an experienced broadcaster myself, and also a lecturer. Some of my books have been published in as many as nine countries.

I married again in 1965, my wife being Miss Diana Bonakis, a highly gifted artist and musician, much younger than myself. The marriage broke up in 1968, since which time I have lived alone, continuing to write books, articles and radio programs, and am still living in northwest England, though in a different house. It is on a lovely site overlooking the estuary of the river Kent in Westmorland, and from my study window I can see the river; from another I catch a glimpse of the Lakeland mountains, in the shadow of which lived Wordsworth and other Lakeland poets.

My hobbies are listening to music, mainly classical though I also like traditional jazz, motoring in fast cars, and fooling about with tape recorders, etc. I reached my sixtieth birthday on May 21, 1973, but still feel young, am still enthusiastic about archaeology and antiquity generally, just as I was when a child. And that is why I enjoy writing for youngsters. But my golden rule is "never write *down* to young people."

SELECTED WORKS: Land of the Pharaohs, 1960; The Secrets of Tutankhamen's Tomb, 1964; Great Leaders of Greece and Rome, 1966; Five Queens of Ancient Egypt, 1969; The Warrior Pharaohs, 1969; Up in a Balloon, 1970; Reading the Past, 1971; Lost Civilizations, 1974.

ABOUT: Author's and Writer's Who's Who, 1971; Contemporary Authors, Vol. 5–6; Who's Who in America, 1972–73; World Authors: 1950–1970.

M. JEAN CRAIG

1915–

AUTHOR OF *The Dragon in the Clock Box,* etc.

Autobiographical sketch of M. Jean Craig:

I WAS born in New York City but grew up in New Brunswick, New Jersey, a small university town, where I was never

M. Jean Craig

more than a five-minute bike ride from fields and woods and a river and a skating pond we called "The Lake." I loved the outdoors, and two early childhood summers at a wonderful camp in Maine clinched it: I was going to become a naturalist.

Well, I didn't. I managed only one year of college and then took a series of dreadful but lucky-to-get-them depression jobs in department stores and offices. But now, all these years later, I note that the nonfiction books I write all have to do with the natural outdoor world, and most of the fiction is full of trees and sunsets and seashores too.

I don't remember ever not knowing how to read. By the time I was eight I'd worked my way through most of my father's sets of Dickens, Poe, Mark Twain, Hawthorne and the like, not to mention the well-beloved *Book of Knowledge* and dozens and dozens of books of my own. (Not to forget, either, that set of de Maupassant on the top shelf, about which my mother said, "That's not for you," so I had to read them all, understanding them not at all, on the afternoons she went out to play bridge.) Then

I graduated to what my father called trash, like the Tom Swift series, which I simply devoured.

I don't think that I ever thought about writing anything myself. Words always went down on paper easily for me, but that was just something I could do, like turning cartwheels or making butterscotch. I did write some poetry in my teens, and once rather shamefacedly sent a short article to the *New Yorker* and felt quite properly snubbed for an upstart when it came back. And during the war (by then I was married to a teacher and had a baby son) I remember coming home from a blue-overall job in an airplane factory and trying to write short stories. I enjoyed doing it, but I didn't think they were very good.

When that marriage ended, I moved to New York and worked for several years in the field of public opinion research. Psychology had fascinated me since I had discovered it at the age of twelve when I read George Dorsey's *Why We Behave Like Human Beings*. I'm still totally fascinated; I'm still trying to learn why we do.

After the war I got married again, this time to a sculptor, and for a couple of years lived in a loft (before people lived in lofts) in the middle of Manhattan's fur district, and worked as a manuscript reader for Twentieth Century Fox. I learned a lot about good and bad writing from that job, willy-nilly.

Then off to Paris for a couple of months, which somehow stretched to seven years. I loved France—the food, countryside, the people, the cities. It was while I was living in France and coping with two new babies and no hot water or phone or bathtub or refrigeration that it came to me that I really wanted to write more than anything else in the world. But I wasn't sure *what* I wanted to write. I tried short stories, articles, more poetry; nothing really worked.

Back in New York eventually, I found a whole new generation of children's books to read to my own children, as well as my own old books to reread, as well as other old ones I'd somehow missed as a child. Some of them were so bad I found myself saying, "I could do better than that!" And some were so wonderful I found myself saying, "What a joy it must be to have written something like that!" And one day I picked up a pencil and tried to write something for children that *I* would want to read, and managed to, and yes it was joy indeed to have written it. So I kept on doing it.

My son is a physicist working in Grenoble now; one daughter is completing her doctorate in psychology in Boston; the other daughter is a talented illustrator and married—and some people have asked why and how I write for children when I no longer have children. I hardly dare tell them that I never wrote for my own children when they were small. All I ever did was try to write what *I* wanted to read, and that's what I still do.

The Dragon in the Clock Box was an American Library Association Notable Book in 1962.

SELECTED WORKS: The Dragon in the Clock Box, 1962; What Did You Dream?, 1964; The Long and Dangerous Journey, 1965; Spring is Like the Morning, 1965; Not Very Much of a House, 1967; Summer is a Very Busy Day, 1967; Dinosaurs and More Dinosaurs, 1968; Pomando, 1969; Where Do I Belong?, 1971; Questions and Answers About Weather, 1973; The Wondrous World of Seedless Plants, with William C. Grimm, 1973; Donkey Prince, 1977; The Little Monsters, 1977.

HELEN CRESSWELL

July 11, 1936–

AUTHOR OF *The Night Watchmen*, etc.

Autobiographical sketch of Helen Cresswell Rowe:

I WAS born the second of three children in North Nottinghamshire, England, in

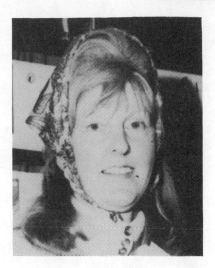

the heart of D. H. Lawrence and Lord Byron country. My father, like D. H. Lawrence's, was a miner during the early part of his life. My childhood was spent in a Nottingham suburb, though I don't remember a time when I did not long to live in the country—as now I do. Nor do I remember a time when I did not know that I was to be a writer. I started writing seriously at seven, and still have exercise books full of my early work, which was almost entirely poetry. As a child I wrote for adults; now I write for children. Is there a moral here somewhere?

During my childhood and teens I put myself through a very rigorous discipline of technical exercises—such as writing epics in the Spencerian stanza, in Gerard Manley Hopkins' sprung rhythm, or in the style of Keats' Odes. I say "discipline" but in fact this gave me the keenest delight. I had then and have now a passion for words as *words*, and never tire of handling them. This long apprenticeship has served me well because I can now write when necessary at a very fast speed with little need for rewriting.

All my books, no matter what they seem to be about, have common springs. They are written out of a sense of the infinite possibilities of life, and of the daily encounter with miracle. I am moved by what Hopkins called "all things counter, original, spare, strange," and at the same time by the richness of the ordinary lives of ordinary people. Again, whatever the outward setting of my stories, the adventures they chart are essentially inner ones, and I travel with my characters to make my discoveries through them. I write with words by Leo Rosten pinned in front of the desk: "When you don't know where a road leads, it sure as hell will take you there." All my books are roads for me, and I hope for my readers too.

Our family lives in a two-hundred-year-old Georgian farmhouse on a hill at the edge of Robin Hood's Sherwood Forest. In 1962 I married Brian Rowe, and we have two daughters, Caroline Jane (December 28, 1963) and Candida Lucy (October 31, 1971). The latter was born at dusk on Halloween and is undoubtedly a white witch. The only time Caroline reads my books is if she takes one out of the library, when it looks, presumably, like a "proper" book with a number, and a stamp at the front. But we read plenty of other books together.

I have now written over forty books, and seven of them have been televised in serial form by BBC television. I have also recently written a series of TV plays about *Lizzie Dripping*, and am about to embark on a second series.

I evidently have unusually sharp hearing and eyesight, and am always amazed that other people never seem to hear the things that go bump in the night, or to see perfectly obvious things like that old gentleman in the fur coat on the TV moon coverage programs, who kept bobbing up from behind lunar rocks and photographing the astronauts last time they were up there. My hobbies are collecting antiques (I hope eventually to become one myself), walking in the country, gardening, exploring new places (or "ticking"), and browsing through graveyards. I love graveyards.

Helen Cresswell earned her Bachelor of Arts in English with honors at Kings College, University of London. Until she turned to writing full time in 1961, she worked at various jobs—as a fashion buyer, an author's literary assistant, a teacher, and for the BBC, for which she still writes.

Helen Cresswell's own favorite book, which has given her the most pleasure in writing of any so far, is *The Piemakers* (England, 1968). In this book, she felt, she successfully fused humor and fantasy for the first time.

The Piemakers was a runner-up for the Carnegie Medal, one of England's top children's book awards, in 1969. The following year *The Night Watchmen* was a runner-up again and also runner-up for Britain's other prestigious prize, the Guardian Award. In 1972, *Up the Pier*, another runner-up for the Carnegie Medal, was designated a Notable Children's Book of the American Library Association. Another Carnegie runner-up was *The Bongleweed* in 1974. *The Winter of the Birds* was an American Library Association Notable Book for Children, 1976.

Writing of Helen Cresswell, a distinguished British critic of children's literature has said: "She feeds two of the child's most precious appetites, the hunger for laughter and the thirst for wonder. . . . The critical reader can surrender totally to the deep pleasure of writing so exquisitely right that it passes almost unnoticed, of ideas genuinely original and developed with satisfying logic, and of a truly comic view of life."

SELECTED WORKS: The White Seahorse, 1970; Pietro and the Mule, 1970; The Night Watchmen, 1970; The Beachcombers, 1972; Up the Pier, 1972; The Bongleweed, 1973; The Winter of the Birds, 1976; A Game of Catch, 1977; Ordinary Jack, 1977.

ABOUT: Author's and Writer's Who's Who, 1971; Contemporary Authors, Vol. 17–18; Something about the Author, Vol. 1; Townsend, John Rowe. A Sense of Story; Junior Bookshelf June 1970.

ERNEST CRICHLOW

June 19, 1914–

ILLUSTRATOR OF *Two Is a Team*, etc.

Autobiographical sketch of Ernest T. Crichlow:

ERNEST CRICHLOW

ALWAYS loved to draw. Started copying comics and illustrations, mostly from *Cosmopolitan* magazine, as a young boy.

Briefly about my training at school: Luckily for me, most of my teachers were professionals enjoying and demanding of themselves the joy that came from turning students onto knowledge, and faulting themselves, as well as the students, when they failed.

In Junior High I had such a teacher who talked about art and what being an artist meant—she also had us copy pencil technique, which I quickly forgot, but not all the comments about art and artists. Then one day she arranged for one of the students to pose for me. Drawing from the model, that did it—I was hooked for life! Later, at Haaren High School, in New York City, Grace Van Allen, Mary Bradley and Florence A. Newcomb, all in the Art Department, greatly assisted me. When I graduated, they went out on their own and arranged a scholarship at Commercial Illustration School of Art and further raised money for my supplies. I was fortunate in having such caring beings for my teachers. They were great ladies, and I thank them all.

After Art School, nothing but depressing times—worked for W.P.A. Art Project and later met Lorraine and Jerrold Beim, writers of children's books, who wanted me to cooperate with them on an idea for a book. We worked jointly, planning, designing, rewriting—finally *Two Is a Team* was born. The publisher offered me nine hundred dollars for the art work, which I was eager to accept, but my friends held out for the royalty arrangement. Reluctantly I went along. We received four hundred dollars each

against royalties, and our first statement paid back the advance, and paid us six hundred dollars more—one thousand the first year. It has earned tens of thousands of dollars since 1945.

Later I worked with Dorothy Sterling. We did *Freedom Train*, *Captain of the Planter* and *Mary Jane*. With Brenda Lansdown I did *Galumph* and with Judith Griffin, *Magic Mirrors*.

Most of my illustrations have been black historical or topical material. I've been able to draw on my experience of black life, as I know it, to assist me. My family and friends have been used over and over again as models.

I enjoyed doing the art work for *Captain of the Planter* because, at that time, I had returned to lithography and the illustrations we had done at school with litho pencils, and it gave me some of the feeling of work on stone.

Galumph, a story about a stray cat in an integrated community, was challenging but worrisome, because I had never drawn a cat before. Again, friends with cats, books about cats, and cat lovers came to my rescue. Not only did I learn to draw cats but became fascinated with cat lore.

Magic Mirrors was indeed a joy. African queens, good and evil godmothers,

Chrichlow: *KRITCH lo*

king fathers, medicine men, gold dust from the sun and silver dust from the moon, and beautiful regal black folk—an illustrator's holiday!

Now I teach, paint, and illustrate when something special comes along.

I've really enjoyed my life—my work has been most rewarding!

———

Ernest Crichlow has participated in group shows and one-man shows throughout the country. He has taught at a number of schools and universities, including Shaw University, Brooklyn Museum Art School, the New York State University at New Paltz, and the City College of New York. His work has often been reproduced in magazines, newspapers and catalogs. Mr. Crichlow is a founder, with R. Bearden and N. Lewis, of the Cinque Gallery and with R. Bearden, a codirector of "15 over 40 black artists" at Saratoga, New York, under the auspices of the State Education Department of Arts and Humanities. Most recently Mr. Crichlow has been engaged on a mural commissioned for the outside of a public school in Brooklyn. He is a member of the Black Academy of Arts and Letters.

Mr. Crichlow and his wife have one son and live in Brooklyn, New York.

SELECTED WORKS ILLUSTRATED: Two is a Team, by Lorraine and Jerrold Beim, 1945; Twelve O'Clock Whistle, by Jerrold Beim, 1946; Freedom Train, by Dorothy Sterling, 1954; Captain of the Planter, by Dorothy Sterling, 1958; Mary Jane, by Dorothy Sterling, 1959; Forever Free, by Dorothy Sterling, 1963; Galumph, by Brenda Lansdown, 1963; Maria, by Joan Lexau, 1964; Lift Every Voice, ed. by Dorothy Sterling and B. Quarles, 1965; We Shall Live in Peace, by Deloris Harrison, 1968; The Magic Mirrors, by Judith Griffin, 1971.

ABOUT: Kingman, Lee and others, comps. Illustrators of Children's Books, 1957–1966.

KEVIN CROSSLEY-HOLLAND

February 7, 1941–

AUTHOR OF *Havelok the Dane*, etc.

Autobiographical sketch of Kevin John William Crossley-Holland:

LEARNING the viola was purgatory, for me and for others. Still, it was the instrument that I had elected to learn and my family was a musical family. Between the ages of ten and, say, eighteen I doubt if I voluntarily picked up more than half-a-dozen books! Notes, not words, seemed to me then and seem to me now by far the purest form of artistic expression.

Still, as things turned out, I have become a writer. I started to write shortly before going to Oxford to read English. That was where I met the Anglo-Saxons, and their world is one of the two mainsprings of my work. At first sight their culture seems so far removed from our own. Of course it is, yet their heroism and doggedness, their love of irony and understatement, their passion for the sea —these and other qualities seem to me as pertinent to the northern world now as they were then. In *Wordhoard*, Jill Paton Walsh and I tried to give a picture of the Anglo-Saxon world; in *The Sea Stranger*, *The Fire-Brother* and *The Earth-Father*, I traced the developing friendship between an Anglo-Saxon missionary and a young boy, Wulf; and in *Storm* I translated many of the riddles that must have defeated all those in the feasting hall who were befuddled by mead.

East Anglia is where I feel at home, and above all on the harsh uncompromising elemental north coast. My work's second mainspring has been a continuing fascination with the folktales associated with that part of England. They are less well known than they should be; at their best—as in *The Green Children* and *That Wilderness*—they are utterly haunting.

I write and rewrite. The thing must sound right to mean right. It's no good

writing about the sea unless you can get something of its rhythms into your prose. That takes me back to music. When I was very small, my father—I remember it so well—once played me to sleep with a reconstruction of the harp found in the great Anglo-Saxon ship burial at Sutton Hoo in East Anglia. That night my three future passions coincided.

———

Mr. Crossley-Holland took his degree in English with honors at St. Edmund Hall, Oxford, and has since traveled extensively in Europe and the U.S.S.R. He is married, has two sons, Kieran and Dominic, and lives in England.

Besides his interpretation of Anglo-Saxon literature for children, Kevin Crossley-Holland has written his own poetry, edited an anthology of Yeats' poetry and several anthologies of stories for children. He has also translated from the Old English for adults, including a modern version of *Beowulf* (1968).

In 1966–68 he received an Arts Council Award for the Best Book for Young Children, and in 1969 he was appointed Gregory Fellow in Poetry in the University of Leeds.

Kevin Crossley-Holland has said of his

translations that they are faithful, "by and large, to the letter of the original," and that it has been the mood he was seeking to pass on to modern readers, "and if I have not caught anything of it, then I have not succeeded in my purpose."

SELECTED WORKS: The Callow Pit Coffer, 1969; Wordhoard (with Jill Paton Walsh), 1969; Storm and other Old English Riddles, 1970; The Peddlar of Swoffham, 1971; The Sea Stranger, 1973; The Fire-Brother, 1975; Green Blades Rising, 1975.

ABOUT: Contemporary Authors, Vol. 41–44; Murphy, Rosalie, ed. Contemporary Poets of the English Language; Something about the Author, Vol. 5.

VÁCLAV ČTVRTEK

April 4, 1911–November 6, 1976

AUTHOR OF *The Little Chalk Man*

Autobiographical sketch of Václav Čtvrtek, written shortly before his death:

I WAS born in the beautiful capital of Czechoslovakia, Prague, as the first of three children in the family of a town clerk. I remember the First World War. I started school in Jičín in 1917. There we lived with my grandfather during the war while my father was in the army. The war over, we moved again to Prague. I studied in the Reformal Realgymnasium in Prague and was graduated from the school in 1933.

I changed my profession several times. I lent the books at the municipal library, worked as an accounting clerk, and for eleven years I was an editor of the juvenile program in the Czechoslovak Radio Prague. Since 1959 I have been a free-lance writer.

I was married three times. From the first marriage I have two children, a son Petr, born in 1939, and a daughter Marketa, born in 1947.

As a boy I was a passionate reader; this led me to an active interest in literature. I wrote for the school magazine and later for the newspapers. My first book

Václav Čtvrtek: *VAHT slahv chiv VUR tek*

VÁCLAV ČTVRTEK

for adult readers appeared before the Second World War. During the war I did not write. Since then I have given my time fully to children's books. I have written quite a few books, plays, radio plays, and TV programs.

My writings include some realistic stories for youth and fairytales for small children.

I think that the center of my production lies in the fairytale. I am convinced the fairytale should be written in a natural way, as a bird sings. Only then it can be fresh, impressive and direct. In my opinion, a story with contemporary people and their problems may find the same response as the classical fairytale with traditional figures and heroes.

For me the most decisive factor in my life was my stay in Jičín in my early impressionable age. Just this historical town Jičín, its romantic neighborhood, my grandfather's old house and large garden are the main sources of my fairytale writings.

———

Václav Čtvrtek received a number of Czechoslovakian prizes for his children's books. In 1967 he was awarded the Austrian State Prize for *Das Kreidemännlein* (The Little Chalk Man). In 1974 his *Rumcajs* was included in the Hans Chris-

tian Andersen Honor List. Mr. Čtvrtek said that he began a book with the assumption that the child is happy and optimistic. Later, when life gets complex and there are problems to solve, the child who has retained his optimism will find them easier to solve. So, said the author, "in my books for the very young reader I try to give them pleasure and strengthen their youthful zest for life. And in my books for the adolescent I try to show them that in this world there are no problems that cannot be solved by one who is convinced that man has a real mission."

SELECTED WORKS: The Little Chalk Man, 1970.

ABOUT: Bookbird No. 4, 1976.

COUNTÉE CULLEN

May 30, 1903–January 9, 1946

AUTHOR OF *My Nine Lives and How I Lost Them*, etc.

Biographical sketch of Countée Porter Cullen:

NEW YORK CITY was Countée Cullen's birthplace; he grew up there and spent much of his adult life in the city. He was born Countée Porter on May 30, 1903. His mother died when he was eleven, and the boy lived with his grandmother until her death in 1918, when he was adopted by the Reverend and Mrs. Frederick A. Cullen, who gave him their name. Mr. Cullen was the founder and pastor of Salem Methodist Church in Harlem. Young Countée attended De Witt Clinton High School, where he was one of the very few black students. He was a leader among his contemporaries and active in school affairs. He edited the weekly newspaper and the senior edition of *The Magpie*, the school literary magazine, and many of his poems first appeared in this magazine. In 1921 one of them, "I Have a Rendezvous with Life," won a prize in a contest sponsored by the Federation of Women's Clubs.

COUNTÉE CULLEN

After graduating from high school, Cullen entered New York University. In 1923 and 1924 he won honorable mention in the Witter Bynner undergraduate poetry contest, sponsored by the Poetry Society of America, and finally in 1925 his "Poems" gained first prize. In the same year, he won another poetry prize, the John Reed Memorial Prize awarded by *Poetry* magazine, for "Threnody for a Brown Girl." That year too, he graduated, Phi Beta Kappa, and his first collection of poems, *Color*, was published by Harper & Brothers, to widespread critical praise. The book won him the first Harmon Award for Literature, awarded by the National Association for the Advancement of Colored People for "distinguished achievement in literature by a Negro."

Cullen received a master's degree in English from Harvard in 1926, and he became assistant editor of *Opportunity, a Journal of Negro Life*, writing a monthly column, "The Dark Tower." The following year two more volumes of his poetry were published, *Copper Sun* and *The Ballad of the Brown Girl*, and he also edited an anthology of black poets, *Caroling Dusk*.

In 1928 Cullen was awarded a Guggenheim Fellowship and he spent two years in France, studying and writing. He loved Paris and like many other black artists, he found his race was no barrier there. He traveled around Europe and made a trip to England, where he met a number of English poets and writers, including John Galsworthy, who became his friends, and whom he visited several times on subsequent trips. A group of Quakers arranged for him to give some poetry readings, and these were very successful. During his stay abroad, Cullen wrote a series of articles for *Crisis*, which was at that time edited by W.E.B. DuBois. Yolande DuBois, the famous writer's daughter, had become Cullen's wife in 1928, but the marriage was not a success and they were divorced two years later. In 1940 Countée Cullen married Ida Mae Robertson.

On his return from Europe in 1930, Cullen made his home in Harlem, which he felt to be his own community. He did, however, make several more trips to Europe until 1938 when the Second World War was imminent. He had begun to feel that his muse was failing, after the productive years of his early twenties, but he continued to write and his work was for the most part well received by the critics. *The Black Christ*, another collection of poetry, came out in 1930; these poems were more somber in mood than his earlier work and may have reflected the unhappiness of his private life at that time. His only novel, *One Way to Heaven*, appeared in 1932. It is a story of Harlem which the author himself described as a two-toned picture. *Medea*, an adaptation in both prose and poetry of Euripides' play, came out in 1935.

In the meantime Cullen had turned down two invitations to teach in black colleges in the South and was teaching English and French at Frederick Douglass Junior High School in Harlem. His poems for "the young, but not too young" were published in 1940 under the title *The Lost Zoo*. They tell in lively and humorous verse of the animals who failed to embark on Noah's Ark. Cullen named as coauthor the cat Christopher, and he made Christopher the central character of the last book to appear during his lifetime, *My Nine Lives and How*

I Lost Them. He died in 1946, at the age of forty-two, and his final collection of poetry, *On These I Stand,* for which he himself had made the selection, appeared posthumously.

Together with Langston Hughes, Countée Cullen was considered the leader of the Harlem Renaissance, though the two poets were not at all alike. Cullen was quieter, gentler, and more introspective than Hughes, and this was reflected in his poetry. As Arna Bontemps wrote, Cullen "was in many ways an old-fashioned poet. He never ventured very far from the Methodist parsonage in which he grew up in New York." Cullen was essentially a lyric poet. He wrote, "Good poetry is lofty thought beautifully expressed. . . . Poetry should not be too intellectual. It should deal more, I think, with the emotions." He often stressed that he wanted to be thought of as just a poet, not as a black poet, and he said, "I wish any merit that may be in my work to flow from it solely as the expression of a poet —with no racial consideration to bolster it up." Despite this, much of his work expressed a pride in his heritage and a keen sense of what it meant to be black. Cullen himself said, on another occasion, "Somehow I find my poetry of itself treating of the Negro, of his joys and his sorrows—mostly of the latter—and of the heights and depths of emotion I feel as a Negro."

SELECTED WORKS WRITTEN: One Way to Heaven, 1932; The Lost Zoo, 1940; My Nine Lives and How I Lost Them, 1942; On These I Stand, 1947; Color, 1969.

SELECTED WORKS EDITED: Caroling Dusk, 1973.

ABOUT: Adams, Russell L. Great Negroes Past and Present; Dreer, Herman. American Literature by Negro Authors; Perry, Margaret. A Bio-Bibliography of Countée P. Cullen, 1903–1946; Rollins, Charlemae. Famous American Negro Poets; Turner, Darwin T. In a Minor Chord; Twentieth Century Authors, 1942; Twentieth Century Authors (First Supplement), 1955; Current Biography, 1946; Newsweek January 21, 1946; New York Times January 10, 1946; Poetry April 1946; Publishers Weekly January 26, 1946; Saturday Review of Literature March 22, 1947; Time January 21, 1946; Wilson Library Bulletin March 1946.

JANE LOUISE CURRY

September 24, 1932–

AUTHOR OF *The Daybreakers*, etc.

Autobiographical sketch of Jane Louise Curry:

I MUST have been eight when I first began to write. The Children's Little Theater group in East Liverpool, Ohio, had set me afire with *The Pied Piper of Hamelin* (I was a straggler in the crowd lured into the mountain by the piper's music), and from then on unnumbered Saturdays were spent in garages or basement playrooms with pins and crepe paper, glue and glitter, and me reworking fairytales for friends (and myself) to play before audiences of tolerant parents and critical infants.

When I was eleven our family moved to Johnstown, Pennsylvania. There, writing took second place to the acting side of make-believe. From a sixth grade role as the mother in Humperdinck's *Hansel and Gretel* to four later summers at the nearby Mountain Playhouse, where I did everything from making papier mâché statues to playing an ingenue lead, I was stagestruck. At the same time, art was sneaking up on me: a passion for doodling had become an interest in drawing, and led eventually to those statues and a job as art technician at the Playhouse. At Penn State I changed my major from theater arts to art education. The "art" was my choice, the "education" from my parents' insistence that with a teaching certificate "you always have something to fall back on." A fainthearted start!

I didn't enjoy teaching art in junior high, but the Los Angeles city schools did introduce me to children as *people.* After a dull semester in a middle-class neighborhood I transferred to the inner city and woke up to a rich and lively mixture of black, Chicano, oriental, white and Indian children. After seven-

teen years I still remember them vividly and think, "Now, *she* (or he) could be in a story about. . . ."

When eventually I went on to graduate school (at UCLA and Stanford), it was in the hope that English literature would be more teachable, and that teaching at the university level would leave some time for my own painting and writing. Along the way I stumbled into children's books when, during a Fulbright year at the University of London, I volunteered to work with a Girl Guide company. At the girls' urging and with their help, the California Indian tales I told (around a campfire of candles set in a pie plate) in the church crypt of Holy Trinity, Brompton, were gathered into a book, *Down from the Lonely Mountain.*

Since then I've been weaving my own stories—fantasies comical and serious, mysterious or mythical—out of places, people, and old tales. After a year on Stanford's English faculty, I "retired" from teaching and began the precarious business of writing full time, shifting from Los Angeles to London, to Pennsylvania, Scotland, Wales, West Virginia, Austria, and back to Los Angeles and London, gathering places and lore. The pleasure of living close to the land, the lore of mushrooms and herbs, the clarity of children, medieval songs, the Shake-

spearean theatre, the archaeology of Arthur's Britain and the kingdoms of pre-Columbian America . . . the things that engage and fascinate me have already suggested scenes and stories enough to keep me busy until eighty. And it doesn't look like stopping there.

———

Jane Curry went to England to study on a Fulbright grant in 1961, and again in 1965 on a Leverhulme Fellowship from Stanford for study at the University of London. She received her Ph.D. from Stanford in 1969. Besides her books for children, Miss Curry has contributed notes to various scholarly journals on her specialty, Middle English poetry, and her painting has been exhibited in various group shows in London. She is a member of the Modern Language Association of America, the Medieval Academy of America, and the International Arthurian Society.

The Change Child was an American Library Association Notable Book in 1969. In 1970, *The Daybreakers* was an Honor Book in the *Book World* Children's Spring Book Festival and in 1972 the same book won the notable book award given by the Southern California Council on Literature for Children and Young People.

SELECTED WORKS: Down from the Lonely Mountain, 1966; Beneath the Hill, 1967; The Sleepers, 1968; The Change Child, 1969; The Daybreakers, 1970; Mindy's Mysterious Miniature, 1970; Over the Sea's Edge, 1971; The Lost Farm, 1974; Parsley, Sage, Rosemary, and Time, 1975; The Watchers, 1975; The Magical Cupboard, 1976; Poor Tom's Ghost, 1977; The Birdstones, 1977.

ABOUT: Contemporary Authors, Vol. 17–18; Something about the Author, Vol. 1.

W. W. DENSLOW

May 5, 1856–March 29, 1915

ILLUSTRATOR OF *The Wonderful Wizard of Oz*, etc.

Biographical sketch of William Wallace Denslow by Douglas G. Greene:

WHEN William Wallace Denslow was

a small boy he noticed that there were few humorous books for children. "I made up my mind," he later recalled, "that some day I'd furnish them the laugh material." It was not until he was forty-three years old that he made his youthful ambition come true.

Denslow was born in Philadelphia in 1856 but soon moved to Manhattan Island. His first pictures were of flowers found by his father, William Wallace Denslow, Sr., who was a botanist. In the early 1870s he studied in New York City at the Cooper Union Institute and the National Academy of Design. Before he had reached the age of twenty his family was no longer able to support him, and he became an office boy for the Orange Judd Company, publishers of several magazines. For the next few years he wandered through New England doing almost anything to survive: painting advertisements on barns, illustrating county atlases, drawing prints of local landmarks, and lecturing on the history of art.

In 1882 he married his first wife, Annie McCartney. Shortly thereafter he opened a studio in New York where he drew illustrations for magazines and designed costumes for plays. Two years later, after separating from his wife, he went to the Midwest to work on the Chicago *Herald* and illustrate books, including *Dollars and Sense* by the great showman and apostle of self-help, P. T. Barnum.

During these years, Denslow could not remain long in one place, and in 1889 he moved to Colorado. He was briefly on the staff of the Denver *Rocky Mountain News* but resigned after a disagreement with the editor and spent five months as a cowboy. Experiences with bucking broncos and wolf packs convinced him that Colorado was still too untamed, and he decided to work for periodicals in San Francisco. He spent much of his time in Chinatown and began a large collection of oriental art. The Japanese Tokumgawa (or Floating World) print, then an international fad,

greatly influenced the development of Denslow's artistic style.

In 1893, the Columbian Exposition, one of the earliest world's fairs, drew Denslow back to Chicago. Rapidly he became one of the most important Midwestern illustrators; it became commonplace to find his signature, "Den," and his small personal "totem," a seahorse, in the corners of illustrations. Besides illustrating books, newspapers and magazines, he participated in the poster craze which swept Europe and America in the 1890s.

In 1896 Denslow married Ann Waters Holden and their home became a gathering place for other artists and writers. Denslow, a friend remembered, was a gruff man with a booming voice and an unusual sense of humor. He was "always grumbling about nothing, always censorious, and laughing uproariously when he had secured his effect." Among his frequent visitors was L. Frank Baum, a newspaperman who was planning to write books for children. Denslow liked Baum's nonsense verse and agreed to illustrate *Father Goose, His Book*, but he had to struggle to realize his hope of publishing humorous pictures for children. Publishers feared that a new book of nursery rhymes could not compete with the traditional Mother Goose verses. Baum and Denslow eventually convinced a small publisher to issue the book in 1899. It was an immediate and astonishing success.

In 1900 Denslow illustrated Baum's *The Wonderful Wizard of Oz*, which has since sold more copies than any other American children's book. Two years later Baum wrote the script and Denslow designed the costumes and scenery for a musical extravaganza version of the *Wizard*. Denslow illustrated only one more Baum book, *Dot and Tot of Merryland*, before personal differences caused the two men to find other collaborators. Denslow, who shared the copyright in *The Wonderful Wizard of Oz* and believed that his pictures were responsible for the success of the Oz characters, wrote and illustrated a booklet entitled *Scarecrow and the Tin-Man* and he produced a series of newspaper stories with the same title. By this time he had been divorced from Ann Waters Holden, and on Christmas Eve 1903 he married Frances Golsen Doolittle in New York City.

With his profits from the *Wizard* and other successful books, Denslow purchased an island near Bermuda. He named it Denslow Island and held court as King Denslow I with a royal entourage of a Chief Steward (his cook) and an Admiral (his boatman). He continued illustrating books, including *Denslow's Mother Goose, Denslow's Night Before Christmas, Billy Bounce, The Jeweled Toad, When I Grow Up*, and a series of eighteen pamphlets under the title *Denslow's Picture Books*. He also prepared a play based on his book *The Pearl and the Pumpkin*. By 1910, however, he had fallen on hard times and he began drinking heavily. He sold his island and subsisted on a small salary from a New York art agency. Occasionally he sold poems and drawings to the children's magazine *John Martin's Book*. He died of pneumonia in March 1915.

SELECTED WORKS WRITTEN AND ILLUSTRATED: Scarecrow and the Tin-Man, 1904; The Pearl and the Pumpkin, with Paul West, 1904; Billy Bounce, with Dudley A. Bragdon, 1906; When I Grow Up, 1909.

SELECTED WORKS ILLUSTRATED: Father Goose, His Book, by L. Frank Baum, 1899; The Wonderful Wizard of Oz, by L. Frank Baum, 1900; Dot and Tot of Merryland, by L. Frank Baum, 1901; Denslow's Mother Goose, 1901; Denslow's Night Before Christmas, by Clement Clarke Moore, 1902; The Jeweled Toad, by Isabel Johnston, 1907.

ABOUT: The Artist's Year Book, 1905; Greene, Douglas G. and Michael Patrick Hearn. W. W. Denslow; Snow, Jack. Who's Who in Oz; Who's Who in America, 1901–1915; Who's Who in New York, 1904–1914; American Artist May 1973; The Baum Bugle Autumn 1963; Spring 1964; Autumn 1972; Journal of Popular Culture Summer 1973.

ARIANE DEWEY

August 17, 1937–

COILLUSTRATOR OF *Milton the Early Riser*, etc.

Autobiographical sketch of Ariane Dewey Dannasch, whose early work appears under the name of Ariane Aruego:

IN fourth grade art class I was asked to paint a picture of something we did during the summer. I painted some bright pink kids swimming in a blue-green lake, but I repainted it so many times that the paper tore and the paint chipped off. My teacher told me later that when she saw my first picture, she thought I was a hopeless student. Things could only get better; I designed and painted stage sets for the school plays, and I wrote, illustrated and handbound my first book as a class assignment. Starting then, I was determined to always paint. Regular school poster paint is still my favorite medium.

I graduated from Sarah Lawrence College where I studied with Ezio Martinelli. He once made me make a graded color chart using red, black and green, and combinations thereof. I hated doing it as it took forever and had to be precise. Little did I know how useful that exercise would be later when I was doing color separations. At the same time I took a course in etching and engraving, and studied woodcut with Antonio Frasconi. Weekends I worked in a New York art gallery. Because I was very fond of folklore and myths I studied anthropology at Columbia University. Then I worked as a Gal Friday for an industrial and graphic design firm and later as an art editor of children's textbooks.

After José Aruego and I were married, we spent a year traveling around the world, mostly in Southeast Asia. I was continually impressed by the brilliant colors that accent the scenery, be it a flower, the sky, a glass inset on a Thai temple, or a sari. I relate just about everything—objects, events, people—to

Ariane: *ary ANN*

color, reacting to color much more than to sound or shape. I suppose I really think in color.

Children are exposed to so much information and such varied visual experiences by television that books are no longer the main source of facts or fantastic images. But a book is still something that can be enjoyed at one's own pace, reread as often as one pleases, looked at for an hour or five minutes. Mainly, picture books are personal and fun!

José Aruego and I have collaborated on twenty-nine books, with more planned. He likes to draw, and I like to paint so that's how we work.

Born in Chicago, Illinois, Ariane Dewey received her Bachelor of Arts degree from Sarah Lawrence in 1959. She met José Aruego while he was painting a mural at International House, Columbia University, and they were married in 1961. Their first books together were listed as by José and Ariane Aruego, but when they were divorced in 1973, Miss Dewey resumed the use of her maiden name, but continued to collaborate with Aruego. Ariane Dewey married Claus Dannasch in 1976. She has a son, Juan Dewey Aruego.

Although they have been working for comparatively few years, Ariane Dewey and José Aruego have achieved a large number of picture books of impressive quality. *Crocodile's Tale*, their first book written and illustrated together, was chosen for the 1973 Children's Book Showcase and the American Institute of Graphic Arts' 1972–73 Children's Book Show. Vladimir Suteyev's *The Chick and the Duckling*, translated and adapted by Mirra Ginsburg, was also a Showcase selection the same year. *Milton the Early Riser*, with text by Robert Kraus, received a Brooklyn Art Books for Children citation in 1975, a Citation of Merit from the Society of Illustrators in 1974, and was included in the Biennale of Illustration Bratislava in 1975. The 1973–74 Children's Book Show mounted by the American Institute of Graphic Arts included Mirra Ginsburg's *Mushroom in the Rain* and Natalie Savage Carlson's *Marie Louise and Christophe*. *Mushroom in the Rain* was an American Library Association Notable Book in 1974, as was Robert Kraus' *Owliver*, which also received a Citation of Merit from the Society of Illustrators and was chosen for Children's Book Showcase 1975. *Herman the Helper* was an Honor Book for the Boston *Globe-Horn Book* Award in 1974.

SELECTED WORKS WRITTEN AND ILLUSTRATED AS ARIANE ARUEGO: Crocodile's Tale (with José Aruego), 1972.

SELECTED WORKS ILLUSTRATED AS ARIANE DEWEY (with José Aruego): Herman Chick and the Duckling, by Vladimir G. Suteyev, translated and adapted by Mirra Ginsburg, 1972; Milton the Early Riser, by Robert Kraus, 1972.

SELECTED WORKS ILLUSTRATED AS ARIANE DEWEY (with José Aruego): Herman the Helper, by Robert Kraus, 1974; Marie Louise and Christophe, by Natalie Savage Carlson, 1974; Mushroom in the Rain, by Vladimir G. Suteyev, adapted by Mirra Ginsburg, 1974; Owliver, by Robert Kraus, 1974; How the Sun Was Brought Back to the Sky, adapted by Mirra Ginsburg, 1975; Marie Louise's Heyday, by Natalie Savage Carlson, 1975; Sea Frog, City Frog, by Dorothy Van Woerkom, 1975; Three Friends, by Robert Kraus, 1975; Boris Bad Enough, by Robert Kraus, 1976; Two Greedy Bears, adapted by Mirra Ginsburg, 1976; Runaway Marie Louise, by Natalie Savage Carlson, 1977; The Strongest One of All, by Mirra Ginsburg, 1977.

ABOUT: Contemporary Authors, Vol. 49–52; Something about the Author, Vol. 7.

PETER DICKINSON

December 16, 1927–

AUTHOR OF *Emma Tupper's Diary*, etc.

Autobiographical sketch of Peter Dickinson:

I WAS born slap in the middle of Africa, within earshot of the Victoria Falls (which has Niagara beat into a cocked hat for splendor). My father was a civil servant in the colonial government of Northern Rhodesia, and my mother the daughter of a South African sheep farmer. He also farmed ostriches, but it was mostly sheep.

In spite of all that, where I *belong* is in the West Cotswolds, among steep little hills with limestone streams cutting along the valley bottoms, and beech-woods lining the ridges like the raised hackles of a dog. I was the second of four boys. We came to live in England when I was seven, but my father died soon after. However, money was somehow raised to send us all to boarding schools at the age of eight. From there I won a scholarship to Eton, bottom of the list, where I specialised in Latin and Greek; and then to Cambridge, where I read English literature. I was quite good at that—but not quite good enough to get a fixed job at the university when I'd finished my studies. But suddenly, for crazy reasons, out of the blue I was offered a job on the editorial staff of *Punch*, which I took (the reasons were so crazy that I was the only candidate, so I can't say I *won* the job) and stayed there for seventeen years.

When I was twenty-five I married an admiral's daughter, a tall, intelligent and artistic girl whom I still like a lot. We have four children—Philippa and Polly who are almost twins at 22 and 21, and John and James who are almost twins at 15 and 14. I like them too.

I can't say why I write children's books—it seems such an obvious thing to do, almost like breathing. I would find it much more unnatural not to write them, and I usually seem to have the next two or three queueing up in my head, waiting to get written. I don't think much in my childhood influenced me, except that I did read hundreds of books. I don't, in fact, remember much about my childhood, which I regret. (It seems stupid that all that's left me of all Africa is a waterfall, a patch of red sand with some thorn trees and a baboon, and the smell of flowering privet.) But I can remember, as if it was yesterday, what it was *like to* be a child. That's the reader I write for.

I don't write children's books all the time; I alternate them with rather curious adult thrillers—the two kinds of book make a change from each other; and I try to write as many different kinds of story as I can, so as not to get typecast. But for some reason I am fascinated—and this keeps coming out—by anything old, really old, and still used and working, if possible. And I like doing things with my own hands too—planting my own potatoes, retiling my own roof, even clearing my own drains. I am fascinated by how things are done, and what it actually feels like to do them, and I think this comes out too.

Peter Dickinson's children's books have several times just missed winning England's top children's book awards. *Heartsease* was commended for the *Guardian* Award in 1970, *The Devil's Children* was on the honors list for the Carnegie Medal in 1970, and *The Dancing Bear* was commended for the *Guardian* Award in 1973. *Emma Tupper's Diary* was designated a Notable Book by the American Library Association in 1971, as was *The Dancing Bear* in 1973.

SELECTED WORKS: Heartsease, 1969; The Devil's Children, 1970; Emma Tupper's Diary, 1971; The Dancing Bear, 1972; Iron Lion, 1972; The Gift, 1974; The Blue Hawk, 1976; Chance, Luck and Destiny, 1976; Annerton Pit, 1977.

ABOUT: Contemporary Authors, Vol. 41–44; Something about the Author, Vol. 5; Signal January 1974.

ALFRED DUGGAN

1903–April 4, 1964

AUTHOR OF *Growing Up in Thirteenth Century England*, etc.

Biographical sketch of Alfred Leo Duggan:

BORN in Buenos Aires, Argentina, Alfred Leo Duggan was the elder son of Alfred Hubert Duggan, a wealthy Argentine of Irish descent. His mother, Grace Hinds, was the daughter of an American diplomat, Joseph Monro Hinds, who had fought in the Civil War. When Duggan was two years old his mother took him to England. From then on England was his home, and despite his mixed heritage he always regarded himself as an Englishman.

At his father's death, Duggan inherited a considerable fortune. When he was fourteen his mother married Lord Curzon, at that time a member of the Inner War Cabinet, and Duggan grew up in influential political and social circles. He developed a strong interest in military history—particularly of the time of the Crusades—when his stepfather purchased and restored Bodiam Castle in Sussex. As he went on to investigate other medieval fortifications, armor and tactics, scenes of men fighting in mail came vividly alive to him. It was an interest he retained all his life, his imagination so touched by the worlds of the Romans and the Normans that he seemed to feel as much at home in past centuries as in his own.

Duggan was educated at Eton and at Balliol College, Oxford. Something of the maverick in his nature showed early. At Eton he left the Roman Catholic faith to embrace Anglicanism, and then while at Oxford he turned to Marxism and atheism. He had shown little appetite for schoolwork, and since he had the means to indulge his desire for pleasure, he did so to the fullest. A young man-about-town, he lived flamboyantly: in winter there were night clubs and fox hunting, in summer adventuring in Greece and Turkey. Archaeology and sight-seeing were Duggan's recreations. After Oxford he traveled in the Levant, searching for the remains of Crusaders' monuments and castles and collecting specimens for the Natural History Museum of London. It was on such a specimen-collecting trip that he shipped on a 600-ton barkentine for a voyage across the Atlantic under sail, going from England by way of Madeira, Trinidad and Panama to the Galapagos Islands. He went along without salary, for the pleasure of the trip.

By 1931, between the Great Depression and his own extravagances, Duggan's personal fortune had been exhausted. He had never capitalized on his early advantages, and he now accepted his changed circumstances with the same unconcern. He still managed to travel. In 1935 he visited the Middle East and helped excavate Constantine's palace in Istanbul for the University of St. Andrews (Scotland). He spent hours reading in the library, his acute mind and remarkable memory recording the atmosphere and details of the remote periods that were later to form the background of his novels.

Duggan had abandoned Marxism and returned to the Catholic church after only a few years. He then became fervently patriotic toward his adopted country. In 1939, at the onset of World War II, he enlisted in the London Irish Rifles (Territorial Army). He saw active service in the arduous expedition to Norway in 1940. He was discharged as medically unfit in 1941 and for the rest of the war years worked in an airplane factory.

When in 1946 Duggan wrote his first book at the age of forty-three, he was able to draw upon a store of detailed information and impressions he had gathered over the years of reading and traveling. *Knight with Armour* begins at Bodiam Castle with a young knight riding forth to the first Crusade in 1099. It did not find a publisher until 1950. After that, however, books followed in a steady stream, all historical novels or biographics treating of the Roman Empire or the early Middle Ages. Later periods were strange to Duggan and even not to his taste. He himself said: "I feel most at home in the period when Rome was collapsing. That is because I am myself a citizen of a civilization in collapse."

Alfred Duggan wrote seven books of popular history for young readers, among them *The Story of the Crusades, 1097–1291* and *Growing Up in Thirteenth Century England*. He never wrote down to his younger readers, and so the books are equally appealing to adults. Among his adult novels was *Conscience of the King*, published in 1951, which Evelyn Waugh, his friend from Oxford days, has called the most characteristic of Duggan's works. It is set at the time of King Arthur—not the Arthur seen in the great romances but one who lived in a time of advancing shadow, when the Romans had withdrawn from Britain and the barbarians were moving in on all sides. Duggan saw parallels between those darkening ages and our own. And because the past was very vivid to him, he tried to bring that vivid life before his readers.

He was a careful and thorough craftsman, typing each chapter at least three times and cutting and polishing as he worked, with the final version ending up almost half the length of the first draft. He tested his sentences by considering how easily they would go into Latin prose and used words with careful attention to their precise meaning. He held a satirical view of man and politics and expressed it tersely, with a wry humor. Simplicity of character and narrative style marked his work.

Even with his success as an author, Duggan avoided publicity and literary gatherings that might have promoted him personally. He preferred living almost in seclusion—a transformation from the wild youth into a quiet family man, his sole occupation writing books. He had married Laura Hill in 1953. Until his death, at sixty-one, he lived in complete domestic happiness with his wife and one son in his sixteenth century house in Herefordshire.

SELECTED WORKS: Julius Caesar, 1955; The Cunning of the Dove, 1960; The Castle Book, 1961; Growing Up in Thirteenth Century England, 1962; The Romans, 1964; The Story of the Crusades, 1097–1291, 1964; Count Bohemond, 1965; The Falcon and the Dove, 1966.

ABOUT: Twentieth Century Authors (First Supplement), 1955; Who's Who, 1964; America October 24, 1964; History Today June 1964; New York Herald Tribune Book Review January 17, 1954; October 24, 1954; The Spectator July 10, 1964.

ALLAN W. ECKERT

January 30, 1931–

AUTHOR OF *Incident at Hawk's Hill*, etc.

Biographical sketch of Allan W. Eckert:

BORN in Buffalo, New York, Allan W. Eckert was raised in the Chicago area

ALLAN W. ECKERT

State Prize for Children's and Juvenile Literature.

Allan Eckert married the former Joan Dowling on May 14, 1955. They have a son Joseph, born in 1964, and a daughter Julie, born in 1965. The Eckerts live in Englewood Beach, Florida.

SELECTED WORKS: Bayou Backwater, 1968; The King Snake, 1968; Blue Jacket, 1969; In Search of A Whale, 1970; Incident at Hawk's Hill, 1971; The Court Martial of Daniel Boone, 1973; Tecumseh! A Play, 1974.

ABOUT: Contemporary Authors, Vol. 13–14; Who's Who in America, 1972–73.

and went to school there. He spent four years in the United States Air Force, from 1948 to 1952, and was discharged with the rank of staff sergeant. Widely traveled through North and Central America and the West Indies, Eckert, like many writers, held a number of jobs before settling to a life of writing. He has been, at one time or another, a postman, private detective, fireman, cook, dishwasher, laundryman, trapper and draughtsman, as well as a worker in factories and on farms. From 1957 to 1960 he worked on the Dayton (Ohio) *Journal-Herald* as a reporter, columnist and editor, and during this period he also attended the University of Dayton and Ohio State University. In 1960 Eckert turned to free-lance writing for magazines. His articles and short stories have appeared in most of the major magazines in the United States and he has also written scripts for the NBC television series "Wild Kingdom."

Eckert's areas of speciality are natural history and American history. Of his books for young people, the best known is *Incident at Hawk's Hill*, which was a Newbery Honor Book in 1972 and was on the American Library Association's List of Notable Books for 1971. In 1976 the German language edition, *Es geschah in der Prärie*, won the Austrian

BENJAMIN ELKIN

August 10, 1911–

AUTHOR OF *Why the Sun Was Late*, etc.

Autobiographical sketch of Benjamin Elkin:

A BOOK-JACKET blurb has me telling stories to my nine brothers and sisters in my native Baltimore, Maryland. That would have been quite a feat since my family left Baltimore before I was one year old. We lived in several other cities before settling down in Chicago, Illinois, where I attended high school and college. I received a B.S. degree from Chicago's Lewis Institute, a teaching certificate from the Chicago Normal College, and M.A. and Ph.D. degrees from Northwestern University in nearby Evanston, Illinois.

Except for three years with the Veterans Administration and the Social Security Board in Washington, D.C., and three years in the U.S. Army during World War II, my work has also been concentrated in Chicago. I taught English and economics at the Harrison and the Von Steuben high schools until 1948, when I became principal of the Philip Rogers elementary school on Chicago's north side. There I remained for twenty-four satisfying years until my retirement

in 1972. Our school received national recognition for its program of curricular enrichment.

It is true that I have always enjoyed telling stories, and that other children on the block would join my own brothers and sisters in listening to my fantastic tales. But I made no serious attempt to write these stories until my army service. Then writing became an enjoyable way of occupying dull evenings in camp. I first wrote a story about army life, which fortunately was never published. As a civilian I wrote more interesting stuff, and my first published book was *The Loudest Noise in the World*. Since then I have had about fifteen other books published but *The Loudest Noise* is still my favorite.

Like most writers, I have frequently been asked, "Where do you get your ideas?" Many of my books are based upon folk tales which have stood the test of time. But I have found that another good source of stories is jokes and riddles. Riddles are particularly good because they pose problems with ingenious solutions. For instance, how do you get out of a locked room without opening the door? Read *The King's Wish* and find out.

Besides storytelling, my hobbies in the past have included bicycling, square dancing, and entering prize contests. I have taken bike trips through a number of states and have "called" square dances for many, many groups. As for prize contests, I specialized in jingles and slogans. Among other prizes I won thirteen wristwatches, a fur coat and a pony.

More recently I have been interested in traveling. I have taken a freighter to Yugoslavia and a cargo liner around the world. On this latter trip I was happy to find copies of my books in such places as Singapore and Hong Kong. Best of all was to stop in unannounced at a plantation home while on safari in Zululand to find a child reading my *Six Foolish Fishermen*.

In my thirty-four years as a school teacher and principal I have enjoyed almost limitless opportunities to share my enthusiasm for stories. I have even taped a series of thirteen television programs for broadcast by the Chicago Public Schools over closed circuit. And children have been generous in expressing their appreciation. But I recently received a letter from an adult, referring to stories which I told him back in 1936:

> Could you possibly be the same Ben Elkin who sat on the steps at Rock Creek Church Road in Washington about a thousand years ago and delighted us kids with your wonderful stories? I ran across your name in *Books in Print* by accident and am eager to know if you're the same man.

It is this lasting attraction of stories and storytelling that makes writing for children so rewarding.

Now that I have retired from teaching I still plan to visit schools and classrooms by invitation, just for the fun of being with the children. And as long as I can, I shall continue to tell them stories through books.

SELECTED WORKS: The Loudest Noise in the World, 1954; Six Foolish Fishermen, 1957; The King's Wish and Other Stories, 1960; Lucky and the Giant, 1962; Why the Sun Was Late, 1966; How the Tsar Drinks Tea, 1971; The King Who Could Not Sleep, 1975.

ABOUT: Author's and Writer's Who's Who, 1971; Contemporary Authors, Vol. 4; Something about the Author, Vol. 3.

SYLVIA LOUISE ENGDAHL

November 24, 1933–

AUTHOR OF *Enchantress from the Stars,* etc.

Autobiographical sketch of Sylvia Louise Engdahl:

I WAS born and grew up in Los Angeles, and received my degree from the University of California at Santa Barbara with the intent of being a teacher. Before long, though, I found I wasn't well suited to teaching; and in 1957 I left the field of education for computer programming, a profession that was then quite new. That absorbed all my time and energy for the next ten years. I liked the work, and it gave me a chance to live in different parts of the country, for I was transferred several times before moving to my company's main office back in Santa Monica, California, where I eventually became a computer systems specialist.

As part of my job I did some writing, but it wasn't the kind I really wanted to do. Throughout my life—since I was twelve years old, in fact—I'd had a deep interest in space travel: not so much in its technical aspects as in the thought of what exploring the universe and settling new worlds will mean to mankind's future. I'd developed the main ideas for my earliest novels—especially *The Far Side of Evil*—in the year before our first artificial satellites were launched. More and more, I wanted to express those ideas. I believed strongly, as I still do, that space exploration is the most significant challenge facing the human race and the only long-range goal that will unite mankind in peace. Then too, I felt that young people were becoming very much interested in the question of man's place in a universe possibly inhabited by other sentient peoples. So I was happy when the opportunity came for me to devote full time to writing books.

I now live in Portland, Oregon, which is my favorite region of the United States; and my mother, who is also a writer, lives with me. She writes about past centuries while I write about future ones and about the hypothetical worlds of other stars. However, I study past centuries too: through extensive scholarly research I discovered some fascinating facts about what scientists and philosophers of the past believed about planets outside our solar system. It's often assumed that science fiction writers originated the concept, but actually it was discussed more in nonfiction by well-known men of the eighteenth and nineteenth centuries than by those of the twentieth. I wrote about the history of such speculation in my book *The Planet-Girded Suns,* as well as about modern scientific theories.

From the beginning I've directed my books not so much to science fiction enthusiasts as to readers of varying tastes. I'm convinced that stories about future or hypothetical worlds appeal to young people who are concerned about today's world; the problems of today can't be seen in perspective unless they're related to yesterday and tomorrow. Almost all teen-agers have an interest in tomorrow.

Since I don't think that a gloomy view of it is realistic, I believe that fiction with a positive view is desperately needed.

Naturally, I don't really imagine that the inhabitants of other solar systems are as much like us as I portray them in my novels. But I do feel that they probably exist as most scientists do today. And if that is true, then their basic feelings must be similar to ours, whatever they may look like, whatever their customs may be. Writing is my way of exploring ideas that, to me, seem universally valid.

———

Enchantress from the Stars was an American Library Association Notable Book in 1970 and was a Newbery Honor Book in 1971. *This Star Shall Abide* received the Christopher Award for children's and young adult books in 1973.

SELECTED WORKS WRITTEN: Enchantress from the Stars, 1970; Journey Between Worlds, 1970; Far Side of Evil, 1971; This Star Shall Abide, 1972; Beyond the Tomorrow Mountains, 1973; The Planet-Girded Suns, 1974; The Subnuclear Zoo (with Rick Roberson), 1977.

SELECTED WORKS EDITED: Universe Ahead (with Rick Roberson), 1975; Anywhere, Anywhen: Stories of Tomorrow, 1976.

ABOUT: Contemporary Authors, Vol. 29–32; Something about the Author, Vol. 4; Horn Book October 1971; June 1972; School Media Quarterly Fall 1972; English Journal February 1975.

"THOMAS FALL"

September 14, 1917–

AUTHOR OF *Wild Boy*, etc.

Autobiographical sketch of Donald Clifford Snow, who writes under the name of Thomas Fall:

I WAS born in the Ozark Mountains of Arkansas. My parents moved to Oklahoma when I was an infant. I attended public schools and graduated eventually from the University of Oklahoma in Business Administration. The idea of becom-

ing a writer was no more than a very private dream. Brilliant, romantic people did such things—not practical, down-to-earth young fellows like me.

I went to work for an oil company in Tulsa and soon realized that I was going in the wrong direction. Searching to discover what I really wanted to do, I took up the guitar but didn't especially like the sound of my own voice. I tried to play jazz on the piano but that didn't satisfy me. The idea of writing stories stirred all the while, but I continued putting it down as something too impractical; my sideline interest in music was irresponsible enough, wasn't it?

For some reason I decided to go to law school. I returned to the campus early that summer and got a student job operating the university switchboard on the night shift. After midnight the phones were dead except for nightwatchmen's routine calls to record their rounds among the buildings, and I spent my time reading. Short stories at first, and then, more specifically, adventure stories. I remember the night I took my dictionary and portable typewriter to work. I told myself that I was going to write some letters, but I knew the truth. I didn't need a dictionary to write letters. I already had a plot in mind; I had been thinking about it for weeks.

When I rolled in the first sheet of paper I sat for several moments simply shattered by the utter blankness of it, and I quickly typed "Dear. . . ." intending to write to someone, anyone, it didn't matter. And then I calmed myself with the zany thought that all I had to do was take whatever words I needed out of the dictionary and transfer them to the blank paper *in the right order* and I'd be a writer. So I began typing again: "Dear Andrew Jackson," and wrote my first story in the form of a fan letter from a dragoon officer to the retired soldier-president at the Hermitage. I completed a draft that night, revised it the next, typed it up on the third, and mailed it to a magazine editor in New York on the fourth morning. It was promptly accepted for publication.

Well. So that's all there was to it. Genius undoubtedly lay wrapped tightly in the center of all my studied practicality. So I would let it out.

I forgot about law and enrolled in the graduate school to study creative writing and literature. Three years and dozens of inept manuscripts later, I finally sold my second story. Meanwhile to support myself I applied for a job with another oil company and made the mistake of revealing that I was, on the side, a fledgling fiction writer. Needless to say, they didn't hire me. They wanted someone who could concentrate for thirty years on drilling costs and depreciation schedules. So I went to Texas, got a job with yet another oil company, and began writing under a pseudonym. I would go to bed sometimes before dark and set my alarm for 3:00 A.M. so that I could get up and work on my stories before going to the office.

After I wrote my first novel I moved to New York. The novel did not earn very much money so I went to work again for money, this time as a writer in the financial department of a large public relations firm—an activity that I continued on a free-lance basis for many years. But my principal interest is in fiction writing. I have published several adult novels and magazine stories. I wrote my first

children's book in 1962 after meeting Mary Cosgrave at a party in Brooklyn. She was children's editor for a prominent publisher and her approach to children's literature excited me greatly. I have since written eight children's books and plan soon to devote all my efforts to that field.

My wife and I bought and renovated a hundred-year-old brownstone several years ago and lived in it until recently. During the summers we camped upstate on a plot of land we bought in the 1950s. Now we live there most of the time, in a house we built ourselves. It happens that she, too, was born in Arkansas and lived in both Oklahoma and Texas before moving to New York where we first met. Our mountain beginnings no doubt stayed in our blood, for we now live in the Shawangunk Range of New York, about half way between the Catskills and the Poconos.

———

My Bird is Romeo, Wild Boy, and *Canalboat to Freedom* were all named by the New York *Times* as among the best of the year of their publication. *Canalboat to Freedom* was also an American Library Association Notable Book in 1966.

SELECTED WORKS: Eddie No-Name, 1963; Edge of Manhood, 1964; My Bird is Romeo, 1964; Wild Boy, 1965; Canalboat to Freedom, 1966; Dandy's Mountain, 1967; Goat Boy of Brooklyn, 1968; Jim Thorpe, 1970.

PENELOPE FARMER

June 14, 1939–

AUTHOR OF *The Summer Birds*, etc.

Autobiographical sketch of Penelope Farmer Mockridge:

I WAS born near London three months before World War II, second of twin girls, hence by English law the younger, which has left me with a secret desire to be French—for there, the one born last is

PENELOPE FARMER

reckoned with impeccable logic to have
been conceived first, hence is in law the
elder. Twins, you see, are notoriously
competitive, and I am no exception to
that rule. My sister and I grew up in
continual mortal combat, from which
our mother had the greatest difficulty in
separating us. But peace has been declared a long time ago now; we fight
only with words and then not often, unless we are thrust on each other's company excessively. Apart from being a
twin, which in most people's eyes makes
you slightly freaky, we had a normal
English middle-class childhood, pro-
gressing from private prep school
through private boarding school, the
only notable events in the course of it,
once the war ended and apart from my
once nearly falling through a glass roof,
being my spending six months in bed at
the age of eight nursing some kind of
incipient tuberculosis, caught from
drinking that supposedly healthy drink,
milk. I suppose it was there that I started
to read as voraciously as I have always
done since. Then it was an Arthur Ransome book a day, usually, because they
gave me vicariously the nice, healthy,
gregarious outdoor life which was denied, though at any other time I wouldn't
have wanted it. In fact I spent the
greater part of my childhood alone, in-

doors and reading, being described vari-
ously as solitary or antisocial, according
to prejudice or lack of it.

Initially I wanted to be an artist and
expressed myself through pictures rather
than words. But I have always written
too, beginning with unfinished sagas
about rabbits and so forth. Before and
after I left university (St. Anne's College,
Oxford) I tried various alternative jobs,
ranging from teaching to waiting in restaurants, but none with such success,
and in betweenwhiles, though I had
given up drawing, I continued to write.
The first stories I had published—modern fairy stories—I started to write when
I was still at school. They were not published in America, but my first book was
commissioned by Margaret McElderry,
then of Harcourt Brace, on the strength
of them, and was in fact based on a story
I had rejected for the original collection. This was *The Summer Birds*. I've
gone on from there, the books growing
up as I've grown up, painfully. Much of
the earlier stuff, indeed, I would happily
see buried. What I'm writing now—or
about to write—sits on a line between
adult and children's fiction. I don't myself much care how the books are categorized, but admit my preoccupations
are probably changing.

Most of my books have been fantasies
and will continue to be so, though as
they creep toward the adult market they
get called science fiction sometimes instead—not that they *are* science fiction.
Again I don't mind the labels. I'm just interested in the impossible event and its
effect on people—I don't think many
writers allow sufficiently for the total
sense of disorientation anyone would
feel who was actually faced by magic;
like Charlotte in *Charlotte Sometimes*,
who finds herself forty years back in
time, or like the four teen-agers in *A
Castle of Bone* faced by a cupboard
which converts objects or people to
earlier states of being. I think the reactions you describe in fancy are more revealing and interesting—often not only
of the characters, but of people in general in an ordinary world—than more

realistic situations could ever be, at least any that I could describe; just as, say, a poetic image says far more, often, than a direct statement. I'm no good at direct statements myself. (I find writing a piece like this total pain and grief.) I couldn't describe the problems of potential delinquents or drug addicts in those terms if I wanted to. But I can, occasionally, write well in the kind of extended image that fantasy allows—whether to do with flight or time travel or anything else that I can come up with.

It is not easy, ever. I don't have many ideas; I'm slow, disorganized, gloomy, and hopelessly lazy. I am married to a lawyer and have two children, a boy and a girl, born in 1964 and 1965. I write as full-time as I can; that is, I used to retire to a separate bed-sittingroom two miles away and stare at a typewriter all day, or else out of the window. I knew all the comings and goings of the neighbors, and very occasionally I managed to write something as well. But in 1974 I broke out further, took a cottage in Somerset two hundred miles out of London, where I'm setting a book, and commute there for part of every week. Whether or not that will be productive remains to be seen.

Penelope Farmer's first book, *The Summer Birds*, was contracted for before she was twenty-one. Though it was recognizably the work of a young writer who still had much to learn about her craft, there was never any doubt that it introduced an original imaginative talent. *The Summer Birds*, about what happens to a group of ordinary village children when a strange boy teaches them all how to fly, was an American Library Association Notable Book in 1962 and a runner-up for England's Carnegie Medal in 1963. Each subsequent book showed the author's growth in skill and power and deepening range until a critic reviewing *A Castle of Bone* could describe it as "necessary writing. What a writer 'must write—or burst,'" as C. S. Lewis said, "what readers' lives are changed

by." Penelope Farmer says that she is "more likely to understand myself through my books than any other way. . . . I suppose I want to be read—who doesn't?—but can only achieve that to the extent I manage to convert private images into narrative and public ones."

Before her marriage Penelope Farmer taught school in London's East End and took a degree in social work from London University. She now lives with her husband and children in a Victorian house in a London suburb. She reviews books for the *Times Literary Supplement* and the New York *Times*. She collects old children's books, is intensely interested in politics, both British and American, and travels to the United States whenever she can.

SELECTED WORKS: The Summer Birds, 1962; The Magic Stone, 1964; Emma in Winter, 1966; Charlotte Sometimes, 1969; A Castle of Bone, 1972; The Serpent's Teeth, 1972; The Story of Persephone, 1973; William and Mary, 1974; August the Fourth, 1976; The Year King, 1977.

ABOUT: Contemporary Authors, Vol. 15–16; Jones, Cornelia and Way, Olivia R. British Children's Authors. Interviews at Home, 1976; Elementary English September 1974; Junior Bookshelf January 1963.

NANCY FAULKNER

January 8, 1906–

AUTHOR OF *Small Clown*, etc.

Autobiographical sketch of Anne Irvin Faulkner, who uses the pen name Nancy Faulkner:

I WAS born and raised in Lynchburg, Virginia, at a fortunate time, for during my early childhood the town was small and homogeneous and peaceful and there were neither wars nor rumors of wars. (As you can see, I came late to the pleasure and business of writing. I was warned away from what I'd always hoped to do by a college professor of English who told me in my sophomore year I'd better give up the idea of writ-

ing because my vocabulary was too big!)

After graduating from high school, I went to the Baldwin School in Bryn Mawr, to Wellesley College and, eventually, to graduate study in history at Cornell University. My interest in history stemmed, I've always thought, from my early reading. In my growing-up years there were few fine books being published for young people. But I had *St. Nicholas* of blessed memory. And I had grandfather's library stocked with complete sets of Dickens and Thackeray, Walter Scott and Robert Louis Stevenson. Certainly those books stimulated, for me, a delight in times past, and that in turn probably sparked my long love affair with books about history, both books to read and books to write.

Between the end of my periods of study and the time when I, at last, came to fulfill my earliest wish "to be a writer," I held a variety of jobs. I started my working life as a clerk in the local tax collector's office. Later I worked in the business offices of the National Geographic Society; as a teacher in high school and college; as head of the Drama Bureau of the School of Continuing Education at the University of Virginia; as editor for the National Recreation Asso-

ciation—where, incidentally, I finally learned to control that too-large vocabulary—and at Walker & Company, on their Companion Books series; finally as vice-president of Chandler Records, which adapted and produced books for young people for radio broadcast.

It was while I was helping with those recordings that, as an experiment and in order to find out just how difficult it was to produce a book for youngsters, I wrote my first historical novel, *Rebel Drums*. I had no thought of publication until a friend urged me to show it to an editor. To my enormous surprise the book was accepted and became the first of a list of historicals, mysteries and picture books for young people.

One of the serendipities that have come to me with writing has been the necessity for travel. My historical books range in locale from ancient Crete (*Traitor Queen*) to the island of Rhodes (*Knight Besieged*) to Glastonbury and Stonehenge (*The Sacred Jewel*) and London at the time of Chaucer (*The Yellow Hat*) and in the age of Christopher Marlowe (*Great Reckoning*) and back to the mountains of North Carolina and Vermont and, of course, my native Virginia. Since I seem to need to get the feel of a place *in situ* as it were, each of these books has taken me afield to see for myself. And I have loved each necessary jaunt.

In 1968, after some twenty-five years of living in New York City, I moved back to Virginia, to Charlottesvillle. It is, for me, very pleasant to be living in this university city where life moves calmly, where there is relatively little pollution and where, upon a half-acre lot, I can "cultivate my garden" (chiefly roses) and come, again, to recognize the songs of the many birds that live among us.

SELECTED WORKS: Rebel Drums, 1952; The Yellow Hat, 1958; Small Clown, 1960; The Sacred Jewel, 1961; Traitor Queen, 1963; Knight Besieged, 1964; Small Clown and Tiger, 1968; Undecided Heart, 1969; Great Reckoning, 1970; Second Son, 1970; The Witch with the Long, Sharp Nose, 1972.

ABOUT: Author's and Writer's Who's Who, 1971; Contemporary Authors, Vol. 4; Foremost Women in Communications, 1970; Wilson Library Bulletin April 1956.

ANITA FEAGLES

February 28, 1926–

AUTHOR OF *Me, Cassie*, etc.

Autobiographical sketch of Anita Mac-Rae Feagles:

I CAN'T remember why I started writing, only that I always wrote and I thought of myself as a writer (but did not so describe myself) about fifteen years before I sold my first story. Kids ask me "where the idea came from" for some of my books and I can't really say; I just know when I'm ready to write about something, and I think it through carefully ahead of time so that it goes fast once I begin to work.

I was an only child, and very much resented people taking my feelings or opinions lightly because I was young. I had four children to make up for the loneliness, and I don't take anyone's opinions or feelings lightly, and now I don't want to be categorized because of age any more than I did then, only now I'm middle-aged. This is a very comfortable time for me to be alive because I'm much happier with the current views of life than I was with the older ones. Most of the changes do not shock me but make me feel that my views are finally being verified.

Our household strikes people as odd because there is quite a variance of attitudes and interests. What we have in common is a genuine interest in people and animals, and all of us bring home an assortment of both. As a result, our house has always been an interesting place to be, if only because it is full of surprises.

I was told early on that creative work might not bring in enough money for a livelihood so I took a master's degree, which was supposed to prepare me to be a school psychologist. The advice was sound but I was not well suited to psy-

chometrics or the authority role, so I floundered and went back to writing. I also did not learn anything in school that helped me in writing. The sort of perception and turn of mind one needs in order to write is not made available in a formal education. It's only fun to know those things because one is less disputable in an argument and more confident of facts.

Because of my husband's work I have been lucky enough to accompany him on business trips that have taken me to some thirty-five countries. It is possible to visit several countries without learning anything, but after thirty-five one almost has to make a few discoveries. I suppose my major one has been that people are much more alike than they are different.

Like many other writers, I look forward to starting a new book. I am only contented when I have a project underway. I hope the next one will be major. If not the next, the one after that . . . so it always goes in my plans. And I hope that whatever I write, it will strike a responsive chord in someone. That is what other authors have done for me, and what I hope to do for someone.

———

Born in Chicago, Anita MacRae Feagles earned her Bachelor of Science degree at Knox College and, after her marriage to Robert W. Feagles, her Master of Science degree at City University of New York. The Feagles' four children are Wendy, Cuyler, Priscilla and Patrick.

Though Mrs. Feagles can't always pinpoint the source of her ideas, she could in the case of *The Tooth Fairy*. One day she overheard thirteen-year-old Wendy and seven-year-old Priscilla. Priscilla had found the wooden box in which Wendy had kept all her old teeth. "So *you're* the Tooth Fairy!" the outraged Priscilla exclaimed. "No," Wendy insisted. "I'm saving these for the Tooth Fairy because she's making a necklace." From these promising beginnings grew the tale of what happens to the newly lost teeth the Tooth Fairy collects from under the pillows of their owners.

SELECTED WORKS: Casey the Utterly Impossible Horse, 1960; The Genie and Joe Maloney, 1962; The Tooth Fairy, 1962; A Stranger in the Spanish Village, 1964; Twenty-Seven Cats Next Door, 1965; He Who Saw Everything: The Epic of Gilgamesh, 1966; Autun and the Bear (retold), 1967; Me, Cassie, 1968; Queen Sara and the Messy Fairies, 1968; Thor and the Giants, 1968; Addicts: Young Men and Women Kicking the Drug Habit, 1971; The Year the Dreams Came Back, 1976.

Muriel L. Feelings

MURIEL FEELINGS

July 31, 1938–

AUTHOR OF *Moja Means One*, etc.

Autobiographical sketch of Muriel L. Gray Feelings:

I WAS born in Philadelphia, the elder of two children. Both my brother and I had artistic ability, which gladdened the heart of my maternal great-uncle, John Harris, who hoped we'd carry on the family artistic tradition of several generations. Keeping us supplied with art materials, he and my mother sponsored my art training at the Philadelphia College of Art's Saturday classes for children.

As a child, I loved reading. I recall many times reading a book even while setting the table, and with a flashlight reading in bed secretly when I was supposed to be asleep.

In high school, art, English and Spanish were my favorite subjects. I recall a bittersweet experience of an English class in which the instructor gave me a C grade on an essay I wrote on *The Old Man and the Sea*, though few red correction marks appeared on the paper. When I queried the reason, she replied, "You must have read some critics—why didn't you name them?" Hurt by the accusation, I explained that I had not read any criticisms of the novel. "Well," she replied, "you have a remarkable insight, young lady," and changed the grade.

After graduation and a year of employment as a clerk-typist, I entered the Philadelphia College of Art where I attended for one year on partial scholarship.

Due to financial constraints I returned to work and studied at PCA in the evenings. The following year I went to California and, in 1963, graduated from California State University at Los Angeles, where I had prepared to be a teacher of art and Spanish. It was there in California that I came to know students from Africa, and my interest in reading about and traveling to Africa was great.

I worked as a teacher in New York,

where again I came to know people from Africa and made plans to go there. In 1966, through recruitment by the Uganda Mission to the U.N., I went to serve as an art teacher in a high school in Kampala, the capital of Uganda. There I spent some of the most purposeful, happy years of my life, in and out of work. It provided the opportunity to use both my art and writing abilities. One of the most rewarding school projects was one in which my students wrote a story of their choice, mainly folk literature, which they then illustrated. The results were illustrated booklets for which I typed the text opposite their illustrations. I presented samples to the Ministry of Education which they considered as bases for future publishing of indigenous literature for schools.

On a voluntary basis I designed flats and background sets for the Educational Television Unit, which was an exciting learning experience.

In Africa I learned more than I could ever teach. The travels and visits with families in the rural areas of Uganda and Kenya, to Dar es Salaam and Zanzibar in Tanzania and to various parts of Zaire (then, Congo-Kinshasa) were like a homecoming and brought many understandings, insights and warm feelings about the people and the life of my ancestors. Upon my return to the United States, I found the Afro-American community in great ferment—politically, socially and culturally, and increasingly knowledgeable about the African experience.

I married Tom Feelings. He was engaged in illustrating books on African life and had (in our correspondence while I lived in Uganda) suggested I bring back folk literature based on the school project I had described.

It was the desire to share the African experience that sparked my writing for children. Despite the growing body of information available, many children, due to the miseducation in the media and public schools, still were starved for a positive and realistic image of Africa. My first story, *Zamani Goes to Market,*

was begun in 1969, a few months after the birth of my son Zamani, and was based on collective experiences of rural African familyhood. I attempted to portray that sense of family, orderliness, and collective work and responsibility that so impressed me.

In the years following I taught in Brooklyn schools and introduced African crafts and, informally, a little Swahili language to the interested black students. During this time I wrote *Moja Means One: Swahili Counting Book*, to bring the concept of African language and concepts to children of African descent, as there was then, to my knowledge, nothing available for children on the subject of Swahili language.

In 1971 my family and I went to work and live in Guyana, South America. There I taught art in two high schools, and in the second year worked for the Guyana Government textbook project to assist in editing and writing booklets for use in the schools. Here again, I found a setting for use of both areas of art and writing.

Upon my return to the United States, I completed a Kishwahili companion to *Moja—Jambo Means Hello: Swahili Alphabet Book*—which I had initiated before moving to Guyana.

I have been living in Philadelphia where I have worked for Afro-American organizations, the most recent being an international manpower training organization with branches of training in African countries. My occupational work has involved cultural orientation training for personnel going to work in Africa and technical writing. I have continued in my (sparse) spare time to write fiction for children between my job and caring for my two sons. Presently I am working on folk tales and a story for older children.

Muriel Feelings' two Swahili books, with illustrations by Tom Feelings, have acquired honors and accolades from all sides. Besides being distinguished as Notable Books by the American Library Association, included in the *Horn Book*

Fanfare list, and being named best of the year by *School Library Journal*, both books were Caldecott Honor Books and both books were named Brooklyn Art Books for Children, a citation made for works that are excellent both as art and as literature. *Jambo Means Hello* won the Boston *Globe-Horn Book* Award (picture book category) for 1974.

SELECTED WORKS: Zamani Goes to Market, 1970; Moja Means One: Swahili Counting Book, 1971; Jambo Means Hello: Swahili Alphabet Book, 1974.

DALE FIFE

AUTHOR OF *Who's in Charge of Lincoln?* etc.

Autobiographical sketch of Dale Fife:

WHEN I was about eight, I wrote a letter to the editor of a children's magazine. It was published. Perhaps seeing my name in print at such a young age influenced what happened later. I wrote rhymes, monologues and stories to fit all occasions—such as birthdays, the Fourth of July, graduations. That none of these survived to this day is a blessing, no doubt. Later I wrote movie scenarios. My favorite setting for these was a London drawing room, notwithstanding the fact I had not been very far from my hometown. They came back promptly, often unopened, from glamorous Hollywood.

My home seemed very ordinary to me. It did not strike me that my mother was an especially interesting character. The eldest of nine orphaned children, she had come from her native Alsace to the United States, expecting to be able to send for her brothers and sisters within a short time. She was still sending for them when she had her own children. I did not think it unusual that our dining room table was stretched end to end with young aunts and uncles who came to stay in our home before gathering the necessaries for their own "nests."

It took a friend to point out to me, when I complained about rejection slips,

DALE FIFE

that my mother was a most unusual person and why didn't I write about *her*? Finally I wrote a short story about her. It sold immediately to a top market. I wrote others. They sold. Finally, these stories and others were published as a book by Farrar, Straus & Giroux. The title was *Weddings in the Family*. This book was followed by another collection of Alsatian stories, *The Unmarried Sisters*, published by the same firm.

The two books were concerned with growing up in an Alsatian-American family. I wanted to write a third, comparing the lot of the immigrants with that of relatives who had not come to America. For this research I went to Alsace. When I returned, the memory of the storybook quality of my mother's village in the Vosges mountains prompted me to write a book for children. It was *A Stork for the Bell Tower* and was published by Coward-McCann. A second followed it, *A Dog Called Dunkel*.

The adult book I intended writing was published later as a teen-age novel. Called *Walk a Narrow Bridge*, it won the Ohioana Award in 1967.

I lived for a time in Nevada, in the mining community of Tonopah. This was near Goldfield, an "almost" ghost town. Many of my early short stories were set in this background. I have also written two books for children using this setting,

The Boy Who Lived In the Railroad De-pot and *Ride the Crooked Wind*. This latter book was the most difficult I have written. Getting into the mind of another culture was an extremely delicate matter for me. But I had known the Paiute Indians as a young girl living on the desert, and I considered them a noble people and wanted to tell their story, so I kept with it. The book was a Junior Literary Guild selection.

At present I am doing a revision of my fourth Lincoln book. Lincoln and Po (of *Ride the Crooked Wind*) are my two favorite characters to work with.

I travel when I can afford it timewise and moneywise. I have just returned from a two-month freighter trip around South America. There are still many places in this world I have not seen, but now I am interested in seeing more of my own country, beginning with the place I was born—Toledo, Ohio—at the beginning of this century, and where I attended Sacred Heart School in East Toledo. I came to San Francisco as a bride. I am a widow and live in San Mateo, a suburb of "the city." I have a son Duncan who lives in New York City and Connecticut.

After my marriage I attended San Francisco State College.

My mornings are spent writing, and often I meet with fellow authors in the afternoons and evenings.

I have no hobbies, as such, but I do work in my garden if I can manage the time.

When young people tell me they are interested in becoming writers, I caution them that it is probably the most difficult way to make money, if that is what their goal is. But for an interesting life, there can be no surer way of obtaining it.

SELECTED WORKS: A Stork for the Bell Tower, 1964; Who's in Charge of Lincoln?, 1965; Bluefoot, 1968; The Boy Who Lived in the Railroad Depot, 1968; Joe and the Talking Christmas Tree, 1968; What's New, Lincoln?, 1970; Adam's ABC, 1971; What's the Prize, Lincoln?, 1971; Ride the Crooked Wind, 1973; Who Goes There, Lincoln?, 1975; Who'll Vote for Lincoln?, 1977.

ATI FORBERG

December 19, 1925–

ILLUSTRATOR OF *Boys Are Awful*, etc.

Biographical sketch of Beate Gropius Forberg:

BEATE GROPIUS FORBERG (she is known as Ati, the diminutive form of Beate) was born in Germany on December 19, 1925. She attended strictly traditional German schools until she was nine, when she left for England to join her parents. Her father was Walter Gropius, the famous architect, founder and director of the Bauhaus in Germany, who later became chairman of the School of Architecture at Harvard University. In England she entered the Bertrand Russell School, a radically progressive school founded by the English philosopher. In addition to adjusting to the contrast between the rigidly formal system of education she had previously experienced and the new freedom, she had to grapple with a new language. She was just beginning to settle down in the school and to enjoy being there when, at the age of eleven, she had to move again, this time to the United States. There she attended Concord Academy, in Massachusetts, and again adapted herself to a traditional system of education.

As a child Ati Forberg enjoyed reading, her favorite books being fairy tales, but drawing was much more important to her and she drew from a very early age. At sixteen, after a summer visit to the experimental community and liberal arts college of Black Mountain, North Carolina, she became so fascinated by it that she left Concord Academy for good and spent the next four years continuously at Black Mountain. She studied art under the painter Josef Albers. Through his teaching she feels that she learned a fundamental approach to the elements of art: color, structure, design, and a heightened awareness of these elements in all aspects of living. When she completed her art studies she decided that her primary interest lay in two-dimensional rather than three-dimensional art,

ATI FORBERG

siderable success. She works in a variety of styles and mediums, but she is happiest working in pen and ink.

Interested in moviemaking and any art form that will create an atmosphere in which a child's imagination can develop freely, Ati Forberg believes that even everyday objects can be presented in such a way that they become magical and evoke a sense of wonder. When her two daughters, Sarina and Erika, were small, they made masks and hand puppets together and created miniature villages out of natural materials.

With her younger daughter, Ati Forberg now lives in Brooklyn Heights where she does free-lance work, concentrating mainly on illustrating children's books.

SELECTED WORKS ILLUSTRATED: Boys Are Awful, by Phyllis McGinley, 1962; Erec and Enid, by Barbara Schiller, 1970; The Key, by Florence Parry Heide, 1971; Persephone, Bringer of Spring, by S. F. Tomaino, 1971; . . . if You Lived with the Circus, by Anne McGovern, 1972; A Friend in the Park, by Anne Norris Baldwin, 1973; Josie's Handful of Quietness, by Nancy Covert Smith, 1975; Cupid and Psyche: A Love Story, retold by Edna Barth, 1976; A Game of Catch, by Helen Cresswell, 1977.

ABOUT: Kingman, Lee and others, comps. Illustrators of Children's Books: 1957–1966.

and she specialized in graphics. She married another former Black Mountain College student, Charles Forberg, and traveled and worked with him in Europe extensively.

Back in the United States, the Forbergs settled in Chicago where they stayed for many years. Charles Forberg taught architecture at the Institute of Design, and Ati Forberg pursued postgraduate studies there. She worked in many different areas, sometimes with her designer husband, sometimes alone. She designed typography, exhibition and window displays, and she worked on a magazine and in advertising agencies. She enjoyed the variety of any work that drew on visual experience. When the Forbergs moved to New York she found fewer opportunities to do such widely varied work, and she became a children's book illustrator almost, as she says, by default. The first children's book she illustrated was *Benjy* by Edwin O'Connor, in 1957.

Ati Forberg believes it is important for a book she is illustrating to have an atmosphere she enjoys, and among the many books she has worked on she remembers *Erec and Enid* with particular affection. She feels black and white is her natural medium, and says that she has never been a painter, though she does full-color picture books with con-

PEGGY FORTNUM
December 22, 1919–

ILLUSTRATOR OF *A Bear Called Paddington*, etc.

Autobiographical sketch of Margaret Emily Noel Nuttall-Smith, who illustrates under the name of Peggy Fortnum:

I WAS born at Harrow-on-the-Hill, Middlesex, England.

My first creative experience may have occurred when I was four years old. I painted my black cat with green house paint, thinking I was giving it a new lease of life. Fortunately the cat was rescued and recovered.

I became an illustrator through a series of accidental happenings rather than by design. When I was a baby, I was nursed—when my mother was ill in the hospital—by a young country girl who lived with us until my twelfth year. Through her I came to love the country. She told me casually of two visions she had—one of her soldier boy who had been killed, and one of angels. This stirred my imagination. My mother, who had spent her childhood in Trinidad, thrilled me with stories of a more exotic kind, and my sister used to invent stories to relieve my fear of the dark. All this storytelling gave me an addiction to reading and books, which may have helped to shape my career.

I remember vividly our holidays in Equihen, France, which was in those days beautiful, and remote. An artist friend living there described in his pictures and sculpture the life of the village peasants and fishermen, thereby giving me another stimulus to draw.

When I was fourteen my father retired from the sea to Crowborough, Sussex, which was on top of a high hill. When war broke out five years later, we had a pretty clear view of the Battle of Britain, part of which was fought overhead. I shall never forget seeing so much heroism. At that point I decided to join up, which indirectly led to my studying book illustration at the Central School in London.

Before the war I had been studying at the Tunbridge Wells School of Art. Having got the Industrial Design Certificate, I started teaching children of all ages. During Dunkirk, I was at a school on the East Coast marshes. Archery was one of the school sports. We practised earnestly and hoped for the best. A year later I was a signals operator in the Auxiliary Territorial Service, thereby jumping—as it were—from the Stone Age to the twentieth century. I cannot say I contributed anything to the war effort, as I was invalided out a year later when my leg was crushed under the wheel of a troop carrier. For some reason this was considered an error on the part of the service, and I was given a pension and a government grant to study at the Central School of Art. I was persuaded to join the illustration class, which was at the top of the building, and attendance was erratic owing to the raids. Hearing bombs and pilotless planes and rockets exploding was rather distracting, but I illustrated my first children's book during this time, a commission given to me by my teacher, John Farleigh, who had just become editor of the Sylvan Press.

When I left the Central in 1945, I worked part-time as a designer in a firm of furnishing fabrics, teaching and illustrating children's books in between. I must have illustrated approximately eighty books.

I married Ralph Nuttall-Smith, painter, sculptor and teacher, who encouraged my ambition to paint and write, which I prefer to do. Now his two sons are grown up and married, we live at West Mersea in Essex. Mersea is an island, being surrounded by marshland and tidal water. The causeway that connects us to the mainland dates back to the Roman occupation.

———

The youngest of six children, Peggy Fortnum loved to paint and write ballads and then to dress up like the characters she invented. She received much encouragement from an older sister who was also a storyteller and artist, from a family friend, and from Sir Frank Brangwyn, who awarded her a prize at a Young Artists exhibition of painting.

Peggy Fortnum is best known for her characterization of Michael Bond's bear called Paddington, whom she has also drawn for the British children's television program "Jackanory," but besides Paddington she has drawn for other children's television shows and illustrated for a number of magazines. Her illustrations to Kenneth Grahame's *The Reluctant Dragon* were exhibited at the British Museum.

She prefers to work "from imagination, memory and references more than direct studies," and will usually make a number of sketches in pen and ink when she has finished reading a story. From these she selects the illustrations she will use, sometimes even choosing the first drawing.

SELECTED WORKS ILLUSTRATED: A Bear Called Paddington, by Michael Bond, 1960; Children's Bells, by Eleanor Farjeon, 1960; Paddington Helps Out, by Michael Bond, 1961; Paddington at Large, by Michael Bond, 1963; The Reluctant Dragon, by Kenneth Grahame, 1965; Paddington at Work, by Michael Bond, 1967; The Happy Prince and Other Stories, by Oscar Wilde, 1968; Paddington Goes to Town, by Michael Bond, 1968; Paddington Takes the Air, by Michael Bond, 1971; Paddington Abroad, by Michael Bond, 1972; Paddington on Top, by Michael Bond, 1976; Paddington on Stage, by Michael Bond, 1977.

ABOUT: Kingman, Lee and others, comps. Illustrators of Children's Books: 1957–1966; Ryder, John. Artists of a Certain Line; Viguers, Ruth Hill and others, comps. Illustrators of Children's Books: 1946–1956.

PAULA FOX

1923–

AUTHOR OF *The Slave Dancer*, etc.

Autobiographical sketch of Paula Fox Greenberg:

Paula Fox

I WAS born in New York City in 1923. When I was eight I lived on a Cuban plantation for two years where I went to a one-room school with eight other students who ranged in age from six to fourteen, a classroom situation which required great agility on the teacher's part to prevent the youngest of us from lapsing into comas while the older children learned their arithmetic, or to stop the older ones from assaulting each other out of boredom while the youngest children learned to read. Before and after Cuba I seldom lived any place longer than a year or so. I attended nine schools before I was twelve, by which time I had discovered that freedom, solace and truth were public libraries.

I wrote a detective story when I was seven. It was so bloody that, appalled by my own invention, I saw to it that various corpses were magically restored to life by the end of the story. I began to write—less criminally—when my two sons were ten and twelve. My first book for children was *Maurice's Room*, the idea for which grew out of a conversation with a friend about the quantity of objects that surround American children. My first novel for adults, *Poor George*, was written at the same time.

I taught school for a number of years and found a special pleasure in fifth graders, who seemed to have the true sophistication of childhood undiluted by the uneasy and painful pseudosophistication of adolescence. I often write about children between nine and twelve when they have a kind of balance, a sense of placement from which life, inevitably, jars them loose.

I have been especially interested in writing about children as they encounter the daily surprises of life, its frequent periods of loneliness, the inexplicability of events and the feelings they evoke.

My sons are now young men. Only recently I found the oldest, who is twenty-six, grinning over a book I had just finished for very young children. I was pleased and grateful.

***

Half-Spanish, half-Irish, Paula Fox went to live with her grandmother in Cuba in 1931, where she learned to speak Spanish from the children she played with. When Batista came to power in 1934 she returned to New York. She seldom saw either of her parents. At seventeen she went to work. She has held a number of jobs—on newspapers, as a machinist for Bethlehem Steel, for the British publisher Victor Gollancz, as a reader for a movie company, and for a British news service in Paris and in Warsaw. She says her most unusual job was punctuating Italian madrigals of the fifteenth century.

Miss Fox studied at Columbia University and has taught emotionally disturbed children, taught English to Spanish-speaking children, and taught at the Ethical Culture Schools in New York City. She is married to Martin Greenberg, a college professor, and has two sons by a previous marriage, Adam and Gabriel, who are now grown.

Paula Fox has written adult novels and written for television, but the body of her work so far has been novels published for children. She does not herself make a strong distinction between writing for children or adults. "Any story is a metaphor," she has said. "It is not life. . . . What applies to good writing is,

I think, absolute, whether for children or grown-ups." Eloquent, striking, original, imaginative, perceptive, uncommon are the adjectives that have greeted her work since her first publication. *How Many Miles to Babylon?* was an American Library Association Notable Book in 1967; *Blowfish Live in the Sea* was a finalist for the National Book Award in 1971.

Miss Fox received an Arts and Letters Award from The National Institute of Arts and Letters in 1972 and a Guggenheim Foundation Fellowship the same year. In 1974 she won the Newbery Medal for *The Slave Dancer*. This powerful historical novel recounts the horrors of the slave trade through the eyes of a white street musician who has been shanghaied by slavers to play while slaves are "danced" for exercise. Answering critics who felt a white woman should not have written about slavery, Paula Fox said, "I write to find out. I write to discover, over and over again, my connections with myself, with others. Each book deepens the question. It does not answer it."

Paula Fox was the American nominee, chosen by the American Library Association, for the 1978 Hans Christian Andersen Award.

SELECTED WORKS: Maurice's Room, 1966; A Likely Place, 1967; How Many Miles to Babylon?, 1967; The Stone-Faced Boy, 1968; Portrait of Ivan, 1969; Hungry Fred, 1969; The King's Falcon, 1969; Blowfish Live in the Sea, 1970; Good Ethan, 1973; The Slave Dancer, 1973.

ABOUT: Townsend, John Rowe. A Sense of Story; Horn Book August 1974.

RUTH FRANCHERE

November 10, 1906–

AUTHOR OF *Willa: The Story of Willa Cather's Growing Up*, etc.

Autobiographical sketch of Ruth Franchere:

I WAS born in Mason City, Iowa, but soon we moved to Waterloo, Iowa. How-

Ruth Franchere

ever, my memories are chiefly of my long summers at Lake Okoboji in the northwestern corner of the state. There my parents had a house to which we joyfully moved the day after the school year ended and which we regretfully left the day before school started again.

I loved the clear, blue water with a real passion; I was on it or in it most of the day. I soon came to know the wild flowers and small animals around it. There is no doubt that my summer experiences made it possible for me later to write with ease and pleasure of the early years of Willa Cather and Carl Sandburg and to be at home in the environment of the fictional characters in *Hannah Herself* and *The Travels of Colin O'Dae*.

Exciting stories about my beloved lake fed my imagination. Indian legends abounded. The great massacre which took place directly across the water from our house (admirably chronicled and embellished by MacKinlay Kantor in his *Spirit Lake*) was a story that I heard many times.

Closer to me were the mysterious accounts of the sea captain who had come so far inland to build the very house in which we lived. The secret panels that we discovered one by one, the captain's large sailboat that had gone down in a

violent storm and could still be seen on a quiet day far offshore, and many stories, real or fancied, sent my imagination in unrestrained directions.

I have always been a story spinner. In my early teens I became storyteller for a group of neighborhood girls. Each day, no doubt prompted by the Saturday movies that we all attended, I concocted wild episodes to keep my friends agape.

My first attempt at publication came when I was in the eighth grade. My teacher encouraged me to submit one of my written yarns to a magazine. Almost paralyzed with excitement, I imagined myself already launched on a writing career. On my father's old typewriter, using pale pink typing paper, I slowly tapped out the story, all two pages of it. I sent it to a popular women's magazine, it was returned promptly, and so ended my early writing career.

I met my future husband, Hoyt Franchere, during my last year at the University of Iowa. He was working toward his master's degree in literature. We were married in the fall.

Illinois College in Jacksonville, where my husband served as an instructor, was the first college founded in the state. My natural curiosity led me to learn as much as possible about its origins. Years later, some of my information became the nucleus for my fourth book, my first fiction, *Hannah Herself*.

The following years were too full for serious writing, although I did work on some short stories until I decided that such stories were not my media. Besides keeping house and caring for a young daughter, I occasionally took on other jobs. I was a book buyer. For seven years I taught English composition to college freshmen.

In time the job of correcting other people's writing palled. My husband was then a university dean. Our daughter Julie had finished college, was on her own, and was soon to be married. At last I could have unlimited hours for total concentration. I could write!

I settled down at my desk at nine o'clock each morning and, with few exceptions, have held to a strict routine of writing through more than sixteen years and twelve published books.

———

Ruth Franchere's *Willa* was an American Library Association Notable Book in 1958. Her *Stephen Crane* was designated an Honor Book in the New York *Herald Tribune* Spring Children's Book Festival in 1961.

SELECTED WORKS: Willa: The Story of Willa Cather's Growing Up, 1958; Stephen Crane, 1961; The Travels of Colin O'Dae, 1961; Jack London, 1962; Hannah Herself, 1964; Stampede North, 1969; Carl Sandburg, 1970; Cesar Chavez, 1970; Tito of Yugoslavia, 1970; Westward by Canal, 1972; The Wright Brothers, 1972.

BERNIECE FRESCHET
August 4, 1927–

AUTHOR OF *Bear Mouse*, etc.

Autobiographical sketch of Berniece Louise Speck Freschet:

I WAS born in Miles City, a small town in Montana which owed its early existence to the large cattle, sheep, and horse ranches around it.

My feeling for nature and wildlife started with my dad, who loved the outdoors. As a young boy, he ran away from his home to come out West and be a cowboy. He was a bronco buster and horse wrangler to some of the biggest cattle and horse spreads in eastern Montana. Later he homesteaded on the Mizpah and at one time drove the Powderville Stage Line.

The log home he built there on Strevel Creek still stands and is lived in today. Sometimes my dad would let me go with him when he hunted pheasants. I'd trail along behind him through cactus and sagebrush, remembering to keep a lookout for rattlesnakes—and then the terrible leap of my heart at the sudden whirr of a pheasant's flight. There were also times when we hiked up brush mountainsides to fish in streams so cold

BERNIECE FRESCHET

that the water numbed your legs—and how they ached when you came out and stood on the bank. My father was one of the first members of the Range Riders Reps, a group of old-time western cowboys, and I was very proud when, as his daughter, they asked me to become a member.

It was my mother who first brought books into my life, reading me stories at bedtime—Peter Rabbit, Reddy Fox, Grandfather Frog, and all of Thornton Burgess's wonderful books—my earliest favorites. Then, when I began to read on my own, I would hide for hours down in the basement by the old warm furnace where I lived in the world between the covers of those books.

When I finished high school in Miles City, I attended the University of Montana for two years and then left for San Francisco to work. I held various jobs, including salesgirl, receptionist, dance instructor and employment interviewer. It was in San Francisco that I met and married Ferucio Freschet, who was attending San Francisco State College. He took a teaching position in San Mateo, California, where we lived with our five children until my husband accepted a job in Lexington, Massachusetts, with the Educational Development Center. We later moved to Rockville Center on Long Island, where my husband is now principal of the senior high school and where we presently live.

When my children were all in school and I felt my life needed another focus, it was my husband who suggested that I try writing. I write for children largely because of the joy books gave to me during my childhood, and because there have always been children around me. . . . I suppose it was a natural thing for me to write for children.

It is a great challenge to write a book that some child might feel as strongly about as some of the books I read when I was young. I write nature stories because I want children to know the beauty of the earth and its creatures—to feel a part of it, and to preserve that beauty.

———

The Web in the Grass was included in the American Library Association's list of Notable Books in 1972.

SELECTED WORKS: The Old Bullfrog, 1968; Beaver on the Sawtooth, 1969; The Flight of the Snow Goose, 1970; The Jumping Mouse, 1971; The Web in the Grass, 1971; Turtle Pond, 1971; Bear Mouse, 1973; Pronghorn on the Powder River, 1973; The Ants Go Marching, 1973; Year on Muskrat Marsh, 1974; Grizzly Bear, 1975; Bernard Sees the World, 1976; The Happy Dromedary, 1977.

ABOUT: Contemporary Authors, Vol. 19–20; Foremost Women in Communications, 1970.

ROBERT FROMAN

May 25, 1917–

AUTHOR OF *The Many Human Senses*, etc.

Autobiographical sketch of Robert Winslow Froman:

I WAS born May 25, 1917, on a ranch near Big Timber, Montana, and grew up in Caldwell, Idaho. The town had a wonderful Carnegie Public Library which was one of my favorite places from the time I learned to read. There I soon discovered the great difference between textbooks and real books. Text-

books came to seem to me utterly false, intended to stuff me with dull facts so that I could pass examinations, after which I could forget the facts. Real books—the shelves and shelves of library books—were full of pleasure and excitement and endlessly varied information and ideas that were fascinating when I discovered them for myself.

By the time I was eleven I had found that I liked to write, mostly poems and stories. My seventh-grade classmates and I put on a play I wrote a couple of times (it was called *The Duke's Lost Brother* and the title is all I remember about it). After that I never had any idea of earning my living any way except as a writer. By the time I was able to do so, I had found that I also liked to write about science.

For several years I wrote on science and other subjects for magazines, but that eventually got to be discouraging. Most magazine editors seemed to feel that their readers did not want to learn about anything that took any effort to understand. What I enjoyed about writing on science was learning about and then explaining exciting and sometimes difficult ideas and discoveries. The effort to understand was what made this enjoyable.

At that point I had the good fortune to discover the possibility of writing for children. Adult readers of magazines may not want to make any effort to understand, but many children do. Some children, to be sure, are so overwhelmed with school busywork and so bored by the textbooks inflicted on them that they lose much of their natural excitement about learning new things. But a real book can help them feel that excitement again.

For many years I've been wandering from one field of science to another—from physics to botany to psychology to chemistry to paleontology to sociology and others—learning about things that intrigue me. Sometimes they are new discoveries, sometimes ideas that have been around a long time but that I never looked into before. Then I try to tell young readers about what I've learned and why it seems so interesting.

Lately, I've been fascinated by mathematics (though definitely *not* by the so-called New Math, a fad that will soon pass). I'm trying to pass on what I've discovered in a series of picture books for very young readers and some longer books for older ones. And I've started writing stories again, too. Among my latest books are *The Wild Orphan*, a story about an Idaho boy and a mountain lion, and *Thomas the Tiger Teacher*, a picture book (the first published by the Scholastic Arrow Book Club and the second by the Scholastic See-Saw Book Club).

But one of the best things writing for children has done for me has been to open me up to poetry again. I went to a supposedly "good" college—Reed College in Portland, Oregon—where the heavily academic approach completely destroyed my childhood interest in poetry. For many years after leaving Reed I did not even read poems. Then, not long after I started writing for children, I also started scribbling, just for fun, what I thought were haiku. One day one of them suddenly turned into something different. The words scrambled all over the page and took a shape that was part

of the poem. Others like it have been popping into my mind ever since. My first book of them, *Street Poems*, was published in 1971 and was a Junior Literary Guild choice. My second, *Seeing Things*, was published in 1974.

SELECTED WORKS: The Many Human Senses, 1966; The Science of Salt, 1967; Spiders, Snakes and Other Outcasts, 1967; Science, Art, and Visual Illusions, 1970; Bigger and Smaller, 1971; Street Poems, 1971; Mushrooms and Molds, 1972; Racism, 1972; Less than Nothing Is Really Something, 1973; Seeing Things, 1974; A Game of Functions, 1974; Arithmetic for Human Beings, 1974; Angles Are as Easy as Pie, 1976.

ABOUT: Contemporary Authors, Vol. 4.

ERICH FUCHS

March 16, 1916–

AUTHOR AND ILLUSTRATOR OF *Journey to the Moon*, etc.

Autobiographical sketch of Erich Fuchs, translated from the German:

EVEN in my childhood and schooldays I passionately loved to paint and draw. Not even my schoolbooks were spared, to the annoyance of my teacher. When this drawing enthusiasm was forbidden me, I drew with ink on blotters. Since I entirely neglected the subjects useful for a solid middle-class professional education, I had to leave school early. My father had to give up the hope that I would complete a course of study that was suited to our class. He was now concerned to direct me to an occupation that would provide me with a living, and after a huge row I had to sign on as an apprentice in a goldsmith's workshop. Two years later, my former drawing teacher arranged for me to attend art school—if not the academy of fine art, still at least the commercial art school in my home town, for the "Heil Hitler" people had decreed that only realistic subjects could be drawn.

I had freed myself of the Hitler Youth when, during an argument with the squad leader, I had punched him in the

Fuchs: FOOKS

jaw and silently fled. In 1937 I was drafted into labor service and immediately after into military service. From 1939 to the end of the war I was stuck at the Front.

At the war's end I buried my war uniform, weapons, medals and papers in a forest somewhere and made my way back home. There I immediately began to paint and draw in a very scantily furnished studio. Later I studied with Professor Willi Baumeister at the Stuttgart Academy of Fine Art.

Since 1947 I have exhibited in international modern art exhibitions. From 1949 to 1958 I had a teaching post at the Stuttgart Academy, and in 1961 a sojourn in Paris.

I married my pupil, Hilde Hermann, in 1952. My wife is a tapestry weaver. My daughter Andrea was born in 1953, and in 1956, my son Olaf.

I had always told stories to the various children of relatives and neighbors. Now it was Andrea and Olaf who wanted to hear stories from Papa. One day my children asked for the story of *Nawai* as a picture book for Christmas. This book was printed in 1964 by Ellermann Verlag. This moved me to make other books,

Journey to the Moon (1969); *Vom Fischer und Seiner Frau* (The Fisherman and His Wife); *What Makes a Nuclear Power Plant Work* (1971); *Hier Studio 7* (This is Studio 7).

As long as people are fed and the stomach works, the brain stands still and the imagination rests. In my books I want to stir the imagination of our children, and I want to show our modern scientific technological world as fantastic as it is on the one hand and, on the other, as realistic as it is, and through my drawings and paintings make modern art understandable to children. I often use different perspectives so that I can show many things. Because the children always ask "What's in this building, what do they make in this factory?" I show them, by taking away the facade, what is behind it.

I concern myself with artistic nonfiction because I believe that the creative element essential to all the discoveries of technology as well as of science must not be lacking in a children's book. Through the picture book we can depict for them, as well as for their parents and teachers, our complicated technical world in a simple, objective and understandable way. A children's book is, and should be, the first art book that contributes to the education of our children. I see it as my task, therefore, to catch the movement of our modern world in an artistic form. Evaluation can begin only if we understand our environment in its charm and its danger; if it is clear to us, we can explain it to our children.

———

Erich Fuchs was born in Stuttgart, where he lives and works today. He is a qualified architect as well as a teacher, painter and illustrator of children's books.

Journey to the Moon was chosen a Notable Children's Book by the American Library Association in 1970 and was also designated one of the best books of the year by the New York *Times Book Review*, *School Library Journal* and the *Horn Book*.

SELECTED WORKS WRITTEN AND ILLUS-TRATED: Journey to the Moon, 1970; What Makes a Nuclear Power Plant Work?, 1972; Looking at Maps, 1976.

ABOUT: Contemporary Authors, Vol. 29–32; Something about the Author, Vol. 6.

GYO FUJIKAWA

AUTHOR AND ILLUSTRATOR OF *Babies*, etc.

Autobiographical sketch of Gyo Fujikawa:

THE name Gyo is masculine. But I am a female, an American of Japanese ancestry, born in California. I was named after an ancient Chinese emperor. My father loved Oriental history and favored and admired this emperor, and he named me even before I was born. It stuck even though I was not the son he secretly hoped for. So, Japanese as well as Americans take for granted I am a male, just as if my name had been Charles, until they find out otherwise.

People constantly ask if I knew from childhood that I would become an artist. I don't think so. As a matter of fact, I know that I had not the faintest idea what I wanted to become. I did love to draw, and much later on, at a time when I should have been thinking about the future, I'm afraid I was a bit vague and not particularly concerned. Only because of the interest of my art teacher in high school did I find myself catapulted into an art school. She sent portfolios of my work to two art schools in Los Angeles for scholarship consideration, and I was fortunate enough to get scholarships from both. I selected Chouinard Art Institute and under the influence of teachers, most specifically Mrs. Chouinard, I slowly found myself. My association with the school lasted many years, first as a student and later as an instructor in color and design.

After that, I free-lanced in New York and Los Angeles. Also, I worked for about a year for Walt Disney, a most memorable and profound experience. I designed promotional material for *Fantasia*. Among many things, I designed

Gyo Fujikawa: *GHEE o FOO je KOW a*

the book on *Fantasia* written by Deems Taylor and published by Simon & Schuster.

To recount my work and experiences in capsule: I have designed movie and pharmaceutical ad campaigns, served as art director on the staff and, as a free-lance for various advertising agencies, and prepared many illustrations of food, animals and children in the magazine, advertising and greeting card fields.

Book illustration is relatively new to me. I love the work, and in the past I've done the work on each book as a self-gratifying and permissive effort, like delicious dessert after the necessary entree of commercial illustration. So far, I have illustrated seventeen books, which I also designed from layout through type specification. Since I love doing these things for children, I dearly hope I can do many more.

———

Gyo Fujikawa, who gives her age as "over twenty-one years," credits Walt Disney with impressing upon her the need for attention to small details. Her illustrations for children are very detailed indeed, filled with the small objects and variety that she knows children appreciate. She takes pains to include everything that has been mentioned in the text so they will be there when children look for them, as they inevitably do. Miss Fujikawa was one of the first artists to use children of many races in her illustrations.

She has executed a number of major commercial commissions and has also designed two United States postage stamps.

SELECTED WORKS ILLUSTRATED: Mother Goose, 1968; A Child's Book of Poems, 1969; Fairy Tales and Fables, 1970; A to Z Picture Book, 1974; Let's Eat, 1975; Let's Play, 1975; Puppies, Pussy Cats and Other Friends, 1975; Sleepy Time, 1975; Gyo Fujikawa's Oh What a Busy Day!, 1976; Can You Count? Babes of the Wild, 1977.

ABOUT: Kingman, Lee and others, comps. Illustrators of Children's Books: 1957–1966; Publishers Weekly January 4, 1971.

RUTH STILES GANNETT
August 12, 1923–

AUTHOR AND ILLUSTRATOR OF *My Father's Dragon*, etc.

Autobiographical sketch of Ruth Stiles Gannett Kahn:

I WAS born and raised in New York City, which you might not guess from my books as they have so little city life in them. But it's important, nonetheless, because I went to a wonderful school in that city where children are encouraged to write and make all kinds of things and learn in creative ways. I remember using my allowance to buy notebooks for writing stories in, not because I was odd or a budding author, but because most of us liked to write—it was fun. It's not surprising that when I grew up I wrote for fun, to amuse myself.

I spent most of my summers in the Connecticut countryside. With my friends I built a small village in our barn, with houses big enough to crawl into, wooden birds suspended between the rafters, a horse and a dog. They are all still there.

Following the grade school years I left New York City for a Quaker boarding school in Pennsylvania, which was followed by Vassar College (class of 1944) with a chemistry major. This was during World War II, and I went to Boston to work as a technician in medical research and, later, in radar research at Massachusetts Institute of Technology.

With the signing of the peace I joyfully switched to making felt toys, writing and waiting on table in a Boston restaurant. Then winter came on, and I took a job at a ski lodge in Vermont. I had never spent a winter in the country, and I thought I might learn how to ski. Well, I didn't learn much about skiing, but between washing dishes and making beds there was time to walk out into the nighttime landscape, lit by the flickering Northern Lights; time to see and feel the early spring coming on as the fields discarded their snow blankets and sent water plummeting down the brooks. I was thrilled, but the skiers were not, and I returned to my father's house in Connecticut while looking for another job. It rained for the next two weeks, and it was during that time that I wrote the first draft of *My Father's Dragon* just for fun and with no thought of publication. I read it to my family and was amazed at their enthusiasm. I did not then nor do I now consider myself a writer. That first book practically wrote itself. The ones that followed, when I was trying, were much harder.

In searching for an illustrator for *My Father's Dragon* I met my husband, Peter Kahn. While my stepmother eventually did the illustrations, he helped with the lettering of the maps and designing the book. He is an artist, printer and designer and has been teaching at Cornell University for the last twenty years. We have lived in New York City, in Baton Rouge, Louisiana, in Hampton, Virginia, in Etna, New York, in Victoria, British Columbia, Canada, and now just outside Trumansburg, N.Y. Meanwhile we have had seven splendid daughters, only the youngest of whom is still at home, in high school.

I have not written anything for quite a while, but I hope to again some day. For the past six years I worked in an innovative elementary public school trying to make possible for others a joyous experience of education, the sort that encourages children to write their own stories, to make all kinds of things, and to learn in creative ways. Now I've retired to the country and I am learning how to spin, to dye, and lots more. I serve on the local school board, still trying to help bring the joy of learning into the classroom.

———

Ruth Gannett married H. Peter Kahn in 1947. Their daughters are Charlotte, Margaret, Sarah, Hannah, Louise, Catherine, and Elizabeth.

My Father's Dragon, which was illustrated by Ruth Chrisman Gannett, took first place in the New York *Herald Tribune* Children's Spring Book Festival in 1948 and was runner-up for the Newbery Medal in 1949. It has been translated into Japanese, Danish and Swedish.

SELECTED WORKS: My Father's Dragon, 1948; Elmer and the Dragon, 1950; The Dragons of Blueland, 1951; Katie and the Sad Noise, 1961.

ABOUT: Contemporary Authors, Vol. 21–22; Something about the Author, Vol. 3.

LEON GARFIELD

July 14, 1921–

AUTHOR OF *Devil-in-the-Fog*, etc.

Biographical sketch of Leon Garfield:

LEON GARFIELD was born at Brighton, Sussex, England. His early ambition was to be an artist, but World War II interrupted his art studies, scarcely begun, and he enlisted in the Army Medical Corps. While serving in Belgium, he met a young ambulance driver, Vivien Alcock, whom he later married. It was she who most influenced his decision to become a writer—an artist herself, she at once recognized that his art was "too literary." Both husband and wife claim a literary ancestor: he, Heinrich Heine, she, Charles Lamb.

After the defeat of Germany, Garfield was employed by the British as an investigator to prepare evidence for the war crimes trials. This work involved him in a macabre visit to the concentration camp at Belsen. He drew on these experiences as well as those of the next five years, spent as a biochemist in hospitals in England (including a period of service in a mental hospital), for material for the darker side of his stories.

With no special age group in mind he started work on a long novel, *Jack Holborn*. A neighbor encouraged him to show it to a literary agent, and it eventually came to the attention of Grace Hogarth, the children's book editor at Constable. She saw it as a story for older children and persuaded Garfield to cut it considerably with this in mind. At the same time she offered him a contract for a second story.

Jack Holborn, published in England in 1964, in the United States in 1965, won a Gold Medal from the Boy's Clubs of America. The second book, *Devil-in-the-Fog* (1966), received the first *Guardian* Award, one of England's most prestigious children's book awards, in 1966. Garfield was a runner-up for the Car-

LEON GARFIELD

negie Medal three times, with *Smith* in 1967, *Black Jack* in 1968, and *The Drummer Boy* in 1970. In 1970 he won the medal with his collaborator, Edward Blishen, for *The God Beneath the Sea*, a retelling of the Greek myths. In addition, *Smith* received an Arts Council of Great Britain Award for the best book for older children published between 1966 and 1969. Garfield's books have frequently appeared on the American Library Association's lists of Notable Books for Children. Both *Smith* and *Devil-in-the-Fog* were serialized on British television, and *Black Jack* was dramatized on radio. Penguin Books has made a full-color film on Garfield himself.

Garfield has written of his beginnings, "I always wanted to write. . . . I seemed to drift to writing for children; or rather, I drifted to the sort of writing I like—which can have wildly exciting adventures *and* something of character and morality. Really what I try to write is that old-fashioned thing, the family novel, accessible to the twelve-year-old and readable by his elders."

Garfield's stories are usually set in the eighteenth century, with characters from the period such as pickpockets, strolling players, body snatchers, pirates, highwaymen and foundlings, and scenes such as Newgate Prison and Bedlam Hospital.

Even the style has an eighteenth century flavor, for Garfield does not write down to his audiences, believing that in a gripping story unfamiliar words and difficult sentence structure will be no barrier. His characters are alive and piquant. Smith, the twelve-year-old pickpocket in the story that bears his name, would make Dickens' Artful Dodger look like a tyro. "A rat was like a snail beside Smith and the most his thousand or more victims got of him was the powerful whiff of his passing and a cold draft in their dexterously emptied pockets."

From the appearance of his first book Garfield has received excellent notices on both sides of the Atlantic. Critic John Rowe Townsend is impelled to superlatives, calling him the "richest and strongest" of the British children's writers of the 1960s and characterizing his stories as "the tallest, the deepest, the mildest, the most spine-chilling, the most humorous, the most energetic, the most extravagant, the most searching, the most everything."

Garfield lives in Highgate, London, with his wife and their young adopted daughter, Jane (named for Jane Austen), and a bearded collie called Tolly after the hero of *Black Jack*.

SELECTED WORKS: Jack Holborn, 1965; Devil-in-the-Fog, 1966; Smith, 1967; Black Jack, 1968; Mister Corbett's Ghost, 1968; The Drummer Boy, 1969; The Restless Ghost, 1969; The God Beneath the Sea (with Edward Blishen), 1971; Child O'War (with David Proctor), 1972; The Ghost Downstairs, 1972; The Golden Shadow (with Edward Blishen), 1973; The Sound of Coaches, 1974; The Prisoners of September, 1975; The House of Hanover: England in the 18th Century, 1976.

ABOUT: Author's Choice, 1970. Contemporary Authors, Vol. 17–18; Doyle, Brian. Who's Who of Children's Literature; Something about the Author, Vol. 1; Townsend, John Rowe. A Sense of Story; Junior Bookshelf August 1971.

MARGERY GILL

April 5, 1925–

ILLUSTRATOR OF *Dawn of Fear*, etc.

Autobiographical sketch of Margery Jean
   Gill Jordan:

I WAS born in Coatbridge, Scotland,
where my maternal grandparents lived,
but the whole of my childhood except
for the first six weeks was spent in or
near Harrow-on-the-Hill, Middlesex,
England.

I can't remember a time when I didn't
draw. My aunts, who were schoolteachers, used to send me half-used exercise
books for drawing paper. These I filled
with pictures of dogs, cats and rows of
little girls. I bent the legs of the little
girls to make them skip or dance. I
thought they looked graceful and pretty,
and very like myself, but nobody ever
noticed the resemblance.

I once took my precious wax crayons
to bed with me. It was a pity we were on
holiday at the time because the sheets
were permanently decorated, and the
landlady of the boarding house didn't
like children much even before that.

When we went on family outings to
the Chiltern Hills I used to collect the
loose lumps of chalk that lay on steeper
slopes. I could carve these into animals
with a pocket knife. I once made a beautiful polar bear but he got badly discol-
ored when the knife slipped, and I still
have the scar.

I decorated all my school textbooks,
which was about the only use I put them
to, and at the age of thirteen I found myself a junior art student at Harrow School
of Art. This was a cheerful system, now
discontinued, whereby we received a
general education in the mornings and
attended art classes in the afternoons.
Our dedicated teacher read plays aloud
to us by the hour—most of Shakespeare,
all of Shaw and Sean O'Casey—and for
the first time my school days were completely happy. After two years thus, we
became full-time art students.

MARGERY GILL

I liked being a student and prolonged
the life by moving on to the Royal College of Art in Kensington, London. I
married when in my second year there.
Our elder daughter was born just weeks
after I graduated and our second three
years later.

I'd always been interested in book illustration and had done the drawings for
a couple of books while I was still a student. Now it seemed to be a job which
I loved doing, could be fitted in with
family life, and added to the family income.

We lived in London for many years,
but now, our daughters are grow up and
married, we have a small cottage in Suf-
folk. I've discovered to my surprise that
I like working in the garden, but I'm
still illustrating books and continue to
find it an exciting job—the only way to
do as I please *and* get paid for it!

———

Margery Gill, who works mainly in
black and white, is today one of the best-
known illustrators for children on either
side of the Atlantic. The list of books she
has illustrated since she began in 1956
is long and impressive, including some of
the favorite titles of the last two decades.

From 1955 to 1963 Miss Gill taught
drawing at Maidstone College of Art but

gave it up when her own illustration work grew too heavy.

She is married to Patrick Jordan, and they have two daughters: Tessa, born in 1948, and Rosalind, born in 1951.

SELECTED WORKS ILLUSTRATED: Dragon Summer, by Ruth M. Arthur, 1963; The Castle of Yew, by L. M. Boston, 1965; Over Sea, Under Stone, by Susan Cooper, 1966; Requiem for a Princess, by Ruth M. Arthur, 1967; What Katy Did, by S. C. Woolsey, 1969; Dawn of Fear, by Susan Cooper, 1970; A Flock of Words, David McKay, ed., 1970; The Little Dark Thorn, by Ruth M. Arthur, 1971; Briar Rose, by the Brothers Grimm, 1972; Talking of Horses, by Monica Dickens, 1974; Jack and the Beanstalk, by Joseph Jacobs, 1975; On the Wasteland, by Ruth M. Arthur, 1975; An Old Magic, by Ruth M. Arthur, 1977.

ABOUT: Kingman, Lee and others, comps. Illustrators of Children's Books: 1957–1966; Ryder, John. Artists of a Certain Line; Junior Bookshelf October 1966.

PAUL GIOVANOPOULOS

November 12, 1939–

ILLUSTRATOR OF *How Many Miles to Babylon*, etc.

Autobiographical sketch of Paul Ciova nopoulous:

I WAS born in Macedonia, Greece, in November of 1939, and I have been an artist for as long as I can remember. My father was a furrier and gave me a thorough training in that business, but World War II interrupted my studies. My father went to France (where my older brother had been born), and it was sixteen years before my family was reunited in the United States.

I was fourteen or fifteen when we moved to Washington Heights in upper Manhattan; it was a very difficult period in my life. I spoke no English whatsoever and although we lived in a totally Greek-speaking community, I still felt like the proverbial stranger in the strange land. The differences between my native land and New York were almost too vast to imagine; being thrust into an English-speaking society was a terribly hard adjustment for a teen-ager to make.

Upon my graduation from George Washington High School I entered New York University's competition for high school artists—and won a two-year scholarship. Although I was still having problems with the language, I continued studying, and when I wasn't studying, I was drawing and painting.

From New York University, I entered the School of Visual Arts and continued to study there for three and a half years. By now I was a full-fledged struggling artist, making a very meager living from the paintings I could sell. I persevered and in 1964 and 1965 won the John Armstrong Chaloner Foundation Fellowship, which permitted me to work and study abroad. I traveled to Spain, Italy and France; while I was in Rome, many of my drawings were sold to Vincent Price. I was finally able to establish a permanent studio in Athens, and my homeland was the inspiration for many of my works of that period.

I came back to New York City and began my career in illustration. In 1968 I illustrated *The Real Tin Flower*, and in 1969, *Free As a Frog*; both volumes were judged among the ten best-illustrated

Giovanopoulos: *JO va NA poo los*

children's books of their respective years by the New York *Times*. I have since illustrated ten other books, and have seen my drawings on the pages of such publications as *Playboy* magazine, *New York Magazine, Fortune, Seventeen, Ladies Home Journal*, the New York *Times*, and *Intellectual Digest*. My works have been shown in many collections, galleries and museums, including the Lacarda Gallery of New York, the National Academy of Design, New York, the Philadelphia Academy of Fine Arts, the Corcoran Gallery in Washington, D.C., and the School of Visual Arts collection.

My horizons have been broadened to include teaching, first at the School of Visual Arts, and presently at Parsons School of Design.

MILTON GLASER

Mr. Giovanopoulos' work is frequently chosen for exhibit at the Society of Illustrators, which awarded him a Gold Medal in 1961. *The Real Tin Flower*, by Aliki Barnstone, was judged one of the ten best-illustrated books of 1968 by the New York *Times*. Mr. Giovanopoulos's illustrations for *Free As a Frog*, by Elizabeth Hodges, achieved the same honor in 1969. *Learning to Say Good-bye*, by Eda LeShan, was judged an American Library Association Notable Book for Children.

SELECTED WORKS ILLUSTRATED: How Many Miles to Babylon, by Paula Fox, 1967; Gallant Women, by Margaret C. Smith and Paul Jeffers, 1968; The Looking-Down Game, by Leigh Dean, 1968; The Real Tin Flower, by Aliki Barnstone, 1968; Free As a Frog, by Elizabeth Hodges, 1969; George and Red, by Elizabeth Coatsworth, 1969; Time for Watching, by Gunilla Norris, 1969; Toto and the Aardvark, by Freda Linde, 1969; Rufus Gideon Grant, by Leigh Dean, 1970; Learning to Say Good-bye, by Eda LeShan, 1976.

ABOUT: Who's Who in the East, Vol. 12; Vol. 13.

MILTON GLASER

June 26, 1929–

ILLUSTRATOR OF *If Apples Had Teeth*, etc.

Biographical sketch of Milton Glaser:

MILTON GLASER was born in New York City and grew up in the Bronx. "The only thing I ever wanted to be was an artist—I was always drawing, drawing, drawing," he told an interviewer. When he was four years old, he recalled, a cousin asked him if he wanted to see a pigeon and then drew one for him on a brown paper bag. "That was a miracle for me," said Glaser, and the beginning of his ambition. His family encouraged him, but he has said that he probably would not have become an artist if he had not been confined by a long illness when he was ten years old.

Glaser attended the High School of Music and Art in New York City, then went on to Cooper Union Art School, graduating in 1951. A Fulbright Scholarship took him to Italy to study etching with Giorgio Morandi at the Academy of Fine Arts in Bologna. He has characterized the experience as "crucial to [his] development." In 1958 he returned to Italy, this time to Rome, where he studied lithography for eight months. With him was his wife, the former Shirley Girton, whom he had married on August 13, 1957.

In 1954, with Seymour Chwast, Glaser had formed the Push Pin Studios, a design studio that quickly gained a reputation for innovative approaches in all

phases of visual communication. Celebrated in magazines devoted to the interests of the field such as *Graphis, Print*
and *Gebrauchsgraphik,* the studio and its
principals also received attention in more
general publications like *Time* and
Newsweek. In 1970 the Louvre's Museé
des Arts Decoratifs honored Push Pin
with a two-months' retrospective show,
the first the Louvre had ever mounted
devoted to the work of a commercial design studio. Later the show tourned major European cities and went to Tokyo
and São Paulo.

While Push Pin's success was shared
with the other artists associated with it,
the variety and flexibility of the studio's
approach to graphic problems reflect the
eclecticism of Glaser himself, who was
termed by one admiring critic the "guru
of Push Pin." Certainly it has been Glaser
who has consistently articulated the doc-
trine of variety, which he practices in
life as in his work. "The whole issue is not
to limit yourself," he has said. He tries to
"disrupt expectation," remaining unclas-
sified and free to try whatever solution
seems the most effective. As one critic
wrote, Glaser is "essentially pragmatic in
his approach—i.e., each problem is seen
as constituting its own body of truths and
in consequence every graphic product
must in some way surpass or modify a
previous achievement and if possible
bring forth a new strain of visual language."

Graphically Glaser has concerned himself with advertising, book and magazine
illustrating and design, murals, architectural design and children's toys. Children's book illustration has occupied a
small corner of his attention, proportion-
ately, but he has applied his same standard to his children's books. They have
been consistently included in the Children's Book Shows of the American Institute of Graphic Arts. One, *Rimes de
la Mère Oie,* a French translation of
Mother Goose, on which he shared the
design and illustration with Seymour
Chwast and Barry Zaid, was also chosen
for the AIGA's Fifty Books Show in 1971.
Help, Help the Globolinks was one of

the New York *Times*' choices for best-
illustrated book of the year in 1970. *Cats
and Bats and Things With Wings* received an award for excellence from the
Society of Illustrators and in 1973 earned
a Brooklyn Art Books for Children citation. Not surprisingly, Glaser has strong,
articulate opinions about the art in children's books. In an interview he deplored
what he considered the ordinariness of
children's books today, scoring publishers for not producing books that change
sensibilities, that show "imagination,
flair, an attempt for excellence." He saw
a trend toward simplifying—possibly an
effect of television, he felt—that over-
looks the fact that books are not a one-
time experience but can be returned to
again and again. Consequently they can
afford to be rich, "denser, subtler, more
generalized than a work that has been
experienced within a defined time frame-
work." As a child he himself "loved dealing with books I didn't thoroughly understand, with a world slightly beyond
my grasp. What I want is something very
literal—a specific body of clear technical
information—and simultaneously some
essential mystery that offers the possibilities of looking at phenomena in a variety
of ways."

In 1975 Glaser severed his twenty-
year partnership in Push Pin Studios,
explaining that "it had too much history." Until 1977 he remained art director and chairman of the board of *New
York Magazine* and art director of *Village Voice.* He teaches at the School of
Visual Arts in New York City. He is coauthor of *The Underground Gourmet,*
a guide to inexpensive good eating in
New York and in 1976 designed and illustrated *The Cook's Catalogue,* a com-
pendium of cooking utensils from all
over the world. In 1975 the design department of the Museum of Modern Art
mounted a show that included some
fifty of his works.

Glaser has received an impressive
number of awards: the Philadelphia
Museum Medal, the Art Directors Club
Gold Medal, the Society of Illustrators
Gold Medal, the St. Gaudens Medal for

Outstanding Achievement from Cooper Union, and the American Institute of Graphic Arts Medallist Award. He is a member of the Alliance Graphique International.

SELECTED WORKS ILLUSTRATED: The Smallest Elephant in the World, by Alvin Tresselt, 1959; If Apples Had Teeth, with Shirley Glaser, 1960; Cats and Bats and Things With Wings, by Conrad Aiken, 1965; Fierce and Gentle Warriors, by Mikhail Sholokhov, 1967; Help, Help the Globolinks, by Gian-Carlo Menotti, 1970; Rimes de la Mère Oie, translated by Ormonde de Kay, Jr., 1971.

ABOUT: Contemporary Authors, Vol. 17–18; Kingman, Lee and others, comps. Illustrators of Children's Books: 1957–1966; Penrose Graphic Arts International, 1975; American Artist September 1958; Art and Artists September 1970; Art News September 1975; Gebrauchsgraphik May 1964; Graphis No. 92, 1960; No. 168, 1973–74; New York Times Book Review May 6, 1973; Print March 1968; January 1969; November 1973; Publishers Weekly May 11, 1972; Wilson Library Bulletin November 1961.

Paul Goble.

PAUL GOBLE

September 27, 1933–

AUTHOR AND ILLUSTRATOR OF *Red Hawk's Account of Custer's Last Battle*, etc.

Autobiographical sketch of Paul Goble, who writes in collaboration with his wife, Dorothy Goble:

THE creative world of make-believe seems most memorable from my childhood days. When looking for birds and animals in the woods and hills of Surrey, I lived every chapter of Ernest Thompson Seton, Grey Owl, and *Hiawatha* which my mother had read to me. When the family went digging for Stone Age flint implements, I used to like to imagine that the people who made them were probably just like Indians. And then I think most of my early pictures were of Indians; never fighting in the cowboy-and-Indian sense because I hated cowboys. My Indians had a romance and nobility above fighting. This interest grew with scrapbooks made up of pictures cut from books and magazines until one Christmas I received the two volumes of the original edition of George Catlin's *Letters and Notes on the North American Indians*. It was the beginning of serious study which still continues.

I was twelve when my parents moved their harpsichord-making workshops to Oxford. There I went to public school; boarded during the week and was free to bicycle home to enjoy the country at the weekends. School was followed by two years' military service in Germany where I spent my time in shooting competitions for the regiment—my expertise resented by some old soldiers—and horse-riding when and where I chose in the beautiful Hartz Mountains.

I went to art school when I was twenty-three. It was at the Central School of Arts and Crafts in London that I met my wife Dorothy. Upon completing my design studies I spent the summer of 1959 fulfilling my dreams visiting the Indians. I was given a name and adopted into the Yakima tribe by Chief Alba Shawaway, and later another name by Chief Edgar Red Cloud, great-grandson of the famous war chief.

The following year I was appointed a visiting lecturer in the industrial design

department at the Central School. My
wife and I ran our own design practice
for ten years and during that time we
won prizes in three industrial design
competitions. But gradually the teaching commitment grew in time and interest until today I am senior lecturer
in three-dimensional design at Ravens-
bourne College of Art and Design in
south London. Having had considerable
industrial experience, I feel able to bring
some (not too much) reality to teaching
in an art college atmosphere.

In the mid 1960s, books about Indians,
for my two children were hard to find.
Those I found were mostly misleading
and so also were the majority of western
films. I think it was a dreadful American
TV serial glorifying General Custer that
finally made me want to tell a few facts:
*Red Hawk's Account of Custer's Last
Battle* was the outcome, a joint effort between my wife and me. We dedicated it
to our son.

He and I spent the summer of 1972 in
Montana, Wyoming and South Dakota.
He was only ten years old but quickly
became a seasoned camper in the national parks and forests and on the reservations. I renewed old acquaintances
and we made new friends.

As a teacher, holidays give me time to
paint and lately to write. I have been
fortunate to meet kind publishers who
have let me do as I like. Industrial design does not allow much scope for one's
own likes and dislikes; it is largely concerned with reconciling conflicting view-
points. Therein lies the satisfaction,
more than in the final result. I find that
I enjoy seeing a small book on a shelf
more than a range of furniture in the
shops.

———

In the covering letter with his sketch,
Paul Goble writes further: "I have to
admit . . . that I hardly think about
children. I never liked children's books.
I found most of them unreal. Beatrix
Potter lasted for years because I loved
the Lake District and knew how real her
stories were. And then I have always

had rather a one-track mind on Indians
—and who bothered in those days to
write books on Indians? If I am honest
I think that I would only have liked my
own books as a child for the reason that
it would have been easy to copy the
style of the childlike drawings."

Each of Paul Goble's books has been
included on the various critical lists of
outstanding books that are compiled
yearly. *Red Hawk's Account of Custer's
Last Battle* was an American Library
Association Notable Book of 1970, as
was *The Sound of Flutes* in 1976.

Dorothy Goble's part in the books
being primarily that of adviser and en-
courager, she did not feel that she war-
ranted a sketch, despite her husband's
wish to share the credit of authorship.

SELECTED WORKS WRITTEN AND ILLUS-
TRATED: Red Hawk's Account of Custer's
Last Battle, 1969; Brave Eagle's Account of
the Fetterman Fight, 1972; Lone Bull's
Horse Raid, 1973; The Friendly Wolf,
1975.

SELECTED WORKS ILLUSTRATED: The
Sound of Flutes: And Other Indian Leg-
ends, transcribed and edited by Richard
Erdoes, 1976.

M. B. GOFFSTEIN
December 20, 1940–

AUTHOR AND ILLUSTRATOR OF *Goldie the
Dollmaker*, etc.

Autobiographical sketch of Marilyn
   Brooke Goffstein Schaaf, who writes
   and illustrates under the name M. B.
   Goffstein:

MY father, an electronics manufacturer,
hummed at the dinner table after every
meal I can remember, sometimes breaking into an impassioned whistle, always
with a warm but distant look in his eye.
He was thinking about his business.

My mother was going to college, and
my little brother and I grew up in St.
Paul, Minnesota, feeling that work was
the only real dignity, the only real happiness, and that people were nothing if

M. 13. goffstein

their lives were not dedicated. My choice was art—a talent which shows up early.

When I went away to Bennington College in Vermont, at seventeen, my "dedication" to my art saved me. Understanding nothing, at first, of the sophisticated talk around me, I stayed at my desk and drew. I made tiny, detailed pictures in pen and india ink: people floating through the air, resting on tree tops, standing in alarm on the backs of strange animals.

I signed up for fiction writing in order to get assigned reading I would like and began to write short stories, which became more and more condensed. Then I went on to study poetry.

By the time I was graduated from Bennington in 1962, I had put in a good apprenticeship. I had worked for printers in New York, during two winter work terms, and had one-woman showings of my drawings and watercolors in New York, St. Paul, and Bennington. I had even carved some small wooden figures and a large cherry log in preparation for writing *Goldie the Dollmaker*, one day.

I worked selling children's books in two stores, and showed my drawings to every publisher in New York, trying to get a job illustrating. Many editors liked my work, and one even bought a picture, but there didn't seem to be any book for me to illustrate.

Several times it was suggested that I write my own book, and I felt ready to do it—to take the responsibility for the meaning of my work, to know what I wanted to say, and to make it clear to others. This, combined with the picture book form, is my discipline, and I feel lucky to have it, because it is hard and flexible enough to last a lifetime.

I married Peter Schaaf, a photographer and concert pianist, in August 1965, and my first book, *The Gats*, came out the following March. So right from the start, an important part of our marriage has been the production of my books. My husband, with his fine sense of design and mechanical ability, is always ready to help.

One of the main things I have tried to show in my books is the beauty and dignity of a life of hard work to make something good, that you believe in.

———

The Gats! was an Honor Book in the *Book Week* Children's Spring Book Festival in 1966. *Sleepy People* and *Across the Sea* were in the American Institute of Graphic Arts' Children's Book Exhibits in 1965–66 and 1967–68 respectively. *Goldie the Dollmaker* was nominated for the Dorothy Canfield Fisher Award in 1970. *Fish for Supper* was both an American Library Association Notable Book for Children and a Caldecott Honor Book for 1976.

SELECTED WORKS WRITTEN AND ILLUSTRATED: The Gats!, 1966; Sleepy People, 1966; Brookie and Her Lamb, 1967; Across the Sea, 1968; Goldie the Dollmaker, 1969; Two Piano Tuners, 1970; The Underside of the Leaf, 1972; A Little Schubert, 1972; Me and My Captain, 1974; Daisy Summerfield's Style, 1975; My Crazy Sister, 1975; Fish for Supper, 1976.

ABOUT: Contemporary Authors, Vol. 21–22; Something about the Author, Vol. 8; Who's Who of American Women, 1974–1975.

ROBERT CONROY GOLDSTON

July 9, 1927–

AUTHOR OF *The Negro Revolution*, etc.

Autobiographical sketch of Robert Conroy Goldston, who has also written under the names Robert Conroy and "James Stark":

I WAS born on Manhattan Island and spent my early childhood on the run between New York, Chicago and Los Angeles. I have fonder memories of the Pennsylvania Turnpike, of the old Lincoln Highway (Route 66), of truck stops and roadside diners, of Last Chance filling stations than I do of any of the city neighborhoods in which my family found temporary refuge. Pursued by enraged landlords and collection agencies, my father (a traveling salesman) kept turning corners hoping to bump into prosperity. Perhaps because of this I have never thought of myself as having been born or raised in geography—but rather in time. I came into the world on the cutting edge of the Great Depression and grew up during the Roosevelt decades. I had almost all the experiences proper to those years: abject poverty; a Little Orphan Annie mug; fervent belief in the New Deal; anguished suspense between episodes of "The Lone Ranger"; a newspaper route and, later, work in a printing plant to help pay my way through a private school in Woodstock, Illinois; collecting pennies for the Spanish Republic—all of it, including, at last, two years with the army in France and Germany.

After the war I returned to New York where I spent several years attending Columbia University. Along with a handful of other students I was a political activist at Columbia in the lonely years (the late forties) before that role became popular. One of my fondest memories is marching in the last May Day Parade ever held in New York City, in 1949: "One, two, three, four! We don't want another war!" How quaint it all seems now.

Since the age of sixteen I had "known" I would one day write, but it seemed natural for an ex-printer's devil to get into publishing through the back door as a production assistant, typographer, book designer and, finally, art director (I flattered myself that I was one of the very few in the industry who could actually set type by hand, run an intertype, manage a press, etc.). I worked in various of these capacities for Oxford University Press, Henry Schuman, Inc., and Henry Holt & Co. from 1948 to 1955.

In 1952 I married a beautiful, elusive, redheaded Greenwich Village neighbor named Marguerite Garvey, with whom I now have, at last count, six children. My escape from Madison Avenue prosperity to the semipoverty of free-lance writing was made at her insistence. Accordingly, in 1955 I signed up for unemployment insurance and began writing the Great American Novel. Eventually I published four Great American Novels, some of which won critical acclaim, one of which helped me get a Guggenheim Fellowship in 1958, and none of which earned much money. But that didn't matter very much since we had fled the economic pressure of New York for the then unspoiled and amazingly cheap life of the Balearic Islands in 1956. Since then (with years out for good behavior in England, New England and Mallorca) the Spanish Mediterranean island of Ibiza has been our home.

I started writing for children as my own children began to read—Spanish and French legends first, history later. Studying history had always been a favorite pastime, but it was not until I saw the kind of indigestible, frequently misleading and usually irrelevant history materials provided for my own children by international schools in Mallorca and England and public schools in Vermont that I felt absolutely compelled to try to provide something better. Since then I have written some thirty-five "supplementary" history texts and taught both American and European history myself. I suppose one of my prime motives has been an urge to pass on to my children and others, not simply the truth, but also the feel and urgency of the troubled decades of my own youth. I write for my (largely) high school and college student audience as I would for adults—pulling no punches, making no historical or verbal concessions. Their eager—and adult—response has been reward enough.

Robert Goldston's books have frequently been included on the various critics' lists of the best of the year, and *The Negro Revolution* was an American Library Association Notable Book in 1968. Goldston held a Guggenheim Fellowship in fiction in 1957–58. Besides more than twenty-five books for young people and four adult novels, he has written for television, for the Canadian Broadcasting System.

Goldston lists his avocations as plumbing, birdwatching, hiking and mountain climbing. His children are Rebecca, Gabrielle, Sarah, Francesca, Maximilian, and Theresa.

SELECTED WORKS: The Legend of the Cid, 1963; Song of Roland (with Marguerite Goldston), 1965; The Civil War in Spain, 1966; The Russian Revolution, 1966; The Life and Death of Nazi Germany, 1967; The Rise of Red China, 1967; The Negro Revolution, 1968; The Vietnamese Revolution, 1972; The Death of Gandhi, 1973; The American Nightmare: Senator Joseph R. McCarthy and the Politics of Hate, 1973; The American War of National Liberation, 1763–1783, 1976.

ABOUT: Author's and Writer's Who's Who, 1971; Contemporary Authors, Vol. 17–18; Something about the Author, Vol. 6; Who's Who in America, 1972–73.

JOHN S. GOODALL
June 7, 1908–

AUTHOR AND ILLUSTRATOR OF *The Adventures of Paddy Pork*, etc.

Autobiographical sketch of John Strickland Goodall:

I WAS born in the small village of Heacham, Norfolk, England, where my family had a country house. My father was Joseph Strickland Goodall, M.B., F.R.C.S. Ed., M.R.C.P., who was the first physician in England to specialize in diseases of the heart. He lived in Harley Street, and my family has been connected with the medical profession for seven generations. He was therefore very puzzled when his only son showed no interest, inclination or ability to do anything but draw and paint. So, after leaving Harrow, the few specimens of my work which were available were shown to three of his friends who, in his opinion, were most suitable to advise me in what I should do next. Sir Arthur Cope, R.A., K.C.V.O. (the eminent Edwardian portrait painter), kindly said I could work in his studio. Sir Leister Harmsworth suggested I should learn the process of printing in one of his printing works in case I took up illustrating or advertising. I really do not know what Viscount St. Cyres, the third of this distinguished company, had to offer but I do know that he, and particularly Lady St. Cyres, were wonderfully kind in introducing me to relations and friends who were brave enough to allow me to paint them.

But first I was sent as a private pupil to John Watson Nicol, who was the brother-in-law of Sir Arthur Cope, and with whom he had run an art school in South Kensington at the beginning of the century. It was while I was working with him that I first met his granddaughter Margaret who in 1933 was to become my wife.

After a year I was moved (still as a private pupil) to Mr. Harold Speed's studio where I learned to paint in oils. After another year I went to the Royal Academy School of Art where I was a student for four years.

On leaving, in order to earn a living (as by this time I was engaged to Margaret Nicol, who had joined me at the R.A. School), I commenced illustrating —and owing to my almost Victorian training, usually period subjects—for the *Radio Times*, and for various books and magazines as well as advertising.

In 1939, as I was in the Territorial Army, I was called up at the beginning of the war and for most of its duration I was serving in the Far East and in India. On one of my leaves, in the Kulu Valley, I started painting landscapes in watercolour for the first time. I held successful exhibitions of these in Delhi and Calcutta and on my return to England was asked by a mutual friend to paint

H.R.H. Princess Marina, Duchess of Kent, and her family at Coppins. This was the first of several "Conversation Pieces" which I painted with a mixture of watercolour and gouache, a medium I have found most satisfactory ever since.

I continued illustrating other people's books and painting landscape when on holiday until I decided to do a book of my own for our granddaughter Lavinia, the child of our only daughter Sarah. *The Adventures of Paddy Pork* was the first of a successful series which are published in England by Macmillan and in America by Harcourt, Brace Jovanovich, Inc., and now by Atheneum Publishers.

Recently, too, I have held exhibitions of "Victorian Pastiche," gouache paintings inspired no doubt by my early training, and have exhibited both in London and in America.

We live now in a secluded cottage in Wiltshire, one of the most beautiful counties in England, where I have a studio in the garden.

———

John Goodall had illustrated books by many other authors before he devised the first of the little wordless books that have so fascinated children and adults alike. Alternate half and full pages, filled with detail, move the usually melodramatic stories along so that the reader is scarcely conscious that no words are being used. The first of these, *The Adventures of Paddy Pork*, won the Boston *Globe-Horn Book* Award for excellence in illustration in 1969, and was an American Library Association Notable Book in the same year. In 1973 *The Midnight Adventures of Kelly, Dot, and Esmeralda* was an Honor Book in the picture book category in the *Book World* Children's Spring Book Festival. Several of Goodall's books have been selected for inclusion in the Children's Book Showcase: *Paddy's Evening Out* in 1974, *Creepy Castle* in 1976, and *Paddy Pork's Holiday* in 1977.

Goodall's work has been represented in the American Institute of Graphic

Arts Shows in 1967–68 and again in 1971–72. He has also exhibited in London, Paris, India and America, and his work hangs in many private collections, including H.R.H. Prince Philip's. He is a member of the Royal Institute of Water Colour Painters, the Royal Society of British Artists, the National Society of British Artists, and is also a Freeman of the City of London.

SELECTED WORKS WRITTEN AND ILLUSTRATED: The Adventures of Paddy Pork, 1968; The Ballooning Adventures of Paddy Pork, 1969; Shrewbettina's Birthday, 1971; Jacko, 1972; The Midnight Adventures of Kelly, Dot, and Esmeralda, 1972; Paddy's Evening Out, 1973; Naughty Nancy, 1975; Creepy Castle, 1975; An Edwardian Summer, 1976; Paddy Pork's Holiday, 1976; The Surprise Picnic, 1977.

ABOUT: Contemporary Authors, Vol. 33–36; Something about the Author, Vol. 4; Viguers, Ruth Hill and others, comps. Illustrators of Children's Books: 1946–1956.

EDWARD GOREY

EDWARD GOREY

February 22, 1925–

ILLUSTRATOR OF *The Shrinking of Treehorn*, etc.

Biographical sketch of Edward St. John Gorey:

EDWARD ST. JOHN GOREY was born in Chicago on February 22, 1925, the son of Edward Lee Gorey, a journalist for the Hearst newspapers, and Helen Garvey Gorey. Gorey's parents were divorced when he was eleven; they remarried sixteen years later. Gorey's interest in drawing showed when he was a very young child. His work appeared in school publications while he was growing up, but his only formal art training was occasional attendance at classes at the Chicago Art Institute.

From June 1944 to February 1946 Gorey served in the United States Army.

He then went to Harvard, where he majored in French. After graduating in 1950 he remained in Boston for three years, supporting himself with a variety of jobs including book-jacket design and working in a bookstore. He was also involved with F. R. Lang's Poet's Theater. Gorey has always considered himself a writer rather than an artist, and during this period he was trying to get a novel going, but none of his beginnings was ever completed. In 1953 he moved to New York, where he still lives for part of the year. For a while he worked in the art department at Doubleday. That same year his first book, *The Unstrung Harp; or, Mr. Earbrass Writes a Novel* was published and was followed a year later by *The Listing Attic*, a collection of illustrated limericks. In 1957 came *The Doubtful Guest* and *The Object Lesson*. While Gorey had begun to develop a small but loyal group of admirers, he received no critical notice until Edmund Wilson published a review of his work in the *New Yorker* in December 1959. Later the article was included in Wilson's *The Bit Between My Teeth*. Wilson, who admired Gorey's drawings, felt that his little books of scant text illustrated by macabre drawings had the same kind of appeal as works by Aubrey Beardsley and Max Beerbohm.

Gorey has published a number of collections of his drawings, both with and without text, many of them under his own imprint, The Fantod Press, so named because fantod is a Victorian word for heebie-jeebies. Since 1964 he has illustrated books for children as well as adults, including Edward Lear's *The Dong With a Luminous Nose* and *The Jumblies*. His drawings have appeared in *Esquire, Playboy*, and *Evergreen* magazines and as cartoons in the New York *Times*. An anthology of fifteen of his early little books, published in 1972 under the title of *Amphigorey*, was extremely successful in this country and in Europe, where Gorey's work appears in German, Italian, Dutch and Swedish editions. The title *Amphigorey* is typical of the puns and anagrams on his own name that are a hallmark of Gorey productions. An amphigory is a nonsense verse or composition which appears to have meaning and turns out not to have. Gorey has written under a number of pseudonyms, some of the most colorful of which are "Eduard Blütig," "Mrs. Regera Dowdy," "Redway Grode," "Ogdred Weary," and "Dreary Wodge."

Edward Gorey is a music and ballet enthusiast, but he has a special passion for the New York City Ballet. He has attended almost every performance given in New York since 1956, with his greatest enthusiasm reserved for works choreographed by George Balanchine. Says Gorey, "Virtually my life is arranged around the New York City Ballet. I leave New York to work at Cape Cod the day after the season closes and I arrive back the day before it opens." A tall, bearded man, he usually wears a fur coat and sneakers to the ballet, and a photograph of him in this distinctive costume has accompanied articles on Gorey and the ballet which appeared in the New York *Times* and in *Playbill* magazine. His book *The Lavender Leotard* is a tribute to the New York City Ballet.

Gorey's books have become collector's items for a coterie of admirers. The distinctive style and highly individual humor that go to make up what Edmund Wilson called "a whole little personal world, equally amusing and somber, nostalgic and claustrophobic, at the same time poetic and poisoned," are used to great effect in Gorey's books for children. His precise pen-and-ink drawings with their telling details frequently establish the mood of the story and sometimes add his own comment in a way that intrigues young readers. He can range from the delicate charm of his watercolor and pen-and-ink pictures for *Sam and Emma*, a delightful story by Donald Nelsen about the friendship between a dog and a cat, to the starkness of the illustrations for Florence Parry Heide's *The Shrinking of Treehorn* and the grisly but never overstated details of *Red Riding Hood* (retold by Beatrice Schenk de Regniers), the version in which the wolf swallows Little Red Riding Hood. *The Shrinking of Treehorn* is doubtless the best known of Gorey's books for children. The story of a little boy who shrinks day by day instead of growing has garnered a number of honors and awards, among them listing as an American Library Association Notable Book, a New York *Times* best illustrated book of 1971, inclusion in the Fifty Books Exhibit and in the Children's Book Show, 1971–72, mounted by the American Institute of Graphic Arts, and selection for the 1972 Children's Book Showcase. The Swiss edition, entitled *Schorschi Schrumpft*, was awarded the prize for the best picture book at the Bologna Children's Book Fair in 1977.

Edward Gorey lives in a small apartment in Manhattan with thousands of books and five cats named Agrippina, Kanzuke, Kokidan, Murasaki and Fujitsubo, the last four names being derived from Lady Murasaki's *The Tale of Genji*, which is one of Gorey's favorite books. His summers are spent on Cape Cod, in the town of Barnstable, where he has an aunt and cousins. He lives in the attic of their house and does the cooking and chauffeuring for the family. Besides book illustration and drawing for magazines, Gorey creates jackets, posters, magazine illustrations and theater scenery.

When a reviewer once asked him why his work is so apt to focus on violence and horror, Gorey replied simply, "I write about everyday life."

SELECTED WORKS WRITTEN AND ILLUS-TRATED: Fletcher and Zenobia (with Victoria Chess), 1967; Why We Have Day and Night (with Peter F. Neumeyer), 1970.

SELECTED WORKS ILLUSTRATED: You Know Who, by John Ciardi, 1964; The Very Fine Clock, by Muriel Spark, 1968; The Jumblies, by Edward Lear, 1968; The Dong With a Luminous Nose, by Edward Lear, 1969; Someone Could Win a Polar Bear, by John Ciardi, 1970; Sam and Emma, by Donald Nelsen, 1971; The Shrinking of Treehorn, by Florence Parry Heide, 1971; Red Riding Hood, adapted by B. S. De Regniers, 1972; Rumpelstiltskin, adapted by E. Tarcov, 1974.

ABOUT: Contemporary Authors, Vol. 7–8; Kingman, Lee and others, comps. Illustrators of Children's Books: 1957–1966; Wilson, Edmund. The Bit Between My Teeth; American Book Collector May 1974; Current Biography November 1976; Esquire June 1974; New Republic November 26, 1966; New Statesman November 3, 1967; New York State Theater Magazine May 1973; New York Times May 7, 1961; November 13, 1973; New York Times Book Review May 7, 1961.

CONSTANCE C. GREENE

October 27, 1924–

AUTHOR OF A Girl Called Al, etc.

Autobiographical sketch of Constance Clarke Greene:

I WAS born in Brooklyn, brought up in Larchmont, New York, and have nothing but the happiest memories of my childhood. My father, mother and grandfather were all newspaper people, and from the earliest time, that was what I wanted to be too. Books were very much a part of our life style and the local library a second home. My family moved to New

York City when I was fifteen, where I attended Marymount School and then Skidmore College. After two years of college, I dropped out, as the euphemism goes, and got a job at the Associated Press due to the extreme shortage of young men, this being 1944. It was a marvelous, wonderful job which paid $16.50 a week, but I had realized my ambition to be a writer and a newspaperwoman. After two years at the AP, I married and had five children, one right after the other. When I sold my first book in 1968, my daughter Philippa, then in college, said, "Why didn't you do this ten years ago, Mom?"

My answer was "I would've if I could've." There was too much activity, too many little bodies under foot. I'm grateful to my children for many things, not the least of which is the fact that from them came a great many of my ideas for books. As my father said, I milked them. Why not? They didn't mind and often argue about what character in a book is modeled after which child.

After having lived in Connecticut for seventeen years, my husband and I have moved to a farm in Maine. We have a horse, two dogs and quite a few cats. I would very much like to write a book about Maine but I feel I must learn more about the state before I attempt putting anything down on paper.

Probably the most exciting day in my life came when I got word that Viking had bought *A Girl Called Al*, my first book. I shall never forget the sense of triumph and elation and just sheer pleasure that at last I had written a book that someone actually thought enough of to publish. And each time some child writes to tell me how much he or she enjoyed something I've written, I get the feeling all over again.

A Girl Called Al was a runner-up in the *Book World* Spring Book Festival in 1969 and was also an American Library Association Notable Book that same year. *Beat the Turtle Drum* was an American Library Association Notable Book of 1976.

SELECTED WORKS: A Girl Called Al, 1969; Leo the Lioness, 1970; The Good Luck Bogie Hat, 1971; The Unmaking of Rabbit, 1972; Isabelle the Itch, 1973; The Ears of Louis, 1974; I Know You, Al, 1975; Beat the Turtle Drum, 1976; Getting No-where, 1977.

ABOUT: Contemporary Authors, Vol. 61–64.

TED GREENWOOD

December 4, 1930–

ILLUSTRATOR OF *Sly Old Wardrobe*, etc.

Autobiographical sketch of Edward Alister Greenwood, who writes and illustrates as Ted Greenwood:

BORN the third and last child to a couple struggling as so many others struggled during the Great Depression, I must have been a somewhat mixed blessing. Yet, despite this, my childhood was rich and varied, brought about mainly by contact with any number of unusual adults. At thirteen I didn't think it very odd to be handed by my grandfather a copy of *The Socialist Sixth of the World*,

a glowing account of life in the Soviet Union, and then be expected to discuss it with him not long after. He himself was a frustrated artist and musician, intensely concerned with the injustices of social systems which, by the nature of their structures, limit human potential. Both my mother and my father were products of a time in this country when opportunities for "risk" occupations were more limited than now. Each would have followed a different occupation if they had been born in my time. They made sure that we children were free to follow our own particular stars, even if these journeys carried the risk of disaster.

Humor and optimism were qualities in my father which most influenced me, although, like everyone else, I have my moments of despair. He was an excellent oral reader and actor, never losing an opportunity to "play" with words. He delighted in a Victorian flowery turn of phrase, but he also had a special affection for the Australian vernacular of the post-World War I period, particularly the exaggerated forms in *The Sentimental Bloke* by C. J. Dennis, which was ideal material for oral reading with a broad Australian accent.

Many such backgrounds have influenced children to value books. For my grandfather, books were the key to the education of the working class. For my father, books were a vehicle of escape into a world of eccentric characters which literature so often portrays. For my mother, books were for self-improvement and the exploration of one's belief. Couple this background with a long period of illness as a thirteen- and fourteen-year-old when I spent most of my time reading or inventing elaborate indoor games, and my interest in the book was cemented. I later added an interest in drama as a form of expression, but my belief in the book as a unique window of communication between two people remains strong.

To make books for young people is to be an optimist, and that is sometimes difficult in a world torn apart. In contrast to drama, the indirect nature of the book as an agent is both its strength and its drawback—it is like throwing seeds to the wind, but, as in the parable, you hope for one to fall on fertile ground. If the wavelengths of the author and reader happen to coincide, then hopefully the moment will be magic.

Ted Greenwood trained as a primary schoolteacher and taught from 1948 until 1956, when he became a lecturer in art education at Melbourne (Australia) Teacher's College. He took a diploma in art from the Royal Melbourne Institute of Technology in 1959. In 1968 he gave up teaching to write, illustrate and paint. His first book, *Sly Old Wardrobe* by Ivan Southall, won the Picture Book of the Year Award of the Children's Book Council of Australia in 1968. The first book he wrote as well as illustrated, *Obstreperous*, was commended by the Council in 1969, as were his illustrations for *Joseph and Lulu and the Prindiville House Pigeons*, which he also wrote, in 1973. Mr. Greenwood received Australian Book Publishers' Design Awards in 1970 and 1973, and in 1974 was on the Honor List for the Hans Christian Andersen Award with *Joseph and Lulu and the Prindiville House Pigeons* which has

not yet been published in the United States.

SELECTED WORKS WRITTEN AND ILLUSTRATED: Obstreperous, 1970.

SELECTED WORKS ILLUSTRATED: Sly Old Wardrobe, by Ivan Southall, 1969.

ABOUT: Contemporary Authors, Vol. 29–32.

HELEN GRIFFITHS
May 8, 1939–

AUTHOR OF *The Wild Horse of Santander*, etc.

Autobiographical sketch of Helen Griffiths Santos:

I WAS born in London just before the start of the Second World War so that, at an early age, I was evacuated to the north of England to a small, industrial town near the Brontë country. I imagine that my love of the country and of animals springs from those early days when I spent a very free and happy childhood wandering round the local farms and across the moors, as well as keeping all kinds of pets at home.

When I was eleven I moved back to London. I planned on a secretarial career, although my heart was set on farming. However, my secretarial training stood me in good stead for the books I was to write later, and the short farming experience I gained when I was sixteen gave me a great insight into animal mentality, so that I don't think it was chance alone that led me to having a book accepted at an early age. I had really learned something.

It was chance, however, that got me interested in Argentina—the present of a book called *Tschiffely's Ride*. From then on I read every book I could lay my hands on that dealt with Argentina, and I began to learn Spanish with the idea of preparing myself to visit that country when I had saved enough money for my passage there.

I didn't get to Argentina. My eagerness to learn Spanish brought me into contact

HELEN GRIFFITHS

with a Spaniard who was in London learning English. For a year we exchanged lessons, and fell in love and married. By then I had three books published, and the letter from my publisher accepting the fourth arrived while I was in hospital having my first baby. I was just twenty-one.

My husband was in the hotel business and as he progressed in his career we had to move frequently from place to place—Lausanne, Madrid, Mallorca, London. We saw lots of places, met lots of people, had two more daughters, and I still found time to write books. We collected and parted with numerous animals on the way—cats, rabbits, sparrows, dogs—because for some reason or another I can never be anywhere for very long without having some furred or feathered creature about the house; and my husband seemed to catch the habit, for one day he came home with a parrot which had flown in through his office window.

I wrote a book about our cats—*Moshie Cat*—and another story about a stray dog who is now a member of the family. Most of my stories have factual backgrounds, and I try to make them as genuine as possible, even at the risk of sometimes making my readers unhappy.

Many children send me letters asking me to write sequels to my stories but I never do as, in my own experience, I have never found a sequel that lives up to the expectations produced by the original story. I like to leave the "What happened next?" to my readers' imaginations.

———

The Wild Horse of Santander was commended for England's Carnegie Medal in 1967.

Helen Griffiths married Pedros Santos de la Cal in 1959. They had three daughters: Elena, born in 1960, Cristina, born in 1962, and Sara, born in 1966. Since her husband's death in 1973, Helen Griffiths has continued to live in Madrid.

SELECTED WORKS: The Greyhound, 1966; The Wild Horse of Santander, 1967; Leon, 1968; Moshie Cat, 1970; Stallion of the Sands, 1970; Russian Blue, 1973; Just a Dog, 1975; The Mysterious Appearance of Agnes, 1975; Running Wild, 1977.

ABOUT: Contemporary Authors, Vol. 19–20; Something about the Author, Vol. 5.

JAAP TER HAAR

March 25, 1922–

AUTHOR OF *Boris*, etc.

Biographical sketch of Jaap ter Haar:

JAAP TER HAAR was born in Hilversum, Holland, where he still lives, with his wife, the former Rudi Schurink. Ter Haar had always wanted to be a writer, but he was not a particularly good student in school and was afraid he would not be able to fulfill his ambition. He was just finishing high school when the Germans overran Holland in 1940; after working in an office for two months, ter Haar had to go into hiding to escape conscription. He attempted to flee to England but instead was stranded in France. Eventually he joined the Resistance.

In May 1945 ter Haar enlisted in the Royal Netherlands Marines and served as a correspondent in Scotland, the United States, Malacca and Indonesia.

Jaap ter Haar: YAAP ter HAHR

JAAP TER HAAR

After two years he received a medical discharge and went to work with the Dutch Radio Overseas Service, preparing foreign language programs for radio stations abroad. He wrote short stories in his spare time and in 1953 began a radio play, "Saskia and Jeroen," about his own twins, which developed into a series of ten children's books. The books enabled Jaap ter Haar to give up his broadcasting job in 1954, and he has been a full-time writer ever since. "For me," he has said, "writing is not so much a gift as a profession. The harder you work at it, the better you learn your trade. (I probably work harder than most people in offices.)" Ter Haar's biggest problem, he says, is getting started. He rewrites the first chapter a number of times—maybe twenty or thirty—until he feels completely at home with his characters who then are apt to take over and carry the book to its conclusion.

Ter Haar has written documentaries, radio and television plays for children and adults; film scripts and novels for young people and adults. The best known in this country is *Boris*, a story about a Soviet Russian boy during World War II, which earned the author a City of Rotterdam award for the Best Book of the Year in 1966. He had earlier won the same award, in 1958, for *Noord-*

weer op de weissbarn, which was published in the United States as *Danger on the Mountain.*

Jaap ter Haar has traveled in the United States at the invitation of the State Department and in the Soviet Union under the sponsorship of the Soviet Writers' Union. He has also traveled extensively in Africa.

He married Rudi Schurink in November 1945 and has four children, Jaap, Bart, and twins, Saskia and Jeroen.

SELECTED WORKS: Danger on the Mountain, 1960; Duck Dutch, 1962; The Story of America, 1967; Boris, 1970; The World of Ben Lighthart, 1977.

ABOUT: Contemporary Authors, Vol. 37–40; Something about the Author, Vol. 6.

VIRGINIA HAMILTON
March 12, 1933–

AUTHOR OF *M. C. Higgins the Great*, etc.

Autobiographical sketch of Virginia Hamilton Adoff:

I WAS born the fifth child of Etta Belle and Kenneth James Hamilton in the village of Yellow Springs, Ohio. At six months of age I fell from my cradle on the porch to the ground and landed on my back. Ever since, I have been particularly fond of Ohio skies.

My childhood and youth I remember as being mostly pleasant, my family having considered me "the baby" until the time I went off to college. My four brothers and sisters flattered me and my parents spoiled me, thus instilling me with an abundant sense of my own importance.

By age six I sang solos in the local African Methodist Episcopal church. This coincided neatly with my discovery of, and extreme fascination with, public school. I fairly ran the mile to school each morning and quickly cracked the mysteries of math and reading. Where my family left off in paying me atten-

Virginia Hamilton

tion, the schools now took on the burden. For the next twelve years my career as one of many teacher's pets was marked by overachievement. I had those old-fashioned teachers who seemed to indulge every child with liberal doses of warmth and discipline. I graduated from high school with honors and had no thought of attending university when Antioch College offered me a full scholarship.

Somewhere along the line, and at an early age, I started to write. It soon became a pleasant habit but I don't remember ever making much of a fuss about it. When I entered college it seemed natural to drift to the departments of literature and creative writing, where at once my prose was given respect. Such attention now induced feelings of claustrophobia; and after three years I dutifully left Antioch for Ohio State University. Many writing courses and literature classes later, I struck out for New York City where, I was told, a great, gold kettle of publishers was waiting just for me.

No rockets exploded in air on my arrival. More writing courses, more study, and after ten years my first book was published. In that time I learned about city life and self-survival. I also learned how to write the best way—by living.

I am extremely fond of children and of singing. But for the most part, I write and sing for myself. My greatest pleasure is sitting down and weaving a tale out of the mystery of my past and present. I'm only thankful that children like my stories as well, my own children included. I have a son, Jaime, and a daughter, Leigh. Leigh often comes home with the news that she has discovered a book that I must read— "Mommy, it's as good as one of yours!"

I met Arnold Adoff in 1957 and we were married in New York, March, 1960. We describe ourselves as a two-Olivetti family. We live with our children, ten cats and one dog, in a great modern house smack in the middle of a cornfield, the last remaining section of that farm belonging to my family. Writing is our staff of life. Home and hearth is the medium by which it grows.

———

Virginia Hamilton began to receive recognition as soon as her books were published, and her list of honors and awards is impressive. All of her books have been chosen Notable Books by the American Library Association in the year of their publication. *Zeely* received the Nancy Bloch Memorial Award of the Downtown Community School of New York in 1968. *The House of Dies Drear* received the Edgar Allen Poe Award in 1968, given by the Mystery Writers of America for the best juvenile mystery of the year. The same book also won the Ohioana Award in 1968. *The Planet of Junior Brown* was an Honor Book for the Newbery Medal in 1974 and a nominee for the National Book Award in 1972. *Time-Ago Lost* was an Honor Book in the eight-to-twelve category in the 1973 *Book World* Children's Spring Book Festival in 1973. And in

1975 Virginia Hamilton received both the 1974 Newbery Medal and the National Book Award for *M. C. Higgins, the Great. M. C. Higgins* was also chosen to represent the United States on the International Honors List for the Hans Christian Andersen Award.

Miss Hamilton has written much about herself and her family roots, which are deep and strong and nourishing. She has described herself as loving "freedom, lazing around and daydreaming," and reading "all the time—everything from Bullfinch to seed catalogs." And again, as "a loner; an introvert, with no companions other than my immediate family. . . . Writers never tell the truth; that is, they tell more than one truth, depending on what they had for breakfast or what they dreamed about the night before. I am fond of telling lies, about my age, creations, the past, and my husband!" About her art, however, Virginia Hamilton is serious: "Whatever else I do . . . I write each morning and night. I think I dream writing, and writing is who I am. . . . I write of the black experience . . . I attempt in each book to take hold of one single theme of the black experience and present it as clearly as I can. . . . You might well ask, what is it I'm getting at. Not actually knowing, I sense that finding out is the reason I persist. I sense also that finding out is far less important than the quest and the pleasure of writing along the way."

SELECTED WORKS: Zeely, 1967; The House of Dies Drear, 1968; The Time-Ago Tales of Jahdu, 1969; The Planet of Junior Brown, 1971; W. E. B. Dubois, 1972; Time-Ago Lost: More Tales of Jahdu, 1973; Paul Robeson, 1974; M. C. Higgins, the Great, 1974; The Writings of W. E. B. Dubois, 1975; Arilla Sun Down, 1976.

ABOUT: Contemporary Authors, Vol. 25–28; Hamilton, Virginia. Illusion and Reality. Library of Congress speech (GPO: 1976). Hoffman, Miriam, and Eva Samuels. Authors and Illustrators of Children's Books; Something about the Author, Vol. 4; Who's Who of American Women, 1974–1975; Elementary English April 1971; Horn Book December 1972; April 1975; August 1975.

LEIF HAMRE

August 9, 1914–

AUTHOR OF *Leap Into Danger*, etc.

Autobiographical sketch of Leif Hamre:

I WAS born and grew up in a small town called Molde, on the west coast of Norway. Quite early in life I decided to be a painter, but I am still not—so chances to succeed are probably faint. After high school I worked for some years as a clerk, saved some money, and finally entered an art school in Oslo. However, the war came to my country and to make a long story short, a few years later I flew as a navigator on Catalina flying boats, stationed with a Norwegian squadron in Scotland. When the war ended I was retrained as a pilot and held, among many other jobs, the position of commander of the first helicopter squadron in the Norwegian Air Force. I have now retired with the rank of lieutenant colonel.

I married in 1947 and have a son, Geir, who is also a pilot in the air force. In 1950 I completed my civilian education by passing matriculation examination. Air Force Staff College in the United States and Defence College in Norway have completed my military education.

I started writing quite early and had my first short story published at the age of eighteen. During the war I had a short story published in the United States. The famous Norwegian author, Sigrid Undset, who lived in New York at that time, happened to read it and sent me a letter urging me to continue writing. But I didn't. I planned to write a book but seemed never to get time to write it. Then in 1956 I saw an advertisement in a newspaper about a competition for writers of juvenile books. The idea struck me that I might find time for a short children's book based on my flying experience. I wrote it in my spare time in three months and delivered the manuscript of *Leap Into Danger* an hour before the deadline for submission. Half

Leif Hamre: *Lafe HOM reh*

a year afterwards, I won the first prize of the competition, and the book sold almost thirty thousand copies in Norway within three months. Subsequently it has been translated into seventeen languages and is on sale in more than twenty-five countries around the world. Hence I got, quite to my surprise, a "rocket start" and continued writing flying stories for young boys and girls. So far I have written five.

Even if I try to make my stories as thrilling as possible, I always keep them within the limits of reality. My main characters are not born heroes but very ordinary young men with average strengths and weaknesses. However, in the face of demanding tasks, they grow equal to them because they have the strength of will to fight them through and are also members of teams that are able to "move mountains" when really needed.

I don't believe in unconquerable heroes but think any of us, even the seemingly weakest, may grow brave and strong by devotion to tasks that demand our utmost effort.

Colonel Hamre not only served as commander of the first helicopter service in the Norwegian Air Force but organized it as well. Out of that experience came his novel *Contact Lost*, which is set at a helicopter unit based in the Arctic. Hamre trained in Canada in 1944, and in 1954 attended the U.S. Air Force Staff College at Maxwell Field, Alabama. He speaks English and German and lists his hobbies as painting and gardening.

Leap Into Danger won a Norwegian State Award as the best book for young people in 1957, as did *Edge of Disaster* in 1958 and *Perilous Wings* in 1959. *Operation Arctic* has been made into a movie and has also been adapted by the author for the Norwegian stage.

SELECTED WORKS: Leap Into Danger, 1959; Edge of Disaster, 1960; Perilous Wings, 1961; Contact Lost, 1967; Operation Arctic, 1975.

ABOUT: Author's and Writer's Who's Who, 1971; Contemporary Authors, Vol. 5–6; Something about the Author, Vol. 5; Publishers Weekly June 18, 1973.

CHRISTIE HARRIS
November 21, 1907–

AUTHOR OF *Once Upon a Totem*, etc.

Autobiographical sketch of Christie Irwin Harris:

ALTHOUGH born in Newark, New Jersey, I came to British Columbia as an infant and—apart from a year now and then in Atlantic Canada, the United States, or Europe—I have lived here ever since.

Growing up on a small farm, I never really thought of writing stories, though I did take the odd swat at verse while keeping the cows or the turkeys out of mischief. Stories were my father's department. His youthful escapades in Ireland were the delight of the neighbors and us children, and the despair of my mother, who was concerned for the image of the Irish.

I trained for teaching. And it was while telling other people's stories to the class that it struck me—I could tell my

Christie Harris

own stories. In a frenzy of excitement I wrote nine little nothings, sold them to a Vancouver newspaper's weekend children's page, and never looked back.

By the time I was married in 1932, the exciting market was radio; friends were getting two dollars for a script. So I began bombarding the new Canadian Broadcasting Corporation with sample scripts for children's programs. They did not appear to notice. But when Vancouver was asked to produce a one-hour juvenile musical fantasy for the official Coronation Day Programme (George VI), I was called in to meet a composer. And together we turned out the first of seven "Special Occasion" shows for the national network.

The Canadian Broadcasting Corporation was a great market for the young mother of five children. Domestic calamities became humor sketches. Past and present happenings in the Fraser Valley became women's talks or adult plays. And my children became "the Harris guinea pigs" for British Columbia School Broadcasts. (They were willing to have the scripts tried out on them because they lived in fear of having to cringe at school when the announcer said, "Script by Christie Harris.")

My interest in the early Canadian West—so different from, yet so tied to the American West—resulted in the weekly CBC juvenile adventure serial that became my first book, *Cariboo Trail*.

On the side, for six years I was woman's editor of a small-town weekly newspaper.

When the Canadian Immigration service transferred my husband to the Northwest Coast, the original home of totem poles, Indian cultures began to corner my attention. And Atheneum began to publish what I wrote about them: *Once Upon a Totem, Raven's Cry,* and *Once More Upon a Totem.*

My continuing interest in the early Canadian West produced *West with the White Chiefs* and *Forbidden Frontier.* In these books it was my husband, not my children, who helped me. Having served for five young years as a "Mountie," he was my authority on trails and horses, boats and adventuring males.

Even after they left home, my children continued to be concerned with cringing over what Mom was turning out. So three of my five gave me their own case histories, though we pretended it was fiction. Moira, a New York fashion artist, gave me *You Have to Draw the Line Somewhere.* Sheilagh, a rebel, gave me *Confessions of a Toe-Hanger.* And Michael, an aeronautical research engineer and test pilot, gave me *Let X Be Excitement.*

Moira, deeply interested in the clothing revolution of the sixties, and long dubious about the accepted psychology of dress, coauthored and illustrated *Fig-leafing Through History; The Dynamics of Dress.*

One family of grandchildren, plus my fascination with Indian lore, plus Cleve Backster's amazing discoveries about the occult life of plants added up to *Secret in the Stlalakum Wild.* While my husband's youthful struggles with a mule in the First World War became our co-authored *Mule Lib.*

My writing is a family affair.

———

Raven's Cry and *Mouse Woman and the Vanished Princesses* received the Canadian Association of Children's Librarians' Medal for the Book of the Year for Children, the Canadian equivalent of the Newbery Medal, in 1967 and 1977, respectively. The same book was chosen a Notable Book by the American Library Association for 1966 and also received the Pacific Northwest Booksellers' Award.

SELECTED WORKS: Once Upon a Totem, 1963; You Have to Draw the Line Somewhere, 1964; West with the White Chiefs, 1965; Raven's Cry, 1966; Confessions of a Toe-Hanger, 1967; Forbidden Frontier, 1968; Let X Be Excitement, 1969; Figleafing Through History (with Moira Johnson), 1971; Secret in the Stlalakum Wild, 1972; Once More Upon a Totem, 1973; Mouse Woman and the Vanished Princesses, 1976; Mouse Woman and the Mischief-Makers, 1977.

ABOUT: Contemporary Authors, Vol. 7–8; McDonough, Irma, comp. Profiles from In Review; Something about the Author, Vol. 6.

ROSEMARY HARRIS

February 20, 1923–

AUTHOR OF *The Moon in the Cloud*, etc.

Autobiographical sketch of Rosemary Jeanne Harris·

I WAS born in a London hotel—suitably; for my family, having a long Services tradition, was constantly on the move. From the eighteenth century onwards all members of it were always going somewhere—to the Northwest Frontier, or Afghanistan, or around the world. I have not myself traveled beyond Europe, but I have spent much time circuiting the British Isles. Once I counted up to thirty-nine moves, and then lost count! For the last ten years Chelsea has been my home, and to stay so long in one place seems almost abnormal.

But Chelsea is familiar ground. After the war I trained there as a painter. I was lucky with my teachers: life classes with Ceri Richards, sculpture with F. E. McWilliam and Henry Moore. Then I studied picture-restoring at the Cour-

tauld Institute. During childhood I wrote a lot, as well as painted, and later wrote plays in my spare time. When one of these nearly reached West End production, I staked everything—rashly!—upon writing, left picture-restoring, and wrote an adult novel called *The Summer-House*. It was published immediately and was followed by other novels and some thrillers (now being published in America). Then I turned to completing a book which had been abandoned for some years.

The decision to finish that rather curious children's book was an important moment for me. When I was seven my parents were in Egypt and sent us back wall hangings of the strange gods, Nut and Osiris, and intriguing pocketknives shaped like mummy cases. Some fascination for the ancient Egyptians must have lain dormant in me after that. (Or perhaps I was merely influenced later by the magnificent Old Kingdom sculpture.) Anyway, *The Moon in the Cloud*, with its partly Egyptian background, erupted years later, unexpectedly, when I was feverish with flu. The first ten thousand words were scrawled in pencil; notes, too, about Reuben, Thamar, his wife, the animals that cynically commented on the scenes, the young Egyptian king. When it was published eventually as the first part of a trilogy, it launched me happily into the world of children's books.

Children are responsive; and they don't pretend. If they like a series their identification with it is complete. (If they don't like it, they say so. A child who asks for a sequel really means it.) In my godchildren and friends' children I have a captive audience—captive critics, too. I enjoy writing these books so much that my publishers have to bully me gently when they want an adult novel. One of the best things about this form of writing is the scope. So many things, even dreams, can start things rolling: some odd historical fact; a chance meeting; a legend—particularly a legend. . . .

Several years ago, Faber asked me to rewrite a famous Japanese legend for a picture book. Soon I was so hooked on beautiful, weird legends that I was searching endlessly for some that could be interpreted in a larger book for older children. Ten of these were published in America under the title of *Sea Magic* and eighteen in England as *The Lotus and the Grail.*

My imagination is usually several books ahead. At the moment I'm working on one with a closely-linked sequel, set in future England and Southern Germany. The first, "A Quest for Orion," is done, and I'm embarking on the second. It would be exciting if this double bill were published in America, nothing would please me more, particularly as so much of my writing has been set in the past, or based on legends, so that these new books have been a completely fresh departure for me. Working on them has been—and is—a stimulating adventure.

But it can be painful working on one book while the plots of others are emerging, especially when they clamor to be born, like all difficult babies, at one o'clock in the morning. (This is where cassette recorders are so useful: a new plot can be sleepily recorded in half an hour.) Sometimes past experiences demand a hearing too. While jet planes roar over London, time does a vanishing trick, and I'm listening instead to the slow be-rrum, be-rrum of German bombers, and waiting for falling flares to light up the sky; and I think immediately—yes, that's it: one day—perhaps next time, I'll write a book about the war. . . .

———

The Moon in the Cloud, Miss Harris's first book for children, was awarded the British Library Association's Carnegie Medal in 1968. In this country it was designated a Notable Book by the American Library Association in 1970 and was an Honor Book in the 1970 *Book World* Children's Spring Book Festival. *The Moon in the Cloud* was followed by *The Shadow on the Sun* and, eventually, *The Bright and Morning Star,* to form a trilogy set in ancient Egypt. Miss Harris has said that she was influenced by Thomas Mann's *Joseph and his Brethren,* but only after she had written *The Moon and the Cloud.* "Then I think it was a strong influence on my writing two other books to complete the trilogy."

SELECTED WORKS: The Moon in the Cloud, 1970; The Shadow on the Sun, 1970; The Seal-Singing, 1971; A Wicked Pack of Cards, 1971; The Bright and Morning Star, 1972; The Child in the Bamboo Grove, 1972; The King's White Elephant, 1973; Sea Magic and Other Stories of Enchantment, 1974.

ABOUT: Author's and Writer's Who's Who, 1971; Contemporary Authors, Vol. 33–36; Something about the Author, Vol. 4; Library Association Record June, 1969.

VIRGINIA HAVILAND

May 21, 1911–

AUTHOR OF *Favorite Fairy Tales Told in England,* etc.

Autobiographical sketch of Virginia Haviland:

I WAS born in Rochester, New York, but moved to New England so young that my "upstate" accent disappeared

Virginia Haviland

quickly in favor of near-to-Boston
speech. Today I live in Washington,
D.C., but even after eleven years I am
teased for continuing to say "Boston," as
if I still lived where I spent some decades.

Always an omnivorous reader as a
child, I fell on whatever came to hand—
in the public library where I read from
A to Z and on piles of books from neighbors' attics. I grew up to enjoy the study
of languages and found my courses in
these at Cornell University an especial
delight—and highly useful later.

It was natural enough that I should
become a librarian. For the first six years
of my library career, I worked on adult
book selection lists at the Boston Public
Library, but among my library science
courses were two—in children's literature and library work with children—
taught by Alice M. Jordan, then the famous head of work with children at the
Boston Public Library, who steered me
firmly in the direction of service to children. I became a children's librarian,
then head of a branch library (retaining
responsibility for children's work), and
finally, still in Boston, the Readers Advisor for Children, which meant having
system-wide direction of the selection of
new books for the library's children's
rooms and the editing of booklists.

In 1949, when I did research for the
second Caroline M. Hewins lecture on
American children's literature—which
became a book entitled *The Travelogue
Storybook of the Nineteenth Century*—a
children's book editor who was in the
audience when I gave this as a lecture
asked me to write a biography for
younger children on a subject of my
choice. This led to *William Penn,
Founder and Friend.*

It was at the library that in 1957 a
need became apparent for books of traditional fairy tales in volumes attractive
to very young readers who were listening to Shirley Temple's introduction of
fairy tales on the air and wanted to read
them for themselves. Discussing this
with Helen Jones, then editor of children's books for Little, Brown and Company in Boston, led to my retelling and
translating, from the German and the
French, many of the favorite old tales
for publication with clear print, ample
margins, and illustration by the best
artists available. By 1973, the series had
grown from three initial volumes to sixteen because of demands for more and
more of these "Favorites." I had been
enjoying foreign travel for some time
and was able to secure in Japan and in
Sweden English translations of tales
available in their languages, which I
turned into tellable versions for children. For some of the Czech and Russian tales I also had help from persons
adept in those languages.

Other writing also has been done on
request—reviews and articles and books
about children's literature and authors.
For example, I was asked to write about
my friend Ruth Sawyer, a great storyteller and the author of *Roller Skates*
and other books.

In 1963 I was invited to the Library of
Congress, to set up a children's book
section for assistance to those with reference and research interests in children's literature. I found myself increasingly involved with writing *about* children's books and reading hundreds of
them, in order, with a committee, to
compile a selected list published each

year by the Library of Congress. Thus children's literature became, even more than when I was a librarian working with children, the center of my working life. Traveling abroad each year has contributed to enlarging my book world, through my participation in international conferences and meeting with authors, illustrators and librarians overseas. Thus in spring 1974 I went around the world giving lectures in Hawaii and Australia, and, in Athens, presiding over the Hans Christian Andersen Jury for international awards in children's literature. Five months later I journeyed to South America to present these awards in Rio de Janeiro. Along the way, on these jaunts, I enjoyed vacationing on a houseboat in Kashmir and traveling in the Andes and up the Amazon. In 1975 I enjoyed participating in a children's book seminar in Teheran.

Virginia Haviland's record of professional accomplishments is nearly as long as her list of books in print. Besides lecturing at Simmons College School of Library Sciences (1957–1962), she has been a lecturer at Trinity College (Hartford, Conn.), an associate editor of *Horn Book* (1952–1963) and a regular reviewer for the magazine. She has been an active member of the American Library Association, also serving on the Newbery-Caldecott Awards Committee, which she chaired in 1953–54. She has also served as a judge—for the New York *Herald Tribune*'s Children's Spring Book Festival and for its successor, the *Book World* Children's Spring Book Festival, for the National Book Award, and on the International Hans Christian Andersen Award Jury, over which she presided in 1972 and 1974. In 1976 Virginia Haviland was awarded the Catholic Library Association's Regina Medal, presented for "continued distinguished contribution to children's literature."

SELECTED WORKS: William Penn, Founder and Friend, 1952; Favorite Fairy Tales Told in England, 1959; Favorite Fairy Tales Told in France, 1959; Favorite Fairy Tales Told in Russia, 1961; Favorite Fairy Tales Told in Poland, 1963; Favorite Fairy Tales Told in Italy, 1965; Ruth Sawyer, 1965; Favorite Fairy Tales Told in Czechoslovakia, 1966; Favorite Fairy Tales Told in Japan, 1967; Favorite Fairy Tales Told in Denmark, 1971; Favorite Fairy Tales Told in India, 1973; Children and Literature: Views and Reviews, 1973.

SELECTED WORKS EDITED: The Fairy Tale Treasury, 1972.

ABOUT: Contemporary Authors, Vol. 17–18; Something about the Author, Vol. 5; Who's Who in America, 1974–75; Who's Who of American Women, 1974–75.

JOHN HAWKINSON

November 8, 1912–

AUTHOR AND ILLUSTRATOR OF *Collect and Paint from Nature*, etc.

Autobiographical sketch of John Samuel Hawkinson, who writes and illustrates on his own and formerly in collaboration with his wife, Lucy Ozone Hawkinson:

ANY kind of formal education had very little to do with what I do. And I must tell you that I had very little to do with education since I found out at the age of six that school was not made for restless little boys.

For many years I worked on the lower rung of society's labor forces and accepted the meager salary and what all that went with that kind of life. Then I got married. My wife sold the first book I wrote, and we became partners in illustrating and writing children's books. For many years we worked hard, raised two children, and were always one step from poverty, but even so, they were happy years because we were determined to keep our children first in our thoughts and attention.

Those years are gone now. My beloved wife died in 1971. I miss her very much. My two daughters, Anne and Julia, and I now live on a two-acre farm in an old house whose architecture I can describe as Michigan built-on. We have a dog, two goats and three horses. The horses mow the lawn, the goats wake me

ART

JOHN HAWKINSON

JOHN HAWKINSON

up in the morning and give milk, and the dog takes care of things when we're gone. The land here is soft and lovely. Song sparrows sing most of the year. There are thousands of bees, and come springtime the population increases with all the birds who come back to raise their young—orioles, vireos and many kinds of sparrows. But when the bobolinks come back to the field behind us, this is the only place to be.

I look forward to each season. Now is the harvest time in our garden, with all its produce to be canned, frozen, dried or put in the cellar. Fruits and nuts both wild and domestic everywhere await us. I tell you, I make the best cider in these parts, and our dried pears—oh boy!

Of course it's not all beer and skittles. There's wood to be cut for the winter. We use wood to cook with and to heat the house. Ruffy, our biggest, smartest horse, hauls the wood in a sled that I made.

At each season the children from the local school come on field trips: in the fall to collect apples and make cider and hike in the woods; in the winter to ski, toboggan and sugarbush; and in the spring, there is so much to see, smell and touch. There's no better place to learn about our world than right out there in it. Our little creek furnishes the most fun and the best introduction to nature study. In it the children can catch and identify many kinds of fish, insects, crustaceans, snakes, frogs, etc. Of course everything is returned to its home before the children come back to the bus all wet and happy.

And once in a while I do a little painting.

John Hawkinson was born in Chicago, Illinois, where he lived and worked for many years. He served in the U.S. Army during World War II and was awarded a Bronze Star. On September 20, 1954, John Hawkinson married author-illustrator Lucy Ozone (1924–1971). Mrs. Hawkinson was born in California and studied at the Chicago Academy of Art. At one time she had worked for a publishing firm. Both wrote and illustrated their own books, together and separately, as well as illustrating the work of other authors. The happy collaboration was ended by Mrs. Hawkinson's death on December 6, 1971.

SELECTED WORKS WRITTEN AND ILLUSTRATED: Robins and Rabbits (with Lucy Ozone Hawkinson), 1960; Collect and Paint from Nature, 1963; More to Collect and Paint from Nature, 1964; Birds in the Sky, (with Lucy Ozone Hawkinson), 1965; The Old Stump, 1965; Where the Wild Apples Grow, 1967; Little Boy Who Lives Up High (with Lucy Ozone Hawkinson), 1967; Pastels are Great, 1968; Who Lives There? 1970; The Mouse that Fell Off the Rainbow, 1971; Let Me Take You on a Trail, 1972; A Ball of Clay, 1974.

SELECTED WORKS ILLUSTRATED: Mystery of the Farmer's Three Fives (with Lucy Ozone Hawkinson), by Margaret Friskey, 1963; Indian Two Feet and His Eagle Feather (with Lucy Ozone Hawkinson), by Margaret Friskey, 1967; Things Are Alike and Different (with Lucy Ozone Hawkinson), by Illa Podendorf, 1971; Every Day is Earth Day, by Illa Podendorf, 1971; Indian Two Feet and The Wolf Cubs, by Margaret Friskey, 1971; Indian Two Feet and the Grizzly Bear, by Margaret Friskey, 1974.

ABOUT: Contemporary Authors, Vol. 5–6; Something about the Author, Vol. 4.

FLORENCE PARRY HEIDE
February 27, 1919–

AUTHOR OF *The Shrinking of Treehorn,*
etc.

Autobiographical sketch of Florence
Parry Heide:

I WAS a late bloomer, so I had to hurry
to make up for lost time. I'd done the
other things: college (UCLA) and
working (in New York—a dream come
true!) and getting married to a wonderful man (another dream) and having
five children (another) but I had never
written anything except letters home.

Then after the children started off to
school I started thinking I should do
something. *Something* was writing lyrics
for which a friend, the late Sylvia Van
Clief, wrote the music. Wonderful, wonderful songs—but where to send them?
We didn't know. While we were finding
out, we wrote a musical. Where to send
that? While making up our minds, we
wrote some children's television musicals (where to send those?) and then
finally children's books. We sent those
off and to our surprise and delight sold
them. So then we kept writing—more
books and more songs. Over a hundred
and twenty-five songs have been sold
and published, and now there are many
books.

One good thing that came out of all
that—one good thing among many—was
that our children could finally write
something besides Housewife when they
had to fill in forms. Author sounds better
—particularly since I never was much of
a housewife. I hope to become much
of a writer, but I'll have to get busy.

Florence Parry Heide was born and
grew up in Pittsburgh, Pennsylvania. Although her mother was a journalist—she
wrote a daily column for the *Pittsburgh
Press* for thirty years—and although she
herself majored in English in college,
she never really intended to become a
writer. After graduating from the Uni-

versity of California at Los Angeles in
1939, she went to New York where she
worked first in the advertising department of RKO, and later for an ad agency
and public relations firm. Then she returned to Pittsburgh and worked as public relations director for the Pittsburgh
Playhouse until her marriage to Donald
C. Heide, a lawyer, in 1943.

The Heides live in Kenosha, Wisconsin. They have five children: Christen
P., born in 1944; Roxanne and Judith,
born in 1948; David C., born in 1950;
and Parry W., born in 1951. One son is
a writer for newspapers and magazines,
the other an editor and writer.

Mrs. Heide explains that she never
cared much for housework or clubs and
shopping or the things women were supposed to do in those days before wom-
en's liberation. She and a neighbor-
friend, Sylvia Van Clief, decided to start
a business. At first it was to be a hot-
fudge-sauce-making operation. They
were already embarked on it when it
occurred to them that they were engaged
in a business that was more of the sort
of housework they disliked. At that point
they happened to hear an operatic aria
to which new words had been written.
"We can do better, we said, and we

Heide: *HIGH dee*

started playing around," says Mrs. Heide. "And we discovered we wanted to do this more than anything." At first they wrote adult songs—Mrs. Heide the words and Mrs. Van Clief the music. They wrote a musical for a movie, then books with records—songs for children— and mysteries. The happy collaboration lasted until Mrs. Van Clief's death as the result of an auto accident. Now Florence Heide is collaborating with her daughter Roxanne on the mysteries and is embarking on an older series with her as well.

Mrs. Heide has, she says, "just drifted" into writing for older children. The ideas come, and she writes. One of these novels, *When the Sad One Comes to Stay*, won second place in the competition for the Council of Wisconsin Writers' Award. The other, *Growing Anyway Up*, was an Honor Book for the Golden Kite Award in 1976. To date her most successful book has been *The Shrinking of Treehorn*, with illustrations by Edward Gorey. Among a number of honors, it was included in the American Library Association's 1971 list of Notable Books for Children and the New York *Times* list of best-illustrated books for 1971.

SELECTED WORKS: Benjamin Budge and Barnaby Ball, 1967; Alphabet Soup, 1970; Giants Are Very Brave People, 1970; Little One, 1970; Sound of Sunshine, Sound of Rain, 1970; The Key, 1971; The Shrinking of Treehorn, 1971; My Castle, 1972; God and Me, 1975; You and Me, 1975; When the Sad One Comes to Stay, 1975; Growing Anyway Up, 1976.

SELECTED WORKS WRITTEN WITH SYLVIA VAN CLIEF: Maximilian, 1967; How Big Am I?, 1968; It Never Is Dark, 1968; Sebastian, 1968; That's What Friends Are For, 1968; The Day It Snowed in Summer, 1969; The New Neighbor, 1970; The Mystery of the Missing Suitcase, 1972; The Hidden Box Mystery, 1973; The Mystery of Macadoo Zoo, 1973; The Mystery of the Whispering Voice, 1974; The Mystery of the Tennis Menace (under the pseudonym "Alex B. Allen"), 1975.

SELECTED WORKS WRITTEN WITH ROXANNE HEIDE: Break-in, 1971; The Mystery of the Melting Snowman, 1974; The Mystery of the Bewitched Bookmobile, 1975; The Mystery of the Vanishing Visitor, 1975; The Mystery of the Lonely Lantern, 1976;

The Mystery at Keyhole Carnival, 1977; Mystery of the Midnight Message, 1977.

FRISO HENSTRA
February 9, 1928–

ILLUSTRATOR OF *The Practical Princess*, etc.

Autobiographical sketch of Friso Henstra:

IN 1928 I was born in Amsterdam. It was bitterly cold, even so cold that I was freezing to my cradle, diaper and all.

I grew up in the old center of Amsterdam, an adventurous place for a kid. In those days that center was still undamaged, a seventeenth-century town with narrow streets, canals and a network of alleys, sailors' pubs and brothels. The quarter was populated mainly by handworkers, thieves, artists, and Jewish merchants with their humor and exuberance.

I was always all eyes, there was always so much to see. I think this was a good training for an illustrator.

At the age of four I started to draw, and I have never stopped making pictures since. When I was fourteen I made my first real painting outside, standing in the street with a canvas and pallet.

Nineteen-forty to 1945: that was the end for the greater part of the population of our quarter—a violent ending.

Later on I decided to become a sculptor: that was in the period after the war—a gay and chaotic period.

I was attending the College of Art in Amsterdam, but this period was interrupted because I had reached the age for compulsory military service, and I landed in the tropics. I was in Indonesia for two years as a soldier. After that it was difficult to find a new beginning. The world had changed. I had my years of poverty and all kinds of jobs, but in 1952 I started as an illustrator.

I was doing cartoons for a weekly sports magazine; later on, pictures for weekly and daily papers, children's books, advertisements, TV, etc.

After years of doing illustrations only, I try to find time again for my old love,

Friso Henstra: *FREE zo HEN stra*

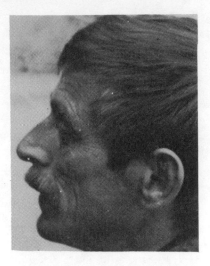

friso henstra

sculpturing. For that reason I have a big cargo boat transformed into a studio. A boat, because room is very scarce in Amsterdam, but there is water enough to moor a ship.

In 1968 I became a teacher at the College of Art in Arnhem, and in this period I got acquainted with Jay Williams. I have illustrated a number of his tales. He visited Holland several times, and we became good friends. One of his books tells about a little boy and an ancient boat (*The Youngest Captain*). The story is more or less inspired by my boat, an ancient boyer with leeboards and carvings.

Sailing and boats are a hobby for me and my wife, and it's difficult for us to live without the nearness of water.

We have a grown-up daughter and are living in a house on a canal near the river Amstel in the center of town. These romantic and baroque environs, a strange mixture of old houses, with stone animals and nymphs on the top of the facades, and modern buildings, have always had a great influence on my work.

———

Friso Henstra's illustrations for *The Practical Princess* earned him the Golden

Apple at the Biennale of Illustrations Bratislava in 1969, and subsequently his work has received a number of awards and citations for excellence. *Stupid Marco* won a Citation of Merit from the New York Society of Illustrators in 1970 and was among the top honor books in the Twenty-second Annual Chicago Book Clinic Exhibition in 1971, as was *The Round Sultan and the Straight Answer* the same year. *The Round Sultan* also took a Gold Medal at the New York Society of Illustrators Show in 1971. The American Institute of Graphic Arts picked *The Silver Whistle* for its list of Fifty Books of the Year (composed of adult and children's titles) for 1971. *Petronella* was in the 1974 Children's Book Showcase and, along with *Forgetful Fred*, exhibited in the 1973–74 Children's Book Show mounted by the American Institute of Graphic Arts.

SELECTED WORKS ILLUSTRATED: The Practical Princess, by Jay Williams, 1969; School for Sillies, by Jay Williams, 1969; The Round Sultan and the Straight Answer, by B. K. Walker, 1970; Stupid Marco, by Jay Williams, 1970; The Silver Whistle, by Jay Williams, 1971; Seven at One Blow, by Jay Williams, 1972; Petronella, by Jay Williams, 1973; Forgetful Fred, by Jay Williams, 1974; The Little Spotted Fish, by Jane Yolen, 1975; (with other illus.) Six Impossible Things Before Breakfast, by Norma Farber, 1977.

E. W. HILDICK
December 29, 1925–

AUTHOR OF *Manhattan is Missing*, etc.

Autobiographical sketch of Edmund Wallace Hildick, who has also written under the name Wallace Hildick:

I WAS born in Bradford in the industrial north of England and spent my childhood in various manufacturing towns in the region: sooty, overcrowded, unlovely places physically, but teeming and richly varied in population and therefore an ideal background for embryonic fiction writers. Not that I was

E. W. HILDICK

one of those kids who scribble away at stories as soon as they learn how to string sentences together. My favorite creative occupation was drawing and coloring.

At age twelve, however, my artistic ambitions received a sharp setback when I was transferred to a school that did not include art in its curriculum. Instead, the bias leaned heavily toward mathematics and science. Again, somewhat forbidding; again, immeasurably useful for the embryonic writer, for the setback proved more of a cutback, a pruning, and the creative juices became concentrated in the one channel left to me: writing—not only in formal English work, but also in describing chemistry experiments, making free translations in Latin and French, and putting some life into history essays. By fifteen, when I left school, I knew for sure what I wanted to be.

Fortunately (though I didn't think so at the time) there are no jobs for apprentice fiction writers at such an early stage. So there followed the usual drifting—again bad for most people but excellent for writers; in my case from public library assistant, to storekeeping in a trucking garage, to radio/radar laboratory assistant with the Admiralty, Na-

tional Service in the RAF, and, after a two-year training course, teaching. The course was excellent and it came just at the right stage in my career.

For the next four years I taught general subjects to backward twelve- to fourteen-year-old boys, who in turn taught me the paramount importance of clarity, concision and concreteness when writing for children. During this period I began to have short pieces published in magazines, and in 1954 I decided to take the plunge and become a free-lance writer. At first all my fiction was for adults, but in 1956 I was sent to cover an educational conference at which speaker after speaker deplored the lack of fiction that would reflect for children in working-class industrial areas something of their own background. I went back home, wrote my report, and began my first children's book, *Jim Starling.*

Since then, I have had over fifty children's books published, seven adult novels, several volumes of literary criticism, and a number of school texts. The interaction between adult work and children's has proved mutually beneficial. Writing adult fiction ensures that one doesn't overburden the children's stories with psychophilosophical complexities, while the practice of writing for children ensures that one's feel for narrative is kept fresh and limber and capable of sustaining the heaviest loads in the adult books.

Unexpectedly, my work as reviewer and literary critic was instrumental in changing the whole course of my career as a children's writer. When, in 1965, I wrote an article on Virginia Woolf for the *Kenyon Review,* I had no idea that it would lead to a cabled invitation the next year to go to Ohio as temporary associate editor of that journal. Naturally I accepted, and my wife Doris, who by this time had given up her teaching post to become my agent, was free to go with me. This meant that we were able to make regular personal contact with American publishers, and whereas my children's books had always previously been turned down as "too British for the

American market," they now began to be accepted, with the sort of modifications an author and editor can soon work out when face to face. The next step was being asked to write children's books specifically for American children, with American settings, and since 1968 this is what I have been doing.

The first two books of this phase were *Manhattan Is Missing* and *Top Boy at Twisters Creek*, and naturally we were very apprehensive as to how well I'd managed to make the transition. But when both titles appeared on the Books Across the Sea committee's spring 1970 list of American Ambassador Books, "chosen to interpret the lives, background and interests of American young people," we knew the test had been passed with honors. In fact no formal award or honor I've received or might hope to receive could ever eclipse that one. Since then I have written a number of all-American books, some of which British publishers have turned down as being "too American for the British market."

E. W. Hildick won the Tom Gallon Award, Britain's top short-story award, in 1957. *Louie's Lot* was a Hans Christian Andersen Honor Book in 1968. Among his books for adults is one of criticism, *Children and Fiction: A Critical Study*. Hildick's children's books have also been translated into French, German, Swedish, Danish, Dutch, Polish, Portuguese, Spanish, Russian, Serbo-Croat, Icelandic, and Italian.

Hildick married Doris Clayton in 1950; they are now permanent residents of Canada.

SELECTED WORKS: Louie's Lot, 1968; Manhattan is Missing, 1969; Top Boy at Twisters Creek, 1969; The Dragon That Lived Under Manhattan, 1970; The Secret Spenders, 1971; Kids Commune, 1972; The Active-Enzyme Lemon-Freshened Junior High School Witch, 1973; Birdy Jones and the New York Heads, 1974; Louie's Snowstorm, 1974; Deadline for McGurk, 1975; The Case of the Nervous Newsboy, 1976; The Great Rabbit Rip-off, 1977; The Top-Flight Fully-Automated Junior High School Girl Detective, 1977.

ABOUT: Author's and Writer's Who's Who, 1971; Contemporary Authors, Vol. 25–28; Doyle, Brian, comp. Who's Who of Children's Literature; Something about the Author, Vol. 2.

S. E. HINTON
1949–

AUTHOR OF *The Outsiders*, etc.

Autobiographical sketch of Susan Eloise Hinton Inhofe:

I WAS born in Tulsa, Oklahoma, where I have lived most of my life. There is nothing to do there, but it is a pleasant place to live if you don't want to do anything. I am now living in California. It has a nice climate. In Oklahoma we had weather.

I started reading about the same time everyone else did, and began to write a short time later. The major influence on my writing has been my reading. I read everything, including Comet cans and coffee labels. Reading taught me sentence structure, paragraphing, how to build a chapter. Strangely enough, it never taught me spelling.

I've always written about things that interest me, so my first years of writing (grade three through grade ten) I wrote about cowboys and horses. I wanted to be a cowboy and have a horse. I was strange for my era, but feel quite comfortable in this one, when everyone wants to be a cowboy and have a horse.

I began the first draft of *The Outsiders* when I was fifteen. Nobody believes that, so I usually say sixteen. My editors say seventeen, just in case. I had written two books before *The Outsiders*. They were about cowboys and horses. I had read all the cowboy and horse books in the library, so I wanted something to read.

I didn't know what I was doing. I happily wrote *The Outsiders* over and over again, not knowing what I was doing. During my junior year in high school, when I was doing most of my work on *The Outsiders*, I made a D in

S. E. HINTON

creative writing. My revenge is to print that fact as often as possible.

The Outsiders is part true and part not true. It's been so long ago I've forgotten which is which. Before it was published I thought I knew how to write. Afterwards I knew I couldn't. I was a teen-age writer, which is similar to being a teen-age werewolf, only it doesn't last as long.

I attended the University of Tulsa where I received a fairly good education, a B.S. in education and my husband, David Inhofe.

David made me write *That Was Then, This Is Now*. When I was writing for fun, I loved it; when it turned into a profession it scared me. I kept thinking, "You don't know what you're doing." I wrote *That Was Then* over a period of three or four months, two pages a day, never looking back. David was my boyfriend at that time; if I didn't get my two pages done, we didn't go out.

I think *That Was Then* was the better written book, but *The Outsiders* will last longer.

After *TWT, TIN* was finished I married David and we went off to Europe where we lived for six months on the southern coast of Spain. We had some strange experiences, and I hope to get a book out of that trip someday.

In case I've left anything out, I will try to put it in now. My favorite authors are Jane Austen and Mary Renault and Scott Fitzgerald and Shirley Jackson. My favorite books are *The Haunting of Hill House* and *Fire From Heaven* and *Emma* and *Tender Is the Night*. I like Vonnegut, Jr.'s novels but not his short stories, and the other way around for Salinger. I don't read Hemingway.

I am a Cancer on the cusp of Leo. I have a horse I raised from a colt and trained myself. I love cats but my husband doesn't, so we don't have one. Yet.

I don't like teen-age romance novels, most of the new movies, running the vacuum, liver-and-onions, or writing about myself. I do like history (ancient), some of the new movies, taking walks, lemon-with-salt, and playing slot machines.

I don't plan to limit my writing to the teen-age audience, but I don't plan to desert them, either. It scares me to look back and realize how little I had to read when I was through with the horse books and not ready for adult novels.

It is certainly harder to write now, though—now that I know what I'm doing.

The Outsiders, a novel about gang warfare, was characterized by one critic as "rare to unique among juvenile books . . . by a writer not yet practiced in restraint, perhaps, but nevertheless seeing and saying more with greater storytelling ability than many an older hand." It was an Honor Book (twelve-to-sixteen years) in the 1967 *Herald Tribune* Children's Spring Book Festival as was *That Was Then, This Is Now* in 1971, when the Festival was sponsored by *Book World*. Both *That Was Then* and *The Outsiders* were included on the American Library Association's list of young adult books published between 1960 and 1975, entitled The Best of the Best, Alive in '75. In addition *The Outsiders* received a *Media and Methods* Maxi Award in 1975 as "material that educational professionals themselves rate maximum in educational effectiveness." Miss Hinton's most recent novel, *Rumble Fish*, was named one of the Best Books for Young Adults, 1975, by the American Library Association.

Extremely popular with young adults themselves, Miss Hinton's books have been published in Denmark, England, Finland and Germany.

SELECTED WORKS: The Outsiders, 1967; That Was Then, This Is Now, 1971; Rumble Fish, 1975.

TANA HOBAN

AUTHOR AND ILLUSTRATOR OF *Look Again*, etc.

Autobiographical sketch of Tana Hoban Gallob:

I WAS born in Philadelphia of Russian parents. Before I started first grade, we moved to a house in the country, in Lansdale, Pennsylvania. There we grew flowers and raised pigeons and bees. My interest in health and health foods must have started then because I remember that we slept on a screened porch until it got quite cold and we raised vegetables and chickens on our two acres.

I was strongly influenced by my father. He must have been a feminist because he believed that I should have my own career so that I wouldn't have to be dependent on anyone. He enrolled me in Saturday morning art classes when I was a little girl. Although I was the youngest in my sketch and life classes, the teachers always picked out my work to talk about.

I sketched all through school. I attended Moore College of Art on a scholarship. After graduation, I went to Europe to paint as a recipient of the John Frederick Lewis Fellowship.

When I returned to Philadelphia, I worked as a free-lance artist, doing advertising and magazine illustration. Before we were married, my husband, Edward Gallob, bought me my first camera. After our daughter Meila was born, I started to do professional photography. I had taken only one photography course in college, so I learned by doing.

I'd always been interested in child development and I became known for my pictures of children. They are easy to shoot naturally. I've made my reputation on the use of natural light. For years I worked in . advertising. One year my photographs appeared on the covers of sixteen magazines.

For a long time I wanted to do a beautiful book. I wondered who would design and write it. Then the time was right and I did it myself. *Shapes and Things* and *Look Again!* were published in 1971, and since then I have been writing and photographing my own books and enjoy it very much.

My books are about everyday things that are so ordinary that one tends to overlook them. I try to rediscover these things and share them with children. But there is more to each picture than a first look reveals. I always try to include something new, something to reach for.

I believe certain things happen when the time is right. I also believe that anybody can do anything he or she really wants to.

Tana Hoban had won more than a dozen gold medals and other prizes as a film maker, photographer and commercial consultant before she turned to making books for children. Her photographs are in the permanent collection of the Museum of Modern Art and have appeared in such magazines as *Life, Look, McCall's* and *Harper's Bazaar*. From 1966 to 1969 she taught photography and graphics at the Annenberg School of Communications at the University of Pennsylvania. With her husband she has been partner-owner of the Hoban-Gallob studio in Philadelphia since 1946. She also keeps a studio in New York, dividing her time between the two cities.

In 1975 *Circles, Triangles and Squares* earned an Honorable Mention award in the Fourth Annual Children's Science Book competition sponsored by the New York Academy of Sciences.

SELECTED WORKS WRITTEN AND ILLUSTRATED: Shapes and Things, 1970; Look Again, 1971; Count and See, 1972; Push, Pull, Empty, Full, 1972; Over, Under and Through and Other Spatial Concepts, 1973; Circles, Triangles and Squares, 1974; Where Is It?, 1974; Dig, Drill, Dump, Fill, 1975; Big Ones, Little Ones, 1976.

SELECTED WORKS ILLUSTRATED: The Wonder of Hands, by Edith Baer, 1970.

ABOUT: Who's Who in America, 1970–1971.

MARGARET MOORE HODGES
July 26, 1911–

AUTHOR OF *The Making of Joshua Cobb*, etc.

Autobiographical sketch of Margaret Moore Hodges:

I WAS born into a bookloving family in Indianapolis and must have had print in my blood from the start. As early as the seventh grade I wrote a paragraph for the school magazine called "Miss Matty's Library." The description clearly shows that I thought it was bliss to be in a library. I still do.

Margaret Hodges

All through high school (Tudor Hall School for Girls) in Indianapolis, and at Vassar College, I went on writing and contributing to school magazines. Luckily I had consistently good sympathetic teachers and I gravitated toward friends who liked to write.

In 1932 I was launched into a new life with a husband and, later, three children, who were and are more important to me than anything else, but part of my domestic happiness was due to the chance I had, through the Junior League of Pittsburgh, to keep on writing. I had a column in the monthly magazine, met regularly with a group of Junior League "Scribblers," and adapted children's books for a Junior League radio program, "The Children's Bookshelf."

I owe a great deal to that constant practice, especially to the "Bookshelf" radio scripts, which were responsible for my first job, as radio storyteller for "Let's Tell a Story," a program sponsored by Carnegie Library of Pittsburgh and the Pittsburgh Public Schools.

At this point a new pattern of life was set out for our family: our three sons were away at school; my husband continued his work of many years as curator and business manager of the Stephen Foster Memorial at the University of Pittsburgh; and I began to work as children's librarian and storyteller at Carnegie Library. I earned a master's degree in Library Science at Carnegie Library School in 1958. *One Little Drum,* my first book, was published that same year. It was followed by others based on experiences of my childhood or of our sons, at home, at camp, at boarding school.

In 1964, after twelve years in the Boys and Girls Room at Carnegie Library, I began four years as story specialist for the Head Start program of the Pittsburgh Public Schools, going from school to school with a book bag in one hand and an autoharp in the other. Meanwhile, "Let's Tell a Story" had become "Tell Me a Story" on WQED, Pittsburgh's educational TV station, and a series was taped for National Instructional Television, which distributes the program nationally. At the same time I began to teach a course in storytelling at the Library School, now the Graduate School of Library Information Sciences at the University of Pittsburgh. From then on, I have taught other courses in children's literature as full-time work, continuing to write on weekends and during vacations.

Our sons are now married and have children for whom I tell stories and play the autoharp. Another new pleasure has been travel, often connected with what I happen to be writing. My husband and I have explored Mexico, the British Isles, Greece, Italy and Iceland, but there is so much more to be seen! "The sea is so vast, and our boat so small." History has become an absorbing interest as I see with my own eyes the places where great events happened and then try to convey for young readers the excitement I have felt. Mythology has become more and more important to me. I understand the need for myth in our modern world and hope to go on retelling myths so that the young can respond to them.

I expect to end my days happily surrounded by books.

The Wave, with illustrations by Blair Lent, was an American Library Associa-

tion Notable Book in 1964 and a runner-up for the Caldecott Medal in 1965. *The Fire Bringer* was also chosen a Notable Book, in 1972. Besides being a personal milestone for the author in turning her toward the pleasures of history, *Lady Queen Anne* was designated the best book for young adults by an Indiana author in 1970. *The Making of Joshua Cobb* was also singled out by critics as a book of special merit, appearing on the New York *Times* list of Outstanding Books the same year in 1971. In 1976 Mrs. Hodges was named the year's Distinguished Alumna by the University of Pittsburgh and Carnegie Library Schools Alumni Association.

SELECTED WORKS: A Club Against Keats, 1962; The Wave, 1964; The Hatching of Joshua Cobb, 1967; Sing Out, Charley!, 1968; Lady Queen Anne, 1969; The Making of Joshua Cobb, 1971; The Fire Bringer, 1972; Persephone and the Springtime, 1973; Baldur and the Mistletoe, 1974; The Freewheeling of Joshua Cobb, 1974; Knight Prisoner: The Tale of Sir Thomas Malory and His King Arthur, 1976.

SELECTED WORKS EDITED: Constellation: A Shakespeare Anthology, 1968.

ABOUT: Contemporary Authors, Vol. 1; Something about the Author, Vol. 1; Who's Who of American Women, 1974–1975.

ANNE HOLM

September 10, 1922–

AUTHOR OF *North to Freedom,* etc.

Autobiographical sketch of Anne Rahbek Holm:

I WAS born in Denmark, in a county in Jutland, where my father's family had lived for more than four hundred years; my mother, coming from the green and smiling island of the Danish capital, hated the dark, silent moors, and when I was eight months old my parents emigrated to America. My father stayed there until his death, but my mother developed in the new climate a germ of tuberculosis and had to return to Denmark where she died when I was three

years old, leaving me with her widowed mother.

My father and my grandmother then began a fight to prevent the other from getting custody; they both won . . . and I grew up with strangers, a nice, well-meaning elderly couple, who loved me very much and believed that "because Mummy says so" was an adequate answer to all whys.

I was a very obedient and well-mannered little girl and soon taught myself to escape from all the fears and bewilderment of a lonely childhood into a world of my own, consisting of books, flowers and fantasies.

One of my teachers persuaded my foster parents to let me train as a journalist, and I married very young.

Those two notes really spell my life—I have been married ever since, very happily, to the numismatist Johan Christian Holm. And I have been writing for as long as I can remember.

My books seem to come in threes; the first—poetry of course—was published when I was twenty, and I continued in this vein with the next two; then, after a pause, I wrote three romances . . . it was great fun! And then three books for older children, of which the one I called *David* brought me, surprisingly, world fame—at

least, how else can one describe it, when the story has been televised, radio broadcast and translated with success in sixteen countries and on four continents. . . . And surprisingly, because when I gave it to my publisher at that time, he liked it, but dared not risk the investment. I put it away and forgot about it; saw, a year or so later, that a prize was to be awarded for the best story in Scandinavia for youngsters, thought up a pseudonym, sent the thing in, and forgot about it again. I also forgot what pseudonym I had put, but as I turned out to be the winner, it did not matter.

Perhaps David's loneliness and fear ring true because I knew both as a child. . . . It might also be just inheritance: one of my family, Knud Lyne Rahbek, around the year 1800 was a professor of literature at the University of Copenhagen. He was also one of the lions, although a good-natured one, of intellectual life in Denmark in his period. Being at ease with a blank sheet of paper and a pen perhaps runs in the blood.

I have for many years lived in an old-fashioned house just outside the royal deer park a few kilometers north of Copenhagen; but we enjoy traveling, and have also a small house in Italy, on the Ligurian coast. I am a grandmother now and like it.

I am still writing—but I think I must start a new batch of three; all my publishers want me to write a *David* a year, and no book can be written more than once.

———

David was the winner of the 1963 Gyldendal Prize for the best Scandinavian children's book. Publication in the United States, Britain and Germany, as well as in the Scandinavian countries, resulted. Published in the United States as *North to Freedom*, the book was an American Library Association Notable Book in 1965 and a Gold Medal Winner in the Boys' Club of America Junior Book Award.

The Holms have one son, Rudi Benedek.

SELECTED WORKS: North to Freedom, 1965; Peter, 1968.

ABOUT: Contemporary Authors, Vol. 19–20; Something about the Author, Vol. 1.

FELICE HOLMAN
October 24, 1919–

AUTHOR OF *Slake's Limbo*, etc.

Autobiographical sketch of Felice Holman Valen:

I CAME to life in New York City and was taken quite soon to Long Island where I grew up. It was immediately known that I was to be a writer and this is how: I had an aunt who was a mystic. Just about the time I was born she received an unsolicited message from outer space which she communicated by letter to my mother. I still have this letter in which my aunt declared her clear knowledge that I was the reincarnation of a prolific, though not too well known, writer of the nineteenth century. Thus nobody turned a hair when I started to write poetry at about age six and at that age my first volume of verse appeared. It was a very limited edition of one, illustrated by my mother who was (and is) a very good painter.

My predestination was augmented by another family influence (other than genetic). The maternal side of my family is given to a trait called "hotchenizing"—a word derived from the family name (Hotchner). Freely translated, "hotchenizing" means to embroider the facts for the sole purpose of improving the effect of an otherwise ordinary narrative. Thus, if a member of the family had to run a block to catch a bus, the story could be built into a dramatic incident which involved several bizarre and costumed characters. It could take the whole dinner hour to tell. It was only a short step from that to the written story, and I was one of the members of the family who took the step.

I went from private to public to private schools in Long Island in search of

I don't know what and was sent to boarding school (Drew Seminary in Carmel, N.Y.) where I most definitely did not find it, though I did find material for a book. From there I went to Syracuse University where I studied English and journalism and met a young journalism student who became my husband. We were married as soon as I finished school. (He was a year ahead of me.) I think we were both going to be newspaperpeople but before we could manage it World War II happened and he went off to take care of that. I went to Washington, D.C., to work for the Office of War Information, which I felt could use my writing abilities. They did not. What they needed was another clerk-typist. I could type abominably and could clerk not at *all* and so I was hired. (Probably the often satirical treatment of public figures and government machinery that appears in my stories is related to this year of my life.) After a year I came to New York and entered the make-believe world of fashion copywriting. When I wasn't writing fantasies about some fashionable madness, I was writing poetry and short stories and putting them in suitcases.

When the war ended my husband came home and went back to gag-writing, and a few years later we had a girl child and moved to Connecticut where we kept two typewriters going. It soon became clear that our child believed that any family without a typewriter must be without a means of livelihood. It was, of course, when I began to see things again through a child's eyes that stories for children began to emerge from the pink typewriter. The first books were taken from life—the child and something in nature—and they were the first three Elisabeth books. After that I could see that there were no limits, and the pleasure of writing for children became apparent and the privilege clear. That's why I keep doing it.

Felice Holman married Herbert Valen in 1941. They have one daughter, Nanine Elisabeth, with whom Felice Holman collaborated on a collection of French stories entitled *The Drac.*

Slake's Limbo was an American Library Association Notable Book for 1974.

SELECTED WORKS: Elisabeth the Bird Watcher, 1963; Elisabeth the Treasure Hunter, 1964; Elisabeth and the Marsh Mystery, 1966; Professor Diggins' Dragons, 1966; The Cricket Winter, 1967; At the Top of My Voice and Other Poems, 1970; The Future of Hooper Toote, 1972; I Hear You Smiling, 1973; The Escape of the Giant Hogstalk, 1974; Slake's Limbo, 1974; The Drac: French Tales of Dragons and Demons (with Nanine Valen), 1975.

ABOUT: Contemporary Authors, Vol. 7–8; Something about the Author, Vol. 7; Horn Book October 1976.

JAMES A. HOUSTON

June 12, 1921–

AUTHOR AND ILLUSTRATOR OF *Tikta'liktak*, etc.

Autobiographical sketch of James Archibald Houston:

I HAVE been drawing madly since I was old enough to stand upright. When I was nine years old, my aunt (then president of the Canadian Authors' Association) brought me a short story and sug-

JAMES A. HOUSTON

gested that I illustrate it in ink. I did so with delight, and a little later received a real check from a children's magazine for three dollars. I decided at that moment that I would make my living at art.

By the time I was twelve I was a student at the Toronto Art Gallery, but I had not yet chosen a particular field in art. My friends and I laughed and painted and happily hit each other over the heads with rulers. Then one morning Dr. Arthur Lismer, Canada's greatest art teacher, who had just returned from a trip to the Congo, played African music through the halls of the Art Gallery. He danced among us, his face covered with a great carved mask. It shook me to the core, and I was hooked forever on the art and lives of primitive peoples. I wanted to go to all the farthest corners of the earth.

I had the luck to live a good part of my youth near two Ojibway reservations. Sometimes I fished and gathered wild rice with these Indians. I was always keenly aware of them and admired their life so close to nature. My best Ojibway friend was Nels, a warmhearted grandfather who appeared to be about a hundred years old. On summer mornings I went roaming with Nels over the land and the lake. It seemed to me then that the only education I wanted was to be gained sitting in his ancient boat or stalk-

ing with him through the woods. From
Nels I learned such invaluable things as
how to catch whitefish the Indian way
and how to whistle to a groundhog and
have him whistle right back.

My formal education at the Ontario
College of Art was interrupted after the
first year by Canada's entry into World
War II. For five years I served with the
Toronto Scottish Regiment, stationed
part of this time in British Columbia,
near the villages of the great Northwest
Coast Indians.

With the war over, I went to Paris in
1947 to complete my studies in life drawing. Back in Canada again, in the autumn of 1948, I was looking for subjects
to draw and, by a piece of unbelievable
luck, I was transported to an Eskimo
hunting ground called Inukjuak. It was
on the northeast coast of Hudson Bay, a
gateway to the Eskimo world.

The Eskimos I first lived with spoke
only their own complicated language,
used snow igloos in winter and tents in
summer, hunted for a living in whale-
boats and sealskin kayaks, and had not
yet experienced the use of money. I
found them to be a warm, friendly people, living in a vast, cold and hauntingly
beautiful world. They were short, vital
and oriental in appearance. Their re-
moteness in Canada had protected them
from the onslaught of western civilization. I became a devoted friend, as they
taught me how to survive in their harsh
climate.

When I returned to southern Canada,
I took with me small sculptures—true Eskimo folk art, carved in stone, bone and
ivory. The carvings were eagerly bought
by admirers of this unique art, and, during my twelve years of living in the Arctic, I did everything I could to encourage
carving by the Eskimos and the sale of
these carvings throughout the world. I
also introduced printmaking to the Eskimos of Cape Dorset on Baffin Island.
Now prints are made in a number of
Arctic areas and sold through Eskimo
cooperatives.

I was appointed the first civil administrator of West Baffin Island, a post I
held for eight years. My base was in
Cape Dorset and I traveled throughout
that territory of sixty-five thousand
square miles by dog sled. In the scattered camps I exchanged stories with the
hunters and carvers and I heard the Eskimo legends. I left the Arctic only to
study printmaking: in 1957 with Unichi
Hiratsuka in Tokyo and in 1961 with
William Hayter at Atelier 17 in Paris.

Feeling that the Eskimos should begin
to take a larger part in governing themselves, I moved in 1962 to New York to
become associate director of design for
Steuben Glass. It was then, after meeting
Margaret K. McElderry, at that time
children's book editor at Harcourt Brace,
that I began writing each morning before going to work and on the weekends.
The legends and stories I had heard in
the snowhouses and thought about during the long Arctic nights became the
core of the eight children's books and one
adult novel I have written since 1964.

My wife and I moved recently to an
eighteenth-century farmhouse in New
England. I presently do free-lance work
on books, glass designs and films. We try
to visit the Arctic each year, for we consider it to be our second home.

———

James Houston has twice received the
Canadian Library Association's Book of
the Year Award, in 1966 for *Tikta'liktak*
and in 1968 for *The White Archer*. The
American Library Association designated
The White Archer a Notable Book in
1967, and in 1968 *Akavak* achieved the
same distinction. In addition to his books
for children, James Houston wrote a
novel for adults, *The White Dawn*,
which was a Book-of-the-Month Club
selection and was made into a film for
which the author wrote the script. He
has also written widely about Eskimo
and Indian art.

Houston holds an honorary Litt. D.
from Carleton University in Ottawa and
is an officer of the Order of Canada. He
is deeply involved in the promotion and
protection of Indian and Eskimo arts and
is a member of a number of organiza-

tions for that purpose, including the Canadian Eskimo Arts Council, Canadian Arctic Producers, the American Indian Arts Center in New York, and Indian and Eskimo Art of the Americas. He is a member of the Trustees' Committee on Primitive Art of the Metropolitan Museum of Art and is honorary vice-president of the West Baffin Eskimo Cooperative.

James Houston has two grown sons by his first marriage.

SELECTED WORKS WRITTEN AND ILLUS-TRATED: Tikta'liktak, 1965; Eagle Mask, 1966; The White Archer, 1967; Akavak, 1968; Wolf Run, 1971; Ghost Paddle, 1972; Kiviok's Magic Journey, 1973; Frozen Fire, 1977.

SELECTED WORKS EDITED: Songs of the Dream People, 1972.

ABOUT: Kingman, Lee and others, comps. Illustrators of Children's Books: 1957–1966.

LANGSTON HUGHES

LANGSTON HUGHES

February 1, 1902–May 22, 1967

AUTHOR OF *Dream Keeper*, etc.

Biographical sketch of James Langston Hughes:

JAMES LANGSTON HUGHES was born in Joplin, Missouri, in 1902, the son of James Nathaniel Hughes and Carrie Langston Hughes. Because his parents separated when he was very young he spent much of his time until he was twelve with his grandmother in Lawrence, Kansas. Hughes's grandmother, who was part Cherokee, had gone to college at Oberlin and had married a freeman who was killed in John Brown's raid on Harper's Ferry. She then married John Mercer Langston, who was also a passionate believer in freedom. Hughes loved and admired his grandmother, who raised him on stories of John Brown's raid and taught him "the uselessness of crying about anything." Later he wrote in his autobiography, "Then it was that books began to happen to me, and I began to believe in nothing but

books." He had never written poetry until, in eighth grade, he was elected class poet because, as he liked to tell it, everyone knew the blacks had rhythm—except blacks themselves—and poetry had to have rhythm. Whatever the reason, young Hughes wrote his first poem, to be read at graduation.

When his mother remarried, Hughes went to live with her and his stepfather in Cleveland. He attended Central High School there, wrote poetry, edited the school yearbook, read widely and deeply, and graduated filled with an enthusiasm for life and its possibilities that poverty, racial prejudice, and a disrupted home life had not dampened.

After graduation Hughes went to visit his father, who had moved to Mexico to escape the color line and gone into business there. Hughes found the experience so profoundly upsetting that he became physically ill. Materialistic, middle class, vociferously racist, the elder Hughes contrasted with every ideal his son held and utterly repelled him. Resisting his father's pressure to enter engineering school, he fled north again. He attended Columbia University for one year, but then decided to travel and see the world. In leaving college he made complete the break with his father and the Establishment values he represented, an event he celebrated as soon as he left New York harbor by throwing overboard all the books he had been studying. The next few years were spent working in Europe and Africa, doing a variety of jobs and writing when he could.

His desire to become a writer strengthened, Hughes returned to the United States in 1924, determined to go to college to get the background he felt he needed. He took what jobs he could find. One day Vachel Lindsay, a poet he much admired, visited the hotel in Washington, D.C., where Hughes was working as a busboy. The young man left three of his poems at Lindsay s table with a note. Vachel Lindsay was impressed by the poems, read them at a lecture he was giving that night, and wrote to Hughes, encouraging him to persevere with his writing. The next year, 1925, Hughes's poem "The Weary Blues" won first prize in a contest sponsored by the black magazine *Opportunity*. Thus his work came to the attention of the publisher Alfred A. Knopf, and in 1926 Knopf published Langston Hughes's first book, also called *The Weary Blues*.

One result was that Hughes received a scholarship to Lincoln University in Oxford, Pennsylvania, and in 1929 he graduated. During that year, he had begun his first novel, *Not Without Laughing*, which was published in 1930.

Langston Hughes received a number of awards and fellowships, including a Guggenheim Fellowship in 1935 and a Rosenwald Fellowship in 1941. He traveled extensively in the United States, lecturing and working with students, and he was particularly concerned with encouraging talent in young black writers. His travels also took him to Russia, Japan and Spain, and to Mexico where he translated a number of Cuban and Mexican stories. His Russian trip and his coverage of the Spanish Civil War for the Baltimore *Afro-American*, together with his political activism during the thirties, made him an object of suspicion in the cold war years of the late forties and early fifties, and he was prevented from appearing on public programs in many places.

Hughes earned his living as a writer and was proud of the fact. "Shortly poetry became bread," he wrote. "Prose, shelter and raiment. Words turned into songs, plays, scenarios, articles and stories." After his first book, his poetry continued to be published, and in 1932 his first book of poems for young people, *Dream Keeper*, appeared. He wrote plays and founded community theater groups in Harlem, Los Angeles and Chicago. He also wrote his autobiography, in two parts—*The Big Sea* was published in 1940 and *I Wonder as I Wander* in 1956. Hughes's best-known character, Jess Simple, first appeared in a weekly column Hughes was writing for the Chicago *Defender*. Simple was a black laborer who spent his evenings in Harlem bars and who gave his opinions and advice on all aspects of American life with earthy and pungent humor. Several collections of tales about Simple were later published in book form, and several other volumes of short stories appeared. Hughes wrote a number of books for children, beginning with *The First Book of Negroes*, published in 1952, and he edited collections of black folklore, humor and poetry. He said of his own work: "My writing has been largely concerned with the depicting of Negro life in America."

Langston Hughes was elected to membership in the National Institute of Arts and Letters in 1946. In 1947–48 he was appointed Visiting Professor of Creative Writing at Atlanta University, and in 1949–50, Poet in Residence at the Laboratory School, University of Chicago. Lincoln University awarded him an honorary Litt. D. in 1946, and in 1963 Howard University also awarded him an honorary doctorate, as did Western Reserve University in the following year. He died in 1967, at the age of sixty-five.

Hughes did not hesitate to criticize smugness and hypocrisy wherever he perceived it, whether among blacks or whites, and whatever the personal cost might be to him. He was welcome in many circles of black and white society, but he felt that middle-class people striving for upper-class status constricted his creativity. Because he employed humor and irony, rather than bitter polemic, and because his voice was usually quiet, it was possible for the militant activists of the sixties to overlook Hughes's lifelong dedication to improving the lot of the American black and to call him old-fashioned and even ambivalent about his own color and the role of black people in American society. Nevertheless he was, in the words of one critic, "the poet-laureate of his people. Their life was his life, and he wrote about it as it was." Calling him "an American original," Arna Bontemps considered Hughes one of the brightest stars of the Harlem renaissance, smoothing the way for younger black poets to receive recognition as American rather than black poets.

SELECTED WORKS WRITTEN: Dream Keeper, 1932; The First Book of Negroes, 1952; The First Book of Rhythms, 1954; The First Book of Jazz, 1955; I Wonder as I Wander, 1956; Famous Negro Heroes of America, 1958; Selected Poems of Langston Hughes, 1959; The First Book of Africa, 1964; Simple's Uncle Sam, 1965.

SELECTED WORKS EDITED: African Treasury, 1960; Poems from Black Africa, 1963; The Best Short Stories by Negro Writers, 1967.

ABOUT: Adams, Russell. Great Negroes Past and Present; Barton, Rebecca Chalmers. Witnesses for Freedom; Contemporary Authors, Vol. 25–28; Dekle, Bernard. Profiles of Modern American Authors; Dickinson, Donald C. A Bio-bibliography of Langston Hughes, 1902–1967; Dreer, Herman. American Literature by Negro Authors; Harte, Barbara and Carolyn Riley. 200 Contemporary Authors; Patterson, Robert and others. On Our Way; Richardson, Ben. Great American Negroes; Rollins, Charlemae. Famous American Negro Poets; Something about the Author, Vol. 4; Tappin, Edgar A. A Biographical History of Blacks in America since 1528; Twentieth Century Authors, 1942; Twentieth Century Authors (First Supplement), 1955; Who's Who in America, 1966–67; Current Biography 1940; 1967; Negro History Bulletin March 1964; Newsweek June 5, 1967; New York Times August 1, 1960; May 23, 1967; Phylon Fall 1960; Saturday Review of Literature March 22, 1947; Wilson Library Bulletin November 1969.

KRISTIN HUNTER

September 12, 1931–

AUTHOR OF *The Soul Brothers and Sister Lou*, etc.

Autobiographical sketch of Kristin Elaine Eggleston Hunter Lattany, who writes as Kristin Hunter:

I WAS born in Philadelphia and grew up in the towns of Camden and Magnolia in Camden County, New Jersey, the area to which, without conscious design, I recently returned. My father was an elementary school principal and, during World War II, an Army officer; my mother, a former teacher who had, when I was born, been forcibly retired by a medieval local law that forbade mothers to teach. Our life seemed comfortable to me as a child, but it was, after all, the depression, and my arrival had reduced my parents to living on a single salary. Secure and comfortable as things seemed, I was always aware of money worries rumbling like ominous thunder in the distance, all the more disquieting because they were so vague and remote. I believe I had a tendency to feel it was all my fault, and I did not wonder at all why I was my parents' only offspring. Most of their friends were schoolteacher couples who produced no children at all until the Catholic Church-inspired law was repealed, by which time I was into my teens.

I think my resultant loneliness—and my onliness—led to the fantasizing and omnivorous reading that I believe helps, more than anything else, to produce a writer. Another circumstance that probably dictated the nitty-gritty nature of my later material was, paradoxically, our middle-class status, which set me apart from and made me self-conscious around the only children available to me as playmates, those of relatively poor blacks. Many of our values and habits were simply different from theirs, and they seemed far happier and freer people. I was a "deprived" child in the reverse sense; I was not permitted to chew gum,

KRISTIN HUNTER

buy penny candy or read comic books, and, after I started piano lessons, playing Bach at home was acceptable, but blues and jazz were discouraged. These simple pleasures, taken for granted by other kids my age, took on the allure of the forbidden for me. In addition, though my parents had to scrimp and save, we seemed enormously privileged in comparison with the other black kids I knew, which probably added an element of guilt to the fascination they held for me.

A schoolteaching and sociable aunt, Mrs. Myrtle C. Manigault Stratton, who spent a great deal of time with me until the repeal of that repressive law allowed her to have a daughter of her own, made it possible for me to write a "youth column" for a black weekly when I was fourteen, giving me an early start on a writing career that later included ten years of advertising and public relations jobs but no "real" writing (except for one television play) until the publication of my first novel, *God Bless the Child*, in 1964.

At about that time I finally achieved my other lifelong aim, to become an insider in the ghetto instead of a wistful, alien onlooker. I moved to an apartment a block below South Street, Philadelphia's liveliest black strip. Five years later, I had seen all I needed to see of

South Street, but it had left an indelible imprint on my work.

South Street appears in virtually every one of my books, from my first adult novel, *God Bless the Child*, to my latest, *The Survivors*, as well as in my first book for young people, *The Soul Brothers and Sister Lou*. In each book it is simply called The Avenue, but it is almost a character in its own right; endowed with a life and a personality of its own, it is the focal point of everything that happens in the urban black community. South Street will probably not appear in any more of my books, since my attention has shifted to suburban and even rural aspects of black life as evidenced in my forthcoming book for adults, *Lakestown Rebellion*, but it was generous with material, yielding up information and experience without any digging on my part. I think the so-called ghetto is an exhausted mine now, ravaged greedily by too many writers and students and sociologists, and that we should all leave it alone to either die in peace or renew itself—which is what I think will happen if the ghetto is given half a chance.

Oddly enough, I never intended to write for children. *The Soul Brothers and Sister Lou* came about only because my publisher's juvenile editor asked me to consider writing a children's book. I considered this an outlandish suggestion at first, but something in the back of my mind filed it away and went to work on it without any conscious knowledge. Then came a summer of listening to some talented young street singers under my window in the South Street apartment, and the story of *The Soul Brothers and Sister Lou*, a young singing group, followed.

Two more children's books, *Boss Cat* and *Guests in the Promised Land*, have appeared since, and I am planning a fourth as a sequel to *The Soul Brothers and Sister Lou*. I have long since resolved the class conflicts of my youth, and simply identify with everything that is positively (as opposed to negatively) black. I am living a full but slow-paced life in a semi-suburban cottage with my husband, John I. Lattany, a craftsman and photographer who is the most helpful and loyal enthusiast and partner a writer could hope for. My other work, teaching writing at my alma mater, the University of Pennsylvania, is so enjoyable I am often mildly surprised at being paid for it. The present is rich, and the future looks promising, as long as part of me never grows up—the part that is still childlike enough to get excited about learning and discovering new things, to hope, and even to believe in occasional miracles.

————

Kristin Hunter received her Bachelor of Science degree in education from the University of Pennsylvania in 1951. After a year's trial, however, finding the classroom discipline required for teaching distasteful, she turned to writing. For bread and butter she worked as an advertising copywriter and in public relations.

In 1955 her television play, *Minority of One*, won the Fund for the Republic's television script competition and was produced on national television the following year. In 1959–60 she held a John Hay Whitney Opportunity Fellowship. Her *The Soul Brothers and Sister Lou* was widely acclaimed for its warm yet honest picture of ghetto life and was among the first children's books dealing with black concerns whose worth depended upon their literary value as much or more than their sociological value. *The Soul Brothers and Sister Lou* was awarded the 1968 Council on Interracial Books for Children Award and, in the same year, the Mass Media Award for the National Conference of Christians and Jews. Translated into Dutch, it received a Silver Slate-Pencil award from the Dutch Publishers Association. *Guests in the Promised Land*, a collection of short stories, won the prize for the best book in the older age category in the 1973 *Book World* Children's Spring Book Festival. It also received a Christopher Award and was nominated for the Na-

tional Book Award. *The Survivors* was designated a Best Book for Young Adults by the American Library Association for 1975.

Kristin Hunter's marriage to John Hunter ended in divorce. She married John Lattany on June 22, 1968.

SELECTED WORKS: The Soul Brothers and Sister Lou, 1968; Boss Cat, 1971; Guests in the Promised Land, 1973; The Survivors, 1975.

ABOUT: Contemporary Authors, Vol. 13–14; Foremost Women in Communications, 1970; Hoffman, Miriam and Eva Samuels. Authors and Illustrators of Children's Books; Who's Who of American Women, 1974–1975; Top of the News January 1970.

PAT HUTCHINS

June 18, 1942–

AUTHOR AND ILLUSTRATOR OF *Rosie's Walk*, etc.

Autobiographical sketch of Patricia Hutchins:

I WAS born in 1942, in an army training camp on the moors in the North Riding of Yorkshire. The commando training course was a full-time playground for us children. We could soon swing the gun turret on a tank and manage the assault course as well as any commando.

When my brother and I were discovered wandering across a rifle range during target practice, my mother decided it was time to move.

Our new home was in a quiet little village, a safe five miles away from the army camp. There we spent our time running wild in the surrounding woods and fields. Mother was forever providing food and lodging to fledgling birds who had fallen from their nests, injured animals rescued from traps, and kittens saved from drowning in the farmer's bucket. They were nursed until they recovered, or were buried with great solemnity under the black currant bush in the garden if they didn't.

One survivor, a crow, decided to stay

Pat Hutchins

and became the bane of my mother's life because of his passion for tinned meat; we were still on rationing then, and coupons were precious. He would sit for hours in front of the fire, wings outstretched and gazing into the flames, stubbornly resisting any attempts to shift him so the warmth could be shared by the rest of us.

Apart from the crow and the seven children, there was a kitten who was terrified of the crow, five pigeons until the kitten grew and climbed into their loft, several white mice belonging to my younger brother, a hedgehog, and a dog who eventually went mad. It was very cheerful and in spite of the overcrowding, everyone was welcome there.

To escape from the noise occasionally, Sooty the crow and I would set off across the fields, and while he rooted for grubs and worms, I sketched. At sixteen I won a scholarship to the local art school. From there I moved to Leeds College of Art to specialize in illustration, very much in awe of the fact that Henry Moore and Barbara Hepworth had studied there.

To have any chance of getting a job it was necessary to go to London, and after six months of part-time shop assisting I did get a job, in an advertising agency. There I met my husband Laurence.

He was to be transferred to his company's head office in New York. Five days after our marriage we arrived in New York where I tried to get work illustrating.

The Macmillan Company liked my work and encouraged me to write my own stories. *Rosie's Walk* and *Tom and Sam* were written and illustrated while we were in New York.

In 1968 we returned to London, where our first son, Morgan, was born—a new source of ideas for stories.

We live in Hampstead, close to the Heath. Our second son, Sam, was born in 1973.

Pat Hutchins' books have received critical accolades and appeared on lists of outstanding books ever since the publication of her first, *Rosie's Walk*, in 1968. *Rosie's Walk* was an American Library Association Notable Book in 1968 as were *Changes, Changes* in 1971 and *Good-Night Owl* in 1972. *Changes, Changes* was an Honor Book in the *Book World* Children's Spring Book Festival in 1971 and was chosen for the Children's Book Council's 1971 Children's Book Showcase. The same title was also included in the 1971–72 Children's Book Show mounted by the American Institute of Graphic Arts. In 1975 Pat Hutchins received the 1974 Kate Greenaway Medal, presented by the British Library Association for the most distinguished work in the illustration of children's books, for *The Wind Blew*.

Speaking of her work, Pat Hutchins says, "I try to keep my stories logical, even if a story is pure fantasy. I used to get terribly frustrated as a child if I couldn't understand the reasoning behind a plot, if someone waved a wand and everything fell into place with no explanation. . . . When I have an idea, I sit down and work out the best way of putting the idea across in book form; then I write the story and design the layout. It's very satisfying to know it's all your own work, from the original idea to the finished artwork."

Pat Hutchins' favorite pastimes are painting and collecting Victoriana, and she loves to watch birds. One of her dreams is to have a cottage and some land in her native Yorkshire. In an interview with Elaine Moss, the noted British book critic, she said, "There's a word that describes people like me, but I can't for the life of me think what it is." The reason, the interviewer concluded, is because Pat Hutchins "is a person, not a type."

SELECTED WORKS WRITTEN AND ILLUSTRATED: Rosie's Walk, 1968; The Surprise Party, 1969; Clocks and More Clocks, 1970; Changes, Changes, 1971; Good-Night Owl, 1972; The Silver Christmas Tree, 1974; The Wind Blew, 1974; And Don't Forget the Bacon, 1975; Follow That Bus, 1977.

SELECTED WORKS WRITTEN: The House That Sailed Away, 1975.

ABOUT: Signal January 1973.

TRINA SCHART HYMAN

April 8, 1939–

ILLUSTRATOR OF *King Stork*, etc.

Autobiographical sketch of Trina Schart Hyman:

I WAS born in Philadelphia, Pennsylvania, on April 8, 1939, thanks to my mother, who is a gingery, independent, capable lady with red hair, and my father, who was a quiet, funny man who liked to go fishing and play the accordion. I grew up in a little tiny town north of the city. There was a beautiful farm across the road from our house, and lots of woods and streams and backyards all around. I also had a little sister who soon grew to be six feet tall and wise and beautiful, but we were always good friends in spite of that. I had a very nice childhood, and I enjoyed myself very much most of the time. I liked best to be under the kitchen table with the dog, and for one whole year I really believed that I was Red Riding Hood—but my family never seemed to mind, so I grew up encouraged.

After I graduated from high school I

went to the Philadelphia Museum School of Art to learn to be an illustrator, which is what I had in mind to do since I was about six. I had a lovely time in art school, and Henry C. Pitz was my favorite teacher.

In 1959 I married my friend Harris and we lived in Boston for a year, where I went to the Boston Museum School and learned about etching and lithography and serigraph. Then we went to Stockholm so that Harris could learn about statistics, and I went to the Swedish state art school for a year. Towards the end of that year I went looking for work, and met Astrid Lindgren who was editor at Rabén and Sjögren and who gave me my first real illustration job. It took me two months to read the book (it was in Swedish) and two weeks to illustrate it.

Then Harris and I took a three-thousand-mile bicycle trip through south Sweden, Denmark, Norway and England. We arrived back in the States with fifty-six cents between us. I had illustrated my first book, learned Swedish, and learned how to pedal a bicycle up mountains and then carry it down on my back. We lived in Boston for the next five years, and after a very discouraging year of pounding New York and Boston pavements with my portfolio, I finally got to illustrate a Little Golden Book. Gradually I got more work, and one of these first important books was for Helen Jones at Little, Brown, who subsequently taught me more about children's books and book publishing and being a good illustrator than anyone or anything else ever has. In 1963 I did my first picture book, for Houghton Mifflin, and had a baby. The baby turned out to be a very articulate and strong-minded little girl, who is now fifteen years old and my severest and most frequent critic. The picture book turned out rather dreadful, but I learned a lot from it.

In 1967 Harris and I parted company and I escaped to New Hampshire along with Katrin, an artist friend, and her twin daughters and some cats, where we all lived very happily in a little stone house on the banks of a big river, with a farm next door and the mountains all around. I wrote my first children's book during that first winter, and fell in love with the countryside, and started to illustrate books at the rate of six or eight a year. The long snowy winters are fine weather for working hard in, and I worked hard, and read children's books when I wasn't working, and sometimes did a painting or used a friend's etching press to do a few etchings. Work is my main vice and my only virtue.

At the present time I live in a big 150-year-old wooden farmhouse, not too far from the river, with falling-down barns and cobwebs in the corners and mice in the attic and huge mossy ancient sugar-maple trees on the front lawn. There are three people, me and Katrin and Dilys, who gives us tea and something to read, and two dogs, and five or six or eight cats, depending on the season, and ten chickens who walk around and lay eggs, and twenty sheep in the back field. We grow flowers and a few vegetables, and our best friend Mr. O'Donnell, who lives across the road, takes care of us and the sheep, and gives us news of the world. Mostly we do our work—Dilys paints and Katrin writes poetry and I fight with drawings and stories and write to some faraway fascinating and friendly artists who help me with a magazine for children called *Cricket*. Our house is filled with books and pictures and stories. We live with them and work with them and learn from them and relax with them, and someday I'll be able to draw it all with some degree of accuracy.

———

Trina Schart Hyman's work has been included in the American Institute of Graphic Arts shows of best-illustrated children's books, and *Greedy Mariani* was in the 1975 Children's Book Showcase of the Children's Book Council as was *Magic in the Mist* in 1976. *King Stork* was a Caldecott Honor Book in 1974 and an American Library Association Notable Book for Children.

In addition to her own book illustration, Trina Schart Hyman is art director for *Cricket* magazine.

Selected Works Written and Illustrated: Sleeping Beauty (retold from Grimm), 1977.

Selected Works Illustrated: Curl Up Small, by Sandol Stoddard Warburg, 1964; Stuck with Luck, by Elizabeth Johnson, 1967; The Moon Singer, by Clyde Robert Bulla, 1969; The Pumpkin Giant, by Ellin Greene, 1970; Magic Heart, by Jan Wahl, 1972; The Popular Girls, by Phyllis Krasilovsky, 1972; King Stork, by Howard Pyle, 1973; Snow White, by Jacob and Wilhelm Grimm, 1974; Why Don't You Get a Horse, Sam Adams?, by Jean Fritz, 1974; Greedy Mariani and Other Folktales of the Antilles, by Dorothy Sharp Carter, comp., 1974; Magic in the Mist, by Margaret Mary Kimmel, 1975; Jane, Wishing, by Tobi Tobias, 1977.

About: Contemporary Authors, Vol. 49–52; Kingman, Lee and others, comps. Illustrators of Children's Books, 1957–1966; Something about the Author, Vol. 7; Cricket September 1975.

S. R. VAN ITERSON

Author of *Pulga*, etc.

Autobiographical sketch of Siny Rose van der Breggen van Iterson:

WHEN I was two years old my father

Siny van Iterson: *SEEN ee van EETER son*

and I traveled from the island of Curaçao, where I was born, to Holland. There
we lived for a long time, although we
traveled a lot and never were in the
same place for long. But when I was
eight or nine years old we settled for a
time in a small historical town, which
still had the old walls and moats of the
stronghold it had been in the Middle
Ages.

To me it seemed that our big rambling
house must have been built around that
time too. The rooms were huge, the hall
cold, the walls always damp. Everywhere
there were dark corners, small rooms
without light, creaky doors and stair-
cases. No room was at the same level
with the next, and some windows had
deep sills where I could sit for hours.

In that house I started to write. I wrote
all kinds of stories—fairy tales, love stories with happy endings, and even poetry. (A child dares to undertake everything.)

After we left town again, my pen
stayed quiet for a long time. I was busy
growing up. War came and ended. Now
married and with my small family, we
went again to Curaçao, that small island
I had always dreamed of, although I had
not the faintest recollection of this place
where I was born.

There in a lonely country house, far
from town, I started to write again, intrigued by this life as it was lived on
those lonesome farms. The superstition
of the people, their customs and behavior, everything I encountered under that
hot and burning sun.

On a whim I sent off the manuscript
and it was accepted, although they kept
me waiting six months before answering.
The second story I wrote about Curaçao
was accepted within two weeks.

It was during the time we lived in
Curaçao that we made a trip to Colombia, never dreaming that it would become my second homeland, or is it my
third? In the end you do not know where
you do belong anymore!

We went back to Holland for a few
years, our family grew, and one day we
packed up our three children and started

S. R. VAN ITERSON

a new life and a new baby in Colombia.
The consequence was that I had to start
a new book, too, as I wanted to dedicate
a book to each of them. Colombia is a
fascinating country. Nature is over-
powering. It seems to form its people.
They are hard and resigned, they are
simple, cruel, human and good. The
more I found out about their culture,
customs, legends and beliefs, the more I
wanted to tell about it. They are part of
their surroundings; one could not put
these stories or the characters in another
setting. They would not fit. At one time
I dedicated one book to my four children
together, Foyita, Victor, Loretta and
Marnix. It brought me a literary award
in Holland and translations in other
countries. So on our first trip to the
United States I decided to take this book
along and see if I could combine pleasure with business. (Not that anybody
gave me the smallest hope, but still I
thought the least I could do was to try
to see a publisher.)

The most difficult people to crack, I
found, were the doorman and the receptionist. Once you have safely passed
them by, everybody is nice and kind and
friendly. I sold my story *Pulga* to William Morrow. The second one, *Village of
Outcasts*, followed a year later. And the
year after that came *The Curse of La-*

guna Grande. Then two more. Is more
to follow? One never knows. In Colombia there is a saying that some people
have a *don*, a gift of God one could call
it. I am quite aware that that gift can be
taken away from me any moment.

De Adjutant van de Vrachtwagen,
published in the United States as *Pulga,*
received the Dutch Juvenile Book Prize
in 1969 and was on the Hans Christian
Andersen Honor List in 1970. *Pulga* was
an American Library Association Notable Book in 1971, and in 1973 earned the
Mildred L. Batchelder Award for its
publisher.

SELECTED WORKS: Pulga, 1971; Village
of Outcasts, 1972; The Curse of Laguna
Grande, 1973; The Smugglers of Buenaven-
tura, 1974; In the Spell of the Past, 1975;
The Spirits of Chocamata, 1977.

ABOUT: Bookbird No. 2, 1970; School
Media Quarterly Summer 1973.

JACQUELINE JACKSON
May 3, 1928–

AUTHOR OF *The Taste of Spruce Gum,*
etc.

Autobiographical sketch of Jacqueline
Dougan Jackson:

WHEN I was eight my parents took a
trip. We children wanted to do something to surprise them on their return.
My sisters' projects I forget, but my little brother determined to get over his
"lithp" and I decided to write a book.
We both succeeded, and our parents
were surprised and very pleased. I think
the immediate cause of my idea was the
finding of a large blank notebook just
begging to be filled, and a homeless
poem I'd composed the year before. I
placed "Five White Ducks" on the second page, since any author knows
enough to leave the first for the Table
of Contents, and I was off—on a miscel-
lany of short stories, poems, anecdotes,

pictures, jokes—and also, I realize now,
on a writing career.

Background causes included a long
and passionate relationship with books,
for my parents read to us from the
cradle; I was a preschool reader; my
older sisters were voracious print-eaters;
and we were surrounded by stimulating
adult and children's books, the latter including Kipling, George Macdonald,
Kingsley, Jules Verne and Frances Hodgson Burnett, not merely the ubiquitous
Nancy Drew, whom we also enjoyed.

Other causes were my family's wide
interests and my rich environment. I
grew up on a dairy and hybrid seed-corn
farm in southern Wisconsin, where I had
a lot of outdoors, animals, interesting
activities to watch, and interesting people to listen to. I took for granted the
University of Wisconsin Agronomy professors who showed up frequently for
noonday dinners, and visiting concert
artists who stayed the night, friends of
my mother in the music world.

I was not only an avid watcher and
listener but, whenever I could be, a par-
ticipator. I detasseled corn. I delivered
milk all over Beloit one summer as a
milkman's helper and got to know every
dog in town, as well as many kitchens. I
had my first conscious awareness of the
contrasts in people and in their circum-

stances, for I unloaded my carrier on the rotting steps of tarpaper hovels that were flooded by the river each spring, and I obeyed the inconspicuous signs that instructed Deliveries in the Rear at the spacious mansions on Sherwood Drive. Sometimes people swore at me; sometimes they invited me in for cookies.

In the fourth grade I wrote a collection of stories about two dog brothers, Bumpy and Billy Bones, and in fifth grade an Oz-ish novel which was published in installments in a weekly newspaper. It ran for four months and could have run four more, but I ended it abruptly when the printed word caught up with my unfinished manuscript. In sixth grade and the years following I turned to scholarship and music, for I was discovering that writing, as I did it, didn't fit the rules.

I'll never forget my incredulous joy when I arrived at Beloit College and found that creative writing had a respectable place in the curriculum. I grabbed every course offered, and owe an unrepayable debt to my first writing professor, Chad Walsh, and later to his and my teacher at the University of Michigan, Roy Cowden. *Julie's Secret Sloth* was written at Michigan, when I was twenty-two. My major was not English or composition, though, but Latin and Greek, a strong foundation for an author which I've never regretted. My major professor, Don King, felt everything was related to the classics, so I was able to take all the other things that delighted me: art, music, literature, biology, history, religion, anthropology.

Then marriage, babies, and no money for sitters or household help brought my writing to a near standstill for too many years, but I slowly produced *The Paleface Redskins* and *The Taste of Spruce Gum*, and then more rapidly my later titles. I love all my books; like my children each is unique, and each, whether a chicken's life in an egg factory, or a girl in a lumber camp atop a Vermont mountain in 1903, or a Wisconsin lake saga of my childhood, or a futuristic horror story where humans are bolted into wheels from birth, has its individual integrity, depth, humor and truth.

My girls, Damaris, Megan, Gillian and Elspeth, are all readers, writers and exacting critics. Our favorite author is Ursula LeGuin. I'm a professor at Sangamon State University in Springfield, Illinois, and the courses I enjoy teaching most are writing, fantasy (I mix "adult" and "children's" fantasies), a Public Affairs Colloquium on "Aspects of Women's Liberation" with special emphasis on children's conditioning, and history of children's literature. Horatio Alger is back, in paperback, but I'm waiting impatiently for an Elsie Dinsmore revival, so that my students can moan with Demi, "I *know* it's a soupy book, but I still weep buckets every time I read it!" or chortle with Megan "Elsie's so awful she's *great!*"

———

Jacqueline Jackson earned her Bachelor of Arts degree *summa cum laude* from Beloit College in 1950 and her Master of Arts from the University of Michigan in 1951. She is a member of Phi Beta Kappa.

In addition to her writing and teaching, Mrs. Jackson is a cellist. She studied at the Wisconsin School of Music in Madison for ten years, and for the last five was the principal cellist with a local chamber music group, with one summer out for study at Tanglewood. She is also an artist and has illustrated several books, including two of her own, *The Paleface Redskins* and *The Ghost Boat*.

Mrs. Jackson has written numerous articles and short stories for young people and frequently lectures around the country on the subject of writing and especially writing for children.

The Taste of Spruce Gum was chosen a Notable Children's Book of 1966 by the American Library Association and received the Dorothy Canfield Fisher Children's Book Award in 1968.

SELECTED WORKS WRITTEN: Julie's Secret Sloth, 1953; The Taste of Spruce Gum, 1966; Missing Melinda, 1967; Chicken Ten Thousand, 1968; Spring Song, 1969; The

Orchestra Mice, 1970; The Endless Pavement (with William Perlmutter), 1973; Turn Not Pale Beloved Snail, 1974.

SELECTED WORKS WRITTEN AND ILLUSTRATED: The Paleface Redskins, 1968; The Ghost Boat, 1969.

ABOUT: Contemporary Authors, Vol. 45–48; Who's Who in America, 1972–1973.

"JANOSCH"

March 11, 1931–

AUTHOR AND ILLUSTRATOR OF *Just One Apple*, etc.

Autobiographical sketch of Horst Eckert, who writes and illustrates under the pseudonym "Janosch":

"JANOSCH"

I WAS born in 1931 in Zaborze, a place more Polish than German. Until I was thirteen years old I went to school there. After that I worked in a blacksmith's shop, and after that in some factories. In 1953 I tried to study at the Academy of Art in Munich, because I wanted to be a painter, because I would be free. But I didn't succeed. I had to leave the academy. I had no talent. However, from that time I lived free in Munich or near there, beside a lake, and I lived by doing odd jobs, painting textiles or papering walls. But it was too much work and I looked for other jobs, until by chance a friend (we were sitting in a coffeehouse) said, "Try to make a children's book. I know a girl who works in a publishing house. She will arrange it."

I tried, but the girl could not arrange it because the book wasn't good. I tried once more. Then another girl arranged it. She worked in another publishing house. That was in 1960, and this first book was *Valek*. This book sold eight hundred copies in thirteen years, but it was translated into Spanish. And now bookmaking was a good job—except for the first six books—because the seventh book sold ninety thousand copies, and some of the following fifty or sixty books were like this. Last time I counted, there were twenty-one translations, but the number of books I don't count any more.

I write and paint the books myself, because it is more trouble to find an author or painter who suits me than to do it myself in the same time.

And now I succeed too in painting. I have had many exhibitions, and it doesn't matter so much whether the pictures are all sold every time because now I don't need money. But to be a painter—that was what I wanted to become when it began.

———

Janosch's pictures are known to children all over the world, for his books have been translated into Dutch, French, English, Spanish, Catalonian, Italian, Russian, Swedish, Afrikaans and Japanese. Altogether more than half a million copies have been sold.

Janosch has been on the Honor List for the German Children's Book Prize, and in 1972 he was cited as Highly Commended by the Hans Christian Andersen jury for the body of his work.

In addition to writing and illustrating his own picture books and those of other authors, Janosch has illustrated textbooks, readers and poetry collections and drawn book jackets and posters. He has written a novel for adults, *Cholonek, oder*

der liebe Gott aus Lehm (Cholonek, or the God of Clay), which has been very successful in Germany.

SELECTED WORKS WRITTEN AND ILLUS-TRATED: Just One Apple, 1966; Tonight at Nine, 1967; Joshua and the Magic Fiddle, 1968; Dear Snowman, 1970; The Thieves and the Raven, 1970; The Crocodile Who Wouldn't Be King, 1970; The Magic Auto, 1971; The Yellow Car Named Ferdinand, 1973.

SELECTED WORKS ILLUSTRATED: The Magic Paintbrush, by Mischa Damjan, 1967; Lazy Blackbird and Other Verses, by Jack Prelutsky, 1969; How Does a Czar Eat Potatoes?, by A. K. Rose, 1973.

ABOUT: Contemporary Authors, Vol. 37–40; Hürlimann, Bettina. Picture Book World; Something about the Author, Vol. 8; Bookbird No. 2, 1973.

ANNE MARIE JAUSS

February 3, 1907–

AUTHOR AND ILLUSTRATOR OF *Discovering Nature the Year Round*, etc.

Autobiographical sketch of Anne Marie Jauss:

I WAS born in Munich, Germany. With my father the landscape painter Georg Jauss, I grew up among artists. I have been drawing as long as I can remember and was always writing something. Reading was one of the great pleasures of my childhood, especially the classics. I was always deeply interested in nature. After studying at the State Art School in Munich, I lived temporarily in Berlin. While there I wrote for the women's page of a Berlin newspaper, and my early paintings were exhibited in various places. This promising beginning came to an end when, with the approach of Hitler, I left Germany in 1932 to live in Lisbon, Portugal. There I made a living mainly as a designer, did some book work, had several one-man shows and exhibited with the modern Portuguese artists group at their annual show.

In 1946 I came to the United States and lived in New York City. In 1947 I had a one-man show of animal paintings at Portraits Inc., called "Portraits of Pets," and received a lot of publicity. I had always desired to do children's books. I finally realized the ambition when Pantheon Books commissioned me to illustrate *The Stars in Our Heaven* by Peter Lum in 1948. This book is still in print. The first book of my own was a book of proverbs, *Wise and Otherwise*. The book of *Legends of Saints and Beasts* followed. In 1955 I had written my first nature book, *Discovering Nature the Year Round*, also still in print. Including my own, I have illustrated some sixty books.

About defining my approach: I try to do something which is essentially simple and timeless. My inspiration comes from the past and from folk art, never from contemporary art.

Since 1962 I have been living in rural northern New Jersey, enjoying the closeness of the woods.

———

Anne Marie Jauss is widely traveled in the United States and Europe, and her work is in many private collections as well as in the Print Collection at the New York Public Library. She has had several one-man shows in New York and Pennsylvania. *The Pasture*, which she wrote

Jauss: *JOWSS*

and illustrated, received the Author's Award of the New Jersey Association of Teachers of English in 1968. In 1972 *Tracking the Unearthly Creatures of Marsh and Pond*, with text by Howard G. Smith, received a Christopher Award. In 1974 her water colors were exhibited at the Larcada Gallery in New York.

SELECTED WORKS WRITTEN AND ILLUSTRATED: Wise and Otherwise, 1953; Legends of Saints and Beasts, 1954; Discovering Nature the Year Round, 1955; River's Journey, 1957; Under a Green Roof, 1960; The Pasture, 1968; The Little Horse of Seven Colors (with Patricia Lowe), 1970.

SELECTED WORKS ILLUSTRATED: The Stars in Our Heaven, by Peter Lum, 1948; Stubborn Donkey, by C. Grantoff, 1949; Some Dogs, by E. M. Parker, 1950; Experiments With a Microscope, by Nelson F. Beeler and Franklyn M. Branley, 1957; Magnets and How to Use Them, by T. S. Pine and J. Levine, 1958; The Falcon and the Dove, by Alfred Duggan, 1966; Piñatas, by Virginia Brock, 1966; The Valiant Little Tailor, by Jacob and Wilhelm Grimm, 1967; The Nightingale and the Emperor, by Hans Christian Andersen, 1970; Collecting Small Fossils, by Lois J. Hussey and Catherine Pessino, 1971; Tracking the Unearthly Creatures of Marsh and Pond, by Howard G. Smith, 1972; The Easy Book of Numbers and Numerals, by David C. Whitney, 1973.

ABOUT: Contemporary Authors, Vol. 1; Foremost Women in Communications, 1970; Kingman, Lee and others, comps. Illustrators of Children's Books: 1957–1966; Viguers, Ruth Hill. Illustrators of Children's Books: 1947–1956.

SUSAN JEFFERS

1942–

AUTHOR AND ILLUSTRATOR OF *Three Jovial Huntsmen*, etc.

Autobiographical sketch of Susan Jeffers:

MY career as an artist began in a tiny school in Oakland, New Jersey, when I was chosen to paint a history mural with the usual Egyptians harvesting in muddy tempera fields. I suspect that I was selected as much for my ability to keep poster paint from running, as for my drawing talent. Yet I was on my way. I

went on to Valentine's Day calendars, fire prevention posters, and Easter bunnies.

Happily for me, I had a very kind mother. She spent hours teaching me how to look at things. She showed me how to make objects appear round or flat and how to mix paint. Best of all she gave me a feeling of immense joy in my work.

In my senior year of high school I chose Pratt Institute for my art education. There I associated with dedicated artists for the first time in my life. I remember slipping into Richard Lindner's illustration class twenty minutes late one day hoping to be unobserved. He stopped the class and with great deliberation turned to me and said reproachfully, "Young woman, art is a love affair." I had never thought of art in those terms before, but that is how I have thought of it since.

After graduation in 1964 I worked in three publishing houses beginning with the simplest jobs; repairing type, pasting up illustrations, and designing books and jackets. I developed a concrete knowledge of children's books there and began to feel again the love I had for them as a child. As I worked on other artists' books,

I became more and more impatient to create them myself.

It was rather frightening to think of working free-lance but it was the only alternative. I needed the freedom of my own time. I managed to make enough to live on and soon began my first book in 1968, *The Buried Moon*. At about this time I also began a studio with Rosemary Wells. Together we worked on jackets and books, pooling our talents and ideas. It was wonderful for inspiration and encouragement and especially laughter.

My next book was *The Three Jovial Huntsmen* which took three years to complete. I actually did the book from start to finish twice. The first version was a terrible disappointment on press and the decision was made not to publish it. I took the next year off to mull things over and teach art at the Wiltwyck School for Boys. There was something compelling to me about that book, however, that I could not forget, and I decided to begin again. The second version was a success and was wonderfully rewarded with a Caldecott Honor Book citation in 1974.

All the Pretty Horses followed. Surely the most effortless book I may ever do, it flowed directly from the talks I used to have with my sister when we were very young just before we dropped off to sleep.

I have just finished a Scottish folktale called *Wild Robin* and a beautiful poem, *Close Your Eyes*, by Jean Marzollo. I am presently working on the magnificent poem by Robert Frost "Stopping by Woods on a Snowy Evening," and a collection of Mother Goose rhymes *If Wishes Were Horses*.

I live and work in Westchester County in a small house on a lake. Around me are the woods and animals that I love to draw, including a Siberian husky named Sitka, who is a hilarious model for my dogs, and a beautiful mare called Antigone. Aside from my books, I love to be outdoors, paint, horseback ride, and spend time with good friends.

———

An instant success, *Three Jovial Huntsmen* brought to its creator awards and honors that might be the envy of artists with a far longer list of works to their credit. The book was a Caldecott Honor Book in 1974, included in the American Institute of Graphic Arts' 1974 Children's Book Show and in the 1974 Children's Book Showcase, and twice cited as a Brooklyn Art Book for Children. In 1975 the jury of the Biennale of Illustrations Bratislava awarded Susan Jeffers a Golden Apple for her *Huntsmen* illustrations. *Wild Robin* was one of the *Horn Book*'s seven best books for 1976.

SELECTED WORKS WRITTEN AND ILLUSTRATED: Three Jovial Huntsmen: A Mother Goose Rhyme, 1973; All the Pretty Horses, 1974; Wild Robin, 1976.

SELECTED WORKS ILLUSTRATED: Everyhow Remarkable, by Victoria Lincoln, 1967; The Buried Moon, by Joseph Jacobs, 1969; (with Rosemary Wells) The Shooting of Dan McGrew (and) The Cremation of Sam McGee, by Robert W. Service, 1969; (with Rosemary Wells) Why You Look Like You, Whereas I Tend to Look Like Me, by Charlotte Pomerantz, 1969; The Spirit of Spring, by Penelope Proddow, 1970; The First of the Penguins, by Mary Q. Steele, 1973.

ABOUT: Top of the News January 1975.

JAMES WELDON JOHNSON
June 17, 1871–June 26, 1938

AUTHOR OF *Lift Every Voice and Sing*, etc.

Biographical sketch of James William Johnson, who wrote as James Weldon Johnson:

JAMES WELDON JOHNSON was born in Jacksonville, Florida, in 1871. His father, James Johnson, was an enterprising, self-educated man, the head waiter at the St. James Hotel in Jacksonville. Helen Louise Dillet Johnson, his mother, was a native of Nassau in the Bahamas. An intelligent woman of considerable musical talent, she was the first black woman to teach in the Florida public schools. She gave both James and his

JAMES WELDON JOHNSON

younger brother Rosamond piano lessons when they were very small, but although James was to enjoy music all his life, it was Rosamond who displayed real musical ability.

James Johnson was educated at Stanton School, Jacksonville's only school for blacks. After finishing grade school, he attended the high school department of Atlanta University, since there were no black high schools in Jacksonville at that time, and he then entered the college program. There he was first confronted with the problems of race. Although he himself had not experienced injustice or cruelty, many of his classmates had. Johnson wrote at this time: "I began to get the full understanding of my relationship to America and to take on my share of the peculiar responsibilities and burdens which every Negro in the United States is compelled to carry. Here was an experience so harrowing that the inner problem of a Negro in America becomes that of not allowing it to choke and suffocate him."

After graduating in 1894, Johnson accepted a job at Stanton School, and on the retirement of the former head, he became principal. He decided to expand the school, and without consulting the board, he gradually added advanced grades, often teaching the classes him-

self until his students were receiving a high school education. Besides his work at the school, Johnson and a friend founded and edited the first black daily paper in the United States, the *Daily American*, though unfortunately it lasted only a few months. He also studied law in a lawyer's office, and in 1897 he became the first black to be admitted to the Florida bar through open examination.

In the meantime Rosamond Johnson had graduated from the Boston Conservatory of Music and returned to Jacksonville. The brothers collaborated on musical entertainments, James writing the words and Rosamond the music. Together they wrote "Lift Every Voice and Sing," a song which achieved widespread popularity and in time became known as the Negro national anthem. They decided to try their luck in New York. At first James only spent his summers there and returned each fall to Stanton School, but in 1901 he moved permanently to New York. The Johnson brothers and another black musician, Bob Cole, formed a highly successful songwriting team.

While Rosamond Johnson and Cole toured as a vaudeville act, James stayed in New York, studying at Columbia University, writing poetry, and gradually becoming involved in politics. His support for Theodore Roosevelt's presidential campaign brought him to the attention of Charles W. Anderson, a member of Booker T. Washington's "Black Cabinet," who was looking for blacks to enter the U.S. Consular Service. Johnson was offered the job of U.S. Consul at Puerto Cabello, Venezuela, and accepted.

In Venezuela Johnson continued to write poetry, much of which was published in the *Century* magazine and *The Independent*. One of his most famous poems, "O Black and Unknown Bards," which is addressed to the anonymous authors of the spiritual, was written during this period. Johnson also finished his novel, *The Autobiography of an Ex-Colored Man*, which was published anonymously in 1912.

This book caused a considerable stir

when it first appeared. Its central character is a black man who, as a child, passes for white. When he is forced to recognize that he is black, he attempts to come to terms with his heritage, but he changes direction again after witnessing a lynching. He becomes obsessed with material success and marries a white woman, renouncing his blackness. Later Johnson had repeatedly to deny that the story was autobiographical. The book, which was described by Jessie Fauset in *The Crisis* as "the epitome of the race situation," is considered a forerunner of the Harlem Renaissance, anticipating later novels both in its use of a detailed New York setting and in its middle-class hero. It shows penetrating insight into the problem of dual heritage.

In 1927 the book was reissued, this time under Johnson's name. Meanwhile, Johnson had been appointed U.S. Consul at Corinto, Nicaragua, and had married Grace Nail of Brooklyn who shared with him the dangers of revolution-torn Nicaragua for three years. Johnson resigned from the Consular Service when he realized his race would prevent him from receiving the promotion he merited. After returning to New York he accepted the post of Field Secretary of the National Association for the Advancement of Colored People. He was determined to arouse blacks to action, and he increased the number of the NAACP's branches from 68 to 310, many of them in the deep South. In 1920 he investigated complaints of brutality by U.S. troops occupying Haiti and wrote a series of articles which appeared in *The Crisis* and the *Nation*. Later that same year he became executive secretary of the NAACP, the first black to take charge of all the association's work. His friend W. E. B. Du Bois commented on his ability "to meet and please all manner of men," which proved of great value in dealing with the many different people he met in the course of his work for the NAACP.

During this time Johnson compiled the first collection of poems by black writers, *The Book of American Negro Poetry*, published in 1922, and with his brother Rosamond he edited *The Books of American Negro Spirituals*. This appeared in 1925 and was followed by a second volume the next year. In 1927 *God's Trombones: Seven Negro Sermons in Verse* was published. This book won Johnson the Harmon Award. He also received the NAACP's Spingarn Medal "for the highest or noblest achievement by an American Negro." Both Talledega College and Howard University awarded him the degree of Doctor of Literature.

In 1931 Johnson left his post with the NAACP and joined the faculty of Fisk University in Nashville, Tennessee, to become professor of creative literature. *Black Manhattan*, a history of blacks in New York, especially those active in the theater, appeared in 1930, and in 1933 his autobiography *Along This Way* was published. James Weldon Johnson died in an automobile accident near his summer home in Maine on June 26, 1938, at the age of sixty-seven.

SELECTED WORKS: God's Trombones, 1927; Black Manhattan, 1930; St. Peter Relates an Incident, 1935; The Books of Negro American Spirituals (with J. Rosamond Johnson), 1940; The Book of American Negro Poetry (ed.), 1969; Lift Every Voice and Sing (with J. Rosamond Johnson), 1970.

ABOUT: Adams, Russell L. Great Negroes Past and Present; Barton, Rebecca. Witnesses for Freedom; Dictionary of American Biography, Supplement 2; Richardson, Ben. Great American Negroes; Rollins, Charlemae. They Showed the Way; Sterling, Dorothy and Benjamin Quarles. Lift Every Voice; Toppin, Edgar A. A Biographical History of Blacks in America Since 1528; Journal of Negro History July 1967; Phylon Summer 1968; Winter 1971.

JOHANNA JOHNSTON

AUTHOR OF *Sugarplum*, etc.

Autobiographical sketch of Johanna Voigt Johnston:

I WAS born in Chicago, Illinois, a city that seems not to have excited me very much as a child. I was more impressed by various small towns in southern Illi-

Johanna Johnston [signature]

nois, where we visited relatives and where I was fascinated by the slower rhythms of life and a certain sense of the past. However, I am grateful for two years at the University of Chicago and two years of study at the school of the Art Institute of Chicago. The last was a brief fling at finding another destiny than that of a writer. I had been writing from earliest childhood—themes that were read aloud in grammar school, reporting for the high school newspaper, contributing to the literary magazine— all that, along with a great many poems written in secret.

I'm sure that I was drawn finally to writing for children because all the really good children's books are very closely related to poetry, saying a great deal in a few words, echoing with overtones of larger meanings. I had moved to New York and was married when my first children's book was published, *The Littlest Reindeer*. After that, I detoured for a while into writing for radio (which also has ties with poetry in its reliance on words alone to create any wonderful or fantastic image desired).

It was several years after my daughter was born before I returned to children's books. And cliché though it may be, the story of *Sugarplum* came into being to beguile her boredom in helping do the dishes.

As my daughter grew older, my own interest in past family history, American history—human history, really—plus a desire to pass on to her a sense of continuity, led me to write on historical themes. Making the past more vivid and immediate gives a sense of solidity to the very fluid present, offering us something to stand on as we make the next steps into the unknown.

As I became more involved in historical research, it was logical that I found various personalities who inspired me to write their biographies for adult readers. But no matter what the age of the readers I write for (and I seem to have addressed all ages from the picture book group on up) my aim has been the same—to evoke a sense of reality and continuity, and an echo, at least, of poetry.

———

Johanna Johnston wrote for the children's radio program, "Let's Pretend," from 1953 to 1956. She married John DeWitt in 1938, and in 1956 married Scott Johnston. She has one daughter, Abigail DeWitt Johnston.

SELECTED WORKS: (as Johanna DeWitt) The Littlest Reindeer, 1946; Sugarplum, 1955; Penguin's Way, 1962; Edie Changes Her Mind, 1964; The Connecticut Colony, 1969; Paul Cuffee: America's First Black Captain, 1970; Together in America, 1973; Who Found America?, 1973; Women Themselves, 1973; Speak Up, Edie!, 1974; Frederick Law Olmsted: Partner with Nature, 1975; Harriet and the Runaway Book: The Story of Harriet Beecher Stowe and "Uncle Tom's Cabin," 1977.

ABOUT: Contemporary Authors, Vol. 57–60.

WEYMAN B. JONES
February 6, 1928–

AUTHOR OF *Edge of Two Worlds*, etc.

Autobiographical sketch of Weyman B. Jones:

I WASN'T born in Oklahoma, but I came there so young that I remember nothing earlier. I haven't lived in Oklahoma since I grew up and began to write, but my writing keeps going back there.

It doesn't often go back to the literal pattern of my youth, which seems special only to me: public schools, high school wrestling team and fraternity (which permanently soured me on "joinings" in general), Saturday and summer jobs at an aircraft company during World War II. More often, I've found myself writing about the frontier society that, incredibly, my own mother remembered because she was born in Oklahoma when it was still Indian territory.

A scholarship took me to Harvard where I encountered literary minds (once, briefly, Robert Frost), the discipline of regular writing, and a tentative sense of talent, which someone has defined as "the ability to find pleasure by working hard in some field." My undergraduate writing there kept going back to Oklahoma: fiction set in hayfields with tornado funnels on the horizon and, eventually, a thesis examining the myth and folklore of the Cherokee.

After that came the Navy during the Korean War, marriage and a family, business, writing and rejection slips.

When my job took me to Washington, D.C., with frequent trips to Cape Kennedy and Houston for the manned space shots, I seemed to have nothing of my own to say about politics or government or men in orbit. Instead, I went back to Oklahoma again with my first book for children, a novel about the Cherokee called *The Talking Leaf*. One of its minor characters is Sequoyah, who developed a kind of alphabet for the Cherokee language that was so efficient a child could learn to read and write in three days.

After that, one day on a visit to Oklahoma, I found in a collection of old books left by my grandfather an account of Sequoyah's *walk* across most of what is now Texas in search of a lost Cherokee band. Thinking about a trip by a seventy-year-old man, who was alone and sick and who never said *why* he was searching for the scattered remnants of the Cherokee, gave me the basis for my next book, *The Edge of Two Worlds*.

Since then, I've written other things, some that worked and some that didn't. The ones that worked did not always involve Oklahoma, but I've come to realize that they all do involve in some way my own beginnings.

———

Edge of Two Worlds was on many of the lists of outstanding books published in 1968, including the American Library Association's list of Notable Books for Children. The novel received the Western Heritage Award for Juvenile Fiction.

Weyman Jones married the former Marilyn Ann Blasio on February 6, 1954. They have two daughters, Lynn and Paula, and live in Connecticut.

SELECTED WORKS: The Talking Leaf, 1965; Edge of Two Worlds, 1968; Computer: The Mind Stretcher, 1969.

ABOUT: Contemporary Authors, Vol. 19–20; Something about the Author, Vol. 4.

JUNE JORDAN

July 9, 1936–

AUTHOR OF *His Own Where*, etc.

Autobiographical sketch of June Jordan Meyer:

HARLEM, U.S.A. was where I was born to Granville and Mildred Jordan, immigrants from the British West Indies. From infancy my mother took me, on Sundays, to the Universal Truth Center on West 125th Street, just beyond Eighth Avenue; there the unifying ground belief was that *the word* is *the truth*. For example, if you couldn't find your wallet, you would "declare the truth"; you would say: "There is no loss in Divine Mind." And/or if somebody such as a bus driver refused to smile/act friendly, you would "declare the truth about him," meaning you would say, "I see the Christ in you." The consequences generally confirmed the premise that *the word* is really powerful—or that choosing the right word(s) would result in the creation of the right/desirable/wished-for reality.

That was probably the beginning of my obsessive dependency on and interest in words—as a means of creating a desirable, wished-for reality. The poem has always seemed to me the fundamental, most intense and devoutly precise use of words, and so I have always regarded myself as a poet, first and essentially.

Children have always seemed to me the most vulnerable, willing and beautiful of all people. And so I have persistently undertaken the writing of poetry and stories and even history that could be accessible and helpful to these most beautiful, open lives, to the best of my understanding and capacity.

But, clearly, the power of good and evil conduct and consequences rests with the grown-up folk of the world. And so it has seemed necessary, in the continuing spirit of my wish to serve children, to undertake poems and stories and essays and whatever else might reach and move my peers, for the sake of the younger ones among us.

I went to Barnard College and left one semester before graduation. I married another student in my junior year, and we became divorced ten and a half years later. We remain close friends, however, and the very proud parents of our son, Christopher David Meyer, who was born July 25, 1958, in the Bedford-Stuyvesant section of Brooklyn, New York, which is also where I grew up and which is where the story of my first novel, *His Own Where*, takes place.

Thinking on the effects that poems and books have wrought upon my own life, I feel simply confirmed to pursue my efforts to abet positive, and radical, and loving, social change—through my work with words.

———

June Jordan has taught English at City College (New York), Connecticut College and Sarah Lawrence College. She has also worked for Mobilization for Youth and helped to found a creative writing workshop for black and Puerto Rican children in Brooklyn. The Rocke-

feller Foundation awarded her a fellowship for creative writing. Miss Jordan
has also received a Prix de Rome award
to study environmental design. Her concern for the physical environment led
her to work with Buckminster Fuller to
plan a new physical community for Harlem after the summer riots of 1964. The
plan was considered utopian but she
had meant it to be taken seriously.

Who Look At Me was conceived when
the Academy of American Poets recommended June Jordan to complete a project begun by Milton Meltzer and Langston Hughes and interrupted by the
latter's death. The text is a long poem
accompanying paintings of black people
throughout their history in America. It
was an American Library Association
Notable Book in 1969. *His Own Where*,
a love story of two ghetto teen-agers,
was June Jordan's first novel for young
people. Widely praised for its realism
and its poetry, the book was a nominee
for the National Book Award in 1972.
Speaking of her hero in an interview,
she said, "Buddy acts, he moves. He is
the man I believe in, the man who will
come to lead his people into a new community. . . . Nothing that Buddy under-
takes in the book is impossible." June
Jordan's passionate commitment to improving the quality of ghetto life, her
belief that change can be effected and
will be, have made her voice a notable
and influential one among writers for
children today. *New Life, New Room*
was designated a 1975 Notable Book for
Children by the American Library Association.

SELECTED WORKS: Who Look At Me,
1969; Soulscript, 1970; The Voice of the
Children (ed., with Terri Bush), 1970; His
Own Where, 1971; Some Changes, 1971;
Dry Victories, 1972; Fannie Lou Hamer,
1972; New Days, 1973; New Life, New
Room, 1975.

ABOUT: Contemporary Authors, Vol. 33–
36; Something about the Author, Vol. 4;
New York Times Book Review September
3, 1972; Publishers Weekly February 21,
1972.

NORTON JUSTER

June 2, 1929–

AUTHOR OF *The Phantom Tollbooth*, etc.

Autobiographical sketch of Norton Jus-
ter:

WE live on an old farm in northwestern
Massachusetts—my wife Jeanne, my
daughter Emily, my cat Louise, and a
large number of nameless creatures
(mice, squirrels, shrews, an occasional
bat, etc.) who also claim rights in our
house. I was born and grew up in Brooklyn, New York, which seems, and is, the
exact opposite of where I now live, but
far from being contradictory, all seems
part of a very natural evolution. My love
of the country is influenced and heightened by my city experience and, con-
versely, my appreciation of the city has
grown through the time spent here.

I studied architecture and practice it
still. My sense of myself is as an architect, and I am always a little embarrassed to call myself a writer since I
don't engage in it with the same consistency and commitment. The way I see
things and think about things is as an
architect, and my writing is totally influenced by this. In many ways I came
to writing by accident. I had always
enjoyed writing but never allowed myself to consider doing it until 1959 when,
as a relaxation from an arduous planning
project, I began to write what I thought
was a short story—for my own relaxation. Before I knew it, it had created
its own life and I was hooked. *The
Phantom Tollbooth* was the result. Since
then I have written *The Dot and the
Line*, *Alberic the Wise* and *Stark Naked*,
and am at present working on a book
about rural living in the late nineteenth
century. I don't ever remember making
a decision to write books for children;
that just seemed to be the way I wrote.
Along with this I carry on my architectural practice, teach architectural design
at Hampshire College in Amherst, Massachusetts, and do a lot of gardening.

Writing and architecture work well together; one acts like a relaxation from the other, so I guess I'll keep doing it that way.

By way of some hard facts: I attended P. S. 99 and James Madison High School in Brooklyn, and the University of Pennsylvania, graduating in 1952. Then I attended the University of Liverpool (England) in 1953, studying city planning on a Fulbright scholarship. I received a Ford Foundation grant in 1960 for work in urban aesthetics and a Guggenheim Fellowship in 1967. I was in the Civil Engineer Corps of the U.S. Navy 1954–1957, building airfields in Morocco and Newfoundland.

My wife is a book designer who has worked for several publishers and now runs her own free-lance design practice as the Quince Press. My daughter, born in 1971, does a lot more than I can describe here.

The Phantom Tollbooth tells the story of a bored schoolboy who, after passing through a magic tollbooth with a toy car, finds himself in a fantasy land where he becomes involved in a war between those who believe that words are more important than numbers and those who believe numbers are more important than words. The boy overcomes sloth and ignorance and manages to bring peace to the Kingdom of Wisdom, and in so doing becomes an alert and active boy. The book was on the New York *Times* list of best selling children's books in 1962 and was also included in that paper's 1966 list of the fifty best books in the previous five years. It was made into a full-length cartoon feature, released in 1970. *Alberic the Wise* was one of ten children's books included in the American Institute of Graphic Arts' Fifty Books of the Year Show, 1966.

SELECTED WORKS: The Phantom Tollbooth, 1961; The Dot and the Line, 1963; Alberic the Wise, 1965; Stark Naked, 1969.

ABOUT: Author's and Writer's Who's Who, 1971; Contemporary Authors, Vol. 13–14; Doyle, Brian. The Who's Who of Children's Literature; Something about the Author, Vol. 3; Time March 22, 1971.

EROS KEITH

June 24, 1942–

AUTHOR AND ILLUSTRATOR OF *Rrra-ah*, etc.

Autobiographical sketch of Eros Keith:

I WAS born in Fulton, Missouri. I didn't live there long however. I was three years old when the doctors discovered I had chronic asthma and possibly tuberculosis. They suggested a dry climate and *we* moved to Denver, the *we* being my mother and her parents, my grandparents. My grandparents moved with us because my father was away. It was World War II and he was in Europe with the U.S. Army.

Denver proved to be an almost instant cure for my illnesses. My mother and grandfather worked during the day and my grandmother took care of me and the house. It was about this time I remember drawing. I was not yet in kindergarten. Grandmother's teaching me to draw was one of the many things she did to entertain me. She also had an endless number of stories, and I was soon drawing pictures illustrating them.

When my father returned from the war a similar thing happened. He told me at bedtime a story that was continued from one night to the next. He was an accomplished storyteller and he made the story up as he went along. The three main characters, Snake Doctor, Alligator Baker and Big Big Bear soon became my favorite creatures to draw.

Kindergarten was a delight to me because it seemed as if all we did was draw, paint with brushes and our fingers, and play with clay. Who could ask for more!

After kindergarten something happened . . . first grade! First grade was lots of discipline and very little drawing! I hated school. I wanted to be a hermit at six. I was a horrible student.

[]

EROS KEITH

My poor parents were constantly being called to visit my teachers.

This hate, fear and distaste for school continued until high school. There my attitude slowly changed for the better. *Beowulf* was the first thing to make me interested in what a teacher was teaching; it was a story, it was magical, and it was very, very visual to me. Another reason, and a good one, was I had several extraordinary teachers.

Between my college board exam scores and my parents' being so poor in those days, it was a miracle that I got into college. I received scholarships my sophomore and junior years, which were a great help.

The years at the University of Chicago and the Art Institute of Chicago were wonderful ones. I cannot put enough emphasis on that. The AIC, when I attended, was still in the actual museum itself. Students had liberties to be envied. We could walk alone, uninterrupted, through the museum from gallery to gallery, closed to the public for the benefit of the students.

I had several part-time jobs while I was in college, in the evenings during the week and full time in the summer. I mention these jobs because most of them proved to be valuable after college. I was an apprentice for a package-design firm, an usher at the Chicago Symphony Hall, and a color transparency retoucher. I even did a little potboiling under a different name for a gallery.

After graduation a friend and I decided New York was where we had to be. We rented a car and a trailer and we were off. Soon after reaching New York, I discovered two terrible things. One, it required more money than I had saved, and two, I was showing a very unprofessional portfolio. I got a job retouching until I had put together a new portfolio. After several months I was ready to pound the pavement once more. I don't remember how many people I showed my work to, but it was many. I wasn't overloaded with work but managed to pay the rent if I stayed on a pizza budget. Gradually work increased. I got a couple of magazine assignments, a few record albums, and many book jackets.

Then I had a couple of very exciting breaks: first, the opportunity to exhibit my paintings with a gallery, and next, meeting a children's book editor. She liked my work and felt I might have the imagination to write a children's book. I made several attempts and failed. She very patiently showed me where I failed. I learned much from our meetings and finally I succeeded in writing an acceptable children's book for publication. The name of this first book was *Nancy's Backyard*. It was slightly autobiographical but I didn't realize that when I wrote it. As the years have flown by I have done fewer and fewer commercial art assignments and concentrated on children's books and my paintings.

SELECTED WORKS WRITTEN AND ILLUSTRATED: A Small Lot, 1968; Rrra-ah, 1969; Bedita's Bad Day, 1971; Nancy's Backyard, 1973.

SELECTED WORKS ILLUSTRATED: The House of Dies Drear, by Virginia Hamilton, 1968; The King's Falcon, by Paula Fox, 1969; Twenty-Two Russian Tales for Young Children, by Leo Tolstoy, 1969; The Plant Wizard, by Marian Murray, 1970; The Donkey Prince, by Angela Carter, 1970; Kevin, by Robert Moery, 1970; Peas in a

Pod, by Miriam Young, 1971; The Moon Is Like a Silver Sickle, by Miriam Norton, 1972; The Other World, by Margaret Hodges, 1973; In a Blue Velvet Dress, by Catherine Sefton, 1973; The Slave Dancer, by Paula Fox, 1973; Mama's Ghosts, by Carol Lee Lorenzo, 1974; From New Bedford to Siberia, by Jerome Beatty, Jr., 1977.

STEVEN KELLOGG

October 6, 1941–

AUTHOR AND ILLUSTRATOR OF *Can I Keep Him?*, etc.

Autobiographical sketch of Steven Kellogg:

I WAS born in Norwalk, Connecticut, and I have lived in Connecticut most of my life. During my early years my best friend, and the most important influence on my decision to become an artist, was my grandmother. She was much more at ease with children than adults, and I loved the hours I spent listening to the stories of her childhood in the late nineteenth century. She taught me to know the plants, birds and animals of the New England woods, and she enthusiastically shared and transplanted her appreciation for the variety of trivial and wonderful treasures that comprised the Victorian clutter of her room. It pleases and surprises me to realize how often the images that appear in my writing and illustrations harken back to the experiences I shared with her.

Some of my earliest memories involve loving to draw, and during my elementary school days, I particularly loved drawing animals and birds. My favorite drawings were thumbtacked in my room from floor to ceiling, and the place had the appearance of a crayoned aviary-bestiary. I made up stories for my younger sisters in which the characters were their stuffed animals and the ceramic animal figures that sat on a shelf in the living room. My sisters called the procedure "telling stories on paper," because I would sit between them with a pad in my lap and busily draw the illus-trations as I chattered along. I am sure that those sessions were the first symptoms of what was to become an adult specialization in the picture book field.

During my high school years I continued to spend a great deal of time painting and drawing, and after graduating I received a Pitney-Bowes Scholarship and attended the Rhode Island School of Design. The best part of that experience came with my senior year and a European Honors Fellowship that sent me to Italy. I was in Florence during the second semester, and I remember the experience of living in that magic city as one of the most meaningful and wonderful of my life.

Upon my return I did some graduate work at American University where I taught etching. I exhibited my etchings and paintings in the Washington area. At the same time I became increasingly interested in children's books, and I began submitting illustrated manuscripts to publishers in New York. During 1966 I was commissioned to illustrate *Gwot!* by George Mendoza, and then, newly married and having acquired six stepchildren, I moved back to Connecticut to devote myself full time to the writing and illustrating of children's books.

Since then I have illustrated many

books, several film strips, and I've written and illustrated a number of books
of my own. Among my favorites are
Margaret Mahy's *The Boy Who Was
Followed Home*, and *The Island of the
Skog*. I am fascinated by the picture
book as an art form, and I love writing
and illustrating for children. They are
an observant and a responsive audience
and I enjoy the challenge that comes
with knowing that the picture book is an
art form that is an important factor in
the foundation of their aesthetic judge-
ment.

———

As one born into a large family and
now with a large family of his own,
Steven Kellogg brings much firsthand
experience to his depiction of children's
behavior. *Can I Keep Him?* and *The
Orchard Cat* were both chosen for inclusion in the American Institute of
Graphic Arts' Children's Book Show in
1971–72. Kellogg's illustrations for Belloc's *Matilda Who Told Lies and Was
Burned to Death* made it one of the
New York *Times* best illustrated books
in 1970, and in 1973 the book received a
Brooklyn Art Books for Children Citation. In 1975, *There Was an Old Woman*
was selected one of the ten Best Illustrated Books of the year by the New
York *Times*. *The Mystery of the Missing
Red Mitten* was included in the Children's Book Showcase the same year.
Kellogg's *Yankee Doodle* was an American Library Association Notable Book
for 1976.

SELECTED WORKS WRITTEN AND ILLUS-
TRATED: Can I Keep Him?, 1971; The Mystery Beast of Ostergeest, 1971; The Orchard Cat, 1972; Won't Somebody Play
With Me?, 1972; The Island of the Skog,
1973; The Mystery of the Missing Red
Mitten, 1974; There Was an Old Woman,
1974; Much Bigger Than Martin, 1976;
The Mysterious Tadpole, 1977.

SELECTED WORKS ILLUSTRATED: Horribly
Funny Hairticklers, by George Mendoza,
1967; The Rotten Book, by Mary Rodgers,
1969; Matilda Who Told Lies and Was
Burned to Death, by Hillaire Belloc, 1970;
Crabapple Night, by Jan Wahl, 1971; The

Castle of the Two Brothers, by Aileen
Friedman, 1972; Here Comes Cat, by Joan
M. Lexau, 1973; Kisses and Fishes, by
Liesel M. Skorpen, 1974; The Boy Who
Was Followed Home, by Margaret Mahy,
1975; Awful Alexander, by Judith Choate,
1976; Yankee Doodle, by Edward Bangs,
1976; Gustav the Gourmet Giant, by Lou
Ann Gaeddert, 1976; Grouchy Uncle Otto,
by Alice Bach, 1977.

ABOUT: Contemporary Authors, Vol. 49–
52; Something about the Author, Vol. 8.

BARBARA KER WILSON
September 24, 1929–

AUTHOR OF *Path-Through-the-Woods*,
etc.

Autobiographical sketch of Barbara Ker
Wilson Tahourdin:

I WAS born in the north of England,
in a provincial city of which my chief
memory is tramcars: yellow-painted
monsters grinding along rails on which
street urchins used to deposit toy pistol
caps. Most of my childhood, however,
was spent near London, with unforget-
table intervals of holidays spent tramp-
ing and climbing in the Lake District.
I was educated at the North London
Collegiate School, an educational establishment of exceptionally strong traditions. The 1939–45 war dominated my
childhood and adolescence: nights of
bombing and gunfire, compulsory silence for radio news bulletins, domestic
upheaval and scarcities of all kinds—
and, all the time, a quiet social revolution taking place in Britain.

After leaving school, I joined the Oxford University Press in London in a
secretarial capacity, then became an editor in the Children's Book Department.
But did I really want to publish other
people's books or to write my own?—a
question I have never stopped asking
myself! Subsequently, I was appointed
as editor of the children's books departments, first at the Bodley Head, then at
William Collins, in London.

In 1956 I had married Peter Tahourdin, the composer, and in 1964 we left

BARBARA KER WILSON

England with our two daughters, Julia and Sarah (born in 1959 and 1961) to live in Australia. Here, I was appointed Children's Book Editor with Angus and Robertson; in 1973, I left A & R to join Hodder and Stoughton's Australian Company, to start a brand-new children's and adult general books list.

As a child, I was an insatiable reader and compulsive writer. As an adult, the novels and stories I have written for young readers are firmly rooted in my childhood experience and memories, especially *In Love and War*. My main interests as a writer lie in the areas of social history (evident in my teen-age novels *Path-Through-the-Woods*, *The Lovely Summer, In the Shadow of Vesuvius*, and *The Biscuit-Tin Family*) and folklore. My first collection of folktales was *Scottish Folk-Tales and Legends* (1954) for the Oxford University Press Myths and Legends series, and my most recent is *Tales Told to Kabbarli*, a collection of Australian Aboriginal folktales. I am now working on a collection of folktales from Papua, New Guinea.

As a publisher, I have worked closely with many leading authors and illustrators: a rich experience. I have also travelled widely in Asia and Europe. The collective impressions and experiences of the last decade or so have led me, I be-

lieve, to a point where I hope to enter a new phase of creative work as a writer. I live now in Melbourne—a city dominated by tramcars: green-painted monsters grinding along rails that all lead into the heart of a busy metropolis founded in the fabulous days of Australia's gold rush.

SELECTED WORKS: Scottish Folk-Tales and Legends, 1954; Path-Through-the-Woods, 1958; The Lovely Summer, 1960; In Love and War, 1963; In The Shadow of Vesuvius, 1965; The Biscuit-Tin Family, 1968; Australia: Wonderland Down Under, 1969; Tales Told to Kabbarli: Aboriginal Legends, compiled by Daisy Bates, retold and edited, 1972.

ABOUT: Contemporary Authors, Vol. 7–8.

"M. E. KERR"
May 27, 1927–

AUTHOR OF *Dinky Hocker Shoots Smack!*, etc.

Autobiographical sketch of Marijane Meaker, who uses the pseudonym "M. E. Kerr" when writing for young people:

I WAS born in Auburn, New York. From the time I was a small child I was aware of a man in our town called Samuel Hopkins Adams. I had never met him, but I knew one thing about him that made me fascinated by him. He was a writer. He was the only writer in our area.

I can't even remember when I first became aware of the notion I wanted to be a writer. It seems that I always did. My father was an ardent reader of everything. Our living room was lined with bookcases. I was always borrowing books from them to take up to my room and devour.

Anything about writing or writers interested me. I romanticized them as other children did movie stars or royalty.

The idea of pseudonyms fascinated me too . . . the idea that you could invent

M. E. Kerr

an entirely new name for yourself and use it as your name when you wrote. I'd always hated the name Marijane.

I attended Stuart Hall in Staunton, Virginia. I was an unruly, rebellious child—a troublemaker with low marks. I was suspended in my senior year for throwing darts at a dartboard decorated with the pictures of faculty members cut out of an old yearbook. My mother's pleas to the bishop (it was an Episcopal school) got me reinstated long enough to graduate.

I went to the University of Missouri, thinking I would study journalism. I switched plans and studied English literature. I was always writing and submitting my work to magazines. I had many, many rejection slips.

But I was right to have switched from journalism. I would have made a bad reporter of any kind. I was more suited to fiction. I lived in fantasy. My grades were always bad. I daydreamed and read and partied. I was a member of a sorority but I liked less conforming friends. I fell in love with a Hungarian boy and hung around with other would-be writers—a motley crew—and dreamed of going to New York, where all the publishing houses were.

I did just that. For a while I was some kind of assistant to the assistant file clerk

at E.P. Dutton. I didn't know short-hand and I was a self-taught typist. These skills were all but essential in 1950 for a young career girl.

Again—I was always sending out stories. I sold my first short story to *Ladies' Home Journal*. I thought I'd received a check for eighty-five dollars. I was delighted when one of my roommates came home and pointed out it was for eight hundred and fifty dollars. I was more than delighted. I was in business as a free-lancer. That was 1951.

In 1952 I published my first novel. I had a pseudonym: "Vin Packer." I wrote mystery and suspense—about twenty books under that name. Then, as M. J. Meaker I wrote a book (nonfiction) about famous suicides, *Sullen Endings*, the inevitable book about one's home-town, *Hometown*, and on and on until as Marijane Meeker I wrote *Shockproof Sydney Shate*. The paperback sale provided enough money for me to experiment.

The late Louise Fitzhugh was a dear friend. I'd read *Harriet the Spy*—and I decided to try a book for young adults. *Dinky Hocker Shoots Smack!* was the result.

I live in East Hampton, New York. I read a lot. I love animals. I love writing, still. And other writers, still.

———

The publication of *Dinky Hocker Shoots Smack!* indicated the presence of a new and interesting voice in contemporary children's literature. Widely acclaimed by critics and specialists and readers themselves, the book was one of *School Library Journal's* Best Books of the Year in 1972 and an American Library Association Notable Book. It was optioned for film and has also been published in a paperback edition. The second book by M. E. Kerr, *If I Love You, Am I Trapped Forever?* was chosen an Honor Book in the older-age category in the 1973 Children's Spring Book Festival. So far her subsequent books have not had quite the same impact as *Dinky Hocker*, in which a bright, overweight teen-ager attempts to come to grips with herself and her surroundings. However, *Is That You, Miss Blue?* was on the American Library Association's list of Notable Books for Children in 1975 as well as its list of Best Books for Young Adults.

SELECTED WORKS: Dinky Hocker Shoots Smack!, 1972; If I Love You, Am I Trapped Forever?, 1973; The Son of Someone Famous, 1974; Is That You, Miss Blue?, 1975; Love is a Missing Person, 1975; I'll Love You When You're More Like Me, 1977.

ABOUT: Janeczko, Paul B. In Their Own Words, English Journal December 1975.

ERIC KNIGHT

April 19, 1897–January 14, 1943

AUTHOR OF *Lassie Come Home*, etc.

Biographical sketch of Eric Mowbray Knight:

ERIC MOWBRAY KNIGHT was born in the town of Menston, Yorkshire, England, the third of four sons in the Quaker family of Frederick Harrison and Marian Hilda (Creasser) Knight. His father was a diamond merchant inclined to extravagance, such as taking the family to the Riviera for the winter. When, two years after Eric's birth, he died suddenly in South Africa, he left his young family without funds. His widow, a purposeful woman, obtained a post in Russia as English governess to Princess Xenia's children. The Knight children were scattered among relatives, and Eric lived with an uncle who was a carter. The boy was very happy there, but when his uncle died, Eric went on to other relatives. By the time he was thirteen he was working full time at various industrial jobs. He formed a kinship with working people that remained with him all his life.

His mother emigrated to America in 1905 and, in an effort to bring the family together again, sent for her sons one by one. In 1912 Knight joined them in Philadelphia. After so many years of separation they were strangers to him. He

worked in mills and factories for a time and then was a copyboy on the Philadelphia *Press*. Then his family sent him off to Cambridge (Massachusetts) Latin School. Later he attended the Boston Museum School of Fine Arts and the National Academy of Design in New York (1916–17) where he won the Elliot Silver Medal for drawing. He found schooling less interesting than the bobbins and looms, rivets and bolts, and power belts of the factories, however, and when World War I began, he enlisted in the Princess Pats, a regiment of the Canadian Light Infantry. He was sent overseas and served as signaler in France until the end of the war.

Knight returned to Philadelphia in 1919, but soon there was no more family. His youngest brother had died in childhood, and his two older brothers, serving with the American Army, had been killed on the same day in June 1918. His mother died not long after.

Knight drifted for awhile. He tried painting, only to find that he was colorblind; turned to newspaper cartooning for the Stamford (Connecticut) *Advocate* and worked on various other newspapers in Connecticut and for the Bronx *Home News*. At loose ends, he joined the U. S. Army and became a captain in the reserve. Later he resumed newspaper work, with interludes for travel to Mexico and Europe. From 1926–34 he was drama critic and columnist for the Philadelphia *Public Ledger*. When he offered, as a feature, six columns of stories behind small news items, the editor "could not use them." Knight sent one of them, "The Two-Fifty Hat," to *Liberty* magazine, where it appeared June 28, 1930—his first published story. In 1932 his first marriage, to Dorothy Hall, ended in divorce and he married again, Jere Brylawski, also a writer.

An autobiographical novel *Invitation to Life* was published in 1934, and when the Philadelphia *Ledger* ceased publication the same year, Knight went to Hollywood as a script writer for Fox and Paramount. He continued to contribute to magazines, *Saturday Evening Post, New Yorker, Colliers, Cosmopolitan*. Many of his stories have appeared in anthologies.

While working for films Knight was encouraged to write fiction by Ernest Hemingway and Whit Burnett. A short story about mill life in Yorkshire was enlarged into a novel, *Song on Your Bugles*, and published in the United States in 1937.

Knight was full of contradictions. He was earnest and serious, yet he was successful at humor and burlesque. Original in thought and theme, he wrote *The Flying Yorkshireman*, based on the amusing notion of a man who believed he could fly. It first appeared in *Story* in July 1937, and later became a selection of the Book-of-the-Month Club.

Always at odds with his employers in his views on film-making and independent criticism, Knight left Hollywood in 1938. For a time he worked on an alfalfa ranch. Then he decided to return East and continue writing. His burlesque satire on Hollywood, *You Play the Black and Red Comes Up*, was published under the pseudonym "Richard Hallas."

Knight was an intense man, indignant at injustice. Much of his subsequent writing was charged with the drama of the events of the thirties—the depression in America, unemployed colliers in Britain,

the distressed areas in Yorkshire. His years in America had destroyed any British acceptance of social strata and class distinction. Yet his British heritage was strong in him. He was a man of two countries, living in America, writing of Yorkshire. Listening to his talk, his friends sometimes asked, "Who is 'we' now?"

The Knights had settled on a farm in Pleasant Valley, Pennsylvania, near Valley Forge. He was soon absorbed in country living. At five feet eleven inches, weighing 160 pounds, he had red hair and a striking smile, and his ruddy English complexion made him look younger than he was. With family, dogs, horses, riding, farming, making furniture and working wood, and with leisure to write whatever he chose to—it was a good life!

Eric Knight was a born storyteller. His mind tended to range until often fact and fancy merged. At the farm he had a favorite collie Toots (originally called Lassie) that accompanied him everywhere. One day, while the Knights were riding a long distance from home, Toots had chased a rabbit into the woods. She did not come back, and searching for her was futile. But Toots came home. She had found her way alone over many miles of strange country. Knight thought about her blind, unquestioning devotion and wrote a story about a come-home dog. "Lassie Come-Home" was the moving story of a dog's struggle against terrible obstacles to keep her habitual appointment with the boy who loved her. It was published in the *Saturday Evening Post* December 12, 1938, as a short story. Knight was persuaded to expand it and have it published as a book for children in 1940. Absorbing and exciting, it was a selection of the Junior Literary Guild and became one of the favorite books for boys and girls and for anyone who has ever loved a dog. Lassie's story was made into a feature film that was so popular that several sequels resulted, including *Lad, Son of Lassie*, and eventually the character became the focus of a popular television serial.

In 1941 came *This Above All*, a best

seller of World War II and a very successful movie. Knight followed that in 1942 with a book of ten short stories in the best tall-tale tradition about Sam Small, the Yorkshireman who had mastered the art of levitation.

But now there was another war on. Knight returned to England to lecture and contribute to war information films. Back in the United States in 1942 he was commissioned in the U.S. Army Special Services Division. He was a captain in the film unit, promoted to major in January 1943. When a U.S. military transport bound for Africa crashed in the jungles of Surinam (Dutch Guiana) Knight was killed on January 14, 1943. He was buried in Jefferson National Cemetery in St. Louis and posthumously awarded the U.S. Legion of Merit.

SELECTED WORKS: This Above All, 1966. Lassie Come Home, 1971.

ABOUT: Current Biography, 1942; Knight, Eric. Portrait of a Flying Yorkshireman, Paul Rotha, ed.; Magill, Frank N., ed. Cyclopedia of World Authors, 1958; Montgomery, Elizabeth Rider. Story Behind Modern Books; The National Cyclopedia of American Biography, Vol. 40, 1967; Twentieth Century Authors, 1942; Twentieth Century Authors (First Supplement); Van Gelder, Robert. Writers and Writing; Who's Who in America, 1942–43; New York Times January 22, 1943; Saturday Review February 6, 1943; Scholastic October 27, 1941; Wilson Library Bulletin March 1941.

HILARY KNIGHT

November 1, 1926–

ILLUSTRATOR OF *Eloise*, etc.

Biographical sketch of Hilary Knight:

HILARY KNIGHT was born in Hempstead, Long Island, to parents who were both artists and writers—his mother, Katharine Sturges, was a fashion- and book-illustrator, and his father, Clayton Knight, a well-known illustrator of aviation books. Art was Hilary Knight's preoccupation from boyhood, and although his parents exerted no pressure on him

to follow an artistic career, they supported and encouraged his interest. "As a child," Knight recalls, "I loved to look at a set of books which belonged to my mother. They were illustrated by Edmund Dulac in a romantic, wonderful, detailed manner. I know he has influenced my style."

Knight began his formal art training at the Art Students League under George Grosz and Reginald Marsh. His studies were interrupted by a period of service in the United States Navy—as a ship's painter. He was discharged after more than eighteen months and continued his training by studying architectural drafting at the Delehanty Institute. Eventually he found the meticulous, detailed work too restricting and left to study interior and theater design. One summer was spent as an assistant designer at a theater in Ogunquit, Maine, and Knight still retains his interest in theatrical design.

Some of his humorous drawings were accepted for magazine publication in 1952 and appeared in *House and Garden*, *Gourmet* and *Mademoiselle*. A few years later, Knight was introduced by a mutual friend to Kay Thompson, the singer and entertainer. Miss Thompson had been using an imaginary character named Eloise in her nightclub act for some time. Eloise was a sophisticated little girl who lived at the Plaza, in New York, and took full advantage of the huge hotel's resources. Together Knight and Miss Thompson worked up a dummy for a book about Eloise's adventures. It was accepted for publication and appeared in 1955 with enormous success. Four sequels followed—*Eloise in Paris*, *Eloise in Moscow*, *Eloise at Christmastime* and *Eloise Takes a Bawth*. Hilary Knight was able to travel to Europe to acquire background material for the first two books.

Knight admits that the success of Eloise was not an unmixed blessing. He says, "There was no real struggle for me. The success of *Eloise* spoiled me a little. Perhaps I had too much, too soon. My technique was not quite mature at the time of *Eloise's* publication. I believe my work has improved since that initial success."

He has done a number of other books since the Eloise titles and has worked hard to prove that he can successfully draw characters other than Eloise. Knight regards himself as primarily a children's book illustrator, and he has shown himself master of a variety of styles and mediums. He says that he works fast and makes no preliminary sketches, doing any preparatory work that is needed in his head. Among the many books he has illustrated, Knight is especially fond of *Tortoise and Turtle* by Evelyn Gendel, which has black and white drawings executed in grease pencil on acetate. He did his research for this book at the Bronx Zoo, an assignment he enjoyed because he loves zoos and always makes a point of visiting the local ones when he is traveling. Knight also looks back affectionately on two books whose texts he wrote. One is *Hilary Knight's ABC*, a large, full-color alphabet book that uses unexpected words for each letter as well as familiar ones. The other is *The Land of Mother Goose*, a collection of over one hundred nursery rhymes, illustrated lavishly with double spreads that would, if put end to end, form an enormous, continuous frieze.

Hilary Knight lives in Manhattan but he has traveled widely in Europe and also in Central America.

SELECTED WORKS WRITTEN AND ILLUSTRATED: Beginning with Mrs. McBee (with Cecil Maiden), 1960; Hilary Knight's ABC, 1961; The Land of Mother Goose, 1962; Speaking of Mrs. McCluskie (with Cecil Maiden), 1962; Sylvia McSloth, 1969; Where's Wallace?, 1964.

SELECTED WORKS ILLUSTRATED: Eloise, by Kay Thompson, 1955; Eloise in Paris, by Kay Thompson, 1957; Hello Mrs. Piggle-Wiggle, by Betty MacDonald, 1957; Eloise at Christmastime, by Kay Thompson, 1958; Eloise in Moscow, by Kay Thompson, 1959; Tortoise and Turtle, by Evelyn Gendel, 1960; Eloise Takes a Bawth, by Kay Thompson, 1964; When I Have a Little Girl, by Charlotte Zolotow, 1965; The Jeremy Mouse Book, by Patricia Scarry, 1969; The Book of Wishes and Wish-Making, by Duncan Emrich (ed.), 1970; I'm a Monkey, by Robert Kraus, 1975; That Makes Me Mad, by Steven Kroll, 1976; The Good Housekeeper, by Robert Kraus, 1977.

ABOUT: Kingman, Lee and others, comps. Illustrators of Children's Books: 1957–1966; Who's Who in American Art, 1973; American Artist March 1963.

FERNANDO KRAHN
January 4, 1935–

AUTHOR AND ILLUSTRATOR OF *Journeys of Sebastian*, etc.

Autobiographical sketch of Fernando Krahn:

IT'S not easy to find out what elements, what circumstances motivated me to be an author-illustrator of children's books. Born and raised in Santiago, Chile, my chances to see good picture books were minimal compared to those possibilities children had at that time in Europe and the U.S.A.

Nevertheless, my German grandmother (I'm a descendant of Germans and Spaniards) still kept the old books that had belonged to my father when he was a child. I nurtured myself with the classic but rather black-humored Wilhelm Busch's collection. Also, deep in a closet, I discovered some scrap books of last century's magazines: lithographed pictures of the news helped me to fantasize a little with Napoleon III or Queen Victoria.

I must say I had a happy childhood. My only brother, two years senior, was a good friend. My mother, a soprano singer excellent in Mozart's operas, motivated my interest in music. (Not too long ago I started my first music lessons, playing the baritone recorder!) My father, a severe-looking lawyer, was a good amateur cartoonist. He wrote many operettas and operas buffa, and organized summer circuses that travelled around small towns in Chile. The whole family came along. He was the clown, a very funny clown. Undoubtedly he was an important influence, though he never understood that I could be a professional artist: I studied

FERNANDO KRAHN

law for three years before he died in 1953. My brother and I decided to make long trips, adventurous style. We prepared an old 1946 Ford and crossed jungles, rivers and deserts of South America. My brother died in 1955 in a car accident we had while going back to Chile.

After three more years of university I became a stage designer. I had much to do at the theater but decided to quit after taking second place in an international contest in Paris, 1961, competing with "Rhinoceros" of Ionesco. It wasn't the "second" that affected me. Actually it was a secret portfolio I had, wordless cartoons, which I wanted to try in New York. . . . There, three months after my arrival in 1962, my first try, *Esquire*, was a success. Then came the *New Yorker*, *Horizon*, *Show*, *Evergreen*, *Atlantic Monthly*, the *Reporter*. . . . I worked as exclusive cartoonist for the *Reporter* until the magazine closed forever. Such an event, plus other hazardous episodes, made me try the children's book field. I got married to a Chilean, Maria de la Luz Uribe, herself a writer, essayist and author of many theater plays for children. She, a Montessori educator, has stimulated me from the beginning. Now our three children, Fernanda, Santiago and Matias, are indeed my most severe critics.

Well, I'm living now with my family in Sitges, Spain, devoting my time to children's books, most of them wordless. I manage also to keep working on my adult cartoons and other more or less "serious" drawings. In 1973 I got a Guggenheim Fellowship to work in film animation, experimenting with new devices I've been inventing since. My first film, *The Perfect Crime*, done completely in my new method, was presented recently at the Oberhausen Film Festival, Germany.

———

Uncle Timothy's Traviata was included in the 1967–68 Children's Book Show of the American Institute of Graphic Arts as was *Hildegarde and Maximilian* in 1970. The latter title was also named by the Institute as one of the Fifty Books of the Year in 1969. The New York *Times* chose *The Life of Numbers* as one of the Outstanding Books of 1970. And in 1974, *April Fools* was selected for Children's Book Showcase.

SELECTED WORKS WRITTEN AND ILLUSTRATED: Journeys of Sebastian, 1968; Gustavus and Stop, 1969; Hildegarde and Maximilian, 1970; How Santa Claus Had a Long and Difficult Journey Delivering His Presents, 1970; A Flying Saucer Full of Spaghetti, 1970; April Fools, 1974; The Self-Made Snowman, 1974; Who's Seen the Scissors?, 1975; Sebastian and the Mushroom, 1976; Little Love Story, 1976; The Family Minus, 1977; A Funny Friend from Heaven, 1977; The Mystery of the Giant Footsteps, 1977.

SELECTED WORKS ILLUSTRATED: Uncle Timothy's Traviata, with words by Alastair Reid, 1967; The First Peko-Neko Bird, by Maria de la Luz Krahn, 1969; The Lioness Who Made Deals, by Fred Gardner, 1969; The Life of Numbers, by Maria de la Luz Krahn, 1970; Abe Lincoln's Beard, by Jan Wahl, 1971; Lorenzo Bear and Co., by Jan Wahl, 1971; Hardlucky, by Miriam Chaikin, 1973; Mooza, Mezi, Mekki, by Jan Wahl, 1974; I Hear America Singing, by Walt Whitman, 1975; Simon Boom Gets a Letter, by Yuri Suhl, 1976.

ALBERT LAMORISSE

January 13, 1922–June 2, 1970

AUTHOR OF *The Red Balloon*

Biographical sketch of Albert Lamorisse:

"I HAVE always preferred to do my writing with a camera, using the inks of natural color: a white mane; a red balloon; a green and yellow field . . ." wrote Albert Lamorisse, the French film maker whose movies, *Bim, Crin Blanc* (White Mane), *Le Ballon Rouge* (The Red Balloon) and *Le Voyage en Ballon* (Stowaway in the Sky) have delighted children and adults throughout the world. They have all appeared in book form in the U.S., illustrated with stills from the films.

Albert Emmanuel Lamorisse was born in Paris on January 13, 1922, the son of Albert Gusman Lamorisse, a businessman of Flemish descent, and his wife Elise. The boy grew up in Paris and in the country town of Verneuil, some fifty miles west of the capital. He did not do well in school—the Lycée Stanislas in Paris and the Ecole des Roches in Verneuil—but after he finished his secondary education he audited classes at the Institut des Hautes Etudes Cinématographiques.

Lamorisse began work as a scriptwriter and photographer, and in 1946 his job as technical assistant on a feature film took him to Tunisia. He became fascinated by the country and its people, and made a documentary film, *Djerba*, about an island off the Tunisian coast. In 1949 he returned to Tunisia to make *Bim*, the story of a small Arab boy and his goat. The film required a year of preparation and four months of shooting.

Lamorisse's reputation was established with his next film, *Crin Blanc*, which he wrote, directed and produced, and which was released in 1953. Set in the Camargue region in the South of France, an area noted for its beautiful wild horses, it told how a boy tamed one of these horses and protected it from the ranchers who wanted to capture it. The

ALBERT LAMORISSE

film received many awards, including the Grand Prix for short films at the Cannes Film Festival.

While he was working on a new film, about a little bear in the Gap region of France, Albert Lamorisse was caught in an avalanche. He was badly injured and had to spend five months in the hospital. The accident immobilized him for a year, but he returned to film-making as soon as he could. He wanted to make a film in color, and he set about learning the techniques of color photography and gaining experience in them by working as a cameraman on a documentary about Guatemala. All he had learned was put to use in *The Red Balloon*, perhaps his best-known film. He wrote forty-two scenarios before he produced one that satisfied him. Lamorisse's own small son Pascal was the star in this enchanting tale of a Parisian boy and his red balloon which follows him everywhere he goes. The film was released in 1956, to great critical acclaim, and again won many awards, including the Grand Prix for short films at Cannes, and the American Academy's Oscar for the best original screenplay.

Lamorisse's next film was a full-length feature, *Le Voyage en Ballon*, released in Europe in 1960 and in the U.S. as *Stowaway in the Sky* in 1962. Again Pascal Lamorisse played a leading part, that of a boy who floats all over France with his grandfather in a homemade balloon. The film took two years to make, and Lamorisse invented a special technique for it, Helevision, which enabled him to photograph from a helicopter without being affected by the machine's vibrations.

Albert Lamorisse was an enthusiastic sportsman who enjoyed physical danger. He loved skiing, riding, swimming and fencing, and he was a licensed helicopter pilot as well as a balloonist. In 1947 he married a dancer, Claude Jeanne Marie Duparc, and they had three children—Pascal, Sabine and Fanny. The Lamorisses lived in Paris in an apartment on the Left Bank, and they also had a country home in the mountains behind St. Tropez, in the South of France, where they made wine, created ceramics and printed their own fabrics. Albert Lamorisse was the inventor of the parlor game Risk, which has achieved great popularity in both Europe and the U.S.

Besides constantly improving his photographic skills, Lamorisse also developed as a director. "When I began I thought that the cinema was above all visual. Today I think that the story is primordial. One evolves you see," he wrote in 1964. He worked with deliberate slowness, saying, "I make films in my own way. I am not a professional, I am an amateur." He said that he made films in order to bring to life his childhood dreams, and in 1962 he told an interviewer, "I'm still dreaming. I'm a little bit *en retard*. When I'm eighty I'll be making pictures about the things I'm dreaming now." It is everyone's loss that he died when he was only forty-eight, killed in a plane crash near Teheran in June 1970.

SELECTED WORKS: White Mane, 1954; The Red Balloon, 1957; Stowaway in the Sky, 1962.

ABOUT: Sadoul, Georges. Dictionary of Film Makers; Who's Who in America, 1970–71; Current Biography, 1963, 1970; New York Herald Tribune June 17, 1962; New York Times June 17, 1962; June 4, 1970; Time October 24, 1960.

JACOB LAWRENCE
September 7, 1917–

AUTHOR AND ILLUSTRATOR OF *Harriet and the Promised Land*, etc.

Biographical sketch of Jacob Lawrence:

"THE human subject is the most important thing," Jacob Lawrence once said, in relation to his work, and certainly this concern of his for the lives, the hopes and suffering, the very ordinariness, even, of human beings, animates everything he has done. Some critics have considered Lawrence America's first authentic black artist, because he has been nurtured entirely on the black experience and owes little or nothing to the white world for his artistic direction.

Jacob Lawrence was born on September 7, 1917, in Atlantic City, New Jersey; the child of a broken family, he was for years shunted hither and yon between his mother and his foster parents. In 1930 he moved with his mother to New York. Jacob had his first contact with art at the Utopia Children's Center in Harlem, where he also gained the invaluable support of the leading black artist and teacher, Charles Alston.

Through Alston, Lawrence began to study at the Harlem Art Workshop, housed in the 135th Street Public Library. Later he also attended classes taught by members of the Works Progress Administration Federal Art Project at its studio on 141st Street.

Between 1936 and 1937, unable to find any other employment, Lawrence joined the Civilian Conservation Corps, but in 1937 he was awarded a full-time scholarship to the American Artists' School. He worked there in the mornings and spent his afternoons in the 135th Street Library, where the famous Schomberg Collection of books by and about blacks is housed. He soaked up everything he could about various historical black figures. After a year, he had finished a series of twenty gouaches telling the story of Toussaint L'Ouverture, the liberator of Haiti; he followed this with another

JACOB LAWRENCE

series of paintings on Frederick Douglass, the great black orator, and Harriet
Tubman, the black Civil War heroine.

At the end of 1938 Lawrence was accepted for employment in the WPA Art
Project. This was an important period for
him, as he recalled later—"[The Project]
was my education. I met people like Sa-
royan before he got famous. They all
used to talk about what was going on in
the world. Not only about art, but everything."

In 1940 and the two succeeding years,
Lawrence was granted fellowships by
the Rosenwald Foundation that allowed
him to travel and paint. In 1941 he was
in New Orleans, researching and also
celebrating his recent marriage to the
West Indian painter Gwendolyn Knight,
when word came of the success of his
first big one-man show in New York and
with it an invitation to join Edith Halpert's Downtown Gallery. Though he
didn't realize it at the time, Halpert was
one of the top art dealers in the nation.
A young artist starting out couldn't have
been launched under better auspices.

Lawrence's trip through the South was
of great importance to him, emotionally
and artistically. In the course of studying
the population shift of impoverished
blacks from the rural South to the indus-

trial North after World War I, he learned
to understand the roots of the urban
blacks whose lives he documented. The
result was a series of sixty panels entitled
The Migration of the Negro that showed
the suffering and disillusion of these immigrants in their struggle for survival.
The series generated great interest in the
art world. The Museum of Modern Art
and the Phillips Gallery in Washington,
D.C., each competed to buy the whole
series and finally compromised by dividing it between them.

Lawrence returned to New York and
plunged into work on paintings of the
metropolitan black community that became the *Harlem* series.

During the war, Lawrence joined the
Coast Guard; in 1946 he was granted a
Guggenheim Fellowship and began work
on a series of fourteen paintings (*War*),
a distillation of his wartime experiences.
Fortune magazine commissioned Lawrence to travel through the South in 1947
to record the effects of the new indus-
trialization on the black population.

In 1949 Lawrence, suffering from a
depressive illness, voluntarily entered the
Hillside mental hospital in New York.
After he was discharged he worked on
a series of paintings depicting life in the
hospital. In these paintings, as in all of
Lawrence's work, the sense of tightly
controlled, disciplined emotion, impris-
oned by an extraordinary compositional
skill, makes them strongly memorable.
"[These] paintings," said one commenta-
tor, "bring into vivid focus the dark underside of man's emotional life as it is
revealed under clinical conditions."

In the fifties, the enormous sixty-panel
series *Struggle: From the History of the
American People* brought Lawrence his
greatest acclaim. Like much of his work,
it is an intensely personal history, encompassed by extended visual narration,
often with quite lengthy written texts.

In 1968 Lawrence painted a series of
illustrations describing the life of Harriet
Tubman which were made into a children's book, *Harriet and the Promised
Land*. It was named an outstanding book
of the year by the New York *Times* and

was also one of the *Times*'s choices of the ten best-illustrated children's books for 1968. It was included in American Institute of Graphic Arts Children's Book Show for 1967–68 and in 1973 received a Brooklyn Art Books for Children citation.

Lawrence originally worked in gouache, but later changed to egg tempera as his chief medium. He has described it as "a brisk medium that cannot be manipulated like oil. You have to get it all right down; you cannot linger over it."

His colors have occasioned much comment; *Time* Magazine once called them "dirty, sometimes neon-bright, always arbitrary." And his style is distinctive in its angularity and often disturbing distortions. Aline B. Loucheim wrote of him that, "although his style with its brilliant color, abstract form and patterned surface is wholly 'modern,' Lawrence is like a medieval artist in wanting to teach by means of pictures and being able to paint only what he deeply knows and feels."

Throughout his career, Lawrence has been a teacher—at first at the famous Black Mountain College in North Carolina in 1946, later at Brandeis University and at Pratt Institute in Brooklyn. Recently he has been teaching at the University of Washington in Seattle.

In 1970 the National Association for the Advancement of Colored People awarded Jacob Lawrence its highest award, the Spingarn Medal, for "his eminence among American painters" and "the compelling power of his work, which has opened to the world . . . a window on the Negroes' condition in the United States."

SELECTED WORKS WRITTEN AND ILLUSTRATED: Harriet and the Promised Land, 1968.

SELECTED WORKS ILLUSTRATED: Aesop's Fables, 1970.

ABOUT: Adams, Russell L. Great Negroes Past and Present; Bearden, Romare and Harry Henderson. Six Black Masters of American Art; Brown, Milton W. with Louise A. Parker. Jacob Lawrence; Current Biography, 1965; Illinois University College of Fine and Applied Arts. Contemporary American Painting and Sculpture; Richardson, Ben. Great American Negroes; Rodman, Selden. Conversations with Artists; Who's Who in America, 1970–71; Who's Who in American Art, 1970; 1973; Negro History Bulletin October 1957; Nordness, Lee, ed. Art USA Now, Vol. 2, 1963; New York Post March 22, 1961; New York Times Magazine October 15, 1950; Time December 22, 1947; February 24, 1961.

MARIA LEACH

April 30, 1892–May 22, 1977

AUTHOR OF *How the People Sang the Mountains Up*, etc.

Autobiographical sketch of Alice Mary Doane Leach, written shortly before her death:

I WAS born in Brooklyn, New York, April 30, 1892. I live in Barrington, Nova Scotia, because my father's family has belonged here since the arrival of the first Cape Cod settlers in 1761.

I wrote my first story before I could write, when I was four. I had wanted my mother to tell me a bedtime story. She said, "Not tonight. You can make up a story yourself in bed." When I called her back, I said:

> Oh, hear those cowbells tinkle
> And see those snowflakes fall
> Upon the stones
> Of the stone, stone wall.

I remember this vividly. We had just returned from a summer in Barrington.

I went to the Barnard School for Girls in New York City, through the 9th grade and graduated from the Plainfield, New Jersey, high school in 1910. After this I went to Earlham College in Richmond, Indiana (1910–1914), where I received my A.B. degree, as Alice Mary Doane. These were childhood first names which stuck to me until after my marriage to MacEdward Leach, whom I met at the University of Illinois, where we both received M.A. degrees in 1917. We both held graduate scholarships in English at Johns Hopkins University, in Baltimore, the following school year.

After that I was head worker at the Friends Neighborhood Guild, a settle-

MARIA LEACH

ment house in Philadelphia. Here in Philadelphia, too, my husband began his career in the English department at the University of Pennsylvania, where he taught until his death in 1967. My son Macdonald Hervey Leach was born in 1924.

I drifted into writing for school readers for the Winston Publishing Company in Philadelphia and also did a year's stint on the Winston elementary school dictionary.

From there I went to Funk and Wagnalls Publishing Company in New York, and from that time on I worked under my real name, Maria Leach. First I wrote definitions for their children's dictionary. Later I was American-English editor for their *New College Standard Dictionary*.

While I was an undergraduate at Earlham I became intensely interested in the works of Fiona McLeod, and this sparked my involvement with folklore and mythology. I began to compile entries for a folklore dictionary.

Hence, when the *New College Standard Dictionary* was completed in 1947, Funk and Wagnalls undertook to publish my idea. The job took four years. This was the *Standard Dictionary of Folklore, Mythology, and Legend*, in two volumes. I was the compiler and got

hold of the distinguished four consultants and twenty-nine contributors. I edited it and wrote about one fourth of it. I cannot continue without mentioning my brilliant and hard-working associate editor, Jerome Fried. There is now an unabridged one-volume edition containing a key to 2405 countries, regions, cultures, culture areas, peoples, tribes, ethnic groups, and twelve major religions, which I compiled.

———

Maria Leach was a member of the American Folklore Society, of which she had been a councilor, of the American Anthropological Association, the American Dialect Society, the Northeast Folklore Society, the Canadian Folksong Society, and the American Indian Ethnohistoric Conference.

SELECTED WORKS: The Soup Stone: The Magic of Familiar Things, 1954; The Thing at the Foot of the Bed, and Other Scary Tales, 1959; Noodles, Nitwits, and Numskulls, 1961; How the People Sang the Mountains Up, 1967; Riddle Me, Riddle Me, Ree, 1970; Whistle in the Graveyard: Folktales to Chill Your Bones, 1974; The Lion Sneezed, 1977.

ABOUT: Who's Who of American Women, 1964–65.

URSULA K. Le GUIN

October 21, 1929–

AUTHOR OF *A Wizard of Earthsea*, etc.

Biographical sketch of Ursula Kroeber Le Guin:

THE youngest of four children and the only girl in the family, Ursula Kroeber Le Guin was born in Berkeley, California, in 1929. Her father Alfred Kroeber was an anthropologist and her mother Theodora a writer. Mrs. Le Guin says that her parents were totally nonsexist and that their expectations for her were the same as for her brothers. She has been writing almost since she can re-

Le Guin: *le GWINN*

URSULA K. Le GUIN

member. "I think it was when I learned the alphabet. I always wrote. I didn't *want* to be a writer. I *was*." From the beginning she wrote mainly fantasies and science fiction, the genre in which she has established herself as an outstanding writer.

Majoring in French, Ursula Kroeber graduated from Radcliffe College with a B.A. in 1951, earned an M.A. at Columbia University and held a Fulbright Fellowship to France in 1953–54. She married Charles A. Le Guin, a historian, in 1953. Her first short science fiction stories were published in the early 1960s. Two of them were set on islands and dealt with, among other things, the rules of magic. In 1967 the publisher of Parnassus Press suggested to her that she might try her hand at writing for young people, giving her complete freedom to write down anything she liked, in whatever way she pleased. As she let her imagination roam, Mrs. Le Guin found herself remembering the islands and magic of her earlier stories, and she began to wonder how wizards—traditionally depicted as wise, white-haired old men—learned their magic arts. From this came *A Wizard of Earthsea*, Ursula Le Guin's first book for young people, published in 1968. The first volume in a trilogy, it was followed in 1971 by *The Tombs of Atuan*, and a year later by *The Farthest Shore*. The trilogy is, in one aspect, about the artist, Mrs. Le Guin has said, "the artist as magician. . . . Wizardry is artistry. The trilogy is then, in this sense, about art, the creative experience, the creative process. There is always this circularity in fantasy. The snake devours its tail. Dreams must explain themselves."

All three books were critically acclaimed. *A Wizard of Earthsea* won the Boston *Globe-Horn* Book Award in 1968 and was on a number of selected lists including the American Library Association's List of Notable Books for Children. *The Tombs of Atuan* was also a Notable Book, was a finalist for the National Book Award for children's books in 1972, and a Newbery Honor Book that year. The last in the trilogy, *The Farthest Shore*, received the National Book Award in 1973. In her acceptance speech, Ursula Le Guin said: "I am not only a fantasist but a science fiction writer, and odd though it may seem, I am proud to be both. We who hobnob with hobbits and tell tall tales about little green men are quite used to being dismissed as mere entertainers, or sternly disapproved of as escapists. But I think that perhaps the categories are changing, like the times. Sophisticated readers are accepting the fact that an improbable and unmanageable world is going to produce an improbable and hypothetical art. At this point, realism is the least adequate means of understanding or portraying the incredible realities of our existence. . . . The fantasist, whether he used the ancient archetypes of myth and legend or the younger ones of science and technology, may be talking as seriously as any sociologist—and a good deal more directly—about human life, as it is lived, and as it might be lived, and as it ought to be lived. For, after all, as great scientists have said and as all children know, it is above all by the imagination that we achieve perception, compassion, and hope."

Mrs. Le Guin is also distinguished as a writer of science fiction for adults—though in fact in the world of good fantasy writing, the boundary between writing for children and writing for adults is a fuzzy one, if it can be said to exist at all. Of her six adult novels, *The Left Hand of Darkness* is probably her best known, in which she explores a world of androgynes from the point of view of an off-world male. The book won the two most prestigious awards for science fiction: The Hugo Award, given by the International Science Fiction Association, and the Nebula Award, given by the Science Fiction Writers Association, both in 1969. When asked why she chose to write from a male point of view, Mrs. Le Guin answered that she didn't want to write autobiographies, an exercise to which she is firmly opposed, that she wanted to "distance" herself from her books. "That's one of the reasons why I write science fiction. I write about aliens. Men are aliens, too. I like the alien point of view."

A contemporary novel for young people, *Very Far Away From Anywhere Else*, was published in 1976. It was named an American Library Association Notable Book for Children as well as a Best Book for Young Adults for 1976 and included on a number of other lists of critics' choices. Ursula Le Guin and her husband Charles have three children, Elisabeth, Caroline and Theodore, and live in Portland, Oregon.

SELECTED WORKS: A Wizard of Earthsea, 1968; The Tombs of Atuan, 1971; The Farthest Shore, 1972; Orsinian Tales, 1976; Very Far From Anywhere Else, 1976.

ABOUT: Author's and Writer's Who's Who, 1971; Contemporary Authors, Vol. 21–22; Something about the Author, Vol. 4; Who's Who of American Women, 1974–75; Algol No. 21, November 1973; No. 24, May 1975; Biography News October 1974; Horn Book April 1971; Top of the News April 1972.

JULIUS LESTER

January 27, 1939–

AUTHOR OF *To Be A Slave*, etc.

Autobiographical sketch of Julius Bernard Lester:

I WAS born January 27, 1939 in St. Louis, Missouri. Moved to Kansas City, Kansas, at age two and to Nashville, Tennessee, at fourteen and finished Fisk University there with a B.A. in English in 1960.

Perhaps the most important influence in my growing up was my father, a Methodist minister from the South and a good storyteller. From him I absorbed so much of Southern rural black traditions, particularly music and stories. Equally important were the summers spent at my maternal grandmother's in Arkansas as well as the adolescent years of my life in Nashville. The South is different in its way of life, and for me that was not wholly negative, despite segregation and discrimination.

I guess I always wanted to be a writer, though I was drawn to music and art as careers. But I never doubted, I guess, that it would be writing. I'm not sure that one can even *want* to be a writer; you are one or you aren't, which is an innate knowledge. Of course, if one stops with that knowledge, he/she will never be a writer, because writing is, more than anything else, work, constant work.

I never thought of writing for children until the editor of my first book said that she thought I could write for children. Amused, I asked her why. She couldn't explain but asked me if I'd be interested in meeting the children's book editor. I did and out of our conversation came the idea for *To Be A Slave*. Since then I have found writing for children of all ages more rewarding than writing for adults, primarily because I like the audience and the responses I get from children. I don't find it any easier to write for children, however, and in some ways

JULIUS LESTER

it is more difficult. Children are a very critical audience.

I have two children, a girl and a boy, and that undoubtedly has been an important factor in my writing children's literature. I want them to have books that I would have liked to have had when I was growing up.

Besides writing, I also teach at the University of Massachusetts. I like to do jigsaw puzzles and figure skate.

I lead a rather solitary life, generally preferring to be alone than with people. I have a dog, a Russian Wolfhound, named Misha, and two cats, Carmen and Greensleeves. I live with my son who is a very good hockey player.

———

Besides his books for children and adults, Julius Lester has written for the *Village Voice, New York Free Press, Sing, Broadside*, and the New York *Times Book Review*. A musician, he joined with Pete Seeger to write *The Twelve-Stringed Guitar as Played by Leadbelly* (1965). He has also edited poetry anthologies and had his own poetry in other people's anthologies.

Lester's books for children have made his name a notable one in the field. His first book, *To Be A Slave*, was a Newbery Honor Book in 1969, won the Nancy Block Award for 1968, and ap-

peared on every major recommended list in its year of publication. *Black Folktales* was on the New York *Times'* list of outstanding books of the year, as was *Long Journey Home*, which was nominated for a National Book Award in 1973.

Lester joined the Student Non-Violent Coordinating Committee in 1966 as head of the photo department and later became a field secretary. He traveled to North Viet Nam in 1967 to photograph the effects of the U.S. bombing there and later went to Cuba with Stokely Carmichael to the Organization of Latin American Solidarity Conference. As he wrote and spoke about his experiences and beliefs he became increasingly identified with black radical politics, and although he did not himself think he was a black militant, he found himself labeled one. He was able to live with the label until the summer of 1969. Increasingly, however, he grew uncomfortable with the stereotypes forced on him by blacks and whites. In resigning his radio talk show (WBAI, New York), of which he was host from 1969 to 1972, he said, "One of my attributes is blackness, but that is not the sum total of my existence, and I refuse to allow society to make it so." And in his autobiography, *All Is Well*, "I am almost fatally ill with people trying to impose their idea of me on me. . . . And anything anyone ventures to say about me will not be true. I will not be pinned by anyone's words, particularly my own."

Julius Lester was married to the former Jane Steinau on December 22, 1962. His daughter, Jody, was born in 1965, and a son, Malcolm, in 1967. The Lesters are divorced.

SELECTED WORKS: To Be A Slave, 1968; Black Folktales, 1969; The Knee-High Man and Other Tales, 1972; Long Journey Home, 1972; Two Love Stories, 1972; Who I Am, 1974.

ABOUT: Contemporary Authors, Vol. 17–18; Julius Lester. All Is Well: An Autobiography; Who's Who in America, 1972–73; Library Journal May 15, 1969; Publishers Weekly February 23, 1970; School Library Journal May 1969.

JOAN M. LEXAU

AUTHOR OF *Benjie*, etc.

Autobiographical sketch of Joan M. Lexau, who also uses the pen name of "Joan L. Nodset" when writing for children:

I WAS born in St. Paul, Minnesota (on March 9), moved as an infant to Washington, D.C., and returned to St. Paul when I was about five. My father was a bridge engineer and free-lance book reviewer and worked in many parts of the country. My mother, my brother (now editor of the *Catholic Digest*) and I lived in a small apartment near the Mississippi River, and a great deal of my time was spent outdoors. I remember hiking along the river, playing hide and seek, football, baseball, marbles, jacks, jumping rope, climbing trees, and indoors, playing with dolls, paper dolls or listening to mystery stories my brother, a year older, made up for me and my friends. And always losing myself in books—the Bobbsey Twins, Nancy Drew, fairy tales, Sue Barton, and a variety of fiction. At thirteen I was exploring all the odd corners and rooms of the St. Paul Public Library, discovering browsing treasures like the philosophy of mathematics.

School to me was dull, senseless and endless, in spite of many kind teachers. During high school I worked as a sales clerk, permanent-wave-kit stuffer, and did light bookkeeping. After graduating, I took a few college courses here and there, mostly in philosophy, and worked at such jobs as waitress at a resort, library clerk, dictaphone operator, bookkeeper and secretary, changing jobs frequently. Finally, after doing secretarial work at a magazine, I moved to New York City to "get into publishing." I began as an advertising production manager and secretary for a trade magazine, and was roped into teaching an evening course in journalism to high school students (I was trying to eavesdrop and learn), which I taught from all the journalism books I could get hold of at the

Forty-second Street Library. This led to a job as reporter-secretary for a weekly religious newspaper. After quitting this job over low pay at the beginning of a severe recession, I lived on temporary typing jobs and free-lance reporting for a news service until I was rescued by Ursula Nordstrom in the children's book department at Harper & Row, where I arrived as a temp and stayed four years as production liaison.

As a child, beginning about seven, I knew I wanted to be a writer. Someday. I constantly wrote in my mind but seldom put anything on paper. A couple of my poems were published, but for the most part I waited to wake up as a writer some magic morning. Until one day at Harper's, having already decided to spend my life working in the children's book field, I was thinking about the authors and how great it must feel to be one (it does), and I suddenly realized I wanted to write children's books myself. So I wrote my first manuscript that weekend, based on a story my mother had told me about her childhood. This was never published but years later Phyllis Fogelman at Dial suggested I take it out and see if it had possibilities. I completely rewrote it with new characters and it was published as *Emily and the Klunky Baby and the Next-Door Dog.* But it was a couple of years after I began seriously writing before my first children's book, *Olaf Reads,* was published by Jeanne Vestal at Dial. This was suggested by a news item about a first grader who saw a sign that said Pull and obediently pulled the fire alarm. I was shocked when it became a controversial book, some adults refusing to believe that a six-year-old could be that innocent. *The Trouble With Terry* was very roughly based on my childhood. *Cathy Is Company* was based on childhood visits with my cousins. My constant lateness led to *Olaf Is Late,* and as a child I was as shy as Benjie in the story of that name. A librarian's remark that there were no books about children who had to sleep more than two to a bed was the germ of *Striped Ice Cream,* and a couple of weeks of cat-sitting led to *Come Here, Cat.* My childhood fear of dogs is reflected in *Go Away, Dog.* I wrote *A House So Big* after remembering the things my brother and I told my mother we would do for her after we grew up. My one adult book is mercifully out of print—a book on nuns researched before Vatican II and coming out just after. I have also written articles on children's books (some under the name of "Marie Seth"), and remedial reading material for adults and teenagers, as well as stories for children's magazines and textbooks.

After more than ten years of living in various parts of New York City, I moved to an abandoned parsonage and church built in 1849, in a village of around one thousand people about ninety miles upstate from New York City. I have a cat, Amy Lou, and a toy fox terrier, Helen Ellen, both named after characters in my books. I spend a lot of time turning the former parking lot into a yard and garden and enter photographs in the county fair. My reading is adult mysteries, which I want to write someday, and nonfiction.

I like to write on different age levels for variety's sake but always return to the easy readers, remembering the joy I felt as a preschooler when my mother was reading a "story-a-night" book to me and I discovered that the printed word *button* was always *button* no matter how many times I asked her, and the ecstasy later of reading my first real book from the first-grade library shelf from blue cover to blue cover in one evening.

———

The Trouble With Terry won the Child Study Association's Children's Book Award in 1962. In 1971, *Striped Ice Cream* was voted the winner of the Charlie May Simon Children's Book Award by the school children of Arkansas.

SELECTED WORKS: Olaf Reads, 1961; Cathy Is Company, 1961; The Trouble With Terry, 1962; Olaf Is Late, 1963; Go Away, Dog (by Joan L. Nodset), 1963; Benjie, 1964; Striped Ice Cream, 1968; A House So Big, 1968; Benjie on His Own, 1970; Emily and the Klunky Baby and the Next-Door Dog, 1972; Come Here, Cat, 1973; I'll Tell on You, 1976.

ABOUT: Contemporary Authors, Vol. 19–20; Hopkins, Lee Bennet. Books Are by People; Something about the Author, Vol. 1.

GUNNEL LINDE
October 14, 1924–

AUTHOR OF *The White Stone,* etc.

Autobiographical sketch of Gunnel Geijerstam Linde:

I WAS born in Stockholm, the capital of Sweden, October 14, 1924. I was the only child and my father died when I was half a year old or so. My mother and I lived by ourselves in a small flat among pieces of furniture that were odd personalities, all of them. My bed was a high mountain during daytime, made by sedimentary stuff wherein dolls and teddy bears sometimes were found like fossils between the layers. They probably got stuck there in the early morning when my mother was busy piling

Gunnel Linde: *GUN nel LIND eh*

[signature]

her bedclothes on top of my bed. I used to dig them out in the evening when I came back from my Montessori school and awaken them to a new and better life. We rode across the room on a captured armchair, passing the ghastliness in the dark between the pedestals of mother's desk close by, and we reached the look-out point at the Windowsill-Shore, where one could see Mother coming on the other side of the traffic stream —when at last she came. Sometimes we passed the time having people race with unsuspecting passing people on the opposite pavement. Who would be first to the corner? The man with the nose or the lady in red? Sometimes I made the teddy bears go to high school—on the top of a high ladder—and sit there waiting while I wrote their school books for them. Sometimes I just wrote long stories in my own homemade handwriting, for fear I might forget them before I had learned to spell. To make the story short: flats, streets and high houses were the landscapes of my childhood, and I rather liked it. I can still feel the thrill of lingering adventure when confronted with an empty room. Beauty to me is the sight of the ever flowing waterfalls on the inside of the fishmonger's windowpane. I like towns.

As soon as I was grown up, I asked for a year free. I wanted to ponder the problem which profession to choose. Before I had made up my mind I had spent two years in an art school and become an illustrator. I also worked as a journalist for some years. I got married to Einar Linde and we had three daughters: Liv, Vysse and Sunniva. I began to write the books I had not had time to write in school and then, as a TV producer and author, I found I had the profession I was looking for.

I have written over twenty books for children, a children's opera for the Royal Swedish Opera in Stockholm, made a sculpture for Bodens Sjukskoterskeskola, Boden, and the films and TV programs asked for by the Swedish Radio-TV, where I have been employed since 1957. My book *The White Stone* was broadcast as a TV-series in thirteen parts on Swedish Television in 1973.

There is so much to be done. I hope I won't die young, that is before 100 years of age, and that at the last minute I will be able to write on my tombstone, as I intend to: It was wonderful to be alive.

———

Gunnel Linde has received a number of awards in Sweden in recognition of her ability to capture the fantasy to be found in the most ordinary everyday surroundings. In addition, in 1969 she received a Diploma of Merit from the international Hans Christian Andersen jury for *Till Aventyrs i Skorstensgränd*, which was a sequel to *Tacka vet jag Skorstensgränd* (*Chimney-top Lane*), Mrs. Linde's first book to be published in the United States. In 1965, *Den Vita Stenen*, published in the United States as *The White Stone*, won the Nils Holgersson Medal, the Swedish equivalent of the Newbery Medal. Of all Mrs. Linde's books, *The White Stone* is perhaps the most successful with American audiences, for in the story of two unhappy children who imbue an ordinary stone with magical powers she has achieved a perfect tension between an often unpleasantly tangible real world and the excitingly potential one of the imagination into which the children escape and gain power to deal with reality. *The White Stone* was an American Library Association Notable Book in 1966.

In contrast, *Pony Surprise*, a translation of *Med lill-Klas i Kappsäcken*, a zany story about a pony, won secretly as a prize and smuggled home from Copenhagen in a suitcase, was apparently too whimsical for American readers and met with little success.

Gunnel Linde married Einar Linde, also a television producer, on January 6, 1949. She joined the Swedish broadcasting company, Sveriges Radio, in 1957 and worked with the children's program section until 1964, when she moved over to Swedish television.

SELECTED WORKS: Chimney-top Lane, 1965; The White Stone, 1966; Pony Surprise, 1968; The Invisible League and the Royal Ghost, 1970.

ABOUT: Contemporary Authors, Vol. 21–22; Something about the Author, Vol. 5.

JEAN LITTLE
January 2, 1932–

AUTHOR OF *Mine for Keeps*, etc.

Autobiographical sketch of Flora Jean Little:

Some people walk on straight roads
And see to both ends
- But my road dips and loops and swoops
And crooks and bends.

I've heard some people tell the world
That they know where they're going
- But that's a thing I couldn't bear
Always knowing.

WHEN I wrote that rhyme one New Year's Eve, I was trying to say how much I love life to be an adventure, inviting you to days full of unexpected delights, sorrows, jokes, problems, times of loneliness, friendships. In another poem, I wrote

JEAN LITTLE

. . . I like to wake up in the morning
And wonder what I'll do.

If I spend my time writing, and I know ahead of time that is what I plan, I still won't know what I'll do till I do it. Often the people I write about startle me by quarreling when I thought they were going to get along just fine or by absolutely refusing to do whatever I had in mind for them. This makes them utterly real to me, much more so than actual flesh-and-blood people I know, and I'm always lonely when I finish a book and send the people away to be published.

Although I'm a Canadian, I was born in Taiwan, where my parents, both doctors, were serving as medical missionaries. I was the second child in a family of four. When I was born, they thought I was blind although they soon found out that I could tell light from darkness. My earliest memories are all of sunny days with myself either singing or being told a story. My mother tells me that my first three words were *Mama*, *Dada* and *book-a*. From the beginning, I liked stories to be about people. I still do. I didn't like fairy tales or legends much because the people weren't real enough.

Mother taught me to read. She has given me the three finest gifts I've had, my life, her love, and the ability to make sense out of words.

When my family returned to Canada in 1939, I attended a sight-saving class in Toronto for one year. Then we moved to Guelph, where I now live. There were no special classes here for children with very poor vision and my eyesight was so limited that I was eligible to attend a school for blind children. My parents decided to enroll me in a regular school and see if I could manage. I did manage, all the way up to a B.A. in English language and literature from the University of Toronto, even though I couldn't read what was written on the blackboard. It was hard, lots of times, but I grew up thinking of myself as a person just like everyone else rather than as a blind girl. Although my left eye is now plastic, I still mostly forget that I don't see well. I can read if I hold the book close enough, and that's what really matters.

When I was a child, because of my limited vision and because my eyes looked peculiar, I was teased a lot and left out of games. I did not feel unloved, though, because our family was a close and happy one and because I found so many friends in the books I read. I went to the library every single day it was open, unless I was sick in bed—and then, I sent my mother.

When I wasn't reading, I was making up a story in my head. When I was ten, I wrote my first "book"; it filled a scribbler, was *not* written for school and was as close as I could get to *Lad of Sunnybank*. I was twelve when I began to write poems. My father gave me much criticism, attention and praise. He had a booklet of my poems privately printed when I was fifteen. He also told me, in no uncertain terms, that I was to be a writer.

I thought writers lived in garrets and starved, so I began to teach school, a special class for crippled children. Then I met Virginia Sorensen at a writer's workshop or some such thing and she not only said writers should do everything I already thought I did but she looked well nourished. I took a chance and wrote *Mine for Keeps*. I put it in a competition, won, and went on writing.

I do lots of other things between and around books. I travel. I go to camp and lead various youth groups. I have three dogs to walk and eleven nieces and nephews to keep track of.

But what my life is really all about is writing. It's a terrible way to make a living but I wouldn't do anything else. I get to live so many extra lives this way.

———

Miss Little writes that she lives in a small gray house with her mother and aunt and that she owns a tiny island and a point of land in Lake Muskoka. Recently she lived in Japan for two and a half years. "It never entered my head to use a pen name," she continues, "I want every bit of credit (or blame) that's coming.

"I do a lot of speaking to kids. A second grader once asked me the only question I have been unable to answer. 'How do you know how to do it?' she said. I stammered around for a while and finally had to admit that although I do know how, I don't know how I know how. That's the big mystery about writing."

Jean Little's first book, *Mine for Keeps*, won the Little, Brown and Company's Canadian Children's Book Award in 1961. The published book was an American Library Association Notable Book for 1962.

SELECTED WORKS: Mine for Keeps, 1962; Home From Far, 1965; Spring Begins in March, 1966; Take Wing, 1968; When the Pie Was Opened, 1968; One to Grow On, 1969; Look Through My Window, 1970; Kate, 1971; From Anne, 1972; Stand in the Wind, 1975; Listen for the Singing, 1977.

ABOUT: Contemporary Authors, Vol. 23–24; Something about the Author, Vol. 2; Horn Book April 1966.

PENELOPE LIVELY
March 17, 1933–

AUTHOR OF *The Ghost of Thomas Kempe*, etc.

Autobiographical sketch of Penelope Low Lively:

I WAS born in Egypt and grew up there, in a house on the edge of the desert, a

few miles from the Pyramids. At the end of the Second World War I was sent to England—a place I scarcely knew, except for summer visits as a small child—to go to boarding school. The next few years, through being thirteen, and fourteen and so on, were a private hell of trying to adapt (entirely unsuccessfully, I'm now proud to say) to the barbarities of an English girls' boarding school, and trying to end the yearning for the place in which I had grown up and make myself some roots in this new country. For years —far into adulthood—I was tormented two or three times a year by a dream in which I returned to the house and garden where I grew up, rediscovering it all with intense joy and relief, only to wake up and find it all untrue. It's a common enough dream—to do with the recovery of childhood just as much as being transplanted from one country to another— but it has been a great relief to me, over the last ten years or so, to feel that I no longer have it. The roots, I suspect, have grown properly at last. Which may be why everything I write is very tightly related to the landscape of England, and why it all seems to be about the importance of memory, and the continuity of people and places.

After the horrors of that boarding school (which I drove past this summer —it had shrunk, as so many nasty experiences can do, given time) I went to Oxford to read history at St. Anne's College. Three entirely happy and profitable years there almost made up for all those wasted years of adolescence. Then I married Jack Lively, who is a university don, and spent the next eight years bringing up our two children, Josephine and Adam, until they were both at school during the day and I found myself once more with time to myself. I hardly know now what led me into writing for children. It was not at all what I had in mind —I had thought of going back to history, and perhaps doing some historical research, but somehow one thing led to another, or, more precisely, the books I started to read and the places I went to somehow fused together into an obsession with the importance of memory, and out of this have come seven novels for older children, and a couple of books for younger ones.

We live in a sixteenth century farmhouse in the countryside outside Oxford, where, digging the garden, I turn up all the evidence of the people who have lived in it before me—the broken pieces of eighteenth century wine bottles, seventeenth century pottery, the bowls and stems of clay pipes from the last couple of hundred years. They are heaped into a bowl on my desk as a suitable reminder of how things are—very appropriate for a writer concerned about memory. The books that I have written so far have all been to do, in one way or another, with the way in which English landscape preserves memory or continuity. I think though that perhaps I have now worked out this obsession with historical memory for myself and become more interested in the workings of memory within the context of people's own lives. But I think I shall always need to draw heavily on the places I move about in for everything I write—this is an inexhaustible country, and I shall never have seen enough of it.

After receiving her degree in 1956, Penelope Lively worked as a research assistant until her marriage to Jack Lively on June 27, 1957.

In 1973 *The Driftway* was an Honor Book in the *Book World* Children's Spring Book Festival, and the following year she was awarded the 1973 Carnegie Medal, England's prestigious children's book award, for *The Ghost of Thomas Kempe*. The book was named to the Hans Christian Andersen Honor List for 1976. *The House in Norham Gardens* was on the American Library Association's list of Notable Children's Books of 1974. In accepting her Carnegie Medal Mrs. Lively remarked, "I do not think children can be doing with solemnity, and neither can I."

SELECTED WORKS: Astercote, 1971; The Wild Hunt of the Ghost Hounds, 1972; The Driftway, 1973; The Ghost of Thomas Kempe, 1973; The House in Norham Gardens, 1974; Boy Without a Name, 1975; Going Back, 1976; A Stitch in Time, 1976; The Whispering Knights, 1976.

ABOUT: Author's and Writer's Who's Who, 1971; Contemporary Authors, Vol. 41–44; Something about the Author, Vol. 7; Junior Bookshelf June 1974.

MYRA COHN LIVINGSTON

August 17, 1926–

AUTHOR OF *Whispers and Other Poems*, etc.

Autobiographical sketch of Myra Cohn Livingston:

I WAS born in Omaha, Nebraska, and enjoyed the sort of happy childhood with family and friends that I would wish for every child. Ever since I can remember I loved books and reading and started to write poems and stories as soon as I could read. My mother always encouraged me to write simply, about the things I knew best, and as a teacher of creative writing today, I still feel that young people should write what is closest to them, a way of looking at the things they feel and love.

I savoured art, sculpture and music, and started to play the French horn at eleven. My family moved to California that year and by the time I was thirteen I was a professional musician. My worlds were writing for the school newspaper, my own poetry and plays, and playing the horn. I played with the California Junior Symphony for five years, won trophies and competitions in both fields, and did some work in the movies. I was strongly torn between music and writing; I studied the horn, the piano and even counterpoint with Darius Milhaud while I was still in high school. By the time I entered Sarah Lawrence College in Bronxville, New York, writing had won out, for there was no orchestra at college with which to play. I wrote my first book of poems, *Whispers*, when I was a freshman at college, although it was not published until twelve years later. My first poems were published in *Story Parade*, a magazine for children, when I was a freshman. I later studied with the poets Horace Gregory and Robert Fitzgerald who furthered my intense love for poetry and writing.

After college graduation, I returned to

California and worked for several magazines, did book reviews for newspapers and later personal public relations work for Hollywood personalities. On a visit to Dallas, Texas, I met Richard Livingston, whom I married in 1952. We lived in Dallas for thirteen years. Our children were born there; Josh in 1953, Jonas in 1957 and Jennie in 1962. In Dallas I started to work with young people teaching creative writing in the Dallas Public Library, and began to love the teaching which has become an important part of my life.

Whispers was published in 1958 and since that time I have written twenty-six other books; some are my own poetry, some are rhythmic prose. After reading and sharing poetry with children all over the country I soon discovered I had a great interest in putting together some anthologies, seven of which are now published. I spend a lot of time in classrooms and libraries, working with children in creative writing and sharing the poetry I love with them. One of my books for adults is about my own experiences as a teacher, and I have written one picture book. I also teach at the University of California where I work with teachers and librarians who are interested in furthering a love for poetry in young people.

I still love classical music and a few years ago had the pleasure of playing the Brahms Horn Trio with Jascha Heifetz, one of my closest friends. I am an avid book collector—Joyce, Yeats, Randolph Caldecott—and have a large library, and I also collect bookmarks. I enjoy bookbinding, raising camellias and iris and nasturtiums, and beach-bumming at Malibu. We have lived in California, in the mountains overlooking the Pacific Ocean, for the past thirteen years. Josh graduated from M.I.T. and is doing graduate work in classical music and engineering. Jonas is an antique and classic car buff and in college and Jennie, in high school, is pursuing her interest in art, writing and music. Our family life is very important to us—we enjoy being together, yet each of us has a very private life. It is in this way that we each continue to grow, to learn.

————

Myra Livingston's *Whispers and Other Poems* was an Honor Book in the New York *Herald Tribune* Children's Spring Book Festival in 1958. In 1962 Mrs. Livingston received an award from the Texas Institute of Letters for *I'm Hiding*, and in 1972 an award from the Southern California Council on Literature for Children. In 1974 *The Way Things Are* was named a Golden Kite Honor Book by the Society of Children's Book Writers.

Mrs. Livingston's teaching of creative writing has assumed a larger and larger place in her life in recent years, though she gives much time to P.T.A. work as well. She has written, "I believe the most important contribution I can make is to guide the young to become aware of their sensitivities and individuality and find a form in which to communicate these strengths to others. My faith in the potential, still largely undeveloped, of the human being, grows with the years."

Out of her teaching have come several anthologies and a book for adults about teaching creative writing, *When You Are Alone, It Keeps You Capone* (1974).

SELECTED WORKS: Whispers and Other Poems, 1958; Wide Awake and Other Poems, 1959; I'm Hiding, 1961; Happy Birthday, 1964; The Moon and a Star, and Other Poems, 1965; The Malibu and Other Poems, 1972; Come Away, 1974; The Way Things Are, and Other Poems, 1974; 4 Way Stop and Other Poems, 1976.

SELECTED WORKS COMPILED: A Tune Beyond Us, 1968; Speak Roughly to Your Little Boy, 1971; Listen, Children, Listen, 1972; Poems of Lewis Carroll, 1973; What a Wonderful Bird the Frog Are, 1973; One Little Room an Everywhere, 1975; O Frabjous Day!: Poetry for Holidays and Special Occasions, 1977.

ABOUT: Contemporary Authors, Vol. 3; Something about the Author, Vol. 5; Who's Who of American Women, 1975–76; Horn Book December 1975; February 1976.

ULF LÖFGREN

October 31, 1931–

AUTHOR AND ILLUSTRATOR OF *The Wonderful Tree*, etc.

Autobiographical sketch of Ulf Löfgren:

I WAS born in Umeå, a little town in the north of Sweden, and I had my elementary education there up until my matriculation examination, which I passed in 1952. Even during my time in school I took an interest in drawing and painting, and this interest dominated my spare time. Some successful efforts to have my drawings published in papers impelled me to think of a career as a drawer and illustrator. But after my matriculation examination I set about a university education in Uppsala, and I studied among other things history of art and history of literature. After earning a Bachelor of Arts degree, I decided to devote myself to advertising and therefore I finished off my university career with training at the Swedish Institute of High Advertising Education. But after two days at the institute I realized that I would never devote myself to advertising. Instead I sat down at a suitable table with my gouache colours and brushes and started to draw my first children's book, which I did with the author Leif Krantz. During my time at the University of Uppsala I had made many drafts of children's books.

My first picture book was called *Barnen i djungeln* (*The Children in the Jungle*), and this book was immediately licensed in nine countries. The year after, I received the Elsa Beskow award for the book, and this distinction is of course very desirable for an illustrator of children's books. This introduction inspired me to proceed with children's books as an illustrator and later on even as an author. And I am still on that track. I have now written and illustrated a number of books of my own and have illustrated more than twenty. I have also done a lot of children's programmes for Swedish television.

I married in 1959 and have two children, Cecilia and Tomas. My wife, Birgitta, is a special teacher and we live in Lidingö, a little island and suburb of Stockholm.

I am represented in the Swedish National Museum with several works. I have been a member of the Board of the Swedish Society of Authors for Youth and a member of the board in the Swedish section of the International Board on Books for Young People (IBBY), member of the board of the Swedish Authors Fund, and president of the Swedish Society of Illustrators.

Ulf Löfgren received the Elsa Beskow Plaque for his illustrations for *The Children of the Jungle* in 1960. In 1969 he received a scholarship from the Swedish Society of Literature for *The Wonderful Tree* and in 1971, for the same title, a silver medal at the Leipzig Book Fair and a gold medal at the international Biennale of Illustrations Bratislava. He received another gold medal at Bratislava in 1973 for *Den förtrollade Draken* (*The Magic Kite*) and again, in 1975, a gold

Ulf Löfgren: *OOLF LERF gren*

medal for *The Tough Lady*, published in Sweden in 1974.

Löfgren's books have been published in translation in Austria, Colombia, Denmark, Finland, France, Germany, Great Britain, Holland, Iceland, Japan, Norway, Spain and the United States.

SELECTED WORKS WRITTEN AND ILLUSTRATED: Felix Forgetful, 1969; The Wonderful Tree, 1970; What * Ever * You * Want, 1972; The Color Trumpet, 1974; The Flying Orchestra, 1974; One-Two-Three, 1974; The Traffic Stopper that Became a Grandmother Visitor, 1974.

SELECTED WORKS ILLUSTRATED: The Children in the Jungle (with Leif Krantz), 1961; The Children in the Water (with Leif Krantz), 1967.

ABOUT: Contemporary Authors, Vol. 25–28; Hürlimann, Bettina. Picture Book World; Something about the Author, Vol. 3; Bookbird No. 2, 1972.

BEMAN LORD

November 22, 1924–

AUTHOR OF *The Trouble With Francis*, etc.

Autobiographical sketch of Harold Beman Lord:

THE small New York farm in Delaware County where I was born no longer exists. It is now covered over by a vast reservoir supplying water for New York City. Those memories of my first eight years there are still very real—as real as the scar I still carry where an ugly rooster pecked me. We had him for Sunday dinner. I grew up with four sisters, a brother, and my mother and father, who moved us seven times in sixteen years. My dad just liked to change jobs, and being a Methodist minister's son, he was used to moving. I liked school well enough but I don't think I was pushed sufficiently. As I had read a great deal—particularly in history—those textbooks were rarely opened.

After high school, I joined a theater group, touring the country for eight months in a car. I think I learned more about life in those eight months than at any other time. We discussed everything—politics, sex, religion, art—and, as the other members of the group were much older, each one became a personal tutor. The woman who gave me my first job in the theater also gave me my first job in the book world: I became head of the New York *Times*-Children's Book Council Reading Is Fun exhibit. I suppose I would not have entered the book field if it had not been for Anne Carroll Moore, who encouraged me to become interested in children's books. For many years I had a sales organization representing numerous publishers. I was then Director of Institutional Promotion and Assistant Vice President for Charles Scribner's Sons. I am now eastern regional sales manager for Scribner. My wife Patricia is also in publishing; for many years she was Vice-President and Editor-in-Chief with Henry Z. Walck, Inc. We have two children, Edwin Beman and Patricia Duffy. We live in New York City, but fortunately we have a house in Connecticut where we can be "country people" on weekends and enjoy the outdoors. (We do not have roosters, ugly or friendly.)

I have always been interested in sports and consider myself a frustrated sports player. This strong interest is reflected in my books, as I feel sportsmanship and participation are very important. Sports should be fun and you don't have to be the hero to enjoy them. I am always happy to hear that both boys and girls enjoy reading my books and find them useful because they too have the same problems as one of the characters.

Once the story idea is firmly fixed in my mind, the writing comes easily. However it takes months for the story to really develop, and I always seem to be thinking about several stories at the same time. Usually they become one. The rewriting is the difficult part as it is not as easy to recapture the same sympathy and mood for the characters as in the first writing. Fortunately, I have not had to do too much of that.

My job requires a great deal of reading but in my free time I love to read mysteries. Someday I hope to write one. Reading should be fun and as soon as we get back to thinking of it as a pleasure, I believe we will have better readers.

Beman Lord headed the New York *Times*-Children's Book Council Reading Is Fun Exhibit from 1949 to 1954. He married Patricia Cummings on September 26, 1959.

SELECTED WORKS: The Trouble With Francis, 1958; Quarterback's Aim, 1960; Look at Cars, 1962 (revised, 1970); The Day the Spaceship Landed, 1962; Rough Ice, 1963; Look at Guns, 1963; Mystery Guest at Left End, 1964; The Perfect Pitch, 1965; Shot-Put Challenge, 1969; Shrimp's Soccer Goal, 1970; The Spaceship Returns, 1970; On the Banks of the Hudson, 1971.

ABOUT: Contemporary Authors, Vol. 33–36; Something about the Author, Vol. 5.

WALTER LORRAINE

February 3, 1929–

ILLUSTRATOR OF *Sir Gawain and the Green Knight*, etc.

Biographical sketch of Walter Henry Lorraine:

WORCESTER, MASSACHUSETTS, was Walter Lorraine's birthplace and the town in which he grew up. As a child he drew whenever he could—"the settings for these creative efforts were usually my mathematics and English classrooms." He remembers being fascinated by the steel engravings in an old family Bible, and he recalls too an early interest in Edgar Allan Poe; he read everything that Poe wrote.

After elementary school in Worcester, Lorraine spent two years at Seaver Street Preparatory School, which he found the most stimulating period of his formal education. The school was a progressive one which encouraged extracurricular intellectual activities as well as sports, and the students were able to put on plays, magic shows and musicals as part of school projects. From there he went to the Classical High School in Worcester.

At that time Lorraine was convinced that he would become either a mechanical or an aeronautical engineer, but after graduating from high school he spent two years in the Navy, where he had enough of an introduction to engineering for him to realize that he would find the work too cold and impersonal. He began to think for the first time about a career in art.

Since he had had no formal art classes in high school, he had no portfolio of work to show to art schools. However, he applied to the Rhode Island School of Design in Providence, which based its admissions on aptitude and psychological testing, and he was accepted. The school laid more emphasis on artistic problem solving than on technique, believing that technique would come later, and Lorraine found this approach stimulating and exciting. His first year at the school was a very satisfying one. He found that everything fell into place and that "art or its application was the only way of life for me."

A job as book designer and production manager of juvenile books at Houghton Mifflin Company in Boston followed his graduation. The first book of significance that he illustrated was *I Will Tell You of a Town* by Alastair Reid. This was published in 1956, and since that time Lorraine has illustrated a number of other books, mostly picture books and stories for younger children.

The medium he prefers is black pen line, though he has used a variety of techniques. He says: "I do not like to think of myself as employing any particular style or approach to my illustrations, though I realize inevitably a personal flavor comes through. I prefer to let the text word dictate the approach." He develops a characterization and style that seem appropriate to the text. When he is preparing to illustrate a book, Lorraine does a great deal of research, and he makes copious notes and jottings rather than doing preliminary sketches. It is this preparatory work, he says, that takes most time. Only when it is completed can he begin the final artwork, and this, once started, is done quickly and spontaneously.

Walter Lorraine is now manager of children's trade books at Houghton Mifflin. He lives with his wife and one of his four children in Newton, Mass. He also teaches a course in book design at Northeastern University. In the past he has taught book illustration at the School of the Museum of Fine Arts and typography under the graphic arts executive training program at Boston University evening school.

Besides his teaching, Walter Lorraine has designed posters and catalogs for the Boston Arts Festival; assisted Bill Hunt when he was establishing the Cambridge Drama Festival; done work in advertising; and once drew a regular cartoon strip for the house organ of Howard Johnson's employees. He is interested in all aspects of children's books, and in 1975 he gave the Showcase Lecture at the Children's Book Council Showcase program in Cleveland on the illustrators of Grimms' *Household Tales*.

———

Lorraine's illustrations to *I Will Tell You of a Town*, by Alastair Reid, won a place among the ten best illustrated children's books of 1956, chosen by the New York *Times*, and his pictures for Julia Cunningham's *Dear Rat* earned the same distinction in 1961.

SELECTED WORKS ILLUSTRATED: Little Laughter, edited by Katherine Love, 1957; One Snail and Me, by Emilie W. McLeod, 1961; David McCheever's 29 Dogs, by Margaret Holt, 1963; The Boy Who Thought He Was a Dog, by Cora Annett, 1965; Sir Gawain and the Green Knight, by Constance B. Hieatt (retold), 1967; From Ambledee to Zumbledee, by Sandol Stoddard Warburg, 1968; My Daddy Longlegs, by Judy Hawes, 1972; McBroom Tells a Lie, by Sid Fleischman, 1976.

ABOUT: Kingman, Lee and others, comps. Illustrators of Children's Books, 1957–1966; Children's Book Council Calendar March–August 1977.

CECIL LUBELL
June 6, 1912–

AUTHOR OF *The Tall Grass Zoo*, etc.

Autobiographical sketch of Cecil Lubell:

I DO the writing. My wife does the drawing. She edits my copy, and that drives me up the wall. I edit her drawings, and she accepts that with only minor hostility. I have noticed, however, that this tends to have a negative effect on the cooking, which she otherwise does brilliantly.

But those are the workaday hazards of being a man-and-wife team. We have learned to live with them.

I write to fit. Especially when we are working on a nature book. This is the way it works:

We agree on the number of pages for each subject. Then my wife designs the pages, marking out the space for text and the space for drawings. Then I calculate the number of lines she has left me. Then we argue. I say that it's ridiculous to think that in thirty lines I can explain how amphibians breathe under water. She says she needs at least a full page for drawings. Then we compromise. I get thirty-five lines. I am not happy. But I write it. It comes to fifty lines. I rewrite it. Not yet. Still a third rewrite and it

clocks in neatly at thirty-five lines. Now I am happy. Thus we take our major satisfactions from minor achievements.

This writing to fit impresses some people and horrifies others. The horrified ones seem to think it diminishes creativity. Nonsense. It challenges creativity. And it's the only way I know of bringing text and pictures into a single, communicable whole. Which is what I assume an illustrated book is all about.

———

Cecil Lubell also writes of himself: "Cecil Lubell was born and raised in Leeds, England, was transplanted to Boston when he was eleven and educated there at the Boston Latin School and Harvard University. Most of his professional life has been spent working on trade journals in the textile and apparel fields. For eleven years, until mid–1973, he was editor of *American Fabrics* magazine and the *AF Encyclopedia of Textiles*. He has now broken away from trade journalism and devotes his time to writing and teaching. Since 1960 he has been writing children's books illustrated by his wife. Most of them are nature

books—*The Tall Grass Zoo, Green Is for Growing, By the Seashore*, etc."

Cecil Lubell earned his B.A. from Harvard in 1933 and his M.A. in 1935. He married Winifred A. Milius in September 1939 and they have two grown sons, David, an archeologist, and Stephen, a graphic designer. The Lubells live on Cape Cod.

SELECTED WORKS (with Winifred Lubell): The Tall Grass Zoo, 1960; Green Is for Growing, 1964; A Zoo for You, 1970; Birds in the Street, 1971; Clothes Tell a Story, 1971; Picture Signs and Symbols, 1972; By the Seashore, 1973; Street Markets Around the World, 1974; Exploring a Brook: Life in the Running Water, 1975.

ABOUT: Contemporary Authors, Vol. 9–10; Something about the Author, Vol. 6.

WINIFRED LUBELL

June 14, 1914–

ILLUSTRATOR OF *The Tall Grass Zoo*, etc.

Autobiographical sketch of Winifred A. Milius Lubell:

OFTEN children from up the road drop in to check on what I am doing, to see what book or film strip is in process. They look with solemn eyes at the drawings on my board, at all the colored inks, brushes, pens and pencils, at all the intriguing paraphernalia of my trade. Then they stare at the lineup of technical books on the shelves surrounding me, many of them propped open at specific illustrations.

"Why do you need so many books?" they ask.

"I need them for research," I say.

"Oh . . ." and their voices trail off in disappointment.

"Do you just copy?" the children want to know.

"Not exactly," I say, and I try to explain the difference between live research and book research.

There is a difference and for me it always comes down to the business of snakes. Snakes are not for me.

So I tell them: "You know about me

and snakes. But I do draw them, though all the research comes from books." Then I show them some snake drawings I did for *Birth of an Island* and *See Through the Jungle*.

"Not very convincing snakes, are they?" I say.

"No," the children agree, "they look lumpy."

"That is because I don't like to watch them," I explain. "So I really don't know how a snake moves, how it looks in action. I can only draw them from books or photos and I'm afraid I don't do that too well. But I can draw you a beautiful praying mantis, eating, hunting, or cleaning its nose. I've looked at them very carefully."

And that's the way it goes for me. Of course, I make very good use of the local libraries, the picture file collection at the Forty-second Street Library in New York, the Library of the Museum of Natural History and my own extensive library. But nothing can take the place of live research.

In a Running Brook, which my husband and I did together, was a luxurious piece of research. We were able to explore our brook for an entire year, visiting it each week, keeping notes and records. I was able to watch and draw each seasonal phase of the brook's life. We learned as we watched and examined. It was the same for our *Green Is for Growing* and *The Tall Grass Zoo*. And it was the same with our recent *A Zoo for You*, though there all the live research was done indoors at home.

Obviously our field research is supplemented by book research. It would be naive not to take advantage of the specialized adult works in any particular field of expertise. But that alone will never make a subject come alive.

There's a danger in over-researching a book. This often happens to me. I lose my sense of proportion. I become so fascinated with each creature and plant that I can't bear to leave anything out. But I must, because I always have twice as many sketches as the average children's book will hold. So I must rely on the more objective editing skills of husband or coauthor or editor.

Another recurring problem for any illustrator of children's nature books is the matter of scale, the need to show the actual size of the things you are drawing. Adult field guides have various ways of showing scale but those are too complex for children. So I must devise other ways to show size.

In *The Tall Grass Zoo*, for example, there is an ant drawn on every page in the same scale as the animal we are discussing. In *Green Is for Growing* I used mice and birds and familiar insects in the same way. In the brook book, I introduced scale drawings of deer, children, plants and trees. In each nature book, this matter of scale must be resolved differently.

As an illustrator of nature books, the biggest challenge I face is how to make my animals or plants look alive, not pinned to a board, not stiff dead specimens. For this, photographs or "scientific" drawings, no matter how brilliantly done, can only be supplements to careful observation of the living creatures or plants.

For me the key problem is to understand the articulation of the plant or the animal. How is it joined? How do the parts fit together? How are the legs of the lizard different from the legs of the pigeon, or the hamster? How do the wings of the damselfly join its thorax?

Always my hope is to sum up in a drawing the concentrated essence of a creature or a plant, to project it almost like a caricature.

Colette puts it so beautifully. She writes: "After all, there is only one creature."

———

Cecil Lubell writes of his wife: "Winifred Lubell was born and raised in New York City, mostly on the upper West Side. She was educated at the Ethical Culture Schools, at the Art Students' League in New York City, and at the Duncan Phillips Museum School in Washington, D.C.

"She began her art career with wood-cut and lithography but soon turned to book illustration where she found her happiest medium. At this writing she has illustrated more than thirty-three books for children, ten of them written by her husband, Cecil Lubell. She has also made record-album covers, been a teacher of art to both adults and children, has worked rewardingly with disadvantaged children at Grasslands Hospital in Westchester, and she has headed an active committee which arranges for continuing displays at the library in Croton-on-Hudson, New York.

"She considers herself one of the incredibly lucky people whose work has been a pleasure. And in her own small way she long ago found a solution to the woman problem, since she has been able to do her work at home, while running a household and raising children. Her favorite quote comes from the German woman artist Kaethe Kollwitz, who said, 'Tell all women artists that I had help in the house.'"

The Lubells were married in 1939.

SELECTED WORKS WRITTEN AND ILLUSTRATED (with Cecil Lubell): The Tall Grass Zoo, 1960; A Zoo for You, 1970; Birds in the Street, 1971; Clothes Tell a Story, 1971; Picture Signs and Symbols, 1972; Street Markets Around the World, 1974; Exploring a Brook: Life in the Running Water, 1975.

SELECTED WORKS ILLUSTRATED: See Through the Sea, by Millicent E. Selsam, 1955; The Story of Caves, by Dorothy Sterling, 1956; See Through the Forest, by Millicent E. Selsam, 1956; See Through the Jungle, by Millicent E. Selsam, 1957; See Through the Lake, by Millicent E. Selsam, 1958; The Birth of an Island, by Millicent E. Selsam, 1959; Caterpillars, by Dorothy Sterling, 1961; Ellen's Blue Jays, by Dorothy Sterling, 1961; Spring Is Here, by Dorothy Sterling, 1964; Fall Is Here, by Dorothy Sterling, 1966; The Moon of the Mountain Lion, by Jean George, 1968.

ABOUT: Contemporary Authors, Vol. 49-52; Kingman, Lee and others, comps. Illustrators of Children's Books: 1957–1966; Viguers, Ruth Hill and others, comps. Illustrators of Children's Books: 1946–1956; Something about the Author, Vol. 6.

EMILY ARNOLD McCULLY

July 1, 1939–

ILLUSTRATOR OF *The Mean Man*, etc.

Autobiographical sketch of Emily Arnold McCully:

I THOUGHT of myself as a midwesterner, while growing up on Long Island —this was a distinction none of my schoolmates shared. I really *was* born in Galesburg, Illinois, and returned there often after we moved, when I was four. But living near New York City, where my father wrote and produced radio programs, was a far greater influence than nostalgia for the prairies. It bred many lavish and unfocused ambitions for success in the theater, in publishing, and in art.

Most of my energy went into writing and illustrating stories, most of them with boy heroes who were my age, which allowed me vicarious participation in adventures at sea, at the racetrack, on a farm, and in the sports arena. The books were bound and embellished with finishing touches like copyright date and flap copy. My mother encouraged my drawing but ushered me in haste through the abstract, inventive period which affords children such freedom of expression. I was, at three, diligently copying both nature and art, and already thinking of the latter as something serviceable.

Pretty soon, too, I stopped doing children's stories and styled myself a writer for adults and a scholar. For a student in a middle-class high school in the fifties, much of the future was predictable: I went away to college, at Brown University, was elected to Phi Beta Kappa, wrote book and lyrics for the annual musical, and acted in many plays. It was a time of varied pursuits, good friends, and none of the freakishness of being "class artist," because I hardly drew at all.

I met my husband at Brown, and we married the day I graduated. I had once planned to go to graduate school, but

that seemed now to be my husband's department, and by contrast I lacked commitment. I was faced instead with a renewal of all the old vague ambitions, all of New York City supposedly at my disposal and no training or experience to do anything in particular. After a long, discouraging job search, I finally decided to fall back on drawing and apply to a studio. They made me errand girl. While I watched the men do paste-ups and surreptitiously practiced them myself, I was in turn regarded with extreme suspicion by the management because of my restlessness. You can't keep a good woman down, so I left the studio to become a mat-cutter at a large advertising agency. There I occupied free moments by writing letters to the president condemning his misuse of the power of persuasion.

Promotion never came, so I finally got up nerve to quit and make a portfolio. It was a ragged thing, which no one took seriously, but I made the rounds for months, encouraged by the fact that at last I had decided what I wanted to be. College paperback covers were using avant-garde illustrations while everyone else seemed to be phasing them out, and so the kindly art director at

Harper and Row gave me my first commission.

That job couldn't keep me busy forever, though, and I began to feel that my current career might be causing my mind to atrophy while my husband's, as he earned a doctorate and began to teach, was expanding in exciting ways. Accordingly, I enrolled at Columbia, at the graduate school of art history. We spent a year in Europe, and I researched a thesis on seventeenth century iconography. But there seemed to be a painful conflict between the making of art and the study and criticism of it, and I wanted badly to stop just talking about the creative process and to get to experiencing it. I free-lanced at book-jacket design and magazine illustration, and finally produced a poster that was seen in the subway by an editor in the junior books division of Harper and Row. She contacted me and boldly offered a chance to illustrate a children's book. This stroke of luck was doubly significant because my husband had accepted a teaching job in Pennsylvania, and it had seemed impossible for me to continue my career outside New York.

Illustrating children's books has made me feel I've returned to what my first instincts told me to do. It wasn't easy re-creating the sensibilities and curiosity of childhood, and only recently, as my own children grow more articulate, do I feel myself on firmer ground. I have enjoyed the challenge of interpreting other people's texts, but it is often a cerebral exercise, and my hope is to write stories myself and achieve the complete synthesis that a good picture book has.

I was fortunately chosen to illustrate *Journey from Peppermint Street*, by Meindert DeJong, the first National Book Award winner for children, the fiftieth anniversary poster for National Children's Book Week and manuscripts like *Maxie*, *That Mean Man*, *Gertrude's Pocket*, *Hurray for Captain Jane*, and *Ma nDa la*. In between restoring two eighteenth century houses, managing organic vegetable and flower gardens, baking bread, changing addresses frequently, and attending to the needs of two young, exuberant boys, I've illustrated more than thirty-five books. Now that my children are readers, I try to make use of some of their gaiety, complexity and mutability in my pictures. One of my keenest interests, too, is to ensure that books no longer mistreat, mislead or misrepresent girls. I participated in a shocking study, conducted by the Women on Words and Images of Princeton, New Jersey, which demonstrated that until recently, most books have.

I have now illustrated over fifty books. I have been writing fiction and my first published story for adults was selected for the O'Henry Collection; Best Short Stories of 1976. I am no longer married and have moved to Brooklyn, New York, to a brownstone.

———

Emily Arnold McCully's children are Nathaniel, born in 1968, and Thaddeus (Tad), born in 1971.

Mrs. McCully received a gold medal from the Philadelphia Art Director's Club in 1968. Her illustrations for Arnold Adoff's Ma nDa la won a place for the book among the 1975 Brooklyn Art Books for Children. Hurray for Captain Jane, by Sam Reavin, was included in the 1972 Children's Book Showcase. In 1969 Mrs. McCully was invited to design the poster celebrating the fifth anniversary of Children's Book Week.

SELECTED WORKS ILLUSTRATED: The Seventeenth Street Gang, by Emily C. Neville, 1966; Journey from Peppermint Street, by Meindert DeJong, 1968; Gertrude's Pocket, by Miska Miles, 1970; Ma nDa la, by Arnold Adoff, 1971; Hurray for Captain Jane, by Sam Reavin, 1971; Girls Can, Too, edited by Lee Bennet Hopkins, 1972; When Violet Died, by Mildred Kantrowitz, 1973; Her Majesty Grace Jones, by Jane Langton, 1974; Stand in the Wind, by Jean W. Little, 1975; The Bed Book, by Sylvia Plath, 1976; My Street's A Morning Cool Street, by Ianthe Thomas, 1976; Martha's Mad Day, by Miranda Hapgood, 1977.

ABOUT: Kingman, Lee and others, comps. Illustrators of Children's Books: 1957–1966; Something about the Author, Vol. 5.

ANN McGOVERN

AUTHOR OF If You Sailed on the Mayflower, etc.

Autobiographical sketch of Ann McGovern Scheiner:

THE rhythm and colors of New York City became part of my bloodstream at birth, for though I've been living in the country quiet of Westchester for seven years, I find I still need the tempo of the city and make the one-hour trip often.

As a shy, stuttering child I don't recall a time when I didn't satisfy my need for creative expression by writing, or my strong escapist needs by reading. In my high school (five thousand girls) there was one English teacher who made me feel my writing was worthy of being shared, and with her encouragement I wrote many stories and poems. Some years later I began working in a children's book publishing company and turned my writing to the most challenging and stimulating audience imaginable.

My need for writing jelled with practical needs, for I was divorced and bringing up a child alone. For more than ten years I worked in publishing by day and wrote children's books when I could. My publishing career ranged from reading manuscripts and writing book-jacket blurbs to editing books, producing children's records and originating the See-Saw Book Club (Scholastic Book Services). By 1967, after I had published sixteen books, I was ready to take a chance at earning my living as a full-time author and I went abroad, first to Paris, then to London where I was also a consultant for Penguin Books. My love of travel is even stronger today, and my husband and I have been around the world twice.

Looking backwards (and forwards) to my books, I realize they reflect my life in three parts: 1) ideas I strongly believe in; 2) desire for knowledge (I never finished college); 3) exciting personal experiences—scuba diving, for example or exploring Mayan ruins or

camping out in Africa, and photographing everywhere.

Black Is Beautiful was written right after Martin Luther King's murder. I went to a rally in the city and heard a young man say in anger and grief: "Black is beautiful, baby. Know it. Feel it." I knew it and I felt it but I also knew that the word "black" had held negative images for far too long. The next two days I wrote pages of positive images about blackness and it became a kind of poem. Because I was strongly against the Vietnam war, I wrote *Little Wolf* to show how one person rejected violence even though the world around him condemned pacifism. In *Runaway Slave: The Story of Harriet Tubman* I chose a woman in history whom both black and white girls could admire. There are still too few heroines in today's children's books. To help fill the void I wrote *The Secret Soldier: The Story of Deborah Sampson* about a young woman in Revolutionary times who was denied adventure because of her sex and poverty.

In my recent *Half A Kingdom*, the peasant girl wins both prince and kingdom and sets out to right the social wrongs of the kingdom where the rich don't work and the poor have to work too hard.

In my historical books I try to ferret out the truth; even though the truth may not be popular. I think it important to tell it like it was; to show, for example, that the Pilgrims got seasick on the Mayflower and threw up like ordinary folk. Trying to crack stereotypes, I emphasized the Sioux nation's peaceable nature in *If You Lived With The Sioux Indians*.

I married Martin Scheiner in 1970 and we joined families (now we are six). We all learned scuba diving and we dive on family vacations. I've had the thrill of diving with sharks and other magnificent sea creatures. I wrote *Sharks* and *The Underwater World of the Coral Reef* to share my joy and knowledge and also to point out that this underwater world is in danger of being destroyed by pollution. My next book, *Shark Lady*, is about the life of courageous Eugenie Clark who has made startling discoveries about sharks.

For my future writings, I plan to concentrate on events in our history long ignored, and to produce books that reinforce humanistic values such as love, individuality, and honesty to each other.

Ann McGovern married Martin Scheiner on June 6, 1970. Their children are Peter McGovern and Charles, Ann and James Scheiner. Besides her many books for children Ann McGovern has written reviews for children's books, a movie, and children's songs. She also writes adult short stories, poetry and travel articles.

SELECTED WORKS: The Story of Christopher Columbus, 1963; Little Wolf, 1965; Runaway Slave: the Story of Harriet Tubman, 1965; If You Lived in Colonial Times, 1966; Black is Beautiful, 1969; If You Sailed on the Mayflower, 1970; Stone Soup, 1971; Squeals and Squiggles and Ghostly Giggles, 1973; If You Lived with the Sioux Indians, 1974; The Secret Soldier: the Story of Deborah Sampson, 1975; Sharks, 1976; The Underwater World of the Coral Reef, 1977; Half a Kingdom, 1977.

ABOUT: Contemporary Authors, Vol. 49–52; Hopkins, Lee Bennet. Books Are by People; Something about the Author, Vol. 8.

STAN MACK

AUTHOR AND ILLUSTRATOR OF *10 Bears in My Bed*, etc.

Autobiographical sketch of Stanley Mack:

I WAS born in Brooklyn, that hotbed of folklore, although I really should have been born in Providence, where I grew up.

One thing about Brooklyn: my second grade teacher sent home a note saying I had talent in drawing, and when we moved to Providence I began to attend Saturday morning art classes at the Rhode Island School of Design.

After high school I gravitated to RISD and spent four years not worrying about preparing for a job. I went to New York for the same reasons kids have always been drawn to the city and knocked around from job to job without making the slightest dent in the art world. After two years in the Army, creating audiovisual materials at the United States Military Academy at West Point, I returned to New York.

I landed a job on the *Herald Tribune*, which was being redesigned, and for a few years until it folded, I was part of one of the most creative and influential publications in the city. As art director of *Book Week*, the *Trib*'s Sunday book section, I also had a crash course on the illustrating and writing of children's books.

At that time I married a *Trib* reporter. On our lunch hours, over sandwiches and coffee, we created a nonsense-verse animal alphabet book, from aardvark to zebra. Harlin Quist published it as *The ABC of Bumptious Beasts*.

When the *Tribune* folded in 1966, I went to the New York *Times* as art director for their expanding book and education divisions. In my spare time, I illustrated Lear's *Four Little Children Who Went Around the World* for Harlin Quist. I started illustrating *Potato Talk*, about the time my first child was born. Some of those illustrations I'll never forget; they were done at 3:00 A.M. while my wife gave the baby his bottle.

A year or so after the baby was born, we moved out of the city and I began to free-lance full time. It's been the everyday world of kids, houses, dogs, etc., that has given me an awareness and interest in children and children's books quite different from simply viewing juvenile literature as a good vehicle for illustration.

I hope to continue to create books that reflect my own children's growth and changing view of the world.

Stan Mack has illustrated more than ten books for children. *One Dancing Drum* was one of the New York *Times'* choice of ten best-illustrated children's books in 1971 and was included in the 1972 Children's Book Showcase. *The Preposterous Week* was chosen for inclusion in the 1971–72 Children's Book Show mounted by the American Institute of Graphic Arts.

Mr. Mack has made animated films, which have been shown on "Sesame Street" and at the Animated Film Festival in Zagreb, Yugoslavia. He has contributed to many magazines and had work exhibited in the Museum of Modern Art (New York) and the New York Society of Illustrators.

SELECTED WORKS WRITTEN AND ILLUSTRATED: (with Gail Kredenser) One Dancing Drum, 1971; 10 Bears in My Bed: A Goodnight Countdown, 1974; The King's Cat is Coming! An Alphabetical Tale, 1976; Where's *My* Cheese?, 1977.

SELECTED WORKS ILLUSTRATED: The Little Man and the Big Thief, by Erich Kästner, 1969; Potato Talk, by Ennis Rees, 1969; Star Bright, by Boris V. Zakhoder, 1969; The Preposterous Week, by George Keenan, 1971; Jethro's Difficult Dinosaur, by Arnold Sundgaard, 1977.

ALLAN CAMPBELL McLEAN

ALLAN CAMPBELL McLEAN

November 18, 1922–

AUTHOR OF *The Year of the Stranger*, etc.

Autobiographical sketch of Allan Campbell McLean:

DESPITE my six-cylinder Scottish name, I was born in England. A place called Walney Island, Lancashire. About as well known in the States, I guess, as Walpole, Massachusetts, is in Great Britain.

Walney was a dormitory for the shipbuilding town of Barrow-in-Furness. The shipyard bossed the town. Even the street I lived in was named after a battleship, which may account for my lifelong distaste for the armed services.

At fourteen—educated largely on Hollywood movies—I became an apprentice motor mechanic. After a couple of months I was fired by an outraged management. I had been caught committing the equivalent of matricide on the internal combustion engine—topping up batteries from the faucet instead of using distilled water. It was an aspect of esoteric craft wholly beyond my comprehension.

An accountant gave me a job as his office boy because the prose style of my letter of application amused him. I graduated to junior clerk until the war provided a convenient means of escape. As soon as I was eighteen, I joined the Royal Air Force and saw service in Egypt, the Western Desert, Tripolitania, Tunisia, Sicily and Italy. My overseas tour ended on a note of drama—a court-martial for insubordination. I spent fifty-six days in "The Glasshouse," which provided the material—and title—for a novel in later years.

Back in England, demobilized from the Air Force, I bought a secondhand typewriter and set up shop as a writer in a cottage in Kent. I had also acquired a wife who was accustomed to eating at reasonably regular intervals.

My first break came from the States. *Liberty*—long-since defunct, alas—paid me five hundred dollars for a short short story. I also had published a couple of paperback thrillers and—in collaboration with my wife—a children's book. I thought I had hitched my pseudonym to the gravy train, but it was simply beginner's luck. Before long the rejection slips threatened to create a garbage problem.

My wife was in a nursing home awaiting the birth of our first child. I was broke. In desperation, I scanned the

McLean: *ma CLAIN*

pages of the *Writers and Artists Year Book* looking for a means to earn a quick buck. There was the answer. *"Christian novels required. 30,000 words. One pound per thousand. No controversy. No sex."*

I dashed off a magnificent Christian novel. Not a whisper of controversy marred a single page. Sex was buried deeper than the War Room in the Pentagon. Characters of the opposite sex were kept so far apart they had almost to communicate by semaphore.

I went to see my wife at the nursing home and told her what I had done. "Ah, well," she said, "I suppose we can live on the immoral earnings for a time."

The manuscript was back by return of post, complete with rejection slip. Formula junk, I decided, was not for me. And if I was going to be broke, I'd be broke in a place where there was no stigma attached to poverty. Back to the land of my forbears, the Highlands of Scotland.

We settled in a remote croft in the Isle of Skye. The croft was perched on the side of a hill looking across the waters of the Minch to the great mountains of Wester Ross. A ring of hills circled us to the west. One of them was Sgurr a' Mhadaidh Ruaidh—The Hill of the Red Fox. It became the title of my first novel for young people set in Skye. The last has yet to be written.

———

Allan Campbell McLean's novels for young people were highly praised when published in the United States. *Master of Morgana* and *Ribbon of Fire* were both named Notable Children's Books by the American Library Association. However, they never achieved wide readership, perhaps because of the unfamiliar setting and the daunting amount of the difficult Gaelic language. The first books, *Hill of the Red Fox*, *Storm over Skye* and *Master of Morgana* are primarily adventure stories with a contemporary setting. Then because of his interest in the local history of Skye, McLean turned to historical novels, set at the time of the Crofter's War in the late nineteenth century. *Ribbon of Fire, A Sound of Trumpets* and *The Year of the Stranger* are rousing partisan pictures of the struggles of poor crofters, for the most part impotent against the superior forces of the lairds and the government that represented their interests. McLean clearly identifies with the poor working man against the established powers of wealth and privilege in his books and in his life, so it was a natural development for him to translate his principles into politics. He stood for Parliament for the Labor Party in 1964, and although he was unsuccessful, he has remained deeply involved in politics, eventually removing from the Isle of Skye to the mainland town of Inverness to be closer to the center of action.

Allan McLean married Margaret Elizabeth White in 1946. They have three grown children, Angus, Catriona and Alasdair.

SELECTED WORKS: Hill of the Red Fox, 1956; Storm Over Skye, 1957; Master of Morgana, 1959; Ribbon of Fire, 1962; A Sound of Trumpets, 1966; The Year of the Stranger, 1972.

ABOUT: Author's and Writer's Who's Who, 1971; Jones, Cornelia and Olivia R. Way. British Children's Authors. Interviews at Home; Contemporary Authors, Vol. 3.

JANET McNEILL

September 14, 1907–

AUTHOR OF *The Battle of St. George Without*, etc.

Autobiographical sketch of Janet Mc-Neill Alexander:

JANET McNEILL is my maiden name. I was born in Dublin in 1907, the third child of a clergyman, in the days of nurses and maids, long skirts and elastic-sided boots, gaslights in the nursery and horse-drawn vehicles going by in the road. One of my earliest memories is that of being carried to the front door to see a Motor Car proceeding past the

house! When I was seven my father was appointed to a large church in England, and I was at a day school at Birkenhead, Cheshire. My father's health broke down, and for a few years, while I was at St. Andrews University, Scotland (M.A. in classics) he was in charge of a small country church back in our native Ireland. I hoped to be a publisher's reader and then start to write myself, but I couldn't find a publisher who wanted to employ me, so I worked for two years as secretary in a Belfast newspaper office, and then very happily married Robert P. Alexander, a civil engineer, and lived for thirty-two years in County Antrim, learning the domestic arts (these were not included in my school curriculum), raising four children, and making a garden. I also served as a member of the Northern Island Advisory Council of the British Broadcasting Corporation, as a Child's Guardian on the local Juvenile Court, and took an interest in Girls' Clubs.

In 1964 we moved to Bristol, England, to be nearer our scattered family. In August 1972 we sustained the loss of one of our sons in a climbing accident and in March 1973, my husband died.

I have always written and hoped to be published. As a child I wrote odes for family celebrations, and later contribu-ted to school and university magazines. When my family were little I neglected writing altogether. Then I found time and opportunity to enter a radio play for a BBC competition and was surprised and delighted to win a second prize. After this, other plays and short stories for radio followed, then adult novels, then children's books. I also contributed to a number of periodicals, including the *Horn Book*.

I write now mostly for children. I find as I get older that my appreciation for children becomes sharper and is more real to me than the confusing adult world in which I live. I can return to the childhood world and am delighted to discover that today's children seem to recognize that I have a right to be there. I enjoy talking to young people and try to keep in touch with them so that my appreciation of how they feel is maintained. Of course the conditions in which today's children live are very different from those in which I grew up, but there is, I am sure, a link in our experience of discovering the world, learning the range of our emotions, respecting our differences, and marvelling at the interest and stimulus which personal relationships bring. Life is made up of relationships. I am always pleased to think that what I write may help a child to understand this and may enable him to think and to laugh. Laughter is always valuable.

———

Janet McNeill has written further: "I was one of a happy family with a great sense of family identity. But my father's long illness haunted my childhood and seemed to make nonsense of the over-simplified religious teaching I had learned. My rebellion against this is certainly part of my adult novels. . . . As soon as I could write I wanted to, but my early efforts were very bad. I don't think I was taught with much imagination at school; my father knew what I was trying to do. When I married he gave me a typewriter, which in those days of cut glass and embroidered tablecloths was a most unconventional wedding gift."

One critic wrote of Miss McNeill's work that though she deals with "universals as old as time" she is "a sensitive observer who sees them afresh."

Besides books, plays, articles and reviews, Janet McNeill has written librettos for a children's opera and an adult one.

Although she has never yet received one of the major awards for children's books, Janet McNeill's books often appear on the yearly lists of books distinguished for their excellence. *The Other People, Goodbye Dove Square,* and *The Battle of St. George Without* were all American Library Association Notable Books.

SELECTED WORKS: The Giant's Birthday, 1964; The Battle of St. George Without, 1966; The Mouse and the Mirage, 1966; Up Tom's Tower, 1967; Goodbye Dove Square, 1969; The Other People, 1970; Various Specs, 1971; A Monster Too Many, 1972; The Prisoner in the Park, 1972; We Three Kings, 1974; Ever After, 1975; The Three Crowns of King Hullabaloo, 1976.

ABOUT: Author's and Writer's Who's Who, 1971; Contemporary Authors, Vol. 9–12; Something about the Author, Vol. 1; Horn Book August 1972; Junior Bookshelf Fall 1967.

MARGARET MacPHERSON

June 29, 1908–

AUTHOR OF *The Rough Rider*, etc.

Autobiographical sketch of Margaret MacLean MacPherson:

I WAS born in a small village called Colinton, near Edinburgh, in 1908, a fourth daughter. I was educated in various Edinburgh schools, but every summer we came home to my father's birthplace in Skye. I used to run wild on the hills, help on the crofts, and try to catch the ponies which were allowed to roam the hills in summertime. When I was lucky I used to ride one barebacked down to the crofts to do a bit of work.

I took a degree of Master of Arts at Edinburgh, was capped in the morning, and married in the afternoon. I always

Margaret MacPherson

wanted to live in the country and farm. As I could not farm myself—no money, no land—I married a farmer against my father's wishes. He never spoke to me again. My husband was a cattle and sheep dealer. We came north to Skye, which has been my home ever since. That was in 1929. We struck a bad patch, prices fell, and we had to find a place of our own. Near the Coolin Hills we rented a remote peninsula of five thousand acres from the Forestry Commission, which didn't want it for tree planting. There was no road. We crossed the loch in a small motorboat, and our boxes and cases were carried up the steep brae to the house. It was a corrugated iron bungalow, too hot in summer, too cold in winter, but that May evening it had a touch of enchantment swathed in spiders' webs. Rabbits looked out from underneath.

We lived there for ten years, first grazing cattle and then building up a sheep stock. We were two and a half miles from the nearest house. Our own rocked like a cradle in every gale of wind. We had it tied down with great boulders to prevent it from becoming airborne. The nearest shop was seven miles away but with the sea at our door we ferried our groceries across in bulk—it was always a red-letter day when the boxes were unpacked. Apart from that we lived off the land—our own mutton and vegetables, deer on the hill and fish in the sea. During the war it became impossible to get help, so we took a croft near Portree.

We reared a family of seven sons, three of whom are farmers now. As you may imagine I had no time for anything but house or farm work. There was hardly time to think, let alone write, but when the boys had grown up and scattered, married, I found myself out on a limb. I had always wanted to write a book. I had done articles and talks for the BBC.

"Well," I said to myself, "it's now or never. No use saying you've no time. Make time." I had about two spare hours in the afternoon, and once started, I scribbled madly, usually outside, on a green shelf above the shore or in the shelter of some birches. When it came to typing, I had to stay indoors, which I didn't much like. The book is called *The Shinty Boys*. Shinty is a very fast game played in the Highlands of Scotland and in Ireland where they call it hurley. No one wanted to take a chance and publish it but finally, in 1963, when I had become a grandmother five times over, it came out. That encouraged me to write another book called *The Rough Road* about when times were bad before the war.

So you see I was a very late starter but better late than never and I now have five books published. My grandchildren read and like them. I have had nice letters from children in America telling me they liked them too. I have made friends of Americans and will always be glad that I made the effort and managed to write a whole book. It feels very long when you are at page one.

———

So far Mrs. MacPherson has always set her stories on the Isle of Skye, in the Hebrides of Scotland. Her backgrounds are authentic and vividly re-create the sound and color of that very special locale. Perhaps for this reason, her first book, *The Shinty Boys*, and later *The New Tenants* failed to find a strong following in the United States. With *The Rough Road*, which depicts the struggles of an adolescent boy to escape an unpleasant home during the hard times of the 1930s, Mrs. MacPherson struck a more universal chord. The book was an American Library Association Notable Book for Children for 1966 and was included in the *Horn Book* magazine's Fanfare, an honor list of the best books of the year. A fifth book, *The Battle of the Braes* (1972), was published in Great Britain.

Soon after the publication of her first novel, Mrs. MacPherson took a degree in teachers training and began teaching in the high school at Portree, the largest town on Skye.

Margaret MacLean married Duncan MacPherson June 28, 1921. Their children are Lachlan, Alasdair, Neil, William, Allan, Andrew and Kenneth. Mr. MacPherson died in 1971.

SELECTED WORKS: The Shinty Boys, 1963; The Rough Road, 1966; Ponies for Hire, 1967; The New Tenants, 1968.

ABOUT: Contemporary Authors, Vol. 49–52; Jones, Cornelia and Olina R. Way. British Children's Authors. Interviews at Home.

MARGARET MAHY
March 21, 1936–

AUTHOR OF *A Lion in the Meadow*, etc.

Autobiographical sketch of Margaret Mahy:

"ONCE upon a time there was a big black-maned Abyssinian Lion. . . ." Perhaps this is more truly a beginning than the actual date of my birth, 21st of March 1936 in a small New Zealand town called Whakatane. The Abyssinian Lion was the invention of my father, a building contractor and bridge builder. The lion's adventures were rather trivial, but his existence was not. He became a creature of my inner landscape, bounding, brilliant and forever Abyssinian.

Mahy: *MAR hee*

MARGARET MAHY

I was the oldest of five children, all of whom were loved, who still occupy strongly individual places in the structure of our family. My mother read us Beatrix Potter and A. A. Milne, L. M. Montgomery and Charles Dickens. My father read us Ballantyne and Marryat and Rider Haggard. He recited ballads and told stories.

Inside the family everything made sense. Outside of it, I now realize, all was confusion. I spent the first twenty-one years of my outside life in a state of unconscious bewilderment. But during that time, from the time I was seven, I wrote stories, filling notebook after notebook. I had poems published in a local paper, and my parents were proud and encouraged me. The notebooks were saved and have recently been given back to me. I am amazed that I am still anxious to protect these stories from the ridicule they deserve, which shows perhaps that I am still involved with them even thirty years later.

School, university and library school were the sources of my exterior education. Omnivorous reading, writing, illustrating my own stories, reading J. R. R. Tolkien, and watching the stars through a home-made telescope helped to educate me in my dreams. Falling in love

caused a tremendous, if slow, crystallization to take place. For the first time the basic bewilderment began to break up. Things began to make a sort of sense. I began to make a sort of sense to myself. I began to know who I was. (Mind you, I am still finding out.) I found that the stories I wrote were inevitably stories for children, but I am still not sure why this is. I don't feel like anything except an adult, and I don't want to return to childhood.

My stories were first published in the *School Journal*—a magazine produced by the School Publications Branch of the Department of Education. Encouraged by this success, and also needing money, I wrote widely, using lots of words. I still like many of the words I used then, although nowadays I try to use fewer.

The miracle that all writers are urged never to expect occurred. An American editor, Sarah Chokla Gross, found a story of mine in a copy of the *School Journal* that was in New York in a printing exhibition. She passed it on to Helen Hoke Watts, who erupted into my life like a volcano. It pleases me to think that the first story they found was *A Lion in the Meadow*. My father had set the great big black-maned Abyssinian Lion bounding over the tawny plain of my inner landscape to good effect. The first five books were *A Lion in the Meadow*, *The Dragon of an Ordinary Family*, *Mrs. Discombobulous*, *The Procession*, and a horror story, *Pillycock's Shop*. They were published in the U.S. by Franklin Watts, Inc. Since then there has been *The Little Witch*, *The Princess and the Clown*, *Sailor Jack and the Twenty Orphans* and others.

It is very exciting to have such a thing happen to one, but disconcerting too. Print removes the story from me. I see my name there, but what is this, this neat pattern of words framed in glowing pictures? . . . Only when I read it aloud am I certain that it is my story. Translation makes it still more remote. These words can never be my own, I do not know what they say. Yet at the same time I know it *is* mine in some ways, and

I feel excited and very grateful to Helen Hoke Watts.

My children enjoy the stories in entirely different ways. Penny is pleased for me in the same way that I am pleased when she gets into the "A" team at net ball. Bridget, on the other hand, sits down to write her own stories. "Once there was a king who would not eat porridge. . . ." "Once a king met a terrible lion. . . ." There it is again, that golden lion, leaping from summer to summer down through time, making our ears sing with its roaring. I wish I had thought to ask my father where he got his lion. Perhaps all storytellers are receivers and transmitters of images. Hopefully they enrich the image as it passes through them.

Bound along, old lion, laughing as you go, finding other people to tell about you.

———

Margaret Mahy is currently librarian in charge of School Library Service in Christ Church, New Zealand. She lives with her daughters Penelope and Bridget in a house by the sea and "hills covered by dense New Zealand bush." In 1970 *A Lion in the Meadow* won New Zealand's Esther Glen Award for the "most distinguished contribution to New Zealand literature for children by an author who is a citizen or resident of New Zealand." In 1973, she won the award again (the first time since the establishment of the award in 1945 that an author has won twice), this time for *The First Margaret Mahy Story Book. A Lion in the Meadow* was among *School Library Journal's* choices for best books of the year in 1969. *The Boy Who Was Followed Home* was an American Library Association Notable Book for Children in 1975.

SELECTED WORKS: The Dragon of an Ordinary Family, 1969; Mrs. Discombobulous, 1969; A Lion in the Meadow, 1969; Pillycock's Shop, 1969; The Procession, 1969; The Little Witch, 1970; The Princess and the Clown, 1971; The Boy With Two Shadows, 1972; The Man Whose Mother Was a Pirate, 1972; The Boy Who Was Followed Home, 1975; Leaf Magic, 1977.

ABOUT: Publishers Weekly April 7, 1969.

ANTONY MAITLAND

June 17, 1935–

AUTHOR AND ILLUSTRATOR OF *James and the Roman Silver*, etc.

Biographical sketch of Antony Jasper Maitland:

BORN in Andover, Somerset, England, in 1935, Antony Maitland was one of six brothers. Since his father was a career officer in the air force, the family moved about a great deal.

Maitland got off to a good start. He studied at the West of England College of Art in Bristol, from which he received the National Diploma in Design in 1957. He won a Leverhulme Travelling Scholarship upon graduation, but was allowed by the administrators of the scholarship to fulfill his two years' National Service before making use of the grant. He traveled in Holland, Spain, Germany, Sicily and France, and in the Middle East, where he made invaluable contacts. He has worked for an architect in Beirut, designed a crest for a bank in Teheran, and has painted a portrait of the Shah of Iran and his family. Maitland's description of his arrival at the Shah's palace in his blue jeans and long hair, portfolio under his arm, is lively, as are his accounts of his face-to-face interviews with the Shah. The actual sittings were few, and Maitland worked largely from photographs.

In England Maitland designed sets for the Quadricentenary Shakespeare Festival at Stratford-on-Avon, and new wall paintings for Madame Tussaud's Exhibition of waxworks. Such work calls for executive ability and the delegating of work to others; but the more private side of his nature draws him to the world of illustration—a world where every detail is the artist's responsibility and he must have complete mastery of the subject.

In this field too he started well. The first book he illustrated was *Mrs. Cockle's Cat* by Philippa Pearce (England, 1961), for which he won the Kate Greenaway Award in 1962. Writing of his prize-winning illustrations, the critic Marcus Crouch praised Maitland's "great technical resourcefulness," "exuberance," "warmth and humor" and the "strength and tenderness of his vision of town and country," placing him alongside Randolph Caldecott. *Mrs. Cockle's Cat* was followed by *James and the Roman Silver* for which Maitland also wrote the text.

But new vistas opened when Grace Hogarth, the children's editor at Constable Young Books, asked him to illustrate *Jack Holborn*, a book by Leon Garfield. It is almost with awe that Maitland talks of the contrast between the world of *Mrs. Cockle's Cat* and the murky, twilight atmosphere of Garfield's eighteenth century setting. But he was beginning to see the role of the illustrator becoming clearer. It was, he has said, as though he were being led along a corridor with rooms on either side to which he alone held the key; he alone could solidify and make convincing the scenes and details. His illustrations for Garfield's *The Ghost Downstairs* earned a commendation for the Kate Greenaway in 1973.

Maitland feels free to pick and choose as far as illustration is concerned and talks of doing one book a year of which he is "not ashamed." "But," he says, "I can never resist adventure" and adventure is sure to arise.

Recently a film company embarked on a full-length film of a Grimm fairy tale and asked Maitland to design the sets and the costumes, giving him the choice of stories. He chose *The Goose Girl* and fulfilled his contracts, but snags developed and the film has not been released.

Maitland owns a Victorian house in London and he also has a little cottage on the Norfolk-Suffolk border. He has said that he wants to be more than just a "weekend tenant arriving with a case of gin." But to a man who can't resist adventure anything may happen, and he may never get a chance to cultivate his garden.

SELECTED WORKS WRITTEN AND ILLUSTRATED: James and the Roman Silver, 1965; Idle Jack, 1977.

SELECTED. WORKS ILLUSTRATED: Jack Holborn, by Leon Garfield, 1965; Devil-in-the-Fog, by Leon Garfield, 1966; Black Jack, by Leon Garfield, 1968; The Drummer Boy, by Leon Garfield, 1969; The Ghost Downstairs, by Leon Garfield, 1972; The Ghost of Thomas Kempe, by Penelope Lively, 1973; Book of Ghosts and Hauntings, by Aidan Chambers, 1974; The Phantom Cyclist & Other Ghost Stories, by Ruth Ainsworth, 1974; The Wonder-Dog, by Richard Hughes, 1977.

ABOUT: Hürlimann, Bettina. Picture-Book World; Kingman, Lee and others, comps. Illustrators of Children's Books: 1957–1966; Who's Who in America, 1972–73; Library Association Record May 1962.

W. T. MARS

September 1, 1912–

ILLUSTRATOR OF *Calico Captive*, etc.

Autobiographical sketch of Witold Tadeusz Josef Mars:

I CONSIDER myself to be exceptionally lucky, having spent my childhood and early young age in one of the most beautiful European cities—Cracow. A city partly surrounded by walls and towers, with seventy-three old churches, squares and streets lined with historic structures, and with the massive Gothic-Renaissance royal castle high on a hill and towering above the entire town.

My mother was an author of children's books and had a marvellous quality of sharing with me the joy of living amidst so much beauty and in a unique atmosphere. Thanks to her I first entered the magic world of Andersen, met Peter Pan, read the *Arabian Nights*, and took part in the adventures of the Nutcracker. Later, when I grew up, she introduced me to the Greek legends and the Scandinavian sagas, to the *Song of Roland*. Together we penetrated the circle of King Arthur's knights. Solitary walks with a

Witold T. Mars

small sketchbook under his arm became the favourite pastime of the little boy who tried to cram into it all the fascinating discoveries he was making on his own. At that time I developed the cult of the book. I started to collect books, to lose them, and to collect them once again.

Books have a magic power of multiplying without our even noticing it; they grow in numbers, fill all possible shelves, cupboards, closets—take over our entire apartment. Finally, they force us to strike back, to defend ourselves against their total victory.

I illustrated my first book at the age of nine, the next one when I was thirteen, and several more before I finished school.

During my studies at the Academy of Fine Arts in Warsaw, I discovered modern painting and new trends in painting. I was overwhelmed with the joy to have discovered form and color. The hectic years of studies passed quickly. So did the dazzling moments of confrontation with Great Art in the museums and galleries of Paris, in Italian and German cities. Next came the period of endeavor and search for my own way, and evaluation of my possibilities. I painted a lot, exhibited both in my own country and abroad. I tried not to think about the

possibility of the approaching war, the way one tries not to think of the coming death.

I spent the war years in the army, in Great Britain, then crossed over to the Continent with the Allied Forces. During brief periods of the war I was able to paint and exhibit in England. On the Continent, during military action, my sketchbook remained my usual faithful companion.

When the war was over I settled in London, trying to resume the old way of life that had been interrupted, and to go back to painting. My old infatuation with books woke once again and grew stronger. I started to illustrate books and magazines.

In 1951 I arrived in this country and immediately executed several assignments which had been waiting for me. Since that time their number has been growing steadily and totals about two hundred books illustrated by me. Nevertheless, I still have a strong feeling of excitement and emotion each time I start to work on a new book.

My very private world of books, painting and illustrations is shared with me by my wife, Helene. She is the author of many unwritten stories and tales. Her sensitivity and appreciation of beauty bring us a lot of joy.

When browsing through my illustrations I fully realize how they vary, both in style and in my approach to each subject. Such treatment is the result of my deep conviction that every single book represents a different experience, since it constitutes a different problem. This dissimilarity should be, and is, reflected in my illustrations. In my opinion, illustrations should be an integral part of the story rather than allowing the reader to identify the artist at first sight.

———

W. T. Mars was born in Rzesna, Poland, the son of a landowner and lawyer. He graduated from the Academy of Fine Arts in Warsaw in 1934 and exhibited his works in Poland and abroad until 1939. During World War II he served with the

Polish forces in Great Britain and was decorated twice. He also participated in group shows in London, Edinburgh, Glasgow, Sheffield and Bristol. Mars became a naturalized American citizen in 1957. He married Helene Bohusz on December 29, 1960.

W. T. Mars has painted murals for the British Industry Fair and the Festival of Britain, and his work is included in the permanent collection of the Polish State Collection, London. He has received painting awards both in Poland and the United States where he won a special merit award in the seventh annual book jacket competition in New York, 1961. Mr. Mars was elected to the Polish Institute of Arts and Sciences in America in 1965. He is also a fellow of the Institute of Design.

SELECTED WORKS: Calico Captive, by Elizabeth C. Speare, 1957; Boomerang Hunter, by Jim Kjelgard, 1960; Dangerous Journey, by Laszlo Hamori, 1962; High Wind for Kansas, by Mary Calhoun, 1965; Great Leaders of Greece and Rome, by Leonard Cottrell, 1966; The Hatching of Joshua Cobb, by Margaret Hodges, 1967; Trouble in the Jungle, by John Rowe Townsend, 1969; Circle of Seasons, by Ann N. Clark, 1970; The Making of Joshua Cobb, by Margaret Hodges, 1971; Barney's Lake, by Nan Agle, 1972; Greenhorn on the Frontier, by Ann Finlayson, 1974; Outdoor Things to Do, by William Hillcourt, 1975.

ABOUT: Contemporary Authors, Vol. 25–28; Kingman, Lee and others, comps. Illustrators of Children's Books: 1957–1966; Something about the Author, Vol. 3; Who's Who in the East, 1974–75.

JAMES MARSHALL

October 10, 1942–

AUTHOR AND ILLUSTRATOR OF *George and Martha*, etc.

Biographical sketch of James Edward Marshall:

JAMES MARSHALL was born in San Antonio, Texas, and lived on a farm until he was in his teens. When he was small, his mother, a confirmed Anglo-

JAMES MARSHALL

phile, read to him a great deal, not from children's books, which mostly he disliked, but from adult books by such writers as Charles Dickens. She bought her six-year-old son a history of England in twenty-four leather-bound volumes, and these became his favorite reading. He drew to amuse himself until he was discouraged by the unsympathetic comments of a first grade teacher.

From the age of nine James Marshall was preoccupied with music. He played both the violin and the viola, and after high school he won a scholarship to the New England Conservatory of Music in Boston, where he studied the viola under Joseph Di Pasquale, the principal violist with the Boston Symphony Orchestra. In 1961 he was in a plane crash, and a severe hand injury put an end to his hopes for a professional music career, though he still plays for his own pleasure.

Marshall attended various colleges and graduated with a degree in history. While he was teaching French and Spanish in a high school in Boston's South End he began to draw for his own enjoyment. The sketches were expanded into sequences of drawings, and a friend persuaded him to take his portfolio to Houghton Mifflin in Boston. A few weeks later he was commissioned to illustrate *Plink, Plink, Plink* by Byrd Baylor.

In 1971 he was sitting on a patio in Texas, drawing idly while *Who's Afraid of Virginia Woolf?* was playing on television. The rough sketches gradually evolved into recognizable characters—hippopotamuses—who required names. Edward Albee's play supplied them, and *George and Martha* was published in 1972.

Marshall says that he prefers to write his own stories, but if he does work with someone else's text, it is important that there should be "the kind of meeting of the minds that means I can do justice to the story." He feels that a strong plot is essential and that the humor of the text must be in tune with his own individual style. For his own books, he always starts with the characters, developing them until they can be put into a situation that can then be expanded into a story. He has used a variety of techniques, including pen and ink with overlays, pencil, and full color. He has no particular preference but feels that the medium should be whatever the subject requires.

Two illustrators in particular have influenced him—Maurice Sendak and Edward Gorey. He says that he became involved in picture books after seeing one of Sendak's books, and he feels he has learned much about the question of scale from Sendak's work. He admires Gorey for his "visual genius that is absolute because he has a particular point of view that is sui generis," and for his talent for making everything happen within the page without any wasted space. Marshall believes that adults and children don't differ greatly on what constitutes a good book, and that good editors have an instinct for the books that children will like.

Since *George and Martha*, Marshall has written or illustrated a considerable number of other picture books, all distinguished by his particular style and humor. He is especially fond of *Mary Alice, Operator Number 9*, a story by Jeffrey Allen, published in 1975.

Writing and illustrating are now his full-time occupations. He lives in Charlestown, Massachusetts, within sight of the Bunker Hill Monument, with an English bulldog and a large family of cats.

———

With the publication of *George and Martha* in 1972, James Marshall achieved immediate recognition; the book was chosen by the New York *Times* as one of the ten best-illustrated children's books for 1972, was an American Library Association Notable Book that year, and was included in the 1973 Children's Book Showcase, a collection of books selected for "high quality of design, illustration, and production." Marshall's illustrations for Charlotte Pomerantz's *The Piggy in the Puddle* and Lore Segal's *All the Way Home* earned him two entries in the American Institute of Graphic Arts Children's Book Show, 1973–74. *All the Way Home* was also included in the 1974 Children's Book Showcase. In 1975 the Showcase committee chose another Marshall book, *The Stupids Step Out*, written by Harry Allard, and in 1977 *Bonzini! The Tattooed Man*, by Jeffrey Allen, was selected. *Dinner at Alberta's*, with text by Russell Hoban and illustrations by James Marshall, was an American Library Association Notable Book for 1975.

SELECTED WORKS WRITTEN AND ILLUSTRATED: George and Martha, 1972; What's the Matter with Carruthers?, 1972; Yummers, 1972; George and Martha Encore, 1973; Miss Dog's Christmas Treat, 1973; Willis, 1974; Four Little Troubles, 1975; The Guest, 1975; George and Martha Rise and Shine, 1976; Speedboat, 1976; A Summer in the South, 1977.

SELECTED WORKS ILLUSTRATED: All the Way Home, by Lore Segal, 1973; The Stupids Step Out, by Harry Allard, 1974; The Piggy in the Puddle, by Charlotte Pomerantz, 1974; The Frog Prince, retold by E. H. Tarcov, 1974; The Tutti Frutti Case, by Harry Allard, 1975; Mary Alice, Operator Number 9, by Jeffrey Allen, 1975; Dinner at Alberta's, by Russell Hoban, 1975; A Day with Whisker Wickles, by Cynthia Jameson, 1975; Bonzini! The Tattooed Man, by Jeffrey Allen, 1976; Lazy Stories, retold by Diane Wolkstein, 1976; It's So Nice to Have a Wolf Around the House, 1977; Miss Nelson is Missing, by Harry Allard, 1977.

ABOUT: Contemporary Authors, Vol. 41–44; Something about the Author, Vol. 6.

SHARON BELL MATHIS

February 26, 1937–

AUTHOR OF *The Hundred Penny Box,*
etc.

Autobiographical sketch of Sharon Bell
Mathis:

I WAS born in Atlantic City, New Jersey. It was there that I spent the first years of my life, posing for the endless photographs taken of a firstborn child, swallowing not quite enough—at least to my liking—of the salty sea, and enjoying afternoon naps snuggled against the walls of sand castles I had tried to build. But for reasons they understood best, my parents, John W. and Alice Frazier Bell, moved the family to the Bedford-Stuyvesant section of Brooklyn, New York, where I saw—and was thoroughly fascinated by—our very own fire escape.

I was more than happy to trade my sand castles for rusty iron railings stuck up into the air higher than nearby tree-tops.

Latin, American History, English, mathematics and any other subjects were all studied—or ignored—on my beloved fire escape. Sometimes I pretended to be the beautiful Lena Horne, created poems for English classes at St. Michael's Academy in Manhattan, or opened library books I had run home to read.

It was there on the fire escape, one magic day, with my skinny legs swinging over the railing and my face pressed against the chipped iron bars—bumpy with years of corroded paint—that I read for the first time, Richard Wright's *Black Boy.*

I was to read it six times that year!

After *Black Boy* I read everything I could find by and about Richard Wright. He became a very important *happening* in my life and I was driven to read works by other black writers. I discovered Willard Motley, Ann Petry, Langston Hughes, Frank Yerby, John Oliver Killens and others. Through their writing, I was helped to see my world more

clearly than ever before. I "borrowed" *The Negro Caravan,* an anthology compiled by three great black editors—Sterling A. Brown, Arthur P. Davis, and Ulysses Lee—from the Brooklyn Public Library for almost two years before I, guiltily, returned it!

English classes at St. Michael's were never the same again for me—a result of my outside reading. The writers whose works I most enjoyed were missing from the literature we studied. Not even Ralph Ellison was mentioned. I understood then, thoroughly, why he had named his great work *Invisible Man.* Eight other young black women graduated from St. Michael's when I did. I, for one, was glad to leave.

I don't know when I actually started writing. I think, probably, that I first tried to create poems—copying my mother. I still have many of the poems she wrote when she was a teen-ager. The aged, yellowed paper is as precious to me as the carefully chosen, beautifully scripted, words. At some point, while I created poems, I began to try short stories. But most of all, I kept reading.

Reading has always helped me. When I am writing a new novel and the images will not work, and I am feeling awful, I get away from my typewriter—for a few days—and read one, two, or three books. Later, perhaps in a week, I am able to create again.

People help me as well as books. My *fairy* godmother, Bertha Reed McDonald, helped me to attend Morgan State College though not in a pumpkin carriage. Then I married Leroy Franklin Mathis and we had three beautiful daughters—Sherie, Stacy, and Stephanie. They were my first living poems.

Today, largely because of my writing, I am able to travel frequently. I have met many people in the publishing world but I am still most fascinated by other black writers. Because of them, I have been led forward and out of myself and into a new understanding of the importance of a literature.

In the relatively short time since her first book was published Sharon Bell Mathis' work has received wide critical notice and many citations for its quality. In 1969 her *Sidewalk Story* was the winner in the seven-to-eleven-year-old category of The Council on Interracial Books for Children's manuscript competition. The award carried a cash prize and resulted in publication by Viking Press, who have remained her publishers ever since. *Teacup Full of Roses* was an American Library Association Notable Book for 1972 and a runner-up for the Coretta Scott King Award in 1973. The next year she won the award for her biography of *Ray Charles. The Hundred Penny Box*, a story of a very, very old lady and a small boy, was a Boston *Globe-Horn Book* Honor Book, a Newbery Honor Book in 1976 and an American Library Association Notable Book for Children, as well as on the leading lists of the best books of the year. *Listen for the Fig Tree* was also an American Library Association Notable Book.

Mrs. Mathis attended the Bread Loaf Writer's Conference in 1970 on a fellowship awarded by the Weekly Reader Children's Book Club. She was writer-in-residence at Howard University from 1972 to 1974 and has been active in many community and professional affairs as well. In 1975 she earned a Master's degree in library science from Catholic University.

She married Leroy F. Mathis on July 11, 1957. She and her husband and three daughters live in Washington, D.C.

SELECTED WORKS: Brooklyn Story, 1970; Sidewalk Story, 1971; Teacup Full of Roses, 1972; Ray Charles, 1973; Listen for the Fig Tree, 1974; The Hundred Penny Box, 1975.

ABOUT: Contemporary Authors, Vol. 41–44; Something about the Author, Vol. 7; Who's Who of American Women, 1974–75.

MASAKO MATSUNO

July 12, 1935–

AUTHOR OF *Taro and the Bamboo Shoot*, etc.

Autobiographical sketch of Masako Matsuno Kobayashi:

WHENEVER I think of the small town where I was born, I remember one late afternoon when I was in a barber shop. It was the first time I had gone to a barber shop alone. I was six years old. The barber asked me what cut I liked. There were a few general types of haircut, but I could not recall the one I usually had.

"Straight," I said.

"Straight?" the barber said, puzzled.

"Yes, very straight," I repeated.

"All right," said the barber uncertainly and began cutting.

"Straight, please," I said at each clip. There was a cut that I did not like. I was afraid that he would cut my hair that way. What I wanted was a Dutch cut. Only, because I could not recall the name, how uneasy and fretful was I all the while he was cutting! This experience still works on me and makes me nervous when I talk with young children. "Do I understand what he really means?" I often ask myself. I think this experience influenced my choice of career somewhat.

I was born on July 12, 1935, as the sec-

Masako Matsuno

ond child of my parents in a quiet town of Ehime Prefecture. I have one elder brother and two younger ones. We moved to Tokyo when I was eight.

I have many things for which I am grateful to my parents. Among them all, I am most thankful to them for educating me without regard for my being a girl. I could study as much as I liked, whatever I wanted to. I was allowed to study at a coeducational university to which, at that time, many parents still hesitated to send their daughters. I majored in Japanese literature at Waseda University. I liked to write, but I did not have a clear idea of writing for children until the day a friend of mine showed me an American picture book. I do not remember the title of the book, but I was impressed to see that the moon was carefully illustrated at a different position on each page according to time. This made me interested in American picture books. After graduating from Waseda, I went to the United States to study at the School of Library Science, Columbia University. I spent one and a half years there and received a master's degree.

At Columbia I met many teachers and friends who kindly led me and guided me in the wonderful world of children's books. It was through their kind help and friendship that I could continue studying there. I was assigned many children's books to read. While reading, I noticed that there were few good books on my country and people. One day, as I was riding along a highway in the suburbs of New York, I suddenly felt like walking in wooden clogs. How do they sound on this smooth asphalt road, I wondered. I wondered also how American children would like that clatter of wooden clogs. Then I got an idea, or rather, I should say, a wish to tell a story about real Japanese children to American children. *A Pair of Red Clogs* was born that day.

After graduating from Columbia I came home and have been writing in Japanese and in English ever since. I do translating (Japanese-English, English-Japanese) too. My first book in Japanese, *Taro and the Bamboo Shoot*, was published in English and in Danish, and it also was included in a Swedish anthology. I hope that, through my work, children, whether they are Japanese or foreign, feel that children are all the same regardless of their races or culture.

I was married in 1960 to Toshiro Kobayashi. We have three children; two sons, Ryosaku and Kenjiro; and a daughter, Satoko. We live in Osaka.

———

Mrs. Kobayashi lists her interests as Japanese Noh plays, tea ceremonies, gardening, reading, music and walking.

SELECTED WORKS: A Pair of Red Clogs, 1960; Taro and the Bamboo Shoot, 1964.

ABOUT: Contemporary Authors, Vol. 5–6; Something about the Author, Vol. 6.

MARIANNA MAYER

November 8, 1945–

COAUTHOR WITH MERCER MAYER OF *A Boy, a Dog, a Frog, and a Friend*, etc.

Autobiographical sketch of Marianna Ammirati Mayer:

I grew up in New York, and I was rather an isolated lonely child. My parents and I lived in a middle-aged neighborhood so there were very few children my own

Marianna Mayer

ter horse and all winter, when it was too cold to ride, I drew pictures of him.

As I got older my love of drawing didn't wane. I pursued drawing and painting more seriously in school and in private instruction. Art was my major in high school as well as college. There was one art teacher in particular who urged me to go on professionally. She thought highly of the Art Students League and tried to persuade my father to send me there full time. But he was determined I attend college first. Reluctantly I did only to leave after a year deeply disappointed with the school's art courses. Returning home I promptly enrolled in the League, where the unmistakable smell of oil paints, turpentine and linseed oil made me feel right at home. It was there that I met my husband Mercer Mayer. That was back in 1964 and in the years that followed I went to work first as a commercial artist in an advertising agency, a copy writer and finally a freelance writer and illustrator of children's books. In the early 1970s I helped organize a women's liberation movement on Long Island, New York. We were a handful of women at first who formed the first Women's Center, in Nassau County. I had the job of developing our first twelve-page monthly newsletter, which was a forum for women to express themselves in writing and illustrating as well as a news bulletin. It was exciting to work with others towards this goal. Usually my work requires me to work solely on my own; a writer's or an illustrator's life very often is a lonely profession. Most of the time you are sitting in your quiet room in front of a drawing board or your typewriter trying to dream up ideas or sweating it out as you bring an idea to completion. But working with these women was a completely different experience for me. As a team we all had something special to offer each other. The newsletter at first started with few subscribers and the Women's Center supported it. Subscribers increased to a rousing 500 eventually enabling the bulletin to support itself and adding to the financial benefit

age to play with. I attended private schools a long distance from my home and so the friends I made at school did not live nearby. My closest companion was Tony, my small black and white shaggy dog. When I wasn't devising and playing games with her I poured over my large collection of children's books. My favorites were fairytales and folktales. I loved the illustrations. Even before I learned to read I would tell myself the stories from the pictures. I also spent a lot of time drawing, making up my own pictures to stories my parents read to me or copying the pictures in picture books. My parents didn't mind my having pet animals and they put up with quite a collection through the years; stray dogs, cats and their litters of kittens, a huge turtle, snakes, frogs, birds, and even ducks. I drew pictures of them all and very often told them stories. When I was seven a friend of the family's, an illustrator, took an interest in my drawing. His enthusiasm and encouragement of my talent made a tremendous impression on me. I wanted to grow up to be just like him. At eight years old my father bought me my first horse, this marked another turning point for me. My first love was drawing but a fast second was certainly horses from then on. Every summer I rode my chestnut quar-

of the Center. Beyond its success there was the additional satisfaction of being a help to talented women who previously had no outlet for their writing and drawing abilities. This was in no small measure a source of inspiration for me personally.

I now live in the country in Connecticut. Besides working on books for children I've realized another childhood dream. I own four horses: two Arab mares, one thoroughbred stallion, and one gelding halfbreed thoroughbred. A lot of my time is taken up with the responsibility of caring for them. That's something I didn't have to think about as a child and barn chores are hard work, but it still gives me a thrill when I look out my kitchen window and see them in their paddocks. That makes all the work worthwhile.

SELECTED WORKS WRITTEN AND ILLUSTRATED (with Mercer Mayer): A Boy, a Dog, a Frog, and a Friend, 1971; Me and My Flying Machine, 1971; One Frog Too Many, 1975.

SELECTED WORKS ILLUSTRATED: Mine!, by Mercer Mayer, 1970.

MERCER MAYER

December 30, 1943–

AUTHOR AND ILLUSTRATOR OF A Boy, a Dog, and a Frog, etc.

Autobiographical sketch of Mercer Mayer:

FIRST of all, I find it quite odd to be included amongst authors. For it is hard to conceive of myself as one. I tell stories with pictures, and quite often I even add words. I am and always have been mostly visual. My verbal skills are practically nil.

I was born in Little Rock, Arkansas, but as my father was in the Navy, I could just as easily have been born in Michigan or Rhode Island. I finally saw my father when I was two years old and the war was over.

My early life is a maze of pictures. I

poured over any illustrated book that I could find. Rackham, Tenniel, Beardsley, Ford and others showed me very clearly what I wished to do. I was in love with the world, or should I say worlds, they depicted. Pen-and-ink was always quite magical for me and still is. I was amazed that a bottle of black ink and a scratchy pen point could create such wonderful things.

My family lived a number of years in the South. We lived on a Navy base surrounded by thick forests and swamps. And if I wasn't drawing or reading science fiction novels, I was catching frogs, crawdads, lizards and snakes. It was a great childhood, very much the American, Tom Sawyer life.

When I entered my early teen-age years, my family moved to Hawaii. I loved Hawaii. It's a wonderful place. But it was there I turned into a typical teen-age wiseacre. After graduation from high school, I decided to take things a little bit more seriously. I studied art for one year at the Honolulu Academy of Arts. It was there that the magic of book illustration came back to me. All my instructors said that I would make a very good book illustrator but that it was a shame there was so little of it done anymore. That effectively squelched that, and it was five years later that book illustration entered my life again.

In 1964 I left home for the big city (New York). I wormed my way in as monitor of one of the painting classes at the Art Students League, as I had no money to pay for classes. It was there I met my wife, Marianna. A monitor's duty is to assist the teacher, set up the model, and take care of anything when the teacher is not there. One day I was told by the downstairs office that there was a new student in class. I walked into class with the student's card in my hand and there, sitting on a stool, she was.

"You must be the new . . . ," I began to say, and then promptly tripped over a light cable, falling flat on my face. A week later we were married. She was eighteen and I was twenty.

An art school portfolio, no matter how good in potential talent it is, is one of the most pathetic things in the world, or at least mine was. I pounded the streets of New York looking for illustration jobs —and received a polite smile everywhere I went. Finally I received some good advice from an art director. He told me to throw my portfolio away because it was so bad.

I can remember sitting there in his office wanting, very simply, to kill him. But I was so crushed that I took his advice and started over. I was working at an advertising agency at the time, and in my spare time I sketched scenes from my childhood, animals, strange and funny creatures that I thought up. As I did them I would throw these little sketched-on odds and ends into a manila envelope. One day I quit my job and marched around dumping my drawings on the desks of a number of children's book publishers in New York. I was asked to illustrate *The Gillygoofang*, published by Dial Press, and *Outside My Window*, by Harper and Row. The first book under my authorship, though it had no words, was *A Boy, a Dog, and a Frog*, published by the Dial Press. Slowly but surely with other books like *There's a Nightmare in My Closet*, I began to add words as well.

I have illustrated about forty books for children, eighteen of which I have written. My wife Marianna is my first critic and best editor. She has co-authored *A Boy, a Dog, a Frog, and a Friend*, and *Me and My Flying Machine*, and has illustrated *Mine*.

I am now at home in what I do. Children's books are a good place to call home.

————

Mercer Mayer's illustrations for Jane Yolen's *The Bird of Time* and Jan Wahl's *Margaret's Birthday* were included in the American Institute of Graphic Arts 1971–72 Children's Book Show. *While the Horses Galloped to London*, with text by Mabel Watts, was chosen for the 1974 Children's Book Showcase. Several of Mercer Mayer's own books have received the Brooklyn Art Books for Children Citation: *A Boy, a Dog, and a Frog*, in 1973, *What Do You Do With a Kangaroo?* in 1975, and *Frog Goes to Dinner* in 1976. *Everyone Knows What a Dragon Looks Like* was cited as a New York *Times* best-illustrated children's book in 1977.

SELECTED WORKS WRITTEN AND ILLUS-TRATED: A Boy, a Dog, and a Frog, 1967; There's a Nightmare in My Closet, 1968; Frog Where Are You?, 1969; A Silly Story, 1972; What Do You Do With a Kangaroo?, 1973; Frog Goes to Dinner, 1974; One Monster After Another, 1974; You're the Scaredy-Cat, 1974; The Great Cat Chase, 1975; Ah Choo, 1976; Hiccup, 1976; Oops, 1977; The Poison Tree and Other Poems (comp.), 1977.

SELECTED WORKS WRITTEN AND ILLUS-TRATED WITH MARIANNA MAYER: Me and My Flying Machine, 1971; A Boy, a Dog, a Frog, and a Friend, 1971; One Frog Too Many, 1975.

SELECTED WORKS WRITTEN: Mine!, 1970.

SELECTED WORKS ILLUSTRATED: The Great Brain, by John D. Fitzgerald, 1967; The Gillygoofang, by George Mendoza, 1968; Outside My Window, by Liesel M. Skorpen, 1968; More Adventures of the Great Brain, by John D. Fitzgerald, 1969; The Bird of Time, by Jane Yolen, 1971; Grandmother Told Me, by Jan Wahl, 1972; The Great Brain at the Academy, by John D. Fitzgerald, 1972; Amanda Dreaming, by

Barbara Wersba, 1973; While the Horses Galloped to London, by Mabel Watts, 1973; The Figure in the Shadows, by John Bellairs, 1975; The Great Brain Does It Again, by John D. Fitzgerald, 1975; Everyone Knows What a Dragon Looks Like, by Jay Williams, 1976.

VICTOR MAYS

July 2, 1927–

AUTHOR AND ILLUSTRATOR OF *Dead Reckoning*, etc.

Autobiographical sketch of Lewis Victor Mays, Jr.:

RECOLLECTIONS of open-decked buses, horse-drawn vans, Washington Square earth yielding to my toy steam shovel and a wildly progressive kindergarten are about all I can mine of the few years spent in my birthplace, New York, before my Hoosier parents withdrew to the Westchester greenbelt. In Bronxville I grew for twelve pleasant years, spending summer vacations in Indiana—an idyllic, fertile change of pace for a suburban boy.

For as long as I remember I've liked to draw—a pastime stimulated in part by childhood illness and by the illustrations in favorite books. The works of N. C. Wyeth, Gordon Grant, Arthur Rackham, and Anton Otto Fischer still trigger excitement and admiration. In school I soon discovered that assigned papers were less onerous if I began by illustrating them. I continued this practice through college and attribute my reasonable academic progress largely to the relief my pictures brought to tired-eyed teachers wading through the class's expository efforts.

Proximity to a wide spot in the Bronx River, Long Island Sound, New York's great liner piers, and Indiana lakes inspired an early, lasting fascination with water and boats—abetted on rainy days by Howard Pease, Stevenson and Conrad. I was on water at every opportunity and happily enlisted in the Navy shortly before World War II ended in 1945, an association I have proudly continued on active and reserve status. Later it seemed natural that my senior thesis at Yale was directed at the technology of New England whaling under sail and that after graduation I should incorporate the material in a yarn for boys, *Fast Iron*, which became both my first book and first illustrating assignment.

I am not a rapid writer, and following a second hitch of Naval service in the Korean War, I elected to concentrate as a free-lance illustrator to keep my family fed and sheltered, writing when other assignments permitted. Except for one book written as a history of my former hometown, subsequent books have shared the background of the sea and foreshore. In them I've tried to write good adventures incorporating lore of the sea and their historical period—flavor which I found so interesting as a boy.

An illustrator's research challenges parallel those of a writer, especially in the area of historical depiction. The quest leads to constantly varying subjects, sources and personal education with each new job. Trips to libraries, museums—even the locale of the book when time and funds allow—these are the joys of the work and they balance the initial agony of blank drawing board and seven-day work weeks when deadlines press.

My lovely wife and three children patiently tolerate my irregular hours. We live (and I work) in a shingle cottage on the shore of Long Island Sound. A southerly wind fetches the toll of the buoys and the moan of foghorns, renewing the spirit on desk-bound late nights.

———

Victor Mays attended Ohio State University as a naval midshipman and received his B.A. from Yale University in 1949. The summer after his graduation he hitchhiked through England, sketching and doing watercolors, and then turned to writing and illustrating *Fast Iron*, which was published in 1953. *Fast Iron* received a gold medal from the Boys' Club of America in their Junior Book Awards program in 1954. *Action Starboard*, then *Pathway to a Village*, and *Dead Reckoning* followed at widely spaced intervals.

During the Korean War, Mays returned to active duty and during 1952–54 served as an intelligence officer in Panama. He is now a commander in the U.S. Naval Reserve.

Victor Mays married Lynnabeth Olwin on July 14, 1954. They have three children, Peyton Anderson, Sara Louise, and Lewis Jefferson. Mays has been a justice of the peace, a library board member, and is active in his local historical association. He is also a member of the U.S. Naval Institute and the Mystic Marine Historical Association. Besides jacket designs and magazine illustrations to his credit, Victor Mays has illustrated more than eighty books.

SELECTED WORKS WRITTEN AND ILLUSTRATED: Fast Iron, 1953; Action Starboard, 1955; Pathway to a Village, 1960; Dead Reckoning, 1967.

SELECTED WORKS ILLUSTRATED: Patrick Henry, Firebrand of the Revolution, by Nardi Campion, 1961; Phantom of the Blockade, by Stephen Meader, 1962; One by Sea, Scott Corbett, 1965; Walk in My Moccasins, edited by Mary P. Warren, 1966; Meet Christopher Columbus, by James T. DeKay, 1968; When Men First Flew, by James McCague, 1969; What Makes a Boat Float?, by Scott Corbett, 1970; Sojourner Truth, Fearless Crusader, by Helen S. Peterson, 1972; Rachel Carson, by Jean L. Latham, 1973; The Nargun and the Stars, by Patricia Wrightson, 1974; Willie Mays: Baseball Superstar, by Sam and Beryl W. Epstein, 1975; William Beebe: Underwater Explorer, by Wyatt Blassingame, 1976.

ABOUT: Contemporary Authors, Vol. 25–28; Something about the Author, Vol. 5; Viguers, Ruth Hill and others, comps. Illustrators of Children's Books, 1946–1956.

ANNE SINCLAIR MEHDEVI
September 12, 1918–

AUTHOR OF *Rubies of the Red Sea*, etc.

Autobiographical sketch of Anne Marie Sinclair Mehdevi:

I WAS born in Manila, the Philippine Islands, on September 12, 1918, where my mother and father, both from Kansas pioneer families, were schoolteachers. When my brother was born three years later, the family moved to Wichita, Kansas, where I grew up. I remember nothing of Manila and have never returned, yet my birth in such an exotic-sounding place had a great influence upon my life. Our house in Wichita was filled with many souvenirs bought in the Philippines—a bowie knife, necklaces of old beads, some cup decorated with pictures of Mount Fujiyama. These fascinated me and I would finger them for hours, making up stories in my head about them. I used to question my mother about life in Manila, so different from the dull routine of Kansas, and her talk of monsoons and Ingote tribesmen and trips to Shanghai infected me with a disease I have never recovered from—the longing to travel, to see for myself the places I heard about.

There was never any doubt about what I would be when I grew up, and I was scribbling poetry almost as soon as I learned to write. This, too, was largely due to my mother. She knew hundreds of poems by heart and would wash the dishes reciting "East is East and West is West" in a loud, joyous voice that rang through the house. She scrubbed my back at bath time, wielding the wash-

Mehdevi: *MAY da vee*

Anne Sinclair Mehdevi

cloth in rhythm with "Wynken, Blynken and Nod." Some time during these years my future was decided: I would travel the world over and then write books about my adventures.

However, I was in some doubt about my talent. I was too shy to show my secret compositions to anyone. Then, when I was in the fourth grade, our town was struck by a cyclone. I was in school, where the window panes blew in and oak trees crashed against the walls. We children became excited and frightened, and the teacher, to calm us, began to make up a story. After she had spoken for a few minutes she pointed to me and said, "Now, Anna Marie, you continue for a bit, and then point to someone else to carry on. In that way, we'll each add to the story." I had been listening closely and so had no trouble at all in making up a new episode. Just as I reached a place when all the clocks in a magic house were striking midnight, I paused and pointed to John. "You continue," I said. Everyone in class shouted, "No, no! What happened next?" And so I had to carry on. Every time I pointed to someone, my classmates clamored for me to go on. My imagination was still spinning a gruesome tale of ogres and bottomless wells when a squadron of police arrived to take us safely to our homes.

After that I was sure I could write stories and waited impatiently to grow up and begin. And everything turned out just as I planned. After working for *Newsweek* and as a journalist, I married a Persian when I was in my twenties, and traveled to Persia. I wrote my first book about my introduction to my fascinating Persian family. As my husband was a diplomat, I was lucky to live in many countries and wrote more books about the new things I saw and did.

I didn't begin to write books for children until I had to teach my own three, Rafael, Alexander and Florence. Our constant moving about made their schooling very difficult, so I taught them at home. The arithmetic and spelling and grammar books I got through a correspondence course were fine; but the story books seemed not very interesting. "Why don't you write books for us?" my children asked, and so I did, and have been doing so ever since.

———

Mrs. Mehdevi attended the University of Rochester on a scholarship, graduated *magna cum laude*, and was elected to Phi Beta Kappa. Then she went to New York where she landed a job on a magazine for teen-agers. "From then on, for five years, I lived just like the slick magazine stories said that people in New York lived. I changed jobs, moved up, made more money, attended first nights at the theater . . . and had lots of boyfriends whose names were in the papers." When she married Mohamed Mehdevi, a young Persian diplomat, on June 5, 1945, she gave up writing. It was not until she returned to New York five years later, when her husband was with the United Nations, that an old publishing friend encouraged her to write about her experiences upon marrying into a Persian family. The resulting book, *Persian Adventure*, was a critical and financial success and established Anne Mehdevi on the literary scene. Her first book for children was *The Leather Hand*.

Persian Folk and Fairy Tales was named a Notable Book in 1965 by the

American Library Association, was listed among the New York *Times* seventy-five recommended titles that year, and included in the *Horn Book's* 1966 Fanfare. *School Library Journal* considered *Parveen* one of the best books of 1969.

Mrs. Mehdevi's son Alexander is also an author of books for children, and her husband is now an author and management consultant. The Mehdevis live in Majorca, Spain.

SELECTED WORKS: The Leather Hand, 1961; Rubies of the Red Sea, 1963; Persian Folk and Fairy Tales, 1965; Parveen, 1969.

ABOUT: Contemporary Authors, Vol. 5–6; Something about the Author, Vol. 8; World Authors: 1950–1970.

"MISKA MILES"

November 14, 1899–

AUTHOR OF *Annie and the Old One*, etc.

Autobiographical sketch of Patricia Miles Martin, who also writes under the name of "Miska Miles":

I WAS born in Cherokee, Kansas, and grew up in the Midwest. I was fortunate in spending all my summers on a farm which belonged to my paternal grandparents. They had lived in the Cumberlands and were among the few who were able to find their way to a kinder environment. They carried with them the attractive and expressive phrases and the particular superstitions from their old home in Kentucky. A rifle was a rifle-gun. A spider's web seen in the morning brought good luck, provided it was left undisturbed. This influence found its way into books—*Hoagie's Rifle-Gun* and *Gertrude's Pocket*, both written under my pseudonym of Miska Miles and published by Atlantic-Little, Brown.

For a time my family lived in Oklahoma. It was there that I first met Indian children, and since that time I have been tremendously interested in the first Americans. I grew up reading everything I could find about their culture. I am deeply influenced by the philosophy ex-

pressed in their poetry. As a result of this sustained interest, I wrote *Annie and the Old One*, again under the pseudonym of Miska Miles.

After attending many schools in Kansas, Oklahoma, Missouri and Colorado, I taught school for four years. The memories of teaching came out in several books; among them *Trina's Box Car* (under my own name of Patricia Miles Martin) and *Teacher's Pet* and *Pony in the Schoolhouse* (by Miska Miles). I have always spent a great deal of time reading and writing. I like the smell of a new book and the feel of a pencil in my hand. My earliest memory of anything connected directly with books goes back to a house where we lived in Fort Scott, Kansas. I remember standing on barren ground under a big apple tree. There was a rocking-horse affair beside me— two flat wooden horses with a seat between. I leaned against the tree trunk and held an open magazine in my hand. I decided that each letter was a word, and, pointing to each letter, I read my own story.

And after that came real reading. Since I was the only child in our family, I spent my childhood either reading or writing. I remember the first time I set about writing deliberately. I was about seven. I sat in the hayloft of the old farm, listening to the rain on the roof, the cheeps of protesting chickens in the barnyard below. I wrote a description of the things I saw that moment, of the things I smelled and heard.

I have written over eighty books for boys and girls. And perhaps the biggest reward in writing comes from receiving letters from children who write about the books they have read.

Presently, my husband and I live in San Mateo, California, and many of my books about children of today stem from incidents that happened here in our own neighborhood.

———

Patricia Miles married Edward R. Martin on October 24, 1942.

Mrs. Martin has written that before she starts a story she needs one line, a thought she considers important enough to share with her readers. From that one thought she can choose the proper setting and protagonist for what she has to say. She writes every day, starting early in the morning and working for at least six hours. Such concentrated effort has helped her to produce a long list of books under both her own name and her pseudonym. The Miska Miles books, all published by Atlantic-Little, Brown, are the ones that have garnered her awards and honors, with one exception: *The Pointed Brush*, issued under her own name, which was an Honor Book in the *Herald Tribune* Children's Spring Book Festival in 1960. *Fox and the Fire*, *Nobody's Cat* and *Annie and the Old One* were all named Notable Books for Children by the American Library Association. *Mississippi Possum* was on the New York *Times* list of seventy-five recommended titles for 1965. *Hoagie's Rifle-Gun* and *Wharf Rat* were both listed among the best books of the year of their publication by *School Library Journal*, and *Wharf Rat* received Honorable Mention in the Second Annual Children's Science Book Awards (1973), sponsored by the New York Academy of Sciences. By far the most honored of Miska Miles'

books, however, is *Annie and the Old One*. Winner of a Christopher Award and a silver medal from the Commonwealth Club of California in 1971, it received the Woodward School Annual Book Award and was named a Newbery Honor Book in 1972.

SELECTED WORKS BY PATRICIA MILES MARTIN: The Pointed Brush, 1959; Happy Piper and the Goat, 1960; The Raccoon and Mrs. McGinnis, 1961; The Lucky Little Porcupine, 1963; Calvin and the Cub Scouts, 1964; Jump Frog Jump, 1965; Jefferson Davis, 1966; John Marshall, 1967; Indians; The First Americans, 1970; Chicanos: Mexicans in the U.S., 1971; Be Brave Charles, 1972; How Can You Hide an Elephant?, 1974.

SELECTED WORKS BY MISKA MILES: Pony in the School House, 1964; Mississippi Possum, 1965; Fox and the Fire, 1966; Teacher's Pet, 1966; Rabbit Garden, 1967; Nobody's Cat, 1969; Gertude's Pocket, 1970; Hoagie's Rifle-Gun, 1970; Annie and the Old One, 1971; Wharf Rat, 1972; Otter in the Cove, 1974; Chicken Forgets, 1976; Swim, Little Duck, 1976; Aaron's Door, 1977.

ABOUT: Contemporary Authors, Vol. 4; Foremost Women in Communications; Something about the Author, Vol. 1; Who's Who of American Women, 1971–72; 1974–75; Top of the News April 1972.

MITCHELL MILLER

February 22, 1947–

ILLUSTRATOR OF *One Misty, Moisty Morning: Rhymes From Mother Goose*, etc.

Autobiographical sketch of Mitchell Alexander Miller:

I WAS born in New York City on February 22, 1947, and grew up in Stony Point, New York. I was the youngest of three children. My childhood reading consisted mainly of books about trains, though I was also fond of comic books. The first drawings I remember doing were of the Army-McCarthy hearings; I still have some of them, with cryptic cap-

Mitchell Miller [signature]

began that year when my friend Alec Wilder composed a book of lullabies that Maurice Sendak illustrated. This was the first really good children's book I had seen, and it suggested to me the best use for my own pictures. The discovery of Maurice Sendak's work was very important to me. His trust in the soundness of the most personal parts of his imagination gave me an idea of how to work. His use of the overall appearance and feeling of a book, in addition to the pictures themselves, was something new to me. Since 1969, when I graduated from Harvard, I have lived in Cambridge, Massachusetts. I have always loved music (my father is a musician). When I'm not drawing I like to sing and play the piano.

---

tions, probably fed to me by the grown-ups gathered round the TV set. For the next several years I drew almost nothing but locomotives. In retrospect my childhood seems to have been spent in bed (I was very lazy) under a pile of frayed railroad magazines and comic books. I also had an unaccountable taste for books of photographs of news events, although I was completely uninterested in the news. I was unaware of the existence of Mother Goose, Beatrix Potter, and children's literature in general until I had grown up.

In 1959 my family moved to New York City. At about this time the subject matter of my pictures began to branch out a little. The locomotives were replaced by people. In 1961 I went away to an awful boarding school, where I began to draw really in earnest, probably to escape my surroundings. It was there that I discovered the existence of what seemed to be a very solid fantasy world that had little apparent connection with what was going on around me. I left after two years and finished high school in New York, at Horace Mann, in 1965. That summer I did my first professional work, background drawings for the credits of a CBS documentary about airplanes. My interest in children's books

Mitchell Miller's work received appreciative attention as soon as it appeared in 1968. Maurice Sendak has called him "one of the most gifted of the new generation of illustrators," who "instinctively does only what is original and personal . . . [so that his work is] contemporary without being ostentatiously so and traditional without quaintness or sentimentality." Miller's work was included in shows of the American Institute of Graphic Arts in 1967–68 and in 1970. *The Magic Tears* was one of the New York *Times* ten best-illustrated books of 1971 and was included in the 1972 Children's Book Showcase.

Miller, who so far has worked only in black and white, is currently preparing an illustrated edition of Edward Lear's *Incidents in the Life of My Uncle Arly.*

SELECTED WORKS COMPILED AND ILLUSTRATED: One Misty, Moisty Morning: Rhymes From Mother Goose, 1971.

SELECTED WORKS ILLUSTRATED: Martze, by Jack Sendak, 1968; A Monkey's Uncle, by W. Hauff, retold by Doris Orgel, 1969; How the Children Stopped the War, by Jan Wahl, 1969; The Magic Tears, by Jack Sendak, 1971.

LILIAN MOORE

Author of *I Thought I Heard the City,* etc.

Autobiographical sketch of Lilian Moore Reavin:

I WAS born in New York City, grew up in its world of infinite promise, went to its schools, was nourished by its human diversity, took for granted its intellectual excitement, and found there a richly satisfying work life. And somewhat on the still undeveloped outskirts of that city was an important meadow in which I spent magical summer days.

The world of childhood was a dreamlike world of books. I think I wore my own special path to the public library on those hard city pavements. There must have been a Beneficent Librarian who watched over me as, books piled on my arm, I read all the way home. Even today I enter a children's library with a rush of love.

I was a child yarn-spinner who entertained my friends with stories, and writing was always the easiest way to express ideas and feelings. Like all such avid readers and "English Majors" I too wrote chapters of the inevitable when I was of college age.

But the real world into which I was graduated as a young adult was anything but dreamlike or literary. It was a world so ravaged by economic depression that it is a peculiar experience to try to describe the quality of life then to those who have known only our affluent society. I was lucky to get a makeshift job teaching truant children who couldn't read. It changed my life. I found that I had a gift for and a pleasure in helping children to learn to read that must have come from deep in my own childhood delight in books. In the years that followed I taught in the New York City elementary schools and then was appointed to the Bureau of Educational Research. It doesn't sound as exciting as it was. I worked for thirteen years with children who couldn't read and with teachers who wanted to help them.

There was so little reading material that I liked for these children that I began to write my own stories. I never did get back to the novel, but I did go on writing for children.

Do we all feel that we have led several different lives? I do. And the search for the connections between them goes on absorbingly.

When my son Jonathan was born I did not return to teaching. And when some years later his father and I were divorced, I found myself in a wholly new work life.

I became an editor for Scholastic Book Services at a historic time. Scholastic was about to pioneer in the field of quality paperbacks for elementary school children. I became editor of the Arrow Book Club, and for the next ten years helped to make available to the middle graders of America good, inexpensive paperbacks they could own, reread, dog-ear and love. It was a joyful experience to be able to bring together—to connect!— to such a program what one had learned as a teacher and writer for children.

About the time I gave up being editor of the Arrow Book Club, I began writing poems for children. I am surprised that it moves me so much—city-bred in the bone that I am—to write the nature poems that I do. So there is some connection between that meadow of my childhood and these poems.

Since most coincidences are connections of a kind, I think of a book I wrote in 1967 called *Just Right*. It was quite different from anything I had written before. Where did it come from? It's the story about a farmer and the land he lives on and loves—the meadow and the pond and the woods where the white-tailed deer live.

Well, in 1969 I married a man I had known long days ago as a young girl, Sam Reavin. He's been a farmer, and we live on the beautiful farm he loves. And the poems in my book *Sam's Place* are about our pond and our meadow and the woods where I first saw a white-tailed deer.

———

Old Rosie was on the list of one hundred best books of the year singled out by the New York *Times* in 1960.

Mrs. Reavin is a keen gardener and loves to listen to music, especially Mozart and "almost any good chamber music."

SELECTED WORKS: My Big Golden Counting Book, 1957; Old Rosie, the Horse Nobody Understood (with Leone Adelson), 1960; Little Raccoon and the Thing in the Pool (with Gloria Fiammenghi), 1963; Little Raccoon and the Outside World, 1965; The Magic Spectacles, 1966; Just Right, 1968; I Thought I Heard the City, 1969; Little Raccoon and No Trouble at All, 1972; Sam's Place: Poems from the Country, 1973; Little Raccoon and Poems from the Woods, 1975; See My Lovely Poison Ivy, and Other Verses About Witches, Ghosts and Things, 1975; Hooray for Me! (with Remy Charlip), 1975.

SELECTED WORKS COMPILED (with Lawrence Webster): Catch Your Breath; A Book of Shivery Poems, 1973; To See the World Afresh, 1974.

ABOUT: Hopkins, Lee Bennet. Books Are by People.

PATRICK MOORE
March 4, 1923–

AUTHOR OF *Your Book of Astronomy*, etc.

Autobiographical sketch of Patrick Moore:

DURING the 1930s, when I was growing up, all astronomers were regarded as slightly crazy. The idea of travelling to the moon was greeted with scornful laughter, and the thought of sending a probe to Mars was enough to send the average critic into hysterics. But from the age of six I was fascinated by astronomy; it all began when I read a book about it, belonging to my mother—who was (and still is) an enthusiast. Subsequently I obtained a small telescope and began studying the moon. I joined the British Astronomical Association when still a schoolboy; I think my first scientific paper was published when I was thirteen.

I had a good deal of illness when I was young, and then, just when I was all set for my university career at Cambridge, a gentleman named Adolf Hitler came upon the scene. In order to do my mild bit in trying to cope with him, I abandoned Cambridge and joined the RAF, flying around in a bomber until things calmed down again in 1945. So, alas, I never did get to Cambridge—something I will always regret. Instead, I continued observing, and also writing.

I was actually born in Pinner, just outside of London; but from the age of six months I have lived in Sussex, and today I am firmly established in an old thatched house in Selsey, on the Sussex coast. With me is my mother; the household is completed by a Very Important Cat. In the garden I have my observatories; the largest telescope is my 15½-inch reflector.

I began broadcasting in the 1950s, and since April 1957 I have presented a monthly programme on television called "The Sky at Night." Among the people who have joined me on the programme from time to time are Dr. Harlow Shapley,

whose recent death is so regretted; Dr. Bart J. Bok, and other great astronomers. One problem is that of answering mail. I have about thirty letters a day, of all kinds—some sane, some eccentric; but many from young enthusiasts, and I always answer them personally, though it does take a great deal of time.

Among my other hobbies are music, chess, and our strange English game of cricket; I am secretary of our local village cricket club, and also its leg-spin bowler (if that means anything to readers outside of Britain!).

When asked what I am, I say that I am essentially a writer. My role, if I have one, is encouraging others to do things that I could never have the ability to do myself. When I meet a professional astronomer or a serious amateur who began by seeing me on TV or reading something I have written—as does happen quite often nowadays—it all seems very worthwhile.

Besides his many books for children and adults, Patrick Moore co-edited, with Laura E. Salt, the twenty-volume Oxford Children's Reference Library, has translated the work of several French astronomers, and conducted children's television programs. He is a fellow of the Royal Astronomical Society, a member of the British Astronomical Association and a former director of its lunar section and of its Mercury and Venus sections, a fellow of the Royal Society of Arts, and a member of the Children's Writers Group of London.

In 1962 Moore was awarded a Lorimer Gold Medal for his services to astronomy and in 1968 he received the Order of the British Empire.

SELECTED WORKS: The World Around Us, 1956; The Earth, Our Home, 1957; The Book About Man, 1960; The Observer's Book of Astronomy, 1962; Exploring Weather (with Henry Brinton), 1964; Your Book of Astronomy, 1966; Exploring Maps (with Henry Brinton), 1967; Exploring Other Planets (with Henry Brinton), 1967; Exploring the World, 1968; Stories of Science and Invention, 1972; Comets, 1976; New Guide to the Moon, 1977.

ABOUT: Author's and Writer's Who's Who, 1971; Contemporary Authors, Vol. 13–14.

URSULA MORAY WILLIAMS

April 19, 1911–

AUTHOR OF *The Three Toymakers*, etc.

Autobiographical sketch of Ursula Moray Williams John:

MY twin sister and I, with a younger brother, were brought up in the depths of country in a very old house of the kind known as a "folly," since two hundred years before we went there it had been built very pretentiously, with a maximum of pillared terraces and halls, by an owner who could never really afford to finish it, and by the time my father rented it much of the house was in ruins, so that we lived only in the central part, with a natural playground of empty rooms and wild parkland all around us.

My father worked with the British Red Cross and ran a local convalescent home in the same park. His great interest was in archaeology, while my mother was a

Moray: *MURRY*

Ursula Moray Williams

homemaker, but she was Froebel-trained and had also studied in Germany.

My brother (now a free-lance journalist in Denmark) went to boarding school, but my sister and I were educated at home with a much-loved Scottish governess. We had the happiest of childhoods, surrounded by pet animals that included a pony, and with ample scope for our imaginations to run wild in those unusual surroundings. We had a large library of books, inherited from the childhood of both our parents, and supplemented by modern children's books at every birthday and Christmas.

We wrote and drew from a very early age, and I finished my first full-length book (quite a long one) while staying away from home at the age of seven. It was about a rather horrid little boy, I think, but I can only remember what he looked like in the pictures. I gave it away to my hero of the moment, a young man of twenty who had just given me my first ride on a horse. He was quite embarrassed and I expect he gave it to his horse.

For the next few years my sister and I wrote and illustrated a book for each other on every birthday and Christmas until we were sixteen, when we went to France for a year to study French and

other subjects in a pension on the lake of Annecy in Haute-Savoie. This lovely place with its mountains, chalet and lake, was like a little Switzerland and provided a background for many of my books, including *The Three Toymakers* series.

On returning home we joined an Art College at Winchester, and it was now that our careers took a different course after almost eighteen years of identical interests. My twin sister went on to the Royal College of Art in London, and studied under Sir William Rothenstein. Later she went to Iceland and married an Icelandic sculptor and painter, Magnus Arnason. She is now a well-known artist and designer living in Reykjavik.

I remained at home writing, and published my first book for children when I was twenty. This was *Jean-Pierre* published by A. and C. Black. Four or five other books followed before I married, in 1935, Conrad Southey John, an aircraft engineer and ex-pilot, great-grandson of the Poet Laureate Robert Southey. Many of my earlier books I illustrated myself, and on one or two occasions my sister collaborated in providing the drawings, but when our four sons were born, pressure of time made me leave the illustrating to others, and although I have produced about sixty books for children since I began, I do not often illustrate them myself.

The best known of my books has been *The Adventures of the Little Wooden Horse* which was published by Harrap in England in 1938, and by Lippincott a little later. It has never since been out of print in England and is published in a great many different languages. Many of my books have been broadcast, televised and dramatized, and I have written for various children's magazines.

I live in the country in an old farmhouse frequently visited by our five grandchildren, and besides writing I have a great interest in our garden, in dressmaking for the children, and in my court work as Justice of the Peace in the county of Worcestershire.

The Three Toymakers was an Honor Book in the middle-age group for the 1971 *Book World* Spring Children's Book Festival.

SELECTED WORKS: The Adventures of the Little Wooden Horse, 1939; Island Mackenzie, 1960; The Earl's Falconer, 1961; High Adventure, 1965; The Moonball, 1967; The Cruise of the Happy-Go-Gay, 1968; The Toymaker's Daughter, 1969; Boy in a Barn, 1970; The Three Toymakers, 1971; Castle Merlin, 1972; Jockin the Jester, 1973; No Ponies for Miss Pobjoy, 1976.

ABOUT: Author's and Writer's Who's Who, 1971; Contemporary Authors, Vol. 13–14; Doyle, Brian, comp. The Who's Who of Children's Literature; Something about the Author, Vol. 3.

ROBERT MURPHY

ROBERT W. MURPHY

August 27, 1902–July 31, 1971

AUTHOR OF *Wild Geese Calling*, etc.

Biographical sketch of Robert William Murphy by Jean Warfield Whittle Murphy:

ROBERT MURPHY was born in 1902 in Ridley Park, Pennsylvania, then a small village and now very much industrialized and part of the mcgalopolis along the Delaware River. Summers at the seashore or in the Pennsylvania mountains were part of his early years until his family moved to Richmond, Virginia, when he was about fifteen years old.

At that time his father and three friends bought a large tract of land complete with a large cypress pond and swamp near a little town with the unlikely name of Lightfoot. Here he spent every free moment from school for several years and this is where he learned to truly love the out-of-doors and become well acquainted with birds and animals. In its way and in many variations this place was the locale for many of his short stories and one novel, *The Pond*, for which he is best known.

He was graduated from Friends Central High School in Philadelphia in 1921 and it was there that one excellent English teacher inspired him to write. I wish I knew her name, for she had a great impact on his life. She encouraged him to read the very best authors, and to criticize and study their writing styles. His favorite writer was Joseph Conrad.

He was a tight writer. He never wasted words. The reader cannot skim through his books and get the importance of his words. He was always of the opinion that any fiction should have a beginning and a middle and an end and a very definite plot line. The pointless, plotless vignettes popular today were not for him. There was no anthropomorphism in any of his animal or bird novels.

Over a period of twenty-five years he sold some sixty-five short stories and articles to the *Saturday Evening Post*. For twenty years he was an editor there. These were the *Post's* great years and in this work he met and became well acquainted with some of the finest writers at that time, and the best editorial brains. It was here also that he learned to know many publishers and literary agents, lots of whom became good friends.

His severance from the *Post* was in 1962 when he started to give full time to free-lance writing. His work methods were simple. He sat down and stayed at his desk regardless of what the flow of words might be for four or five hours every morning. There was no telephone in his study, which was in the guest house, which he named "The Shack." He did not want to be disturbed.

The Peregrine Falcon was his first book after retirement from the Post. This was followed by The Pond and after that he wrote The Golden Eagle. Wild Sanctuaries, a book about the federal wildlife refuges, was five years in preparation and was followed by A Heritage Restored, a "boiled down" version of the original for younger readers. During those years he also wrote The Mountain Lion, his only Southwest-oriented novel.

The Warmhearted Polar Bear was a book for the very young, amply illustrated with nonsense pictures. Wild Geese Calling was also for children. Both Wild Geese Calling and The Pond have been televised by Disney. Other Disney purchases have been The Golden Eagle and The Mountain Lion.

A collection of short stories, all from the Post, is called The Phantom Setter. His last book, The Stream, is a novel, ecological in nature, about a fishing club in the Pocono Mountains, Pennsylvania, where we fished for some twenty-five years. There was also camping and shooting at that club.

Bob's hobbies were hunting, fishing, falconry and photography. Photography was consuming, and the pictures he took on his travels gave him perfect records to work from when he wrote. I recently gave the Interior Department about one thousand color slides of the refuges he wrote about in Wild Sanctuaries.

The Haunted Journey was the story of Vitus Bering and the discovery of Alaska. He first became interested in this subject as the result of work he did for an article about sea otters that was in the Post. It, too, has been rewritten for young readers.

Our last years together were here in the Southwest, where he continued to write. Our youngsters and I, as was he, are wedded to this part of the country where things seem to be simpler than they ever were in the East where we'd both been born and lived all our lives until 1967. We were indeed fortunate to have been able to relocate in this country.

———

Robert W. Murphy attended Washington and Lee University in Lexington, Virginia, for two years. In 1928, he married the former Isabel Palmer. After her death he married Jean Warfield Whittle on March 22, 1946. The Murphys have two children, Robert Shane and Molly Jean, both now grown up. At the time of his death, Mr. Murphy was living in Prescott, Arizona.

Murphy joined the Saturday Evening Post in 1942 as an associate editor and stayed until he retired in 1962 as a senior editor. Over the years he conducted courses in writing at the University of Indiana, University of Colorado, and University of Michigan Writers' Conferences. He won the Dutton Junior Animal Book Award twice, in 1966 for Wild Geese Calling, and in 1969 for A Heritage Restored. The Pond was listed by the New York Times in November, 1964, as one of the best-selling children's books.

SELECTED WORKS: The Warmhearted Polar Bear, 1957; The Haunted Journey, 1961; The Pond, 1964; Wild Geese Calling, 1966; A Certain Island, 1967; A Heritage Restored: America's Wildlife Refuges, 1969.

ABOUT: Contemporary Authors, Vol. 9–10; New York Times July 14, 1971; Publishers Weekly September 6, 1971.

OGDEN NASH

August 19, 1902–May 19, 1971

AUTHOR OF Custard the Dragon, etc.

Biographical sketch of Frediric Ogden Nash:

THE light verse of Ogden Nash, poet of the American commuter and P.T.A. meeting, is often described as ingenious

OGDEN NASH

cessful bond salesman in New York and a period as a copywriter in an advertising agency, writing streetcar advertising.

During the period from 1925 to 1933, Nash was on the editorial and advertising staffs, first of Doubleday, Doran, and then of Farrar and Rinehart, book publishers. The first actual breakthrough he achieved with his writing was in 1930 when he scrawled out a poem and sent it to the *New Yorker*. It began in autobiographical vein:

I sit in an office at 244 Madison Avenue
And say to myself, you have a responsible
   job, havenue?

This was the historic first of 352 verses that Ogden Nash was to publish in the *New Yorker* from 1930 to 1971. Briefly, Nash was a member of the *New Yorker* editorial staff before he turned to writing full time.

Nineteen thirty-one was marked by Nash's marriage to Frances Rider Leonard and by the publication of his first book of verse, *Hard Lines*. His reviewer in the London *Times Literary Supplement* remarked frostily that "this verse would be improved if the author took more care with his rhymes"; nevertheless, Nash soldiered on to publish more than thirty further collections of verse over the years and to become the leading American exponent of humorous verse, respected in American poetic circles for just the ingenuity and technical control that his London reviewer accused him of lacking.

His career has been rich and has included, as well as his verse, several stints as editor of various poetry anthologies; a memorable collaboration as lyric writer with S. J. Perelman in 1943 on the musical *One Touch of Venus*; and several screenplays. There were several television appearances, as well as whole series of lectures and public readings, delivered in accents of "clam chowder New England with a little Savannah at odd moments."

Among his books written for a younger

and improbable humor. He became famous not only for his choice of subject matter—the usual, the humdrum, the trivial events and annoyances that are part of most people's daily existence—but also for his lighthearted doggerel style, in which he would top a very long, seemingly never-ending line with a sudden, audaciously invented near-rhyme. In fact, he had a knack for bending language to do whatever he wanted it to do. Even more significant, Nash was one of the few writers to bring poetry to humor rather than simply to wrap a humorous thought in poetic form.

Frediric Ogden Nash, the son of Edmund Strudwick and Mattie Chenault Nash, was born on August 19, 1902, in Rye, New York. The Nash family was a distinguished Southern one: Nashville, Tennessee, was named after one famous ancestor. Ogden was educated at St. George's School, Newport, Rhode Island, and spent one year (1920–21) at Harvard where, he said, "I got just enough of a classical education to interfere with my English."

He returned for a short time to teach at St. George's. In later years he was often fond of saying he "lost [his] entire nervous system carving lamb for a table of fourteen fourteen-year-olds." There followed an interval as a notably unsuc-

audience was *Parents Keep Out: Elderly Poems for Youngerly Readers*, which was followed by his Christmas books, including *Scrooge Rides Again*, as well as the delightful Custard books: *Custard the Dragon* and *Custard the Dragon and the Wicked Knight*, in which Custard is engagingly brought to life by the drawings of Ogden Nash's elder daughter, Linell Chenault.

Ogden Nash brought great pleasure to many people, especially during the years he traveled the lecture circuits. He reflected the essence of American pragmatism and good sense in his "resigned but cheerful verses," as Ned Bradford, his friend and editor at Little, Brown, once described them. He was also that strange animal, the financially successful poet, the reason perhaps being that he remained sensitive to common experience and was, moreover, gifted with the ability to translate his impressions in an uniquely wry and funny way. Ogden Nash's talent flourished unabated until his death on May 19, 1971.

SELECTED WORKS: Parents Keep Out: Elderly Poems for Youngerly Readers, 1951; Custard the Dragon, 1959; A Boy is a Boy, 1960; Custard the Dragon and the Wicked Knight, 1961; Girls are Silly, 1962; Animal Garden, 1965; The Cruise of the Aardvark, 1967.

ABOUT: Author's and Writer's Who's Who, 1971; Benet, Laura. Famous American Humorists; Contemporary Authors, Vol. 13–14; Dodd, Loring Holmes. Celebrities at our Hearthside; Fadiman, Clifton. Party of One; Jones, Evan, ed. The Father Nash; Murphy, Rosalie, ed. Contemporary Poets of the English Language; Something about the Author, Vol. 2. Twentieth Century Authors (First Supplement); Who's Who in America, 1970–71; Current Biography, 1941, 1971; Life October 29, 1951; Newsweek May 31, 1971; New York Times November 9, 1940; May 20, 1971; New Yorker May 29, 1971; Saturday Review June 19, 1971; Scholastic October 2, 1937; March 4, 1940; Seventeen January 1963; Time May 31, 1971.

RUTH NICHOLS

March 4, 1948–

AUTHOR OF *A Walk Out of the World*, etc.

Autobiographical sketch of Ruth Joanna Nichols:

I WAS six years old when I realized I wanted to be a writer. I don't know what it is that creates such a clear feeling of vocation in a child so young: the great encouragement I received from my family was part of it. My mother was a natural teacher who started reading to my sister and me when we were very small, and by the age of five she had introduced me not only to the usual children's classics but to a child's version of the *Iliad* and the *Odyssey*. A "skeleton" of classical myth was thus incorporated into my imaginative life very early and perhaps helped my tendency to turn *backward*, not only to my personal past but to the past of the human race.

As a child I was absorbed in dreams, in parallel worlds, and in the study of the sixteenth century, a period which retains its fascination for me. As a result, at eighteen I produced my first published book, *A Walk Out of the World*. The social skills came later and less easily, but the discovery of friends my own age filled out another dimension and made me very happy.

I took an Honours B.A. in Religious Studies at the University of British Columbia in 1968, and an M.A. at McMaster University in 1972; I am now working on a Ph.D. in Western Religious Thought. Enjoyable as my education has been, I hope to leave academics afterwards and give back a little of what I have received, perhaps by working with children. In 1969 I published an autobiographical novel, and in 1972, my second children's fantasy.

I have great respect for the fantasy form: it expresses the ideal beauty which I believe exists somewhere near the heart of reality and which we forget at our

RUTH NICHOLS

peril. Therefore I feel fantasy is by no means so "childish" as many people assume. But my published books, much as I enjoyed writing them, have been mainly exercises in storytelling: as Professor Tolkien said of the lesser Rings, they are "essays in the craft before it was full-grown."

What my craft will be like when it is full grown I cannot yet tell. Meanwhile, one learns to write by writing; and until I understand more clearly the purpose of my work and of my life, I hope my stories can give pleasure to others.

A Walk Out of the World was an Honor Book in the 1969 *Book World* Children's Spring Book Festival and an American Library Association Notable Book. *The Marrow of the World* was named Book of the Year for children in 1973 by the Canadian Library Association.

Ruth Nichols is married and lives in Ottawa, dividing her time between working on her doctoral thesis and her writing. Her favorite authors are Jane Austen, George Eliot and Charlotte Brontë, whom she rereads and studies often, hoping to improve her own work. "If I have a special quality," she writes, "I think it is the ability to extrap-

olate from my own experience—so ordinary in itself—to other experiences which have a kindred quality: the 'faculty of association by similarity' which is crucial for the transmutation of life into fiction."

SELECTED WORKS: A Walk Out of the World, 1969; The Marrow of the World, 1972; Song of the Pearl, 1976.

ABOUT: Author's and Writer's Who's Who, 1971; Contemporary Authors, Vol. 25–28.

"ROBERT C. O'BRIEN"

January 11, 1918–March 5, 1973

AUTHOR OF *Mrs. Frisby and the Rats of NIMH*, etc.

Biographical sketch of Robert Leslie Conly, who wrote under the name of "Robert C. O'Brien," by Sally M. Conly:

ROBERT C. O'BRIEN was the pseudonym for Robert Leslie Conly who was born Janunary 11, 1918, in Brooklyn, New York. He was the third of five children born to Leslie Marsland and Agnes O'Brien Conly. Both parents were well educated. Agnes O'Brien came from a well-to-do Irish Catholic family of lawyers and doctors in Rochester, New York, and was a graduate of Smith College. Leslie Marsland Conly graduated from the University of Rochester and met his wife when both were school teachers in Rochester. By the time Robert was born, however, his father had given up teaching for a job as a reporter on the New York *Herald Tribune*. He was to stay with the *Tribune* for the rest of his life, later becoming manager of the *Tribune* Fresh Air Fund, a charitable organization that operated summer camps for poor city children.

The mother also worked for the Fresh Air Fund as did the children when they were old enough to be counselors in the camps, and this strong bond with the New York *Herald Tribune* added to the literate, reading-writing atmosphere of the home.

"ROBERT C. O'BRIEN"

When he was still a baby, the family moved to Amityville, Long Island, and Robert grew up there, attending a parochial school and, later, Amityville High School. As a child he was precocious and showed musical talent, but he was also sickly and fearful. He hated school and did not get along with his brothers and sisters, who considered him selfish and spoiled by an overly protective mother; but by the time he reached high school he was happier and more successful both in scholarship and in human relations. He was admired particularly for his wit and for his musical ability. He was not good at contact sports but he was a fast sprinter on the track team and an excellent swimmer. He was editor of the school paper and showed a great facility with words, especially for turning out verse.

In 1935 he entered Williams College, but the new situation brought stress and tensions, and he left college abruptly during his sophomore year. He worked briefly in Albany, New York, before drifting back to his family in disgrace— parents then being less tolerant of dropping out of college than they are now. It was an unhappy time, later referred to as his "breakdown," but in a few months he was feeling better, and he decided he really wanted to be a musician.

Robert had begun taking piano lessons in high school and now he resumed them, taking the train from Amityville into New York City to study at the Juilliard School of Music and to take extension courses at Columbia University. The following year his parents persuaded him to go back to college, this time to the University of Rochester where he could continue his music at the Eastman School but also get a B.A. in English at the university.

In the end, English won out. Although he always devoted much of his leisure time to music, he earned his living and made his greatest contribution writing English.

After graduation from the University of Rochester in 1940, and a brief stint in an advertising agency, he went to work for *Newsweek* magazine in New York City. World War II was imminent, and it was an exciting time for journalists. Protected from the draft by a 4F classification (based on both physical and psychological frailties), he was promoted from the clip desk to researcher to staff writer.

In 1943 he married Sally McCaslin, a researcher in the Books Department of *Newsweek*, and in 1944 they moved to Washington, D.C., where he became a reporter covering Capitol Hill for the old Washington *Times-Herald*.

For the next twenty-nine years—until his death from a heart attack in 1973— he lived and worked as an editor and writer in the Washington area.

He worked as a writer but not as a writer of fiction. He covered national and city news for the *Times-Herald* and later for *Pathfinder News* magazine. Then in 1951 he joined the staff of the *National Geographic* magazine where the stories he wrote or edited encompassed the world. He wrote fiction only in the last ten years of his life.

Before that time he had other interests: a growing family (he had a son, Christopher, born in 1944, and three daughters—Jane, born in 1948, Sarah, in 1952, and Catherine, in 1958), music, reading, furniture making, and, most important to his books, a growing interest in the world of nature.

He came to this interest late. Although he had spent his adolescent summers in camps, as a counselor and swimming instructor, he had grown up surprisingly oblivious to all but man-made creations. He did not know the names of birds or trees, and it was a family joke that he called all flowers hydrangeas. At the same time he was attracted to the quiet of the country and felt the need to escape from the pressures of job and city. In 1950 he bought a weekend place, a small house with seventeen neglected acres on the North Anna River in an isolated section of Spotsylvania County, Virginia. It was here that he began, for the first time, to feel a connection with the river, the woods and the wild animals around him.

After three years of traveling to the country on weekends, he and his family opted for full-time rural living. They gave up the weekend place and bought a small farm near the Potomac River within commuting distance of Washington. Here they grew vegetables and flowers, raised chickens and ducks, chopped wood and built fences, kept horses and a cow. Conly even learned to milk the cow, although he never did get on well with large animals. They made him nervous and he made them nervous (he used to vow the most docile horse bit or kicked if he got in its vicinity). He liked small animals and birds, and his favorite of the many family pets was a small sparrow named Jenny which one of his children had raised from a fledgling and which, for several years, occupied a cage in the dining room.

Robert C. O'Brien, the writer, was to draw on all these experiences and to recreate them in his books with the most painstaking detail. He also, in one of his books, *A Report From Group 17*, used the physical locale of this farm as the setting of the book.

In the ten years spent there, Robert Conly often talked of writing a novel. Sometimes he started a short story. But he already had more work than he could do—his job at the *Geographic*, the daily drive in and out of Washington, the endless chores of a house in the country.

Then in the early 1960s he got an eye disease, glaucoma, the treatment of which affected his eyes so that he could no longer drive after dark. There was no public transportation, and during the winter months he could not get home from work. The problem was resolved in 1963 with another move, this time back to the city.

Robert Conly was now living fifteen minutes from his office, in a modern brick house on a city lot. Although he would again acquire a weekend retreat, on the Cacapou River in West Virginia, he suddenly had time on his hands and he began systematically to plan and to write a novel for children. That book, *The Silver Crown*, was published by Atheneum in 1968. It was followed in 1971 by *Mrs. Frisby and the Rats of NIMH*, which won the Newbery Medal. In 1972 Atheneum published his adult suspense novel, *A Report From Group 17*, which was picked as an alternate by the Book-of-the-Month Club. His latest book, *Z for Zachariah*, was published posthumously by Atheneum in 1975.

He managed this steady output in spite of a full-time job with the *National Geographic* by giving up most social life and by writing at least a few paragraphs *every day*, Sundays and holidays included.

He chose to write under a pen name because the *Geographic* frowned on outside writing by members of its staff; and, until his death, it was not generally known that Robert L. Conly, Senior Assistant Editor of the *National Geographic* magazine and Robert C. O'Brien, fiction writer, were one and the same.

He chose the name O'Brien because it was his mother's name and because in his Irishness, in his Catholicism, and in his complex, creative temperament, he identified very much with that side of the family.

Two aspects of Robert C. O'Brien's writing seem closely related to his actual life—one, his fascination with the lore of nature, which he so lovingly details, and two, his sympathy for and understanding of children. Perhaps harking back to his own struggle to grow up, he never forgot what it was like to be young and vulnerable; and he is able to make the reader share his concern for the weak and defenceless whether his characters are animal or human.

Robert C. O'Brien died March 5, 1973, at the age of fifty-five.

SELECTED WORKS: The Silver Crown, 1968; Mrs. Frisby and the Rats of NIMH, 1971; A Report From Group 17, 1972; Z for Zachariah, 1975.

ABOUT: Contemporary Authors, Vol. 41–44; Horn Book August 1972; New York Times March 8, 1973; Time March 19, 1973; Top of the News April 1973.

DORIS ORGEL

DORIS ORGEL

February 15, 1929–

AUTHOR OF *A Certain Magic*, etc.

Autobiographical sketch of Doris Adelberg Orgel:

I WAS born in Vienna, Austria, and spent my first nine years there. Certain vivid memories remain: At five I wrote a story of which I was inordinately proud. It was about a huntsman in a forest, and had a comma after every word. I read a lot: fairy tales, the more gruesome, the better; Kipling (*The Jungle Book*, in German translation, was my all-time favorite); and Wild West Romances. When I was eight, instead of reading in bed, I started to write a book about dolls coming to life and running away from home. But it was dull; I gave it up and soon went back to reading.

One time my sister and I ran away to our grandparents' to live there with a dog we had just bought, but were doubly betrayed: our grandmother made us return the dog to the pet store; then she took us back home.

I remember my third-grade teacher, her kind voice, the big pores around her nose, and that she cried, but did not say

anything, when I and seven other Jewish girls in her class were thrown out and made to go to an all Jewish school. This was in the spring of 1938, after Hitler came.

I remember people leaving, for any country that would take them in. A friend of mine, also nine years old, who lived in the same apartment house was sent away—to Manchuria. It happened so suddenly, we never said goodbye.

Our family were able to stay together. We fled to Yugoslavia, to England, and came to the United States in the winter of 1940.

We spent one year in St. Louis, Missouri, where I was horrified to find that black kids were excluded from white kids' schools, just like Jews from "Aryan" schools in Vienna. After that we moved to New York.

I went to Hunter College High School, Radcliffe College and graduated from Barnard College in 1950. I was married in 1949; worked in publishing for six years; then had three children, Paul, Laura and Jeremy, and concurrently developed, or rather, re-discovered, a love of children's books. I've been reading, translating, writing, and occasionally reviewing them since.

My husband is a psychiatrist and psychoanalyst. Our three children are grown

Orgel: *or GHEL*

now. One is a pianist. The other two, at this writing, are in college and have not yet decided on careers.

———

Doris Orgel's retelling of Theodor Storm's *Little John*, which was illustrated by Anita Lobel, took first prize in the picture-book category in the 1972 *Book World* Children's Spring Book Festival. *Sarah's Room* was chosen by the New York *Times* as one of the hundred outstanding children's books of 1963. Mrs. Orgel's favorite of all her retellings is Clemens Brentano's *The Tale of Gockel, Hinkel, and Gackeliah. A Certain Magic* was an American Library Association Notable Book for Children for 1976. Of the books she has invented herself, *Next Door to Xanadu* brings her the most letters from readers. Besides her writing, Doris Orgel lists "other joys and endeavors" as "keeping house, spurts of gardening, reviewing children's books for the New York *Times*, tennis, trips, and seeing friends."

She married Shelley Orgel on June 25, 1949.

SELECTED WORKS: The Tale of Gockel, Hinkel, and Gackeliah, by Clemens Brentano (retold), 1961; Sarah's Room, 1963; Cindy's Snowdrops, 1966; The Goodbyes of Magnus Marmelade, 1966; Cindy's Sad and Happy Tree, 1967; In a Forgotten Place, 1967; On the Sand Dune, 1968; A Monkey's Tale, by Wilhelm Hauff (retold), 1969; Next Door to Xanadu, 1969; Phoebe and the Prince, 1969; The Uproar, 1970; The Mulberry Music, 1971; Little John, by Theodor Storm (retold), 1973; Bartholomew, We Love You, 1973; The Child From Far Away, by E. T. A. Hoffman (retold), 1974; A Certain Magic, 1976; Merry Merry Fibruary, 1977.

ABOUT: Something about the Author, Vol. 7.

REGINALD OTTLEY

AUTHOR OF *Boy Alone*, etc.

Autobiographical sketch of Reginald Ottley:

A LIFE, like a story, has to begin somewhere. Mine began in a small house on

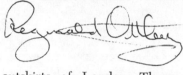

the outskirts of London. There were problems with my birth and I was, apparently, born dead. Caught in the necessity of saving my mother's life, the doctor and midwife put me to one side in the empty firegrate. I heard later in life from the old midwife that I looked a sad sight, being such a bonny boy.

"Twelve pounds, seven ounces," she often said to me. " 'Twas sad to see you dead."

Sufficient is to say my mother was saved and, miraculously, I suddenly squawked. From there on, I was soon tucked in with my mother. Having survived a bad start, I grew into a fairly normal type of boy.

Along with my brothers, I went to a small Church of England school. My only good subjects were English and composition. Whilst there I had more than my fair share of fights because of my "dreamy" ways. I was always imagining being lost on desert islands, or galloping horses across wild terrain. Indeed, the bane of my life was a girl in the girls' half of the school who named me "Dreamy Daniel." She used to shout it after me at the top of her voice, making me feel as if I wanted to shrivel down into the kerbstones.

I left school at fourteen and, though

I loved my mother deeply, ran away to sea. After a year or so, during which I was washed overboard from a ship in mid-Atlantic, then washed back on board again, I sailed for Australia.

There I worked as a "wood-and-water-joey" on a big grazing property, and later became cattle drover, horsebreaker, and general wanderer of the Australian Outback, travelling mostly on horseback.

During this time there was a constant thought in my mind that I should, one day, write about the life that I was living—about the people, the land and the whole environment. Strangely, too, many times it was often said to me over lonely campfires, or in isolated bush huts, "You ought to write about it, Reg. Git it down on paper."

From the Outback I went to Fiji as manager of a large cattle station. I lived there until war broke out, and I returned to Australia to enlist.

I served with the Remount Squadron and was in charge of "breaking in." All told, some five thousand horses passed through my hands. The men were incredible characters, drawn from all parts of the Australian Bush.

After the war I trained racehorses in Sydney. Then I flew to Guadalcanal, in the British Solomon Islands, to try and reinstate the herds of cattle shot out by American and Japanese forces during their respective occupations.

Finally I went to French-governed New Caledonia, to manage a large *d'élevage*, or property, for breeding cattle. It was there that I began to seriously think about writing.

On a visit to London, I submitted a script to the BBC. It was of a personal experience in the Outback, and they liked it immediately. I broadcast the story during the interval of a symphony concert. Over the years I have broadcast quite a number of similar stories, including broadcasts to schools.

Like these stories, my books are based on personal experience, warped on a loom of fictional imagination, as were the dreams of "Dreamy Daniel."

Boy Alone, published in Britain and Australia as *By the Sandhills of Yamboorah*, was by far the most successful critically of Ottley's books. About a young orphan, a wood-and-water boy on an Australian Outback cattle station, it was a prize book in the middle category in the 1966 *Book World* Children's Spring Book Festival, won the Thomas Alva Edison Foundation National Mass Media Award in 1967, was an American Library Association Notable Book of 1966, and was on the *Horn Book* magazine's Fanfare in 1967. The Australian edition was highly commended for the Australian Children's Book Council's Best Book of the Year Award in 1966. The second book in what turned out to be a trilogy about the boy, *The Roan Colt*, published in Australia as *The Roan Colt of Yamboorah*, was commended by the Australian Children's Book Council in 1967. *Rain Comes to Yamboorah*, the last of the three Yamboorah "boy" books was considered one of the best books of 1968 by *School Library Journal*. In 1970 *The Bates Family* received Honorable Mention from the Australian Children's Book Council in competition for the best book of the year.

SELECTED WORKS: Boy Alone, 1966; The Roan Colt, 1967; Rain Comes to Yamboorah, 1968; The Bates Family, 1969; Brumbie Dust, 1969; Jim Grey of Moonbah, 1970; No More Tomorrow, 1971; The War on William Street, 1973.

ABOUT: Author's and Writer's Who's Who, 1971.

PEGGY PARISH
July 14, 1927–

AUTHOR OF *Amelia Bedelia*, etc.

Autobiographical sketch of Peggy Parish:

THE questions I am most frequently asked, as I guess are most writers, are: "Did you always want to be a writer?"

Peggy Parish

and "How did you get started?" Both questions are rather complex to answer. To the first, the answer is "no," I had not a thought in my head as to being a writer. I always enjoyed writing. In fact, during my grade school years, I caught on to the fact that my teachers did not check homework, so I never bothered with it except when the assignment was to write a story. I knew those would be read aloud. But as for becoming a writer, that was something some phantom people did. Being born and brought up in a very small town where there was no cultural exposure, none of the art world was real to me.

Nor did I take college seriously. I had always had a rich fantasy world and was a child who needed time alone. I enjoyed other children, but I was never bored when alone. And I developed a love for reading at an early age. It never occurred to me in college that I was supposed to be preparing myself to do something. My father, having been denied formal education beyond the fourth grade, didn't seem to think of it either. (My mother died when I was young.) So I delayed graduation as long as possible because I was having fun, took a

degree in English because I loved reading, and graduated prepared to do absolutely nothing. And I'm so glad it worked out that way. The teacher shortage was critical at that time, and while visiting my brother, who was a doctor in a coal mining area in Kentucky and had a wife and two children, I was talked into teaching. We stayed there two years. The second year I taught creative dancing to young children and then somehow ended up in Oklahoma. I then went to the Panhandle to teach third grade. And again taught dancing and produced the community shows. By this time I knew I wanted to be in some creative field but still had no sense of direction as to what kind. But New York seemed to be the logical place to find out, so to New York I went. I was fortunate enough to get a job in a progressive experimental school where creativity was stressed. And while helping the children to find themselves, I, in turn, began to find myself. At that time I could not find the material for them and began to write it myself. This set me to thinking that if I had this problem perhaps other teachers were finding the same thing to be true. Thus I wrote my first story thinking in terms of publication and sent it out. Then I waited and finally received the inevitable form rejection slip. I've never been a very patient person where adults are concerned, and this didn't sit well with me. But again I was in an enviable position: because of the nature of our school, many of the parents were in creative fields. One parent, who at that time was an editor of adult books and is now editor-in-chief of a leading publishing house, found out I was trying to break into the field and wanted to introduce me to an editor at Harper. I protested that I wasn't ready for that. But he was persistent, and I finally agreed. And there is where my real training began. What this editor saw in my first feeble offerings I will never know, but she stuck with me and finally managed to get me to shape up. (By this time I had managed to get a couple of books published by other houses.)

Then came the idea for *Amelia Bedelia*. I held that manuscript for awhile after I wrote it because the idea seemed so obvious that I was afraid to submit it for fear it would come right back telling me to do something new. But it turned out to be new, and my editor immediately accepted it and called me in. After blue-pencilling out about three-fourths of it she told me to go home and do it properly. And that was the real beginning of being accepted as a writer for me. *Amelia Bedelia* has reached her teen-age years now and is still going strong. And while I publish with several houses I continue to treasure the guidance and support I constantly receive from this editor. When she moves I follow. And she continues to make me grow until I now work on many different kinds of books as well as for a wide range of reading levels.

I am far from being the model of a well-structured, disciplined writer. I never make notes unless it's a nonfiction book, don't begin a book until it's fully plotted, and work on no schedule. For that reason I need fairly constant prodding or I probably would never produce a book. But fortunately I get that. A lot of it comes from the readers. When I hear from enough of them that they've read all of the books in a particular series and what is the next one, I begin to feel guilty and buckle down. And then there's that editor. I use any excuse I can find at times not to write and I don't listen to many people, but to her I do. My favorite story is once when I had to be in the hospital for a fairly long stay I felt that was excuse enough for not writing. After all I was recuperating. But she paid no attention to that. She gave me the first line of a story and I agreed to do it—in my mind it would be done in the future, the distant future. But then she clamped down. My orders were to write at least one line a day. I could write more, but they wouldn't carry over. She was going to call me each morning at nine-thirty and I had better have something to read to her. And she stuck with it. I was out of the hospital before the book was completed, but those calls still came. And the resulting book is still doing very well.

Peggy Parish was born and grew up in Manning, South Carolina. She graduated from the University of South Carolina with a degree in English, and when she later came to New York she taught third grade at the Dalton School for many years. Now she has returned to South Carolina, to Columbia, where she spends her time doing book review columns, book talks, teacher workshops and teaching children creative writing techniques in school, as well as writing herself. She loves to sew dresses for little girls ("the ones that require a lot of handwork") and do work with her hands, which often results in a new craft book. She has also learned to drive and has bought a car which she uses to explore her new city. However, she writes, "I do not expect to stay here for any long period of time. I . . . am down to basic living and love it. It gives me such a sense of freedom to know I can pick up and go wherever I desire."

School Library Journal named *Dinosaur Time* one of the Best Books of Spring 1974. Many of Miss Parish's books have appeared in children's book club paperback editions, attesting to their popularity.

SELECTED WORKS: Good Hunting, Little Indian, 1962; Amelia Bedelia, 1963; Thank You, Amelia Bedelia, 1964; Key to the Treasure, 1966; Let's Be Early Settlers with Daniel Boone, 1967; A Beastly Circus, 1969; Costumes to Make, 1970; Granny and the Desperadoes, 1970; Granny, the Baby and the Big Gray Thing, 1972; Dinosaur Time, 1974; Good Work, Amelia Bedelia, 1976; Teach Us, Amelia Bedelia, 1977; Hermit Dan, 1977.

ABOUT: Foremost Women in Communications.

DOROTHY D. PARKER
September 22, 1927–

and

ROBERT ANDREW PARKER
May 14, 1927–

AUTHOR AND ILLUSTRATOR OF *Liam's Catch*, etc.

Autobiographical sketch of Dorothy D. Parker and Robert Andrew Parker by Dorothy Lane Daniels Parker:

OUR first visit to Ireland together was in 1964, a short stay of three weeks in which we tried to see as much of that beautiful country as my husband knew from several previous trips there. We hired a car but would often pull off the road for a picnic lunch and a long walk through walled fields where cattle and sturdy horses grazed and farmers greeted us with a word or two about the weather. It wasn't until 1969 when my husband was a Guggenheim Fellow that we traveled there with our children and lived for the most of the summer in a small County Kilkenny town. We watched the salmon netting that year at Inistioge—the inspiration for our first book together, *Liam's Catch*.

Robert was experienced in book illustration, having worked with Marianne Moore in 1958 on a book of her animal poems for the Museum of Modern Art limited edition. Each book was hand colored. More recently, he has done a small hand-colored edition of *The Death of the Ball Turret Gunner* by Randall Jarrell for David Lewis. His drawings illustrated a group of nature poems edited by William Cole for Viking and it was his work for Viking's *Pop Corn and Ma Goodness* that gave him Caldecott honors. Later came *The Trees Stand Shining* and *Zeek Silver Moon* for Dial. He has done the drawings for another book compiled by William Cole, *A Book of Animal Poems* for Viking and *The Mermaid*

and the Whale by Georgess McHargue for Holt, Rinehart and Winston.

But I believe it began long before, when on a trip to Africa he sent picture letters of the people and places he saw to our two oldest boys, then just ten and nine, or perhaps even earlier when, as a child recuperating from tuberculosis in New Mexico, he made picture books.

It was twenty-nine years ago that we met and married in Chicago where I had always lived. Discharged from the U.S. Air Force, Robert was soon to begin study at the Chicago Art Institute on the G.I. Bill. I was a student at Mundelein College. Our family grew quickly with Christopher born in 1950, Tony in 1952, Eric in 1954, Geoffrey in 1956 and Nicholas in 1962. During these years my husband finished art school and we moved to New York where he taught art in Westchester public schools for a few years. His reputation as a painter moved on meanwhile with one-man shows in New York City, representation in national and international shows, a National Institute of Arts and Letters grant in 1962 and the Guggenheim Fellowship in 1969. By 1968 the children required less of my care and I became interested and active in politics. My other published writing is a journal I kept while a delegate to the 1972 Democratic National Convention which was carried by several New York newspapers and one in Connecticut.

We enjoy working together and hope that *Liam's Catch* is the first of many collaborations.

———

Born in Norfolk, Virginia, Robert Andrew Parker had lived all over the country by the time he entered the United States Air Force in 1943. After his term in the service ended in 1946, he went to the Chicago Art Institute, from which he graduated in 1952. Parker was a student at Atelier 17 in New York in 1952–53. He and Dorothy Daniels had been married on November 20, 1948.

The artist has received a number of awards and honors, beginning with a National Arts Council Award in 1959, a Rosenthal Foundation Grant from the National Institute of Arts and Letters in 1962, a Tamarind Lithography Workshop (Los Angeles) Fellowship in 1967, and a Guggenheim Fellowship in 1969–70. His work hangs in the permanent collection of the Museum of Modern Art in New York, the Los Angeles County

Museum, the Whitney Museum and the Brooklyn Museum, and he has showed in group and one-man shows in the United States and abroad. Parker has also made drawings for a Hollywood movie and has designed sets for an opera.

The artist's illustrations for *Pop Corn and Ma Goodness*, by Edna Mitchell Preston, made it a Caldecott Honor Book in 1970; *Liam's Catch* was chosen for inclusion in the American Institute of Graphic Arts Children's Book Show in 1971–72; and *Izzie*, by Susan Pearson, received a Society of Illustrators Citation of Merit in 1976.

SELECTED WORKS WRITTEN BY DOROTHY D. PARKER AND ILLUSTRATED BY ROBERT ANDREW PARKER: Liam's Catch, 1972.

SELECTED WORKS ILLUSTRATED BY ROBERT ANDREW PARKER: Pop Corn and Ma Goodness, by Edna Mitchell Preston, 1969; King Fox, retold by Freya Littledale, 1971; The Trees Stand Shining, compiled by Hettie Jones, 1971; Zeek Silver Moon, by Amy Ehrlich, 1972; A Book of Animal Poems, compiled by William Cole, 1973; The Mermaid and the Whale, by Georgess McHargue, 1973; Izzie, by Susan Pearson, 1975; The Winter Wife, by Anne Eliot Crompton, 1975; When Light Turns Into Night, by Crescent Dragonwagon, 1975; Battle in the Arctic Seas, by Theodore Taylor, 1976; The Great Jazz Artists, by James Lincoln Collier, 1977; Oliver Hyde's Dishcloth Concert, by Richard Kennedy, 1977.

ABOUT ROBERT ANDREW PARKER: Who's Who in America, 1970–71; Who's Who in American Art, 1970; 1973; Art in America August 1964.

JILL PATON WALSH

April 29, 1937–

AUTHOR OF *Fireweed*, etc.

Autobiographical sketch of Gillian Bliss Paton Walsh, who uses the pen name of Jill Paton Walsh:

I WAS born in 1937 in a suburb of north London, Finchley, in or near which I grew up and went to school. Luckily for me, however, the general nastiness of London in the blitz persuaded my step-grandfather to take the family to St. Ives

JILL PATON WALSH

in Cornwall for a while; when my mother went home to London with the other children I was already at school, and so I stayed behind, blissfully happy in that lovely place, which is the setting for *Goldengrove*, my own favorite among my books. After some two years my grandmother died, I came home, and lived in Finchley until I won a place at St. Anne's College, Oxford, where I took a degree in English and met my husband and many of our closest friends. After Oxford I taught in a secondary girl's school for three and a half years till my son Edmund was born, in 1963, and then I gave up teaching and began to write on a battered typewriter inherited from my brother. There followed in quick succession, a daughter, Margaret, *Hengest's Tale*, *The Dolphin Crossing*, and a daughter, Clare. These things are the central element in the life I lead now— half a woman running a family, half a writer, all the time a jumpy compromiser between one mode of living and the other.

I am a practical sort of person, able to build cupboards and keep the freezer stocked up, and liking cooking and social life very much. I have always talked too much, and still do. Being able to write is the best thing that ever happened to me, except being able to make

and keep friends. I have now written ten books, and show no signs of stopping. We live in Richmond, in Surrey, a pleasant and sociable place, and enjoy ourselves more of the time than one has any right to expect.

———

Almost all Mrs. Paton Walsh's books have been well received in the United States, but *Fireweed* and *Goldengrove* have garnered the most accolades. *Fireweed*, which was a runner-up for Britain's prestigious Guardian Award in 1970, was a prize book in the older category in the *Book World* Children's Spring Book Festival in 1970. It was also an American Library Association Notable Book and on the *Horn Book* magazine's Honor List. *Goldengrove* was commended for the Guardian Award in 1972 and was on the New York *Times* list of outstanding books of the year. *Unleaving* won the Boston *Globe-Horn Book* Award for 1976.

SELECTED WORKS: Wordhoard (with Kevin Crossley-Holland), 1969; Fireweed, 1970; Goldengrove, 1972; The Emperor's Winding Sheet, 1974; The Huffler, 1974; The Island Sunrise; Prehistoric Culture in the British Isles, 1976; Unleaving, 1976.

ABOUT: Contemporary Authors, Vol. 37–40; Something about the Author, Vol. 4; Cricket March 1976.

HANS PETERSON
October 26, 1922–

AUTHOR OF *Mickey and Molly*, etc.

Autobiographical sketch of Hans Peterson:

BORN on October 26, 1922, in a worker's family, I started by trying to become a worker too. I started in a factory at the age of fifteen, but at the same time I was writing short stories and similar things for magazines. In 1945 I won a prize in a children's book competition and had my first book published. Two years later my first collection of short stories was published and my first novel.

The children's book reaches the individual at his most sensitive age. I do believe that children's literature is considerably more important than the literature for adults, and if we could only avoid the word "children's book" and instead talk about the "children's novel," I think the status of it would be increased, as would the literary claims of this very important literature.

For the rest, I should like to add that I was married in 1958 to Anne Marie, who used to be a photographer and has now taken up this profession again, since we have been doing some photographic picture books together for different ages. We also have two children, Lena, born in 1962, and Jan, born in 1965, and we live in Gothenberg, one of the more wonderful towns of our earth.

———

Since then I have been writing children's books, picture books, short stories and novels, have done series for children and adults for broadcasting and television. From the start I believed that I wanted to write for adults, but with the Magnus books, which were published here in Sweden at the end of the fifties, I felt that I rather belonged to the children's book writers. The adults have got so many who speak for them and defend them if they can't manage for themselves, while children so often are helpless and stuck with the arbitrariness of adults.

With the Magnus books I had my breakthrough internationally too, and they are now translated into Finnish, Norwegian, Danish, Icelandic, German, French, English, American, Polish, Dutch and Japanese. This stimulated me to further work with the children's book, as a description of the child's situation and as a protest book. I continue writing novels for adults, which I think is a good training for description of individuals and surroundings, something that does not appear so frequently in the children's book. But—my main interest is the children's book and my foremost medium when it comes to reaching the audience.

Hans Peterson's series of stories about a little boy called Magnus was published in the United States during the 1960's. *Magnus and the Wagon Horse*, which received Sweden's highest children's book award, the Nils Holgersson Plaque, in 1958, was also on the Honor List for the Hans Christian Andersen Award. The German edition of *Magnus and the Squirrel* won the German Children's Book Prize.

SELECTED WORKS: Magnus and the Squirrel, 1959; Magnus in the Harbor, 1962; Benjamin Has a Birthday, 1964; Mickey and Molly, 1964; Brownie, 1965; Tom and Tabby, 1965; Magnus and the Wagon Horse, 1966; Magnus in Danger, 1967; Magnus and the Ship's Mascot, 1967; Erik and the Christmas Horse, 1970; When Peter Was Lost in the Forest, 1970; The Big Snowstorm, 1975.

JAN PIENKOWSKI

August 8, 1936–

ILLUSTRATOR OF *Meg and Mog*, etc.

Biographical sketch of Jan Pienkowski:

AN only child, Jan Pienkowski was born in Warsaw, Poland. One of his early

Jan Pienkowski: *YON Pe en KOFF ski*

JAN PIENKOWSKI

memories is of the wartime period when the family lived in the country. Small Jan hated milk, and the cook would bribe him to drink his daily glass by telling him the folktales that she remembered from her own childhood, some of them so frightening that the little boy had nightmares after hearing them. When, many years later, Pienkowski came to illustrate Joan Aiken's collection, *Kingdom Under the Sea*, he was delighted to find it contained some of those same stories that had so enthralled him as a child.

He did not go to school until he was nine, and he says that he spent a lot of time drawing and making things, "especially traditional objects, such as Christmas tree decorations, cribs, puppet theatres, etc." He read a great deal as a boy, but because of the war the only children's books he had were those that had belonged to his parents when they were young. These were mostly Polish translations of such classics as *The Secret Garden*, *Tom Sawyer* and the Dr. Doolittle stories. His father was in the Polish Army, and in 1946, when Jan Pienkowski was ten, the family, like so many other Poles, came to England, at the invitation of the British Government.

There were artists and architects on both sides of Pienkowski's family, and he

assumed that he too would be an artist of some kind. When he entered Cambridge University he planned to study architecture but was persuaded to read English and classics instead. "Even so," he recalls, "it was at Cambridge that I began designing: plays, posters and the greeting cards for friends which afterwards led to the formation of the firm of which I am now a director."

The greeting card designs attracted the attention of a publisher, who approached Pienkowski to illustrate a children's book. Other such commissions followed, though Pienkowski says he tends to regard illustration as a hobby rather than a living. "The silhouette technique evolved out of my first book with Joan Aiken, *A Necklace of Raindrops*—largely because I panicked and blacked in the faces at the last minute. Then, in *Kingdom Under the Sea* I began to experiment with 'marble' backgrounds which produced marvellously unexpected results. It may be that much of this derives from my Central European background . . . although there is also the fact that, being Polish, I tend to get typecast in that direction. Yet the bright colours and two-dimensional shapes I love to use are characteristic of that part of the world and crop up again and again, from the paper cutouts of the Polish countryside to the fretted woodwork of every mountain village from Switzerland to the Tatras."

The *Meg and Mog* books, in which Pienkowski collaborates with Helen Nicoll, are illustrated in a completely different style which uses a thick black line and bold flat color. The books came out of a series called "Watch" which Helen Nicoll produced for BBC Television. Pienkowski used to draw for the camera, and one of the most popular characters was a witch. Eventually the witch became Meg and acquired a cat named Mog. Pienkowski says that he particularly enjoys doing these books because he can make use of all the devices of the comic strip. He has always been attracted to comics, which were not available in Poland during his wartime childhood. When he first came to England, he longed to buy them but was not allowed to do so because his parents disapproved of them. "It seems to me that this form has enormous merits of impact and economy. Instead of describing one another, words and pictures are complementary and the narrative depends equally on both. When Mog says AAAA-TISHO or 'Look! Footprints!' the words are not only instantly clear but also part of the picture, contributing to its total visual effect."

Jan Pienkowski is unmarried and lives in a large Victorian house next to the River Thames, with a dog, three chickens and half a horse. "My principal work consists of running Gallery Five, a publishing company of which I am a founder-director, and doing quite a lot of freelance design in various fields—I would very much like to design for the theatre, which is something I have not done very much of. I spend quite a lot of time working on group projects with young children, usually large mural paintings, and I would like to have time to do more of this kind of work."

Jan Pienkowski's illustrations for *The Golden Bird*, by Edith Brill, were commended for the Kate Greenaway Medal in 1970, and in 1971 he won the medal for his illustrations for Joan Aiken's *The Kingdom Under the Sea*.

SELECTED WORKS WRITTEN AND ILLUSTRATED: Colors, 1974; Numbers, 1975; Shapes, 1975; Sizes, 1975.

SELECTED WORKS ILLUSTRATED: A Necklace of Raindrops, by Joan Aiken, 1969; Jim Along Josie, by John and Nancy Langstaff, 1970; Meg and Mog, by Helen Nicoll, 1973; Meg's Eggs, by Helen Nicoll, 1973; Meg and the Sea, by Helen Nicoll, 1975; Meg on the Moon, by Helen Nicoll, 1975.

ABOUT: Something about the Author, Vol. 6; Books for Young Children, Vol. 9, No. 4, 1974; Junior Bookshelf August 1972.

HARRIET PINCUS

October 13, 1938–

AUTHOR AND ILLUSTRATOR OF *Minna and Pippin*, etc.

Autobiographical sketch of Harriet Pincus:

I WAS born in the Bronx and lived there for twenty-four years. Luckily for me there was a small park behind our apartment building. Since I was a city child I loved this park because of its trees, fences and the chance to see grass instead of concrete sidewalks. Most of the magic and wonder of my childhood is closely linked to this park and to the several summers spent in Amenia, New York. My intoxication for nature was intensely felt then and has always remained with me.

As far back as I can remember I have loved drawing. I became consciously aware of wanting to become an artist in the fourth grade and both my parents encouraged me in that direction.

The Saturday morning art classes at the Art Students League were my first real taste of art instruction. Attending the High School of Music and Art also enabled me to exercise my imagination and explore the various art forms.

During my last year in high school I was stricken with polio and spent almost two years in a hospital for rehabilitation. Afterwards I went back to the Art Students League in a wheelchair to continue with my drawing and painting.

To me, illustrating children's books is something of a miracle because in that world all extraordinary possibilities exist. One has such freedom with which to work, not just in terms of media and technique but also because one can give the imagination such free play. And after all, that is the joy of being childlike.

Harriet Pincus was represented in the American Institute of Graphic Arts Children's Book Show in 1967–68. In 1970

HARRIET PINCUS

COLETTE PORTAL

her illustrations and Lore Segal's text for *Tell Me a Mitzi* took first prize in the picture-book category in the *Book World* Children's Spring Book Festival. *The Wedding Procession of the Rag Doll and the Broom Handle*, Miss Pincus's first picture book, received a Brooklyn Art Books for Children Citation in 1973.

SELECTED WORKS WRITTEN AND ILLUSTRATED: Minna and Pippin, 1972.

SELECTED WORKS ILLUSTRATED: Tit for Tat, and Other Latvian Tales, by Mae Durham (retold), 1967; The Wedding Procession of the Rag Doll and the Broom Handle and Who Was in It, by Carl Sandburg, 1967; Who is Paddy?, by Elizabeth C. Cooper, 1967; The Hunkendunkens, by Richard R. Livingston, 1968; Little Red Riding Hood, by the Brothers Grimm, 1968; Tell Me a Mitzi, by Lore Segal, 1970.

COLETTE PORTAL

March 9, 1936–

AUTHOR AND ILLUSTRATOR OF *The Life of a Queen*, etc.

Biographical sketch of Colette Portal Folon:

A PARISIAN by birth, Colette Portal grew up and studied there, attending the Ecole de Dessin Académique et Clas-

sique for four years. She married designer Jean Michel Folon on March 20, 1961. Now separated, she lives in Paris with her son François.

Colette Portal has drawn ever since she can remember. She says that she was a poor student when young because she filled her notebooks with colored drawings instead of notes.

In 1960 *La Vie d'une Reine* (*The Life of a Queen*), depicting the life of an ant colony, was published in the French periodical *Marie-Claire* and two years later appeared in book form in Germany. In 1964 the book of poetic text and detailed illustrations was published in the United States. It was designated one of the best illustrated children's books of 1964 by the New York *Times*. In 1967 Pantheon published *The Honeybees*, with Franklin Russell's text and Miss Portal's illustrations. Again the New York *Times* selected Miss Portal's work as among the best of the year, and the book was also chosen for the 1967–68 Children's Book Show mounted by the American Institute of Graphic Arts. *The Beauty of Birth* (published in France as *Le Premier Cri*) followed in 1971. To date it is the only other work of Miss Portal's to appear in the United States. She has illustrated two books by Jerome Peignot, *Le Pense Bête* (The Reminder), and *Un Drôle*

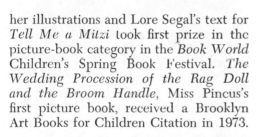

d'Oiseau (A Funny Bird), both appearing in 1974. At the same time she has been working on a series of ten books with a natural history theme for Encyclopaedia Britannica.

Miss Portal uses whatever techniques her projects require, whether pen and ink, gouache, watercolor, oil, crayon or pastel. Besides illustrating children's books, she has executed paperback book jackets, wallpaper and greeting card and advertising designs. Recently she designed sets for a ballet based on *A Thousand and One Nights* for Felix Blaska.

SELECTED WORKS WRITTEN AND ILLUSTRATED: The Life of a Queen, 1964; The Beauty of Birth, 1971.

SELECTED WORKS ILLUSTRATED: The Honeybees, by Franklin Russell, 1971.

ABOUT: Hürlimann, Bettina. Picture Book World; Kingman, Lee and others, comps. Illustrators of Children's Books: 1957–1966; Something about the Author, Vol. 6.

OTFRIED PREUSSLER

October 20, 1923–

AUTHOR OF *The Satanic Mill*, etc.

Autobiographical sketch of Otfried Preussler translated from the German:

I COME from the city of Reichenberg, in Bohemia, where I was born the son of a teacher, where I spent childhood and youth, and where I went through high school. After the war and five years of Soviet imprisonment, I came to Upper Bavaria, and I have stayed here.

My wife and I live with our three daughters and a black cat at Haidholzen bei Rosenheim, a small place on the northern edge of the Alps. There are many small and not-so-small lakes in our vicinity where you can swim in summer and skate in winter. We also have thousands of good places to mountain climb and ski, right at the front door, so to speak.

From 1953 to 1970 I was a teacher in a primary school. I always liked to tell

Otfried Preussler: *OAT freed PROYSS ler*

stories to our daughters and my pupils, and they liked to listen. What was more natural than to write these stories down one day?

My first children's book, *The Little Water Sprite*, appeared in 1956. Since then I have published nine other books and, though I don't know how it happened, they have all had an unexpectedly great success. At present the number of copies in German is about four million. Altogether more than a hundred foreign editions of my books exist in twenty-eight languages, among them not only world languages like English and Russian, but also languages of smaller and smallest peoples like Lithuanian and Gaelic.

Why do I write just for children? Because it gives me the greatest pleasure, and because I have gained the conviction that children are the best, most perceptive, and most grateful audience an author can wish for.

How I came to write one of my most successful children's books, *The Little Witch*, is a story in itself. One evening our daughters, at that time still small, announced before going to bed that they were terribly afraid. Afraid of what? "Of the wicked witch!" I sought to make it clear that these days one need no longer fear wicked witches because there are no more. "And why are there no more?" I admitted that until then I had never thought about it. However, it wasn't long until an answer was found—for my little daughters and for all the children who would like to know why these days one no longer needs to be afraid of a wicked witch.

———

Otfried Preussler is an accomplished translator from Czech and English (he has translated Lloyd Alexander's books into German), and his translations as well as his own books have consistently appeared on the honor lists for the German Children's Book Prize. He received the prize itself in 1972 for *The Satanic Mill* (*Krabat*), while his *The Little Water Sprite* (*Der Kleine Wasserman*)

and *The Wise Men of Schilda* (*Bei uns in Schilda*) were each given special awards by the Children's Book Prize jury in 1957 and 1961 respectively. *Krabat* also received the European Children's Book Prize in 1973. In 1972 Preussler was highly commended by the Hans Christian Andersen Award jury, and in that same year *The Adventures of Vanya* was awarded the Silver Stylus of Rotterdam.

The Satanic Mill, for slightly older readers than Preussler's other books, received widespread critical acclaim upon publication here and was designated a Notable Children's Book by the American Library Association in 1973.

Otfried Preussler has said that he writes with an ear attuned to the boy he once was, who liked stories that helped him "sharpen his understanding and prove his ability to read behind the lines." He tries to give his reader "an opportunity to come a bit further in his life and in the development of his consciousness, to find his way around in his own world a little better." At the same time, he tries to provide fun for his reader and for himself too, since his fun lies in the craft and creation itself. His philosophy, arising from his own experience, is that when life grows difficult, those who will endure will do so because

they learned to dream when young and to laugh sometimes, even in the most critical situations.

Otfried Preussler is a member of the International P.E.N. Club.

SELECTED WORKS: The Little Water-Sprite, 1961; The Little Witch, 1961; The Robber Hotzenplotz, 1965; The Little Ghost, 1967; The Adventures of Vanya, 1970; The Further Adventures of Robber Hotzenplotz; A Story About Kasperl, 1971; The Satanic Mill, 1973.

ABOUT: Bookbird, No. 4, 1972; No. 4, 1975.

LAURENCE PRINGLE

November 26, 1935–

AUTHOR OF *Dinosaurs and their World*, etc.

Autobiographical sketch of Laurence P. Pringle:

I WAS born in Rochester, New York, and grew up on a farm about twenty miles from that city. I attended a one-room schoolhouse until the fourth grade. After high school graduation (1953), I worked in a hospital for a year. Then a friend urged me to go to college, and I began investigating the idea, which had seemed out of the question until then. I was interested in writing and nature, and chose to study wildlife conservation at Cornell University. Later I obtained a master's degree in the same field at the University of Massachusetts in Amherst. During this period I grew—slowly—as a writer and photographer.

Sometimes I wonder what I would be doing today if a certain set of circumstances had not existed in the late fall of 1962. I was studying journalism at Syracuse University, my daughter was about to be born, and I needed a job. I found only one opening, with a new children's magazine to be published at The American Museum of Natural History in New York City. Fortunately I was taken on as an associate editor. Most of what I know about writing, especially writing for children, was learned during the seven years

Lawrence Pringle

that *Nature and Science* existed. If I had found work at another sort of magazine, I might never have written for children.

At *Nature and Science* we took great care that both text and illustrations were clear and accurate, and I apply the same standards to my books. Some editors consider me a nuisance when I insist that an expert read the manuscript, that I see the art, the dummy, and so on. Sure, I'm a nuisance. After all, I write for children—the people most likely to be changed by books and most vulnerable to misinformation and nonsense.

I've written about thirty nonfiction books for children and young adults and will probably write at least thirty more. Recently I tried writing some picture-book fiction, and was disappointed at the results. I would like to write the sort of fiction that my own children (when younger) would ask for again and again. There are personal matters, such as divorce and death, and external ones, such as advertising and television, which affect children's lives and which can be dealt with in books for very young children. So far my efforts have been too heavy-handed, but I'll keep trying.

In the next few years I want to become a good guitar player, tennis player and cook. I especially want my sons

(Sean, born in 1966, and Jeffrey, born in 1964) to join me in the kitchen, and we can probably all learn a few things from my daughter (Heidi, born in 1963). Their mother and I were divorced in 1970. I see them frequently, partly because of obligation, but mostly because Heidi, Jeffrey and Sean are lively, fascinating people whose company I would seek even if we weren't related.

Often in the past I said "no" to new opportunities and challenges. Now I'm more likely to say "why not?" I expect to write more books for adults. I want to become a better photographer, and have some short stories and even cartoons published in the *New Yorker.* I'm not necessarily committed to writing for the rest of my life. For a long time, writing and photography served as means of making a sort of living, expressing my creativity, gaining recognition and acceptance—and keeping people at a distance. Now acceptance of that sort is less important, and I seek greater intimacy with people. In a few years I might have a different career, one with much more direct contact with people and less with a typewriter. Why not?

Listen to the Crows was an American Library Association Notable Book for Children of 1976.

SELECTED WORKS: Dinosaurs and Their World, 1968; The Only Earth We Have, 1969; From Pond to Prairie: The Changing World of A Pond and its Life, 1970; One Earth, Many People: The Challenge of Human Population Growth, 1971; Pests and People: The Search for Sensible Pest Control, 1972; Estuaries: Where Rivers Meet the Sea, 1973; City and Suburb: Exploring an Ecosystem, 1975; Energy: Power for the People, 1975; Listen to the Crows, 1976; The Minnow Family, 1976; The Controversial Coyote, 1977; Death is Natural, 1977; The Hidden World, 1977.

ABOUT: Contemporary Authors, Vol. 29–32; Something about the Author, Vol. 4.

ROBERT QUACKENBUSH

July 23, 1929–

AUTHOR AND ILLUSTRATOR OF *Old Mac-Donald Had a Farm*, etc.

Autobiographical sketch of Robert Mead Quackenbush:

FOR several years I have been teaching courses in writing and illustrating children's books with the premise that each person has a unique story to present and share with children . . . the author's own story; for each of us has lived in a unique way. To awaken this knowledge within the student, I will usually begin the first class by having the student draw or write about the room he or she slept in as a child. From that first assignment it is exciting to watch the student discover his childhood world again and to view in each individual work the self-realized potential not known before by its creator.

The room I slept in as a child was in my home in Phoenix, Arizona. Although I was born in Hollywood, California, I consider myself a native of Phoenix because my parents moved there when I was one week old. My room in the family house took many changes in the seventeen years I lived there, for I was always painting and decorating and building furniture for it. One thing was always the same about the room; it was a place to draw pictures. My pictures filled the room from an early age. Even the windowpanes were painted with see-through pictures of birds and flowers as though they were part of the desert scene I saw through my window. When I graduated from high school, I left Phoenix to pursue my art studies and to live in new rooms.

The school I chose for my art studies was the Art Center College of Design in Los Angeles. After a two-year interruption to serve in the army, I graduated from there with a Bachelor of Professional Arts in 1956 and came to New York. My initial training in New York was as an art director before I became a full time free-lance artist in 1961. At first I was involved in printmaking, and my work was exhibited in leading museums in the United States including the Whitney Museum and the Philadelphia Academy of Fine Arts. Then publishers noticed my work and I illustrated my first children's book in 1962. Since then I have illustrated over fifty books for children and adults including three Junior Literary Guild Selections, and *The Pilot*, by James Fenimore Cooper and Weem's *The Life of Washington* for the Limited Editions Club. Also, I have written and illustrated over twenty books for children including, in the nonfiction area, *Take Me Out To the Airfield! How the Wright Brothers Invented the Airplane*.

In 1968 I opened the Robert Quackenbush Gallery in New York where I could give visitors the opportunity to see how I approach my work and could offer classes in art. That is when I also began writing as well as illustrating books for children. *Old MacDonald Had a Farm* (1971) for Lippincott was my first and its success led to a series of picture-song books for the same publisher that were done with the intention of preserving some of our classic American folksongs

for today's children. One of the pleasures
of working on this series was going back
to that early room again in my mind's
eye and finding something there for my
next book. It was there I found the puzzles and games for *Go Tell Aunt Rhody*,
the wild west show and game of chance
for *She'll Be Comin' 'Round the Mountain*, a disastrous party for *Skip To My
Lou*, etc. There were a total of eight
books in the series and I was most honored in 1976, when I received a citation
for them from the American Flag Institute as an "outstanding contribution to
America's bicentennial in the field of
children's literature." The series also led
to one of the major works of my career
thus far with the publication (fall 1977)
by Lothrop, Lee & Shepard of *The Holiday Song Book* (100 songs for 27 holidays) which I compiled, edited, wrote
lyrics, provided historical data, designed
and illustrated, a project that I would
liken to the accomplishment of climbing
Mt. Everest!

But now I have a "new room." In 1971,
I married Margery Clouser, a fashion
designer. Our son, Piet Robert, was born
in 1974. He is the inspiration for my
books now. As I experience his growth
into each new stage of development, a
flow of ideas emerges that I want to
share with my son and with children
everywhere. *Too Many Lollipops* for
Parents', the Fun-To-Read series I am
doing for Lothrop, which includes the
Pete Pack Rat and *Detective Mole* stories, and many others are all, what I call,
"Piet inspirations." Because of him, my
work is constantly changing as his ma-
turational needs change. And each new
book I am working on with him in mind
is just as exciting to do as the last, because it is a whole new adventure.

Poems for Galloping, a compilation of
Mother Goose verses, was included in
the American Institute of Graphic Arts
Fifty Best Books Show in 1963. In 1967,
Quackenbush received a citation from
the Society of Illustrators for *If I Drove*

a Truck, by Miriam Young, and in 1969,
for *Little Hares*, by Oscar Wilde, and
for his Limited Editions Club edition of
James Fenimore Cooper's *The Pilot*.

Quackenbush, whose name comes
from the Dutch for "duck in the bush,"
teaches classes at his own gallery and is
also a member of the faculty at the
School for Visual Arts in New York City.

SELECTED WORKS WRITTEN AND ILLUS-
TRATED: Old MacDonald Had a Farm,
1972; Go Tell Aunt Rhody, 1973; She'll Be
Comin' 'Round the Mountain, 1973; Clem-
entine, 1974; There'll Be A Hot Time in
the Old Town Tonight, 1974; The Man on
the Flying Trapeze, 1975; Skip to My Lou,
1975; Too Many Lollipops, 1975; Detective
Mole, 1976; Pete Pack Rat, 1976; Take Me
out to the Airfield!, 1976; Detective Mole
and the Secret Clues, 1977; (comp.) The
Holiday Song Book, 1977.

SELECTED WORKS ILLUSTRATED: I Feel
the Same Way, by Lilian Moore, 1967;
Horatio, by Eleanor Clymer, 1968; Little
Hares (The Devoted Friend), by Oscar
Wilde, 1969; If I Drove a Car, by Miriam
Young, 1971; Six Silver Spoons, by Jannette
Sebring Lowrey, 1971; If I Drove a Train,
by Miriam Young, 1972; Lines, Segments,
Polygons, by Maud H. Sitomer, 1972;
Pronghorn on the Powder River, by Ber-
niece Freschet, 1973; The Wizard Islands,
by Jane Yolen, 1973; If I Rode a Dinosaur,
by Miriam Young, 1974; Engine Number
Seven, by Eleanor Clymer, 1975; Horatio's
Birthday, by Eleanor Clymer, 1976.

ABOUT: Contemporary Authors, Vol. 45–
48; Kingman, Lee and others, comps. Illustrators of Children's Books: 1957–1966;
Something about the Author, Vol. 7; American Artist April 1965; Wilson Library Bulletin December 1973.

IAN RIBBONS

April 20, 1924–

AUTHOR AND ILLUSTRATOR OF *Tuesday 4
August 1914; The First Day of World
War I*:

Autobiographical sketch of Harold Ian
Ribbons:

I WAS four when I drew sailing galleons
and trains coming out of tunnels. At nine
I started a novel about pirates. Both occupations, being entirely derivative,

would have signified little had I not, at adolescence, developed a distinct distaste for my surroundings.

I was reared in a South London suburb in the days of gravelled side roads and Wall's ice cream carts; trees shaded sad houses; there was a forlorn park where elders played tennis. School became a womb, lessons and reading a private joy. I suppose I might have gone on to study social history at Oxford—which was what my friends seemed to be doing—if I had not one day opened a book on the Impressionists. For the first time I became aware of the art of painting. I had always drawn, but it was something I never took seriously, or no more so than woodwork or puppet carving or digging an Anderson Shelter (the war had come by then).

In this book were suburbs like Penge, grassy glades, streets covered in snow and dappled sunshine, yet all transfigured and made permanent. The book seemed so wonderful that it never occurred to me, in those culture-starved days, to yearn for the originals. Which was just as well: the National Gallery risked displaying just one picture a month in wartime. And so I gazed at the shadows of railings on pavements and

felt that my own life could be made magical after all.

In September 1941 I enrolled at Beckenham School of Art. I drew plump women and mixed paint and learned the orders of architecture. I etched on copper; I hand-composed type; I made painfully detailed watercolours. I dutifully gained an Exhibition at the Royal College of Art.

Then came my slice of war. "Keep away from everything that goes bang!" was the principal's farewell. Within two months I was training in the wetness of Scotland for the Royal Artillery. Later I "trooped" to India, on E deck below the waterline, and served with an Indian Field Regiment in the final campaign in Burma.

Back in England, at four years at the Royal College, I left to teach in a madhouse called Guildford School of Art.

I perched students along the railings of the cattle market to draw cows and pigs; I ground limestones and made many lithographs and etchings; and I did free-lance work ranging from book jacket design to advertising. Some commissions took me on location: for a week I drew coal miners for a BBC film on Newcastle; once in Amsterdam I made eighty portraits for a company brochure. I chased girls, searching an elusive ideal, and towards the end of my Guildford period the ideal found me. We married (she an Italian) in a San Marino church cellar at midnight in the depths of winter. Ten years later we are still together and, miraculously for this age, happier than ever, with two vociferous children to keep the home noisy. A grown-up son from an earlier marriage drops in to give me advice, and my eight-year-old drives us upriver on a small boat we have.

I now paint when I can, undertake various commissions—recently a bas-relief for a Canadian Mounties' commemorative silver bowl. I teach film animation one day a week and spend an increasing amount of time on my own books. I have rediscovered the delights of historical research; I remember the shock of first seeing Nelson's painful, left-handed scrawl in his original letters in the Public Record Office; I climbed the main mast of the Victory and measured her gun decks. I journeyed to the Meteorological Library to study actual weather reports for 4 August 1914. And I discovered the difficulties of writing to space.

I strive for immediacy. For my last book, on Gettysburg, I traced many manuscript letters and diaries, most of them unpublished. I only quote what seems unaffected, in the witness's normal tone of voice. My illustrations are of real people. For instance, the sailors in my Trafalgar books are all Billingsgate fish porters. I have sketched on many windy corners.

I am as interested in the soldier as in the general, the shopkeeper as the politician: all of them made history. I hope my drawings and my words combine to reflect a complex slice of reality, to make the reader feel he is himself reliving a moment in time. I would like him to put down one of my books with the thought: "So *this* is what it was like!"

Three books that Ian Ribbons wrote as well as illustrated have not yet appeared in the United States: *The Island* (1971), *The Battle of Gettysburg, 1–3 July 1863* (1974), and *Mr. McKenzie Painted Me* (1976).

Besides various other commissions outside his work in children's books, Ian Ribbons recently completed drawings for a Folio Society publication of Kipling short stories entitled *21 Tales*.

SELECTED WORKS WRITTEN AND ILLUSTRATED: Monday 21 October 1805; the Day of Trafalgar, 1968; Tuesday 4 August 1914; the First Day of World War I, 1970.

SELECTED WORKS ILLUSTRATED: Ten Tales of Detection, compiled by Roger Lancelyn Green, 1967; The Sea Gull, by Penelope Farmer, 1968.

ABOUT: Kingman, Lee and others, comps. Illustrators of Children's Books: 1957–1966.

HANS PETER RICHTER

April 28, 1925–

AUTHOR OF *Friedrich*, etc.

Autobiographical sketch of Hans Peter Richter, translated from the German:

AT my birth I could have seen the world-famous towers of Cologne cathedral, though at the time I probably didn't care to look at them. I was baptized with real Cologne water too—though not with the kind in the little bottles; they took it out of the aqueduct for me, doubtless because the other was too strong—perhaps that's why I babble a little sometimes!

What I managed to accomplish in my "exciting" youth is amply described in my book *Ich War Kein Braves Kind* (I Was A Bad Boy). Then one day that beautiful time ended at one stroke: I had to wear a uniform, like everyone else my age. At ten I already felt like a little general. And so I set out to become one. The experiences I gathered on the way are set down in the books I have written about that period. My military profession came to a sudden end when I was twenty years old and the Second World War was over.

For a new profession I looked for something that I thought would be somewhat less dangerous. How often one deludes oneself in life! I studied sociology and psychology at some well-known universities, and today I myself instruct students. In the meantime, however, that has also become a "dangerous" profession.

I also pass the time writing stories: that is healthier! The impetus to do it comes from my own children. I have four of them. It began with stories for the very smallest, *The Uncle and His Merry-Go-Round* or *Hengist the Horse*. As my children grew, so did the scope of my stories; now the children are big and the books thicker, though very thick they will never be, for I myself don't like to read thick books.

People have asked me whether I write

Hans Peter Richter: *HAHNZ PAY ter RICK ter*

SELECTED WORKS: Friedrich, 1970; I Was There, 1972.

ABOUT: Contemporary Authors, Vol. 45–46; Something about the Author, Vol. 6.

KJELL RINGI

February 3, 1939–

AUTHOR AND ILLUSTRATOR OF *The Magic Stick*, etc.

Autobiographical sketch of Kjell Arne Sorensen-Ringi, who shortens his name to Kjell Ringi when writing books for children:

I WAS born in Gothenberg, a seaport on the west coast of Sweden. My whole youth was affected by my nearsightedness and the fact that I consistently refused to wear my glasses. Consequently my studies at school and at college were not too successful, especially as I was rather tall and placed far from the blackboard. Screened off from the world I was often lost in fantasies, writing grotesque figures on the desk top. In spite of the fact that my schoolmates often teased me, my childhood was rather happy, I think. Had I worn my glasses and passed college, I should probably have been an average bank accountant or something like that today, instead of—as I see it—being in the lucky position of creating picture books and pictures.

I recall that I as a child drew pictures on everything that came near me. I did it as a kind of therapy or escape from reality. Even today I can feel a strong uneasiness if I don't hold pen or brush for some days.

After the unsuccessful time at college I went to the Art Industrial School in Gothenberg in 1956 and in 1957–1958 to the Berghs Advertising School in Stockholm. With a certain amount of talent and glasses on, I was given awards as well as self-confidence during this time. The education concerned mostly advertising sketching, but if you go to a school you are allowed to let fantasy flow without restraint. Employed at an advertising

my books thinking of certain children. Not really! Not even my own. Strictly speaking, I simply invent them because it gives me pleasure. And so long as it gives me pleasure, I'll keep on writing.

———

Hans Peter Richter has written more than twenty books, which have been translated into ten languages. His best known book in the United States is *Friedrich* (*Damals war es Friedrich*), which was a runner-up for the German Children's Book Prize in 1964 and in 1972 won the Mildred Batchilder Award, presented by the American Library Association for the most outstanding translated book published in a given year. Besides his books for young people, Dr. Richter writes essays, radio and television plays, school and children's programs, and collaborates on reading texts. He has also written a book about children's literature, *Der jungen Leser wegen* (For the Young Reader).

A specialist in French culture, Dr. Richter was invited to spend a year at the Cité Internationale des Arts in Paris in 1965–66.

Kjell Ringi: *SHELL REENG yee*

agency during 1960 (after military service) I mostly made original drawings on the sketches of others. In 1961 I was more or less fired by the art director, who had the opinion that I was careless. I often saw this man get his inspiration from the famous Swiss journal *Graphis* in which I, some years later, had the honor of being introduced in a "one-man" article.

In order to get to know myself I took an odd job on a cruise liner to New York, the West Indies and South America. In New York (the first port) I was left behind without glasses and only a toothbrush in my pocket. It was a terrible experience, but my visit six years later was to be the more worthwhile.

Perhaps I was given the igniting spark in the West Indies, because when I returned to Gothenberg three months later I started painting (pictures) frenetically day and night until 1967. I had many exhibitions in Scandinavia and was given a lot of publicity in papers and on TV.

People bought my pictures. The same fellows who once had teased me now diffidently came up to me in the street and congratulated me on my latest successes. Very satisfying!

During this time I also made two comic strips, "The Mirror" and "The Cork's Crew," which still continue to be published on a small scale. In 1967 I went to New York to find a gallery in which I could exhibit my pictures.

An acquaintance of mine suggested that I show my pictures to Miss Ursula Nordstrom at Harper and Row, publishers. The night after I'd seen her, I knelt over the hotel bed writing down the idea of my first picture book, *The Magic Stick*, as I had been asked to, with Manhattan's noisy nightlife streaming in through the window. It was a great time!

I have never regretted this step into the field of children's books even though it sometimes has stolen my time from my painting.

The picture books I read as a child I remember better than books I read two weeks ago. Now at late hours, when I am working on a book, I am altogether back in a lost paradise. I can hardly think of a better inspiration than knowing that every night, at least somewhere on earth, a mother and child lean over one of my books.

I have to feel that I have fun myself when I work on a book. If that is the case, there is always a chance that other adults also enjoy the book when they read it aloud to their children.

I am happy if I can give a human message with my books. I don't want to do it with grand airs or masterful manners—just with a discreet tap on the shoulder. As a matter of fact, I am a little bit bashful with children and therefore I am glad and grateful to be able to speak to them through my books.

———

Kjell Ringi received several Swedish design awards while still in school. In 1970 he was awarded a Citation of Merit from the Society of Illustrators for *The Winner*. He has exhibited his paintings and illustrations widely and had work in magazines and on television, both in the United States and in Scandinavia. Both *My Father and I* and *The Parade* were adapted for Swedish television by Mr. Ringi, who also did the animation.

An article in *Graphis* describes Ringi as "a worker of gigantic capacity . . . [with] something of the contained force of a natural phenomenon" and as an artist "not being conscious of those petty rules that bind together our common, smooth-shaven society."

SELECTED WORKS WRITTEN AND ILLUS-TRATED: The Magic Stick, 1968; The Stranger, 1968; The Winner, 1969; The Sun and the Cloud, 1971; My Father and I (with Adelaide Holl), 1973; The Parade (with Adelaide Holl), 1975.

SELECTED WORKS ILLUSTRATED: The Man Who Had No Dream, by Adelaide Holl, 1969.

ABOUT: Contemporary Authors, Vol. 45–48; Graphis No. 112, 1964.

MARILYN SACHS

December 18, 1927–

AUTHOR OF *Veronica Ganz*, etc.

Autobiographical sketch of Marilyn Stickle Sachs:

I WAS born in the Bronx, one of the least celebrated boroughs of New York City. The street I lived on had no trees or flowers, but it had children, lots and lots of children. The street didn't go anywhere important, and cars seldom came through. In the summertime it was frequently closed to traffic.

But every day, after school, and all day Saturday and Sunday, the children spilled out of the tall apartment houses that ran down the block and filled all the empty spaces on the street and sidewalks. Something was always going on outside. Our family was poor but we seldom felt sorry for ourselves because everybody else on the street was in the same financial boat. We children played hard and, as we grew older, roamed comfortably through other parts of the city.

The only fly in the ointment was that I was a shameful coward. Small, skinny and a "cry baby," I was easy prey for the local bullies. My lack of courage was particularly disgusting to my older sister who frequently had to fight my battles for me in order to uphold the family honor. How I admired her! She was the one who introduced me to books. On cold, wet days, or on days when somebody or other was after me, I stayed home or went to the library. My books brought me such comfort (and still do) that I determined quite early to be a writer. I have been writing just about as long as I have been reading. To me the two go hand in hand.

I wrote all through elementary school, high school and college. I worked on school newspapers and magazines. But when I graduated from Hunter College in 1949, I didn't seem to have much to write about. So I took a job with the Brooklyn Public Library as children's librarian, went to Columbia University for a master's degree in library science, and spent ten happy years working with children and books.

It was during this time that I wrote my first book, *Amy Moves In*. It took ten years before it was published, a long, discouraging time. Since then I have had eleven other books published.

My own childhood shapes my books. Growing up in a poor urban neighborhood, I missed out on trees and birds and babbling brooks. But I had people—so many people—fat ones, skinny ones, mean ones, friendly ones, smart ones, scared ones. . . . They all lived on my block, and they are with me when I write my books. They push and shove each other and shout, "I'm next. Look at me!" I doubt if I will ever in one lifetime get around to all of them.

I am lucky to have a lively family with strongminded members. They encourage me and keep me in my place at the same time. There is my husband Morris, a sculptor, my daughter, Anne, my son, Paul. We live in San Francisco now but always enjoy our trips back to New York.

———

A Marilyn Sachs book can nearly always be found on the lists of critics' choices and readers' favorites any year that a new one appears. *Veronica Ganz* was an American Library Association Notable Book for 1968 as was *A Pocket Full of Seeds* for 1973. *A Pocket Full of Seeds* also won an Honor Award in The Jane Addams Children's Book Award, 1974. *The Bears' House* was nominated for the 1971 National Book Award.

Marilyn Stickle married on January 26, 1947. The Sachs have two children, Anne, born May 18, 1957, and Paul, born September 16, 1960.

SELECTED WORKS: Amy Moves In, 1964; Laura's Luck, 1965; Amy and Laura, 1966; Veronica Ganz, 1968; Peter and Veronica, 1969; Marv, 1970; The Bears' House, 1971; A Pocket Full of Seeds, 1973; The Truth About Mary Rose, 1973; Dorrie's Book, 1975; Matt's Mit, 1976; A December Tale, 1976.

ABOUT: Contemporary Authors, Vol. 19–20; Something about the Author, Vol. 3; Publishers Weekly January 8, 1973.

ANTOINE DE SAINT-EXUPÉRY

June 9, 1900–July 31, 1944

AUTHOR AND ILLUSTRATOR OF *The Little Prince*, etc.

Biographical sketch of Antoine-Jean-Baptiste-Marie-Roger de Saint-Exupéry:

"SAINT-EX," as he was known to his friends, began life on June 9th, 1900, as Antoine-Jean-Baptiste-Marie-Roger de Saint-Exupéry, born in Lyons to an aristocratic, though not particularly wealthy, family.

His two great loves in life were to be poetry and flying, and from an early age he showed a marked interest in both: as a child of six he was already writing poems for himself and making little sketches of aeroengines. By 1912 Saint-Exupéry had made his first flight, with the pilot Jules Védrines; and by 1920 he was in the French Air Force, where he soon obtained a civil pilot's license after some hair-raising private lessons in Strasbourg, which he had taken because he was dissatisfied with the snail-like pace of the official air force pilot training.

In 1923, at Le Bourget airport, the first of a series of near-fatal accidents began the legend of Saint-Exupéry's almost magical invulnerability to death. His commercial flying career began on the famous French flying postal service, La Ligne (The Line), started by Latécoère Company and plying between Toulouse and Dakar. His work with the company often involved flying under bad weather conditions and also extremely hazardous night flying over the hostile Spanish-Moroccan deserts, inhabited by warring desert tribesmen.

He was an extraordinarily careless pilot. Many of his crashes were due to his forgetting to check his gasoline gauge, failing to pay attention to his route, or even, once, forgetting to let down the landing gear. It was almost as if he were being deliberately careless in order to provide himself with challenge and excitement, for whenever there was danger

Antoine de Saint-Exupéry: ANN twon de SAN teg Zu pay REE

ANTOINE DE SAINT-EXUPÉRY

he rose superbly to the occasion and flew with incredible skill and daring.

After flying the Casablanca-Dakar route for a time, Saint-Ex was appointed company representative in Spanish Morocco, at the edge of the Sahara. It was a colorful and action-packed period that involved him in air crashes and delicate diplomatic dealings with the Spanish and the Moroccans. Upon his return to France after eighteen months, Saint-Exupéry was awarded the Legion of Honor. His first novel, *Southern Mail*, was based on these experiences.

In 1929, Saint-Exupéry was sent to South America where the Latécoère Company had set up new postal air routes from Buenos Aires to the Tierra del Fuego. For the next two years he was involved in further adventures, including flights through a cyclone and through the Andes mountains at a time when planes flew between the mountains and not over them. After the Latécoère Company's liquidation, Saint-Exupéry returned to Paris, where he married a widow, the Countess Consuelo Manuelo, whom he had met in Buenos Aires. *Night Flight*, based on his experiences in South America, published in 1932, won the Prix Femina in France and made him an international celebrity.

The period of his mid-thirties was un-settled, occupied mainly by writing and occasional flying. He incurred injuries on a poorly prepared Paris-to-Saigon flight in 1934, and later in a flight from New York to Guatemala City. He achieved great critical success with the publication of *Wind, Sand and Stars* in 1939, winning the Grand Prix du Roman, awarded by the Académie Française.

In September 1939, at the outbreak of World War II, Saint-Exupéry was recalled to service, but to his disgust he was assigned to be an instructor at Toulouse, well out of active combat. Despite the attempts of influential friends to prevent it, for he was considered medically unfit, he managed to get reassigned to a reconnaissance squadron based in Champagne. There, rather than stay in the officers' quarters, he lived with a poor family in the village of Orconte. He became especially fond of the children of the family, one of whom later served as a model for the Little Prince.

After the defeat of France, Saint-Ex went to America where, in 1942, he published *Flight to Arras*, reflecting his distress and pain at France's occupation. An underground edition was published in occupied France.

In 1943 Saint-Exupéry published *The Little Prince* in New York, incorporating his own charming and evocative drawings. The story, in the metaphors of childhood but with great depth of feeling that makes it not unlike the work of William Blake, describes the relationship of the little prince and a flower, and later, the little prince and a pilot alone in the desert after a crash. The book describes the transforming power of a simple love, the little prince and the pilot developing a very close and tender relationship. The pilot "felt the need of protecting him, as if he . . . were a flame that might be extinguished by a little puff of wind."

The Little Prince, an international success, sold over three million copies in the United States alone, and five million worldwide.

Soon afterwards, Saint-Exupéry, at forty-three years of age, managed to pull enough strings to get himself a pilot's commission to fight with the Americans in North Africa, making reconnaissance flights over France; on July 31, 1944, he was lost without a trace on one of these flights, leaving behind him a legend as potent and as imaginatively compelling as that of Lawrence of Arabia. To live a life of action was essential to him: "Before writing," he once declared, "one must live, one must learn to see; no literary artifice can cover the lack of these essentials"—and he died in action, as he had lived.

In 1965, *Citadelle (Wisdom of the Sands)* was published posthumously. He had worked on it intermittently for eight years and it required much editing. A long and rather confused parable of a Berber prince who learns wisdom and the use of power, it is not unlike *The Little Prince*, though lacking its clarity and simplicity. Together the two works embody Saint-Exupéry's credo, his search for a meaning to life that transcends the banal, the ugly, and the plain wicked. Though he never acknowledged a belief in a deity, his search is the religious quest of a profoundly moral man.

SELECTED WORKS: Night Flight, 1932; Southern Mail, 1933; Wind, Sand and Stars, 1939; Flight to Arras, 1942; The Little Prince, 1943; Wisdom of the Sands, 1950; Sense of Life, 1965.

ABOUT: Current Biography, 1940; Gray, James. On Second Thought; Pudney, John. Six Great Aviators; Twentieth Century Authors; Twentieth Century Authors (First Supplement); Contemporary Review August 1956; Newsweek June 13, 1960; New Yorker March 18, 1961; New York Times Book Review December 27, 1970; Publishers Weekly August 20, 1973; Time June 13, 1960.

KATHARINE SAVAGE

August 13, 1905–

AUTHOR OF *The Story of the Second World War*, etc.

Autobiographical sketch of Katharine James Sanford Savage:

I WAS born in the quiet county town of Worcester, England, in 1905. My father was British, or more precisely, Welsh. My mother was American from New England. Both had remained true to their Methodist and Puritan upbringing and in consequence my childhood was rigidly regulated. Nevertheless, I enjoyed life, for I always felt that freedom of thought and action lay just around the corner.

As my father had retired from the Merchant Navy where he had ended his career as commodore of the Cunard Line, and my mother never fitted into the pattern of English country life, we moved constantly. Therefore my education was unconventional and international. I went to school in England, the States and on the Continent. I acquired French and German and a facility for fitting into different ways of life—but no formal degrees. I always loved writing, but I lacked a sense of purpose until I went seriously into a job during the Second World War.

In 1938 I had married Oswald Savage, a rising young rheumatologist. In 1941 we had a son, Martin, and by this time my husband was in the army. Five months later he was sent overseas, and for me it was a long war. When my husband first managed to get home leave Martin was four years old. During these years I worked in London at the Ministry of Information, at first in the Middle East Division and later in charge of the Counter Propaganda Section, commonly known as Anti-Lies, where we analysed and summarised Nazi propaganda. It was grim but fascinating work, and I learned a great deal about total war and the human mind.

After the war I joined the foreign department of the *Economist* newspaper and remained there for ten years. I worked on an eight-page confidential publication named *Foreign Report*. Space was at a premium and every word counted. It was magnificent training in concise writing, which has been invaluable to me ever since.

In the summer of 1954 when Martin

Katharine S. Savage

was thirteen years old we spent a family holiday in Brittany. Martin was impressed by the monuments to the heroes of the Free French Resistance and began to ask questions about the war. His ignorance was startling. My husband and I discussed it with our contemporaries and we realized that, once the conflict and bloodshed ended, we had instinctively tried to forget them. We had not wanted to talk about the horrors of war, and as a result our children had grown up not knowing what it was all about. It suddenly seemed to me very important that this particular generation should be aware of the danger of war so that they could strive for peace.

I left the *Economist* and wrote *The Story of the Second World War*. I tried to explain to children why the war had happened and how it was fought. Martin read and criticized every chapter and together we sorted out complicated situations and set them down in simple words. Without his help it would have been far more difficult to hold teen-age interest.

In the following twelve years I wrote six more books, all of them linking the course of history and the development of man to modern ideas and current events. I enjoy both the research and the writing, and I find it immensely satisfactory to stimulate the interest of the young in the world at large. By a former marriage I have three children and eight grandchildren who keep me in touch with teen-age thinking and give me more pleasure than I can ever put into words.

My husband has now retired and we live in the south of France, in an old farmhouse surrounded by olive orchards and vineyards. We have worked hard setting up a new life and getting our home in order. But the time has now come when I feel the irresistible urge to return to my typewriter.

SELECTED WORKS: The Story of the Second World War, 1958; People and Power: The Story of Three Nations, 1959; The Story of Africa: South of the Sahara, 1961; The Story of World Religions, 1967; The Story of Marxism and Communism, 1969; The Story of the United Nations (revised edition), 1970; The Story of the Common Market, 1970.

ABOUT: Author's and Writer's Who's Who, 1971; Contemporay Authors, Vol. 15–16.

BETTY SCHECHTER

February 5, 1921–

AUTHOR OF *The Peaceable Revolution*, etc.

Autobiographical sketch of Betty Goodstein Schechter:

I WAS thirty-eight years old when I first tried writing for publication. It was 1959, and an interest in Jawaharlal Nehru had led to a greater interest in Mohandas Gandhi and the nonviolent struggle for Indian independence he had led. Reading Gandhi's autobiography, I had learned that as he was just beginning a long career of jail-going in the cause of Indian freedom, he was encouraged and greatly influenced by reading Henry Thoreau's *Essay on Civil Disobedience*. And no wonder! When I reread Thoreau's essay, I realized that his "peaceable revolution" against the state of Massachusetts and Gandhi's "satyagraha-soul force" cam-

paign against the British raj were, in essence, one and the same thing.

And then, suddenly, my daily newspaper began printing new installments of the Thoreau and Gandhi story. First in Greensboro, North Carolina, and then in cities all over the South young black men and women were purposefully sitting at lunch counters that had always been reserved for the exclusive use of white people. Asked to leave, they were politely but resolutely refusing. Dragged off their stools and charged with breaking local segregation ordinances, they were cheerfully singing on their way to jail. They told reporters they wanted to do two things: spotlight the injustice of the laws they broke, and afflict the conscience of the American people. They added that they thought jail was a good place to do both.

In 1846 Henry Thoreau, a white American going to jail because he refused to cooperate with a system that used tax dollars to kill Mexicans who had never done Americans any harm and to track down fugitive slaves and return them to their masters; half a century later and half a world away, Mohandas Gandhi, a brown-skinned Indian spending years of his life in British jails before the British

people finally bowed to the might of Indian nonviolent resistance; and now, thousands of young black Americans wearing their jail terms as badges of honor showing their readiness to sacrifice and suffer for American ideals. What a story! It stretched from one era of history to another and to another. It crossed oceans and then recrossed them to show that a single powerful idea could move men and women of different races, different cultures, and different creeds to peaceable feats of great heroism. It was a story that was crying to be told to a generation growing up in the dreadful shadow of the atom bomb.

Since nobody else was telling it, I decided that I would like to make a try at it. My husband and our children, a twelve-year-old daughter and nine-year-old son and daughter, twins, were all agreeable, and they all helped by doing some of the household chores I usually did. It all worked out as we hoped it would and I learned so much in the course of writing *The Peaceable Revolution* and had such a good time in the process that I can't think of a nicer way to spend a couple of years of spare time.

I was born and brought up in New York City. I graduated from Smith College in 1942 and then worked briefly for the Norden Bombsight Company. Then I got a job with the United Nations Information Office, a precursor of the United Nations. In 1944 I married Edward Schechter, who was in the army at the time, and continued to work for UNIO until he came back from overseas in 1946. Claire was born in 1947, and Ellen and Jay were born in 1950. In 1953 we all moved to Kingston, Pennsylvania, a suburb of Wilkes-Barre, and in 1968 we moved to Shavertown, further into the beautiful Pennsylvania Hills.

In 1964 *The Peaceable Revolution* received the Child Study Association's Children's Book Award and the Thomas Alva Edison Foundation Award for character development of children. The book was designated one of the one hundred outstanding titles of the year by the New York *Times* in 1963, and in 1966 was included in the *Time*'s list of the fifty most important children's books of the previous five years. Listed on the *Horn Book* magazine's Fanfare list, *The Peaceable Revolution* was also an American Library Association Notable Book in 1963, as was its successor, *The Dreyfus Affair*, in 1965. *The Dreyfus Affair* was also singled out by the New York *Times* as one of the best books of its publishing year and in 1966 received the Charles and Bertie G. Schwartz Juvenile Award from the Jewish Book Council of America.

SELECTED WORKS: The Peaceable Revolution, 1963; The Dreyfus Affair: A National Scandal, 1965.

ABOUT: Contemporary Authors, Vol. 7–8; Something about the Author, Vol. 5.

ELEONORE SCHMID

1939–

AUTHOR AND ILLUSTRATOR OF *Tonia*, etc.

Autobiographical sketch of Eleonore Schmidlin-Schmid, translated from the German:

IT is not easy for me to speak about my work. I believe that every book should speak for itself. What I like about writing and illustrating children's books is that they are for children. Children are at the beginning of their lives, dependent on their surroundings and able to judge people and things in a very limited way. They see pictures and stories as alive, they compare them with their own observations and experiences. They like to be surprised by the unexpected and to identify with the heroes of children's books. Everything is new and fantastic, and everything is possible.

Children become youths and then grown-ups. We are responsible for their world. And that is what fascinates me in the creation of children's books.

My childhood memories are peopled by dwarfs, goblins, witches, giants, fairies, kings and robbers. Animals and plants led their own special lives there, too, and everyday objects—wallpaper, furniture, carpets—were filled with significance and symbols. I would slip into being different things. I would buzz through the house like a fly and look at the world from above, naturally seeing it from a fly's-eye view. The ceiling was then the floor and the floor the ceiling, making everything upside down. Or as a bird I would take off from the windowsill and fly to the next tree. I was dwarf and giant; there was no barrier. If anything bad ever threatened me, the good people came and rescued me. Reality and fantasy were so intermingled that the one became the other. The world around me could become enchanted at any time. I took my personality from the fairy tale world. I lived in the stories. I wanted to experience them.

After school I spent a year on a farm and learned to know animals, agriculture at work, and the changing of the seasons.

I have always drawn. I wanted to train for a career in art, and I attended the Kunstgewerbe-Schule in Lucerne for five years. I became a graphic artist.

After I had completed my studies, I went to Zurich. Since I didn't want to concentrate exclusively on advertising, I

Eleonore: *ELAYA noreh*

took a job with a newspaper publisher. I also became involved with children's games and books. I illustrated Robert Louis Stevenson's *Treasure Island*. The factual illustrations consisted of ships' charts, sail specifications, tables of knots, tools, weapons, plants and animals.

I went on to Paris and later to New York where my first children's book was published. It was *The Tree* and its seasons. I enjoyed the work and more books followed.

Today I live with my son Caspar Iskander in Zurich. Every evening we tell stories or read fairy tales and legends. We hide everyday happenings in our stories. Mostly they begin, "I know a boy, he's as big as you, who today was. . . ." In this way we can discuss problems as a game and he also tells me his point of view. And he also peoples his fantasies with dwarfs, snowmen, witches, fairies, robbers and many others.

————

Eleonore Schmid was born and grew up in Lucerne, Switzerland. After working for a publisher in Zurich, where she drew for children's magazines, designed toys and illustrated an edition of *Treasure Island*, she spent a year in Paris and then, in 1965, went on to New York where she spent three years. She shared a studio with Etienne Delessert and besides various commercial assignments designed cards for UNICEF, did covers for *Punch* and *Graphis* and began to illustrate children's books in earnest. The first, *The Tree*, written by Delessert, won an Award of Excellence from the Society of Illustrators and a first prize for illustration at the Bologna Book Fair. Then followed another book with Etienne Delessert, *The Endless Party*, and the next year *Horns Everywhere*, which Miss Schmid wrote and illustrated herself. Both books received Awards of Excellence from the Society of Illustrators. Also included in the 1969 Illustrators Show was an illustration from *Fenny*, with text by Hans Baumann.

Miss Schmid returned to Europe on a freighter after a sojourn in Mexico, and

in 1969 she married the painter Aja Iskander Schmidlin. That year *Fenny* was on the Honor List for Picture Books for the German Children's Book Prize. Eleonore Schmid received a medal at the Biennale of Illustrations Bratislava 1969 for her illustrations for *The Tree* and another Bratislava medal for the 1976 publication, *Das schwarze Schaf* (The Black Sheep). Two more books, *Die Geschichte vom grossen A* (The Story of the Big A) by James Krüss and *Passepoil* by Chantal di Marolles, have not been published in the United States.

SELECTED WORKS WRITTEN AND ILLUSTRATED: Horns Everywhere, 1968; Tonia; The Mouse with the White Stone and What Happened on Her Way to See Uncle Tobias, 1974.

SELECTED WORKS ILLUSTRATED: The Tree, by Etienne Delessert, 1966; The Endless Party, by Etienne Delessert, 1967. Fenny the Desert Fox, by Hans Baumann, 1970.

ABOUT: Bookbird No. 3, 1971; Graphis No. 131, 1967.

JOHN SCHOENHERR

July 5, 1935–

AUTHOR AND ILLUSTRATOR OF *The Barn*, etc.

Autobiographical sketch of John Schoenherr:

I WAS born and raised in New York City and attended some usual, and some unusual, public schools. At the age of four I simultaneously learned to speak English, read and draw. Having chronic bronchitis and sporadic attacks of asthma, these abilities were rather well developed by long periods of being bedridden and alone.

I read and made pictures voraciously. At eight years I had done my first oil paintings and by ten was reading some of the works of Jules Verne. The editions illustrated by N. C. Wyeth were my particular favorites, juxtaposing fascinating

JOHN SCHOENHERR

adventures with very appropriate illustration.

For my health I was often sent to relatives who lived in the country. After my faulty eyesight was corrected, I found the vistas of the Catskill Mountains and Hudson River far more compelling than the more easily reached horizons of the city.

I began classes at the Art Students League of New York at thirteen, the same year I entered high school. I produced etchings and lithographs under the direction of Will Barnett whose influence remains with me.

With increasing mobility and maturity, I began spending available free time in zoos and museums, took up spelunking and a bit of rock climbing, and discovered the Adirondack Mountains, where I could be alone for about a week at a time, backpacking in a virtual wilderness.

I entered Pratt Institute, keeping up most of these activities on weekends not devoted to painting. On graduation, I began illustrating for several small magazines and soon was offered my first real hardcover book to illustrate. It was called *Rascal* and was written by Sterling North. It led to a great number of children's books, and eventually my friend Emilie McLeod, editor at Atlantic Monthly Press, cajoled me into writing my only book, *The Barn*.

I had married Judith in 1960, and after the birth of our daughter Jennifer, we bought a small former farm. While doing some watercolors on our neighbor's farm, I had become intrigued by their massive old barn and spent some time poking around and falling through floors. A skunk was a regular visitor of ours, and the story evolved in the evenings, bedding down Jennifer and Ian (our son).

I have written nothing since then, being entirely occupied with painting. The simultaneous total perception of a picture suits me far better than the linear nature of verbal material.

Otherwise, we are growing trees and trout, and make occasional forays to wilder places than ours around the world.

———

After his graduation from Pratt Institute in 1956, John Schoenherr started illustrating science fiction and gradually turned to the nature field, which now concerns him exclusively. He won first prize at the National Speleological Salon in 1963 and in 1965 he received the World Science Fiction Award, which named him best science fiction artist of the year. Schoenherr's paintings hang in a number of private collections. He had a one-man show at the Bronx Zoo in 1968, is frequently included in shows of the Society of Illustrators, and exhibited in the American Institute of Graphic Arts' Children's Book Shows of 1967–68 and 1970. *Simon Underground*, with text by Joanne Ryder, was selected for the 1977 Children's Book Council Showcase.

He is a member of the American Society of Mammalogists, the National Speleological Society, the Society of Illustrators, and the Society of Animal Artists.

SELECTED WORKS WRITTEN AND ILLUSTRATED: The Barn, 1968.

SELECTED WORKS ILLUSTRATED: Rascal, by Sterling North, 1963; Gentle Ben, by Walt Morey, 1965; The Fox and the Fire,

by Miska Miles, 1966; Moon of the Chick-
arees, by Jean C. George, 1968; Nobody's
Cat, by Miska Miles, 1969; Hoagie's Rifle
Gun, by Miska Miles, 1970; Incident at
Hawk's Hill, by Allan W. Eckert, 1971;
Julie of the Wolves, by Jean C. George,
1972; Wharf Rat, by Miska Miles, 1972;
Black Lightning; Three Years in the Life of
a Fisher, by John A. Giegling, 1975; Simon
Underground, by Joanne Ryder, 1976; A
Bat Is Born, by Randall Jarrell, 1977; Kil-
ory and the Gull, by Nathaniel Benchley,
1977.

ABOUT: Kingman, Lee and others, comps.
Illustrators of Children's Books: 1957–1966.

ANN HERBERT SCOTT

ANN HERBERT SCOTT

November 19, 1926–

AUTHOR OF *Big Cowboy Western*, etc.

Autobiographical sketch of Ann Herbert
Scott:

I CAN hardly remember a time when I
wasn't "writing." The only child of overly
appreciative parents, I early discovered
the good feel of words. When I was tiny,
my mother began collecting my stories
and poems in a scrapbook and for many
years she saved anything that was published in our little school magazine.
Later when homework assignments
called for rhymed verse, I can remember
sitting on the livingroom stairs long after
my bedtime while my father (a journalist and amateur poet himself) prodded
me to improve rough places in the meter.
In Chestnut Hill, Philadelphia, where
I was born and spent my first fourteen
years, I lived in a pleasant little house
on a shady, tree-lined street. When I was
five, the depression wiped out my great-
uncle's business and he and my two
great-aunts came to live with us. They
became part of a warm, sometimes sti-
fling, circle of love that undergirded me
throughout my growing up.
When I was six, my family bought an
old farm in Bucks County, a place that
was to be a source of enormous joy for
many years. Summers at the farm meant
hunting for wild strawberries, making
hideouts in the blackberry thickets, ly-

ing awake in my attic bed listening to
the drumming of rain on the tin roof.
Growing up without brothers and sisters, I was fortunate in having good
friends. Our neighborhood in Chestnut
Hill was alive with children and as I
grew older, I found several close school
friends who became like sisters. I was
fortunate, too, in my early education for
I received a solid classical foundation at
Springside, a small girls' school staffed
by clear-minded single ladies of dedication and scholarship. Later, when my
father's heart trouble encouraged a move
to the country, I transferred to George
School, a Quaker boarding school not far
from our farm.
Both at George School and later at the
University of Pennsylvania, I edited the
newspaper, worked on the yearbook, and
dabbled in theater. Probably the greatest single influence in my college years
was my work at the University Camp for
Girls, a camp which provided a life-
changing environment for little girls
from the city slums and for students who
served as their counselors. ·
Years later I returned to university life
and to work with young children. In the
middle fifties I studied social ethics with
Richard Niebuhr at Yale and served on
the staff of Wider City Parish, an experimental ministry attempting to serve the

people of New Haven's most crowded areas. In my work with black and Puerto Rican children, I became aware of the scarcity of library and textbooks reflecting the everyday lives of city youngsters. Some day, I told myself, I'd like to try writing books in which my friends could find themselves.

The day came years later in Reno, where I moved when I married William Scott, a physics professor at the University of Nevada. I had gotten back into writing in the process of typing and editing a book manuscript for my husband. One sunny morning in May, we packed off the results of several years' writing and research, and I sat down in the backyard and wrote *Big Cowboy Western*. Set in a familiar housing project neighborhood in New Haven, the story had been taking shape in my mind all spring. I little realized how extraordinarily lucky I was when the first publisher accepted my manuscript just two weeks after it arrived in New York.

Writing became central in my life for the next few years. Then in 1966 our son Peter was born, and our daughter Katherine (Katie) arrived with the beginning of the new year in 1969. For a number of years the involvements of family life, coupled with concerns of our little Quaker Meeting, the American Friends Service Committee, and other Quaker projects, took most of my energy. Recently, with both children in school, I have been studying art (design, stitchery, print-making) and once again working on my own writing.

My stories for young children seem to come into being when I have the inner space to let the ideas have their way with me. Almost always the central ideas come as gifts from children, and when I am not too preoccupied with more "important" matters I find ideas everywhere. Now and then I have the inward room to let an idea take root, ripen, push me around, and then sometimes a book is born.

———

Ann Herbert received an M.A. from

Yale University in 1958 and married William Taussig Scott on September 29, 1961. She has said that she thinks "the pull toward children's writing comes from something childlike within" her and that wherever she's lived there have been a few small children who have been among her closest friends.

Sam, published by McGraw-Hill in 1967, was an American Library Association Notable Book.

SELECTED WORKS: Big Cowboy Western, 1965; Let's Catch a Monster, 1967; Sam, 1967; Census U.S.A.: Fact Finding for the American People 1790–1970, 1968; Not Just One, 1968; On Mother's Lap, 1972.

ABOUT: Contemporary Authors, Vol. 21–22; Hopkins, Lee Bennett. Books Are by People.

LORE SEGAL

March 8, 1928–

AUTHOR OF *Tell Me a Mitzi*, etc.

Autobiographical sketch of Lore Groszmann Segal:

I WAS born in Vienna. Hitler took over Austria when I was ten years old, and I came to England with a transport of five hundred Jewish children. We were distributed among English families, and I once counted eleven different houses in which I lived over the next seven years.

In 1945 I entered the University of London and, after I got my B.A. degree in English literature, followed my family, who had moved on to the Dominican Republic. I taught English in Ciudad Trujillo until 1951 when my visa to the United States came through. I came to live in New York, worked at several jobs, and began to write my autobiographical novel, which I called *Other People's Houses* and which was published in the *New Yorker*.

I married my late husband David Segal in 1961.

My children's books were accidents. My mother loved to tell my children,

Lore: *LO reh*

Beatrice and Jacob, about a small character called Rudi, a Victorian kind of child who was always getting into trouble for disobeying the grown-ups. The children loved Rudi, but I created a counter character called Mitzi, whose relationship with the adult world was more tentative, who gets into trouble, too, but not much, and is more likely to get into fantasies, though not very far, and out again. Three of these stories were written down—with great difficulty: it took three years to get them right. They were called *Tell Me a Mitzi*, illustrated by Harriet Pincus, and its sequel, *Tell Me a Trudy*, illustrated by Rosemary Wells, and now being published. I've also written a little joke of a book called *All the Way Home*, and translated some fairy tales illustrated by Maurice Sendak under the title *The Juniper Tree and Other Tales From Grimm*.

———

Lore Segal's autobiographical novel, *Other People's Houses*, created an excited stir when it appeared in the *New Yorker* in 1961. Her account of her experiences as a refugee child in Britain earned its young author the sort of interested attention only dreamed of by many writers with a far greater output. *Other People's Houses* has appeared in a paperback edition and was recently reissued in England in an abridged version—containing only part one—as a book for young people. In 1967 the Michigan University Press published *Gallows Songs*, a translation of Christian Morgenstern's poetry by Lore Segal in collaboration with the poet W. D. Snodgrass.

Tell Me A Mitzi, with illustrations by Harriet Pincus, won the *Book World* Children's Spring Book Festival Award for Picture Books in 1970. It was on the American Library Association's list of Notable Children's Books of 1970 and on the major lists of best and recommended books. In 1973 *The Juniper Tree*, Lore Segal's translation of Grimm fairy tales (which included four translated by Randall Jarrell) was published. Illustrated sumptuously by Maurice Sendak, the book received wide critical notice and immediately established itself as one of the important publishing events of the year. Mrs. Segal is currently at work on another novel. She has also published short stories, translations of poetry and reviews.

From 1963 to 1966 Lore Segal held a Guggenheim Fellowship; from 1967 to 1968 a Grant from the National Council on the Arts and Humanities; and from 1972 to 1973 a grant from the Creative Artists Public Service Program. Since 1969 she has been an adjunct associate professor in the School of Arts at Columbia University, teaching writing and translation.

SELECTED WORKS: Other People's Houses, 1964; Tell Me a Mitzi, 1970; All the Way Home, 1973; The Juniper Tree and Other Tales From Grimm (with Randall Jarrell), 1973; Tell Me a Trudy, 1977.

ABOUT: Contemporary Authors, Vol. 15–16; Something about the Author, Vol. 4; Who's Who in America, 1970–71; Who's Who of American Women, 1971–72.

YASUO SEGAWA
April 5, 1933–

ILLUSTRATOR OF *Taro and the Bamboo Shoot*, etc.

Autobiographical sketch of Yasuo Segawa, translated from the Japanese by Herokuni Sugahara:

I WAS born in the town of Okazaki in central Japan in 1933. I cannot say I have ever in my life known real peace of mind without painting, which is something that came to me entirely naturally.

I still remember distinctly the event that first made me aware of this essential part of my nature. One day, soon after the end of the Second World War, as I was returning from school, I passed a small, shabby-looking house. Looking in, I happened to see what looked like a packet of dried fish wrapped in a newspaper. It took hold of my mind and I was consumed with curiosity about this half-glimpsed apparition. Every day as I walked past I would look into the house and wonder what it meant. At last I summoned the courage to step inside and take a look, and I found that without knowing it I had been looking at a painting. The house was owned by a traditional Japanese-style painter named Keisen Yamamoto. As soon as I reached home I prevailed upon my mother to let me become his pupil.

For the next year I was under the tutelage of Yamamoto. This was, however, the only formal artistic training I ever received.

After becoming Yamamoto's pupil I began to take a serious interest in the work of other painters. And the first artist whose work appealed to me strongly was the nineteenth century French realist Daumier. Captivated by the vision I found in Daumier's works, I began to copy his paintings. I would copy each of them in turn and then use them as a model for my own sketches. When I had been through all the Daumier paintings I could find, I shifted my attention to others in the same tradition—Delacroix,

the masters of the Italian Renaissance, and from there to the Impressionists, and eventually almost anything I came across. From this rigorous exercise of copying I acquired techniques I was able to apply in my drawings and sketches.

For over ten years this regimen of copying and sketching served as my principal artistic discipline. While it was not in itself enough to satisfy my creative instinct, it did serve two distinct and important roles in my artistic development: first, it furnished me with my only source of pleasure during the years of my adolescence and early youth, which were otherwise disturbed by the general postwar disorder, a life of extreme poverty in Tokyo, and years of illness from lung disease; second, it provided me with the medium through which my early tensions were channeled and, as it were, cultivated. It heightened the awareness of various contradictions already in me: the mechanical process of drawing against the desire for self-expression; the restriction to a given set of objectives against the irresistible will to the universal; and my own appetite for western

Yasuo Segawa: *ya SOO o say GA wa*

painting against my keen feelings for traditional Japanese painting.

In the course of this period of self-training my feeling of suppressed tension had been building until it came to the breaking point. I spent long and painful days without being able to undertake anything at all. And so it was with inexpressible joy that I broke through the wall of frustration and realized my own purpose.

At that time I was entirely dependent on my wife for financial support, being incapacitated after a long illness. I was suffering, unable to overcome my inner problems or decide which direction I should take as a painter. I would set out from home in the morning and spend the day visiting the various one-man exhibitions in Tokyo. And every day I used to return in the evening with sore feet, no closer to a solution of my problems. One day when I was bored with going to these exhibitions I went instead to the National Museum. And there I discovered what was to be my inspiration—classical Buddhist painting of the Heian period. Standing before one particular painting, my understanding of its spirit was such that I felt, for the first time in my life, that it was I myself who had painted it. Over a gulf of more than a thousand years it confronted me with blinding power, and it came to me in an instant that lines in sketch are deeply connected with the earth from which they were born and that a single black line can take in every color and all of time and space.

Up to this time I had done some portraits and poster designs and a few illustrations as a means of earning a living, but that occasion could be said to represent the beginning of my career as a painter. My maiden work, Kitsune-No-Yomeiri (The Fox Wedding) appeared in 1960, and the work for which I was awarded the Grand Prize in the 1967 Biennale of Illustrations Bratislava, Fushigi-Na-Takenoko (*Taro and the Bamboo Shoot*), was executed in 1963. For ten years I worked steadily. I produced

ten picture books myself and did illustrations for countless other books. But I learned that even the revelation from my encounter with Buddhist painting did not bring with it a release from my agony of mind. In fact, the more engrossed I became in illustrating the stronger it grew, and by the time I went to Europe to receive the prize in 1969, the feeling was stronger than ever.

This time I found temporary relief through a spate of making lithographs in Zurich; but more important, about this time I came to realize that the anguish I felt simply represented the painful process of casting off an old skin in order to reach a new stage in self-realization. I even began to feel that this continuous cycle of tension growing and receding in me is actually an endless process of rebirth on the road to that final state in which one's work is free from all local limitations and can speak for itself. I am driven to recall the Buddhist idea of karma—meaning predestination or necessity. I cannot say whether it will eventually be granted to me, through this long process of change and development, to reach that state of transcendental lucidity that one finds in an anonymous ancient fresco or in old Buddhist paintings. But I have come to believe that instead of trying to escape from tension in my soul, I must learn to live with it in order to approach closer to true self-realization.

Now I live in the city center of Tokyo with my wife and two children.

Yasuo Segawa was the nominee from Japan for the Hans Christian Andersen Award in 1975.

SELECTED WORKS ILLUSTRATED: Taro and the Bamboo Shoot, by Masako Matsuno, 1964; The Witch's Magic Cloth, by Miyoko Matsutani, 1969; How the Withered Tree Blossomed, by Miyoko Matsutani, 1971.

ABOUT: Bookbird No. 2, 1969.

GEORGE SELDEN
May 14, 1929–

AUTHOR OF *The Cricket in Times Square*, etc.

Autobiographical sketch of George Selden Thompson, who writes as George Selden:

GEORGE SELDEN THOMPSON, really, but I use my first two names because at the time I was starting out there was another writer called George Thompson somewhere in the vicinity.

It is difficult to write about one's self. I would much rather write about small animals—good and bad—small children —good and bad—than about a middle-aging author.

The facts are simply stated. I was born in Hartford, Connecticut, educated at Loomis School and Yale University, and then had the great American experience of a year all over Europe. And I'm afraid that all the clichés are true: mind, eyes and, hopefully, hearts open in the splendor of the old continent. (Mine did anyway. Hopefully.)

Came back to New York and started to write. There had never been any question about that, by the way. I remember as a very small boy a day when I felt compelled to write a story about—Good Lord, I think it was mountaineers! Not that I knew a thing about them, except they had been mentioned in a text we were using in school. I simply was driven to the desk, and have been driven there, again and again, ever since.

The first effort—blessedly out of print —was *The Dog That Could Swim Under Water*: a feeble attempt to do justice to a real live dog, Flossy, who could at least retrieve nice stones and white golf balls from a brook even if she couldn't quite swim under water. After that came *The Garden Under the Sea*— also out of print. (But republished under the name *Oscar Lobster's Fair Exchange* by Harper and Row. And it seems to have found a new life. I'm de-

GEORGE SELDEN

lighted that it's also been taken by a paperback company.) I recount these failures not, Lord knows, to boast, but because, if any unpublished or discouraged children's author reads this, I would like to say, as Noel Coward himself once said to me at a monster literary party where I was the least-known writer, "Press on!"

I pressed on. And with *The Cricket in Times Square* came up with a winner. (Thanks largely to Garth Williams' inhumanly beautiful illustrations. Inhumanly, I mean, because they're of animals.)

Since then, there's been *Tucker's Countryside*—more *Cricket* characters, in a different locale—*The Genie of Sutton Place* and *Harry Cat's Pet Puppy*. (More about my cricket characters! I apologize, but I keep getting letters, asking.)

So far as inspiration goes—present, past, and future—I have only one: *The Lord of the Rings* and *The Hobbit*. Tolkien's work, so unbelievably fine and exciting, is both inspiration and desperation. *No one else* will ever again go that high, that far! However, one goes on failing as best one can.

So I guess that's about all. Only this: I hope I will always be driven to the desk. And to those of you who never had the fun and pleasure of meeting Noel Coward—at least remember his advice!

———

The Cricket in Times Square is well on the way to becoming a classic children's book. It was a Newbery Honor Book in 1961 and an American Library Association Notable Book for Children. It has appeared in paperback and been televised, and finally, in response to requests from children for a sequel, Selden wrote *Tucker's Countryside*. The author's own favorite book, it won a Christopher Award in 1969 and was also included on a number of the selective lists of the best books of the year. *Harry the Cat's Pet Puppy*, a third story about the favorite characters, Chester the cricket, Tucker the mouse, and Harry the Cat, was an American Library Association Notable Book.

After studying English and classical literature at Yale, Selden won a Fulbright scholarship to Italy in 1951–52. Besides reading and writing and people, he is interested in archeology and is extremely fond of music, particularly opera.

SELECTED WORKS: The Cricket in Times Square, 1960; I See What I See!, 1962; The Mice, The Monk, and The Christmas Tree, 1963; Heinrich Schliemann: Discoverer of Buried Treasure, 1964; Sir Arthur Evans, Discoverer of Knossos, 1964; Sparrow Socks, 1965; Oscar Lobster's Fair Exchange, 1966; The Dunkard, 1968; Tucker's Countryside, 1969; The Genie of Sutton Place, 1973; Harry Cat's Pet Puppy, 1974.

ABOUT: Contemporary Authors, Vol. 5–6; Hopkins, Lee Bennett. More Books by More People; Something about the Author, Vol. 4.

ZOA SHERBURNE

September 30, 1912–

AUTHOR OF *Almost April*, etc.

Autobiographical sketch of Zoa Morin Sherburne:

I WAS born in Seattle, Washington, where I have resided for all of my life except for those times when I find myself traveling about the country and, these past few years, various parts of the world.

I was the second of four daughters but for many years I was in the unenviable position of being "the middle one." Being not so old and not so pretty as my elder sister and not so young and adorable as the baby, I soon learned that I had to be something *different* and so I became a writer.

My first memory of being a successful writer was when I was no more than nine or ten years old. My sisters and I were determined to do something BIG for our mother on Mother's Day, so while the other two cleaned the house and made the cake I composed a mother's day poem. I wish I could remember it because it was probably terribly sticky and sentimental, but Mother cried when she read it, and I knew that first sweet smell of success.

In the sixth grade I wrote my first "play," which was subsequently produced by the English class.

After high school the Great Depression was with us and any thoughts of going to college had to be shelved. I went to work and forgot that writing was my big love. I was everything from a waitress to a director of a dance school. But in spite of the Great Depression I had a wonderful time. Eventually I found the man who was to make me very happy for over thirty years. We were married on a shoestring and after a while the depression went away and we settled down to raising a family. And I mean a fam-

Zoa: *ZO a*

Zoa S. Sherburne

ily! We had three daughters . . . then three sons . . . and then, to even things up nicely, another daughter and another son. The children, in order of appearance, are: Marie Antoinette, Norene Yvonne, Zoey May, Herbert Junior, Thomas Morin, Philip Gerard, Alice Delores, and Robert.

Somewhere between Herb Junior and Thomas I found myself returning to my writing. I had always written small bits of nonsense verse about my children but one lucky day I turned on the radio (this was before TV) and heard about a national contest that seemed to fit me like a glove. So I sat down in the midst of all my unfinished housework and dashed off "twenty-five words or less" in the shape of a poem.

With the prize money I returned to school—a writer's class, and for four months I absorbed everything I could about the writing craft.

Five months after enrollment I sold my first short story. The sales continued, slowly at first, but I never stopped writing—mostly because my husband was so proud of my efforts and encouraged me in every way possible. (Even to taking

the children on long rides so I could have a quiet house.)

When the short story market started to skid (TV, you know!) my agent and one of my favorite editors, Bryna Ivens of *Seventeen* magazine, suggested that I turn my efforts to books for teen-agers, and that is where I have remained ever since.

My own teen-agers are mostly married and gone. My son Robert is the only one home now, but I still write for this age group because this really is the most fascinating age in the world.

Problem stories, present-day problems that affect the youth of our day, have always been the backbone of my books. Recently I wrote about a girl who is an epileptic in *Why Have the Birds Stopped Singing?* I have used such far-out topics as drug addiction, alcoholism, mental health and ESP. But I have also written about love and warmth and family feeling. If the problems are the backbone, then the family has to be the skin and flesh covering the bones.

Once in a while I get a letter from a new fan and she says something like "I really loved your book . . . I cried and cried. . . ." And once more I know the sweet smell of success.

Zoa Sherburne received the Child Study Association Children's Book Award in 1959 for *Jennifer*, a story about a young girl whose mother is an alcoholic.

SELECTED WORKS: Almost April, 1956; Jennifer, 1959; Stranger in the House, 1963; Girl in the Mirror, 1966; Too Bad About the Haines Girl, 1967; The Girl Who Knew Tomorrow, 1970; Leslie, 1972; Why Have the Birds Stopped Singing?, 1974.

ABOUT: Contemporary Authors, Vol. 3; Foremost Women in Communications; Something about the Author, Vol. 3; Who's Who of American Women, 1971–72.

PAUL SHOWERS

April 12, 1910–

AUTHOR OF *Find Out by Touching*, etc.

Autobiographical sketch of Paul C. Showers:

I AM a retired newspaperman. There is no place I could really call my hometown. I was born in the Yakima valley of Washington, and my parents returned to their native Michigan when I was three and settled in Muskegon. Then we moved to a suburb of Chicago and then to Rochester, New York. After a year in the junior college at Grand Rapids, Michigan, I transferred to the University of Michigan at Ann Arbor, where I graduated in 1931 with an A.B. For most of the depression I shuttled between Grand Rapids, New York, Chicago and Detroit, free-lancing and collecting more rejection slips than checks, acting and doing publicity with a series of short-lived stock companies, constructing out-size crossword puzzles for the old humor magazine *Life* (until Time, Inc., bought it). In 1937 I got a job with the Detroit *Free Press* and in 1940 switched to the New York *Herald-Tribune*. During World War II, fourteen of my forty-four months as an enlisted man were spent at an air base in west Texas, the rest of the time on the staff of *Yank*, the army magazine. In 1946 I joined the New York *Times* Sunday Department where I worked as an editor in the travel section and later the Magazine until 1976, when I retired on July 4. Now that I can devote full time to writing, I am working on books for adult readers as well as children. I am divorced and have two children, a daughter and a son.

Most of my children's books have been nonfiction for beginning readers. I tried my first one at an editor's invitation and promptly discovered that there is more to a good primer than meets the eye. I had watched my own children struggling to learn reading from some monumentally dull books. I think learning to read should be as enjoyable as learning to swim or ride a bicycle. But as I worked I recalled some of the difficulties I had with my first readers back in Muskegon. There was, for example, the story of Mr. Lock digging for clams at the seashore. As a freshwater Midwesterner, I had never seen a clam that had to be dug for, nor, at six, did I know anybody with the same name as the thing a key fitted into. And Mr. Lock was clearly not the same kind of person like Mr. Squirrel, about whom we sang our little song. It was distracting.

Books for beginners, who are just learning to find meaning in unfamiliar patterns of letters and words, are an interesting problem to a writer. The vocabulary should be largely familiar, with dependent clauses used sparingly (they have to be kept in mind while the main clause is being unraveled, or vice versa). Simple sentences but not simple ideas. A beginning reader is far more sophisticated than the text he is capable of handling. His book should be easy to read but it should not be dull. Sometimes when I get tired of constructing simple sentences, I lapse into doggerel verse to keep things moving.

When working on a primer I like to spend time talking to young children. In the suburbs a rope swing used to hang in our garden. When young neighbors came to try it out and I happened to be gardening, our conversations came naturally and easily. Now in my city apartment I keep a cookie jar and candy jar well stocked. At the typewriter I test my sentences with: "Would I say it this way to Jock? . . . Would this make Kate laugh? . . . How would Garry say this?"

SELECTED WORKS: Find Out by Touching, 1961; Look at Your Eyes, 1962; Follow Your Nose, 1963; Your Skin and Mine, 1965; Before You Were a Baby (with Kay Showers), 1968; A Baby Starts to Grow, 1969; What Happens to a Hamburger, 1970; Use Your Brain, 1971; Sleep Is for Everyone, 1974; Where Does the Garbage Go?, 1974; The Moon Walker, 1975; A Book of Scary Things, 1977.

ABOUT: Contemporary Authors, Vol. 1.

HILDA SIMON

November 22, 1921–

AUTHOR AND ILLUSTRATOR OF *Exploring the World of Social Insects*, etc.

Autobiographical sketch of Hilda Rita Simon:

BORN in Santa Ana, California, Hilda Simon had an enjoyable early childhood. The region's wealth of animal life was readymade for a child with a love of nature inherited from her German-English forebears and encouraged by her brilliant and many-talented father. She eagerly began to draw the animals she observed and captured in the garden almost as soon as she was able to hold and use a pencil.

In the late twenties, the family's extended trip to Europe to visit relatives became a more or less permanent stay when the stockmarket crash of 1929 wiped out the tool-manufacturing plant Miss Simon's father had built up in partnership with a friend. Stranded in Germany and plagued by the recurrence of an old respiratory ailment, Mr. Simon managed to support his family by writing and translating scientific and technical material for the famed Zeiss Optical Works in Jena. Young Hilda, who, like her older sister, had grown up bilingual, went to school in Jena. As the Hitler regime consolidated its power, attending classes became an unpleasant ordeal for the American girl, whose family was adamantly opposed to everything the Nazis stood for. When war came, the Simons faced difficult times with the breadwinner gravely ill and the political climate increasingly hostile. Despite the fact that she was at the top of her class, Miss Simon left school two years before graduation because she objected to the politicization of the curriculum. Instead, having perfected a special pastel technique—initially only as a hobby—based upon her studies of eighteenth century French painters, she helped support her family by doing portraits of friends and acquaintances. During those years she also attended lectures at the University of Jena as an unofficial guest student, her main fields of interest being biology and languages.

When troops of the famed American Eighth Army entered Jena in 1945, they were surprised and delighted to find an American family in the heart of Germany. In subsequent days, the Simons welcomed in their home any and all American military personnel from colonel to private. The family's return to the United States was somewhat delayed by the precipitous, overnight transfer of that German region to the Soviets, a transfer that, among other things, cost the Simons the rest of their property.

Having returned to this country, Hilda Simon was faced with the necessity of earning enough to support her family as well as help friends in Europe through the hunger and misery of the postwar years. Having decided that she could best combine her artistic talents and her interest in animals by writing and illustrating nature books, she looked for a job that could further her ambition, and accepted a position as the head of the art department of the Hart Publishing Company in New York. While there, she acquired a great deal of technical know-how and began to develop a special technique for doing fine illustrations that had a halftone look. Her first book illustrated in that fashion was *Exploring the World of Social Insects*. It was chosen as an outstanding book of the year by the New York *Times*, and received high praise from various expert sources.

A few years later, Miss Simon gave up her job and devoted all her time to writing and illustrating, having perfected her technique of doing full-color artwork by hand-drawn separations. These can be reproduced easily, permitting the artist full color-control while substantially reducing printing costs.

Between 1963 and 1976, Miss Simon wrote and illustrated some fifteen books, most of them juveniles. Her *Insect Masquerades* was an American Library Association Notable Book in 1968 and was designated one of the best books of the year by *School Library Journal*. Various others have received awards and commendations by the National Science Teachers' Association, the Children's Book Council, and review media. Although she writes many adult books—her *Splendor of Iridescence* was a Book-of-the-Month Club Special Selection in 1972—she plans to continue writing for young people as well because she sees this as the best way of passing on some of the love, understanding and concern for animals her father fostered in her. Among Miss Simon's present and future projects are a book on the courtship of birds; a history of the datepalm, the "bread of the desert"; and one about animal patterns and their influence on art and culture. Also in the future are plans for biographies of Frederick the Great and the German poet Friedrich Schiller.

Hilda Simon lives and works in her home in New Paltz, New York, where she observes and keeps as pets many specimens of the small wildlife described in her books.

SELECTED WORKS WRITTEN AND ILLUSTRATED: Exploring the World of Social Insects, 1963; Wonders of Hummingbirds, 1964; Insect Masquerades, 1968; Feathers, Plain and Fancy, 1969; Milkweed and Butterflies; Monarchs, Models and Mimics, 1969; Partners, Guests and Parasites: Co-existence in Nature, 1970; Living Lanterns: Luminescence in Animals, 1971; Dragonflies, 1972; Chameleons and Other Quick Change Artists, 1973; Snakes: The Facts and the Folklore, 1973; Frogs and Toads of the World, 1975; Snails of Land and Sea, 1976.

ABOUT: Kingman, Lee and others, comps. Illustrators of Children's Books; 1957–1966.

DONALD J. SOBOL

October 4, 1924–

AUTHOR OF *Encyclopedia Brown, Boy Detective*, etc.

Autobiographical sketch of Donald J. Sobol:

MY mother told me I was born in New York City on October 4, 1924, and I believe her. There may be shinier towns, but none to me is more exciting, and besides, four is my lucky number. My father was a self-made man in the rags-to-riches tradition who once paid me a compliment. I worshiped him.

Before a stint in World War II, I had aspirations to be a tenor, a sculptor, a baseball player. But I discovered that I was tone deaf, that sculptors walked uptown for hot water, and that I couldn't hit a retired major-leaguer's inside curve ball to save my skin.

I was educated at Fieldston School in New York City, where everyone had goals, and at Oberlin College in Ohio, where everyone had chosen a profession by the end of the sophomore year. Such willful self-restrictions astounded me. I craved a life free of repetition and boredom and not a career that spread out ahead of me like a game of dominoes already completed. Writing seemed the proper vehicle to take me where I wanted to go in my years. Everywhere.

Professor Ralph Singleton of the Oberlin English Department encouraged me, and his blue pencil transformed my short story assignments into sales. During the next eight years I wrote under pen names for pulp and slick magazines. Since they never paid me quite enough, I worked as a newsman with the New York *Sun* and the Long Island *Daily Press* and later as a merchant at R.H. Macy's.

At the age of thirty I quit being a jobholder and set myself up as a free-lance writer, though I was told that, lacking experience, insights and a reliable typewriter, I was railroading myself into poverty. My good sense in marrying Rose Tiplitz, an engineer, helped me to survive the shaky years, during which I toiled a hundred hours a week and was partially responsible for four wonderful children: Diane, Glenn, Eric and John.

In 1961 we piled into a station wagon and, pulling a rented trailer filled with books and bikes, drove to Florida for the winter. We have been here ever since. Besides enjoying the outdoors—boating, fishing, tennis, camping—we have traveled together throughout the United States and Europe.

I have written about forty books for young readers. Many have appeared in foreign countries—Denmark, England, Finland, France, Germany, Israel, Japan and Spain—and a few have won prizes. Plot governs in all my work, and I strive to entertain from the first paragraph to the last. My only theme is brotherhood.

———

Donald Sobol married Rose Tiplitz in 1955. His first book for children, *The Double Quest*, appeared in 1957. In the 1960s he wrote the nationally syndicated newspaper feature "Two Minute Mystery Series." Mr. Sobol believes that the function of the author of juvenile stories is to entertain children and that dedication to this purpose frequently incurs the displeasure of editors and reviewers. To illustrate, he points out that his first book about Encyclopedia Brown was rejected by twenty-six publishers before it was finally accepted and published with only two added paragraphs in the opening chapter. The first book and its numerous successors have proven extremely popular, and several have appeared in book club paperback editions. In 1972 *Encyclopedia Brown Keeps the Peace* was given the Pacific Northwest Library Association Young Reader's Choice Award, for which children in grades four to eight vote for their favorite book. *Encyclopedia Brown Takes the Case* was voted the favorite book of the Aiken County (S.C.) schoolchildren and so received the 1976 Aiken County Children's Book Award.

SELECTED WORKS: The Double Quest, 1957; The First Book of Medieval Man, 1959; The Wright Brothers at Kitty Hawk, 1961; Encyclopedia Brown, Boy Detective, 1963; Encyclopedia Brown and the Case of the Secret Pitch, 1965; Secret Agents Four, 1967; Encyclopedia Brown Keeps the Peace, 1969; The Amazons of Greek Mythology, 1972; Encyclopedia Brown Takes the Case, 1973; Encyclopedia Brown Lends a Hand, 1974; True Sea Adventures, 1975; Encyclopedia Brown and the Case of the Midnight Visitor, 1977.

ABOUT: Contemporary Authors, Vol. 1; Something about the Author, Vol. 1.

JIM SPANFELLER
October 27, 1930–

ILLUSTRATOR OF *Where the Lilies Bloom,* etc.

Autobiographical sketch of James John Spanfeller, who works as Jim Spanfeller:

MY background is all Philadelphia. I was born, raised and educated there. I attended La Salle College High School and from there went to the Philadelphia College of Art, and after service in the U.S. Army I spent a year painting at the Pennsylvania Academy of Fine Art. My family and my wife's family all still live in the Philadelphia area. I was married to Patricia Durkin in 1953. We have a son, Jim Jr., a writer, with whom I have just collaborated on a book. We live in Katonah, New York, a small Westchester town north of New York City.

Since illustration is a communication art it is therefore subject to the requirements of marketing problem-solving whether for magazines, advertising or books.

The children's book field is totally dominated by the taste and demands of the librarians and institutions which apparently accounts for such a low aesthetic level in an area which should be the most exciting. Juvenile publishers seem to be completely intimidated by this group. I believe that nothing new and innovative will happen in children's books in this country until this pattern changes.

———

Jim Spanfeller says he was interested in drawing and writing stories from about the fourth grade on but he had no formal training until he entered the Philadelphia Museum School of Art. At first he found the lack of art background a disadvantage, but he has come to feel it was a good thing. "When it comes to art," he says, "overtraining is worse than undertraining."

Spanfeller defines art as "work with a human value, work that says something personal," and he feels that magazine illustration allows an artist much more scope for personal expression. His own work tends to be satirical, although a casual observer may not be quick to perceive it because of his elaborately decorative style. As one critic said, "Even in the most straightforward of his drawings [he] finds room for critical social comment and for exposing what he calls 'the nonsense patterns of modern society.'"

Spanfeller values the opinion of his colleagues and takes great pleasure in having been named Artist of the Year by the Artists Guild of New York in 1964 and in regularly being chosen to exhibit in the Society of Illustrators' Shows. He held a one-man show at the Society of Illustrators in 1965, and his work was included in the 1967–68 Children's Book Show of the American Institute of Graphic Arts.

SELECTED WORKS ILLUSTRATED: The Summer Birds, by Penelope Farmer, 1962; Indian Hill, by Clyde R. Bulla, 1963; O-Sono and the Magician's Nephew and the Elephant, by Henry Morgan, 1964; Dorp Dead, by Julia Cunningham, 1965; Emma in Winter, by Penelope Farmer, 1966; Pink

Puppy, by Flora M. Wood, 1966; Where the Lilies Bloom, by Vera and Bill Cleaver, 1966; God Loves You, by Catherine Marshall, 1967; The Plug at the Bottom of the Sea, by Robert Lamb, 1968; A Tune Beyond Us, edited by Myra Cohn Livingston, 1968; The Malibu and Other Poems, by Myra Cohn Livingston, 1972; 4 Way Stop and Other Poems, by Myra Cohn Livingston, 1976; Doug Meets the Nutcracker, by William Hooks, 1977.

ABOUT: Kingman, Lee and others, comps. Illustrators of Children's Books, 1957–1966; Who's Who in America, 1970–71; Print March 1965.

JOHN STEPTOE

September 14, 1950–

AUTHOR AND ILLUSTRATOR OF *Stevie*, etc.

Autobiographical sketch of John Lewis Steptoe:

I BEGAN living my life in a place where body movement, basketball and big legs were life's greater joys. Where slick talk, slick clothes, a way with women, and the usual sight of cadillacs parked at the curb in a tacky neighborhood were more typical than to sit around the house all day and paint or draw, which caused me to seem rather peculiar. But aside from my desires being atypical to this environment, I was and still am very much in love with this isolated culture I was born from.

I lived in the Bedford-Stuyvesant section of Brooklyn. Born in St. John's hospital and lived at 840 Monroe Street till I was about sixteen. I went to the High School of Art and Design in Manhattan, but just before completion of the twelfth year (three months) I quit, moved off the block, and learned to hitchhike. I found my way to Camden, New Jersey, where I stayed for a few months, and then moved back to New York, where I divided myself between living in Manhattan (125th Street) and Brooklyn, between exploring the society at large and developing my knowledge of the streets. The greater, though less apparent, difference between the two worlds was, in simplistic terms, one world that devoted all too much time to diabolical mind plays and the other (my home world) devoted to a sort of blissful mindless dance. The society's devotion to the mind, and the inner city's devotion to the body left it to me to reside in near seclusion in a town called Peterboro, in New Hampshire, where I'm presently finding a happy medium of devotion to both mind and body.

My career in children's books began just after I had gotten back from Camden. I had idealistically walked out on Madison Avenue as if, just because I might deserve one, I was gonna get a job. Surprisingly enough I did get one. I had gotten some names of some people to see at *Harper's* magazine from a high school teacher, Burmah Burris. As it turned out, none of the people whose names I had worked there anymore. But I did have some things that might work in a children's book in my portfolio, so I went to the children's book department, where I met Ursula Nordstrom, editor-in-chief at Harper Junior Books. She suggested that in addition to illustrating a children's book, I might also write one. By the time I was nineteen my first book, *Stevie*, was published. Within the next two years (70–71) I did *Uptown* and *Train Ride* at Harper's and then *Birthday* at Holt, Rinehart and Winston. In 1970 Bweela, my daughter, was born and then in 1971 Javaka, my son. *My Special Best Words*, published in 1974 with Viking Press, is a story about our relationship in home life.

I've always considered myself to be primarily a painter. *Stevie* was my first literary adventure. One of my incentives for getting into writing children's books was the great and disastrous need for books that black children could honestly relate to. I ignorantly created precedents by writing such a book. I was amazed to find out that no one had successfully written a book in the dialogue which black children speak. So what is important here is not so much how I did it (referring to my environmental background), but the fact that I did do it. The fact that it can be done and that there is an audience of children who are very much a part of this society but who go on relatively neglected as far as literature written for and about them in their language. It's much more than just filling a vacuum though. Black children, all children need good books. Good books are more than a luxury; they are a necessary part of a child's development and it's all of our jobs to see that we all get them.

———

The publication of *Stevie* brought instant recognition to John Steptoe and earned him a gold medal from the Society of Illustrators. The book was chosen a Notable Book by the American Library Association and appeared on a number of lists of the best books of the year, including *School Library Journal* and *Publishers Weekly*. *Train Ride* was on *Horn Book* magazine's 1972 Fanfare list, and was among the New York *Times*'s outstanding books of 1971. *The Birthday* was included in the 1971–72 Children's Book Show mounted by the American Institute of Graphic Arts,

which selected the book as one of twenty American entries to the Biennale of Illustrations, Bratislava, 1973. In 1975, Steptoe shared the Irma Simonton Black Award with author Eloise Greenfield for *She Come Bringing Me That Little Baby Girl*. The award is given by the Bank Street College of Education for an outstanding book for young children combining excellence of text and graphics. The same book was an Honor Book in the competition for the 1975 Boston *Globe-Horn Book* Award for Illustration.

SELECTED WORKS WRITTEN AND ILLUSTRATED: Stevie, 1969; Uptown, 1970; Train Ride, 1971; Birthday, 1972; My Special Best Words, 1974; Marcia, 1976.

SELECTED WORKS ILLUSTRATED: All Us Come Cross the Water, by Lucille Clifton, 1973; She Come Bringing Me That Little Baby Girl, by Eloise Greenfield, 1974.

ABOUT: Contemporary Authors, Vol. 49–52; Something about the Author, Vol. 8; Illustrators XII, 1971; Life August 29, 1969.

SANDOL STODDARD

December 16, 1927–

AUTHOR OF *Growing Time*, etc.

Autobiographical sketch of Sandol Stoddard Warburg:

MY own childhood was spent in a situation divided between two dramatically contrasting cultures—the solemn and lonely, self-conscious world of provincial New England, and the delightfully warm, easygoing atmosphere of an old fashioned home in Birmingham, Alabama. My first attempts to write at a very early age were almost certainly a form of protest against the tensions between the two worlds and a way of creating a world of my own in which nothing could be disrupted. A high-pressure, fiercely academic education in the years that followed taught me many useful litterary and critical skills, but kept me

nervously exhausted and far too constricted, I now feel, under a sort of protective glass, bound to "succeed" in
conventional terms, yet increasingly separated from the sources of my creativity.
The real crunch for females of my particular sort in the 1940s was finally, that
one was supposed to emerge from college terribly well-polished and yet not
to take up any career—not, above all, to
take any risks that might interfere with
one's real duty to marry well and bring
up children properly within the dictates
of the social establishment, north or
south.

Having made up my mind by the time
I was a senior at Bryn Mawr at the age of
nineteen that I was a writer, I left college, married outside the establishment
and moved west. Since that time I have
raised four sons (each of them quite different from the other and from me, and
all free spirits), have continued to write
and to study in my own way at my own
pace, and have survived the struggles involved in countering the systems of my
upbringing. I've been rich and poor, divorced, alone, remarried, homebound
and homeless—finally to realize, now that
I am beginning (in 1977) to publish
both fiction and nonfiction, for adults as

well as for children, that this has all been
a necessary preparation for the works of
my maturity, and a part of the pilgrimage of any dedicated writer.

My early books were, I think, an attempt to get down to the very simplest,
barest bones of things. The presence of
many small children in my life was a
challenge to me to formulate and share
with them the things I knew for certain
to be true and of real value. At the same
time my children helped to free the creative child in me—to introduce me to the
joyous energy within. I am fond of my
early books now, rather as if some interesting younger sister had written
them. But my book *On the Way Home*
is for me what the title implies—the beginning of my fully realized and fully
conscious pilgrimage.

I have been fortunate along the way
in finding the teachers I needed, both in
books (Spenser, Austen, Lewis, George
McDonald, Margaret Wise Brown) and
in person (Lawrence Stapleton of Bryn
Mawr, Matthew Evans and Leonard
Wolf of San Francisco State). And I
have been blessed over the years by
friendships with extraordinary men and
women who have nourished me beyond
measure. These are what seem to me at
present the most important facts and
events of my life. And I hope I may
cheer some fellow pilgrim by mentioning
here that, as a writer and a person glad
to be a woman, I have found whatever
"success" I may have achieved in the
long run to have been far less valuable
to me than what is usually termed "failure." The breaking of the safety glass is
the crucial issue. If I may be pardoned
for quoting my own book, "We who seek
make a journey of mystery together,
though there are times when we may not
touch hands; for those of us who dare,
alone and in the dark, to move forward
on the path toward truth have begun
already, in our various and separate
ways, the long journey home."

———

Sandol Stoddard Warburg's adaptation of Spenser's *Saint George and the*

Dragon was an American Library Association Notable Book in 1963. Both *The Thinking Book* and *Growing Time* were selected as outstanding books in the year of their publication by the New York *Times*. *Free*, with illustrations of Jenni Oliver, was included in the 1977 Children's Book Showcase.

Sandol Stoddard Warburg has four sons by her marriage (to Felix M. Warburg), Anthony, Peter, Gerald, and Jason.

SELECTED WORKS: The Thinking Book, 1960; Saint George and the Dragon, by Edmund Spenser (adapted), 1963; Curl Up Small, 1964; I Like You, 1965; From Ambledee to Zumbledee, 1968; Growing Time, 1969; Hooray for Us, 1970; On the Way Home, 1973; (as Sandol Stoddard) Free, 1976.

ABOUT: Contemporary Authors, Vol. 7–8; Hopkins, Lee Bennett. Books Are by People.

KATHRYN SWARTHOUT

January 8, 1919–

and

GLENDON SWARTHOUT

April 8, 1918–

AUTHORS OF *Whichaway*, etc.

Biographical sketch of Glendon Fred Swarthout and Kathryn Blair Swarthout by Kathryn Swarthout:

WE wrote our first book for children when we were forty and afraid. One sunny, significant morning we stared at each other. What we had feared had come to pass. We were adults, frighteningly and finally. And when that happens, one of the best antidotes is to write a book for the children you once were. We wanted to tell them a story, and in the telling, to find if they were lost forever or if they still resided in the brittling houses of ourselves. If we told the story well, these children would listen. And if they listened, they lived.

Writing it, we discovered, was a healthy experience, for to write a book for children is to take off some of your

creative fat. You have to confront the fundamentals of fiction—story and character and setting. You go to school again and learn how much you've forgotten. Children turn up their noses at reviews and promotion and best seller lists. They make you work. They force you to find out what fiction can and should be and, even more important, to honor it.

We have published five. It has been a collaboration of great joy. For two of them, *The Ghost and the Magic Saber* and *The Button Boat*, we rummaged the attics of our childhoods, both of which were spent in Michigan. A third, *Whichaway*, was made of the distances and silences and history of Arizona, which has been our home for fourteen years. *TV Thompson*, all fantasy and folderol, we conceived and outlined aboard a ship outbound for the South Pacific. And the last, *Whales to See The*, addressed itself to the specific problem of learning disabilities.

Having been an elementary teacher, I fret principally about our readers, those "middle-aged" youngsters of ten to fourteen who I suspect have been too often overlooked by writers. What will the story say *to* them? What will it do *for* them? My chief concern is its ultimate effect. My husband's is that of the novelist; material and method—theme, structure, style, pace—the imposition of order upon the chaos that is life. Together we talk our books into existence, then write and rewrite until, at the end, they resemble our marriage, built of bone and spirit and indivisible of authorship.

We believe that books for children are as crucial as books for adults, if not more so. We write them because we want very much to, and not often, and to them we bring stout hearts and trembling portables. We try to persuade our readers to love the English language. And finally, where we are indomitably old-fashioned, we attempt to invent a story which excites and engrosses.

We hope to write more books together. But only if we find stories to tell ourselves, and children within us to listen.

———

Kathryn Blair Swarthout was born in Columbus, Montana, attended Ward-Belmont (1937–38), the University of Michigan (A.B. 1940), and Michigan State University (M.A. 1956). She was married to Glendon Swarthout on December 28, 1940. They have a son, Miles Hood.

Glendon Swarthout was born in Pinckney, Michigan, attended the University of Michigan (A.B. 1939, A.M. 1946) and Michigan State University (Ph.D. 1955). He served as a sergeant in World War II with the Third Infantry Division. He has taught at the Universities of Michigan, Maryland, Michigan State and Arizona State and has published ten novels. His awards include the Theatre Guild Award in Playwriting, 1947, the Hopwood Award in Fiction, 1948, and selection for O. Henry Prize Short Stories in 1969. *The Shootist* won a Golden Spur Award from the Western Writers of America, Inc. for the best Western novel published in 1975.

SELECTED WORKS WRITTEN BY GLENDON SWARTHOUT: Bless the Beasts and Children, 1970; The Tin Lizzie Troop, 1972; Luck and Pluck, 1973; The Shootist, 1975; The Melodeon, 1977.

SELECTED WORKS WRITTEN BY GLENDON AND KATHRYN SWARTHOUT: The Ghost and the Magic Saber, 1963; Whichaway, 1966; The Button Boat, 1969; TV Thompson, 1972; Whales to See the, 1975.

ABOUT GLENDON SWARTHOUT: Contemporary Authors, Vol. 3.

ABOUT KATHRYN SWARTHOUT: Contemporary Authors, Vol. 41–44; Something about the Author, Vol. 7.

THEODORE TAYLOR

June 23, 1921–

AUTHOR OF *The Cay*, etc.

Autobiographical sketch of Theodore Taylor:

I WAS born in Statesville, North Carolina, a cotton-mill town in the red clay country of the Piedmont. Childhood was rather poor in the material way but so rich in fields and streams; freedom to roam, explore. I found great pleasures on the muddy Catawba; in the creeks and woods.

Books became a part of my life very early and an extension of "pretend" adventures. Sometimes five would go home with me from the public library. They were, almost solidly, adventure tales.

My father was an ironworker, Irish-American. My mother, German-American, was a unique lady, so unlike him. Though frail, she had a tremendous zest for life; was creative. Her bent was drama in her teens, and she'd wanted to go on the stage. I remember many kitchen recitals.

My four sisters were older and were of great influence, connection with a world outside mine. One was living in London; another in New York; another was a schoolteacher in the Carolina foothills. Youngest, Mary, was at home but seemed so sophisticated. She introduced me to Hemingway when I was about eleven. It was a heady experience. She had discovered him and was collecting everything he wrote.

I began writing, painfully, at age thir-

teen, working for the Portsmouth, Virginia, *Star*, reporting high school events. We'd moved there a year earlier. I have never really stopped writing since.

Along the way, I was a copyboy for the Washington *Daily News*, running copy for a man who became a considerable writer, Robert Ruark. I got mixed up in boxing, became a ring second, and then a prizefight manager. Wrote sports copy for Bill Stern at NBC (radio); went off to war in the merchant marine, then in the U.S. Navy. Volunteered for the Bikini atom bomb project just to see the thing go off.

I worked for a newspaper in Florida, then one in the West Virginia coalfields; some public relations work in New York —doing magazine fact and fiction at night. The navy again during the Korean War, and after it, press agentry and finally production work in Hollywood.

Meanwhile, my first book (adult) came along in 1954, *The Magnificent Mitscher*, a biography. *Fire on the Beaches*, also adult, was published in 1957.

Since then, I've been combining books with film work, mostly pictures made overseas. They have afforded the chance to travel while working, Taiwan to Athens, Juneau to Stockholm. Obviously, the backgrounds offer story material.

My first book for young readers was the result of movie work, *People Who Make Movies*. The attempted goal each year is one book for young readers, one for adults and a movie project of some type.

I find it hard to write about what I have not seen or, in some way, experienced. So I am always ready, anxious and willing—at the sound of a jet engine turning on or the blast of a ship's whistle —to go.

By far the best known and, it turned out, the most controversial of Theodore Taylor's children's books is *The Cay*, the story of a prejudiced white boy saved from drowning by a black West Indian sailor, with whom he is afloat on a raft for some days, and in the course of their time together, the boy's attitudes begin to change. The book was hailed by many as a contribution to better racial understanding and received a number of awards and citations, among them the silver medal of the Commonwealth Club of California in 1969 and the Jane Addams Children's Book Award in 1970, which is given for the book that "best combines literary merit and stresses the dignity and equality of all mankind, peace, and social justice." In addition *The Cay* was an American Library Association Notable Book, was on all the major critics' lists of best books, and was made into a film for television. But while there was high praise in many quarters, there was also strong criticism from others. Some black groups felt that because Taylor had presented the black man from the point of view of the white boy, he was reinforcing racist attitudes, and they did not feel that the boy's attitudes were shown to change enough to keep them from considering *The Cay* "racist." In 1975 the then head of the Jane Addams Children's Book Award Committee stated publicly that she felt the award in 1970 had been "a mistake."

Taylor promptly returned his Award to the Jane Addams Peace and Freedom Association. In a long letter to the editors of the American Library Association's *Top of the News* he explained that he had not intended to be racist, was not sure he had in fact been, that what he'd intended had been a "plea for better race relations and more understanding."

SELECTED WORKS: People Who Make Movies, 1967; The Cay, 1969; Air Raid—Pearl Harbor! The Story of December 7, 1941, 1971; The Children's War, 1971; Meldonado Miracle, 1973; Teetoncey, 1974; Teetoncey and Ben O'Neal, 1975; Battle in the Arctic Seas, 1976; The Odyssey of Ben O'Neal, 1977.

ABOUT: Contemporary Authors, Vol. 21–22; Something about the Author, Vol. 5; Top of the News November 1971; April 1975.

KAY THOMPSON

KAY THOMPSON

1912–

AUTHOR OF *Eloise*, etc.

Biographical sketch of Kay Thompson:

SINGER, songwriter, song-arranger, actress, choreographer—the ebullient Kay Thompson has been all of these things, but to succeeding generations of delighted children (and their parents) she is best remembered as the begetter of the inimitable Eloise, terror of the Plaza Hotel in New York.

Born in St. Louis in 1912, Kay Thompson started playing the piano at the age of four and at fifteen made a precocious appearance with the St. Louis Symphony, playing Liszt. At seventeen, she says, "I was a stagestruck kid and I got out of St. Louis fast." She went to California to teach diving, but soon made her debut on the radio, first singing with the Mills Brothers and then later acting as both singer and arranger with Fred Waring.

Miss Thompson then went on to produce her own radio program on the CBS network, "Kay Thompson and Company." Of this, she says candidly, "We didn't, any of us, know *what* we were doing. But despite the fact that we were an instantaneous flop, we all learned a lot from it. It was my first chance at coordinating a whole project, and it enthralled me. After the show, I came to a serious decision. I had to be an actress and I had to be alone. So I went to Hollywood, where I was neither."

During Kay Thompson's spell in Hollywood, she worked with MGM choreographer Robert Alton on such films as *The Ziegfeld Follies*, *The Harvey Girls*, and *The Kid from Brooklyn*. The movie life did not satisfy her, however, and in 1946 she left to put together a very successful nightclub act. The show—"the greatest that ever hit humanity," she has described it—consisted of sophisticated songs in which she was backed by a team of four dancing, singing, clowning young men, the Williams Brothers (Richard, Robert, Donald, and Andy, who is now famous in his own right). The effect of this act, remarked one reviewer, "was a combination of ballet, barber shop, roughhouse and penthouse that never for a moment got out of hand, but always seemed as if it might."

After the act was disbanded in 1953, Kay Thompson's next theatrical success was her one-woman show which opened in January 1954 at the New York Hotel Plaza—a most significant location, for it was here, in 1955, that Eloise was truly born, as far as a wider public was concerned, when Kay Thompson met her ideal Eloise-illustrator in the person of Hilary Knight. "Hilary and I had immediate understanding," she says. "Eloise was a little girl who lived at the Plaza, and she was a very special kind of little girl. We wrote, edited, laughed, outlined, cut, pasted, laughed again, read out loud, laughed and suddenly we had a book." *Eloise*, the first book in the series of five that was to follow, was published by Simon and Schuster in November 1955. It was an instant and loudly hailed success.

The character of Eloise is that of an appealingly awful six-year-old of mind-boggling precocity, the essence of impudence in transit to adulthood. Eloise had been, for a long time, an inside running joke between Kay Thompson and her friends. She had been conceived one day when Miss Thompson had been bawled out for being late to a rehearsal and asked who she thought she was. She replied in a high, squeaky voice, "I'm Eloise, and I'm six."

The Plaza has never quite recovered from the Eloise onslaught; the management was very enthusiastic about the whole idea; for years, Hilary Knight's portrait of the atrocious little girl was displayed in the hotel in a place of honor. Eloise became a whole industry—a flood of Eloisiana, including dolls, records, toys, luggage, clothes and cards became available to her avid fans in the mid-fifties. That first book was followed by *Eloise in Paris*, *Eloise at Christmastime*, *Eloise in Moscow* and *Eloise in the Bawth*.

After *Eloise* and her nightclub act, Kay Thompson went on to movie roles, the most famous of which was her appearance in *Funny Face* with Fred Astaire and Audrey Hepburn.

Single since her second marriage ended in 1947, Kay Thompson now alternates between Rome and New York, where she has not deserted the Plaza. Children have not deserted Miss Thompson's creation either. Originally intended as adult entertainment, Eloise is now firmly entrenched in the galaxy of children's favorite storybook characters.

SELECTED WORKS: Eloise, 1955; Eloise in Paris, 1957; Eloise at Christmastime, 1958; Eloise in Moscow, 1959; Eloise in the Bawth, 1964.

ABOUT: Current Biography, 1969; Who's Who in America, 1970–71; Who's Who of American Women, 1974–75; Harper's Bazaar November 1972; Harper's Magazine July 1948; Life January 26, 1948; McCall's January 1957; Publishers Weekly December 16, 1957; May 12, 1969; Time November 10, 1947.

JOHN ROWE TOWNSEND
May 10, 1922–

AUTHOR OF *Trouble in the Jungle*, etc.

Autobiographical sketch of John Rowe Townsend:

MY first book was written when I was eight years old. It was in five penny-notebooks (you could get penny notebooks in those preinflation days) and was about a family of twelve children: a remarkable family, because they were all aged between nine and twelve and none of them were twins. They cut down a tree in their back yard and made it into a boat in which they rowed around the world annexing new territories to the British Empire. I can't think what made me a (temporary) imperialist at such an early age. My family were not empire builders; I was born in a very ordinary street in the industrial city of Leeds.

I was lucky and got onto the educational ladder, finishing up at Cambridge University where I took an honours degree in English. Then for many years I was a newspaperman, mainly on the Manchester *Guardian*. Eventually I became editor of the weekly international edition. I gave up this job in 1969 to have more time for writing and lectur-

ing, but I still keep a small part-time connection with the *Guardian* as children's book review editor.

Reviewing was what led me to write books of my own. In the late 1950s I came to the conclusion that English children's books were altogether too harmless, hygienic and cozy. I wanted to bring it home to children of the comfortable, reading classes that there were children who got a much rougher deal from life. At least, that's what I thought I wanted to do. Now I'm not so sure. It could be just that there was a book inside me hollering to get out, and I had to provide myself with a reason for writing it.

My first book, *Gumble's Yard,* was set in the "Jungle"—not a real jungle, but a tangled slum district—from which came its American title, *Trouble in the Jungle.* Together with *Pirate's Island* and *Widdershins Crescent* (American title *Goodbye to the Jungle*) it makes up a trio of books that are sometimes called the Jungle Trilogy. The character in them whom I most love is a small girl called Sandra: thin, shrewd, sharp-faced, maybe not too clean, but a splendid, salt-of-the-earth child, endlessly resourceful, used to looking after younger ones, knowing how to mend clothes, or where to buy potatoes a penny a pound cheaper than anywhere else.

Later books have tended to move up the age-range, not by deliberate intention but because that's the way they happened to come. *Good-Night, Prof, Dear* is about a rather square, studious boy who falls in love with the waitress at the local "greasy spoon" and runs off romantically with her towards Gretna Green in Scotland, where he thinks they'll get married. She's not a romantic girl, and marriage is not for her, but she treats him (I think) both well and generously.

Places inspire me enormously. I have a deep love for those English industrial landscapes that tourists never see—so ugly, and yet so sadly beautiful. I like seacoasts, too. *The Intruder,* which was made into a British TV serial, is set in a coastal village where the tide goes out for miles and comes in "as fast as a galloping horse." *The Summer People* has a very different coastal setting: a clifftop village that is slowly crumbling into the sea. I have been to America many times and have always loved it but have not yet dared to set a book there.

I believe that realistic fiction should be more concerned with the enduring truths of human nature than with surface details and fashionable issues (though it should of course get the details right). Human nature is absorbing, inexhaustible, and infinitely strange. In personal life, I believe the best thing in the world is a good, lasting, happy marriage.

———

John Rowe Townsend married Vera Lancaster on July 3, 1948; she died in 1973. Their children are Aletha Mary, Nicholas John, and Penelope Anne.

The three "Jungle" books (*Trouble in the Jungle, Pirate's Island,* and *Goodbye to the Jungle*), *The Intruder,* as well as *The Summer People* and *Noah's Castle* were all American Library Association Notable Books. *The Intruder* has won Townsend the greatest number of awards, having received the Boston *Globe-Horn Book* Award (for text) in 1970 and an Edgar from the Mystery Writers of America in 1971. The same title was on the Honors List for the Carnegie Medal, the British equivalent of the Newbery Medal. The New York *Times* considered *Good-bye to the Jungle, The Intruder*, and *The Summer People* outstanding books in their year of publication, and *School Library Journal* voted *Trouble in the Jungle* one of the best of the year in 1969, and *Noah's Castle* one of the best books for spring in 1976.

Townsend is also well known as a critic and writer about children's literature. *Written for Children: an Outline of English Language Children's Literature* was among the books *Horn Book* magazine chose for its Honor List in 1972. In 1971 Townsend gave the May Hill Arbuthnot Lecture in Atlanta, Georgia, and the Anne Carroll Moore Lecture at the New York Public Library.

SELECTED WORKS: Good-bye to the Jungle, 1967; Pirate's Island, 1968; Hell's Edge, 1969; Trouble in the Jungle, 1969; The Intruder, 1970; Good-Night, Prof, Dear, 1971; The Summer People, 1972; Forest of the Night, 1975; Noah's Castle, 1976; Top of the World, 1977; The Visitors, 1977.

SELECTED WORKS EDITED: Modern Poetry, 1974.

ABOUT: Author's and Writer's Who's Who, 1971; Contemporary Authors, Vol. 37–40; Something about the Author, Vol. 4; Who's Who in America, 1972–73; Signal May 1974; Top of the News June 1970.

PHILIP TURNER

December 3, 1925–

AUTHOR OF *The Grange at High Force*, etc.

Autobiographical sketch of Philip William Turner, pen name "Stephen Chance":

I AM Canadian by birth—not that it adds

PHILIP TURNER

up to much. We came home to Britain when I was six months old, and my earliest received information is of my father having to unload the luggage because Britain was in the middle of a dock strike. The next twelve years mattered, though. My father was first on the staff of Newcastle Cathedral and then later vicar of a parish in Leeds, Yorkshire—and this in the middle of the 1930s slump. One of my most vivid memories as a child is of my father somehow finding the money to pay an out-of-work stonemason to carve the figure of a saint to go in the niche over the church porch. No one who has not experienced the flavour of the north of England can ever understand that. I have tried—imperfectly—to put it into my Darnley Mills books. It is a mixture of high hills, history, industry and determined people. It is beautiful, squalid and altogether engrossing.

It seems to me that we are surprisingly close copies of our background—particularly if it was happy. I am a parson, probably because my father was a parson and I admired him as a good and wise man. If he had been, say, a civil engineer, what should I be now? As it is, I know and love and hate the Church of England. In my writing life I have torn it apart on radio and television, and have written plays making mock of it. In the

Darnley Mills stories—and under other hats—I have, perhaps, repaid a debt of love. It is a damnable institution, and probably one of the greatest institutions men have ever devised. I shall go on hating and loving it until the day that I die.

For the rest, I have worked in prisons, parishes, schools, and for radio and television. Out of it all I remember best the saying of a friend of mine who was a radio producer. "If I could choose I would broadcast nothing but people. People in their wonderful complexity."

People get an increasingly rough deal in this synthetic world of ours—but it does seem to me that not much else matters.

———

The Grange at High Force is one of what Mr. Turner refers to as his Darnley Mills books because of its setting in Darnley Mills in the Yorkshire Dales of England. *The Grange at High Force* received The Carnegie Medal, awarded by Britain's Library Association, in 1965. *Brian Wildsmith's Illustrated Bible Stories*, for which Turner retold the stories, was an American Library Association Notable Book of 1969 and was considered one of the outstanding books of the year by the New York *Times*.

Turner served in the Royal Naval Volunteer Reserve from 1943–46 and after his return went to Worcester College, Oxford, where he read English. He was ordained in 1951 and served in various parishes until 1966, when he joined the BBC Midland Region as religious broadcasting organizer, a post he held until 1970.

Philip Turner married Margaret Dana Samson on September 23, 1950. They have three children: Simon, Stephen and Jane.

SELECTED WORKS: Colonel Sheperton's Clock, 1966; The Grange at High Force, 1967; Sea Peril, 1968; Steam on the Line, 1968; Brian Wildsmith's Illustrated Bible Stories, 1969; War on the Darnel, 1969; Wigwig and Homer, 1970; (as "Stephen Chance") Septimus and the Minster Ghost Mystery, 1974; The Stone Offering: a Septimus Mystery, 1977.

ABOUT: Author's and Writer's Who's Who, 1971; Contemporary Authors, Vol. 25–28; Library Association Record June 1966.

GRANT UDEN

June 17, 1910–

AUTHOR OF *A Dictionary of Chivalry*, etc.

Autobiographical sketch of Grant Uden:

I WAS born in Kent, the county in the southeast corner of England where my ancestors from Holland settled five hundred or more years ago. I am a Man of Kent, not a Kentish Man. Kentish Men are born north and west of the River Medway that bisects the county. Men of Kent (reckoned much the superior breed, for rather dubious reasons) are born south and east. In 1066 they went with green boughs in their hands to greet William the Conqueror and, as a result, were confirmed in all their ancient rights and privileges. I therefore retain all those ancient rights and privileges, though I have never discovered what they are.

Having disposed of my ancestry, I must add that much of my life has been spent outside my home county, in various parts of England, both rural and industrial. It is often said that a writer's work reflects his environment and background. Mine does not. I have written a good deal about knights though I have never been one, my ancestors having been villains and peasants of a troublesome nature; about ships, in which I have never served; and about horses, on which I do not ride.

The controlling interest in my life has probably been collecting old books, documents, letters, countryside relics and a dozen other things that re-create the past for me. These more than anything have provided the material for what I write.

I have rarely attempted to write especially for children, since I do not believe ideas and vocabulary need to be restricted for their benefit. Neither am I

Grant Uden

very proud of, or conceited about, my books. If I ever begin to feel that way, I always remember a small girl who said she had seen me in a television programme. "That must have been a nasty experience for you," I said. She replied, "Oh, no. You weren't as bad as all *that*." I think one of the best books I ever wrote was one of the smallest, a history of the *Fighting Temeraire*, one of Nelson's ships. Three feet of its stern carving are in my study, a case of an author really getting close to his subject. The book I most enjoyed producing was *A Dictionary of Chivalry*, because the illustrations by Pauline Baynes are so beautiful.

The cleverest thing I have ever done, however, is to marry my wife and have two daughters. I have dedicated books to all three. After them, my chief loves are old books, old pieces of paper, the English countryside and the sea.

———

A Dictionary of Chivalry has won Mr. Uden a number of distinctions on both sides of the Atlantic. In England it received the 1968 Kate Greenaway Medal, the equivalent of our Caldecott Medal,

for Pauline Baynes' illustrations, and was a runner-up for the Carnegie Medal, the equivalent of the Newbery Medal. In the United States it was designated an American Library Association Notable Book for 1969 and was a runner-up in the *Book World* Children's Spring Book Festival for 1969.

SELECTED WORKS: Collector's Casebook, 1963; A Dictionary of Chivalry, 1969; Hero Tales From the Age of Chivalry, 1969.

JAMES RAMSEY ULLMAN

November 24, 1907–June 20, 1971

AUTHOR OF *Banner in the Sky*, etc.

Biographical sketch of James Ramsey Ullman:

JAMES RAMSEY ULLMAN, author and theatrical producer, is perhaps best remembered today for his books of adventure, many of them based on his own firsthand experiences as a mountain climber and world traveler.

Born on November 24, 1907, in New York City, he was educated at the Ethical Culture School there, at the Phillips Academy in Andover, Massachusetts, and at Princeton University, from which he graduated in 1929. His senior thesis at Princeton won a prize, and was published in 1930 (*Mad Shelley*, Princeton University Press). "This," he is reported to have said, "had the dubious effect of turning me from the rational life to writing."

From 1929 to 1932, Ullman worked as a reporter and feature writer on the Brooklyn *Eagle*, and then turned his hand to producing plays and to writing them. He produced twelve plays between 1933 and 1939, his biggest success being his production of Sidney Kingsley's Pulitzer Prize-winning play, *Men in White*. Not all his productions were received with rapture, however; the year 1936 saw Ullman with four flops in succession on his hands. "*The Laughing Woman*," said a critic of one production,

JAMES RAMSEY ULLMAN

"has the dramatic content of a hole in a doughnut."

Feeling that Broadway was not his field, Ullman went off on a journey across the Andes and down the Amazon River; *The Other Side of the Mountain*, was the account of his arduous journey. In 1939 he began contributing short stories to the *Saturday Evening Post*, *Story*, *Collier's*, *Esquire* and the *American Mercury*, among others.

During World War II Ullman was an officer in the American Field Service (ambulance unit), and was for fifteen months, in 1942 and 1943, attached to the British Eighth Army in Africa; he was awarded the Star of Africa by Great Britain.

Mountain climbing was, with writing, Ullman's most absorbing interest. He first began to climb in Switzerland in 1927, while still an undergraduate at Princeton, and later feats included climbing Mount Olympus in 110° of heat, the Mexican volcano Ixtaccihuatl through six-foot snowdrifts, the Jungfrau, the Matterhorn, and some of the Andes "foothills." He was a member of the American Alpine Club, which limits its membership to those who can prove they have climbed certain peaks, and he took part as official historian in the first American expedition to Mount Everest in 1963.

Among Ullman's works of nonfiction are a history of mountain climbing, *The Age of Mountaineering* and *Americans on Everest*, the story of the 1963 expedition. His first novel, *The White Tower*, was also about climbing. The tortuous ascent of a fictional Alpine mountain, the Weissturm, that is described in the book is intended by the author to symbolize all the goals in life toward which men strive. Reviewers of the novel, while critical of Ullman's powers of characterization, did appreciate the vivid detail, the sense of reality and immediacy which he was able to bring to his story by means of his own solid first-hand experience of climbing. The book became a national bestseller. Ullman again made good use of his mountaineering experience in his book for young people, *Banner in the Sky*, published in 1954, which was a runner-up for the Newbery Medal.

Ullman was married three times and had two sons by his first wife. He died on June 20, 1971, at the age of sixty-four.

SELECTED WORKS: Banner in the Sky, 1954; Down the Colorado with Major Powell, 1960.

ABOUT: Author's and Writer's Who's Who, 1971; Contemporary Authors, Vol. 3; Who's Who in America, 1970–1971; Current Biography, 1945; Current Biography Yearbook, 1971; Reader's Digest February 1942.

JUDITH VIORST

AUTHOR OF *The Tenth Good Thing about Barney*, etc.

Autobiographical sketch of Judith Stahl Viorst:

I WAS born in New Jersey, grew up in the suburbs of New Jersey, graduated from Rutgers (also New Jersey), and finally realized my wicked dream of moving to Greenwich Village, New York.

Viorst: *VEE orst*

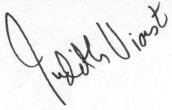

In 1960 I married Milton Viorst, a journalist, and settled more or less permanently in Washington, D.C., where we live in a big white house on a dead-end street with our three sons—Anthony, sixteen, Nicholas, fourteen, and Alexander, ten.

I have always written, starting at about age seven with a poetic ode to my dead mother and father who, at the time, were both quite alive, and quite insulted. I wrote, I sent out, I was rejected, with clockwork regularity—mostly gloomy, suicidal poems, but also some children's books, for which I had and continue to have a very special love.

I worked for a while editing children's books for a publishing house in New York and later edited science books for teen-agers in Washington. And then, finally, I was given the chance to write some paperback science books (on space, on nature, on geology, on scientific experiments), and at last I was a published author.

Since being published seems to beget being published some more, life as a writer got easier and more varied. I did five adult books of humorous verse, a prose book on marriage, many magazine and newspaper articles. I currently write a monthly column for *Redbook* magazine.

And every year, for the past six years, I have published a children's book. The writing of them gives me enormous joy and satisfaction and I'd like to keep writing them as long as I live.

With one exception, all my books have been suggested by my own kids' experiences and needs: a book on death, on sibling rivalry, on manic Sunday mornings, on a rotten day in the life of a small boy, on fear of monsters, zombies, fiends, etc. I find my sons fierce and funny, and these qualities appear in many of my characters, some of whom are named after my boys.

I notice that my books aren't growing any older, even though my children certainly are. Perhaps I'll go on to write for that mid-aged child, but I suspect that an important piece of myself is arrested at that golden age of picture books.

Judith Viorst received an Emmy Award for poetic monologues written for a CBS television special, "Annie, the Woman in the Life of a Man." She has contributed poems and articles to *New York*, the New York *Times*, *Holiday* and *Venture*, among others. From 1970–72 she wrote a syndicated column for Washington *Star* Syndicate.

Alexander and the Terrible, Horrible, No Good, Very Bad Day was cited by *School Library Journal* as one of the best books of 1972. Although she has received no major awards, Mrs. Viorst's books are popular with children and have established for her a secure place in children's literature. In particular, *The Tenth Good Thing about Barney*—in which a child mourns the death of a beloved cat by reciting the good things to remember about it, the tenth being that Barney's buried body will enrich the earth—is often cited as one of the best of the books that deal with the subject of death and grief for a very young child.

SELECTED WORKS: Sunday Morning, 1968; I'll Fix Anthony, 1969; Try It Again, Sam: Safety When You Walk, 1970; The Tenth Good Thing about Barney, 1971; Alexander and the Terrible, Horrible, No Good, Very Bad Day, 1972; My Mama Says There Aren't Any Zombies, Ghosts, Vampires, Creatures, Demons, Monsters, Fiends, Goblins, or Things, 1973; Rosie and Michael, 1974.

ABOUT: Contemporary Authors, Vol. 49–52; Something about the Author, Vol. 7.

"COLETTE VIVIER"

1898–

AUTHOR OF *The House of the Four Winds*, etc.

Autobiographical sketch of Colette Duval, who writes for children under the name of "Colette Vivier," translated from the French:

I WAS born in Paris and I have always lived there, either on the right bank of the Seine in the peaceful district of Batignolles or on the left bank in the Latin Quarter. I have two sisters, Simone and Genevieve, and all three of us had a happy childhood. At night when we were in bed we invented stories in which each one of us had a role to play. Then the next day I would write it down in a thick pink notebook. It was full of spelling mistakes and full of incredible adventures, but this is how I acquired the taste for writing.

When I was six years old, I entered a public school of which my grandmother was principal. I admired her greatly. Her name was Madame Vivier, and this is how I sign my books, in memory of her. I then went to the lycée and later to the faculty of the Sorbonne. When I was twenty years old, I married; my husband was a professor of literature. I have a son, André, and two grandsons, Remi and Yves. Sons, grandsons, nephews and nieces—I have always lived surrounded by children. I like to play with them, follow them to their games: "We got lost . . . we found a house." I have never cut the thread of childhood. When I write a book I am completely caught up in my characters as if I lived with them.

I draw my characters from reality but I fashion them according to my whim and I try to paint the places where the action takes place as true to life as I can. I know the *Maison des Petis Bonheurs* (House of the Little Happiness) where Aline lives. I know the little cafe of *L'Etoile Polaire* (The Polar Star), and the plateau of the daisies where the people of the *La Porte Ouverte* (The Open Door) build their homes themselves to escape their sweltering one room in the old Parisian street. When I found them established up there I was as happy as they were. . . . And the children understand me. When I came to a library to discuss this book with young readers I was assaulted with questions: "Did Francis install the swing? . . . Did Etiennette sow the flowers? . . . And a few little girls cried: "Say Madame, could we go to the new house and see how the people are doing in their new home?"

From time to time I bring some of my personal remembrances to my stories. The drowning of Paul in *L'Étoile Polaire* is my drowning one vacation morning and the stupid stories told by Suzanne in *La Grande Roue* (The Big Wheel) are the stories which I wrote in the famous pink notebook. The one book, however, in which I have invented almost nothing is *The House of the Four Winds* (*Maison des Quatre Vents*) in which the action takes place in 1943 during the Nazi occupation. My husband and I were part of a Resistance network. Everything that takes place is part of my personal experience or that of my close friends. Everything except the execution of young Michel. But, on the contrary, with *La Grande Roue*, which takes place in the year 1900, I have had to engage in research about this period known as the Belle Epoque. This is how I described the marriage of my great-aunt, and I have recopied the menu of the banquet, a meal so plentiful that I cannot understand how the guests were able to reach dessert.

Vivier: VIV *i ay*

I have never practiced a profession. If I have written a few books it was solely for my pleasure.

———

Twice Colette Vivier has been highly commended for her contribution to International Children's Literature by the international jury for the Hans Christian Andersen Award—in 1972 and in 1974.

SELECTED WORKS: The House of the Four Winds, 1969.

LYND WARD

June 26, 1905–

AUTHOR AND ILLUSTRATOR OF *The Biggest Bear*, etc.

Biographical sketch of Lynd Kendall Ward:

LYND KENDALL WARD was born in Chicago on June 26th, 1905, the son of a Methodist minister. He was raised in Illinois, Massachusetts and New Jersey, where he attended high school in Englewood; but from very early childhood he spent the summers with his parents in a remote part of Canada, near Lonely Lake, Ontario, and the Ontario woodlands have, in fact, played a profound part in his thought and artistic development, and continue to do so to this day.

In 1926, immediately after his graduation from Columbia University Teachers College with a degree in fine arts, Ward, with his bride May McNeer traveled to Leipzig to enter the National Academy for Graphic Art; there he studied the traditional print techniques of etching, engraving and lithography.

It was while he was in Leipzig, browsing through a bookstore, that Ward stumbled on a story in woodcuts by the Belgian artist Frans Masereel: from that moment on, Ward knew that his direction as an illustrator lay in wood engraving—a slow, difficult medium, used essentially in the eighteenth and nineteenth centuries before the invention of photomechanical reproduction. The level of instruction at the academy was luckily extremely high, and served to lay the foundation of his whole career in graphic illustration.

After returning to the United States from Leipzig, Ward began his career as an illustrator, his work characterized by his authenticity of detail and locale, strong design, and the compelling mood or emotion he was able to evoke in the reader.

Lynd Ward's woodcut novel, *God's Man*, was the first woodcut novel to be published without text, and it created a sensation in 1929. The same year saw his collaboration with his wife on a children's book, *Prince Bantam*, based on a Japanese folk tale; this was the first of many such joint ventures. Ward has also illustrated books written by his elder daughter, Nanda, and worked with his younger daughter, Robin, who is a book designer.

Besides engraving and lithography, Ward has published illustrations in various other media, including watercolor and pen drawing—but he is best known for engraving over one thousand books in this painstaking medium.

Much of his best work has been done for the Limited Editions and Heritage Clubs; in 1954, he won the Silver Medal of the Limited Editions Club for twenty-five years of excellence in illustration. His work is notable also for the meticulous preparations he makes: over six years of study, for instance, went into the illustrations he executed for *America's Abraham Lincoln*. The total number of illustrated books to his credit is now well over one hundred, in over forty-five years of work. Other awards include the Carteret Book Club Award in 1942, the Library of Congress Award for wood engraving in 1948, a National Academy of Design Award in 1949, the Samuel F. B. Morse medal in 1966, the Rutgers Award for children's literature in 1969 and the University of Southern Mississippi's Children's Collection Medallion in 1973. In 1975 he and May McNeer shared the Regina Medal, awarded by the Catholic Library Association for "continued distinguished contribution to children's literature." Ward is a member of the Society of Illustrators, the Society of American Graphic Artists, over which he presided for six years, and his books have often been chosen for exhibit by the American Institute of Graphic Arts as among the Fifty Books of the year.

One of Ward's best known works is his 1953 Caldecott Medal-winning book, *The Biggest Bear*, the first of the small number of books he has both written and illustrated. The story of a bear that grows and grows utilizes, as do several of his books, the locale and experience of his early years in the Canadian woods. *The Silver Pony* uses no written text: The child must supply this from his own imagination and experience. The book, a runner-up for the Boston *Globe-Horn Book* Award in 1973, was chosen as one of the best-illustrated books of the year by the New York *Times*, and was included in the 1974 Children's Book Showcase.

Lynd Ward remains an active illustrator, occasionally writing articles on illustrating, playing his accordion, and indulging his hobby of stonework building on his property in New Jersey.

Prints by Lynd Ward can be found in the Metropolitan Museum of Art, the Library of Congress, the Victoria and Albert Museum, and in many other important collections.

SELECTED WORKS WRITTEN AND ILLUSTRATED: The Biggest Bear, 1952; Martin Luther (with May McNeer), 1953; Armed With Courage (with May McNeer), 1957; Bible Readings for Boys and Girls, 1959; The Bible Story, 1961; Nic of the Woods, 1965; The Silver Pony, 1973.

SELECTED WORKS ILLUSTRATED: Little Red Lighthouse and the Great Gray Bridge, by Hildegarde H. Swift, 1942; Johnny Tremaine, by Esther Forbes, 1943; America's Paul Revere, by Esther Forbes, 1946; Little Baptiste, by May McNeer, 1954; High Flying Hat, by Nanda W. Ward, 1956; America's Abraham Lincoln, by May McNeer, 1957; The Cat Who Went to Heaven, by Elizabeth Coatsworth, 1958; Gaudenzio:

Pride of the Palio, by Marguerite Henry, 1960; A Peculiar Magic, by Annabel and Edgar Johnston, 1965; The Wolf of Lamb's Lane, by May McNeer, 1967; The Treasure of Topo-el-Bampo, by Scott O'Dell, 1972; Bloomsday for Maggie, by May McNeer, 1976.

ABOUT: Contemporary Authors, Vol. 17–18; Hoffman, Miriam, and Eva Samuels. Authors and Illustrators of Children's Books; Hopkins, Lee Bennett. Books Are by People; Kingman, Lee and others, comps. Illustrators of Children's Books: 1957–1966; Mahony, Bertha E. and others, comps. Illustrators of Children's Books: 1944–1945; Something about the Author, Vol. 2; Viguers, Ruth Hill and others, comps. Illustrators of Children's Books: 1946–1956; Who's Who in America, 1970–71; Who's Who in American Art, 1973; American Artist March 1975; Elementary English November 1962; Horn Book August 1953; February 1964; Library Journal March 15, 1953; Publishers Weekly February 4, 1950; March 14, 1953.

CLYDE WATSON

July 25, 1947–

AUTHOR OF *Father Fox's Pennyrhymes*, etc.

Autobiographical sketch by Clyde Watson:

MY name has always confused people—telephone operators make me repeat it over and over, and once I was almost put in the men's ward of a hospital because of my name. People ask me "Did your parents want a boy?" In fact, no. Some of my ancestors came from the Firth of Clyde in Scotland, and Clyde has been a family name for a long time.

I grew up on a farm in Vermont with seven brothers and sisters, chickens, goats, cats, dogs, horses and an occasional pig or two. My mother, a writer, and my father, an illustrator and writer, both worked at home rather than have offices to which they disappeared daily, and as a result, drawing and writing were part of everyday life in our household. We were able to learn the techniques of their trade whenever we

Clyde Watson

wanted to, and they both encouraged us by responding to everything any of us wrote or drew.

My parents believed in varieties of educational experience, and all of us spent at least one year "having school" at home. I spent three such years, and one in a public school in Switzerland.

After graduating from Smith College in music in 1968, I did graduate work in education at the University of Massachusetts, while teaching full time in a private elementary school in Amherst. From there I went to Princeton, Maine, where I taught Passamaquoddy Indian children for several years.

I believe all children are born natural artists and writers, and one of the things I worked hardest on in teaching was to try to excite children to write and illustrate stories about themselves, their dreams, their friends, and their troubles.

The first book I had any part in was called *Fisherman Lullabies*. It consisted of poems selected by my older sister Wendy, who had already been illustrating books for several years. I set these poems to music and she illustrated the book. I did the work for this during my last year as an undergraduate. The following year I collaborated with my parents, setting to music a Christmas poem written by my mother and illustrated by my father. Thereafter I began the writing of words, starting with *Father Fox's Pennyrhymes* and *Tom Fox and the Apple Pie*, both of which Wendy illustrated.

I can't say that any *one* thing in my life has influenced my choice of writing as a career, or my writing itself, unless it be the excitement and encouragement our parents showed at all of our work. Other than that I believe that everything that ever happens to me contributes to my writing. I remember many parts of my childhood, and memories in general are very important to me.

In addition, I am lucky to be able to work so well with Wendy. Because we share our growing-up memories, we think very much alike. When I write, I see in my head the kind of pictures Wendy will make; and she seems to know just what I have in mind when I describe a scene or a character, and illustrates it just as I would if I could draw what I see in my head.

———

Father Fox's Pennyrhymes brought its author and illustrator high praise from all sides. In 1971 it was chosen one of the best of the year by the *Horn Book*, the New York *Times* and *School Library Journal*; was an American Library Association Notable Book; and a finalist for the National Book Award for the year. It was included in the 1972 Children's Book Showcase and in the Children's Book Show of the American Institute of Graphic Arts, who awarded the book a certificate of excellence in 1973. A Brooklyn Art Books for Children Citation was awarded it for 1973–74.

SELECTED WORKS WRITTEN: Fisherman Lullabies (with Wendy Watson), 1968; Carol to a Child, with Nancy Dingman Watson, 1969; Father Fox's Pennyrhymes, 1971; Tom Fox and the Apple Pie, 1972; Quips and Quirks, 1975; Hickory Stick Rag, 1976; Binary Numbers, 1977.

SELECTED WORKS ILLUSTRATED: How Does It Feel to Be a Tree?, by Flo Morse, 1976.

ABOUT: Contemporary Authors, Vol. 49–52; Something about the Author, Vol. 5.

SALLY WATSON
January 28, 1924–

AUTHOR OF *Linnet*, etc.

Autobiographical sketch of Sally Lou
Watson:

Sally Lou Watson

I WAS born in Seattle, oldest of five
children and a misfit. I never did like
my own age group, preferring to chat
with adults and play with younger children (whom I could teach and boss).
And I always needed solitude. So I spent
my childhood gorging on books, writing,
and leading my siblings into hair-raising
adventures. (We hardly ever *disobeyed*,
mind. We just thought of things that
hadn't been forbidden. Like acrobatics
on the roof ridgepole.) I regarded dolls
simply as heroines for adventures, and
used to wonder why anyone made baby
dolls, who were *much* too young. I was
deeply shocked to discover—much later
—that you were supposed to *mother*
them! Ugh! I *never* had any maternal instinct! . . . Nor marital, either. A life of
housework? Ugh twice! There were so
many important and interesting things to
do! Like reading, writing, climbing
trees, collecting words, handcrafts, gardening, ballet, more reading, and teaching everything I read to anyone who
would listen.

Clearly (not counting a brief unrealistic ambition to be a prima ballerina) I
was destined to teach. Because—though
Mother kept murmuring about why
didn't I try writing books for children,
this was more unrealistic than ballet. No
ordinary person could hope to become a
writer. . . .

So I finished high school and post-
poned college. (There was a war on.) I
joined the navy, where I learned aircraft
instrument repair and the value of personal freedom and privacy. Then to Colorado State College of Education, where
I learned that teaching wasn't for me,
after all. Ugh three times. Then by some
miracle I was accepted at Reed College,
where I learned every mental discipline
I have, including the utter joy of deep
study and research—and a few goals.
("This is the sort of story you might sell
to a slick magazine, Sally . . . if that's all
the higher you're aiming? . . .") That
was from Lloyd Reynolds, whose famous courses in calligraphy I missed,
due to trying to get the required courses
to graduate in a mere two years. This
was a mistake. His course would have
been far more valuable to me than a
B.A., even one from Reed.

So I graduated—to find myself useless
for any job. Over-educated and under-
trained, they told me scornfully. En-
dured three years of boring office work
in San Francisco, fan mail at MGM (ugh
four times), and so on, until I met two
old high school friends (on Hollywood
and Vine, actually) who said one day,
"Why don't you write books for children?"

Just what Mother always said—but
this time it sounded different. So I did.
Started *Highland Rebel* that very night.
It seems I'd been preparing for it all my
life without ever letting myself know.

That was 1953. Presently I moved to
Oakland to work part time helping
Mother run her reading materials, Lis-
ten and Learn with Phonics, on a slen-

der shoestring—and also teaching remedial reading, independently of schools, who approved the results but not the method.

In '63 Americana took over production and sales, Mother no longer needed me, so I fulfilled an old old dream and came to England to live and to write books full time at last. By '67, with seven books and a reading series published, I took up Judo at the idiotic age of 43½. Then I bought a cottage in the country and named it for a type of Judo throw called Sutemi, meaning roughly "full commitment" or "go-for-broke." It seemed appropriate. Especially after I broke a leg having one done on me.

Now, with twelve books published, I am also a Judo Black Belt, a coach, Provisional National Referee, Senior Recorder, and Examiner. My five-to-nine classes a week do tend, alas, to take attention from my writing, as do the various local, area, national and even international events in which I officiate in various ways. It's a part-time profession, providing the social life, exercise, and outlet for healthy aggressions that writing lacks—plus the teaching that I can't seem to escape and find I don't want to.

In my spare time, I teach remedial reading, devote myself to a brand-new-as-of-last-year profession of enamel on copper (I'm currently developing a nice style of landscapes), work on a novel and a judo book for beginners (illustrated), tend a quarter-acre garden and a large-ish house. In the course of all this, something gets awfully neglected. The housework, of course. But who cares?

———

Sally Watson received the Woodward School Annual Book Award in 1959 for *To Build a Land*, which was also named one of the one hundred outstanding books of the year 1957 by the New York *Times. The Mukhtar's Children* was named in *Horn Book* magazine's Honor List in 1968 and included in its Fanfare List for 1966–70.

SELECTED WORKS: Highland Rebel, 1954; Mistress Malapert, 1955; To Build a Land, 1957; Poor Felicity, 1961; Witch of the Glens, 1962; Lark, 1964; Other Sandals, 1966; The Mukhtar's Children, 1968; The Hornet's Nest, 1968; Jade, 1969; Magic at Wychwood, 1970; Linnet, 1971.

ABOUT: Contemporary Authors, Vol. 5–6; Something about the Author, Vol. 3.

WENDY WATSON
July 7, 1942–

ILLUSTRATOR OF *Father Fox's Pennyrhymes*, etc.

Biographical sketch of Wendy McLeod Watson Harrah by Clyde Watson:

WENDY WATSON grew up as the oldest of eight children with an illustrator-father and a writer-mother, on a farm in Putney, Vermont.

Her artistic impulses delighted family and friends early on when she began giving as gifts handbound books of her own creation, framed pen and ink drawings, and handprinted greeting cards.

Her first published work was a children's book which she wrote and illustrated as a senior project in high school. Since then she has illustrated many books and received many honors and awards.

Originally known as an illustrator of children's books, in 1976 she made her debut as an author-illustrator with the publication of *Lollipop*, a story for very young children.

Wendy presently lives in Toledo with her husband and young daughter.

———

Wendy Watson attended the Putney School in Putney, Vermont, and then went on to Bryn Mawr College. She majored in Latin and graduated in 1969, magna cum laude with honors. Her formal art training consisted of summer study with Jerry Farnsworth on Cape Cod during college summers and study at the National Academy of Design in 1966 and in 1967, as well as learning from her artist father. For two years af-

WENDY WATSON

ter her graduation from college she worked as a compositor and designer for a small press in New Hampshire. Since then she has worked as a free-lance illustrator. Miss Watson married the actor and opera singer Michael Donald Harrah in 1970 and has a daughter, Mary Cameron Harrah, born in March, 1973. Besides illustrating and painting, Wendy Watson is an accomplished amateur musician. She plays the piano and has played the cello with chamber music groups.

Wendy Watson is best known for her illustrations to *Father Fox's Pennyrhymes*, with text by her sister Clyde. Besides being an American Library Association Notable Book (1971), and named one of the best of the year by *School Library Journal*, the New York *Times* and the *Horn Book*, it was nominated for the National Book Award and was selected for inclusion in the 1972 Children's Book Showcase. It was also chosen by the American Institute of Graphic Arts as one of twenty American entries in the 1973 Biennale of Illustrations Bratislava. Miss Watson's work was included in the American Institute of Graphic Arts 1967–68 Children's Book Show, and in the 1972–73 show as well.

SELECTED WORKS WRITTEN AND ILLUSTRATED: Lollipop, 1976.

SELECTED WORKS ILLUSTRATED: The Cruise of the Aardvark, by Ogden Nash, 1967; The Lost Toys Witch, by Maybell Lizzie Harmer, 1970; The Hedgehog and the Hare, by J. L. K. Grimm, 1969; Father Fox's Pennyrhymes, by Clyde Watson, 1971; Open the Door and See All the People, by Clyde Robert Bulla, 1972; Tom Fox and the Apple Pie, by Clyde Watson, 1972; Sleep is for Everyone, by Paul Showers, 1974; The Birthday Goat, by Nancy Dingman Watson, 1974; Maps, Tracks, and the Bridges of Königsberg, by Michael Holt, 1975; Quips and Quirks, by Clyde Watson, 1975; Hickory Stick Rag, by Clyde Watson, 1976; Binary Numbers, by Clyde Watson, 1977.

ABOUT: Contemporary Authors, Vol. 49–52; Something about the Author, Vol. 5.

LISL WEIL

AUTHOR AND ILLUSTRATOR OF *Pudding's Wonderful Bone*, etc.

Autobiographical sketch of Lisl Weil:

BORN in Vienna, Austria, I've been blessed in having parents that gave love and understanding to support my talents. I've been fortunate too in having teachers that opened in me a free expression of feelings and a keen eye to see the world.

I've been drawing, dancing and loving music all my life. I might have been the inventor of decorated wrapping paper, because as soon as I could hold a crayon, any sheet of paper in our home was filled with my drawings. When I was eight years old I got very ill. Doctors from afar would come to study my case. I'm told it wasn't medical knowledge, but the will and love of my mother, that carried me over this seizure which took two years, with learning to be active again thereafter. Perhaps one can say I was reborn.

At fifteen my first drawings appeared in a Viennese weekly and a daily newspaper. At sixteen I had my own column in practically every issue, writing and drawing my observations of stage personalities and places of interest. This all

Lisl Weil: *LEE zel WILE*

LISL
WEIL

while I was still a pupil at art school.
I've also been a member of a well-
known dance group.

Via Holland, where for almost one
year I worked as a stage designer and
with a Dutch magazine and newspaper,
I arrived in New York without knowledge of the English language. I got a job
as a girl Friday at a peasant-style store
on Fifth Avenue, doing advertising, fabrics, window display, and building
shelves. At that time I also met my hus-
band-to-be. He guided me into being a
free-lance artist, doing *the* thing I love
best—drawing and writing for young
people.

With my books I want to make youngsters aware of their own feelings and
feelings around us. I love to make them
feel happy and positive, and to make
them laugh with me. I do not art-design
my books. I believe true design to grow
by itself out of the story I am illustrating. I have done over one hundred
books. More than half of them I have
written too.

Twenty-seven years ago, I also became a performer on the concert stage.
As a symphony orchestra plays, I draw

and dance the story of the music, making listening a visual feature and showing the close relation of all art forms. My
colorful huge drawings on easels, eight
by twenty-two feet, translate every
sound into lines, till all becomes pictures
telling the story the composer has set in
his music. I've done Stravinsky's *Fire-
bird*, and Prokofiev's *Cinderella* to mention two. I have performed with many
major orchestras around the country and
perform every season at New York's
Avery Fisher Hall at Lincoln Center
with the Little Orchestra Society at their
sold out Young People's Concerts. NBC
nationwide TV specials have brought
me large audiences in this, my very own
way of drawing music.

Out of these musical and graphic
studies I also made picture books that
brought part of a score into it—the *Sorcerer's Apprentice* by Dukas, for instance. This book led Weston Woods
into filming a movie, in which I draw
the *Sorcerer's Apprentice* just as I do on-
stage.

I am most grateful and happiest working. To me it really is no work, but something that is in me and I must give to
others.

———

Lisl Weil attended the Kunstgewerbe-
schule in Vienna, where she won the
school's highest award for outstanding
ability. After graduating from school she
worked for various Viennese and European periodicals, traveled widely and
made sketches of theatrical subjects,
some of which were selected to represent
Austrian art at the Exposition Internationale in Paris.

Following her arrival in the United
States in 1939, Miss Weil worked as art
director for Lanz of Salzburg, then did
free-lance textile design, interior decorating, advertising, graphic design and
magazine illustration. After she began
writing and illustrating books for children she had a television program called
"Children's Sketchbook," which ran for a
year.

Lisl Weil married Julius Marx on April 11, 1946.

SELECTED WORKS WRITTEN AND ILLUS-TRATED: Pudding's Wonderful Bone, 1956; The Busiest Boy in Holland, 1959; Mimi, 1961; The Sorcerer's Apprentice, 1962; Eyes So-o Big, 1964; The Story of Smetana's Bartered Bride, 1967; The Golden Spinning Wheel, 1969; The Hopping Knapsack, 1970; Fat Ernest, 1973; The Candy Egg Bunny, 1975; If Eggs Had Legs, 1976; Chicken, 1976; Gertie and Gus, 1977.

SELECTED WORKS ILLUSTRATED: Three Birthday Wishes, by Ruth Holberg, 1953; Breakneck Hill, by Doris Hendrickson, 1955; Clancy's Witch, by Emilee W. McLeod, 1959; What Will I Wear? by Helen Diehl Olds, 1961; Miss Polly's Animal School, by Mary Elting, 1961; What Makes Me Feel This Way? by Eda J. LeShan, 1972; The Bed Just So, by Jeanne Hardendorff, 1974; The Case of the Condemned Cat, by E. W. Hildick, 1975; The Great Rabbit Rip-off, by E. W. Hildick, 1977.

ABOUT: Contemporary Authors, Vol. 49–52; Current Biography, 1958; Kingman, Lee and others, comps. Illustrators of Children's Books: 1957–66; Something about the Author, Vol. 7; Viguers, Ruth Hill and others. Illustrators of Children's Books: 1946–56.

ROSEMARY WELLS

January 29, 1943–

AUTHOR AND ILLUSTRATOR OF *Morris's Disappearing Bag*, etc.

Autobiographical sketch of Rosemary Wells:

ACCORDING to my mother, the first things I ever drew with consistency were angry policemen. I think she's probably right, as she's saved some, but I can't imagine ever having seen an angry policeman in Gramercy Park, New York City, when I was only two years old. We didn't stay in New York. My mother had stopped dancing when she had me. She had been in the Ballet Russe de Monte Carlo and the American Ballet. My father was a playwright and so could work in a converted chicken house on a small farm in the New Jersey countryside. I

Rosemary Wells

grew up there, just after the war, at a time when New Jersey was rural and parkways and shopping plazas had yet to come. Mr. Dilkes, our neighbor, supplied us with eggs and owned a woods where I spent much time with my friends.

I drew pictures all day long in school (when I wasn't supposed to be doing it) and every night after supper for at least a couple of hours before bed, when the lights went out but I could still listen to the Dodgers turned very, very low. The house was filled with books and animals, and what time I wasn't drawing, playing baseball, or roaming the woods, I read. We had no television. No one did until it was too late.

My three parents, and that includes a grandmother with a steel-trap mind and another house full of books, by the ocean, abetted my drawing early and constantly, often to the dismay of teachers, who would have preferred that I take notes instead of caricaturing them in my notebook or do math instead of writing little poems. I owe a great deal to my parents. I think as professionals, they treated me as a professional, without ever pushing or condescending, either. Time passed. I graduated from Red Bank High School in 1961.

After a year at another college I went to Boston Museum School, to be as near as possible to Dartmouth College, where Thomas M. Wells was a junior. At museum school I was taught anatomy, perspective, life drawing and printing by a battalion of strict, old-school Germans. To this day I can draw a skeleton in any position and name the bones and muscles in Latin.

I was married after a year at Boston Museum and used this new status as an excuse to get out in the world instead of continuing school. I was such a terrible painter—and the word illustrator was used nearly as an epithet amongst fine artists—that I decided to become a book designer. I got my first job in publishing when I was nineteen, and until I was in my late twenties and on staff at the Macmillan Company, I never lifted a pencil except to sketch page layouts and comp type. I wanted to become an art director.

One day I drew up a dummy, with pictures, of a Gilbert and Sullivan song. I gave it to my boss, Ava Weiss, at Macmillan. Twenty minutes later, Susan Hirschman, the editor-in-chief, told me, "Sit down, Rosemary, you're a Macmillan author now." I never looked back.

To supplement the false starts in writing and illustrating, Susan Jeffers (also on the staff at Macmillan) and I started a book design studio in Susan's Brooklyn apartment. Although neither of us could do bookkeeping or math, and both of us hated making appointments to show our portfolio, those were very palmy days.

Since Tom and I put off having a baby until 1973, I cannot say my love of children's books has much to do with children. It is for the child in myself that I do picture books, and for the adolescent still lurking there that I do novels. My editor, Phyllis Fogelman, and I have worked out a sort of alternating picture book-novel-picture book scheme whereby I can keep working at a great rate and not get stale in either endeavor.

I've had ambitions, at various times in my life, to be an actress, to be the first woman baseball manager, to run a restaurant, and to be a secret agent stationed in London, but book publishing has been my professional home since I was a teen-ager. It is a small world, and not without faults, but to me it is the last bastion of civilization, so I believe I shall continue to try to perfect my abilities writing and illustrating, and let the other things ride.

———

Rosemary Wells' novel for young adults, *The Fog Comes on Little Pig Feet*, was an Honor Book in the twelve- to sixteen-year-old category in the 1972 *Book World* Spring Children's Book Festival. It also appeared on the American Library Association's Bicentennial List. *None of the Above*, also a young-adult novel, appeared on best-of-the-year lists in *School Library Journal* and Kirkus Service, among others. *Leave Well Enough Alone* was one of *School Library Journal's* best books for Spring 1977. It is with her picture books, however, that Rosemary Wells has scored her greatest successes so far. *Noisy Nora, Benjamin and Tulip*, and *Morris's Disappearing Bag* were all American Library Association Notable Books. *Noisy Nora* was one of *School Library Journal's* choices of best of the year and was included in the 1974 Children's Book Showcase. *Benjamin and Tulip* has been designated a Brooklyn Art Book for Children three times—in 1975, 1976, and 1977—by the Brooklyn Public Library and the Brooklyn Museum. The book also received a Citation of Merit from the Society of Illustrators in 1974. In 1975 *Morris's Disappearing Bag* was one of *School Library Journal's* Best of the Year. It won the Irma Simonton Black Award given by the Bank Street College of Education and was also included in the Bias-Free Illustration Show promoted by the American Institute of Graphic Arts. Mrs. Wells' illustrations have regularly been among those selected for the Children's Book Shows of the American Institute of Graphic Arts, with *The Shooting of Dan McGrew*, by Robert W. Service, in 1970, *Impossible Possum*, by Ellen Conford, in 1971–72, and in 1973–74, *Noisy Nora* and *Two Sisters and Some Hornets*, by Beryl Epstein and Dorrit Davis.

Rosemary Wells was married to Thomas Moore Wells, an architect, in 1963. They have two daughters, Victoria, born in 1973, and Marguerite, born in 1977.

SELECTED WORKS WRITTEN: The Fog Comes on Little Pig Feet, 1972; None of the Above, 1974; Leave Well Enough Alone, 1977.

SELECTED WORKS WRITTEN AND ILLUS- TRATED: John and the Rarey, 1969; Michael and the Mitten Test, 1969; The First Child, 1970; Martha's Birthday, 1970; Miranda's Pilgrims, 1970; Unfortunately Harriet, 1972; Noisy Nora, 1973; Benjamin and Tulip, 1973; Abdul, 1975; Morris's Disappearing Bag, 1975; Don't Spill it Again, James, 1977.

SELECTED WORKS ILLUSTRATED: A Song to Sing, O!, by W. S. Gilbert, 1968; Hungry Fred, by Paula Fox, 1969; The Duke of Plaza Toro, by W. S. Gilbert, 1969; The Shooting of Dan McGrew and The Crema- tion of Sam McGee, by Robert W. Service, 1969; Marion's Moonball, by Winifred Rosen, 1970; The Cat That Walked by Him- self, by Rudyard Kipling, 1970; A Hot Thirsty Dog, by Marjorie Weinman Shar- mat, 1971; Impossible Possum, by Ellen Conford, 1971; Two Sisters and Some Hornets, by Beryl Epstein and Dorrit Davis, 1972; With a Deep Sea Smile, by Virginia A. Tashjian, comp., 1974; Tell Me a Trudy, by Lore Segal, 1977.

IRVING WERSTEIN

May 22, 1914–April 7, 1971

AUTHOR OF *I Accuse: The Story of the Dreyfus Case*, etc.

Biographical sketch of Irving Werstein:

IRVING WERSTEIN was born in Brooklyn, New York, and grew up in Richmond Hill, Long Island. From high school days, when he served on the staff of his school paper, he was determined to be a writer. But in the years of the great depression of the 1930s, this goal was a difficult one to attain. Forced by family financial reverses to drop out of New York University after two years, he

IRVING WERSTEIN

supported himself by a variety of jobs— he was a comedian on the Catskill borscht circuit, a factory worker, a "sur- geon" in a doll hospital, a waiter, a sales- man, an actor. It cannot have been an easy life, but his accounts of it were al- ways filled with a wry good humor.

Many years later he wrote of these times more seriously: "I believe that any- one who lived through the 1930s will never forget those trying days. They were a crucible, a furnace—and yet, de- spite the despair, they were days of up- lift and striving, a period of essential honesty and courage. Life was hard for most young people in the 1930s. It was a strange time to graduate from high school, to enter college, to hunt for a job, to come of age—but in the darkness there was still light. As Franklin D. Roosevelt put it, 'Failure is not an American habit.' "

And failure was not his habit, either. All through those difficult days he per- sisted in his writing, and in 1938, at the age of twenty-four, he sold his first story to an adventure magazine for fifteen dol- lars. This was the beginning of his ca- reer as a full-time free-lance writer, which continued, interrupted only by his four years service in the United States infantry during World War II, for the rest of his life. At first he wrote mostly for magazines; his stories and articles appeared in the *Saturday Evening Post, Saga, True,* and other popular magazines of the time. During the war, he was for a time a staff member of the servicemen's magazine, *Yank.* When the war ended, he resumed his magazine writing, and also turned to television, with scripts that were produced in England and Australia as well as in the United States.

The depression years, however, had been more than a time of stern apprenticeship for Werstein. He learned from them compassion for the plight of others, a sense of history, and a conviction that one man's writing can make a difference in the lives of many. Thus it was that he began to write for young readers, discovering what was to prove his real métier. His themes were the great events that have shaped our modern world, and the men and women who were actors in those events. His special gift was an ability to bring those events and persons vividly to life.

Many of his books were concerned with war and battles, both recent and historic. Introducing one of them he wrote: "Only by revealing the actual face of war can young people be made to realize how senseless it is; perhaps another generation will do better than mine did and bring an end to the abomination of war." In writing about battles he always remembered that it was not generals and admirals but men and boys who did the fighting. Meticulous research in combat reports and regimental histories supplied him with the needed information on military strategy, but he turned also to letters and diaries of the participants, and to contemporary magazines and newspapers, for a picture of their time and a feeling for their everyday concerns.

This respect for the individual and the youthful enthusiasm he kept all his life were reflected in several biographies of heroic men and women: Captain Dreyfus, whose trial foreshadowed the rise of antisemitism in Europe; "Mother" Jones, pioneer of the early American labor movement; Tom Smith, "marshall without a gun" in the Abilene of the 1870s; and many more. Research on his biography of Alan Seeger was made specially pleasant for him by the generous cooperation of the poet's sister who shared memories and treasured family snapshots with him. Of all his books, perhaps the most meaningful to him was *The Long Escape,* which dramatized a true story of World War II—the flight of fifty convalescent Belgian children and their nurse from the advancing German forces. The nurse who led those children to safety was a close friend, and his book was a proud tribute to her bravery.

Irving Werstein was a man of lively intelligence and quick wit, with an unpredictable but always engaging sense of humor. One of his editors reports that his telephone calls were a high point of her beginning days in publishing—she might find herself caught up in a fluent conversation in French before she had time to realize that she really couldn't speak that language, or deep in a mock-serious analysis of the day's events with someone who announced himself to be "Herr Doktor Strangelove." Werstein sometimes masked his feeling for his friends with a sort of affectionate mockery, but he never made the slightest attempt to conceal his pride and love for his wife Goldie and their son Jack. The last years of his life were shadowed by Mrs. Werstein's long illness. His friends admired the grave courage that now replaced his natural ebullience, and could not doubt that grief was in large part responsible for his early and sudden death at fifty-seven.

When Irving Werstein died more than forty-five of his books were in print. He would be the first to agree that they were not "great literature," but he was justly proud of his accomplishment. He cared deeply about justice and truth, and was eager to communicate that feeling to young readers. As a Jew he wrote with special pride of the struggle of the defenders of the Warsaw ghetto (*The Uprising of the Warsaw Ghetto*) and of the founding of the new nation of Israel (*All the Furious Battles*). Long before it became fashionable, he had chronicled the injustices done to the American Indian (*Massacre at Sand Creek*). He was in the best sense of the word a patriot—aware of his country's failings and yet confident of its worth. His books have been for many young readers their first introduction to the crucial events of history—history brought alive and imbued with a spirit of hope characteristic of Irving Werstein himself.

SELECTED WORKS: Marshall Without a Gun, 1959; Massacre at Sand Creek, 1963; The Long Escape, 1964; Turning Point for America; the Story of the Spanish-American War, 1964; The Great Struggle: Labor in America, 1965; Sound No Trumpet: The Life and Death of Alan Seeger, 1967; I Accuse: The Story of the Dreyfus Case, 1967; The Uprising of the Warsaw Ghetto, 1968; All the Furious Battles, 1969; The Cruel Years: The Story of the Spanish Civil War, 1969; Strangled Voices: The Story of the Haymarket Affair, 1969; Labor's Defiant Lady: The Story of Mother Jones, 1969; Pie in the Sky, an American Struggle: The Wobblies and Their Times, 1969; Shattered Decade, 1919–1929, 1970; Land and Liberty: The Mexican Revolution, 1971.

ABOUT: Contemporary Authors, Volume 29–32; New York Times May 4, 1969; April 9, 1971; Publishers Weekly April 26, 1971.

ANNE HITCHCOCK WHITE

ANNE HITCHCOCK WHITE

February 22, 1902–June 30, 1970

AUTHOR OF *Junket*, etc.

Biographical sketch of Anne Hitchcock White, by W. Homer White:

SHE was born Anne Wilson Hitchcock in St. Louis, Missouri, and was brought up there. Her father, Judge George C. Hitchcock, was of the third generation out of New England and was solidly rooted in Vermont, thanks to his great-grandfather, Ethan Allen, while her mother was out of Keene, New Hampshire, and Boston. It was not to be wondered at, therefore, that she considered herself a New Englander. Her early summers were spent on the Cape, at Cotuit,

thus fortifying this feeling. There she learned sailing, but she was somewhat overshadowed by two brothers who were crack sailors, and somewhat hampered by the remarkable skirts and middy blouses that the 1910s saw fit to huddle young girls into.

During this early period she developed a strong leaning toward the stage . . . the influence, one supposes, of the glamorous young Ethel Barrymore. Along with this interest went the study of the piano, at which she developed a more than considerable dexterity and which she did not give over until she gracefully retired in favor of her husband.

She attended Milton Academy, where theatricals were once more her point of concentration, to the extent that she wrote and directed the class play at her graduation. She went on to Vassar, and after two years became a statistic, ex-Vassar '25. She retired from college and went to New York, where she studied and trained under Madame Ouspenskaya, and acted and directed with the Neighborhood Playhouse and the American Laboratory Theater.

Then, as an article written some years ago had it, "her theatrical career was cut short by her marriage" with Homer White on May 2, 1932. A honeymoon of two years followed, in Mallorca, where she set up shop as a young housewife in a lovely old windmill, a *molino harinero*, complete with a tremendous tower for the sails. When she and her husband learned from the citizens of Establiments that there had been *another* mad *extranjero*, known to their grandfathers (so they said), who also had made music in the *molino*, both determined at once that it had to be Chopin, before he and Georges Sand moved on to Valldemosa. And in fact, only a few years ago the government found that this was indeed so and declared the *molino* a National Monument.

In 1935 she and her husband returned home and built a house in Essex, Massachusetts, on a hill overlooking the grand Ipswich-Essex marshes. When America entered the war, her husband was posted to our Embassy at Madrid. For her part, she discovered a remarkable talent for things mechanical—she, who used to ask wherever was the gas tank—and for nearly a year served as instructor at the Air Force Training School in Boston. When permission was finally granted, she joined her husband in Madrid, where she remained for two absorbing years. In 1944 her husband was transferred to London, where she joined him as a member of the Reports Board for the Office of Strategic Services.

Back home in the spring of 1945, she set about her writing. In 1948 Little Brown published her first juvenile, *The Adventures of Winnie and Bly*—which became *Snups og Mette* in Swedish, and "The Dear Knows What" in Japanese— stories that she had told to three small children whose father was at the time serving in the Pacific War. Viking Press, who now became her publishers, brought out *Serapina* in 1951. In 1953, *The Ladies Home Journal* in its October issue published a novel, *The Man Who Wouldn't Marry*, her only venture outside the juvenile field. *Junket* appeared in 1955, *The Uninvited Donkey*—which an ebullient young editor at Viking entitled "Donkey Hoe-Tee"—in 1957, and *A Dog Called Scholar* in 1963, the latter

being her favorite, and her husband's also. Another book was on the ways when she fell ill in 1964. She died on June 30, 1970.

It should be added, by way of indicating her quality, that one of the last, almost unintelligible scrawls she was able to make was a quotation from Housman: "What evil luck so ever/For me remains in store,/'Tis sure much finer fellows/ Have fared much worse before."

A Dog Named Scholar was a runner-up in the middle age-group in the 1963 New York *Herald Tribune* Children's Spring Book Festival. *Story of Serapina* was included in *Horn Book's* Fanfare 1952. Of all Mrs. White's books *Junket*, about a dog "who liked everything just so," has been the most long lived. It is still in print and has recently appeared in a paperback edition. It was selected by the New York *Times* as one of the one hundred best books of the year in 1955.

SELECTED WORKS: The Adventures of Winnie and Bly, 1948; The Story of Serapina, 1951; Junket, 1955; The Uninvited Donkey, 1957; A Dog Called Scholar, 1963.

ILON WIKLAND
February 5, 1930–

ILLUSTRATOR OF *Mio, My Son*, etc.

Biographical sketch of Ilon Wikland:

ILON WIKLAND was born at Dorpat, Estonia, and lived for most of her childhood with her grandparents in a small town on the Baltic Sea. She came to Sweden as a refugee in 1944. There she went to two different art schools in Stockholm, Skolan för Bok- och Reklamkonst, and Signe Barth's Painting School. After two years in a decorating studio she had a chance to study in England for six months, and upon her return she began working for a publisher as a layout artist. She married her husband, an officer in the Swedish Navy, in 1951 and at

Ilon: *EE lon*

ILON WIKLAND

that time began working as a free-lance artist, doing magazine illustration. Then a meeting with the noted Swedish author Astrid Lindgren changed her life. Not only did the author become a personal friend, but Ilon Wikland became convinced, after illustrating *Mio, My Son,* that book illustration was her métier. Subsequently she illustrated almost all of Astrid Lindgren's books and Hans Peterson's, as well as those by other authors. Recently she has begun doing her own very simple picture books. She works primarily in black and white or in full color.

In 1966 Ilon Wikland received a government scholarship to pursue her work and in 1969 she was awarded the Elsa Beskow Plaque, Sweden's highest award to an illustrator.

Miss Wikland and her husband and four daughters live outside of Stockholm. Besides her work she loves to travel. She is also a follower of Ernst Idla, a fellow Estonian who directs a gymnastic program.

SELECTED WORKS WRITTEN AND ILLUSTRATED: I Can Help Too! 1971; See What I Can Do! 1974.

SELECTED WORKS ILLUSTRATED: Mio, My Son, by Astrid Lindgren, 1956; Magnus and the Squirrel, by Hans Peterson, 1959; Magnus in Danger, by Hans Peterson, 1961;

Magnus in the Harbor, by Hans Peterson, 1962; Christmas in Noisy Village, by Astrid Lindgren, 1964; Magnus and the Ship's Mascot, by Hans Peterson, 1967; Magnus and the Wagon Horse, by Hans Peterson, 1966; Erik and the Christmas Horse, by Hans Peterson, 1970.

ABOUT: Hürlimann, Bettina, Picture-Book World; Kingman, Lee and others, comps. Illustrators of Children's Books: 1957–1966.

BARRY WILKINSON

April 29, 1923–

AUTHOR AND ILLUSTRATOR OF *The Diverting Adventures of Tom Thumb*, etc.

Autobiographical sketch of Barry Wilkinson:

I WAS born in the small industrial town of Dewsbury, Yorkshire, England, where my father was an inspector of police. The town was a grey tangle of factories, warehouses, coal-pits, and slums, and we lived on the edge of the town. Some of my happiest times were spent in the Yorkshire countryside near Tadcaster with my grandmother, who was the housekeeper of Grimstone Manor in Gilling. I found school life very boring and relied on the escapism provided by the five cinemas, the radio, music, and my everlasting drawing to keep me amused.

I think it was my fascination with the cinema that led to an interest in all the visual arts, particularly those allied to some form of storytelling. I was sent to the local art school and after three years of academic training (and five wartime years in the Royal Air Force) I was accepted by the Royal College of Art in London.

After pursuing a variety of interests I chanced on stained-glass designing and was awarded my diploma in that subject.

After a period working in a stained-glass studio and then teaching the subject at Wimbledon College of Art, I continued teaching but then reverted to my original interest: illustration and graphics. Being a practical sort of person I

found teaching to be unfulfilling and I yearned to paint and draw for my living. So, rather late in life, at the age of thirty, after a session on film animation, I took a chance and with the help of my wife, who went out to work, and started to free-lance, hoping the work would come my way. Luckily it did and, relying heavily on my agent, I have been solely employed in illustrating ever since. Admittedly it has ranged widely from transparent murals and Christmas street-decorations in London and Glasgow, through advertising, down to minuscule drawings in magazines, illustrating stories on television and so on, but my real enjoyment comes from working for books, and children's picture books in particular. When the Bodley Head took a chance with my work I think it was then that I felt a genuine sense of achievement. And although I am a frustrated jazz musician, film director, actor, industrial designer and many other exciting people, I have at least achieved one ambition—to illustrate books.

I met my wife Pam when we were both students at art college where she was studying textile design, but her interests now are in painting and reviving country crafts. We have two children

Joanna (22), social worker, and Tom (21), film maker, and we live at Sevenoaks in Kent.

———

Barry Wilkinson's work was selected for inclusion in the 1967 *Graphis* children's issue.

SELECTED WORKS ILLUSTRATED: The Diverting Adventures of Tom Thumb, 1969; Puss in Boots, by Charles Perrault, 1969; Lazy Jack, by Joseph Jacobs, 1970; The Story of Aladdin, by Naomi Lewis (retold), 1971; My Family, by Felicity Sen, 1977.

BARBARA WILLARD

1909–

AUTHOR OF *The Lark and the Laurel*, etc.

Autobiographical sketch of Barbara Mary Willard:

BEING the first writer in a family has its problems. We had been actors on my father's side but my maternal grandmother and all my aunts clearly found that a curious way of living, and they saw the same suggestion of fecklessness in writing. That girl should be in the open air. Why don't you join a tennis club? You'll get round-shouldered sitting huddled over a desk. . . . No doubt I grew increasingly morose as I insisted on following my bent. By today's standards I had a sketchy education. At the time it was the best a girl could hope for whose parents could certainly not afford to send her to one of the famous girls' schools. However, I had two teachers who did their best to see me through. The first, by describing my school essays as 'glib, but silly' laid the foundations of self-criticism. The second, the nun who taught English at my convent school, who was sister to a distinguished historian, nagged me into a sense of style.

My first novel was published when I was twenty and appropriately earned me twenty pounds. However, I was bound to go on. Reviewers were kind and I did once contrive a novel that sold five thou-

BARBARA WILLARD

I like to write stories about children of all ages, but at present I'm writing a rather older thing—a sort of chronicle of the area where I live. This is in Sussex, my native heath to which I returned to settle some years ago. The place is called Ashdown Forest, it is all that remains of the great Wealden forest that once covered southeastern England. I find it a place full of mystery and excitement, almost weighed down with a sense of the past. Writing about people I have imagined living there in times of crisis from the fifteenth to the seventeenth centuries has given me more pleasure and satisfaction than anything I have worked on before.

————

sand copies. I supported myself with fringe jobs—as a reader for film companies, as a play reader and occasional modest reviewer—half-a-guinea a book, I seem to remember.

I had been an only child until I was twelve, when my parents with some embarrassment supplied me with a brother. I spent so much time with him that I always say I've had my second childhood and only await my third. No doubt at all that it was going over all the old stories with him, finding new ones and making up others, that implanted a desire to write for the young. Goodness knows how many times I made false starts and put the idea away for years at a time. At last I did place a story for children. It must have been turned down by fifty publishers before it found a modest home, and I should now like to forget all about it. All the same, it gave me the necessary determination to plod on. By a lucky chance I hit on a story that suited a new mood in writing for children and somebody gave me an introduction to Grace Allen Hogarth, then with Constable. I had three chapters to show her and to my joy she commissioned the book. It was called *The House With Roots* and came out in 1959.

Since then I have been unable to stop.

Barbara Willard says that she always felt that the years since she began writing for children, were her happiest, but now that she has "Mantlemass in the bag," the happiest years are now. Mantlemass is the name of the manor in the Ashdown Forest of Sussex that has formed the setting for her most recent and best acclaimed novels. The interlocking Mantlemass stories trace the fortunes of the manor families through the most turbulent periods of English history, beginning at the end of the War of Roses. They have brought Miss Willard accolades on both sides of the Atlantic. *The Sprig of Broom* was commended for the prestigious *Guardian* Award in 1972, as was *A Cold Wind Blowing* in 1973. In 1974 *The Iron Lilly* won the *Guardian* Award. It was also chosen a Notable Book by the American Library Association, as was *Storm from the West* (not one of the historical novels) in 1964.

She loves to garden, walk and cook and retains her strong interest in theater and the local Sussex dialects.

SELECTED WORKS: If All the Swords in England, 1961; Hetty, 1963; Storm from the West, 1964; Three and One to Carry, 1965; The Richleighs of Tantamount, 1967; Flight to the Forest, 1967; The Lark and the Laurel, 1970; A Dog and a Half, 1971;

The Sprig of Broom, 1972; A Cold Wind Blowing, 1973; The Iron Lilly, 1974; Harrow and Harvest, 1975; Convent Cat, 1976; The Miller's Boy, 1976.

SELECTED WORKS EDITED: Hullabaloo! About Naughty Boys and Girls, 1969; Happy Families, 1974.

ABOUT: Author's and Writer's Who's Who, 1971; Jones, Cornelia and Olivia R. Way. British Children's Authors. Interviews at Home; Children's Book Review Spring 1975; Signal January 1972.

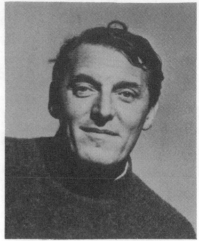

JAY WILLIAMS

May 31, 1914–

AUTHOR OF *The Practical Princess*, etc.

Autobiographical sketch of Jay Williams, who uses the pseudonym of "Michael Delving" for his adult detective stories:

I HAVE been writing books for children for thirty-five years, and reading them for nearly twice as long. My earliest, happiest excursions were to the library and the substance of my games was Pyle's *Robin Hood*, Dumas' *The Three Musketeers*, and Doyle's *Sir Nigel*. My first writing was a feverish version of King Arthur, done at the age of twelve and with the inclusion of a new character —myself. It is anything but surprising that my first books for children were historical tales and that my first adult novel, *The Good Yeomen*, was about Robin Hood.

During the two years that I spent otherwise profitlessly at the University of Pennsylvania, I discovered a wide field of literature to which, during my high school years, I had been largely blind, and which ranged from the Norse sagas through Tolstoy, Proust and Sterne. I began writing in earnest, mostly imitations of Baudelaire's prose poems and pastiches of Lord Dunsany, and my English teachers warned me that I would come to no good unless I first came to grips with reality. Notwithstanding, I could never write a decent essay on *Beowulf* and still can't.

My writing was sidetracked for seven years by a spell in the theater, as a comic, stage manager, and press agent. In 1942 a literary agent I knew told me there was a shortage of books for children between the ages of eight and twelve, "mainly," she added, "in historical novels and mysteries." The words "history-mystery" jingled in my head for a few days, and suddenly a story arrived almost complete, a mystery set in Augustan Rome. I quit my job and began work on it as a gamble. It took me a year, and was published in 1943 under the title *The Stolen Oracle*.

During the war, I served mostly in the infantry and was wounded in Germany. Through the kind offices of a supply sergeant who loaned me the use of a corner of his office and a typewriter, I wrote two children's books with a military inspiration, one about the Roman army, the other about the Peasant's War in Germany. When I got out of the army, I found that I was committed to writing and it has been my profession ever since. I am the author of seventy-five books of fiction and nonfiction, of which fifty-eight are for children.

In 1954, Raymond Abrashkin and I

began work on a science fiction novel for young people, called *Danny Dunn and the Antigravity Paint*. Abrashkin, then almost completely paralyzed from a desperate illness, had taught science and had written newspaper and magazine columns about education. He was a brilliant idea-man; I did the writing. He couldn't speak and would point to letters on a drawing of a typewriter keyboard. We soon developed a kind of shorthand in which a letter or two stood for a whole word. Later, as his illness advanced, we had to invent a code in which he "spoke" to me by winking. He died soon after the fifth of the Danny Dunn books was published, but before his death had the satisfaction of reading nearly a thousand fan letters a year from children, and of knowing that the series was firmly established.

———

Jay Williams was born in Buffalo, New York, the son of Max and Lillian Jacobson. He attended the University of Pennsylvania in 1932–33 and Columbia University in 1933–34. In 1941 he married Barbara Girsdansky. Their children are Christopher and Victoria. From 1941–45 Williams served in the army in Europe and was decorated with a Purple Heart. He held a Guggenheim Fellowship in literature for 1949.

The Roman Moon mystery received the award of the Boys' Clubs of America in 1969. Two of the Danny Dunn books have received the Young Reader's Choice Awards sponsored by the Pacific Northwest Library Association: *Danny Dunn and the Homework Machine* in 1961 and *Danny Dunn on the Ocean Floor* in 1963.

Joan of Arc and *The Question Box* were both selected by the New York *Times* as the best in their year of publication. *The Practical Princess* was judged by *School Library Journal* to be one of the best books of 1969. In addition a number of the picture books for which he has written the texts have been singled out because of the excellence of their illustrations.

Williams divides his time between Connecticut and Europe, and when not traveling or writing indulges his interest in Oriental painting and field archery.

SELECTED WORKS: The Stolen Oracle, 1943; The Roman Moon Mystery, 1948; Tournament of the Lions, 1960; Joan of Arc, 1963; The Question Box, 1965; The Practical Princess, 1969; Stupid Marco, 1970; The Silver Whistle, 1971; Petronella, 1973; Forgetful Fred, 1974; Everyone Knows What a Dragon Looks Like, 1976; The Reward Worth Having, 1977; The Time of the Kraken, 1977.

SELECTED WORKS WRITTEN WITH RAYMOND ABRASHKIN: Danny Dunn and the Antigravity Paint, 1956; Danny Dunn on a Desert Island, 1957; Danny Dunn and the Homework Machine, 1958; Danny Dunn on the Ocean Floor, 1960; Danny Dunn and the Fossil Cave, 1961; Danny Dunn and the Automatic House, 1965; Danny Dunn and the Smallifying Machine, 1969; Danny Dunn, the Invisible Boy, 1975; Danny Dunn and the Universal Glue, 1977.

ABOUT: Contemporary Authors, Vol. 2; Something about the Author, Vol. 3; World Authors: 1950–1970; Current Biography, 1955; McCall's January 1973; Wilson Library Bulletin October 1955.

JAMES PLAYSTED WOOD

December 11, 1905–

AUTHOR OF *Elephant in the Family*, etc.

Autobiographical sketch of James Playsted Wood:

THOUGH I was born of English parents in South Brooklyn, I was brought up in Harlem where I went to the Model School of the New York Training School for Teachers. I was told that there were other places than Manhattan but did not really believe it until we moved to Holyoke, Massachusetts, when I was twelve and I saw some actual woods. In high school I edited the school paper, wrote the school news for the Holyoke *Transcript*, and was janitor of a large private school. As soon as I graduated I returned to New York and minor jobs on the *Sun-Herald* Syndicate, then the New York *Tribune*.

I was still on the *Tribune* when, a year later, I entered Columbia College. As I worked six nights a week on the paper that first year I hardly knew what was going on in either place. After college I spent two years in New York as an advertising copywriter. Somewhere along the line I took an honors M.A. in American literature at Columbia.

I spent seven years teaching English in the du Pont Manual Training High School and writing weekly book reviews for the *Courier-Journal* in Louisville, Kentucky; published my first novel; then became, first instructor, then assistant professor of English in Amherst College. World War II put an end to that. The army made me a newsman again.

After training at Miami Beach and a few months at Maxwell Field I was assigned to the Office of the Chief of Staff in the Pentagon and was based mostly in the Press Branch, War Department Bureau of Public Relations. At various times I wrote press releases, ghosted speeches and official statements, edited a magazine, *Firepower*, and was Officer-in-Charge of *War Times*, the War Department's weekly newspaper. When the war ended I went to the Curtis Publishing Company, which then published *The Saturday Evening Post, Ladies' Home Journal, Country Gentleman, Jack and Jill* and *Holiday*, in Philadelphia. There I ghosted more speeches, articles and books, and worked in editorial, research and circulation. All of this time I was writing books of my own. From 1974–1976 I was contributing editor of the Limited Editions Club.

I have no idea when or how I began to write. I learned to read from Alger books and the novels of the American Winston Churchill, and even then I was as fascinated by the fact that a man could write a book as by the stories. I feel as if I have always written. Though, perforce, I have done other things, nothing else has ever seemed to me worth doing or attempting.

Certainly I do not know how I began to write for children. I have never been able to see any essential difference between children and adults except that children are honest. When one of my books is published I look on the jacket flap where it says "10 up" or "from ages 9 through 90" to find out whom I wrote it for.

James Playsted Wood's books in many subject areas testify to the variety and scope of his interests. Elsewhere he has said, "In writing I try to be clear and tell the truth as I see it. I care little or nothing for editorial opinion or critics' comment. I write to please myself. If the result happens to please a few other people, I'm delighted. . . . Sometimes, when I get tired of careful, scholarly work, I let my imagination go and write *When I Was Jersey* and *The Mammoth Parade.*"

Today Wood lives in Massachusetts and, in his spare time, collects jade and grows hollies. He remarks in the letter sent with his sketch, "I have no real photograph as I object to them, but the snapshot shows me in characteristic pose. The plants are ilex crenata Oconee River, which I brought from Georgia. Out of perversity, my primary motivation, I grow holly in a region where it will not grow."

SELECTED WORKS: Elephant in the Family, 1957; A Hound, a Bay Horse, and a Turtle-dove, 1963; The Man Who Hated Sherlock Holmes, 1965; The Snark Was a Boojum, 1966; What's the Market? The Story of the Stock Exchange, 1966; When I Was Jersey, 1967; Mr. Jonathan Edwards, 1968; The Mammoth Parade, 1969; The People of Concord, 1970; The Admirable Cotton Mather, 1971; Poetry Is: Thoughts about the What, Why and Who of Poetry, 1972; Colonial New Hampshire, 1973; Kentucky Time, 1977.

ABOUT: Author's and Writer's Who's Who, 1971; Contemporary Authors, Vol. 9–10; Something about the Author, Vol. 1; Who's Who in America, 1970–71.

PATRICIA WRIGHTSON

June 19, 1921–

AUTHOR OF A Racecourse for Andy, etc.

Autobiographical sketch of Alice Patricia Wrightson:

AS a child I was one of a family of six and, incredibly, lonely. This was because of being isolated between two older sisters and three younger brothers. My father was a solicitor who preferred the country to law, and I grew up in country areas on the North Coast of New South Wales. My schools ranged from a two-teacher country school to an important demonstration school; and by far my favourite was the State Correspondence School for children isolated in the country. I was really educated by my father in literature, philosophy and wonder; and by my mother in the social sciences. My most profitable year of schooling was the year in which I abandoned formal schooling altogether and spent the year, without permission or guidance, in discovering Shakespeare.

All of my schools assumed I would become a writer, but I very nearly didn't. I wasn't sure how to begin, was awed by the great writers, and couldn't believe there was any excuse for beginning. Only after I had been married and divorced and had two children of my own (Jenny and Peter) did I at last dare to try; and then I realized that my children's lives would be rather arid if I really had nothing to say to them. I was very lucky to begin by accident in so demanding a school, and my work has been a continuing exploration of it. I retired as editor of School Magazine, a literary magazine produced by the New South Wales Department of Education for children in the primary schools. Half a million copies, graded into four parts, are distributed free every month. Since my retirement I can concentrate on writing.

I can only add that I have a powerful disbelief in the point and value of biographical notes of this sort. What are they for? What are they about? It is perhaps a kindly thought to allow a writer to pose for the camera; but if there is a sober need for information about him, why not go to the unimpeachable source of the writer's work? Everything about him that could possibly matter is on record there—at any rate in the case of the committed writer for children. And in the free and lonely world of imagination it is impossible to sustain a convincing pose for long. There is no one there to react and guide the poser.

My conviction about this is probably caused by a very dull set of biographical data. I certainly find the notes of other writers fascinating to read.

———

Patricia Wrightson was born in Lismore, New South Wales, Australia. She worked for twenty years in hospital administration before undertaking her present job. Her novels are few in number, but almost all of them have achieved distinction in their own country and abroad. Although Mrs. Wrightson hopes someday to write for adults, when she has "come to the end of this field, and goodness knows when that will be," she finds that novels for children are more challenging, because there is so little room in them for "worldly thinking" and pretense, which she despises. She chooses themes "involving some mental exploration and a stretching of understanding," with the aim of inducing her readers to think for themselves and reach their own conclusions.

With the exception of *Down to Earth*, all Mrs. Wrightson's novels have reached the final competition for Australia's Book of the Year Award given by the Children's Book Council of Australia. Of her two earliest books, *The Crooked Snake* (1955, Angus and Robertson) and *The Bunyip Hole* (1957, Angus and Robertson), the first won the award in 1956 and the second received a commendation for it in 1959. *The Feather Star*, the delicate exploration of a girl's passage from childish to adult perceptions, was the first Wrightson work to be published in the United States. It was an American Library Association Notable Book in 1963, having been commended for the Book of the Year Award the same year. Mrs. Wrightson's most distinguished book to date is *A Racecourse for Andy* (*I Own the Racecourse* in the Australian and British editions). Andy is a retarded boy who believes he has bought a racecourse for three dollars and proceeds to act accordingly. The story is funny, poignant and compelling, and in the course of it the author gives the reader ample opportunity to weigh the question "How real is reality?" Highly commended for the Australian Book of the Year Award in 1969, *A Racecourse for Andy* was an American Library Association Notable Book in 1968, a prize book in the 1968 *Book World* Children's Spring Book Festival, and appeared on *Horn Book's* Honor List for 1968 as well as its Fanfare List 1966–1970. It was also a runner-up for the prestigious Award in England in 1969 and named to the Honor List for the Hans Christian Andersen prize in 1970. Subsequent books, *An Older Kind of Magic* and *The Nargun and the Stars*, were also distinguished, the first being Highly Commended for the Australian Book of the Year Award in 1973, while the latter won the award in 1974 and was also named a Notable Book by the American Library Association the same year. In 1976 the book was named to the Hans Christian Andersen Honor List by the International Board on Books for Young People.

SELECTED WORKS: The Feather Star, 1963; Down to Earth, 1965; A Racecourse for Andy, 1968; An Older Kind of Magic, 1972; The Nargun and the Stars, 1974; The Ice is Coming, 1977.

ABOUT: Townsend, John Rowe. A Sense of Story. Bookbird No. 2, 1970; Signal No. 19, 1976.

JANE YOLEN
February 11, 1939–

AUTHOR OF *The Girl Who Cried Flowers*, etc.

Autobiographical sketch of Jane Yolen Stemple:

I COME from a line of storytellers. My great-grandfather was the Reb, the storyteller in a small village in Finno-Russia, my father an author, my mother a mostly unpublished writer. From early childhood I have written. In fact, in first grade I was the heralded author of the class musical about talking vegetables. I played the chief carrot and our grand finale was a singing salad.

But if I had to point to my primary source of inspiration, it would be to the folk culture. My earliest readings were the folk tales and fairy stories I took home from the library by the dozens. Even when I was old enough to make the trip across Central Park by myself, I was still not too old for those folk fantasies. My father, who plays the guitar and sings, first introduced me to folk songs, but I went him some better in learning every old English, Scottish, Irish and Appalachian love song and ballad I ever heard. Years later, at Smith College, I made an unhappy college career bearable by singing with a guitar-playing boyfriend at fraternity parties and mixers. We made a little money, a lot of friends, and imprinted hundreds of folk tunes on our hungry minds.

Those folk tales and fairy stories and ballads still find their way into my life. I read fantasy stories and science fiction and folk literature for pleasure. I sing the old songs to my own three children, Heidi and Adam and Jason. And all those fey creatures, merfolk, tree maidens and dragons of the old world find their way into my many tales.

———

Jane Yolen was born in New York City and lived there until she was thirteen, when her family moved to Westport, Connecticut. She received her B.A. from Smith College in 1960 and then went to New York and worked at various publishing jobs until she ended up at Alfred A. Knopf as an assistant juvenile editor. She remained there until 1965, when she left to write and travel in Europe. In the meantime, on September 2, 1962, she had married David W. Stemple, a photographer and computer expert. The Stemples have three children: Heidi Elisabet, born 1966; Adam Douglas, born 1968; and Jason Frederic, born 1970. They live on a farm in Hatfield, Massachusetts.

Besides writing books for children, Jane Yolen is a frequent reviewer of them for the New York *Times Book Review* and a columnist for the *Daily Hampshire Gazette*. She has been on the Board of Directors of the Society of Children's Book Writers and taught courses in writing for children at Smith College and in adult education programs. Those teaching experiences were distilled in a book, *Writing for Children*, published in 1973.

Miss Yolen has a strong personal enthusiasm for kites and is a member of both the International Kitefliers Association and the American Kite Fliers Association, so it is not surprising that kites appear in some of her stories. The best known is doubtless *The Emperor and the Kite* which, with illustrations by Ed Young, was a Caldecott Honor Book in 1968. The same title was an American Library Association Notable Book and was listed among the seventy-five best books of the year chosen by the New York *Times*. A number of Jane Yolen's books have been singled out for the contribution of their illustrations and included in showcases or children's book shows. Besides being praised for its illustrations, *The Girl Who Cried Flowers* was a finalist for the 1975 National Book Award and received the 1974 Golden Kite Award, given by the Society of Children's Book Writers for the book that "best exhibits excellence in writing and genuinely appeals to the interests and concerns of children." *The Transfigured Hart* was a Golden Kite Honor Book in 1975, and *The Moon Ribbon* received the award in 1976.

SELECTED WORKS: The Witch Who Wasn't, 1964; The Emperor and the Kite, 1967; Greyling, 1968; The Seventh Mandarin, 1970; The Girl Who Loved the Wind, 1972; The Boy Who Had Wings, 1974; The Girl Who Cried Flowers, 1974; Rainbow Rider, 1974; The Little Spotted Fish, 1975; The Transfigured Hart, 1975; The Moon Ribbon and Other Tales, 1976; The Giants' Farm, 1977; The Hundredth Dove and Other Tales, 1977.

ABOUT: Contemporary Authors, Vol. 15–16; Foremost Women in Communications; Something about the Author, Vol. 4.

ALKI ZEI

December 15, 1928–

AUTHOR OF *Wildcat Under Glass*, etc.

Autobiographical sketch of Alki Zei Sevastikoglou:

I WAS born and grew up in Athens, Greece. I decided to be a writer one summer when I was ten and was feeling very bored. We were vacationing, my parents, my sister, one year older, and I, on a small Greek Island, Samos, where my mother was born.

After lunch my sister and I were not permitted to run out in the sun or swim; instead we were to have a siesta as the grown-ups did. To pass those dull hours my sister took up painting. I, being unable to draw a single straight line, took up writing poetry.

My career as a poet lasted that one summer. Next summer I took up "publishing" a satirical paper about my family, our friends, and our neighbors. It was issued in one single copy, as I had to write it by hand on large sheets from my copybook.

On October 28, 1940, Mussolini's Fascist army attacked Greece. Hospitals were soon crowded with wounded Greek soldiers. One of our schoolmistresses organized a puppet theatre to entertain them. She taught us how to make and handle puppets. I fell passionately in love with our puppet theatre and started writing short plays for our group to perform.

The fighting lasted five whole months; then the Nazis, too, attacked Greece to help their allies, the Italian Fascists. Greece was occupied by both of them. So our puppet theatre, along with the whole Greek people, took part in the resistance against both of them.

Among our audience were writers, artists and intellectuals. As it turned out, one of them, young playwright and stage director Yorgos Sevastikoglou, was so enthusiastic over our performance, my plays, and me myself that, when Greece was liberated after three and a half years and soon after I graduated from school, he married me and is still married to me.

For two years I studied literature at Athens University and wrote short stories. Then I quit the university for a drama school, graduating with an actor's diploma.

Alki Zei: *AL kee Zee*

I have traveled quite a lot in my life —sometimes of my own volition, sometimes not. I had just taken my first steps on the stage when I left for Italy—Rome —on my way to meet my husband, who by then was living in the Soviet Union, working there in the theatre and the cinema. While I was waiting in Rome for a Soviet visa, I played small parts in Eduardo de Filippo's troupe. My career as an actress stopped there.

In the Soviet Union I had neither the capacity nor the strength to start learning a foreign language anew so as to be able to act on the stage. To be honest, I confess that writing appealed much more to me than acting.

For ten years my husband and I lived in the Soviet Union where our daughter, Irini (pronounced Erene—which in Greek means peace), and our son, Petros, were born. There, in Moscow, I wrote my first novel for children, *Wildcat Under Glass*, and studied film writing at the Moscow Cinema Institute for two years.

In 1964 we left the Soviet Union to settle in Athens again. Three years later, in 1967, we again took the road abroad: a military dictatorship took over Greece. This time we came to Paris where we have since lived. Here in Paris I wrote my second novel for children *Petros' War*.

In 1975 two of my books for children, *Uncle Plato*, a novel, and *Boots and Pumps*, a collection of short stories, were published in Greece. A novel for children, *Along the Rails*, will also be published soon.

I live in France, but my heart, my thoughts, my language, my roots are in Greece, where I shall soon return now that my country is free.

———

Alki Zei's two books for young people were included on all the major honor lists when they appeared here. Both were chosen Notable Books by the American Library Association and each earned for its publisher the Mildred Batchelder Award, given by the American Library Association for the best translated book published in the previous year.

Wildcat Under Glass has been translated into English, Russian, Estonian, French, German, Danish, Finnish, Swedish and Japanese, and *Petros' War* so far has appeared in English and Russian.

The author has also had short stories published in Greek magazines.

SELECTED WORKS: Wildcat Under Glass, 1968; Petros' War, 1972.

Authors and Illustrators Included in This Series

The following list indicates the volume in which each individual may be found:

J—The Junior Book of Authors, second edition (1951)

M—More Junior Authors (1963)

T—Third Book of Junior Authors (1972)

F—Fourth Book of Junior Authors and Illustrators (1978)

Adams, Adrienne—T
Adams, Andy—J
Adams, Julia Davis. See Davis, Julia—J
Adams, Katharine—J
Adamson, Joy—F
Adler, Irving ("Robert Irving")—T
Adler, Ruth—T
Adoff, Arnold—F
Adoff, Virginia Hamilton. See Hamilton, Virginia—F
Adshead, Gladys L.—M
Agle, Nan—F
Aichinger, Helga—F
Aiken, Joan—T
"Akens, Floyd." See Baum, L. Frank—T
Alcorn, John—T
Aldis, Dorothy—J
Alexander, Janet McNeill. See McNeill, Janet—F
Alexander, Lloyd—T
Alexander, Martha—F
Alger, Leclaire Gowans. See "Nic Leodhas, Sorche"—T
"Aliki" (Aliki Liacouras Brandenberg)—T
Allee, Marjorie Hill—J
"Allen, Adam." See Epstein, Samuel—M
Allen, Agnes—F
"Allen, Alex B." See Heide, Florence Parry—F
Allen, Jack. See Allen, Agnes—F
Allen, Merritt Parmelee—J
Almedingen, E. M.—T
Ambrus, Victor G.—T
Ames, Gerald—T
Ames, Rose Wyler ("Peter Thayer," Rose Wyler)—T
Anckarsvärd, Karin—T
Andersen, Hans Christian—J
Anderson, Adrienne. See Adams, Adrienne—T
Anderson, C. W.—J, T
Anderson, Lonzo—T
Angeli, Marguerite de. See de Angeli, Marguerite—J

Angelo, Valenti—J
Anglund, Joan Walsh—T
Anno, Mitsumasa—F
"Arden, Barbie." See Stoutenburg, Adrien—T
Ardizzone, Edward—M
Armer, Laura Adams—J
Armstrong, Richard—T
Armstrong, William H.—T
Arno, Enrico—F
Artzybasheff, Boris—J
Aruego, Ariane. See Dewey, Ariane—F
Aruego, José—F
Arundel, Honor (Honor Morfydd Arundel McCrindle)—F
Asch, Frank—F
Ashmun, Margaret—J
Asimov, Isaac ("Paul French")—T
Atwater, Florence Hasseltine Carroll—M
Atwater, Montgomery Meigs—M
Atwater, Richard Tupper—M
Atwood, Ann—F
Aulaire, Edgar Parin d'—J
Aulaire, Ingri Parin d'—J
Austin, Margot—M
Averill, Esther—J
Avery, Gillian (Gillian Elise Avery Cockshut)—F
Ayer, Jacqueline—T
Ayer, Margaret—M

"Babbis, Eleanor." See Friis-Baastad, Babbis—T
Babbitt, Natalie—F
Bagnold, Enid (Enid Algerine Bagnold Jones)—F
Bailey, Carolyn Sherwin—J
Baity, Elizabeth Chesley—M
Baker, Betty—T
Baker, Margaret—J
Baker, Margaret J.—M
Baker, Mary—J
Baker, Nina Brown—J
Baker, Olaf—J
Baker, Rachel—M

Balch, Glenn—M
Balderson, Margaret—F
Baldwin, James—J
Balet, Jan—T
"Ball, Zachary" (Kelly Ray Masters)—F
"Bancroft, Laura." See Baum, L. Frank—T
Bannerman, Helen—J
Bannon, Laura—M
Barbour, Ralph Henry—J
Barne, Kitty—J
Bartos-Höppner, Barbara—F
Baudouy, Michel-Aimé—T
Baum, L. Frank ("Floyd Akens," "Laura Bancroft," "John Estes Cook," "Captain Hugh Fitzgerald," "Suzanne Metcalf," "Schuyler Stanton," "Edith Van Dyne")—T
Baumann, Hans—T
Bawden, Nina (Nina Mary Mabey Bawden Kark)—F
Baylor, Byrd (Byrd Baylor Schweitzer)—F
Baynes, Ernest Harold—J
Baynes, Pauline—T
"BB" (Denys James Watkins-Pitchford)—T
Beatty, Hetty Burlingame—M
Beatty, John—T
Beatty, Patricia—T
Beckman, Gunnel—F
Beeler, Nelson F.—M
Behn, Harry—M
Beim, Jerrold—J
Beim, Lorraine—J
Bell, Corydon—T
Bell, Margaret E.—M
Bell, Thelma—T
Belpré, Pura (Pura Belpré White)—F
Belting, Natalia Maree—T
Bemelmans, Ludwig—M
Benary-Isbert, Margot—M
Benchley, Nathaniel—F
Bendick, Jeanne—M
Bendick, Robert—M
Benét, Laura—J
Bennett, John—J

361

Bennett, Rainey—F
Bennett, Richard—J
Berg, Björn—F
Berna, Paul—T
"Berry, Erick" (Allena Best)—J
Berson, Harold—F
Beskow, Elsa—J
Best, Allena. See "Berry, Erick" —J
Best, Herbert—J
Beston, Henry (Henry Beston Sheahan)—J
"Bettina" (Bettina Ehrlich)—M
Betz, Betty—M
Bialk, Elisa—M
Bianco, Margery Williams—J
Bianco, Pamela. See Bianco, Margery Williams—J
Bileck, Marvin—F
Bill, Alfred H.—J
Billings, Henry—M
Birch, Reginald—J
Bischoff, Ilse—M
Bishop, Claire Huchet—J
Bishop, Elizabeth—F
Blakely, Gwendolyn Elizabeth Brooks. See Brooks, Gwendolyn—F
Bleeker, Sonia—M
Blegvad, Erik—T
Blegvad, Lenore—T
Bloch, Marie Halun—F
Blough, Glenn O.—M
Blume, Judy—F
Bock, Vera—M
Bolliger, Max—F
Bolognese, Don—F
Bond, Michael—T
Bonham, Frank—T
Bonsall, Crosby Newell (Crosby Newell)—T
Bontemps, Arna—J
Bonzon, Paul-Jacques—F
Borton, Elizabeth. See Treviño, Elizabeth Borton de—T
Boston, Lucy—T
Bothwell, Jean—J
Bourliaguet, Léonce—F
Boutet de Monvel—J
Bowman, James Cloyd—J
Boylston, Helen—J
Bradbury, Bianca—F
Bragg, Mabel Caroline ("Watty Piper")—F
Brandenberg, Aliki Liacouras. See "Aliki"—T
Branley, Franklyn M.—M
Brann, Esther—J
Bransom, Paul—M
"Breck, Vivian" (Vivian Gurney Breckenfield)—M
Breckenfield, Vivian Gurney. See "Breck, Vivian"—M
Brenner, Barbara—F

Brenner, Fred—F
Brier, Howard, M.—M
Briggs, Raymond—T
Bright, Robert—M
Brindze, Ruth—M
Brink, Carol—J
Brinsmead, Hesba Fay—F
Bro, Margueritte—M
Brock, C. E.—J
Brock, Emma L.—J
Brock, H. M.—J
Bromhall, Winifred—M
"Bronson, Lynn." See Lampman, Evelyn Sibley—M
Bronson, Wilfrid S.—J
Brooke, L. Leslie—J
Brooks, Gwendolyn (Gwendolyn Elizabeth Brooks Blakely) —F
Brooks, Walter R.—J
Broster, D. K.—J
Brown, Edna A.—J
Brown, Marcia—M
Brown, Margaret Wise ("Golden MacDonald")—J
Brown, Paul—J
Brown, Roy—F
Bruckner, Karl—F
Brunhoff, Jean de—J
Brunhoff, Laurent de—M
Bryson, Bernarda—T
Buehr, Walter—T
Buff, Conrad—J
Buff, Mary Marsh—J
Bulla, Clyde Robert—M
Burbank, Addison—J
Burch, Robert—T
Burchard, Peter—T
Burgess, Thornton W.—J
Burglon, Nora—J
Burkert, Nancy Ekholm—T
"Burnford, S. D." See Burnford, Sheila—F
Burnford, Sheila ("S. D. Burnford," "Philip Cochrane Every")—F
Burningham, Helen Oxenbury. See Oxenbury, Helen—T
Burningham, John—T
Burton, Hester—T
Burton, Virginia Lee—J
Busoni, Rafaello—J
Butterworth, Oliver—F
Byars, Betsy—T

Caldecott, Randolph—J
Calhoun, Mary (Mary Huiskamp Calhoun Wilkins)—T
Cameron, Eleanor—T
Cameron, Polly—F
Camp, Walter—J
"Campbell, Bruce." See Epstein, Samuel—M
Carigiet, Alois—T

Carle, Eric—F
Carlson, Natalie Savage—M
Carpenter, Frances—M
Carr, Harriett H.—M
Carr, Mary Jane—J
Carrick, Carol—F
Carrick, Donald—F
Carrick, Valery—J
Carroll, Latrobe—M
Carroll, Ruth—M
Carter, Helene—M
Casserley, Anne—J
Caudill, Rebecca—M
Cavanah, Frances—M
Cavanna, Betty (Elizabeth Headley)—M
Chalmers, Mary—T
"Chance, Stephen." See Turner, Philip—F
"Chapman, Walker." See Silverberg, Robert—T
Chappell, Warren—T
"Charles, Nicholas." See Kuskin, Karla—T
Charlip, Remy—T
Charlot, Jean—M
Chase, Mary Ellen—F
Chase, Richard—M
Chastain, Madye Lee—M
Chauncy, Nan—T
Chipperfield, Joseph E.—M
Chönz, Selina—F
Chorao, Kay (Ann McKay Sproat Chorao)—F
Chrisman, Arthur Bowie—J
"Christopher, John" (Samuel Youd)—F
Church, Alfred J.—J
Church, Richard—M
Chute, B. J.—M
Chute, Marchette—M
Chwast, Jacqueline—F
Chwast, Seymour—F
Ciardi, John—T
"Clare, Helen." See Clarke, Pauline—T
Clark, Ann Nolan—J
Clark, Mavis Thorpe (Mavis Thorpe Clark Latham)—F
Clarke, Arthur C.—F
Clarke, Pauline ("Helen Clare") —T
Cleary, Beverly—M
Cleaver, Bill—F
Cleaver, Elizabeth—F
Cleaver, Vera—F
Clymer, Eleanor ("Elizabeth Kinsey")—F
Coatsworth, Elizabeth—J
Cober, Alan E.—F
Coblentz, Catherine Cate—J
Cockshut, Gillian Elise Avery. See Avery, Gillian—F
Coggins, Jack—M
Colby, Carroll B.—M

Flora, James—T

Folon, Colette Portal. *See* Portal, Colette—F

Forberg, Ati (Beate Gropius Forberg)—F

Forbes, Esther—M

Forman, James—T

Fortnum, Peggy (Margaret Emily Noel Nuttall-Smith)—F

Foster, Genevieve—J

Foster, Marian Curtis. *See* "Mariana"—T

Fox, Paula (Paula Fox Greenberg)—F

Franchere, Ruth—F

François, André—T

"Françoise" (Françoise Seignobosc)—M

Franklin, George Cory—M

Franklin, Madeleine. *See* "L'Engle, Madeleine"—M

Frasconi, Antonio—T

Fraser, Claud Lovat—J

Freeman, Don—M

Freeman, Ira Maximilian—M

Freeman, Lydia—M

Freeman, Mae Blacker—M

French, Allen—J

"French, Paul." *See* Asimov, Isaac—T

Freschet, Berniece—F

Friedman, Frieda—M

Friermood, Elisabeth Hamilton—M

"Friis, Babbis." *See* Friis-Baastad, Babbis—T

Friis-Baastad, Babbis ("Eleanor Babbis," "Babbis Friis")—T

Fritz, Jean—T

Froman, Robert—F

Frost, Frances—M

Fry, Rosalie K.—T

Fuchs, Erich—F

Fujikawa, Gyo—F

Fyleman, Rose—J

Gaer, Joseph—M

Gág, Flavia—M

Gág, Wanda—J

"Gage, Wilson" (Mary Q. Steele)—T

Galdone, Paul—T

Gall, Alice Crew—J

Galt, Tom—M

Gannett, Ruth Chrisman—M

Gannett, Ruth Stiles (Ruth Stiles Gannett Kahn)—F

Garfield, Leon—F

Garner, Alan—T

Garrett, Randall. *See* Silverberg, Robert—T

Garst, Shannon—J

Gates, Doris—J

Gatti, Attilio—J

Gay, Zhenya—M

Geisel, Theodor Seuss. *See* "Seuss, Dr."—M

Gekiere, Madeleine—T

George, Jean Craighead—M

"Gibson, Josephine." *See* Hine, Al and Joslin, Sesyle—T

Gibson, Katharine—J

Gill, Margery (Margery Jean Gill Jordan)—F

Giovanopoulos, Paul—F

Gipson, Fred—T

Girvan, Helen—M

Glaser, Milton—F

Glubok, Shirley—T

Goble, Dorothy. *See* Goble, Paul—F

Goble, Paul—F

Godden, Runner—M

Goffstein, M. B. (Marilyn Brooke Goffstein Schaaf)—F

Goldston, Robert Conroy (Robert Conroy, "James Stark")—F

Gollob, Tana Hoban. *See* Hoban, Tana—F

Gollomb, Joseph—J

Goodall, John S.—F

Gorey, Edward—F

Goudge, Elizabeth—T

Goudy, Alice E.—T

Grabiański, Janusz—T

Graham, Lorenz—T

Graham, Margaret Bloy—M

Graham, Shirley—M

Gramatky, Hardie—J

Grant, Susan Mary Cooper. *See* Cooper, Susan—F

Gray, Elizabeth Janet (Elizabeth Gray Vining)—J

Green, Roger Lancelyn—T

Greenaway, Kate—J

Greenberg, Paula Fox. *See* Fox, Paula—F

Greene, Constance C.—F

Greenwood, Ted (Edward Alister Greenwood)—F

Grierson, Elizabeth W.—J

Grifalconi, Ann—T

Griffiths, Helen (Helen Griffiths Santos)—F

Grinnell, George Bird—J

Gripe, Harald. *See* Gripe, Maria—T

Gripe, Maria—T

Guillot, René—M

Gurko, Leo—T

Gurko, Miriam—T

Haar, Jaap ter—F

Haas, Irene—T

Hader, Berta—J

Hader, Elmer—J

Haley, Gail E.—T

Hall, Rosalys Haskell—M

Hamilton, Virginia (Virginia Hamilton Adoff)—F

Hamre, Leif—F

Handforth, Thomas—J

Harkins, Philip—M

Harnett, Cynthia—T

Harrah, Wendy McLeod Watson. *See* Watson, Wendy—F

Harris, Christie—F

Harris, Rosemary—F

Hartman, Gertrude—J

Haskell, Helen Eggleston—J

Haugaard, Erik Christian—T

Hautzig, Esther—T

Havighurst, Marion—M

Havighurst, Walter—M

Haviland, Virginia—F

Hawkinson, John—F

Hawthorne, Hildegarde—J

Hays, Wilma Pitchford—T

Haywood, Carolyn—J

Headley, Elizabeth. *See* Cavanna, Betty—M

Heide, Florence Parry ("Jamie McDonald," "Alex B. Allen")—F

Heinlein, Robert A.—M

Henderson, Le Grand. *See* "Le Grand"—J

Henry, Marguerite—J

Henstra, Friso—F

Hentoff, Nat—T

Herald, Kathleen. *See* Peyton, L. M.—T

Hess, Fjeril—J

Hewes, Agnes Danforth—J

Heyliger, William—J

Hightower, Florence—T

Hildick, E. W. (Edmond Wallace Hildick)—F

Hillyer, V. M.—J

Hine, Al ("Josephine Gibson," "G. B. Kirtland")—T

Hine, Sesyle Joslin. *See* Joslin, Sesyle—T

Hinton, S. E. (Susan Eloise Hinton Inhofe)—F

"Hippopotamus, Eugene H." *See* Kraus, Robert—T

Hirsch, S. Carl—T

Hoban, Lillian—T

Hoban, Russell—T

Hoban, Tana (Tana Hoban Gollob)—F

Hodges, C. Walter—T

Hodges, Margaret Moore—F

Hoff, Syd—T

Hoffmann, Felix—T

Hofsinde, Robert—T

Hogan, Inez—M

Hogner, Dorothy—J

Hogner, Nils—J

Hogrogian, Nonny—T

Holberg, Richard A.—J

Le Guin, Ursula K.—F
Leighton, Margaret—M
Leisk, David Johnson. *See* "Johnson, Crockett"—T
"L'Engle, Madeleine" (Madeleine Franklin)—M
Lenski, Lois—J
Lent, Blair ("Ernest Small")—T
Lent, Henry B.—J
"Leodhas, Sorche Nic." *See* "Nic Leodhas, Sorche"—T
Lester, Julius—F
Le Sueur, Meridel—M
Lewellen, John—M
Lewis, C. S.—M
Lewis, Elizabeth Foreman—J
Lewiton, Mina—M
Lexau, Joan M. ("Joan L. Nodset")—F
Ley, Willy—T
Lifton, Betty Jean—T
Linde, Gunnel—F
Linderman, Frank B.—J
Lindgren, Astrid—M
Lindman, Maj—J
Lindquist, Jennie D.—M
Lindquist, Willis—M
Lionni, Leo—T
Lipkind, William—M
Lippincott, Joseph Wharton—M
Little, Jean—F
Lively, Penelope—F
Livingston, Myra Cohn—F
Lobel, Anita—T
Lobel, Arnold—T
Löfgren, Ulf—F
Lofting, Hugh—J
Longstreth, T. Morris—M
Lord, Beman (Harold Beman Lord)—F
"Lord, Nancy." *See* Titus, Eve—T
Lorenzini, Carlo. *See* "Collodi, C."—J
Lorraine, Walter—F
Lovelace, Maud Hart—J
Low, Joseph—T
Lownsbery, Eloise—J
Lubell, Cecil—F
Lubell, Winifred—F
Lucas, Jannette May—J

McCloskey, Robert—J
McClung, Robert M.—M
McCord, David—T
McCracken, Harold—J
McCrindle, Honor Morfydd Arundel. *See* Arundel, Honor—F
McCully, Emily Arnold—F
"MacDonald, Golden." *See* Brown, Margaret Wise—J
"McDonald, Jamie." *See* Heide, Florence Parry—F

McGinley, Phyllis—J
McGovern, Ann (Ann Weinberger McGovern Scheiner)—F
McGraw, Eloise Jarvis—M
McGraw, William Corbin. *See* Corbin, William—M
MacGregor, Ellen—M
McIlwraith, Maureen Mollie Hunter McVeigh. *See* Hunter, Mollie—T
Mack, Stan (Stanley Mack)—F
Mackay, Constance D'Arcy—J
MacKinstry, Elizabeth—M
McKown, Robin—T
McLean, Allan Campbell—F
McMeekin, Isabel McLennan—M
McNeely, Marian Hurd—J
McNeer, May—J
McNeill, Janet (Janet McNeill Alexander)—F
McPherson, Margaret—F
McSwigan, Marie—M
Mahy, Margaret—F
Maitland, Antony—F
Malcolmson, Anne—M
Malkus, Alida Sims—J
Malvern, Corinne—J
Malvern, Gladys—J
Manning-Sanders, Ruth—T
Mare, Walter De La. *See* De La Mare, Walter—J
"Mariana" (Marian Curtis Foster)—T
Mars, W. T. (Witold Tadeusz Josef Mars)—F
Marshak, I. *See* "Ilin, M."—J
Marshall, James—F
Martin, Patricia Miles. *See* "Miles, Miska"—F
Mason, Miriam E.—M
Masters, Kelly Rae. *See* "Ball, Zachary"—F
Mathis, Sharon Bell—F
Matsuno, Masako (Masako Matsuno Kobayashi)—F
Mayer, Marianna—F
Mayer, Mercer—F
Mayne, William ("Dynely James")—T
Mays, Victor (Lewis Victor Mays)—F
Meader, Stephen W.—J
Meadowcroft, Enid—J
Meaker, Marijane. *See* "Kerr, M. E."—F
Means, Florence Crannell—J
Medary, Marjorie—J
Mehdevi, Anne Sinclair—F
Meigs, Cornelia—J
Meltzer, Milton—T
Mendoza, George—T
Merriam, Eve—T
Merrill, Jean—T

"Metcalf, Suzanne." *See* Baum. L. Frank—T
Meyer, June Jordan. *See* Jordan, June—F
"Michael, Manfred." *See* Winterfeld, Henry—T
Miers, Earl Schenck—T
"Miles, Miska" (Patricia Miles Martin)—F
Milhous, Katherine—J
Miller, Elizabeth Cleveland—J
Miller, Mitchell—F
Milne, A. A.—J
Minarik, Else—T
"Minier, Nelson." *See* Stoutenburg, Adrien—T
Mizumura, Kazue—T
Mockridge, Penelope Farmer. *See* Farmer, Penelope—F
Montgomery, Rutherford—M
Montresor, Beni—T
Monvel, Boutet de. *See* Boutet de Monvel—J
Moon, Carl—J
Moon, Grace—J
Moore, Anne Carroll—J
Moore, Lilian (Lilian Moore Reavin)—F
Moore, Patrick—F
Moray Williams, Ursula (Ursula Moray Williams John)—F
Mordvinoff, Nicolas—M
"More, Caroline." *See* Cone, Molly—T
Morey, Walt—T
Morgan, Alfred P.—M
Mowat, Farley—T
Munari, Bruno—T
Murphy, Robert W.—F

Nash, Ogden (Frediric Ogden Nash)—F
Nesbit, E.—M
Ness, Evaline—T
Neville, Emily—T
Newberry, Clare—J
Newcomb, Covell—J
Newell, Crosby. *See* Bonsall, Crosby Newell—T
Newell, Hope—M
"Nic Leodhas, Sorche" (Leclaire Gowans Alger)—T
Nichols, Ruth—M
Nicolay, Helen—J
"Nodset, Joan L." *See* Lexau, Joan M.—F
Nolan, Jeannette Covert—J
North, Sterling—T
Norton, Alice Mary. *See* "Norton, Andre"—M
"Norton, Andre" (Alice Mary Norton)—M
Norton, Mary—T

Nuttall-Smith, Margaret Emily Noel. *See* Fortnum, Peggy—F

O'Brien, Jack—M
"O'Brien, Robert C." (Robert Leslie Conly)—F
O'Cuilleanain, Eilís Dillon. *See* Dillon, Eilís—T
O'Dell, Scott—M
Olcott, Frances Jenkins—J
Olcott, Virginia—J
Olsen, Ib Spang—T
O'Neill, Mary—T
Orgel, Doris—F
Ormondroyd, Edward—T
Orton, Helen Fuller—J
"Osborne, David." *See* Silverberg, Robert—T
"Otis, James" (James O. Kaler) —J
Ottley, Reginald—F
Oxenbury, Helen (Helen Oxenbury Burningham)—T

Palazzo, Tony—T
Paradis, Adrian A.—M
Parish, Peggy—F
Parker, Bertha M.—M
Parker, Dorothy D.—F
Parker, Edgar—T
Parker, Robert Andrew—F
Parnall, Peter—T
Parrish, Maxfield—J
Parton, Ethel—J
Patch, Edith M.—J
Paton Walsh, Jill (Gillian Bliss Paton Walsh)—F
Paull, Grace A.—J
Pearce, Philippa—T
Peare, Catherine Owens—M
Pease, Howard—J
Peck, Anne Merriman—J
Peet, Bill—T
Perkins, Lucy Fitch—J
Petersham, Maud—J
Petersham, Miska—J
Peterson, Hans—F
Petry, Ann—T
Peyton, K. M. (Kathleen Herald)—T
Phillips, Ethel Calvert—J
"Phipson, Joan" (Joan Margaret Fitzhardinge)—T
Piatti, Celestino—T
Picard, Barbara Leonie—T
Pienkowski, Jan—F
Pier, Arthur Stanwood—J
Pincus, Harriet—F
"Piper, Watty." *See* Bragg, Mabel Caroline—F
Pitz, Henry C.—M
Pogány, Willy—J
Politi, Leo—J

Polland, Madeleine—T
Poole, Lynn—M
Portal, Colette (Colette Portal Folon)—F
Porter, Sheena (Sheena Porter Lane)—T
Potter, Beatrix—J
Poulsson, Emilie—J
Preussler, Otfried—F
Price, Christine—M
Price, Edith Ballinger—J
Pringle, Laurence—F
Proudfit, Isabel—M
Provensen, Alice—T
Provensen, Martin—T
Pyle, Katharine—J

Quackenbush, Robert—F
Quennell, Charles Henry Bourne—M
Quennell, Marjorie—M

Rackham, Arthur—J
Rand, Anne (or Ann)—T
Rand, Paul—T
"Randall, Robert." *See* Silverberg, Robert—T
Rankin, Louise S.—M
Ransome, Arthur—J
Raphael, Elaine. *See* Bolognese, Don—F
Raskin, Ellen—T
Ravielli, Anthony—T
Rawlings, Marjorie Kinnan—T
Reavin, Lilian Moore. *See* Moore, Lilian—F
Reed, Philip—T
Reed, W. Maxwell—J
Reeves, James—T
Rendina, Laura Cooper—M
Renick, Marion—M
Rey, H. A.—J
Rey, Lester del. *See* del Rey, Lester—T
Ribbons, Ian (Harold Ian Ribbons)—F
Richter, Hans Peter—F
Ringi, Kjell (Kjell Arne Sorensen-Ringi)—F
Robbins, Ruth—T
Robertson, Keith—M
Robinson, Irene B.—J
Robinson, Mabel Louise—J
Robinson, Tom—J
Robinson, W. W.—J
Rojankovsky, Feodor—J
Rolt-Wheeler, Francis—J
Roos, Ann—M
Rose, Elizabeth—T
Rose, Gerald—T
Rounds, Glen—J
Rourke, Constance—M
Rowe, Dorothy—J

Rowe, Helen Cresswell. *See* Cresswell, Helen—F
Rugh, Belle Dorman—T

Sabin, Edwin L.—J
Sachs, Marilyn—F
Saint-Exupéry, Antoine de—F
Sánchez-Silva, José—T
Sandberg, Inger—T
Sandberg, Lasse—T
Sandburg, Helga—T
Sandoz, Mari—T
Santos, Helen Griffiths. *See* Griffiths, Helen—F
Sarg, Tony—J
Sasek, Miroslav—T
Sauer, Julia L.—M
Savage, Katharine—F
Sawyer, Ruth—J
Sayers, Frances Clarke—J
Scarry, Richard—T
Schaaf, Marilyn Brooke Goffstein. *See* Goffstein, M. B.—F
Schaefer, Jack—T
Schechter, Betty—F
Scheele, William E.—T
Scheiner, Ann Weinberger McGovern. *See* McGovern, Ann —F
Schindelman, Joseph—T
Schlein, Miriam—M
Schlick, Pamela. *See* Bianco, Margery Williams—J
Schmid, Eleanore—F
Schmidlin-Schmid, Eleonore. *See* Schmid, Eleonore—F
Schoenherr, John—F
Schneider, Herman—M
Schneider, Nina—M
Scholz, Jackson V.—M
Schoonover, Frank—M
Schultz, James Willard—J
Schulz, Charles—T
Schweitzer, Byrd Baylor. *See* Baylor, Byrd—F
Scott, Ann Herbert—F
Scoville, Samuel Jr.—J
Scudder, Mildred Lee. *See* Lee, Mildred—T
Seaman, Augusta Huiell—J
"Sebastian, Lee." *See* Silverberg, Robert—T
Segal, Lore—F
Segawa, Yasuo—F
Seignobosc, Françoise. *See* "Françoise"—M
Selden, George (George Selden Thompson)—F
Selsam, Millicent E.—M
Sendak, Maurice—M
Seredy, Kate—J
Serraillier, Ian—T
"Seuss, Dr." (Theodor Seuss Geisel)—M

Sevastikoglou, Alki Zei. *See* Zei, Alki—**F**
Sewell, Helen—**J**
Shannon, Monica—**J**
Shapiro, Irwin—**J**
Sharp, Margery—**T**
Sheahan, Henry Beston. *See* Beston, Henry—**J**
Shecter, Ben—**T**
Shepard, Ernest—**M**
Sherburne, Zoa Morin—**F**
Shimin, Symeon—**T**
Shippen, Katherine B.—**M**
Shotwell, Louisa R.—**T**
Showers, Paul C.—**F**
Shulevitz, Uri—**T**
Shura, Mary Francis (Mary Francis Craig)—**T**
Silverberg, Robert ("Walker Chapman," "Walter Drummond," "Ivar Jorgenson," "Calvin M. Knox," "David Osborne," "Robert Randall," "Lee Sebastian")—**T**
Simon, Charlie May—**J**
Simon, Hilda—**F**
Simon, Howard—**M**
Simont, Marc—**M**
Singer, Isaac Bashevis—**T**
Skinner, Constance Lindsay—**M**
Slobodkin, Louis—**J**
Slobodkina, Esphyr—**T**
"Small, Ernest." *See* Lent, Blair —**T**
Smith, Jessie Willcox—**J**
Snedeker, Caroline Dale—**J**
Snow, Donald Clifford. *See* "Fall, Thomas"—**F**
Snyder, Zilpha Keatley—**T**
Sobel, Donald J.—**F**
Sommerfelt, Aimée—**T**
Sorensen, Virginia—**M**
Sorensen-Ringi, Kjell Arne. *See* Ringi, Kjell—**F**
Southall, Ivan—**T**
Spanfeller, Jim (James John Spanfeller)—**F**
Spang Olsen, Ib. *See* Olsen, Ib Spang—**T**
Speare, Elizabeth George—**M**
"Spencer, Cornelia" (Grace S. Yankey)—**J**
Sperry, Armstrong—**J**
Spier, Peter—**T**
Spilka, Arnold—**T**
Spykman, Elizabeth C.—**M**
Spyri, Johanna—**J**
"Stanton, Schuyler." *See* L. Frank Baum—**T**
Stapp, Arthur D.—**M**
"Stark, James." *See* Goldston, Robert Conroy.
Steele, Mary Q. *See* "Gage, Wilson"—**T**
Steele, William O.—**M**

Steig, William—**T**
Stein, Evaleen—**J**
Stemple, Jane Yolen. *See* Yolen, Jane—**F**
Steptoe, John—**F**
Sterling, Dorothy—**T**
Sterne, Emma Gelders—**M**
Stevenson, Augusta—**M**
Stoddard, Sandol—**F**
Stobbs, William—**T**
Stolz, Mary—**M**
Stone, Helen—**M**
Stong, Phil—**M**
Stoutenburg, Adrien ("Barbie Arden," "Lace Kendall," "Nelson Minier")—**T**
Streatfeild, Noel—**J**
Suba, Susanne—**M**
Sublette, C. M.—**J**
Summers, James L.—**M**
Sutcliff, Rosemary—**M**
Swarthout, Glendon—**F**
Swarthout, Kathryn—**F**
Swift, Hildegarde Hoyt—**J**
Syme, Ronald—**M**

Tahourdin, Barbara Ker Wilson. *See* Ker Wilson, Barbara —**F**
"Tatham, Campbell." *See* Elting, Mary—**M**
Taylor, Sydney—**M**
Taylor, Theodore—**F**
Teale, Edwin Way—**T**
Tenggren, Gustaf—**M**
Tenniel, Sir John—**J**
ter Haar, Jaap. *See* Haar, Jaap ter—**F**
Tharp, Louise Hall—**M**
"Thayer, Jane." *See* Woolley, Catherine—**M**
"Thayer, Peter." *See* Ames, Rose Wyler—**T**
Thompson, George Selden. *See* Selden, George—**F**
Thompson, Kay—**F**
Thorne-Thomsen, Gudrun—**J**
Thurber, James—**M**
Titus, Eve ("Nancy Lord")—**T**
Todd, Ruthven—**M**
Tolkien, J. R. R.—**M**
Torrey, Marjorie—**M**
Tousey, Sanford—**J**
Townsend, John Rowe—**F**
Travers, Pamela—**J**
Trease, Geoffrey—**M**
Tredez, Alain. *See* "Trez, Alain"—**T**
Tredez, Denise. *See* "Trez, Denise"—**T**
Treece, Henry—**M**
Tresselt, Alvin—**M**
Treviño, Elizabeth Borton de (Elizabeth Borton)—**T**

"Trez, Alain" (Alain Tredez)—**T**
"Trez, Denise" (Denise Tredez) —**T**
Trnka, Jiří—**T**
Tudor, Tasha—**J**
Tunis, Edwin—**M**
Tunis, John R.—**M**
Turkle, Brinton—**T**
Turner, Philip ("Stephen Chance")—**F**
Turngren, Annette—**M**

Uchida, Yoshiko—**M**
Uden, Grant—**F**
Udry, Janice—**T**
Ullman, James Ramsey—**F**
Ungerer, Tomi—**T**
Unnerstad, Edith—**T**
Unwin, Nora S.—**M**
Urmston, Mary—**M**

Valen, Felice Holman. *See* Holman, Felice—**F**
Vance, Marguerite—**M**
"Van Dyne, Edith." *See* Baum, L. Frank—**T**
van Iterson, S. R. *See* Iterson, S. R. van.—**F**
van Stockum, Hilda—**J**
Venturo, Betty Lou Baker (Betty Baker)—**T**
Verne, Jules—**J**
Vining, Elizabeth Gray. *See* Gray, Elizabeth Janet—**J**
Viorst, Judith—**F**
"Vivier, Colette"—**F**
Voight, Virginia Frances—**M**

Waber, Bernard—**T**
Wahl, Jan—**T**
Waldeck, Jo Besse McElveen—**J**
Waldeck, Theodore J.—**J**
Walden, Amelia Elizabeth—**M**
Wallace, Dillon—**J**
Walsh, Gillian Paton. *See* Paton Walsh, Jill—**F**
Warburg, Sandol Stoddard. *See* Stoddard, Sandol—**F**
Ward, Lynd—**F**. *See also* Mc-Neer, May—**J**
Watkins-Pitchford, Denys James. *See* "BB"—**T**
Watson, Clyde—**F**
Watson, Sally Lou—**F**
Watson, Wendy (Wendy Mc-Leod Watson Harrah)—**F**
Weber, Lenora Mattingly—**M**
Weil, Lisl—**F**
Weisgard, Leonard—**J**
Weiss, Harvey—**T**
Wellman, Manly Wade—**M**
Wells, Rhea—**J**
Wells, Rosemary—**F**

Wersba, Barbara—**T**
Werstein, Irving—**F**
Werth, Kurt—**M**
Wheeler, Francis Rolt-. *See* Rolt-Wheeler, Francis—**J**
Wheeler, Opal—**M**
White, Anne Hitchcock—**F**
White, Anne Terry—**M**
White, E. B.—**M**
White, Eliza Orne—**J**
White, Pura Belpré. *See* Belpré, Pura—**F**
White, Robb—**J**
Whitney, Elinor—**J**
Whitney, Phyllis A.—**J**
Wibberley, Leonard—**M**
Wier, Ester—**T**
Wiese, Kurt—**J**
Wikland, Ilon—**F**
Wilder, Laura Ingalls—**J**
Wildsmith, Brian—**T**
Wilkins, Mary Huiskamp Calhoun. *See* Calhoun, Mary—**T**
Wilkinson, Barry—**F**
Willard, Barbara—**F**
Williams, Garth—**M**

Williams, Jay ("Michael Delving")—**F**
Williams, Ursula Moray. *See* Moray Williams, Ursula—**F**
Williamson, Joanne S.—**T**
Wilson, Barbara Ker. *See* Ker Wilson, Barbara—**F**
Winterfeld, Henry ("Manfred Michael")—**T**
Wojciechowska, Maia—**T**
Wood, Esther—**J**
Wood, James Playsted—**F**
Woody, Regina J.—**M**
Woolley, Catherine ("Jane Thayer")—**M**
Worth, Kathryn—**J**
Wrightson, Patricia (Alice Patricia Wrightson)—**F**
Wuorio, Eva-Lis—**T**
Wyeth, N. C.—**J**
Wyler, Rose. *See* Ames, Rose Wyler—**T**
Wyndham, Lee—**M**

Yamaguchi, Marianne—**T**

Yamaguchi, Tohr—**T**
Yashima, Taro—**M**
Yates, Elizabeth—**J**
Yates, Raymond F.—**M**
Yaukey, Grace S. *See* "Spencer, Cornelia"—**J**
"Ylla" (Camilla Koffler)—**M**
Yolen, Jane (Jane Yolen Stemple)—**F**
Youd, Samuel. *See* "Christopher, John"—**F**
Young, Ed—**T**
Young, Ella—**J**

Zarchy, Harry—**M**
Zei, Alki (Alki Zei Savastikoglou)—**F**
Zemach, Harve—**T**
Zemach, Margot—**T**
Zim, Herbert S.—**J**
Zimnik, Reiner—**T**
Zion, Gene—**M**
Zollinger, Gulielma—**J**
Zolotow, Charlotte—**M**
Zwilgmeyer, Dikken—**J**

Picture Credits

Baron of Coronado, Benjamin Elkin; *Jerry Bauer,* Leonard Cottrell; *Baxter,* Philip Turner; *Jack Beale,* Arthur C. Clarke; *Miguel Cerdá,* Anne Mehdevi; *Colin Ballantine,* Barbara Ker Wilson; *Ty Crowell,* Theodore Taylor; *Antony Di Gesu,* Margaret Cosgrove; *Elizabeth Diggs,* Emily McCully; *Terry Dintinfass Gallery,* Jacob Lawrence; *Eclipse* (Zurich), Selina Chönz; *Elliot & Fry, Ltd.* (London), Agnes Allen; *Frederick & Nelson,* Zoa Sherburne; *Freeman,* Patricia Wrightson; *French Cultural Services,* Antoine de Saint-Exupéry; *Mimi Forsyth,* Susan Jeffers; *David Gahr,* Julius Lester; *Barbara Goldberg,* Arnold Adoff, Virginia Hamilton; *Inge Gosney,* Ursula Moray Williams; *Guelph Daily Mercury,* Jean Little; *Hamish Hamilton Children's Books Ltd.,* Honor Arundel; *Harcourt Brace & World,* Margaret MacPherson; *Harper and Rowe,* Gwendolyn Brooks; *B. J. Harris,* Penelope Lively; *Wm. Heineman Ltd.,* Enid Bagnold; *Honolulu Star Bulletin,* Martha Alexander; *Nicholas Horne,* Grant Uden; *Bertil Jigert,* Björn Berg; *Zoa Kamitses,* "M. E. Kerr"; *Jill Krementz,* Edward Gorey; *Little, Brown & Co.,* Ogden Nash; *Alen MacWeiney,* Judith Viorst; *Manchester Guardian,* "John Christopher"; *Oscar Marzaroli,* Allan McLean; *Helen Meurer,* Jane Yolen; *Milwaukee Journal,* Ursula Le Guin; *NAACP,* James Weldon Johnson; *Emily Nelligan,* Marvin Bileck; *Bruce Nicholson,* George Selden; *J. L. Nodset,* Joan Lexau; *Nunawading Gazette,* Hester Brinsmead; *Darcy Panteado,* Elizabeth Bishop; *Joe Panther Enterprises,* "Zachary Ball"; *Arthur Plotnik,* Margery Gill; *Ted Polumbaum,* James Ullman; *Kay Prindle,* Beman Lord; *Robert C. Ragsdale,* Sheila Burnford; *Ramsey and Maspratt,* Mary Ellen Chase; *Roberts,* Scott Corbett; *Roster I Radio-TV* (Stockholm), Gunnel Linde; *Peter Schaff,* Marilyn Goffstein; *Simpson Studios,* Bianca Bradbury; *Robert Smithies,* John Townsend; *United Press International,* Kay Thompson, Eric Knight; *Vacationland Studios,* Paul Goble; *Vivienne* (London), Nina Bawden; *Wagner International Photos,* Weyman Jones; *David Walser* (London), Jan Pienkowski; *Frances C. Ward,* Virginia Haviland; *Watson,* James Houston. *Albert Yamauchi,* Martha Alexander.